HISTORICAL CATALOGUE

OF THE

PRINTED EDITIONS

OF

HOLY SCRIPTURE

IN THE LIBRARY OF

THE BRITISH AND FOREIGN
BIBLE SOCIETY

COMPILED BY

T. H. DARLOW M.A. AND H. F. MOULE M.A.

IN TWO VOLUMES

VOL. I.—ENGLISH

WIPF & STOCK · Eugene, Oregon

Wipf and Stock Publishers
199 W 8th Ave, Suite 3
Eugene, OR 97401

Historical Catalogue of the Printed Editions of Holy Scripture
in the Library of the British and Foreign Bible Society, Volume I
English
By Darlow, T. H. and Moule, H. F.
Softcover ISBN-13: 978-1-6667-5219-9
Hardcover ISBN-13: 978-1-6667-5220-5
eBook ISBN-13: 978-1-6667-5221-2
Publication date 6/27/2022
Previously published by The British and Foreign Bible Society, 1903

This edition is a scanned facsimile of the original edition published in 1903.

PREFACE

THE ORIGIN AND GROWTH OF THE LIBRARY

THE Bible House Library dates back to the year of the Society's foundation. On 17 December 1804, the Committee resolved to issue an appeal 'soliciting donations of Bibles, Testaments, or portions of the Scriptures, in the ancient or modern languages' for the use of agents and members of the Society. One of the first to respond was Mr. Granville Sharp, who promptly sent in between thirty and forty volumes, including versions in Arabic, Dutch, 'Caledonian or Scotch Gaelic,' Gothic, Malabar, Mohawk, Hutter's Matthew and Mark in thirteen languages, and a copy of John Eliot's 'Virginian Indian Bible.' This generous example was followed year after year by numerous benefactors, and a list of 'Donations to the Library' has been a feature in each succeeding Annual Report. Among the donors occur such names as Mr. William Blair, Dr. Adam Clarke, the Rev. Joseph Hughes, the Rev. John Noble Coleman, the Rev. Dr. E. Henderson, Mr. James Thomson, the Rev. John Jones, Mr. George Stokes, General Colin Macaulay, Lord Bexley, Mr. Samuel Bagster, the Baron Silvestre de Sacy, Mr. Josiah Forster, Mr. Edward Dalton, and Prince Louis Lucien Bonaparte. The Library was also gradually increased by copies of new versions and editions published by the Society, and by gifts from other religious, missionary, and learned institutions, at home and abroad. Besides printed editions of the Scriptures, the collection came to embrace a certain number of Biblical and other manuscripts, as well as numerous grammars, lexicons and philological works, chiefly for the use of the Society's translators and revisers.

EARLIER CATALOGUES

The earliest printed list of the Library occupies fourteen pages after the title to Vol. I (1805-10) of the Society's reprinted Annual Reports, and enumerates some 450 volumes. The first catalogue proper was issued in 1822, in pamphlet form, and also appears as pp. 112-144 of the Annual Report for that year. A longer list, filling 86 pages, was published in 1832. At length in 1855 Mr. George Bullen, afterwards Keeper of Printed Books at the British Museum, was commissioned by the Committee to prepare a complete Catalogue of the Society's Library, which by that time had grown to about 5000 volumes in more than 150 different languages. Mr. Bullen followed the plan of the British Museum, arranging all printed editions of the Scriptures under (i) Complete Bibles in various languages, (ii) Old Testaments, (iii) Separate Parts of the Old Testament, (iv) Apocrypha, (v) New Testaments, (vi) Separate Parts of the New Testament. Under each of these headings the books were grouped in the following linguistic order: (*a*) polyglots, (*b*) original languages, (*c*) Latin, (*d*) English, (*e*) other languages in alphabetical order.

THE FRY COLLECTION

Since the publication of Mr. Bullen's Catalogue in 1857, the Library has more than doubled in size, partly by the increase of missionary versions of the Scriptures, until it now includes books in over four hundred different languages and dialects. It has been further enriched by the acquisition in 1890 of the unique collection of English Bibles which had been brought together by Mr. Francis Fry of Bristol. This embraced over 1200 volumes of the Scriptures in English, together with specimens of the principal editions in Welsh, Irish, Gaelic, and Anglo-Saxon, and represented many years of patient research and lavish expenditure. Regarding these books Mr. Bullen wrote: 'So important a collection was, I have no hesitation in saying, never before brought together by a private individual; and for English Bibles, I know of none anywhere existing that can compare with it, whether in public or in private libraries.' Through the persevering zeal of Dr. William Wright, then Editorial Superintendent, this treasure was secured unbroken for the Library, at a cost of 6000*l*. The sum was raised by special contributions from friends of the Society, including munificent gifts from members of Mr. Fry's family.

THE PRESENT CATALOGUE

In 1899, in view of the Society's approaching Centenary, the Committee entrusted the present writer with the task of preparing a new Historical Catalogue of the Bible House Library, and appointed Mr. Horace Moule to assist him in the work. In drawing up their plan, the compilers received valuable advice from Dr. Richard Garnett, C.B., Dr. W. Robertson Nicoll, Dr. J. Rendel Harris, Dr. C. Hagberg Wright, and the late Rev. J. Gordon Watt. It was decided to confine the Catalogue to Printed Editions of Holy Scripture, reserving other books in the Library for separate treatment. Under each language-heading, all editions—whether complete Bibles, Testaments, or separate portions—are arranged in strictly chronological order according to their dates of publication. This method exhibits the history of Bible translation in any tongue, and has peculiar value as tracing the evolution of those missionary versions which the Society specially exists to promote. In order to make the sequence complete, we have endeavoured to note each vital link in the lineage of a version, in its proper place, enclosing between brackets such editions as are not represented in the Library. Commentaries are omitted, unless they contain a continuous text, which is then catalogued under its own language.

The English section of the Library, from its unrivalled importance, demanded exceptional treatment. And it seemed not unfitting that the first volume of the British and Foreign Bible Society's Catalogue should be devoted to the Bible of the English-speaking race. The second volume, which is in preparation and will appear in 1904, enumerates editions of the Scriptures in all other languages, arranged in alphabetical order, with a prefixed list of polyglots. The Biblical Manuscripts in the Library, which include one important Greek palimpsest, will be noted in an Appendix to the second volume. An index of (a) translators and editors, (b) printers and publishers, and (c) places of printing and publication, will be added to each volume. Cross-references in the Catalogue have been made as complete as possible, and for this purpose a distinguishing number is affixed to each edition.

We gratefully acknowledge the ungrudging assistance which we have received from many friendly helpers and critics, some of whose names appear in the introduction to each volume. The publication of the Catalogue has been made possible by special gifts from generous successors of those who founded and built up the Society's Library without cost to its general funds.

Only those who have compiled a Historical Catalogue can appreciate the labour which it entails. The main burden of collation and research has fallen upon my friend Mr. Moule. For some years he has devoted himself ardently and unreservedly to the task. And I rejoice to have this opportunity of placing on record that the credit for whatever has been achieved mainly belongs to him.

Though we have striven after accuracy, it is impossible that we should have escaped errors, and we are acutely conscious how far this Catalogue falls below its ideal. Yet the task has been a privilege, and the toil has brought inspiring compensations. He who sits in the Library of the Bible House and studies that unsurpassed collection of versions of one Book, realises how their sound has gone out into all lands and their words unto the ends of the world. Nay, he has vision of a spiritual multitude which no man can number, of all nations and kindreds and people and tongues, who cry with a loud voice, saying :—*Salvation to our God which sitteth upon the throne, and unto the Lamb.*

T. H. DARLOW.
Literary Superintendent of the Bible Society.

All Saints' Day, 1903.

HISTORICAL CATALOGUE

OF

PRINTED EDITIONS

OF

HOLY SCRIPTURE

VOL. I.—ENGLISH

MEMORIAE
FRANCISCI FRY BRISTOLIENSIS
VIRI MEMORANDO DIGNISSIMI
VT QVI PLVRIMA EXEMPLA
BIBLIORVM ANGLICE TYPIS IMPRESSORVM
TANTO STVDIO TANTA SAGACITATE
EXQVISIVERIT COLLEGERIT CVRAVERIT
VT HODIE THESAVRVS ILLE INCOMPARABILIS
HVIVS BIBLIOTHECAE DECVS SIT PRAECIPVVM
IPSORVM AMANTIS LIBRORVM
AMANTIORIS TAMEN ILLIVS QVEM LIBRI DECLARANT
VOLVMEN PRIVS CATALOGI NOSTRI
DEDICAMUS

INTRODUCTION

TO

THE ENGLISH SECTION

For reasons briefly summarised in the Preface, this Catalogue devotes an exceptional amount of space and attention to English editions of Holy Scripture. Of these books, the Bible House Library, since it acquired the Fry copies, possesses one of the most complete collections in existence. To give some idea of its wealth in this department, we may mention that the Library contains twenty-eight different editions of Tindale's New Testament; five editions of Coverdale's Bible, and nine of his New Testament; four editions of Matthew's Bible; two of Taverner's Bible, one of his Testament, and four of the very scarce portions; twenty editions of the Great Bible (including a complete set of the seven large editions 1539-41); ninety-seven editions of the Geneva Bible, besides twenty-three other editions of the Geneva Testament; eighteen editions of the Bishops' Bible (a complete set), and twenty-four other editions of the Bishops' Testament.

We realised accordingly that this section of our Catalogue demanded an entire volume. It will be seen that we have enumerated nearly a thousand separate editions of the English Bible, or some part of it, published before the close of the eighteenth century. In order to exhibit the historical development as completely as possible, we have noted every issue of significance—even in the very few cases where such an issue was not represented in the Library.

It lay outside our task to undertake serious original research into the problems connected with the genesis and growth of the English text of Scripture. We have attempted, however, to present, under each important version, a digested summary of the results arrived at by the masters in this study, indicating our own conclusions on disputed points. Bishop Westcott's invaluable *History of the English Bible* is not likely to be superseded as an authority, but scholars will rejoice that a revision of it has been undertaken by Mr. W. Aldis Wright.

With regard to the bibliography, we have spared no pains to give full descriptions, including the register of signatures, of all early editions. In the case of later issues, sufficient details are supplied for purposes of identification. The description of each book is taken from a perfect copy—in the Library or elsewhere—which has been carefully examined and collated at first hand. Where no such copy was accessible, we have cited the description given by the best authority. But unless the contrary be stated, all the descriptions and collations represent independent work. The slight differences which so often occur between copies of the same edition of an early printed book compel bibliographers to consider each volume as a selection of sheets. If we could bring home to ourselves the conditions under which a primitive craftsman had to labour—above all, if we could spend a week in some sixteenth-century workshop and watch the actual process of printing there carried on—we might lay hands on the key to most of those typographical puzzles which delight the souls of modern collectors and perplex the compilers of catalogues.

We have sought throughout to give prominence to facts which illustrate the life of the English Bible among the English people. The accessions of sovereigns are noted as a kind of landmark, sometimes of high significance. (See note on p. 59.) The story of the 'Popish Pictures' (see p. 171) gives us a vivid glimpse into the conflict between the Puritans and Archbishop Laud. The rise of Puritanism is reflected in the practice of omitting to bind up the Apocrypha with many early seventeenth-century copies. Although it is not till 1640 that we find an English Bible which deliberately drops them out from its list of books, yet as early as 1615 Archbishop Abbot had forbidden any stationer to issue a Bible without the Apocrypha, under penalty of a year's imprisonment.[1] The prices paid for copies at different periods have been recorded, wherever reliable evidence was forthcoming. (See Nos. 35, 45, 69, 89, etc.; also pp. 264, 403.) Under the date 1641 we have printed the scarce contemporary tract *Scintilla* (p. 189), which throws a flood of light upon the Bible-trade in the reigns of James I and Charles I. The evils of a Bible-monopoly receive further illustration from the immense contraband traffic in English Scriptures printed in Holland which was carried on throughout the seventeenth century. (See note on p. 194, and pp. 184, 188.) The Bible Society's success in multiplying and cheapening copies early in the last century has been summarised in a note (p. 818) under the date 1804.

Our heartiest acknowledgments are due to the numerous Librarians and private collectors who have so readily answered enquiries respecting particular books in their keeping. We are indebted to the Marquis of Northampton, the President of the Bible Society, for a description of his famous copy of Coverdale's first Bible. The Rev. R. Lovett has permitted us to collate his unique copy of

---

[1] See C. R. Rivington's paper 'The Records of the Worshipful Company of Stationers,' printed in Arber's *Transcript of the Registers of the Stationers' Company*, vol. v., p. xlix.

INTRODUCTION TO THE ENGLISH SECTION xiii

Taverner's octavo Testament of 1539. Our special thanks are recorded to the Library authorities at the British Museum, at Cambridge University, at St. Paul's Cathedral, at Lambeth Palace, and elsewhere, for their unvarying courtesy and kindness. Among those who have given us valuable criticism and counsel whenever appealed to, we are bound to mention Mr. A. W. Pollard, of the British Museum, and Mr. Charles Sayle, of the Cambridge University Library. Mr. C. R. Rivington and Mr. E. R. McC. Dix have respectively supplied special information in regard to members of the Stationers' Company, and the earliest English Scriptures printed in Ireland. Mr. Cyril Davenport has lent us his expert advice in describing embroidered and other bindings. Mr. W. Aldis Wright has not only allowed us to consult him on numerous points of difficulty, but has also generously placed at our disposal his notes on such editions as Erasmus' Paraphrase of 1549 and the Geneva Bible of 1560. Dr. James Hastings has kindly furnished us with advance proofs of certain articles in the extra volume of his Dictionary of the Bible.

Some of the choicest volumes which Mr. Fry collected are discussed in monographs which he himself published, and many of the remainder contain descriptive notes in his own handwriting. A manuscript list of the whole Fry collection, giving extracts from these notes, was carefully drawn up by Mr. G. M. Clark, the veteran clerk of the Bible House Library, from whom we have received much willing and useful assistance.

We have done our utmost to secure accuracy, by repeating collations, verifying references, and comparing the proofs with the actual copies described. But in such a catalogue errors are inevitable; and we shall be sincerely grateful for any corrections of those which we cannot hope to have escaped.

T. H. D.
H. F. M.

∵ *An Appendix to this volume contains :—*

(i) *a few editions omitted by mistake, or acquired since the early sheets of the Catalogue were sent to press; together with additional notes on certain editions.*

(ii) *a list of the books of the Bible which were translated into provincial dialects of English for Prince Louis Lucien Bonaparte.*

EXPLANATORY NOTES

Every edition down to 1824 which is represented in the Bible House Library appears in the following pages. After that date mere reprints are omitted, unless they present some feature of importance or interest. Thick square brackets indicate that the edition which they enclose is not represented in the Library.

The *date* stands before each entry. Books which bear more than one date are catalogued under the latest, with cross-references at the other dates.

The *title* in all early editions is given *verbatim et literatim*. Where no title was accessible, the contents of the book are indicated within round brackets. Any words in a 'Description' printed in italics stand for a literal transcript.

In the line following the title are given the *printer* (or *publisher*), the *place*, and the *date*, unless these have been already supplied in the title. When they are not found in the book itself, but ascertained from other sources, they are enclosed within square brackets. When they are conjectural, a query-mark is added.

The same line contains the *size-mark*, f°, 4°, 8°, etc., standing for *folio, quarto, octavo*, etc. These designations are often used inaccurately in early catalogues, where, for example, the octavo Tindale Testaments are generally styled 'duodecimos.' After 1800, for this size-mark are substituted the dimensions of the book in centimètres, measured on the outside of the copy described. This method is now adopted at the Cambridge University Library, in describing books printed after 1900.

The letters 𝔅. 𝔏., after the size-mark, indicate that the book is printed in *black-letter*—'English,' or 'Gothic' type.

In the *description*, 'preliminary' leaves (or pages) mean all those which precede the actual text. A full register of signatures is given, together with the total number of leaves (including blank leaves) in the book. Unless the contrary is stated, A–Z indicates the normal signature-alphabet of 23 letters—A B C D E F G H I (or J) K L M N O P Q R S T V (or U) X Y Z. The recto of a leaf is indicated by *a*, the verso by *b*. In later editions only such details are given as suffice for identification.

After 1611 each edition, unless otherwise described, gives the text of King James' version.

The mark ¶ precedes the description of the copy or copies in the Bible House Library. Down to 1800, the inside measurements of these copies are given in millimètres.

From 1535 to 1800 inclusive each Bible includes the Apocrypha, unless the contrary is stated (cf. note on p. 316). In the case of many seventeenth- and eighteenth-century Bibles it is difficult to determine whether a copy 'wants the Apocrypha.' The words 'No Apocrypha' mean that the list of books omits them; but even then they are occasionally inserted. Very often the Apocrypha are 'included in the list of books but not required by the signatures'; in such a case, if the Library copy omits them, the words 'wants Apocrypha?' are added. Sometimes 'the insertion of the Apocrypha interrupts the signatures.'

The Metrical Psalms have not been catalogued as editions of Scripture. But the following pages show how often they occur bound up with copies of the Bible or New Testament. Unless the contrary is stated, Sternhold and Hopkins' version is meant.

The letters [**F. F.**] signify that the copy belongs to the Fry Collection.

The number which closes an entry is that assigned to the edition in this Catalogue for purposes of reference.

EDITIONS REFERRED TO

The following are the editions of the chief authorities cited:—

Anderson, C. *The Annals of the English Bible.* 2 vols. London. 1845.

Arber, E. *A Transcript of the Registers of the Company of Stationers of London, 1554-1640.* 5 vols. London. 1875-94.

Cotton, H. *Editions of the Bible and parts thereof in English, from the year* MDV *to* MDCCCL . . . Second edition. Oxford, 1852.

Rhemes and Doway . . . Oxford. 1855.

Dickson, R., and Edmond, J. P. *Annals of Scottish Printing* . . . Cambridge. 1890.

Dobson, W. T. *History of the Bassandyne Bible.* Edinburgh . . . 1887.

Fry, F. *A Description of the Great Bible* . . . *also of the editions in large folio, of the Authorized Version* . . . London. 1865.

The Bible by Coverdale . . . London. 1867.

A Bibliographical Description of the editions of the New Testament, Tyndale's version . . . London. 1878.

Herbert, W. *Typographical Antiquities* . . . *begun by* . . . *Joseph Ames* . . . 3 vols. London. 1785-90.

Horne, T. H. *A Manual of Biblical Bibliography* . . . London. 1839.

Kilburne, W. *Dangerous Errors in Several late printed Bibles* . . . Finsbury. 1659. (See W. J. Loftie.)

Lea Wilson. *Bibles, Testaments, Psalms, and other books of the Holy Scriptures in English, in the Collection of Lea Wilson.* London. 1845.

Lee, J. *Memorial for the Bible Societies in Scotland* . . . Edinburgh. 1824. *Additional Memorial* . . . Edinburgh. 1826.

Lewis, J. *A complete history of the several translations of the Holy Bible and New Testament into English* . . . Third edition. London. 1818.

Loftie, W. J. *A Century of Bibles, or the Authorised Version from 1611 to 1711, to which is added William Kilburne's Tract* . . . 1659 . . . London. 1872.

Lovett, R. *The English Bible in the John Rylands Library. 1525 to 1640.* Printed for private circulation. 1899.

O'Callaghan, E. B. *List of editions of the Holy Scriptures and parts thereof, printed in America previous to 1860* . . . Albany. 1861.

Orme, W. *Bibliotheca Biblica* . . . Edinburgh. 1824.

Scrivener, F. H. A. *The Authorized Edition of the English Bible (1611), its subsequent reprints and modern representatives.* Cambridge. 1884.

Smith, W. E. *A Study of the Great 'She' Bible (1613 or 1611).* Printed for private circulation. 1890.

Stevens, H. *The Bibles in the Caxton Exhibition* . . . London. 1878.

Westcott, B. F. *A general view of the History of the English Bible.* Second edition. London. 1872.

*Not least art thou, thou little Bethlehem
In Judah, for in thee the Lord was born;
Nor thou in Britain, little Lutterworth,
Least, for in thee the word was born again.*
    *Heaven-sweet Evangel, ever-living word,
Who whilome spakest to the South in Greek
About the soft Mediterranean shores,
And then in Latin to the Latin crowd,
As good need was—thou hast come to talk our isle.
Hereafter thou, fulfilling Pentecost,
Must learn to use the tongues of all the world.*

                    TENNYSON—*Sir John Oldcastle, Lord Cobham.*

HISTORICAL CATALOGUE

OF PRINTED EDITIONS

OF

HOLY SCRIPTURE

PART I.—ENGLISH

1525. FACSIMILE. (The New Testament.)
[*Peter Quentell: Cologne.* 1525.] 4°. 𝔅.𝔏.

Photo-lithographed from the unique copy, now in the Grenville Collection, British Museum; edited with an elaborate preface by E. Arber (London, 1871).

Nothing but this fragment survives of the earliest, though—so far as is known—unfinished, edition of the New Testament in English. Translated by William Tindale.

Tindale, otherwise Hychyns, born c. 1490, studied at Oxford, and afterwards at Cambridge. By 1523 he had resolved that, if God should spare his life, before many years he would cause plough-boys to know the Scripture. Discountenanced in London, he crossed to Hamburg, and completed his translation on the Continent, using William Roye as an amanuensis. At Antwerp in 1535 he was betrayed to his enemies, and imprisoned in the Castle of Vilvorde, where he died a martyr in October, 1536.

According to Johann Dobneck (Cochlæus), in his *De Actis et Scriptis Martini Lutheri* (1549 ed., p. 132 *f.*), 3,000 copies of the first ten sheets (A-K) of this book had been secretly printed (probably by Peter Quentell) at Cologne, when the editors were obliged to flee to Worms, and there begin work afresh. Possibly the remaining sheets were then printed, and the whole book issued about the same time as the octavo edition from Schoeffer's press.

DESCRIPTION of the Grenville fragment. [Titleleaf, A 1, wanting,] *The . prologge*—7 ff., *The bokes conteyned in the newe Testament*—1 p., on verso a full-page woodcut, representing St. Matthew; text, ff. 2 (not numbered) to xxiiij, ending abruptly in the middle of Matthew chap. xxii. (H 4 *b*). With marginal notes and references. Signatures: A-H⁴; 8 sheets, wanting 1 leaf; 31 ff.

—— Another copy.

1.

VOL. I. B

1525. FACSIMILE. (The New Testament.)
[*Peter Schoeffer: Worms.* 1525.] 8°. 𝕭.𝕷.

A lithographic reproduction of the Bristol copy of this Testament; with an Introduction etc. by Francis Fry. (Printed for the Editor, Bristol, 1862.)

The first edition of Tindale's New Testament definitely known to have been completed; printed, in all probability, by Peter Schoeffer at Worms in 1525.

Fry's No. 1. Of the original issue of 3,000 copies, only two are known to survive. One, a beautiful illuminated copy, preserved in the Baptist College Library, Bristol, apparently wants only the titleleaf. The other, in St. Paul's Cathedral Library, has 71 leaves missing.

DESCRIPTION of the Bristol copy. [Titleleaf, A 1, wanting,] text, ff. j (A ij) to cccliij (Tt 1) *a*; *To the Reder. Geve diligence Reder* . . . —3 pp., *The errours comitted in the prentynge*—3 pp., 1 p. blank.

Signatures: A–Z⁸ AA⁸ BB⁸, Aa–Ss⁸ Tt⁴; 348 ff. A full page contains 33 lines. No prologues, marginal notes, references, or chapter-contents. Outside the text, the volume contains nothing except a short epilogue *To the Reder*, and a list of *errata*.

Small woodcuts, representing the different Evangelists and Apostles, appear at the beginning of the Gospels, the following Epistles—Romans, 1 Peter, 1 John, Hebrews, James and Jude, and Revelation; and another cut (the Day of Pentecost) before Acts.

[The title may have been similar to that dated 1532, found in a copy of a New Testament of 1536 ('Mole' edition). A facsimile of this title (formerly in the possession of Dr. Angus), made from a tracing supplied by Francis Fry, is given at p. 352 in Demaus' *William Tyndale* (revised edition). It runs: *The Newe Testa-|ment in Engly[she] translated | after the [Greek con]tay | ninge these bokes |* . . . (list of books, ending with) *The Epistles taken out of the | olde Testament. | Anno. 1532.*]

2.

THE TRANSLATION. A careful examination of Tindale's version of the New Testament shows that he translated directly from the Greek, using as collateral helps the Vulgate, Erasmus' Latin version (printed alongside his Greek text), and Luther's German New Testament of 1522. The Wycliffite versions seem to have exercised no considerable influence on Tindale or succeeding translators (*cf.* Westcott, *History*, p. 334 etc.). As regards himself Tindale's words are explicit: . . . *I had no man to counterfet, nether was holpe with englysshe of eny that had interpreted the same, or soche lyke thīge ĩ the scripture beforetyme.* . . . (*To the Reder*, octavo edition, 1525). Echoes of the fourteenth-century version in Tindale's work are apparently due to the fact that certain of Wycliffe's phrases had passed into current speech.

The variations from the quarto edition which occur in the text of the octavo are so slight that they may be ascribed to the printer. The octavo Testament contains no marginal notes. Those in the quarto show that Tindale, while adapting some of Luther's notes and transferring others bodily, wrote many himself expressly to accompany his own version. These marginal notes soon came to be described by his opponents as 'pestilent glosses.'

As regards the diction of Tindale's translation, it is remarkable to what an extent this first printed English New Testament fixed the phraseology of all its successors. Even in the Revised Version of 1881 it has been calculated that at least 80 per cent. of the words stand precisely as they stood in Tindale's Testament of 1525. Dr. Westcott thus sums up Tindale's achievement: 'He established a standard of Biblical translation which others followed. It is even of less moment that by far the greater part of his translation remains intact in our present Bibles, than that his spirit animates the whole. He toiled faithfully himself, and where he failed he left to those who should come after the secret of success. The achievement was not for one but for many; but he fixed the type according to which the later labourers worked. His influence decided that our Bible should be popular and not literary, speaking in a simple dialect, and that so by its simplicity it should be endowed with permanence.'

1531. (The Pentateuch.)
Hans Luft : Malborow. ' 17 Jan. 1530 ' [=1531]. 8°. Partly 𝔅.𝔏.

The *editio princeps* of the Pentateuch, and the first portion of the Old Testament printed in English.
This translation, which forms the basis of all subsequent English versions, was the work of William Tindale. There seems no doubt that while freely using the Vulgate, Luther's German Pentateuch (1523) and other versions, he translated from the Hebrew. The most convincing arguments in favour of this view are supplied by internal evidence, and by the translator's direct allusions to the Hebrew text at the end of the Genesis prologue and elsewhere.

DESCRIPTION. Genesis: title : *The fyrst | boke of | Moses called | Genesis* (within woodcut border), on verso begins *W. T. To the Reader. When I had translated the newe testament . . .* —7 pp., *A prologe shewinge the vse of the scripture Though a man had a precious iuell . . .* —4 ff. The text, ff. i to lxxvi, followed on verso by *A table expoundinge certeyne wordes*—7 pp., ending on L 7 b with colophon : *Emprented at Malborow in the lan | de of Hesse, by me Hans Luft, | the yere of oure Lorde. M. | CCCCC. xxx. the. xvij. | dayes of Janu | arij*, 1 f. blank.
Black-letter; generally 31 lines to the full page. Signatures : [unsigned]⁸, B–L⁸ ; 88 ff.
Exodus : first title : *A Prolo | ge in to the secon- | de boke of Moses called | Exodus*, on verso begins *W T Of the preface . . .* (ending with a list of words explained)— 15 pp.; second title : *The secon | de boke of Moses, cal- | led Exodus* (within border), verso blank. The text, ff. II to LXXVI, ending on K 4 a, verso blank.
Roman type (except occasional letters); 28 lines to the full page. Signatures : [unsigned]⁸, A–I⁸ K⁴ ; 84 ff. Many leaves are incorrectly numbered. There are 11 large woodcuts nearly filling the entire page on ff. 43 a and b, 44 a, 45 a, 46 b, 47 a, 48 b, 49 b, 50 b, 56 a, 57 b. These illustrate such subjects as *The forme of the arke of wittnesse . .* , *The forme of Aaron with all his apparell*, etc.
Leviticus : first title : *A pro- | loge in to the | thirde boke of Moses | called Leuiticus* (within border), on verso begins *W T A prologe in to the thirde boke of Moses, called Leuiticus. The ceremonies . . .* —15 pp.; second title : *The Thyrde Bo- | ke of Moses. Cal- | led Leuiti- | cus* (within border), verso blank. The text, ff. II to LII, ending on G 4 b.
Roman type, etc., as in Exodus. Signatures : A⁸, A–F⁸ G⁴ ; 60 ff.
Numbers : first title : *A prolo | ge in to the fourth boke of | Moses, called Nu- | meri* (within border), on verso begins *W T A prologe in to the fourth boke of Moses, called Numeri. In the seconde . . .* —19 pp.; second title : *The four | the boke of Moses called | Numeri* (within border), verso blank. The text, ff. ij to lxvij, ending on K 3 b ; 1 f. blank.
Black-letter, etc., as in Genesis. Signatures : A¹⁰, B–I⁸ K⁴ ; 78 ff.
Deuteronomy : title : *A pro | loge in to the | fyfte boke of Moses, cal- | led Deuteronomye* (within border), on verso begins *W T This is a boke . . .* —7 pp. The text, ff. I to LXIII, ending on I 7 b, followed (on the same page) by a short list of words explained, which runs over on to I 8 a, verso blank.
Roman type, etc., as in Exodus and Leviticus. Signatures : A⁴, B–I⁸ ; 68 ff.
The total number of leaves is 378.
In addition to the prologues many marginal notes occur in each section, some of them keenly controversial for the Protestant cause, *e.g.* the well-known comment on Numbers xxiii. 8 (*How shall I curse whom God curseth not . . .* etc.) : *The pope cā tell howe. Cf.* also the notes on Genesis ix. 5, xlvii. 26, Exodus xxxvi. 6, etc.
The only woodcuts in the volume are the title-borders, a frame with blank shield at base (used seven times) ; and the eleven blocks in Exodus, which Tindale is said to have purchased with part of the money obtained from Tunstall, who bought up Tindale's Testaments in order to burn them (*cf.* Demaus' *William Tyndale*, rev. ed., p. 217). Identical or very similar blocks were used by Vorsterman for his Dutch Bible of 1528, and by Peter Quentell in a Latin Bible of 1529. Similar illustrations appear in Luther's Pentateuch of 1523.
The colophon at the end of Genesis alone supplies date and printer and place. There is no need to treat this colophon as intentionally misleading ; for books extant, bearing a similar colophon, support the view that Hans Luft really was printing books at Marburg about this date, though his chief press was certainly at Wittenberg. Notwithstanding the variations of type, it is probable that all five sections of this volume issued from one press. One woodcut border is used for most of the titlepages, and the watermarks throughout are the same. (*Cf. Athenæum*, 18 April 1885.)

¶ 157 × 103 mm. Imperfect: wanting the first 9 leaves of Genesis (i.e. the Prologues and the first leaf of text), fo. 15 (B 7) of Leviticus, and the first 4 leaves (i.e. the Prologue) and the last leaf of Deuteronomy. These 15 leaves are supplied in facsimile. The blank leaf at the end of Genesis is also missing. The Genesis section appears to have belonged originally to another copy, as its leaves are more closely cut.
Four facsimile leaves of the second edition (1534) of Genesis (*cf.* note below), viz. A 1, 2, 7 and 8, are inserted at the beginning. [F. F.]

——Another copy.

152 × 95 mm. Very imperfect; wanting all Genesis (88 ff.), and 64 ff. of Exodus. Begins at Exod. ch. xxx, fo. 57 (H1), and is perfect on to the end of that book. Leviticus is perfect. Numbers wants the first and last leaves of the prologue (A 1 and 10). Deuteronomy wants the last sheet I (ff. 57–63, and the last leaf). In all, 162 ff. are missing. Genesis may have been in black-letter (1530 edition), or in roman type (1534).
This section, from Exodus fo. 57 to Deuteronomy fo. 56, is perfect, except for the 2 ff. missing from the Numbers prologue. It contains the Deuteronomy prologue, which is missing from the first copy.

A copy (G. 12161) in the B. M. wants only the blank leaf at the end of Numbers.

3.

[In 1534 appeared a second edition, differing only in the first section (Genesis), which was revised and reprinted in roman type, the preliminary leaves being altered as follows:
Title: *The firste| Boke of Moses called | Genesis. Newly | correctyd | and | amendyd by | w.T. | M.D.XXXIIII* (within a border composed of four blocks representing above—the offering of Isaac, below—the crossing of the Red Sea, and at the sides—(left) the brazen serpent, and (right) Moses receiving the tables of the Law), verso blank; prologue: *Vnto the reader W.T. Though a man had a precious Iuell...* —11 pp. (The first prologue in the former edition is here omitted, and the second has certain changes.) The text begins on verso of the last page of prologue, with a woodcut initial letter. Signatures: A–L⁸; 88 ff.; the leaves are numbered from A 8. No list of words at the end of this section and no colophon. There is a perfect copy in St. Paul's Cathedral Library.]

1531? FACSIMILE. The prophete | Jonas⁄ with an introduccio̅ before teachin | ge to vnderstode him and the right vse al- | so of all the scripture⁄ and why it was writ | ten⁄ and what is therin to be sought⁄ and | shewenge wherewith the scripture is loc- | ked vpp that he which readeth it⁄ can not vnderstode it⁄ though he studie therin ne- | uer so moch: and agayne with what keyes | it is so opened⁄ that the reader can be | stopped out with no sotilte or fal- | se doctrine of man⁄ from the | true sense and vnder- | stondynge ther- | of.

[Qu. *Martin de Keyser: Antwerp.* 1531?] 8°. 𝕭. 𝕸.

A facsimile reproduction of the unique copy of this long-lost work of Tindale, discovered in 1861 by Lord Arthur Hervey, afterwards Bishop of Bath and Wells; edited with Introduction etc. by F. Fry (London and Bristol, 1863).

DESCRIPTION. Title (without border or ornament), verso blank; *W.T. vnto the Christen reader*—19 ff. *The Storie of the prophete Jonas* (the text)—7 pp.; 1 p. blank.
Signatures: A–C⁸; 24 ff. Black-letter, like that used by Martin de Keyser of Antwerp in a folio French Bible of 1530. Without date, printer and place. The book appears to be mentioned under the date 3 Dec. 1531, in a list of books denounced by Stokesley, Bp. of London. Tindale's Prologue to Jonah was reprinted with variations in the following editions of Matthew's Bible:—1549, *Daye and Seres*, and *Raynalde and Hyll*; 1551, *John Daye*, and *Nicolas Hyll* (and others).

4.

1534. The ne- | we Testament⁄ dyly | gently corrected and | compared with the | Greke by Willyam | Tindale: and fynes- | shed in the yere of ou | re Lorde God. | A. M.D. &. xxxiiij. | in the moneth of | Nouember.

Marten Emperowr [=*de Keyser*]: *Anwerp.* 8°. 𝕭. 𝕸.

A carefully revised edition of Tindale's New Testament of 1525.

Fry's No. 3. In a second address to the reader Tindale defends with much spirit his own translation against the pretended corrections of Joye, and quotes for the purpose of identification the *tytle* of Joye's unauthorised 16° edition of August 1534 (Fry's No. 2), a copy of which is in the B. M.

DESCRIPTION. Seventeen preliminary leaves: first title (within woodcut border), on verso begins *W. T. vnto the Reader* (ending with notes on *Repentaunce* and *Elders*)—17 pp., *A prologe into the . iiii . Euangelystes* . . . ending with *A warninge to ye reader if ought be scaped thorow necligence of the prynter* . . . and an *erratum* (Matt. xxiii. 26)—2 ff., *Willyam Tindale, yet once more to the christen reader*—9 pp., 1 p. blank; second title: *The ne-| we Testa-| ment,|Imprinted at An-| werp by Marten | Emperowr. | Anno. M.D. xxxiiij.* (within woodcut border), on verso *The bokes conteyned in the newe Testament.* The text, ff. i (really 2, A ii) to ccclxxxiiii (really 384, Bb 6) *b*; followed on the same page by . . . *the Epistles taken oute of the olde testament, which are red in the church after the vse of Salsburye vpon certen dayes of the yere*, which end on fo. cccc (Dd 6) *a*, on verso begins *This is the Table, where in you shall fynde, the Epistles and the Gospels, after the vse of Salsbury*, with a note at the end on certain words ('Infernus,' 'Hell,' etc.) under the heading *These thinges haue I added to fill vp the leffe with all*, ending on Ee 8 *a* (not numbered) with the words *The ende of this boke*, verso blank.

Signatures: ⋆⁸ ⋆ ⋆⁸, A–Z⁸ a–z⁸ Aa–Ee⁸; 424 ff. In the foliation 249 and 250 are omitted, and the last 8 ff. are not numbered. A full page contains 33 lines. References, subject-headings, and notes—a few of the last in roman type—appear in the margins. There are Prologues (chiefly based on Luther's) to all the Epistles; that before Romans fills 34 pp. Two curious misprints occur in the O.T. Epistles: (1) in Gen. xxxvii. 20, *a sand pitte* for *some pitte*; (2) in Isa. liii. 2, *as a sparow* for *as a spraye*.

The woodcut border of the first title is a frame with a blank shield at base. That of the second differs slightly, and the shield bears three graving tools and the initials *M K*, i.e. Martin de Keyser. The 39 woodcuts include small cuts of the Evangelists, the Day of Pentecost, SS. Paul, Peter and James, and 22 larger cuts to illustrate the Revelation.

¶ 154 × 95 mm. Wants only the last leaf, which is supplied in facsimile. In sixteenth-century binding, with goffered edges. [F. F.]

The B. M. possesses Anne Boleyn's copy, printed on vellum.

5.

1534. N. T. 8°. See 1535.

1535. The ne-|we Testament yet once agay|ne corrected by Willyam Tindale: | Where vnto is added a Kalendar | and a necessarye Table / wherin ea|sely and lightelye maye be foun-|de any storye contayned in the|foure Euangelistes and|in the Actes of the | Apostles. | Prynted in the yere of oure|Lorde God. M.D.|&. xxxv.
[Qu. *Martin de Keyser? For Govaert van der Haghen: Antwerp.*] 1535,34. 8°. 𝔅.𝔏.

This edition of Tindale's New Testament is considered to be the last revised by the translator himself, and forms the basis of the text printed in Matthew's Bible of 1537.

Fry's No. 4; known as the 'G. H.' edition, from the monogram on the second titlepage. H. Stevens conjectured that G. H. stands for *Guillaume Hytchins*, the assumed name of Tindale, and the other part of the monogram for *Jacob van Meteren*, as the printer. But H. Bradshaw (*Collected Papers*, p. 354) proved the monogram to be a trade-mark, which indicates that Godefridus Dumæus, *i.e.* Govaert van der Haghen (G. H.), was the publisher of the book. Printed possibly by Martin de Keyser.

DESCRIPTION. [Twenty-nine] preliminary leaves: first title (in black and red, within woodcut border), on verso *An Almanack for . xxi . yeares* (1535-55), [? Kalendar— 6 ff.], *The office of all estates*—1 f., *Willyam Tindale vnto the Christen Reader* (with notes on *Repentaunce* and *Elders*)—15 pp., *A prologe into the . iiii . Euangelystes* . . . —3 pp., *A table for the iiii. Euangelistes* . . . *A table for the Actes of the Apostles*— 21 pp., 1 p. blank; second title: *The ne-| we Testa-| ment,| Anno. M.D. | xxxiiii.* (within woodcut border), on verso *The bokes conteyned in the newe Testament*. The text, ff. i (really 2, A ij) to cccxlvii (really 327, s 7) *a*; on the same page begin . . . *the Epistles taken oute of the olde testament . . . after the vse of Salsburye . . .*—these end on v 4 *b*, and are followed by . . . *the Table, where in ye shall fynde the Epistles and the Gospels, after the vse of Salsbury*—8 ff., ending on ☙ 8 *b*.

Signatures: [signature not known]⁸ *⁸ * *⁸ * * *⁴, A–Z⁸ a–t⁸ v⁴, ☙⁸; 376 ff. The preliminary leaves, and those in the last sheet, are not numbered; the foliation of the rest of the book is most incorrect. Only two leaves before the signature * are extant, containing the first title (dated 1535), Almanack, and *The office of all estates*; probably 6 ff. of Kalendar (mentioned in the title) made up with these the first sheet. It appears from the date 1534 on the second title (A 1 *a*) that the printing of the text was begun in that year, the first title and preliminary leaves being added in 1535. A full page contains 39 lines. References, subject-headings, and notes in the margins. The prologues, as well as part of the marginal matter, are printed in a different and smaller type. The error (Matt. xxiii. 26) noted in the Nov. 1534 edition and the two misprints in the O. T. Epistles do not appear.

The first title-border seems to be that used in the Nov. 1534 edition, with blank shield. The second title-border represents above—Christ preaching, at the sides—(left) Moses receiving the tables of the Law, and (right) the brazen serpent; below is the monogram. The cuts in the text resemble generally those in the Nov. 1534 edition; but those of SS. Paul, Peter, and James are new.

¶ 140 × 89 mm. Contains the only two leaves of the first sheet known to exist. Probably wants only the Kalendar (? 6 ff.) in the preliminary matter. Text perfect. The 21 ff. (s 8 to end) of additional matter, which were missing, have been supplied in facsimile. Recently rebound. Inserted at the end are (1) four leaves (formerly placed after the first title), containing the second address of the Nov. 1534 edition (*Thou shalt vnderstonde moost dere reader . . .* etc.), copied in MS.; and (2) a leaf (fo. xiiii) from Powell's Latin-English Testament (1549), which had been used to back the volume in binding. [F. F.]
6.

[Another octavo edition of Tindale's New Testament, *fynesshed in the yere of oure Lorde God A. M. D. and xxxv.*, exhibits peculiarities of spelling, due perhaps to a Dutch or Flemish compositor. Fry's No. 5. Copies in B. M. and University Library, Cambridge.]

1535. Biblia | The Byble: that | is, the holy Scrypture of the | Olde and New Testament, | faythfully translated in | to Englyshe. | M.D.XXXV. | S. Paul. II. Tessal. III. | Praye for vs, that the worde of God | maye haue fre passage & be glorified. | S. Paul. Colloss. III. | Let the worde of Christe dwell in you | plenteously in all wysdome, &c. | Josue. I. | Let not the Boke of this lawe departe | out of thy mouth, but exercyse thy selfe | therin daye and nyghte, yᵗ thou mayest | kepe and do euery thynge accordynge | to it that is wrytten therin.

[Qu. *Christopher Froschover : Zurich* ?] f°. 𝔅. 𝔏.

The *editio princeps* of the printed English Bible. Translated by Miles Coverdale (1488–1568), a Yorkshireman educated at Cambridge, who spent many years on the Continent. Consecrated Bishop of Exeter, 1551, he was deprived in 1553, and after further exile ended his days in London.

THE TRANSLATION. This Bible, according to the statement on the original title-page (see below), was *faithfully and truly translated out of Douche* [i.e. German] *and Latyn*. And in the Dedication to Henry VIII Coverdale himself says: *I haue . . . purely & faythfully translated this out of fyue sundry interpreters . . .*; so in the Prologue: *And to helpe me herin, I haue had sondrye translacions, not onely in latyn, but also of the Douche interpreters: whom (because of theyr synguler gyftes & speciall diligence in the Bible) I haue ben the more glad to folowe for the most parte*. Thus Coverdale does not profess to have translated directly from the Hebrew and Greek originals. A careful examination of the text itself confirms this view, and enables us to ascertain, almost beyond doubt, that his *fyue sundry interpreters* were the Swiss-German version of Zwingli and Leo Juda (printed at Zurich 1524–29), the

Latin version of Sanctes Pagninus (the first edition of which appeared in 1528), Luther's German version (finished in 1532), the Vulgate, and Tindale. In the main his translation is based on the first two of these.

That Coverdale did translate directly from the original languages has been sometimes argued on the following grounds:—(1) A critical examination shows that he sometimes follows the Hebrew or Greek in preference to the Latin. [But this may quite fairly be ascribed to the influence of the German 'interpreters.'] (2) The omission of the words *out of Douche and Latyn* from the 'English' title (see below) suggests that they were suppressed as misleading. [H. Stevens (*Bibles in the Caxton Exhibition*, p. 70) pointed out an obvious explanation. As the title is in a woodcut border, space is limited. The printer of the new title completed the quotation from Joshua, thus adding two lines. To gain this space he had to save two lines earlier in the title. Consequently the words which could best be spared were dropped—*and truly* and *out of Douche and Latyn*. The facts as to the translation are sufficiently set forth in the Dedication (which first appears along with the changed title) and in the Prologue.] (3) In a letter dated Paris, 23 June 1538, written to Thomas Cromwell, Earl of Essex, by Coverdale and Grafton, when preparing the Great Bible of 1539, these words occur: *We follow . . . not only a standing text of the Hebrew, with the interpretation of the Chaldee and the Greek; but we set also in a private table the diversity of readings of all texts* . . .; and it seems natural to infer that Coverdale used these same helps for his earlier Bible. [Even this is by no means conclusive. And the evidence on the other side, both external and internal, far outweighs it. Coverdale certainly had some knowledge of Hebrew; but his own statement as to his methods of translation cannot be explained away. And so far as his version has been critically examined, almost every rendering can be traced directly to one or other of the five 'interpreters' mentioned above.]

Though his work does not rank beside Tindale's, it was Coverdale's glory to produce the first printed English Bible, and to leave to posterity a permanent memorial of his genius in that most musical version of the Psalter which passed into the Book of Common Prayer, and has endeared itself to generations of Englishmen. (See No. 25.)

We may note two curious renderings, first found in this version, which lent popular names to certain later editions of the English Bible; *So y^t thou shalt not nede to be afrayed for eny bugges by night* (Ps. xci. 5); and *there is no more Triacle at Galaad* (Jer. viii. 22).

PLACE AND PRINTER. Nothing definite is known as to the place of printing. The type of the body of the book has never been satisfactorily identified. Some of the larger letters, however, in the titles and headlines occur in certain contemporary books printed at Zurich, Worms, Mainz, Wittenberg and Cologne. Many minor indications point to *Zurich* as the most likely place, and to *Froschover* (who printed the Coverdale Bible of 1550) as the probable printer.

Symeon Ruytinck in his short Life of Emanuel van Meteren, printed in the latter's *Nederlandtsche Historie* (1614 edition, fo. 672), seems to state that Coverdale's translation was made and printed at the expense of Jacob van Meteren of Antwerp. This is confirmed by Emanuel's affidavit, 1609, cited in Dict. of Nat. Biog., art. *Coverdale*. And Coverdale apparently alludes to such an arrangement in his Prologue: . . . *I was instantly requyred* . . . etc. Henry Stevens (in the Introduction to *Bibles in the Caxton Exhibition*) attempted to base on Symeon Ruytinck's notice the strange theory that Jacob van Meteren was responsible even for the translation itself, using Coverdale merely as his reviser for the press. (*Cf. Athenæum*, July-August, 1884; and Dict. of Nat. Biog. *l.c.*)

DESCRIPTION. [Eight] preliminary leaves (see below): title (within woodcut border), verso blank, Dedication: *Unto the most victorious Prynce and oure most gracyous soueraigne Lorde, kynge Henry the eyght* . . . signed *youre graces humble subiecte and daylye oratour, Myles Couerdale*—5 pp., *A prologe. Myles Couerdale Unto the Christen reader*—6 pp., *The bokes of the hole Byble* . . .—2 pp., *The first boke of Moses, called Genesis what this boke conteyneth*—1 p. The text, divided into six parts:— (1) the Pentateuch, ff. i to xc (p 6) *a*, verso blank; (2) Joshua–Esther, with title: *The seconde parte of the olde Testament. The boke of Josua. . . . The boke of Hester* (within border), on verso the contents of Joshua; the text, ff. ij to cxx (vv 6) *b*; (3) Job–*Salomons Balettes*, ff. i to lij (Ii 4) *a* (on this last page are given two *Fautes escaped in the pryntinge of this parte*), verso blank; (4) Isaiah–Malachi (with Baruch), with title: *All the Prophetes in Englishe. Esay . . . Malachy* (within border), on verso the contents of Isaiah; the text, ff. ij to cij (Rrr 6) *b*; (5) the Apocrypha (except Baruch), with title: *Apocripha . . . The thirde boke of Essdras*.

The seconde boke of the Machabees. Vnto these also belongeth Baruc, whom we have set amõge the prophetes next vnto Jeremy, because he was his scrybe, and in his tyme (within border), on verso a short preface: *The transslatoure vnto the reader*, and the contents of 3 Esdras; the text, ff. ij to lxxxi (really 83, O 5) *b*, 1 f. blank; (6) the New Testament, with title: *The new testament. The gospell of S. Mathew. . . . The Reuelacion of S. Jhon* (within border), on verso the contents of Matthew; the text, ff. ij to cxiij (TT 5) *b*; at the end of the text is *A faute escaped in pryntinge the new Testament*, below which is the colophon: *Prynted in the yeare of oure Lorde M. D. XXXV. | and fynished the fourth daye of October*; 1 f. blank.

The title and preliminary leaves mentioned above are printed in English black-letter, unlike the angular type used in the body of the book. The Marquis of Northampton's is apparently the only copy known which contains this 'English' title of 1535. But the copy preserved in the Earl of Leicester's library at Holkham Hall, has a different title: *Biblia | The Bible, that | is, the holy Scripture of the | Olde and New Testament, faith- | fully and truly translated out | of Douche and Latyn | in to Englishe. | M.D. XXXV. | S. Paul. II. Tessa. III. | Praie for vs. . . . and be glorified. &c. | S. Paul Col. III. | Let the worde . . . in all wyssdome &c. | Josue I. | Let not the boke . . . therin daye and nighte &c.* (within the same woodcut border); on verso, *The bokes of the whole Byble . . .* (ending at the bottom of the page with *Malachias, Malachy the prophet*). In this same copy is also found a unique leaf of preliminary matter, containing on recto the end of the prologue from the words *are able to make satisfaction . . . to the end . . . be glory and domyniō now and ever. Amen.*, and on verso: *The first boke of Moses, called Genesis. What this boke conteyneth*. Now both this title (hence styled the 'foreign' title) and this leaf are printed in the same angular type which is used in the body of the book. No doubt they are relics of the preliminary matter as originally issued, which, in all probability, consisted of four leaves, containing title, list of books (2 pp.), prologue (4 pp.), and contents of Genesis. (One of the two British Museum copies, C. 18. c. 9, has an imperfect title resembling that in the Earl of Leicester's copy.) It appears that the printer who promoted the sale of the edition in England cancelled these leaves, and issued instead a fresh title (slightly altered) and seven other preliminary leaves (including a Dedication to the king), all of which were printed in English black-letter. This printer—no doubt Nycolson, from whose press came the second edition of 1537—probably also inserted the map which is found in some copies of this Bible.

It should be noted that the first page of the Dedication in a genuine copy of this edition contains the words *. . . your dearest iust wyfe, and most vertuous Pryncesse, Quene Anne* (i.e. Anne Boleyn). In some copies is found *Quene Jane* (i.e. Jane Seymour, whom the king married 20 May 1536); Fry has shown that this 'Queen Jane leaf' really belongs to Nycolson's 1537 Bible, and has been substituted for the other.

Varieties of the 1535 title are found in a copy at the University Library, Cambridge, and in another sold by Mr. Quaritch in 1900. Yet another title, very similar to the 1535 English title, but bearing the date M.D.XXXVI, occurs in the copy formerly in the possession of the Earl of Jersey (now Lord Carysfort's), and also in that preserved in the library of Gloucester Cathedral.

Signatures: ✠⁶ (Nycolson's issue), a–p⁶, aa–vv⁶, Aa–Hh⁶ Ii⁴, Aaa–Rrr⁶, A–O⁶, AA–TT⁶; 570 ff. Each part of the text has a separate foliation. The text is printed in angular black-letter; two columns on a page, 57 lines to the full column; no catchwords. In the margins are printed references, a few alternative renderings, and the letters denoting the sections into which each chapter is divided; there are no verse-divisions. The chapter-contents are given together at the beginning of each book. No notes, except a very few in the margins. A short preface occurs before Proverbs, and another before the Apocrypha.

Woodcuts: The border to the general title is composed of four blocks: (1) the top block represents the Sacred Name יהוה, in the left corner a picture of the Fall, *Genesis. 2*, with the words *In vvhat daye so euer thou | eatest therof, thou shalt dye*, and in the right corner the risen Christ, *Mathe. 28*, with the words *This is my deare sonne, in vhom | I delyte, heare him. Matth. 17*; (2) the left-hand block contains representations (above) of Moses on the Mount receiving the Tables of the Law, *Exo. 21*, with the words *These are the lavves, that | thou shalt laye before them*, and (below) of the reading of the Law, *3 Esdre. 9*; (3) the right-hand block shows (above) our Lord giving his last charge to the disciples, *Marci. 16*, with the words *Go youre vvaye in to all the | vvorlde, & preach the Gospell*, and (below) St. Peter preaching, *Actvvm 2*; (4) the bottom block represents Henry VIII seated on his throne, with the royal arms displayed below; the king holds in his right hand a sword, and with his left presents the Bible to a group of prelates kneeling on his right side, while a similar group of nobles are kneeling on his left; in the left corner stands David bearing his harp, with the words *O hovv svvete are thy vvordes vnto my | throte: yee more then hony &c., Psal. 118*, and in the right corner is St. Paul holding a sword in his right hand, with the words *I am not ashamed of the Gospell of | christ. for it is the povver of god. Ro. 1.* The border to the pt. 2 title is composed of eight blocks: (above) three blocks—Joshua viewing the slain, Moses, and the storming of a city; (at the sides) two ornamental blocks—boys blowing horns; (below) three blocks—the Ark crossing Jordan, David, and the fall of Jericho. The border to the pt. 4 title is similar to that of pt. 2, but has different corner blocks, representing Isaiah, Jeremiah, Ezekiel's vision, and Daniel in the lions' den, and an extra block inserted beneath the letterpress of the title—Baruch reading the prophecy. The border to the pt. 5 title is also similar, but the corner blocks represent a priest reading the Law, the return to Jerusalem, the sortie after the death of Holophernes, and the storming of a city. The border to the N. T. title is also similar, but the small central block at the top represents our Lord triumphing over death, and that at the bottom St. John Baptist; while the four corner blocks depict the Evangelists. The woodblocks in the text include two before Genesis (representing the six days of Creation), a large illustration of the Tabernacle, and many small cuts (generally about 70 × 50 mm.) scattered throughout the volume. Altogether 68 separate woodblocks are used, and by repetition these are made to form 158 distinct illustrations.

A map is inserted at the end of the Pentateuch in some copies. It is entitled: *The descripcion of the londe of promes, called Palestina, Canaan, or the holy londe,* and measures 400 × 297 mm. The inscriptions on the two scrolls are in English. According to a MS. note by Fry only two whole copies of this map, and four halves, are known to exist. One of the two copies of this Bible in the John Rylands Library at Manchester possesses a perfect and unique impression of the map, with the inscriptions in Latin, and other peculiarities.

¶ 317 × 202 mm., with original rough edges to some leaves. Like every other copy extant, it is imperfect. Wants title and all preliminary leaves except ✠ 3, also a 3 to 6, and the last leaf of text (TT 5)—12 ff., which are supplied in facsimile. The two blank leaves (O 6 and TT 6) are also missing. And the right half of the map is wanting. Inserted at the beginning of the copy are the following:—(1) Facsimiles of three title-leaves—(*a*) the original, or 'foreign,' title, (*b*) the 'English' 1536 title, (*c*) the imperfect 'foreign' title found in one of the two B. M. copies (C. 18. c. 9), as first mended by Harris, who completed it by copying the right half of the titlepage in the 'Apryll 1540' (Petyt and Redman) Bible, or that of 1549 (Raynalde and Hyll), which gives the legends in Latin, not in English. (2) A facsimile of the unique leaf of preliminary matter (in 'foreign' type) found in the Earl of Leicester's copy. (3) A map (genuine) out of the Bishops' Bible of 1574, being an impression off the same block as that used for the Coverdale map. (4) Harris' facsimile of the 1535 map. (5) A photograph of the 1535 English title (wanting the bottom right-hand corner, which has been incorrectly completed by hand), taken from the Marquis of Northampton's copy. (6) A facsimile of the Prayer printed on verso of the title found in one of the copies in the University Library, Cambridge (this Prayer very closely resembles that printed on verso of the title in the 1537 edition—see below). [F. F.]

—— Another copy.

301 × 196 mm. Imperfect: wanting title and all preliminary leaves, also a 1 to 6, b 1, TT 1, 2, 3 and 5—19 ff., which are supplied in facsimile. The two blank leaves are also missing. Part of the map appears to be genuine, but has been restored. Inserted at the beginning are facsimiles of the three other titles mentioned above, and of the unique preliminary leaf found in the Earl of Leicester's copy.

7.

1536. The Newe Testa-| ment yet once agayne corrected by wil-| lyam Tindale: where vnto is added a | necessarye Table: wherin easely and | lightelye maye be foūde any sto-| rye contaynd in the foure Euangelistes, and in | the Actes of the | Apostles. | The Gospell of {S. Matthew. | S. Marke. | S. Luke. | S. John. | The Actes of the Apostles. | Jesus sayd Marke.xvj. | Go ye into all the worlde, and preache | the glad tydynges to all creatures, | he that beleueth and is bapti-| sed, shalbe saued. | Prynted in the yere of our Lorde | God. M. D. and .XXXUJ.

[Qu. *Antwerp* ?].   4°.   𝕭. 𝕷.

There are three distinct quarto editions of Tindale's New Testament, all bearing this date, which, while agreeing closely, differ throughout in many small points.

They are distinguished from one another chiefly by the variations in a woodcut of St. Paul, prefixed to eleven Epistles. The Apostle's foot rests on a stone, which in one edition is *blank*; in another it bears the figure of a *mole* (or hedgehog); and in the third an *engraver's mark* or monogram, with the initials A. B. K. The text agrees closely with that of the G. H. edition.

F. Fry in his work, *A Bibliographical Description of the Editions of the New Testament, Tyndale's Version*,... (pp. 72–82), deals at length with these three quarto editions. They were probably published independently of the translator, and were printed at Antwerp by one or other of the following printers:—Symon Cowke, Christopher Endhoven, William Vorsterman, Matthew Crom, or Hans van Ruremonde; the last seems to be the most likely name. Herbert (pp. 492–3) suggests John Gowghe of London. All three issues differ in the cut of St. Paul (alluded to above), in the cut of St. Matthew, and (slightly) in the arrangement or spelling of the two titles, etc. There is no conclusive evidence to show their order of publication. But various small differences mentioned below suggest that the 'Mole' edition was the first, and the 'Blank Stone' the last, of the three.

As the corresponding leaves in each edition are generally interchangeable, no doubt many copies have been mixed.

A. Known as the 'Mole' edition. Fry's No. 8.

DESCRIPTION. Four preliminary leaves: title (within narrow woodcut frame), verso blank, *Willyam Tyndale vnto the Christen Reader*—5 pp., *The office of all estates* and *A prayer to be sayd dayly*—1 p. Text: Matthew–Acts, ff. 1 (not numbered) to cxlij (s 6) *a*, verso blank; title: *The epistles of the | Apostle Saynct Paul.... The Epistles of S. Peter.... The Reuelacion of Saynct John the diuine. | The Epistles taken oute of the olde Testament. | A necessary Table for the hole newe Testament. | Prynted in the yere of oure Lorde. | 1 5 3 6* (within same frame as general title), verso blank, *A prologe vpon the Epistle . . . to the Romayns*—13 pp., 1 p. blank (these 8 ff. are not numbered); text, Romans–Revelation, ff. 143 (not numbered) to ccxlvj (H 8) *a*; on verso begin *... the Epistles taken oute of the olde Testament ... after the vse of Salsburye ...*—21 pp., ending on fo. ccliiij (really 256, I 10) *b*; *This is the Table wherein ye shall fynde the Epistles and the Gospels, after the vse of Salsbury*—8 ff., ending on ✠ 8 *b*, with a small cut of the royal arms.

Signatures: [second leaf signed ‡ ij, and third leaf A iij]⁴, a–r⁸ s⁶, A⁸, t–z⁸ A–H⁸ I¹⁰, ✠⁸; 276 ff. The numbers 252 and 253 are repeated in the foliation. A full page contains 38 lines. References, and only two notes (Acts xvii. 28, *Aratus*; Tit. i. 12, *Epimenides*), in the margins; contents at the head of each chapter in the first part; prologues, printed in smaller type than the text. The *necessarye Table* mentioned in the general title and that (probably the same) alluded to in the title to the second part are not found in any extant copy, and apparently were omitted.

Sheet A (containing title to second part and prologue to Romans) seems to have been printed separately from the rest of the book, and afterwards inserted, since it interrupts the foliation and sequence of signatures.

Among the errors may be noted the omission in 1 Cor. xi. 25 of the words *This cup is the new testament in my blood* (fo. clxij, x iiij, *b*).

The numerous woodcuts, many of which repeat the same blocks, include cuts of the Evangelists, 122 small cuts in the Gospels, the Day of Pentecost, the Conversion of St. Paul, SS. Paul, Peter and James, and 21 large cuts in Revelation, as well as the title-border, and a small cut of the royal arms (with dragon and greyhound as supporters) on the last page. Cuts identical with, or very similar to, many of these are found in books printed at various presses.

¶ 235 × 149 mm. A duplicate of fo. clxxxvij (A 5), showing slight variations, is inserted.

[F. F.]

8.

—— ANOTHER EDITION.

B. Known as the 'Engraver's Mark' edition. Fry's No. 9.

The cut of St. Paul, containing the engraver's mark, is found in a book entitled *Storys and prophesis out of the holy scriptur* ... (1535,36), printed by Symon Cowke at Antwerp (Herbert, p. 1545).

This generally agrees closely with the 'Mole' edition. *The office of all estates*, however, is printed on verso of the title, instead of on the last page before the text, which is blank in this edition. The second and third preliminary leaves are signed ✠ ij and ✠ iij, and the first sheet in the second part bears the signature ‡. In pt. 2 title, *Ebrues* occurs instead of *Hebrues* in the 'Mole' edition. The last leaf before the *Table* is correctly numbered cclvj. One new note is added, 1 Cor. xv. 32, *Menander*.

¶ 222 × 139 mm. Imperfect: wanting title and three following leaves. (Fry apparently removed these on the ground that they belonged to the 'Blank Stone' edition.) The second and third leaves of the Prologue to Romans really belong to the 'Mole' edition; they are signed A ij and A iij. All the rest of the volume is 'correct,' according to Fry's note. Inserted at the beginning are a photograph of the titlepage; a reprint (2 pp.) of *A Proclamation for the abolishing of English bookes, after the death of Anne Askew, set forth by the King, Anno 1546, the eighth day of July*; and many MS. notes. [F. F.]

9.

—— ANOTHER EDITION.
C. Known as the 'Blank Stone' edition. Fry's No. 7.

This generally agrees with the 'Mole' and 'Engraver's Mark' editions, but differs in the following points:—The woodcut frame of the titles is shortened by the removal of the bases to the columns. The preliminary matter and the Romans prologue are printed in a different type, with 57, instead of 59, lines to the full page. The lines in the text are slightly longer, and the print shows wider spacing.

Other noticeable points are:—The second preliminary leaf is signed ✱ ij, and the third A iij; while the first sheet in the second part bears the signature A. The pt. 2 title is printed in larger type (the same as the first title). In some copies of this edition the mistake in 1 Cor. xi. 25 is corrected. Variants—incorrect and corrected leaves—are also found of x 5 and y 7. Sig. I 10 is numbered ccliiij, as in the 'Mole' edition.

¶ 203 × 146 mm. The first title is mended. Contains both impressions of the three variant leaves mentioned above. Inserted are many MS. notes by G. Offor and F. Fry. [F. F.]

10.

1536. The newe | Testament yet once | agayne corrected by | Wyllyam Tyndall / Wheare vnto is added an exhortacion | to the same of Erasmus Rot. | with an Englysshe Kalender | And a Table / necessary to fynde | easly and lyghtely any story | contayned in the . iiii . euan- | gelistes & in the Actes | of the Apostles. | 1536.

[Qu. *Antwerp* ?]   8°.   B. L.

There are three, or perhaps four, octavo editions of Tindale's New Testament bearing this date, which, while agreeing closely, differ throughout in many small points. The text in all agrees generally with that of the G. H. edition.

Although we have no direct evidence as to printer or place, they were probably all produced at Antwerp.

A. Fry's No. 10.

DESCRIPTION. Twenty-nine preliminary leaves: first title (in black and red, within woodcut border), on verso *An Almanack for . xxi . yeares* (1535-55), Kalendar—6 ff., *The offyce of all estates*—1 f., *An exhortacion* . . .—23 pp., 1 p. blank, *Wyllyam Tindale vnto the Christen reader*—8 ff.; second title: *The newe | testament | newlye | corrected* (with a rose below title, and ornaments at top and bottom), on verso *The bokes conteyned* . . . (with rose and cornflower at foot of page). Text, A ij to z iiij b; *Here folowe the Epystles taken out of the olde Testamēt . . . after the vse of Salsburye* . . ., which end on bb iiij a ; on the same page begins . . . *the Table wherein ye shal fynde the Epystles and the Gospels after the vse of Salsbury*, ending on cc 4 a, verso blank.

Signatures: [unsigned]⁸ [second leaf marked ij]⁸ ✠⁴ ✱⁸, A–Z⁸ &⁸ ℈⁸ a–p⁸ q⁴ r–z⁸ aa⁸ bb⁸ cc⁴; 428 ff. Leaves not numbered. A full page contains 35 lines. References, subject-headings, and notes, in the margins. Contents before each chapter, in the Gospels and Acts. Prologues to most of the books. *Of S. Marke, what man he was, & of hys auctoryte* is printed *after* St. Mark's Gospel. The *exhortacion* in the preliminary matter is a translation of *Erasmi Roterodami Paraclesis Ad Lectorem Pium* prefixed to the first (1516) and subsequent editions of his Greek Testament.

Among the errors may be noted, Mark v. 27, 30 *preache* for *preace* (or *press*), Phil. iii. 19 *worthely mynded* for *worldely mynded*, and a strange confusion of words in Rev. xix. 15.

This edition may be readily distinguished from Fry's Nos. 11 and 12 by two decisive differences:—(1) The lines in the text are slightly shorter, measuring 57 mm.,

instead of 60 mm. in the other two editions; and the letters are consequently printed more closely. (2) The asterisks referring to marginal notes have 5 points in No. 10, but 7 points in Nos. 11 and 12.
The woodcuts include the title-border, composed of four blocks representing, above, a symbol of the Trinity, with the words *Soli Deo Gloria*; at the sides, figures of St. Peter (left) and St. Paul (right); and, below, emblems of St. Luke (left) and St. Mark (right), and a medallion (in the centre) with the words *Verbvm Caro Factvm*; cuts of the Evangelists, SS. Paul, Peter and James, and the Day of Pentecost; 21 cuts in Revelation (like those in Matthew's Bible of 1537); and a few ornaments.

¶ 129 × 86 mm. Imperfect: wanting both titles (which are, however, supplied in facsimile) and all preliminary matter except Tindale's Address (8 ff.); also 33 leaves of text—H 1, 8 7, X 1 and 8, all sheet ꝑ, a 1, 4 and 5, b 1 and 2, i 3 and 4, t 8, v 1, 2, 3, 6, 7 and 8, x 6 and 8, y 3, 5 and 6, z 2 and 4; and 16 leaves of supplementary matter—z 5, 6 and 7, and aa 8 to end; 70 ff. in all. [F. F.]
There is a large perfect copy in the John Rylands Library.

11.

—— ANOTHER EDITION.
B. Fry's No. 12.

No perfect copy of this edition is known to exist. It agrees closely with Fry's No. 10 described above, and probably contained exactly the same preliminary and supplementary matter, though no leaves before the *Exhortacyon*, or after bb 8, are extant.

DESCRIPTION. [? title, almanack, etc.—8 ff.,] *An Exhortacyon* . . . —23 pp., 1 p. blank, *Willyam Tyndale vnto the Christen reader*—8 ff.; second title: *The newe | testament | newlye | corrected | M.D. xxxvi.* (within woodcut border, with flower above date), on verso *The bokes conteyned* . . . (with ornament at foot of page). Text, A ij to t (really z) iiij b; followed by the O.T. Epistles and Table, ending probably on cc 4, as in No. 10.
Signatures: [—]⁸ [leaves numbered 1 to 12 at foot] ¹² ⁎⁸, A–Z⁸ &⁸ ꝑ⁸ a–p⁸ q⁴ r–z⁸ aa⁸ bb⁸ [—]⁷⁴; probably 428 ff. Generally agrees closely with the other edition, though there are slight variations in the text and woodcuts. Phil. iii. 19 is printed correctly.

¶ 126 × 88 mm. Imperfect: wanting all preliminary matter except Tindale's Address (8 ff.) and second title, and all supplementary matter—z 5 to end; probably 44 ff. in all. The text is perfect. [F. F.]
There is a less imperfect copy in Lambeth Palace Library. (A copy of the very similar edition, Fry's No. 11, may be seen in the Baptist College Library, Bristol; and a copy of Fry's No. 13—the last of this group—in St. Paul's Cathedral Library.)

12.

[The 1536 folio edition of Tindale's Testament (Fry's No. 6), ascribed by H. Bradshaw to T. Godfray, London, is generally considered to be the first portion of the English Scriptures printed on English ground. A perfect copy is in the Bodleian Library.]

1537 ? (The New Testament.)

[Qu. *James Nycolson: Southwark.* 1587 ?] 8°. 𝕭.𝕷.

Coverdale's version.

The only copies known are imperfect, both at the beginning and at the end, and leave us uninformed as to printer, place, and date. But the type, initial letters, etc. agree very closely with those used by James Nycolson of Southwark, especially in his quarto Bible of 1537. The contents of chapters stand in the form of a summary before each book (as in the 1535 folio Bible), and not at the head of each chapter as in Matthew Crom's 1538 New Testament; and only one of Tindale's Prologues appears in this edition. Both these points suggest that this edition preceded M. Crom's, and was printed in 1537 or even earlier. Lea Wilson (p. 143) mentions under 'circa 1535' an edition which appears to resemble this; and J. Dix suggested 1534 or 1535 as the date of the similar edition described below.

DESCRIPTION. [title, etc. ?], Prologue—4 ff., *The summe of this Gospel* (Matthew)—2 ff. text, ff. 1 (not numbered) to ccc.lii (Yy 8) b; . . . *the Epistles of the olde Testament* . . . *after the vse of Salisbury* . . . —31 pp., ending on fo. ccc.lxviii (bb 8) a, on verso begins *The Table* . . . (? pp.) . . .
Signatures: [—] A⁷⁶, A–Y⁸ Aa–Cc⁸, ✠⁸ ⁎⁸, Dd–Yy⁸, aa⁸ bb⁸ [—]; [—] + 6 + 368 + 16 + [—] ff. The two sheets ✠ and ⁎, containing the Prologue to Romans, are not included

in the foliation. A full page contains 36 lines. References in the margins. Coverdale's summaries before each book. *Gloses* at the end of many chapters. No prologues, except that of Tindale to Romans, inserted between sheets Cc and Dd. The woodcuts include cuts of the four Evangelists and St. Paul, like those used in Nycolson's folio Bible of 1537.

¶ 138 × 84 mm. Imperfect: wanting all the leaves before *The summe*, and all after bb 7; also 14 ff. of text—S 1, X 1, 3, 6 and 8, Y 1, 2 and 8, Bb 1, Cc 8, Dd 7 and 8, Ee 1 and 8. The leaf bb 8 is supplied in facsimile, from the copy in the possession of Lord Amherst. The B. M. has also an imperfect copy (C. 51. a. 1.), catalogued under 1538.
At the beginning are inserted 7 pp. of MS. notes by Fry, who mentions that he discovered 14 leaves of this copy bound up with a Greek Testament; the water-stains and other marks show clearly that these leaves originally belonged to the volume in which they are now replaced. [F. F.]

13.

—— ANOTHER EDITION.

This closely resembles the preceding, having the same signatures and agreeing generally page for page throughout the book.

In a MS. note J. Dix quotes G. Offor's opinion that this edition was printed circa 1534, before Coverdale's first folio Bible, and suggests a Paris press. But, like the preceding edition, it was most probably printed by James Nycolson, at Southwark, about 1537. One difference between them is that this has woodcut initials only at the beginning of each book, the former at the beginning of nearly every chapter. Some leaves, e.g. in sheet Aa, are numbered incorrectly in this edition, but correctly in the former.

¶ 147 × 90 mm. Imperfect: beginning with fo. iiii (A iiii), and ending with fo. ccc.lvii (aa v); and the following leaves of text are missing—F 6, K 8, L 1, Q 1, Oo 3, Pp 3 and 4, Qq 8, Rr 7 and 8, Vv 5, aa 1. Many other leaves are badly mutilated, where cuts and initials have been taken out. A minute fragment of the title preserved at the beginning of the volume shows that it had a border of woodcuts. [F. F.]

14.

1537. Biblia | The Byble, that | is the holy Scrypture of the | Olde and New Testament, fayth-| fully translated in Englysh, and | newly ouersene & corrected. | M.D.XXXVII. | S. Paul. II. Tessa. III. | Praye for vs, that the worde of God maye haue for | passage and be glorified. | S. Paul. II. Colloss. III. | Let the worde of Christ dwell in you plenteously in al | wysedome. | Josue. I. | Let not the Boke of this lawe departe out of thy | mouth, but exercyse thy selfe therin daye and nyght, that thou mayest kepe and do euery thynge accordyng | to it that is wrytten therin. | Imprynted in Sowthwarke for | James Nycolson.

f°. 𝕭.𝕷.

Coverdale's version.

The first folio Bible printed in England. It is uncertain whether this, or the quarto also issued by Nycolson in the same year, was the earliest Bible printed on English ground. But probably this is the prior edition; since in the other the words *Set forth with the Kynges moost gracious licence* appear for the first time on the titlepage, and the Summaries are removed from the beginning of the books and placed at the head of each chapter.

The text, in spite of the words *newly ouersene & corrected*, appears to be a close reprint of Coverdale's Bible of 1535.

DESCRIPTION. Eight preliminary leaves: title (within woodcut border), on verso *Because that whan thou goest to studye in holy scripture* . . . (two forms of prayer to be said before and after reading the Scriptures), Dedication: *Unto the moost victorious Prynce* . . . —5 pp., *A prologe* . . . with *Fautes escaped in pryntynge* at the end—6 pp., *The bokes of the whole Byble.* . . . —2 pp., *The fyrst boke of Moses, called Genesis. What this boke contayneth*—1 p. The text, divided into six parts: (1) Genesis-Ruth, ff. j to cxix (really 118, V 4) *a*, verso blank; (2) 1 Samuel-Esther, with title (within border), on verso contents of 1 Samuel, text—ff. ii to c (Rr 4)*b*; (3) Job-*Salomons*

Ballettes, ff. j to lx (kKk 6) *b*; (4) Isaiah–Malachi, with title (within border), on verso contents of Isaiah, text—ff. ii to c.iii (Rrr 7)*b*, 1 f. blank; (5) *Apocripha* (containing Baruch), with title (within border), on verso *The translatoure vnto the reader* and contents of 3 Esdras, text—ff. ii to lxxxix (P 5) *b*, 1 f. blank; (6) N. T., with title (within border), on verso the contents of Matthew, text—ff. ij to Cxix (v 5)*b*, *The table wherin ye shal fynd the Epistles & the Gospels after the vse of Salisbury*—2 ff., 1 f. (? blank, or containing colophon).

Signatures : ✱ ✱⁸, A–T⁶ V⁴, Aa–Qq⁶ Rr⁴, aAa–kKk⁶, Aaa–Qqq⁶ Rrr⁸, A–P⁶, a–t⁶ v⁸; 602 ff. Each part of the text has a separate foliation. The text is printed in bold English black-letter, two columns on a page, 57 lines to the full column; no catchwords. The headlines and folio numbers are printed in fine large type, except in pts. 4 and 5. Fo. 31 (f 1) in pt. 6 differs from the other leaves in the number of lines to the column, and in the spacing of the type. The two forms of prayer (by *Nicolas* [Shaxton] *Bysshoppe of Salisbury*) are like those printed on verso of title in one of the copies of the 1535 Bible, preserved in the University Library, Cambridge. In the Dedication *Quene Jane* supplants *Quene Anne*. As regards the marginal matter etc., the book generally agrees with the 1535 Bible. In the Psalter, the first line of the Latin is given at the beginning of each Psalm; and the Psalms are divided into verses.

The title-borders generally correspond to those used in the 1535 edition, with the following differences:—pt. 2 title: the corner blocks represent Samuel anointing David, David and Goliath, Elijah's sacrifice, and the storming of a city; and the whole is enclosed within an outer ornamental frame; pt. 5 title: the corner blocks at the top represent Moses and the Elders, and Baruch reading the prophecy; with outer frame; pt. 6 title: with outer frame. The cuts in the text do not occur so frequently in this edition. Excluding the title-borders, 57 separate blocks are used for 94 illustrations. Three of the blocks found in the 1535 Bible are not used, but one new cut—Jonah cast into the sea—is introduced. Some of the larger initial letters reproduce designs from *The Dance of Death*. No map appears to have been issued with this edition.

¶ 321 × 213 mm. Imperfect: wanting all preliminary leaves, the first leaf of text, and the two leaves of Table at the end;—11 ff., which are supplied in facsimile. The blank leaf at the end of pt. 4, and the eighth leaf (probably blank) of the last sheet, are also missing.   [F. F.]

According to a MS. note, Fry was able, after many inquiries, to trace no more than eight copies of this edition. The Lincoln Cathedral Library copy wants only the last leaf.

15.

1537. The Byble. | that is the holye Scrypture | of the Olde and Newe Testamente | faythfully translated in Englysh, & newly | ouersene and correcte. | M.V.XXXVII. | S. Paul. II Tessa. III. | Praye for vs, that the worde of God may haue | fre passage and be gloryfyed. | S. Paul. Coloss. III. | Let the worde of Christ dwel in you plenteous | lye in al wysedome. | Josue. I. | Let not the Boke of thys lawe departe oute of | thy mouth, but exercyse thyselfe therin daye and | nyghte, that thou mayeste kepe & do euery thynge | accordynge to it that is wrytten therein. | Imprynted in Sowthwarke in | Saynt Thomas Hospitale by | James Nycolson. | Set forth with the Kynges moost gracious licence.

4°. 𝕭. 𝕷.

Coverdale's version.

The first quarto Bible printed in England.

In spite of the statements on the general and New Testament titlepages, this, like the folio of 1537, appears to be a close reprint of Coverdale's Bible of 1535.

The royal licence, which now appears for the first time, was obtained probably by the influence of Thomas Cromwell, afterwards Earl of Essex.

DESCRIPTION. Eight preliminary leaves: title (in black and red, within woodcut border), on verso begins *The bokes of the hole Byble* . . .—2 pp., Dedication: *Unto the moost victorious Prince* . . . and Prologue: *Myles Couerdale vnto the Christen reader*—9 pp., *An Almanacke for xix. yeares* and Kalendar—2 ff. The text, divided into four parts: (1) Pentateuch, ff. i to xcvii (n i) *a*; on verso (2) title: *The seconde parte of the olde Testamement. The boke of Josua.* . . *The boke of Hester*, text—ff. cxviii (really 98) to cc.xxx (ff 6) a; on verso title: *Apochripha. The bokes and treatises* . . . with list of books and preface, text—ff. cc.xxxi to ccc.xxvii (really 328, ss 10) b; (3) title: *The thyrd part of the olde testamente, whose contentes folowe in the nexte page. Imprynted in Southwarke for James Nycolson* (within border), on verso *The contentes of this boke. Job . . . Malachy*, text—ff. ii to C.lxxix (really 180, Zz 8) a, verso blank; (4) title: *The new testa-|ment faythfully translated | and lately correcte | by Myles Co | uerdale.| Marke . xvi. | Go ye youre waye . . . all creatures. | Paull. Roma. i. | I am not ashamed . . . God* (within border), on verso the list of books, text—ff. 2 (not numbered) to cxxiiii (really 123, Q iii) a; on verso begins *The table wherin ye shall fynde the Epistles and the Gospels after the vse of Salisbury*—4 pp., 1 p. blank, 1 f. blank.

Signatures: ✠⁶, a–z⁸ aa–ee⁸ ff⁶ gg–rr⁸ ss¹⁰, Aa–Hh⁸ Ii⁴ Kk–Zz⁸, A–P⁸ Q⁶; 642 ff. The numbering of the leaves in the text is most incorrect. Pts. 1 and 2 with the Apocrypha contain 328 leaves; pt. 3, 180; and the New Testament, 123;—altogether 631 leaves of text. The text is printed in small but clear black-letter, two columns on a page, 59 lines to the full column; no catchwords. Some titles of the books are in Latin (e.g. *Judicum, Sapientia*). *Quene Jane* in Dedication. Marginal notes etc., as in the folio edition of the same year. The contents are printed at the head of each chapter instead of together at the beginning of each book. At the end of some books the printer has attempted an artistic arrangement of asterisks, pointing hands, and other marks.

The woodcut title-border is composed of four ornamental blocks; that at the top has in the centre a medallion containing two heads. It is used for the general title (in which the line *Set forth . . . licence* is printed outside the border), and for the titles to pts. 3 and 4. Only two illustrations occur in the text, viz. the large cut of the Tabernacle, which fills the recto of fo. 44 (f iiii) in pt. 1, and the small cut, representing Aaron in his robes, a few pages after (fo. 47, f 7, b). Some of the larger initial letters reproduce designs from *The Dance of Death*.

¶ 219 × 156 mm. Very imperfect: wanting all preliminary leaves; in pts. 1 and 2, with Apocrypha, ff. 1–8, 11–14, 19–22, 25, 32, 33, 314, 315; in pt. 3, ff. 87–90, 151; in pt. 4, ff. 41–48, 76, 77, 93–96, 121, 122; and the two last leaves (Q 5 and 6).

The *correct* numbers of the 42 missing leaves of text are given above; as in nearly every case these do not agree with the folio numbers as printed, it is useful to give also the signatures: all a, b 3 to 6, c 3 to 6, d 1 and 8, e 1, rr 4 and 5, Mm 3 to 6, Vv 3, all F, K 4 and 5, M 5 to 8, Q 1 and 2. One leaf, mm 7, is mutilated.

Seventeenth-century binding with brass corners. [F. F.]

The John Rylands Library possesses a large perfect copy.

16.

1537. The Byble, | which is all the holy Scrip-| ture : In whych are contayned the | Olde and Newe Testament truly | and purely translated into En-|glysh by Thomas | Matthew. | Esaye.j. | Hearcken to ye heauens and | thou earth geaue eare : For the | Lorde speaketh. | M,D,XXXVII, | Set forth with the Kinges most gracyous lycēce.

[*Printed for R. Grafton and E. Whitchurch of London.*
Qu. *Antwerp?*] f°. 𝔅.𝔏.

The first edition of the Bible known as 'Matthew's version.'

This version, which welds together the best work of Tindale and Coverdale, is generally considered to be the real primary version of our English Bible.

Thomas Matthew is commonly treated as a pseudonym of John Rogers (1500?-1555), Tindale's intimate friend, and the first martyr in the Marian persecution. But as Rogers only edited what is essentially Tindale's translation, it seems more probable that *Matthew* stands for Tindale's own name, which it was then dangerous to employ. The text in the Pentateuch adheres closely to Tindale's version, and the New Testament follows his G. H. edition. In the portion from Ezra to the end of the Apocrypha (including Jonah) it is substantially Coverdale's. But from Joshua to Chronicles the text differs so much from Coverdale's version that it is supposed to be based on a translation left by Tindale in manuscript form for Rogers' use. Rogers' own share in the work was probably confined to translating the prayer of Manasses (inserted here for the first time in a printed English Bible), and the general task of editing the materials at his disposal, and preparing the marginal notes, collected from various sources, e.g. Tindale, Pellican's Commentary, etc.

As to the place of printing, nothing definite is known. Conjecture points to Antwerp, perhaps at the press of Matthew Crom. The *Kinges most gracyous lycēce* was obtained by Cromwell at Cranmer's request, in spite of, or, it may be, even in ignorance of, Tindale's close connection with the book. Richard Grafton and Edward Whitchurch, the London printers, published the edition of 1,500 copies in England.

DESCRIPTION. Twenty preliminary leaves : title (in black and red, within woodcut border), on verso *These thynges ensuynge are ioyned with thys present volume of the Byble . . . And in the Margēt of the boke are there added many playne exposycyons of soch places as vnto the symple and vnlearned seame harde to vnderstande*, *The Kalender* with *An Almanack for . xviij. yeares* (1538–57)—2 ff., *An exhortacyon to the studye of the holy Scrypture gathered out of the Byble . . .* (with large flourished initials I R at the bottom of the page)—1 p., *The summe & content of all the holy Scripture, both of the olde and newe testament*—2 pp., Dedication : *To the moost noble and gracyous Prynce Kyng Henry the eyght . . .* (with flourished initials H R below the signature *Youre graces faythfull & true subiect Thomas Matthew*)—3 pp., *A table of the pryncypall matters conteyned in the Byble, in whych the readers may fynde and practyse many commune places* (preceded by a short preface *To the Chrysten Readers*)—13 ff., *The names of all the bokes of the Byble . . .* and *A brief rehersall of the yeares passed sence the begynnynge of the worlde, vnto this yeare of oure Lorde. M. ccccc. xxxvij. . . .* —1 p., 1 p. containing a large engraving. The text, divided into four parts:— (1) Genesis—*Salomons Ballet*, ff. 1 (not numbered) to Ccxlvij (Hh 7) *a*, verso blank; (2) title : *The Prophetes in Englysh, Esay. . . . Malachy* (within border), on verso *The Prophete Esaye* (with an engraving, and two pairs of flourished initials R G, E W), the text—ff. j to xciiij (MM 6) *b* (with flourished initials W T) ; (3) title : *The volume of the bokes called Apocripha : Contayned in the comen Transl. in Latyn, whych are not founde in the Hebrue nor in the Chalde. The Regestre therof . . .* (within border), on verso preface *To the Reader*, text—ff. ij to lxxxj (Kkk 9) *b*, 1 f. blank ; (4) title : *The newe Testament of oure sauyour Jesu Christ, newly and dylygently translated into Englyshe with Annotacions in the Mergent to helpe the Reader to the vnderstandynge of the Texte. Prynted in the yere of oure Lorde God.* M.D.XXXVII. (within border), verso blank, text—ff. ij to Cix (O 5) *a* ; on verso begins . . . *the Table wherin ye shall fynde the Epistles and the Gospels, after the vse of Salsbury*—5 pp., 1 f. (O 8) bearing on recto the colophon : *The ende of the newe Testament, and of the whole Byble, To the honoure and prayse of God was this Byble prynted and fynesshed, in the yere of oure Lorde God a, M,D,XXXVII*, verso blank.

Signatures : *⁶ **⁸ ***⁶, a–z⁸ Aa–Hh⁸, AA–LL⁸ MM⁶, Aaa–Iii⁸ Kkk¹⁰, A–O⁸ ; 556 ff. The numbering of the leaves is generally correct. The text is printed in bold black-letter, two columns on a page, 60 lines to the full column ; with catchwords. In the margins are printed references, section-letters, and numerous notes. Contents at the beginning of each chapter. *The Ballet of Balettes of Salomon* is divided into paragraphs, with separate headings printed in red, e.g. *The voyce of the Churche, Christ to the Churche*, etc. Tindale's prologue of 7 pages precedes Romans. The Dedication mentions *Quene Jane*. The *table of the pryncypall matters*, or concordance, is taken from Olivetan's French Bible printed at Neuchatel in 1535 ; and the Apocrypha preface is borrowed from the same book.

The large woodcut which forms the border of the general and N. T. titles represents (in the centre) a tree, supporting a tablet with the letter-press ; (on the left) Moses receiving the Law, the Fall, the brazen serpent, and a tomb bearing a skeleton ; (on the right) the Annunciation, the angels' message to the shepherds, the Crucifixion, and Christ rising from the grave and trampling on death ; at the base of the tree is seated a man, solicited by two figures representing the Law and the Gospel. (The words *Set forth . . . lycēce* in the general title are printed outside the border.) The border of pt. 2 title is composed of sixteen small blocks, and that of pt. 3 title of fifteen blocks. The full-page engraving before the text represents Adam and Eve in Eden, surrounded by many birds and beasts. The large cut on verso of pt. 2 title illustrates Isaiah vi ; and similar cuts, representing incidents in David's life, occur before Psalms and Proverbs. There are 41 distinct cuts (like those of the 1535 Bible) used in the text of pts. 1, 2 and 3 ; and cuts of the Evangelists, SS. Paul, Peter and James, and 21 illustrations to Revelation, in pt. 4. The elaborate woodcut title-border, and the full-page illustration of Adam and Eve, are said to resemble closely engravings found in a Low German Bible, printed at Lubeck in 1533.

The flourished initials I R, H R, R G, E W, and W T, referred to in the Description, no doubt stand for John Rogers, Henricus Rex, Richard Grafton, Edward Whitchurch, and William Tindale.

¶ 364 × 236 mm. Imperfect: wanting the general title, which is supplied in facsimile, the border being taken from a genuine copy of the N. T. title. The last leaf, in which five out of the eight lines of type are genuine, is completed in facsimile. The blank leaf at the end of pt. 3 is missing. The marginal matter is neither cut nor obliterated, as is the case with many copies.

Two extra leaves (ff. 12 and 13 of pt. 3) are inserted, exhibiting variations from their parallels in this copy. Fry suggested that they might belong to a 'pirated edition, of which J. Lenox has the centre of the title and last leaf, as it is supposed.' (*Cf.* Westcott, *History*, p. 73.) [F. F.]

—— Another copy.

347 × 225 mm. Imperfect: wanting all preliminary leaves; in pt. 1, ff. 1 to 10, 12, 13, 15, 16, 26; in pt. 2, title; in pt. 3, last leaf (blank); in pt. 4, ff. 101 to 105, 108, 110, 111, and last leaf (bearing colophon). Of these, five preliminary leaves (✳ 2 to 6), and ff. 105, 110 and 112 in pt. 4, are supplied in facsimile. A duplicate of fo. 93 in pt. 4 is inserted; as well as pt. 2 and Apocrypha titleleaves, taken from a copy of the folio Bible printed at Rouen in 1566.

This copy illustrates how books were mutilated and disfigured by their owners, so as to escape such penalties as were threatened in 1543, 'when Parliament proscribed all translations bearing the name of Tyndale, and required that the notes in all other copies should be removed or obliterated' (Westcott, *History*, p. 87.) The prologues and notes throughout this volume (except in a few leaves supplied from another copy) have been obliterated with reddish-brown paint. (*Cf.* W. Prynne's *Canterburies Doome* . . ., 1646, p. 181.)

Bound up at the beginning is a quantity of matter, both printed and MS., relating to early editions of the English Bible. A former owner states in a note that he found this copy at a farmhouse in Somerset, where it was being 'used to dry flowers and leaves, and press pieces of washed muslin and ribbon, of which it was full.'

17.

1538. The newe | Testament in Englyshe | and Latyn accordyng to the | translacyon of doctour Eras- | mus of Roterodam. | Anno. M.CCCCC.XXXVIII. | Ieremie. XXII. | Is nat my worde lyke a fyre sayeth | the Lorde, and lyke an hammer | that breaketh the harde | stone ? | Prynted in Fletestrete by | Robert Redman | Set forthe vnder the Kynges | moste gracious lycence.

4°. 𝕭. 𝕷.

This diglot is the earliest which contains Tindale's English New Testament, with the Latin of Erasmus. Fry's No. 14. The English agrees generally with the G. H. edition.

DESCRIPTION. Five preliminary leaves: title (in black and red, within woodcut border), on verso *An almanacke for . xxii . yeres* (1539–60), Kalendar (with doggerel rhymes after each month)—3 ff.; second title : *The newe | Testament in | Englyshe & | in Latin | Novvm | Testamentvm | Anglice et | Latine. | Anno Dñi. 1538* (within border), on verso list of books. Text, ff. 2 (not numbered) to CC.LXXXXij (OO 4) *b*; on the same page begin the Old Testament Epistles *after the vse of Salisbury*, in English only, which end on PP 8 *b*; the table of Epistles and Gospels—4 ff., with colophon on the last page QQ 4 *b*: *Thus endyth the Newe Testament bothe in Englyshe & in Laten, of mayster Erasmus translaciō, with the Pystles takē out of y͏ͤ Olde testamēt. Set forthe with the Kynges moste gracious lycēce, and Imprynted by Robert Redman dwellyng in Fletestrete at y͏ͤ sygne of the George nexte vnto saynte Donstons Churche. The yere of our lorde . M.CCCC.XXXviij . and the thyrty yere of the Kynges moste gracious reygne. God saue the kynge.*

At the bottom of the last page of the Kalendar is a catchword *Nota*, but nothing is known of the passage intended to follow, which was probably never printed.

Signatures: [unsigned]⁴, A–Z⁸ AA–NN⁸ OO⁴ PP⁸, QQ⁴; 308 ff. Leaves numbered in the text. The texts are printed in parallel columns, the English in black-letter on the inside of each page, and the Latin in an unusual type outside. A full page of the English text contains 40 lines. References in the margin.

The woodcut title-border is the well-known frame containing the initials H H, and representing above—boys playing, and below—the story of Mutius and Porsenna. (The words *Cvm privilegio ad imprimendvm solvm* are printed outside the border on the first titlepage.) The same design is used for the second title. Two cuts of each Evangelist occur at the beginning of his Gospel.

As this edition of **1538** (Redman's) and those of **1548,47** and **1549** (Powell's) closely resemble each other, and generally read together, mixed copies of the diglot are sometimes found. Redman's has the chapter headlines in black-letter; Powell's Nos. 1 and 2 have them in roman type. The Latin text of Powell's No. 1 is in the same type as the Latin text of Redman's; in Powell's No. 2 this appears in roman. Thus the three editions may be easily distinguished. The passage in 1 Cor. xi is correct in all three; and all have the error in 2 Cor x. 11, *think on his wife*.

¶ 222 × 161 mm. Imperfect: wanting the preliminary leaves, and A 2 and 7; these 7 leaves are supplied in facsimile, and there is also inserted a photograph of the first titlepage taken from the perfect copy in the Bodleian Library. [F. F.]

—— Another copy.

A fragment of 116 leaves, mixed up with a copy of Powell's 1548,47 edition. (See below, No. 41.) [F. F.]
18.

1538. The newe tes-|tament both Latine and | Englyshe ech correspondent to | the other after the vulgare texte, com-| munely called S. Jeroms. Fayth-|fully translated by Myles | Couerdale. | Anno. M.CCCCC.XXXVIII. | Jeremie. XXII. | Is not my worde lyke a fyre sayeth the | Lorde, and lyke an hammer that | breaketh the harde stone? | Printed in Southwarke | by James Nicolson. | Set forth with the Kyn | ges moost gracious licence.

4°.   Partly 𝕭. 𝕷.

The first edition of Coverdale's diglot Testament.

The English text differs somewhat from that in the 1535 Bible, agreeing more closely with the Vulgate.

Before leaving London in the spring of 1538 for Paris, where he had undertaken to prepare, under Thomas Cromwell's patronage, what was afterwards known as the Great Bible, Coverdale had settled that Nycolson should publish for him in London a New Testament with the Vulgate text and his own English version printed side by side. This was determined on in order to reassure his timid friends, and to confute his critics. The book appeared in 1538 in a handsome form, but so full of misprints and errors that Coverdale repudiated it, and immediately arranged for an edition under his own superintendence at Paris. This appeared in November of the same year from the press of Francis Regnault. Nycolson, however, published, also towards the end of 1538, a revision of his first edition; this, according to the titlepage in some copies, was *Faythfullye translated by Johan Hollybushe*.

DESCRIPTION. Six preliminary leaves: title (in black and red, within woodcut border), verso blank, Dedication *To the moost noble, moost gracious, and oure moost dradde soueraigne lord Kynge Henry y͏ͤ eyght* . . . (signed *Youre graces humble and faythfull subiecte. Myles Coverdale.*)—3 pp., To the Reader—3 pp., An Almanack for .xviii. yeares (1538-55) and Kalendar (printed in double columns)—2 ff. The text, ff. 1 (not numbered) to 344 (really 342, Vv 6) b; followed by the table of Epistles and Gospels *after Salysbury vse*—2 ff.

Signatures: ✠⁶, A–Z⁸ Aa–Vv⁸; 350 ff. The Latin text is printed inside in roman type, the English outside in black-letter. A full column of English text contains 41 lines. Marginal references in black-letter. No prologues, chapter-contents, or notes.

The title-border is like that used in Nycolson's quarto Bible of 1537.

¶ 198 × 140 mm. Imperfect: wanting the six preliminary leaves, which, however, are supplied in facsimile. A quasi-facsimile is inserted of the original title of the second edition, which shows the difference in the use of the black and red inks (see next entry). [F. F.]
19.

1538. The newe tes-|tament both in Latine and | Englyshe eche correspondente to | the other after the vulgare texte, com-| munely called S. Jeromes. Fayth-|fullye translated by Johan | Hollybushe.| Anno. M.CCCCC.XXXVIII.| Jeremie. xxii. | Is not my worde lyke a fyre sayeth the | Lorde, and lyke an hammer that | breaketh the harde stone. | Prynted in Southwarke | by James Nicolson. | Set forth wyth the Kyn-| ges moost gracious lycence.

4°.   Partly 𝕭. 𝕷.

The second quarto edition of Coverdale's diglot Testament.

As stated above (see previous entry), Coverdale repudiated Nycolson's faulty first edition, and undertook himself to bring out another in Paris (see next entry). Thereupon Nycolson, on his own account, published this second and corrected issue. The type was reset, and errors are far less common, though many still persist, e.g. in the numbering of the folios. Some copies have a title closely agreeing with that of the first edition, but with many more words in red ink (see previous entry, *ad fin.*); others, like the copy described below, have a title printed entirely in black, with the name *Johan Hollybushe* substituted for Miles Coverdale. In the latter case the titleleaf appears (from its different water-lines etc.) to be a cancel-leaf, inserted in place of the other. [*Cf. Huth Library Catalogue*, iv. pp. 1450–1.] Johan Hollybushe probably stands for the pseudonym, or even the real name, of Nycolson's editor. The text throughout shows signs of revision (e.g., in Matt. xxvi. C. *before the cock synge* is altered into *before the cocke do crowe*). This edition retains Coverdale's Dedication and Address.

DESCRIPTION. Six preliminary leaves: title (all in black, within woodcut border), verso blank, Dedication—3 pp., *To the Reader*—3 pp., Almanack and Kalendar—2 ff. The text, 342 ff.; followed by the table—2 ff.
Signatures, etc., as in the first edition.
Title-border, same as before.

¶ 202 × 138 mm. With the cancel-title bearing the name *Johan Hollybushe*. The title is mounted. [F. F.]
20.

1538. The new testamen both in | Latin and English after | the vulgare texte : | which is red in | the churche. | Translated and corrected by My- | les Couerdale : and prynted in | Paris, by Fraunces Regnault. | M.ccccc.xxxviii | in Nouembre. | Prynted for Richard Grafton | and Edward whitchurch | cytezens of London. | Cum gratia & priuilegio regis.
8°. Partly 𝔅. 𝔏.

Another edition of Coverdale's diglot.

This is the edition issued under his own superintendence in November 1538 (see above), at Paris, where the printer Regnault was busy preparing the first edition of the Great Bible, which appeared in 1539.

DESCRIPTION. [Eight] preliminary leaves: title (in black and red, within woodcut border), verso blank, Dedication *To the ryght honorable lorde Cromwell . . .* (signed, *youre lordshippes humble and faithfull seruytoure. Miles Couerdale.*)—1 f., To the Reader— 1 f., *An Almanack for . xvii . yeares* (1539-55)—1 p., Kalendar—6 pp., 1 p. blank, (1 f. blank?). The text, ff. 1 (not numbered) to cclxxiiij (MM ij) *b*; followed, on the same page, by the table of Epistles and Gospels *after Salysbury vse*, which ends on MM iiii *b*.
Signatures: ✠⁸, A–Z⁸ AA–LL⁸ MM⁴; 284 ff. The Latin text is printed inside in roman type, the English outside in black-letter. A full column of English text contains 49 lines. Marginal references in roman type.
The title-border is an architectural design. There is a cut of St. Mark placed before St. Matthew's Gospel; this cut, similarly misplaced, appears in the folio Great Bibles of 1540 and 1541. The initials exhibit great variety of design.

¶ 161 × 102 mm. Imperfect: wanting the title and following leaf, which are supplied in facsimile. There should also probably be a blank leaf (✠ 8) before the text. Sheets L and M are transposed. Early seventeenth-century binding. [F. F.]
21.

[Another edition of this book seems to have been published by Grafton and Whitchurch in the following year (1539), with reprinted title and dedication (*cf.* Cotton, p. 16 and p. 333).]

1538. The new | Testament of oure | Sauyour Iesu | Christ. | Faythfully translated, & | lately correcte : wyth a | true concordaunce in the | margent, & many neces- | sary annotacions decla- | rynge sondry harde pla- | ces cōteyned in the text. | Eympīt in the yeare | of our Lorde. Mdxxxviij.
Matthew Crom: Antwerp. 8°. 𝔅. 𝔏.

Coverdale's version.

c 2

Some hold this edition to be the earliest separate issue of Coverdale's New Testament, but Nycolson's editions described above (Nos. 13 and 14) are probably earlier.

DESCRIPTION. Eight preliminary leaves: title (in black and red, within woodcut border), on verso *An Almanack for xxxii. yeares* (1539-70), Kalendar—4 ff., *A prologe vnto the newe Testament*—5 pp., *A Prologe of Saynte Matthew* (with cut)—1 p. The text, A 1 to m 8; . . . *the Epystles of the olde Testament* . . . *after the vse of Salysbury* . . . —19 pp., ending on o ij a, the table of Epistles and Gospels *after the vse of Salysbury*— ending on o 7 a, on the same page begins *The summe & content* . . . which ends on o 8 b with the colophon: *Imprynted at Antwerpe, by Matthew Crom. In the yeare of our Lorde M. D. xxxviii.*

Signatures: *⁸, A–Z⁸ a–o⁸; 304 ff. The leaves are not numbered. A full page contains.48 lines. References etc. in the margins. Coverdale's summaries before the chapters; and *gloses* at the end of many. Tindale's Prologues to most of the books.

The title-border represents, on the left, Moses with the tables of the Law, and on the right, the Day of Pentecost; at the top is the legend: *Litera occidit spvs avt vivificat, 2 Cor. 3*, and below *Herken to ye heaues, and thou earth geue eare: For the Lorde speaketh. Esay 1.* The book contains in all about 200 cuts. These include cuts of the Evangelists, and SS. Paul, Peter and James (the two latter being full-page cuts). Before St. Matthew there is a half-page cut with three lines of 14 figures each; and at St. Luke iii occurs a somewhat similar full-page cut, with eight lines containing in all 72 figures and two very small cuts. The text also contains 153 small illustrations (generally 69 × 51 mm.), distributed as follows: 51 in St. Matthew, 22 in St. Mark, 42 in St. Luke, 37 in St. John, and 1 in Acts. These illustrations are said to be by Lieven de Witte, a painter of Ghent, and to have appeared before in a work entitled *Jesu Christi Vita*, printed by M. Crom in 1537. At Acts ii occurs a full-page cut of the Day of Pentecost; and in Revelation there are 21 full-page illustrations. Many tail-pieces, etc.

¶ 146 × 93 mm. Imperfect: wanting title, the eighth preliminary leaf, and the last leaf in the book; these, however, are supplied in facsimile. [F. F.]

22.

—— ANOTHER EDITION.

While generally agreeing closely with the preceding, this exhibits variations in certain sheets, and appears to be a distinct issue. Besides small typographical variations, omissions of some references and *gloses* etc., well-marked differences occur in a few of the cuts—*e.g.* a *full-page* cut of St. John (like that used in R. Harrison's folio Bible of 1562) stands before his Gospel (this alters the arrangement of some succeeding pages), and the cut on k 5 b is placed on k 6 a—while the colophon on the last page reads: *Fynysshed in the yeare of oure Lorde M. D. xxxviii.* As this book shows fewer cracks in the woodblocks, and contains many small errors which are corrected in the preceding volume, probably it is slightly earlier than the issue with Matthew Crom's name in the imprint.

¶ 150 × 95 mm. Imperfect: wanting all preliminary leaves; also A 1, 2, 4, 5 and 8, all sheet C, E 5, all sheet L, and 1 2. The contemporary binding (bearing the initials G. G., sometimes identified with Garret Godfrey) displays the royal arms, with angels as supporters, on one side, and on the other the Tudor rose, with angels as supporters, and the shields of St. George and the City of London; round the rose is inscribed the elegiac couplet:

hec rosa virtutis de celo missa sereno
eternū florens regia sceptra ferct.

This volume was at one time stolen from the Library, and sold to a London bookseller; but it was afterwards recovered, through information given by Mr. Fry to Mr. Bullen, who compiled the Catalogue printed in 1857.

23.

1539. The Most | Sacred Bible, | Whiche is the holy scripture, con- | teyning the old and new testament, | translated into English, and newly | recognised with great diligence | after most faythful exem- | plars, by Rychard | Taverner | Harken thou heuen, and thou earth gyue | eare: for the Lorde speaketh. Esaie. i. | Prynted at London in Fletestrete at | the sygne of the sonne by John Byd- | dell, for Thomas Barthlet, | Cvm Privilegio | ad imprimendum solum. | M.D.XXXIX.

f°. 𝕭. 𝕴.

The first edition of Taverner's Bible. A revision of Matthew's Bible of 1537.

Richard Taverner (1505?–1575), the author of this revision, had high repute for Greek scholarship, and was at this time Clerk of the King's Signet, and in the employ of Thomas Cromwell. In his corrections of the text, Taverner aims at compression and vividness. He substitutes in many places a Saxon for a Latin word, as *spokesman* for *advocate*; and does not hesitate to coin words, as *mercystock* (1 John i. 2). Many marginal notes are omitted, and some new comments added. Taverner's work exercised practically no influence on later revisions (Westcott, *History*, p. 219).

DESCRIPTION. Sixteen preliminary leaves: title (within woodcut border), verso blank, Dedication *To the most noble, most myghtye, and most redoubted prynce, kynge Henry the* .*VIII.* . . .—1 p., *These thynges ensuynge* . . . *and An exhortacion* . . .—1 p., *The contentes of all the Holy Scriptvre* . . .—1 f., *The names of all the bokes of the Byble* . . .—1 p., *A brief rehersall of the yeres passed* . . . *and A table of the principal maters conteyned in the Bible*—25 pp. The text, divided into four parts: (1) *Genesis–Salomons Ballet*, ff. 1 (not numbered) to ccxxx (Pp 8) *b*; (2) with title, *The Boke of the Prophetes. Esaye . . . Malachy*, verso blank, text—ff. II to LXXXXI (PP 7) *b*; (3) with title, *The Volvme of the Bokes called Apocripha* . . ., verso blank, text—ff. I to LXXV (Nnn 3) *b*, 1 f. blank; (4) with title, *The Nevv Testament . . . translated in to English: and newly recognised . . . by Rycharde Taverner. Praye for vs . . . ii. Tessa. iii. Prynted in the yere of oure Lorde God M. D. XXXIX.* (within border), verso blank, text—ff. II to CI (R 5) *b*; *This is the Table wherin ye shall fynde the Epistels and the Gospels after the vse of Salisbury*—5 pp., ending on R 8 *a*, with colophon: *The ende of the newe Testament, and of the hole Byble. To the honour and prayse of God, was this Byble prynted: and fynysshed, in the yere of our Lorde God, a M. D. XXXIX.*; 1 p. blank.

Signatures: ☞⁴ ☞☞⁶ ☞☞☞⁶, A–Z⁶ Aa–Oo⁶ Pp⁸, AA–OO⁶ PP⁸, Aaa–Mmm⁶ Nnn⁴, A–Q⁶ (K is wanting) R⁸; 512 ff. Text printed in double columns, with 68 lines to the full column. Headlines (which include the folio numbers and some subject headings) in roman capitals. Contents of chapters in smaller black-letter. References and some notes in the margins. In pt. 4 sheet K (ff. 55–60) is wanting in all known copies; it must have been used, or intended, for a Prologue to the Epistle to the Romans—probably Tindale's. The Epistles of Peter and John precede the Epistle to the Hebrews. There are many peculiarities in the spelling—e.g. *peax* for *peace*, *hable* for *able*, etc.

The border to the general and N. T. titles is like that used in Nycolson's quarto Bible of 1537, but has an additional outer frame. The other titlepages are quite plain.

¶ 277 × 190 mm. Imperfect: wanting the general title and the last leaf (R 8)—both supplied in facsimile—and the blank leaf (Nnn 4) at the end of pt. 4. Inserted at the beginning is a sheet of MS. containing Taverner's pedigree, as derived from Harl. MSS., Cole's MSS., Hexton Registers, and Wood's *Athenæ*. [F. F.]
24.

[Lewis (p. 130, *n*.) and others mention a quarto edition of this Bible, but no copy can be traced; though the New Testament of Taverner's version was published both in quarto and in octavo, in the same year.]

1539. The Byble in | Englyshe, that is to saye the con-| tent of all the holy scrypture, bothe | of yᵉ olde and newe testament, truly | translated after the veryte of the | Hebrue and Greke textes, by yᵉ dy-| lygent studye of dyuerse excellent | learned men, expert in theforsayde | tonges. | Prynted by Rychard Grafton & | Edward Whitchurch. | Cum priuilegio ad imprimen-| dum solum. | 1539.

f°. 𝕭.𝕷.

The first edition of the 'Great Bible,' *the hole byble of the largyest volume*, which Thomas Cromwell, as the King's vicegerent, in an injunction to the clergy (September 1538), ordered to be *set vp in sum conuenient place wythin the said church that ye haue cure of, where as your parishoners may moste cōmodiously resorte to the same and reade it.*

A revision by Coverdale of Matthew's Bible, which he corrected chiefly by the aid of Sebastian Münster's Latin translation of the Hebrew O. T. (1534,35), and of the Vulgate and Erasmus' Latin version in the N. T., with the collateral help of the Complutensian Polyglot (published about 1520). Coverdale worked under Cromwell's direct patronage; hence the result is sometimes known as 'Cromwell's Bible.' This version and its subsequent editions are often called 'Cranmer's Version,' although that Archbishop had little, if anything, to do with their preparation, beyond adding a Prologue, which first appeared in the second large folio edition, April 1540.

The printing was originally entrusted by Grafton and Whitchurch to Francis Regnault, the Paris printer. But at the end of 1538 the work was suppressed by the French authorities, and many of the sheets confiscated. Coverdale and Grafton, however, were able to save some, and to transport the necessary presses, type and workmen to London, where the edition was completed in April 1539. (See *Athenæum*, 20 May 1871.)

In the Book of Common Prayer the Psalter still follows, with slight variations, the Great Bible; but since 1662 the Epistles and Gospels have been taken from King James' version. The translation of the Canticles, the Lord's Prayer, and the Commandments, with other quotations of Scripture, differs more or less from all our standard versions.

DESCRIPTION. Six preliminary leaves: title (in black and red, within woodcut border), on verso *The names of all the bookes of the Byble . . .*, *The Kalender* with *An Almanach for . xix . yeares* (1539–57)—2 ff., *An exhortacyon . . .*—1 p., *The summe and content of all the holy Scripture . . .*—2 pp., *A prologue, expressynge what is meant by certayn signes and tokens that we haue set in the Byble* (ending with God save the Kynge)— 1 p., *A descripcyon and successe of the kynges of Juda and Jerusalem . . .* followed by *wyth what iudgement the bokes of the Olde Testament are to be red*—1 f. The text, divided into five parts: (1) the Pentateuch, ff. j to lxxxiiij (l 4) a, verso blank; (2) with title: *The second parte of the Byble contaynyng . . . The booke of Josua . . . The booke of Hiob* (within border), verso blank, text—ff. ij to cxxiij (Q iii) b, 1 f. blank; (3) with title: *The thirde parte of the Byble contaynyng . . . The psalter. The prouerbes. Ecclesiastes. Cātica cāticorū. The prophetes. Esay . . . Malachy* (within border), verso blank, text—ff. ij to cxxxiiij (really 132, RR 6) a, verso blank; (4) with title: *The volume of the bokes called Hagiographa. The thyrde boke of Esdras. . . . The seconde boke of ye Machabees* (within border), on verso a note on the Apocrypha: *To the Reader. In consyderacyon . . .*, text—ff. ij to lxj (really 80, Kkk 8) b; (5) with title: *The newe Testament in englyshe translated after the Greke, cōtaynig . . . The Gospelles . . . The actes The Epistles of . S. Paul . . . The Epistle of Saynt James . . . The reuelacion of . S. John* (within border), verso blank, text—ff. ii to ciij (Nn 7) a, followed on the same page by *A Table to fynde the Epistles and Gospels vsually red in the chyrch, after Salysbury vse . . .*, which ends on Nn 8 b with the colophon: *The ende of the new Testamēt: and of the whole Byble, Fynisshed in Apryll, Anno. M. CCCCC. xxxix. A dño factū est istud*.

Signatures: ✱⁶, a–k⁸ l⁴, A–P⁸ Q⁴, AA–PP⁸ QQ⁶ RR⁶, Aaa–Kkk⁸, Aa–Nn⁸; 530 ff. Text printed in bold black-letter, double columns, with 62 lines to the full column. The headlines include short subject headings in the early part of the book. Words not found in the original are printed in smaller type. In the margins are placed references, and many pointing hands and other signs referring to notes which the editor had intended to append (cf. *A prologue, expressynge . . .*), but which never appeared.

The large border to the general title is the well-known woodcut, ascribed to Holbein, which represents Henry VIII, Cranmer and Cromwell distributing Bibles, and the people shouting 'Vivat Rex' and 'God save the King.' This design also appears on the Apocrypha titlepage. The titles to pts. 2 and 3 are enclosed within borders, each formed of 16 small woodblocks, representing Bible incidents. These are repeated in the text, with many similar blocks, having an ornamental border or column on each side. Different cuts are found at the beginning of the Psalter, St. Matthew's Gospel, and the Epistle to the Romans. The N. T. title-border is formed of 8 larger blocks, representing the following: (1) the Annunciation, (2) the Holy Innocents, (3) the Shepherds in the Fields, (4) the Circumcision, (5) the Adoration of the Magi, (6) the Crucifixion, (7) the Stem of Jesse, and (8) the Resurrection. Many woodcut initials also occur scattered throughout the book.

This edition may be readily distinguished from all the six succeeding large folio editions of the Great Bible by many points of difference, e.g. (1) the Apocrypha title has the Holbein woodcut border; (2) the N. T. title has a border of 8 woodblocks; (3) all the small cuts in the text have an ornamental column on each side.

Mr. Fry made a special study of the Great Bibles of 1539–41, and recorded the results in his work *A Description of the Great Bible, 1539, and the six editions of Cranmer's Bible . . .* (1865). Of the seven editions in this series, five have 62 lines to the full page and the remaining two 65 lines. As each corresponding leaf in these two groups contains the same letterpress, though differently set up, the leaves are interchangeable, and most copies appear to be mixed; doubtless, many copies were originally issued in this state. The problem is further complicated by the fact that certain leaves of some editions were reprinted, apparently because the supply of these particular leaves had run short, and they were required to complete copies then being made up. By examining every leaf of a great number of copies, and tabulating his results, Fry attempted to ascertain what leaves properly belonged to each edition, and to make a list of the 'reprinted' leaves. Though his conclusions may not always appear convincing, and it is impossible now to test their accuracy, his work remains a monument of painstaking research, and the tests which he laid down are generally applied to copies of these editions. He himself spared no pains to secure for his own collection 'standard' copies of each edition, and his set of Great Bibles now preserved in this Library is probably the only complete set extant, each copy of which may be considered perfect.

¶ 402 × 272 mm. Wanting only the blank leaf Q 4. The first title and the last two leaves have been mounted. In seventeenth-century binding, with brass plates etc. Inserted are (1) a facsimile of a variant of the fifth leaf of preliminary matter, found in a copy at Lambeth Palace. Fry believed it to have been a rejected proof. (2) A pamphlet, giving different renderings found in the Great Bibles of 1539 and April 1540, drawn up by Fry in 1865.
[F. F.]

A fine copy, printed on vellum and illuminated, which was originally prepared for Thomas Cromwell himself, is preserved in the Library of St. John's College, Cambridge.
25.

1539. The | newe Testamēt | of oure Sauyour | Jesu Christ. | Faythfully translated by | Myles Couerdale : wyth | a true concordaunce / and | many necessary annota- | cyons / declaring sondry | harde places contayned | in the texte. 1539.
M. Crom : Antwerp. 8°. 𝔅.𝔏.

This resembles the former edition printed by M. Crom in 1538. The type, however, is much larger; there are fewer woodcuts, and some are different; while the *Gloses* are omitted in the Epistles.

DESCRIPTION. Eight preliminary leaves : title (in black and red, within woodcut border), on verso *An Almanack for . xxx . yeares* (1540–70), Kalendar—4 ff., Prologue—5 pp., and on last page a cut of St. Matthew and short prologue. The text, A 1 to s iiij *b* ; followed by the O. T. Epistles—15 ff., *Fautes escaped in the pryntynge*—1 p., and table— 9 pp., ending on v 8 *b* with colophon : *At Antwerpe by Matthew Crom. M. D. XXXIX.* (So Cotton, p. 334.)

The arrangement of the preliminary leaves given above is that found in the copy preserved in the John Rylands Library; it corresponds with the order of preliminary leaves in the 1538 edition. But in the copy below the Kalendar ends in the middle of a page; the Prologue immediately follows, and fills 3½ pages, breaking off at the words . . . *as God hath commaunded him* (the rest is omitted) ; and on the last page is the woodcut and prologue (differing slightly in type from the Rylands copy).

Signatures : ✱⁸, A–Z⁸ Aa⁸ Bb⁸, ✠⁸ ✠✠ⁿ, a–vˢ ; 384 ff. The leaves are not numbered. A full page contains 35 lines. On the two sheets ✠ and ✠✠ following Acts are printed Tindale's Prologue to the Romans—27 pp., and *The Summe of the Scrypture*—4 pp., in smaller type ; last page blank.

The title-border is like that in the 1538 edition ; but the text below is omitted, and the words *Cum Gratia & Privilegio Regali, ad imprimendum solum* appear instead. There are over 100 cuts in the book. These include cuts of the Evangelists and SS. Paul, Peter and James ; also 29 small cuts in St. Matthew, 9 in St. Mark, 28 in St. Luke, 24 in St. John, and 2 in Acts, with a full-page cut of the Day of Pentecost ; and 21 illustrations to Revelation, like those used in the quarto editions of Tindale's Testament printed in 1536.

¶ 157 × 97 mm. Imperfect: wanting all preliminary matter except three leaves (containing Kalendar November 8 to end, Prologue, and last page) ; also 10 ff. of supplementary matter, s 5 to 8, and v 3 to 8 ;—15 ff. in all. Four leaves at the beginning, and ten leaves at the end, are printed on yellowish paper, and apparently belong to another copy; they include the three preliminary leaves which differ from the Rylands copy, and are perhaps cancelled leaves.
[F.F.]
26.

1539. The Nevv | Testament in Englysshe: | after the Greke exemplar: | Dilygently translated, | and corrected by | Rycharde | Tauer- | ner. | M. D. XXXIX. | Cum Priuilegio ad Impri- | mendum solum.

Thomas Petyt, for Thomas Berthelet: London. 4°. 𝕭.𝕷.

Two editions of Taverner's version, in quarto and in octavo (see below), were issued in 1539.

DESCRIPTION. Fifteen preliminary leaves: title (in black and red, within woodcut border), on verso *An Almanacke for . xxviii. yeares* (1539–66), Kalendar (two months on each page)—3 ff., *A Table for the foure Euangelystes : Wherein you maye lyghtlye fynde any story conteyned in them* . . .—8 ff., *The table for the actes of the apostles*—5 pp., *The Bokes conteyned in the newe Testament*—1 p. The text, ✻✻✻ 4 to P ii *b* (Acts ends on V 5, and is followed by a blank leaf; Romans begins a new set of signatures in blackletter); followed by the Old Testament Epistles *after the vse of Salysbury*—P iii to Q 7*b*, and *The table wherin ye shall fynde the Epystles, & the Gospels after the vse of Salysbury*—Q 8 to R 8 *b*, ending with the colophon : *Imprynted at London in Paules church yearde, at the sygne of the Maydens heed, by Thomas Petyt, for Thomas Berthelet, Prynter to the Kynges Grace Cvm privilegio ad imprimendvm solvm.*
Signatures [unsigned]⁴, ✻⁸ ✻✻✻⁴ A–T⁸ V⁶, A–R⁸ ; 310 ff. The eaves are not numbered. References in margin ; but no prologues, notes or chapter-contents. A full page contains 34 lines. Headlines in roman type. A wood-cut of the Evangelist appears before each Gospel, and there are smaller cuts before Romans and 2 Timothy. The volume contains many misprints.

¶ 184 × 136 mm. Imperfect: wanting title and 11 following leaves, ¹A 2 to 8, ¹M 7, ²I 3, and ²P 8 to the last leaf ²R 8 ;—38 ff. in all. The blank leaf after Acts (V 6) is also missing. The title and the leaves of text are supplied in facsimile. ¹A 1 and ²N 1, which are mutilated, are completed in facsimile. [F. F.]

The only other copy now known is the fine perfect copy in St. Paul's Cathedral Library, from which the collation given above has been made. Cotton (p. 16) mentions a copy in the Bodleian, but Fry was unable to find it there in 1868.

27.

1539. (The New Testament.)

T. Petyt, for T. Berthelet: London. [1539.] 8°. 𝕭.𝕷.

Taverner's version.

DESCRIPTION. [Title and preliminary leaves unknown.] The text, ff. i to cccv (R 1) *b* (Acts ends on Clxxv—Y 7, and is followed by one leaf—probably blank ; Romans begins a new set of signatures) ; followed by the Old Testament Epistles *after the vse of Salysbury* —ff. cccvi to cccxix (S 7), and . . . . *the Table wherin ye shall fynde the Epystles & the Gospels after the vse of Salysbury*—17 pp., ending on T 8 *a* with the colophon : *Imprynted at London in Paules churche yearde, at the sygne of the Maydens heed, by Thomas Petyt, for Thomas Berthelet, Prynter to the Kynges Grace. Cvm privilegio ad imprimendvm solvm*, verso blank. Lewis (p. 134) quotes the title of a Taverner Testament of 1539, and mentions a Kalendar at the beginning ; but he does not give the size of the edition. Herbert (p. 553) evidently understood it to be the octavo edition.
Signatures : [—], A–Y⁸, A–T⁸ ; [—] + 328 ff. Only the first leaf in each sheet is signed. A full page contains 36 lines. Headlines in roman type. Marginal references.

¶ 142 × 90 mm. A fragment of seven leaves only : —ff. 109 (two impressions), 110 (two impressions), 112, 117 and 118. [F. F.]

The collation given was made from probably the only copy extant, formerly in the collection of the Earl of Ashburnham, and now in the possession of the Rev. R. Lovett. It is apparently the identical copy described by Herbert, and by Cotton (p. 335).

28.

1540. The Byble | in Englyshe, that is to saye, | the content of all the holye | scrypture, bothe of the olde | and newe Testament, truly | translated after the veryte | of the Hebrue and Greke | textes, by the diligent stu- | dye of dyuers excellent | lerned men, experte | in the foresayde tongues. | Prynted at

London by Thomas | Petyt, and Roberte Redman, for | Thomas Berthelet : Prynter | vnto the Kynges grace. | Cum Priuilegio ad impri- | mendum solum. | 1540.

f°. 𝕭.𝕷.

Great Bible version.

A re-issue (dated April, 1540) in smaller size of the Great Bible of 1539. It is not an exact reprint, for the text shows traces of correction and revision.

DESCRIPTION. Four preliminary leaves: title (in black and red, within woodcut border), on verso *An Almanacke for . xxx . yeres* (1540–68); *The Kalender, The names of all the bokes of the Byble* . . . . and *A prologue, expressynge* . . .—5 pp.; 1 p. blank. The text, divided into three parts: (1) Genesis–Job, ff. j to ccxiiij (dd 8) *b*; (2) Psalms–Malachi and Apocrypha, ff. i to CC.xxvij (really 226, Fff 6) *b*; (3) N. T., with title: *The newe Te- | stament in Englysshe after the | last recognicion and settynge | forth of Erasmus, contey- | nynge these bokes. | The Gospels* . . . . (within border), verso blank, text—ff. ij to C.ij (really 110, NNn 6) *b*; the table of Epistles and Gospels *vsually red in the chyrch, after Salysbury vse*—2 ff., ending on NN 8 *b* with the colophon: *The ende of the newe Testament: and of the whole Byble. Finisshed in Apryll. Anno M.CCCCC.XL. Imprynted at London by Robert Redman, and Thomas Petyt, for Thomas Berthelet: Prynter vnto the Kynges Grace. Cvm privilegio ad imprimendvm solvm.* Signatures : ✠⁴, A–K⁸ L⁶ M–Z⁸ aa–dd⁸, Aa–Rr⁸ Ss⁸ Tt⁶ Vv–Zz⁸ Aaa–Eee⁸ Fff⁶, AAa–NNn⁸ (with extra sheet HHh‡⁸ before HHh); 556 ff. Text printed in double columns, with 57 lines to the full column. No subject-headings in the headlines after 1 Esdras (Ezra). Words not found in the original are printed in roman type. References, pointing hands etc., in the margins, as in the 1539 edition. The list of books in the preliminary matter is directly copied from that in the 1539 edition, and accordingly divides the text into five parts. Similarly the second part of this edition (beginning with the Psalter) has the following incongruous title at the head of the first column: *The thyrd part of the Byble conteynyng these Bokes. The Psalter* . . . . *Malachy.* The Apocrypha begins on C.xliij *a* with a similar title: *The volume of the Bokes called Hagiographa* . . . .; though the Prologue stands on the preceding page immediately after Malachi. It appears from its unusual signature and duplicated foliation (57–64) that one sheet (containing Acts xiii to end) had been at first accidentally omitted in printing the New Testament. An odd mistake occurs at the end of the Almanacke: *The yeare . . . hath in all, thre hundred and . lvi. dayes and syxe houres.*

The woodcut border to the general and N. T. titles is the same as that used for the title of the Coverdale Bible of 1535, except that the legends here are in Latin, instead of in English. No other woodcuts occur, except a few ornaments and large initials.

¶ 324 × 213 mm.

Inserted at the beginning is a genuine copy of an Admonition, issued by Bishop Bonner when he 'set up Six Bibles in certain convenient places of St. Paul's Church,' after the King's proclamation in May, 1540 (*cf.* Westcott, *History*, p. 81).

An admonicion and aduertisement

geuen by the Bysshop of London, to all readers of thys Byble in thenglyshe tounge.

To thentent that a good and wholsome thynge, godlye and verteously (for honest entētes and purposes) set forth for many : be not hyndered, or malynged at, for the abuse, defaute and euel behaueour of a fewe. Who for lacke of dyscrecion and good aduisement commonlye (wythout respect of tyme or other dewe circumstaunces) procede rashly and vnaduysedly therin. And by reason therof rather hynder, then set forwarde the thynge that is good of it selfe.

It shall therfore be very expedyent that whosoeuer repayreth hether to reade thys booke (or any soche lyke in any other place) he prepare hym selfe chefelye and principally wyth all deuocion, humilite and quyetnes, to be edefyed and made the better therby. Adioynynge therevnto his perfect and most bounden duetye of obedyence to the Kynges maiestye our moost gracious and drad soueraygne Lorde & supreme heade : especiallye in accomplysshynge hys graces moost honorable iniunctions and comaundementes geuen and made in that behalfe.

And ryght expedient, yee, necessarye it shalbe also that leauynge behynde hym vayne glorye, hypocresie, and all other carnall and corrupt affeccyons : he brynge with hym discrecion, honest intent, charyte, reuerence & quyet behaueour : to and for the edifycacyon of hys awne soule, wythout the hinderaunce, let, or disturbaunce of any other his christen brother. Euermore forseynge, that no nombre of people be specyallye congregate therfore, to make a multitude. And that no exposition be made thervpon, otherwyse then it is declared in yᵉ boke it selfe. And that especiall regarde be had, that no readinge therof be vsed (alowde & wyth noyes) in the tyme of any deuyne seruice or sermonde: or that in the same there be vsed any disputacion, contēcion, or any other mysdemeanour. Or finallye that any man iustlye maye reken him selfe to be offended therby, or take occasyon to grudge or maligne therat.

✠

God saue the Kynge.

The first titlepage bears the signature *Wm. Herbert*. [F. F.]

—— Another copy.

315 × 210 mm. Imperfect: wanting the general title and two following leaves of preliminary matter, and the last two leaves in the book; all of which are supplied in facsimile.

29.

1540. The Byble in | Englyshe, that is to saye the con- | tēt of al the holy scrypture, both | of yᵉ olde, and newe testamēt, with | a prologe therinto, made by | the reuerende father in | God, Thomas | archbysshop | of Cantor | bury, | This is the Byble apoynted | to the vse of the churches. | Prynted by Edward whytchurche | Cum priuilegio ad imprimendum solum. | M. D. xl.
f°. 𝕭. 𝕷.

The second edition (April, 1540) of the Great Bible. The earliest containing Cranmer's Prologue, and bearing on the first title the words *This is the Byble apoynted to the vse of the churches.*

This edition represents Coverdale's continued revision-work on the text of the Bible, and shows the further influence of Münster's Latin O. T., especially in the Prophets, and of Erasmus in the N. T.

In general appearance, typography, etc., this closely resembles the first edition.

DESCRIPTION. Ten preliminary leaves: title (in black and red, within woodcut border), verso blank, *The Kalender* with an *Almanacke for . xviii . yeares* (1540-57)—2 ff., *An exhortacyon* . . .—1 p., *The summe and content* . . .—2 pp., *A prologue, expressynge* . . .—1 p., *A descripcyon and successe* . . .—1 f., *A prologue or preface made by the moost reuerende father in God, Thomas Archbyshop of Canturbury Metropolytan and Prymate of Englande* (ending with *God saue the kynge*, and two pairs of initials H R—one small, the other large and flourished)—3 ff., *The names of all the bookes* . . . —1 p., 1 p. blank. The text, divided into five parts, each with separate foliation, as in the 1539 edition. The colophon reads: *The ende of the newe Testament: and of the whole Byble, Fynisshed in Apryll, Anno . M.CCCCC.XL. A dño factū est istud.*
Signatures: ✱⁶ ✠⁴, . . . etc. (as in the first edition); 534 ff. A full column contains 62 lines.
The general and N. T. titles have the Holbein border. The borders to the titles of pts. 2, 3, and 4 are each composed of 16 woodblocks (one block on the Apocrypha titlepage represents a madman astride a hobbyhorse). There are a few very large initial letters; that before Romans (86 × 87 mm.) contains the initials E. W.
An error (generally corrected in later editions) occurs near the beginning of Cranmer's Prologue: . . . *some there are that be to slowe, and nede not the spurre* . . . (for . . . *nede the spurre* . . .).
In some copies (*e.g.* that in the John Rylands Library), the general title bears the name of *Rychard Grafton* as the printer, and differs slightly in other respects from that described above.

¶ 399 × 269 mm. The general title is mounted; and one leaf, ✱ 5, which was mutilated, has been carefully restored. [F. F.]

The B. M. possesses a magnificent copy, printed on vellum and illuminated. This was presented to Henry VIII by *Anthonye Marler of London haberdassher*, who appears to have defrayed the expense of these editions of the Great Bible (*cf.* Anderson, vol. ii. p. 142).

30.

1540. The Byble in | Englyshe, that is to saye the con- | tēt of al the holy scrypture, both | of yᵉ olde, and newe testamēt, with | a prologe therinto, made by | the reuerende father in | God, Thomas | archbysshop | of Cantor | bury, | This is the Byble apoynted | to the vse of the churches. | Prynted by Rychard Grafton. | Cum priuilegio ad imprimendum solum. | M . D . xl.

f°. 𝕭.𝕷.

The third Great Bible (July 1540); and the second with Cranmer's Prologue.

The text mainly follows that of the second edition, though it contains a number of minute variations.

> DESCRIPTION. [Ten] preliminary leaves: title (in black and red, within border), verso blank, *The Kalender* with *Almanacke for . xviii . yeares* (1540-57)—2 ff., [*qu.* three more leaves, as in the preceding edition?] *A prologue or preface* . . . (ending with two flourished initials H R)—3 ff., *The names of all the bookes* . . . —1 p., 1 p. blank. The text, arranged as in the first edition. The colophon reads: *The ende of the newe Testament: and of the whole Byble, Fynisshed in July. Anno . M.CCCCC.XL. A domino factum est istud This is the Lordes doynge.*
> Signatures: ★⁷⁶ ✠⁴, . . . etc., as before; 534 (?) ff. A full column contains 62 lines.
> The general and N. T. titles have the Holbein border. The titles to pts. 2, 3 and 4 have borders composed of 16 woodblocks. The large initial letter before Romans is without E W.
> Fry notes two errors: (1) in the Apocrypha, fo. 37 *b*, 1st col., l. 57, after *vanitie* this sentence is omitted: *Now he that loueth parell, shall perish therin*; (2) in Romans ii A. (fo. 61) *the kyngdome of God* for *the kyndnes of God.*

¶ 403 × 273 mm. Perfect, according to Fry's collation; but it is probable that there should be, not three but six leaves in the first sheet (as in the April edition), though both the B. M. and Rylands copies (otherwise perfect) lack leaves ★ 4 to 6. Possibly ★ 4 was blank, and completed the sheet. Half of the last leaf has been carefully restored; and the first title is mounted. The blank leaf (Q 4) at the end of pt. 2 is missing. Several sheets are rather smaller than the bulk of the book, and may have belonged to another copy.

[F. F.]
31.

1540. The newe testament in | englyshe, translated after the texte of Master Eras- | mus of Roterodame : in anno | M . D . xl. | Let the worde of Christ dwell in you plen- | teously in all wysdome. | Collos. iii. c | Prynted by Rychard Grafton, and | Edward Whytchurche. | Cum priuilegio ad imprimendum solum.

4°. 𝕭.𝕷.

Great Bible version.

> DESCRIPTION. Four preliminary leaves: title (in black and red, without border), on verso *Almanacke for . xix . yeares* (1540-55), *The Kalender*—3 ff. The text, ff. i to ccxlii (really 240, GG 8) *a*; *A Table to fynde the Epistles and Gospels vsually red in the chyrche, after Salysbury vse* . . . —11 pp., [1 f., probably blank.]
> Signatures: ★⁴, A-Z⁸ AA-GG⁸ HH⁶; 250 ff. A full page contains 39 lines. Marginal references.

¶ 204 × 153 mm. A fragment of 6 leaves only: z 3, 4 and 5, and AA 2, 3 and 4. A facsimile of the titlepage is inserted. In an envelope accompanying this fragment are enclosed :—collations of the text of these 6 leaves with that of various Bibles and Testaments of the same period, by F. Fry and N. Pocock; a transcript of *A prayer for the reader* . . . at the beginning of an octavo edition issued by the same printers in 1539; and photographs of the titlepage and one page of text (h 1 *a*) of the same Testament, taken from a copy at Wolfenbüttel. [F. F.]

The copy in Lambeth Library, from which the above collation was made, belonged to W. Herbert.

32.

1540. Here | begynneth | the Prouerbes of | Salomon. | Wherunto is added | dyuers other Bookes of | the Byble. Uery good | and profytable for | euery Chrysten | man for to | knowe. | Prynted in the yeare of | our Lorde. | 1540.
R. Redman: London. 8°. 𝔅.𝔏.

Great Bible version.

A small octavo edition containing the books of Proverbs, Ecclesiastes, the Song of Solomon, Wisdom, and Ecclesiasticus.

It has been stated (Cotton, p. 17) that this is one part of a five-volume edition of Matthew's Bible. But, as this is the only 'part' known to exist, and two of its books are taken from the Apocrypha, it is evidently a separate publication. Moreover, the text, where examined, does not follow Matthew's Bible (1537), but agrees very closely with the Great Bible version, in the edition issued by T. Petyt and R. Redman, April 1540.

DESCRIPTION. One preliminary leaf: title (within woodcut frame), on verso *The contentis of this Booke. The Prouerbes of Salomon. Ecclesiast. The boke of the precher. Cantica Canticorvm. The Ballet of Ballettes. Liber Sapientie. The Boke of wysdome. Ecclesiasti. The Boke of Jesus Syrac. The nomber of the Chapiters of euery Boke.* . . . The text, A 2 to V 6 b; followed by one leaf containing on recto, in large type: *Here endeth the boke of Jesus, the Sonne of Sirache, which is called in Latine Ecclesiasticus. Finis huius libri*; and on verso the colophon: *Imprynted at London in Flete Strete, by me Robert Redmā dwelling within the Temple Barre at the sygne of the George next vnto Saynte Dunstanes church Anno Domini, M.DDDDDXL.* The last leaf (V 8) contains on recto Redman's device, a flourished Gothic R in white on a black ground; verso blank. (So Lea Wilson, p. 289.)
Signatures: A–V⁸; 160 ff. The leaves are not numbered. A full page contains 34 lines. The headlines are in roman capitals. Short summaries precede each chapter, and references are given in the margins. The explanatory headings (*The voyce of the Churche, The spousesse to her cōpanyons,* etc.) are inserted throughout *The Ballet of Ballettes,* as in Matthew's and Taverner's Bibles.

¶ 128 × 86 mm. Imperfect: wanting B 1 and 2, and the last two leaves V 7 and 8.
On the flyleaf are written in a contemporary hand a number of texts chosen out of the volume, and beneath, in another hand, *hæ sententiæ collectæ & scriptæ fuerunt per Thomam Lathumum patrem meum manu sua propria. Tho: Lathum.* On the titlepage in the second handwriting is the inscription *Sum Thomæ Lathumi eiusque Amicorum Liber. 1575. aⁿ Reginæ Elizabeth: xvij°.*
[F. F.]
33.

1541. The Byble in | Englyshe of the largest and grea-| test volume, auctorised and apoynted | by the commaundement of oure moost | redoubted prynce and soueraygne Lorde, | Kynge Henrye the .viii. supreme head | of this his churche and realme of | Englande: to be frequented and | vsed in euery church w'in this his | sayd realme, accordynge to the | tenoure of hys former In-| iunctions geuen in | that behalfe. | Ouersene and perused at the cō-|maundemēt of the kynges hyghnes, | by the ryght reuerende fathers in God | Cuthbert bysshop of Duresme, and Ni-|colas bisshop of Rochester. | Printed by Rycharde Grafton. | Cum priuilegio ad imprimendum solum. | 1541.

f°. 𝔅.𝔏.

The fourth Great Bible (Nov. 1540); and the third with Cranmer's prologue.

The colophon gives the date Nov. 1540, but the publication seems to have been delayed, as the titlepage bears the date 1541, and is the same as that used for the Great Bible of Nov. 1541.

Though this edition claims to be *ouersene and perused* by Bishops Tunstall (1474–1559) and Heath (1501?–1578), the text shows no sign of careful revision; indeed in many parts it approximates more closely to that of 1539 than to that of April or July 1540. This and the Nov. 1541 edition, though printed in the same style as the five other Great Bibles, have a slightly longer page, which contains 65, instead of 62, lines in a full column.

DESCRIPTION. Six preliminary leaves: title (in black and red, within woodcut border), on verso *The names of all the bokes* . . . , *The Kalender* with *Almanacke for . xviii . yeares* (1540-57)—2 ff., *A Prologue or preface* . . . (ending with two flourished initials H R)—3 ff. The text, arranged as before in five parts:—(1) ff. i to lxxij (i 8) *b*; (2) with title (within border), verso blank, text—ff. ii to cviij (O 4) *a*, verso blank; (3) with title (within border), verso blank, text—ff. ii to cxvi (PP 4) *a*, verso blank; (4) with title (within border), verso blank, text—ff. ii to lxxij (really 70, Iii 6) *b*; (5) with title (within border), verso blank, text—ff. ii to xcij (really 91, Mm 5) *a*. On Mm 5 *b* begins *A table to find* . . . ; this ends on Mm 6 *b* with colophon : *The ende of the newe Testamente and of the whole Byble. Fynyshed in Nouember Anno. MCCCCC . XL. A d̃no factū est istud*.

Signatures: ✶⁶, a–i⁸, A–N⁸ O⁴, AA–OO⁸ PP⁴, Aaa–Hhh⁸ Iii⁶, Aa–Kk⁸ Ll⁶ Mm⁶; 464 ff. A full column contains 65 lines.

The general title and the N. T. title have the Holbein border. From this the arms of Cromwell now disappear; they have been cut out of the block, leaving a blank circle 22 mm. in diameter below Cromwell's figure. (He had been executed in July, 1540.) The titles to pts. 2, 3 and 4 are enclosed within borders, each composed of 16 woodblocks.

The words *and lyfe for euermore* are omitted at the end of Psalm cxxxiii.

In some copies of this edition the name of E. Whitchurch appears on the general title as printer, instead of R. Grafton.

¶ 406 × 275 mm., with the original rough edges to some of the leaves. The 'standard' copy used by Fry in his work on these editions. According to his MS. note, it contains all the 'genuine and correct' Nov. 1540 leaves, except 8 in pt. 1, viz. ff. 65 to 72, which are variant leaves. The eight 'correct' leaves are found in the copy described below, containing the 'reprints.' [F. F.]

—— Another copy.

Fry's 'Nov. 1540 with Reprints.' The following leaves in pt. 5 (New Testament) are reprinted with differences :—ff. 34 to 39, 41 to 72, 81 to 90 (numbered 91), and 92 (the last leaf); and ff. 108 and 109 in pt. 3 are variant leaves; 51 leaves in all.

397 × 271 mm. The general title (bearing R. Grafton's name) has been mounted. A second copy of the titleleaf to pt. 5 is inserted. [F. F.]

—— Another copy.

This copy contains the two variant leaves, and all the reprinted leaves, found in the immediately preceding copy, except fo. 92 in pt. 5. Four leaves, ff. 49, 51, 54 and 56 in pt. 4, belong to the Nov. 1541 edition.

385 × 260 mm. Imperfect: wanting general title and other preliminary leaves; fo. 1 in pt. 1; the titleleaves of pts. 3 and 4; and the last two leaves in the volume. A few leaves are mutilated. Sheets Ii and Kk in pt. 5 are misplaced, coming before sheets Ff, Gg and Hh.

—— Another copy.

'A most remarkable mixed copy, containing parts of all the seven editions, the two November reprints, some variations I have before described, and some new variations' (MS. note by Fry). A full MS. collation is inserted in the volume, giving the edition (according to Fry's tests) to which each leaf belongs.

382 × 251 mm. Imperfect: wanting general title and other preliminary leaves, and last leaf in the volume. The missing leaves are supplied in facsimile (following the Nov. 1540 edition). Three leaves only (ff. 19, 22 and 91 in pt. 5) were inserted by Fry. All the others, representing every large folio edition of the Great Bible, were found thus mixed together in the volume when bought by him. [F. F.]

34.

1541. The Byble in | Englysh, that is to saye the content | of all the holy scrypture, both of the | olde and newe Testament with a | Prologe thereinto made by | the reuerende father in | God, Thomas | archebyshop | of Cantor | bury. | This is the Byble appoynted | to the vse of yᵉ churches | Prynted by Edwarde Whitchurch | Cum priuilegio ad imprimendum solum. | Finished the . xxviii . daye of Maye. | Anno Domini, | M. D. XLI.

f°. 𝕭. 𝕷.

The fifth Great Bible (May, 1541); and the fourth with Cranmer's Prologue.

In this, as in the preceding edition, the revision of the text appears to have been very slight.

In April 1541 Anthony Marler received permission to sell copies of the Great Bible *unbound for x s. sterling, and bound, being trimmed with bullyons, for xii s. sterling* (equivalent to about £6 and £7 5s. to-day). And in the next month a royal proclamation announced the heavy penalties to which each parish was liable which failed to provide its church with a copy by the November following. (*Cf.* Anderson, vol. ii. pp. 142-3.)

DESCRIPTION. Six preliminary leaves, as in the Nov. 1540 edition. Text, etc., as in the other editions with 62 lines to the full column. The colophon reads: *The ende of the newe Testament: and of the whole Byble, Fynysshed in Maye, Anno M.CCCCC.XLi. A dño factū est istud.*
Signatures: ✱¹ ✱ ✱², . . . etc., as before; 530 ff.
According to Fry there are no pointing hands in the margin or text.
The general title and N. T. title are enclosed within the Holbein border with Cromwell's arms erased. The titles to pts. 2, 3 and 4 each have a border composed of 16 woodblocks.
The 'variations' in this edition are:—two varieties of the list of books on the back of the general title; pt. 2, fo. 117; pt. 5, ff. 12 and 13. Slight variations have also been found in copies of the general title, the second leaf of the Prologue, and the N. T. title (Fry's *Description*, p. 16.)

¶ 398 × 273 mm. Contains one variant leaf, fo. 117 in pt. 2. [F. F.]

—— Another copy.

376 × 255 mm. Imperfect: wanting general title and two following leaves; pt. 3, title-leaf; pt. 5, fo. 40 and last leaf of the volume;—6 ff. in all.
The following leaves belong to other editions: To the 1539 edition—pt. 2, fo. 33; pt. 3, fo. 50; pt. 5, titleleaf and ff. 12, 13, 32, 62 to 74, 76 to 80, 89 to 91, and 94 to end. To the April 1540 edition—pt. 5, ff. 92 and 93. To the Dec. 1541 edition—the first leaf of Prologue, and pt. 1, ff. 11 to 14. As a general titleleaf is inserted a specimen of the 1539 pt. 4 title, with the centre cut out, and a quasi-facsimile from the Dec. 1541 title put in its place.

—— Another copy.

378 × 240 mm. Imperfect: wanting general title and two following leaves; pt. 1, fo. 81 and last leaf (84); pt. 3, fo. 17; pt. 5, titleleaf, ff. 8 and 100 to the end (the last 5 leaves)—13 ff. in all. Many leaves at the beginning and end are mutilated.
Two of the variant leaves, viz. pt. 5, ff. 12 and 13, occur in this copy. The following leaves belong to other editions: To the April 1540 edition—one leaf of preliminary matter (*A descripcyon and successe* . . .); pt. 1, ff. 66 and 71; pt. 3, ff. 18, 23, 49 and 56. To the July 1540 edition—pt. 3, ff. 50 and 55. To the Dec. 1541 edition—five leaves of preliminary matter (containing the Prologue, *An exhortacyon* . . . and first page of *The summe and content* . . ., and *The names of all the bookes* . . .); pt. 3, ff. 24, 51 and 54; pt. 4, ff. 1 to 80 (the whole of the Apocrypha); pt. 5, ff. 59 and 62.

35.

1541. The Byble in | Englyshe of the largest and grea- | test volume, auctorysed and apoynted | by the commaundemente of oure moost | re-doubted Prynce, and soueraygne Lorde | Kynge Henrye the . viii . supreme heade | of this his churche and Realme of | Englande: to be frequented and | vsed in euery churche w'in this his | sayd realme, accordynge to the | tenour of his former In- | iunctions geuen in | that behalfe. | Ouersene and perused at the cō- | maundemēt of the kynges hyghnes, | by the ryghte reuerende fathers in God | Cuthbert bysshop of Duresme, and Ni- | colas bisshop of Rochester. | Printed by Edwarde Whitchurch. | Cum priuilegio ad impri-mendum solum. | 1541.

f°. 𝔅. 𝔏.

The sixth Great Bible (Nov. 1541); and the fifth Bible with Cranmer's Prologue.

DESCRIPTION. Six preliminary leaves, text, etc., as in the Nov. 1540 edition. The colophon reads: *The ende of the newe Testament and of the whole Byble. Fynyshed in Nouember. ·Anno .M.CCCCC.XLJ. A dño factū est istud.* Signatures etc. as in the Nov. 1540 edition. A full column contains 65 lines.

The general and N. T. titles have the Holbein border with Cromwell's arms erased; the titles to pts. 2, 3 and 4 are enclosed within borders composed of 16 woodblocks.

The general title, the Prologue, and fo. 86 in pt. 3, according to Fry, are common to this edition and that of Nov. 1540.

A general title is found in some copies bearing the name of R. Grafton (the same as that which appears in the first two copies of the Nov. 1540 edition, described above).

¶ 384 × 267 mm. [F. F.]

—— Another copy.

Fry's 'Nov. 1541, with Reprints.' The following leaves are reprinted with differences: pt. 1, ff. 65, 66, 71 and 72; pt. 2, ff. 57, 64 to 67, 70 to 108; pt. 3, ff. 41 to 43, 46 to 104, 106 to 110, 113, 115; pt. 4, ff. 57 to 70; pt. 5, title, and ff. 25 to 27, 30 to 87, 89, 90, 92;—in all 196 different leaves. The general title is that described as 'Variation Nov. 1541' in Fry's book; it bears the name of E. Whitchurch, differs slightly in the setting-up of the type, and has verso blank. (Apparently Fry inserted it in this copy.) The N. T. title also differs slightly from that usually occurring in this edition. Two lines omitted at the top of fo. 57 in pt. 4 (where the reprinted leaves in the Apocrypha begin) are printed on a slip and pasted at the bottom of the last column of fo. 56.

401 × 266 mm. The general titleleaf, which was mutilated, has been carefully restored.

[F. F.]
36.

1541. The Byble in | Englyshe, that is to saye the con-|tent of all the holy scrypture, both | of the olde & newe testament with | a prologe therinto, made by | the reuerende father in | God, Thomas | archebysshop | of Cantor-| bury. | This is the Byble appoynted | to the vse of the churches | Printed by Rycharde Grafton ¦ Cum priuilegio ad imprimendum solum. | An. do. M.D.xl.

f°. 𝔅. 𝔏.

The seventh Great Bible (Dec. 1541), the last of the 1539–41 series; and the sixth with Cranmer's Prologue.

The colophon gives the date Dec. 1541.

DESCRIPTION. Ten preliminary leaves: title (in black and red, within woodcut border), verso blank, *The Kalender* with *Almanacke* . . . —2 ff., *An exhortacyon* . . .—1 p., *The summe and content* . . . —2 pp., *A Prologue, expressynge* . . . —1 p., *A description and successe* . . . —1 f., *A prologue or preface* . . . (with two large flourished initials H R at the end)—3 ff., *The names of all the bookes* . . . —1 p., verso blank. The text, arranged as in the four similar editions. The colophon reads: *The ende of the newe Testament, and of the whole Bible, Finysshed in December. Anno. M.CCCCC.XLi. A domino factum est istud. This is the Lordes doynge.*

Signatures: ✱ ⁶ ✠⁴, . . . etc., as before; 534 ff. A full column contains 62 lines. A very few pointing hands.

The general and N. T. titles have the Holbein border, with Cromwell's arms erased. Those to pts. 2, 3 and 4 have borders composed of 16 woodblocks. The large initial P occurs before Romans.

According to Fry, four leaves in pt. 3—ff. 28, 92, 93 and 124—are common to this edition and that of July 1540. Very slight variations are found in some leaves. Some copies have another general title, exactly like that described above, except that *Edward Withchurch* is substituted for Richard Grafton.

¶ 393 × 266 mm. Inserted at the beginning is a genuine copy of the centre of the alternative general title, mentioned above. [F. F.]
37.

1545? The Epi- | stles and Gospelles wyth a brief | Postil vpon the same from Aduent | tyll Lowe sondaye whiche is the | (Wynter parte) drawen | forth by diuerse learned | men for the singuler | cōmoditie of all | good christen | persons | and namely of Prestes and | Curates newly re- | cognized. | Cum priuilegio ad impri- | mendum solum. *Etc.*

Rycharde Bankes: London. 1545? 4°. 𝖁.𝕷.

A volume of sermons on the Liturgical Epistles and Gospels, with the text; edited by R. Taverner.

According to J. Holmes (Brit. Mag. vol. xxix. p. 361) the original draft of this work is contained in a MS. (Harl. MSS. 6561) now in the British Museum. It is a translation, believed to have been made by Henry Parker Lord Morley, for the use of his kinswoman Anne Boleyn, and to have been presented by him to her, when Marchioness of Pembroke, in 1532. Taverner alludes in his preface to a certain *brefe postil*, which had been placed in his hands, as the basis of the volume; and states that he revised and augmented it with the aid of *other sobre men*. Two of the sermons were adopted by Archbishop Parker, and published in the second book of Homilies.

A modern reprint was issued by the Oxford University Press in 1841, edited with a preface by E. Cardwell.

DESCRIPTION. (1) (Winter part) title (within woodcut border), on verso *The copy of the kinges graciovs privilege, Rycharde Tauerner clerke of the Signet to our soueraigne lorde the kynge wyssheth to the christen reader* . . . —1 f., *A table of the Exhortacions* . . . —2 ff. Text, First Sunday in Advent–St. Athanasius' Creed, ff. i to cliiii (really 155, Qq iii) *b*, ending with colophon: *Imprynted at London by Rycharde Bankes, and are to be solde in Powles churche yarde by Thomas Petyt. Cum priuilegio* . . ., 1 f. blank.

Signatures: [unsigned]⁴, A–Z⁴ Aa–Qq⁴; 160 ff.

(2) (Summer part) (*a*), title: *The Epi- | stles and Gospelles with a brief Po- | stil vpon the same from after Easter | tyll Aduent, which is the Somer | parte, set forth for the singuler | cōmoditie of all good chri- | sten men and namely | of Prestes and | Curates | Roma. i. . . . Cum priuilegio* . . . (within border), on verso begins *The preface of Richarde Tauerner to the reader* . . .—2 pp., *A table of the exhortacions* . . .—5 pp. Text, First Sunday after Easter–Wednesday in Whitsun week, ff. i to lxx (really 72, S 4) *b*, ending with colophon: *Imprinted at London by Rychard Bankes. Cum priuilegio* . . . (*b*), title: *The Epi-|stles and Gospels with a brief Po-|styll vpon the same from Trinitie | sonday tyll Aduent, drawen forthe | by diuers learned men for the sin-|guler cōmoditie of al good chri | stians and namely of Pre-|stes and Curates. | Christus Mat. iiij . . . Cum priuilegio ad impri-|mendum solum* (within border), on verso *The copy of the kinges graciovs privilege.* Text, Corpus Christi Day–The Twenty-fifth Sunday after Trinity, ff. lxvij (R ij) to Clxxxvj (&& iij) *b*, ending with colophon: *Imprinted at London by Richarde Bankes, and solde in Fletestrete at the sygne of the whyte Harte by Anthony Clerke. Cum priuilegio* . . . , 1 f. blank.

Signatures: [unsigned]⁴, A–S⁴; R–Z⁴ Aa–Zz⁴ &&⁴; 76 + 124 = 200 ff.

(3) (Holy Days) Begins: *The Gospels with | brief sermons vpon them for | all the holy dayes in the | yere.* St. Andrew's Day–At Buryings, ff. i to lxiii (really 64, hh 8) *b*, ending with colophon: *Imprinted in London by Rychard Bankes, and are to be soulde in Paules church yarde. Cum priuilegio* . . .

Signatures: aa–hh⁸; 64 ff.

Total number of leaves—424.

A full page contains 32 lines.

The woodcut border used for the titlepages of parts 1 and 2 (*a*) is the frame containing the initials H H, and representing below the story of Mutius and Porsenna. That employed for the titlepage of part 2 (*b*) is composed of four ornamental blocks.

The above collation is taken from the copy C. 10. a. 5. in the B. M. There are many varieties of the book, which read generally with one another, but differ in many small particulars. It is probable that the sections, each of which has a distinct colophon, were at first issued separately, but subsequently combined to form a complete volume. Some copies are mixed; e.g. in the B. M. copy mentioned a large section of (1) and all the second part of (2) belong to an impression in which the headlines, marginal matter, and Bible text are printed in roman type instead of black-letter.

The date is uncertain. A title to the first portion of the Summer part, found in what is probably the earliest issue of the book, bears the date 1540. It has on verso *The copy of the kynges graciouse priuilege*, and is placed with seven following leaves, containing the sermon on the Resurrection, immediately before sheet A. In subsequent editions this title is dropped, and the sermon is inserted near the end of pt. 1. Pt. 3 cannot have been published before 1542, since in the sermon *On the day of weddyng* there is an allusion to an *acte of parlimēt made in the . xxxii . yeare of the reygne of our mooste drad Soueraygne lorde the kyng that now is Henry the eyght*. Probably the complete book, in the form above described, was published about 1545.

¶ 203 × 142 mm. Imperfect: wanting in (1) eight leaves at the beginning, and the last leaf (blank); all (2); and the last sheet in (3). It exactly agrees with the copy C. 10. a. 5. in the B. M. The sheets B–L in (1) belong to an impression in which the headlines etc. are printed in roman type. [F. F.]

38.

—— ANOTHER EDITION.

With headlines, etc., in roman type.

¶ A fragment, containing only sheets B–L in (1) mentioned above. [F. F.]

39.

ACCESSION OF KING EDWARD VI: 28 JANUARY 1547.

1547. The new testa | ment in Englyshe | accordyng to the trā | slacion of the great | Byble. | Imprynted at London in | Fletstrete at the sy-|gne of the Sunne | ouer against the | cōduyt, by Ed | ward Whit | churche. | 1547.

8°. 𝕭. 𝕷.

Great Bible version.

This appears to be the earliest edition of Scripture printed in the reign of Edward VI, and the only issue in the year 1547. (W. Powell's diglot Testament is dated in the colophon 1547, but on the title-page 1548.)

DESCRIPTION. Sixteen preliminary leaves: title (in black and red, within woodcut border), on verso *An Almanacke for . xxv . yeres* (1546–70), *The Kalendar*—8 ff.; *A Table for the foure Euāgelistes, wherin thou maist lightly fynde any story contayned in them . . . in four sections* :—*S. Mathew*—3 ff., *S. Marke*—3 pp., *S. Luke*—5 pp., *S. Jhon*— 3 pp., *Here foloweth the Actes of the Apostles*—5 pp.; *A compendious and brief rehersall of all the contentes of the bokes of the newe testamente* (in rhyming couplets) —1 f. The text, a i to R 4 a ; *A table to fynde the Epistles and Gospelles vsuallye red in the Churche, after Salisbury vse* . . . —6 pp., ending on R 7 a ; on verso, the colophon : *Imprynted at Londō | in Flete strete at the sy-|gne of the Sunne ouer a-| gainst the Cōduit by Ed | warde whitchurche | the first day of De | cember. | M.D.XLVII. | Cum priuilegio ad impri- |mendum solum* ; 1 f. (probably blank). Signatures : ✠⁸ †⁸, a–z⁸ A–R⁸; 336 ff. Leaves not numbered. A full page contains 36 lines. No prologues, chapter-contents, or notes. References in the margins.

There are two serious typographical errors in this edition: (1) N 8 b (2 Pet. iii) ends with the words . . . *the daye of God, by* [*whom* omitted] *the heauens* (catchword *shall*), and on the next page (O i a) the printer repeats 20 lines of text from *the heauens & yearth whyche are now . . . to . . . the day of God, by whō the heauens*; (2) O 8 b (Rev. i) ends . . *I Jhon your brother, and cōpanion in tri* (catchword *bula-*), and the next page begins *and the seuen golden candlestickes* . . . , omitting eleven verses (about a page of text).

The titleborder contains a small tablet at the base bearing the initials N H. No illustrations. An initial A contains the letters I R.

¶ 144 × 95 mm. Wanting only the last leaf, probably blank.

Apparently unique; perhaps the impression was withdrawn, owing to the above-mentioned errors.

On the titlepage are written in an early hand the words *I pray you be good to this poore man the bearer hereof*. [F. F.]

40.

1547. N. T. 4°. See 1548.

1548. The Newe | Testa- | ment | in Englishe and in | Latin | Novvm Testamen- | tvm Anglice et | Latine. | Anno Dñi. 1548.
William Powell: London. 1548,47. 4°. 𝕭. 𝕷.

The second edition of the diglot of Tindale's version of the New Testament in English, with the Latin of Erasmus.

Fry's No. 16. Closely resembling the first issue, printed by R. Redman in 1538. Dated 1547 in colophon.

DESCRIPTION. One preliminary leaf: title (within woodcut border), on verso the list of books. The text, O. T. Epistles, and table, as before. The colophon closely agrees with that of the 1538 issue; but the name of *Wyllyam Powell* (at the same sign) is substituted for Robert Redman, and the date is given as *M. CCCCC. xlvii. and the fyrst yere of the Kynges moste gracious reygne.*
Signatures: A–Z⁸ AA–NN⁸ OO⁴, PP⁸ QQ⁴; 304 ff. Headlines in roman type. Latin text printed in same type as 1538 edition.
The titlepage has the Mutius and Porsenna border as in Redman's issue, but without red ink, or words printed below. The cut of St. John before his Gospel (English text) is new. The others are similar in design to those used before.

¶ 205 × 149 mm. Imperfect: wanting the titleleaf (supplied in facsimile), and NN 8. Five duplicate leaves (MM 7 and 8, NN 2, 3 and 4) are inserted at the beginning.
[F. F.]

—— Another copy.

A mixed copy, containing many leaves of Redman's 1538 edition. A former owner (J. Dix) in a MS. note states his belief that this copy was issued by Powell in a mixed state. But Fry in another note doubts if the printer would thus mix the editions, as the headlines differ so greatly. The following leaves belong to the 1538 edition: all C; D 3, 4, 5 and 6; E 3, 4, 5 and 6; F 1, 2, 7 and 8; H 1, 2, 7 and 8; all K; Q 1, 2, 7 and 8; R 3, 4, 5 and 6; S 1, 2, 7 and 8; all T; V 1, 2, 7 and 8; Z 3, 4, 5 and 6; AA 3, 4, 5 and 6; CC 3, 4, 5 and 6; DD 1, 2, 7 and 8; all HH; all II; KK 1, 2, 7 and 8; all LL; MM 3, 4, 5 and 6; NN 3, 4, 5 and 6; all PP;—116 ff. All the rest belong to Powell's edition of 1548,47.
229 × 116 mm. Imperfect, wanting titleleaf and ff. 2 to 16, i.e. sheets A and B. The quasi-facsimile title inserted is incorrect; it is a copy of Redman's second title with the date altered.
[F. F.]
41.

1548. The newe | Testamēt of the last trās- | laciō. By Wylliam Tyndal wyth | the Prologes & Annotacyons in | the margēt, declaring many hard ¦ places conteyned in the text, | also in the latter ende fo- | loweth the Epistles | of the olde Te- | stament | Imprinted in the yeare | of oure Lord God M.CCCCC. | XLviii. And in the seconde | yeare of the Reygne of our | moste dread souerayne | Lorde Kynge Ed- | warde the . vi. | Cum Priuilegio.
[Qu. T. Petyt: London?] 4°. 𝕭. 𝕷.
Tindale's version.

Fry's No. 17. The earliest edition which bears on its titlepage the words *of the last translation by William Tindale.* We may assume accordingly that the editor followed some revision which he believed to be *the last.* Now this agrees more closely with the G. H. edition than with the others; thus affording a further proof that the G. H. Testament was the last revised by Tindale himself.

DESCRIPTION. Twenty preliminary leaves: title (within woodcut border), on verso Almanack (1549–70), Kalendar—3 ff., Table ending with *A compendyous and brief rehersal of al ye contētes of the bokes of the new testamente*—7 ff., *W. T. vnto the christē Reader*—17 pp., 1 p. blank. The text, B 1 to Qq 1 *a*; O. T. Epistles, Qq 1 *b* to Rr 5 *b*; table of Epistles and Gospels, Rr 6 *a* to (Rr 10?—Rr 9 is the last leaf known).
Signatures: [unsigned]⁴ ✠⁸ A–Y⁸ Aa–Qq⁸ Rr⁷¹⁰; 326 (?) ff. Leaves not numbered. A full page contains 34 lines. References, subject-headings, and notes in the margins. Prologues to some books.

The latter half of v. 13 in 1 Pet. ii (*whether it be unto the king as unto the chief head*) is omitted in this edition.

The title-border has on each side a figure, holding a basket of fruit; the initials T P (i.e. probably Thomas Petyt) occur twice. No illustrations.

¶ 195 × 138 mm. Imperfect: wanting title and preliminary leaves; all sheets B, C and D; E 1 to 5, 7 and 8; F 1 and 8; L 1 and 8; S 8; V 1 to 7; X 4 to 8; Y 1; Ee 4; Ii 8; Oo 1, 2 and 8; and all subsequent leaves;—probably 100 leaves in all. Inserted in the book are facsimiles of the title and the first leaf of text, as well as a photograph of the titlepage in the copy at Lincoln College, Oxford (which is the best copy known). [F. F.]

42.

1548. The newe Testa | ment of our Sauiour Christ, newly | set forth after the beste copie of Wyllyam Tin- | dales translation. Whereunto are added | the notes of Thomas Mathewe | wyth other, healpynge verie | muche to the vnder- | standynge of | the text. | Imprinted at | London by John Daye | and William Seres, dwelling | in Sepulchres parish at the | signe of the Resur- recti- | on a litle aboue | Holbourne | cōduit. | Anno M.D.xlviii. the . xxvii. | of October. | Cum gratia & priuilegio | ad imprimendum solum.

8°. B. L.

Tindale's version.

Fry's No. 19. The text is based on the 1534 and G. H. editions, and shows signs of careful editing.

Notwithstanding the statements in the title and printer's address, very many of the notes of Matthew's Bible have been omitted, and others much altered. The compilation of these notes, which include many fresh comments, was perhaps the work of John Day himself (*cf.* the printer's address); or possibly of Bale, Bishop of Ossory, whose commentary *The Image of both Churches* (printed by Day and Seres about this date) is several times referred to in the notes on Revelation.

This is the first edition issued with notes at the end of the chapters.

DESCRIPTION. Sixteen preliminary leaves: title (in black and red), on verso, a woodcut, *The Printer to the Reader*—1 p., *An almanake for . xxix . yeres* (1549–77), *The kalender* (including *The table of the Epistles and Gospelles*)—6 ff., *Uvilliam Tindale vnto the christian reader* with list of books—15 pp., *A prologe* . . .—1 p. The text, C i to EE iiii *b*; followed on the same page by the O. T. Epistles *after the vse of Salisbury*, which end on FF 8 *b*.

Signatures: [unsigned]^8 B–Y^8 Aa–Yy^8 AA–FF^6; 400 ff. Leaves not numbered. A full page contains 38 lines. References, subject-headings and notes, in the margins. Also contents before the chapters, and (in most of the books) notes at the end of the chapters. Prologues before the Gospels and Epistles. The position of the table of Epistles and Gospels in the Kalendar is unusual.

The woodcut on verso of title displays within a border the arms, apparently, of Sir Thomas Willoughby (*cf.* Fry, *A Bibliographical Description*, pp. 110–1). It occurs in other books printed by Day. Herbert (p. 618) describes the arms as those of Katherine Duchess of Suffolk, who belonged to the Willoughby family. The illustrations include cuts of the Evangelists, and 20 cuts in Revelation.

In this Testament first occurs the well-known 'wife-beating' note to 1 Pet. iii (see below, 1549 folio Bible by the same printers).

An elaborate article in the *Athenæum*, 12 August 1893, emphasises the historical importance of this edition in connection with its appearance just before the First Prayer Book of Edward VI (1549).

¶ 134 × 91 mm. Imperfect: wanting title and other preliminary leaves; also C 1 and 8; F 1 and 8; all N; O 1 and 8; R 1; Aa 1; Ff 8; Yy 4 and 5; CC 1; EE 8; all FF. All these are supplied in facsimile (some are photographs), except FF 1 and 2. Inserted is a photograph of the flyleaf of the copy in the Library of the Dean and Chapter of Windsor, containing a MS. letter by John Careless (*cf.* Fry, *A Bibliographical Description* . . ., pp. 111–2). [F. F.]

43.

1548. N. T. 4°. See 1549.

1549. The newe Te | stament of the last trans- | lacion. By Wylliam Tyndall with | the Prologes and annotacions in | the mergēt, declaryng many harde | places conteyned in the texte, | also in the later ende folo- | weth the Epistles | of the olde Te-| stament. | Imprinted in the yere of oure Lorde | God. M.D. xlix. And in the thyrd | yere of the reigne of our moost | dreade soueraygne Lorde | Kynge Edwarde | the syxte. | Cum priuilegio ad impri- | mendum solum.

Wyllyam Tylle : London. 1549, 48. 4°. 𝔅. 𝔏.

Tindale's version.

Fry's No. 18. The text generally agrees with the G. H. edition. Probably printed in 1548; the title and preliminary leaves being added in 1549.

DESCRIPTION. Ten preliminary leaves: title (in black and red, within woodcut border), on verso *An Almanacke for . xxii . yeare* (1549-70), Kalendar (with quaint verses below each month)—3 ff.; *Wyllyam Tyndall vnto the Christen Reader,* followed by the contents of the Gospels and Acts,—6 ff. The text, B i to Mm 6 b; followed on the same page by the O. T. Epistles *after the vse of Salisburye,* which end on Nn 8 b with the colophon: *Imprinted at London wythin Aldrichgate in the parisshe of Sayncte Anne and Agnes by Wyllyam Tylle in the yeare of oure Lorde God. 1548. Cum priuilegio* . . . Added at the end are two leaves containing *A table to fynde the Epystles and Gospels vsuallye reade in the Churche, according.vnto the booke of Common prayer* . . . ending with the colophon: *Imprynted at London by Thomas Petet*—3 pp., 1 p. blank.

Signatures: [unsigned]⁴ A⁶, B-Z⁸ Aa-Nn⁸, Ii²; 292 ff. Leaves not numbered. A full page contains 35 lines. References, subject-headings, and notes, in margins. Prologues before St. Matthew, and all the Epistles. The book is carelessly printed and abounds in errors and omissions.

The title-border is an architectural design, with two supporting figures, and below under an arch a recumbent figure writing. No cuts in the text.

The two leaves containing the table of Epistles and Gospels do not properly belong to the book; their signature is Ii, and they were printed by T. Petet, not by W. Tylle. Apparently they were borrowed from some edition in which Ii was their correct signature (such as that printed by T. Gaultier *pro I. C.*, 1550), and added just before publication, in order to give the Epistles and Gospels according to the Prayer Book of March 1549. The rest of the book is adapted to the Salisbury Use.

¶ 176 × 121 mm. Imperfect: wanting title and other preliminary leaves; also all B, C 7, and the two last leaves. These are supplied in facsimile—14 leaves (sheets A and B) being photographs. [F. F.]

44.

1549. The first tome or vo- | lume of the Paraphrase of | Erasmus vpon the newe | testamente. | Enpriented at London in Flete- | strete at the signe of the sunne by | Edwarde Whitchurche the | last daie of Januarie. | Anno Domini. | 1548.

The second tome . . .

'31 Jan. 1548' [=1549], 1549. f°. 𝔅. 𝔏. 2 vols.

An English version of Erasmus' Latin Paraphrase or Commentary. With the text of the New Testament, Great Bible version.

Four of the dedicatory epistles are addressed to Queen Catherine (Parr), *by whose good meanes & procuremente this present weorke hath been by soondrie mennes labours turned into our vulgare toungue.* Among the translators were Nicholas Udall, Thomas Key, Miles Coverdale, John Olde, and Leonard Coxe; while Princess (afterward Queen) Mary translated the greater part of the Paraphrase upon St. John's Gospel. The Paraphrase on Revelation, omitted by Erasmus, was the work of Leo Juda, translated by Edmund Alen.

ENGLISH

The injunctions issued by Edward VI in 1547 ordered that a copy of this book should be placed in every church within a year after the date of the visitation which was about to be made (Cardwell, *Documentary Annals*, vol. i. p. 9). The contemporary churchwardens' accounts contain references to the purchase of the book—*e.g.* in those of St. Margaret's, Westminster:

> 1548. Paid for the half part of the Paraphrases of Erasmus, 5s.

and again, in those of Wigtoft, Lincolnshire:

> 1549. It. paid for the Paraphrases of Erasmus, 7s.
> It. paid for a chain for the Paraphrases, 4d.

DESCRIPTION. Vol 1: title (within woodcut border), verso blank, *To the moste puissaunt prince . . . Edwarde the sixthe . . . Nicolas Udal wisheth . . .*—25 pp., *To the Ientill christian reader Nicolas Udall wisheth . . .*—4 pp., 1 p. blank, *To the moste vertuous Ladie Quene Katherine . . . Nicolas Udall . . . wisheth . . .*—2 ff., St. Matt.—ff. 1 (not numbered) to cxxi (really 110, S 8) *a*, verso blank; *To the most excellent . . . princesse Quene Catherine . . . Thomas Key . . . wisheth . . .*—3 pp., 1 p. blank, *To the moste christian prince Frauncys the Frenche kyng Erasmus of Roterodame sendeth gretyng* (dated 1523)—11 pp., *The lyfe of s. Marke . . .*—1 p., St. Mark—ff. i to xciiii (Qq 4) *b*; *To the moste vertuous . . . Quene Katerine . . . Nicolas Udall wisheth . . .* (dated 1545)—6 ff., Erasmus' preface (dedicated to Henry VIII, and dated 1523)—7 ff., *The life of saincte Luke . . .* —1 p., 1 p. blank, St. Luke—ff. 1 (not numbered) to cxciiii (ii 8) *a*, verso blank; *To the moste vertuous . . . Quene Katerine . . . Nicolas Udall . . . wisheth . . .*—2 ff., *To the moste renouned prince, Ferdinando Archduke of Austriege . . . Erasmus of Roterodam wisheth health* (dated Jan. 1523, i.e. 1524)—5 ff., *Sainct Johns life . . .* 1 p., 1 p. blank, St. John—ff. 1 (not numbered) to cxiiii (really 117, T 9) *b*, 1 f. blank; Acts—ff. 1 (not numbered) to lxxxvii (P 3) *a*, on verso a small cut, 1 f. blank.

Vol. 2: title: *The seconde tome | or volume of the Paraphrase of | Erasmus vpon the newe testament: contey- | nyng the Epistles of S. Paul, and other the | Apostles. Wherunto is added a Para- | phrase vpon the Reuelacion | of S. John. | Imprinted at London in Flete- | strete at the signe of the Sunne by | Edwarde Whitchurche, the | xvi. daye of August. | Cum priuilegio ad imprimen- | dum solum. | Anno do. 1549.* (within border), verso blank, *To the most Excellent Prince . . . Kyng Edwarde the sixte . . .* (signed *. . . Myles Couerdall*)—2 ff.; Tindale's Prologue to Romans—9 ff., Erasmus' Argument—4 ff., text (Romans)—ff. 1 (not numbered) to xliiii (H ii) *b*; 1 Cor., Argument—2 ff., text—ff. iii to xliiii *a*, verso blank; 2 Cor., Arg.—1 f., text—ff. xliiii (really 46) to lxiiii (really 66, Ll 4) *a*, verso blank; Gal., Arg.—3 pp., text—ff. ii *b* to xxi (dd 3) *b*, 1 f. blank; *To the Christian reader, Iohn Olde wysheth . . .*—5 ff., 1 f. blank; Ephes., Arg.—1 f., text—ff. ii to xv (CC 3) *a*, verso blank, 1 f. blank; Phil., Arg.—1 p., 1 p. blank, text—ff. ii to x (BBb 4) *b*; Col., Arg.—1 p., 1 p. blank, text—ff. 1 (not numbered) *b* to x (bbbb 4) *a*, verso blank; 1 Thess., Arg.—1 p., 1 p. blank, text—ff. ii to viii *a*, on the same page 2 Thess. Arg., 1 p. blank, text—ff. ix to xi (BBBb 5) *b*, 1 f. blank; *Erasmus of Roterodame to the Right reuerende Byshop and mooste excellent Prynce of Traiecte, Philip of Burgundye, sendeth gretyng* (dated 1519)—1 f., 1 Tim. Arg.—1 p., text—ff. ii *b* to xviii *b*, 2 Tim. (with Arg. at beginning)—ff. xix to xxv *b*; *To the right worshipfull master John Hales, his seruaunt Leonarde Coxe wysheth . . .*—1 p., Titus, Arg.—1 p., text—ff. iii (really 27) to xxxi (really 32, FFFF ii) *a*; Philemon, Arg.—1 p., text—ff. xxxii and xxxiii (really 33 and 34); Hebr., Arg.—1 p., text—ff. 1 (not numbered) *b* to xxvii (EEEEe 3) *a*, verso blank, 1 f. blank; *To the right Excellent . . . Lady Anne, Duchesse of Somerset . . . John olde wisheth . . .* (dated 1549)—3 pp., short list: *The Canonicall Epistles*—1 p.; 1 Peter, Arg.—1 p., text—ff. 1 (not numbered) *b* to xv *a*, on the same page 2 Pet., Arg., text—ff. xv *b* to xxi *a*; Jude (with short Life and Arg.)—ff. xxi *b* to xxiiii *a*; James (with short Arg.)—ff. xxiiii *b* to xl *b*; 1 John (with short Arg.)—ff. xli to liiii *b*; 2 John—1 f.; 3 John—1 f. (ℭ 18); *A paraphrase or comentarie vpon the Reuelacion of S. John, faythfullye translated by Edmond Alen*—ff. i to xl (ℭℭ G 4) *a*, ending with the words: *The ende of the Reuelacion of S. John thus brefely expounded by the seruaunt of Christ Leo Jude, a minister in the churche of Tigury and, translated out of the high Duche by Edmonde Alen*, on verso a cut.

Signatures: Vol. 1: a⁸ B⁸, ℭ², A–R⁶ S⁸, ℭ², ℭ⁶, Aa–Pp⁶ Qq⁴, ℭ⁶, (∴)⁸, a–z⁶ aa–hh⁶ ii⁸, ℭ², ( )⁶, A–S⁶ T¹⁰, A–O⁶ P⁴; 652 ff. Vol. 2: ✠⁶ ✠✠⁶ ℭ⁴, A–G⁶ H², Aa–Ff⁶ Gg⁸ Hh–Kk⁶ Ll⁴, aa–cc⁶ dd⁴, ℭ⁶, AA⁶ BB⁶ CC⁴, AAa⁶ BBb⁴, aaaa⁶ bbbb⁴, AAAa⁶ BBBb⁶, AAAA–EEEE⁶ FFFF⁴, AAAAa–DDDDd⁶ EEEEe⁴, ✲² ℭA–ℭH⁶ ℭI⁸ ℭℭ A–ℭℭ F⁶ ℭℭ G⁴; 362 ff.

Total number of leaves—1014.

A full page contains 48 lines. Text of N. T. divided into sections, and printed in smaller type. With marginal headings. Dedications, Arguments, etc., as mentioned above.

The woodcut border used for both titles contains the royal arms above, and another coat of arms below with the initials E and W on two tablets. The cut at the end of each volume illustrates Rev. xii.

W. Aldis Wright has distinguished no less than six varieties of Vol. 1. No doubt, owing to the demand for copies at an early date, several presses were employed at the same time, and the work of printing was pushed on as rapidly as possible. Some copies are mixed. There appear to be no such varieties of Vol. 2.

The description given above applies to the variety represented by the copy No. 4 in Mr. Wright's collection.

¶ 280 × 192 mm. Wants only the blank leaf at the end of Vol. 1. Owing to the wear and tear of public use, perfect copies are uncommon. This copy appears to have belonged to a private library. Vol. 2 contains many notes written in a contemporary hand on the blank pages. On the last page is written p$\bar{r}\bar{m}$ huius libri .vj^s.

45.

—— ANOTHER EDITION.

W. Aldis Wright's No. 1.

In this variety St. Matthew ends on fo. cxxvii (Q 7) b, St. Mark on xcviii (m 10) b, St. Luke on cci (Bbb 9) b, St. John on cxxiii (PPp 11)b, and Acts on xc (LLL 10) a. In the other varieties the Paraphrase on St. Luke xxii ends with the words . . . *conuerted and chaunged*; but this edition contains two pages more, ending with the words . . . *to put Jesus to death.*

¶ 280 × 197 mm. Vol. 1 only; imperfect: wanting several leaves.

46.

[In 1551,52 appeared a second edition, in which the leaves in each volume are numbered consecutively throughout, and tables are added. The Paraphrase on St. Luke xxii ends with the words . . . *to putte Jesus to deathe.* The N. T. text is printed in roman type.]

1549. The Byble, that | is to say all the holy Scri- | pture: In whych are cō-|tayned the Olde and | New Testamente, | truly & purely trā-|slated into En-| glish, & nowe | lately with | greate in-| dustry & diligē-| ce recognised. | Esaye. i. | Hearken to ye heauens, and thou | earthe geue eare: For the | Lorde speaketh. | Imprynted at | London by Jhon Daye, dwelling | at Aldersgate, and William | Seres, dwelling in Peter Colledge. | Cum gratia et Priuilegio ad Impri-|mendum solum. | xvii . day of August . M.D.XLIX.

f°. 𝕭. 𝕷.

A reprint of Matthew's Bible of 1537, with the notes, etc., revised; edited by Edmund Becke. (*Cf.* No. 66.)

Tindale's prologue to Jonah (see above, No. 4) is reprinted for the first time in this edition of the Bible.

DESCRIPTION. Twenty preliminary leaves: title (in black and red, within woodcut border), on verso *An Almanacke for . xxix . yeares* (1549-77), *The Kalendar* with a short note at the end *These thinges ensuynge are ioyned with thys present volume of the Byble* . . . — 2 ff., *An exhortacion* . . . and *The summe and content* . . . —1 f., the address *To the moost puisant and mighty prince Edwarde the sixt* . . . (signed *Your graces faythfull & humble subiect Edmunde Becke*)—3 pp., *A description and successe* . . . —1 p., *A Table of the principall matters* . . . (with short preface *To the Christen Readers*)—23 pp., *A perfect supputacyon* . . . *A Prologe shewynge the vse of the Scrypture* and *The names of all the bokes* . . . —4 pp., *A Regyster or a bryefe rehersall of the names of the moost famous & notable persons, mencyoned in the olde and newe Testamente*—1 p. The text, divided into five parts:—(1) Pentateuch, ff. i to lxxxvi (really 88, S 4) b; (2) Joshua–Job, with title (within border), on verso begins text—ff. 1 (not numbered) b to cxiij (really 114, Tt 6) b; (3) Psalms–Malachi, with title (within border), on verso begins text—ff. 1 (not numbered) b to cxlv (really 147, AAa 7) b,

1 f. blank; (4) Apocrypha, with title (within border), on verso begins text (preceded by prologue)—ff. 1 (not numbered) *b* to lxxvi (Nnn 4) *b*; (5) N. T., with title (within border), verso blank, text (with long prologue and list of books)—ff. ij to c.xxi (really 120, V 6) *a*; on verso begins *This is the Table wherein ye shal fynde the Epistles and the Gospels, after the vse of Salsburye*—5 pp., ending on c.xxiii (really 122, V 8) *b* with the colophon: *The ende of the newe Testament, and of the whole Byble. To the honoure and prayse of God was this Bible printed & fynyshed, In the yeare of oure Lorde God. Anno M.D.xlix. Imprinted at London by John Daye dwellynge at Aldersgate, and Willyam Seres dwellynge in Peter colledge towarde Ludgate. These bokes are to be solde by the lyttle conduyte in Chepesyde. Cum Priuilegio ad imprimendum solum.*

Signatures: AA⁶ BB⁶ CC⁶, D–R⁶ S⁴, Aa–Tt⁶, AA–GG⁶ HH⁸ II–ZZ⁶ AAa⁸, Aaa–Mmm⁶ Nnn⁴, A–T⁶ V⁸; 568 ff. The numbering of the leaves is often incorrect; two leaves (HH 7 and 8) are omitted in the foliation. Printed in rather peculiar black-letter; double columns, with 65 lines to the full column. References, and a few notes etc., in the margins; contents before each chapter. The majority of the notes are printed together after the chapters. With Tindale's prologues, etc., including the long prologues to Jonah and Romans and that to the New Testament.

The general title is enclosed within a border composed of 14 cuts: two above—the creation of Eve, and crossing the Red Sea; two below—Abraham and Isaac, and the worship of the golden calf; the remaining 10, arranged 5 on each side of the letter-press, illustrate New Testament incidents. The borders to the other titles are each composed of 6 blocks—an ornamental block (boys blowing horns, like the blocks used for title-borders in the Coverdale Bible of 1535, etc.) on each side, and four cuts—two above and two below the letterpress; those on the N. T. titlepage represent the Evangelists. The illustrations in the text include: two large half-page engravings before the Psalms and Isaiah; many cuts in pts. 1 to 4; cuts of each Evangelist; and 20 small *figures* in Revelation, with rhyming couplets, printed either below or at the sides of each cut (e.g. *By the starres in hys hȧd we may wel se, What maner of mē our preachers should be*).

This Bible contains the well-known note at the end of 1 Pet. iii on the words *To dwell ıb a wyfe accordinge to knowledge*, in which occurs the sentence *And yf she be not obedient and healpfull vnto hym endeuoureth to beate the feare of God into her heade, that therby she maye be compelled to learne her duitie and do it*. It is often called the 'Bug Bible,' though the rendering *bugges* in Ps. xci. 5 is first found in the Coverdale Bible of 1535, and occurs in many others.

¶ 299 × 192 mm. Wants only the blank leaf (AAa 8) at the end of pt. 3. [F. F.]

—— Another copy.

280 × 184 mm. Imperfect: wanting general title, and the fifth and sixth leaves of preliminary matter; also D 3 and 4, AAa 4 and 5, and the blank leaf AAa 8. Three leaves from a Geneva Bible of 1579 are inserted in place of the missing leaves in pt. 1 (D 3 and 4). In seventeenth-century binding.

47.

1549. The Byble, | whych is all the holy Scrip | ture : In whych are contayned the Olde | and Newe Testament, truelye and | purely translated into Englishe | By Thomas Matthewe. | 1537. | And now Imprinted in | the Yeare of oure Lorde. | M. D. XLIX. | Esaye. i. | Hearcken to, ye heauens, and thou | earth geue eare : For the Lord | speaketh. | Imprinted at London By Thomas | Raynalde, and William Hyll dwelling | in Paules Churche yeard.

f°. 𝕭. 𝕷.

A reprint of Matthew's Bible of 1537.

DESCRIPTION. Forty-three preliminary pages, title (in black and red, within woodcut border), on verso *These things ensuinge are ioyned wyth thys present volume* . . ., *The Kalender* with *An Almanack for .xii .yeares* (1550–61)—2 ff., *An exhortacyon* . . .—1 p., *The summe and contente* . . .—2 pp., *A descripcion and successe* . . .— 2 pp., 1 p. blank; *A table of the pryncypal matters* . . . (with short preface)—27 pp., *The names of al the Bokes* . . . and *A brief rehersal* . . .—1 p.; *Unto the Reader W. T.* —3 pp. On verso of the last preliminary leaf (A ii) begins the text (the following leaf is numbered *ii.*—probably it should be *iii.*):—(1) Genesis–Job, ends on ccxliiii (really 256, vv 4) *b*; (2) Psalms–2 Macc., subdivided as follows: (a) Psalms–*Salomons Ballet*, ff. j to Lxiii (really 60, Kk 6) *a*, verso blank; (b) *The Prophetes in Inglysh. Esay. . . . Malachy*, ff. LXiiii (really 61) to CCxix (really 190, KK 4) *a*; (c) on KK 4 *b The volume of The Bokes Called Apocripha . . . The Registre therof . . ., To the Reader*—1 p., text—ff. CCXvii (really 191, KK 5) *b* to CccXl (really 291, DDd 7) *a*, verso blank. 1 f. blank; (3) and (4), New Testament, with title (within woodcut border), verso blank; (3) Gospels and Acts, ff. ij to lxxvi (really 74, I 10) *a*, verso blank; (4) prologue to Romans (in small type)—4 ff. (not numbered), text—Romans–Revelation, ff. i to Xlviii (really 57, i 3) *a*; on the same page in the second column begins the Table of Epistles and Gospels *after the vse of Salysbury*, which ends on LJ (really 60, i 6) *a*, with the colophon: *The ende of the new testament and the whole Byble To the Honoure and Prayse of God was this Byble prynted and fynisshed, in the yeare of oure Lorde God A. MD.XXXVII And nowe agayne accordyngly imprented, and finyshed the laste daye of Octobre. In the yeare of oure Lord God M.D.XLIX. At London. By Wylliam Hyll, and Thomas Reynaldes Typographers. God saue the kynge. Cum priuilegio*, verso blank.

Signatures: ⁂⁂ ⁂ ⁂ ⁂ ⁂⁶, A–Z⁶ aa–tt⁶ vv⁴, Aa–Yy⁶ AA–YY⁶ AAa⁶ BBb⁴ CCc⁶ DDd⁸, A–H⁸, I¹⁰, a–c⁶ d–h⁸ i⁶; 706 ff. Text printed in double columns, with 54 (sometimes 53) lines to the full column. The book is badly printed with worn type, though the paper is good. The numbering of the leaves is extraordinarily inaccurate. Prologues, notes at the end of the chapters, chapter-contents, marginal references, etc.

The woodcut border used for the general and the N. T. titles is the same as that found in the April 1540 (Berthelet) Bible, viz. the border used in the Coverdale 1535 Bible, with, however, the legends in Latin instead of English. No woodcuts in the text. Two very large and curiously flourished initials occur before the prologues to Leviticus and Deuteronomy.

¶ 296 × 191 mm. Wants only the blank leaf Ddd 8. The general title is mounted.

[F. F.]

—— Another copy.

305 × 192 mm. Imperfect: wanting general title; also I 10, h 8, and all sheet i; 9 ff.; the blank leaf (DDd 8) is also missing. Bound in undressed calf-skin.

—— Another copy.

292 × 191 mm. Imperfect: wanting the general title and five following leaves; also H 8, h 8, and all sheet i; 14 ff.; the blank leaf (DDd 8) is also missing. The title and some of the preliminary leaves are supplied in facsimile.

—— Another copy.

285 × 180 mm. Imperfect: wanting all matter before C 4 (Gen. xxx); also Aa i, AA 6, b 6 and the last leaf in the volume (i 6); 39 ff. A great part of the missing matter is supplied in manuscript (copied from Day and Seres' 1549 Bible), and a facsimile of the last leaf (supplied by Mr. Lea Wilson) is inserted. It has the blank leaf DDd 8. Bound in two volumes.

48.

1549. The Byble in | Englishe, that is, the olde | and new Testament, after the | translacion appoynted to | bee read in the Churches. | Imprynted at London in Flete- | strete, at the signe of the Sunne, ouer a- | gaynste the conduyte, by Edwarde | Whitchurche. The . xxix . day of Decem- | ber, the yeare of | our Lorde. | M.D. XLIX. | Cum priuilegio ad imprimen- | dum solum.

f°. 𝕭.𝕷.

Great Bible version.

DESCRIPTION. Six preliminary leaves: title (within woodcut border), verso blank, *A Prologue or preface . . .* —7 pp., *The summe and content . . .* —2 pp., *An exhortacion . . . and The contentes of the first parte of the Byble*—1 p. The text, divided into five parts:—(1) Pentateuch, ff. j to xcviii (m 10) *b*; (2) Joshua–Job, with title (within border), verso blank, text—ff. ij to cxlij (S 6) *a*, verso blank; (3) Psalms–Malachi, with title (within border), verso blank, text—ff. ii to cxlviii (TT 4) *a*, verso blank; (4) Apocrypha, with title, on verso begins text—ff. 1 (not numbered) *b* to xcvi (Mmm 8) *b*; (5) N. T. with title (within border), on verso begins *A Table to finde the Epistles and Gospels vsually read in the Churche, accordyng vnto the booke of Common prayer* .. 3 pp., text—ff. i to cxvi (O 12) *b*.

Signatures: [the 2nd signed ✻✻✻, and the 3rd ✻✻✻✻✻]⁶, a–l⁸ m¹⁰, A–R⁸ S⁶, AA–SS⁸ TT⁴, Aaa–Mmm⁸, [unsigned]², A–N⁸ O¹²; 608 ff. The six preliminary leaves, the latter portion (ff. 89 to end) of pt. 2, and all pts. 3 and 5, were probably printed by E. Whitchurch, whose name appears on the general titlepage. The rest of the book (pt. 1, pt. 2—as far as fo. 88, and pt. 4) is printed in a different, though somewhat similar, type, and perhaps came from another press; the chief characteristics of this portion are—the flourished initials before the chapters, the flourished capitals in the headlines, and the names God and Lord printed in Roman capitals. A full column contains 57 lines.

The general title-border is like that used for Whitchurch's edition of Erasmus' Paraphrase printed in the same year (see above). The border to the pt. 2 title is composed of 11 woodblocks:—two above and two below are like those used in the Great Bibles, a smaller cut is placed immediately beneath the letter-press, and the remaining 6 small cuts representing N. T. incidents are arranged 3 on each side. The pt. 3 and pt. 5 title-borders are similarly arranged, save that in the former a larger cut appears immediately beneath the letterpress, and in the latter this block is omitted. The titlepage to pt. 4 has no woodcut border, but is printed in bold and curious type: *Apogrypha. The fourth parte of the Bible: contayninge these Bookes* ... There are only two cuts in the text; these occur on ff. 9 *b* and 13 *b* in pt. 1, and represent Abraham and Isaac, and Jacob's Ladder. A large initial letter appears at the beginning of Genesis.

¶ 308 × 190 mm. The general title is mounted. [F. F.]

49.

1549. The Newe | Testa-| ment | in Englyshe and in | Latin of Erasmus | Transla-| cion. | Novvm Testamen-| tvm Anglice et | Latine. | Anno dñi. 1549.

W. Powell: London. 4°. 𝕭. 𝕷.

The third edition of the diglot of Tindale's version of the New Testament in English, with the Latin of Erasmus, first published by R. Redman in 1538.

Fry's No. 21. Powell's second issue of the book.
In arrangement, signatures, etc., this closely agrees with Powell's first issue. The colophon reads the same, with the alteration of the date and the addition of the words *Cum priuilegio ad imprimendum solum.*
Headlines and Latin text printed in roman type.

¶ 220 × 162 mm.
With the Metrical Psalms (1630).
Seventeenth-century binding, stamped E. G. L. [F. F.]

50.

1549. The Newe Te- | stament of oure Sa- | ueour Jesus Christ translated by | M. Wil. Tyndall, yet once agay- | no corrected with newe Annota- | cyons very necessary to better on- | derstondynge. Where vnto is ad- | ded an exhortacion to the same of | Erasmus Rotero. with an En | gelshe Calender. And a Ta- | ble, necessary to fynde ea- | sly, and lyghtly any sto- | ry contayned in the | fowre Euangeli- | stes, & in the | Actes of | the Apo- | stles. | M.CCCCC. xlix.

[Printer and place unknown.] 8°. 𝕭. 𝕷.

Tindale's version.

Fry's No. 23. The text agrees generally with the G. H. edition.
The names of place and printer are not given; they may have appeared on another title, now lost. This issue strikingly resembles the three octavo editions of 1536 in many points:

e.g. the wording of titles, Erasmus' Exhortation, and many peculiar readings and errors. So that it was probably printed about 1536, perhaps at a continental press; and issued later with a new title, in 1549. Possibly Day and Seres were the publishers, as the type of two reprinted leaves in the text is identical with that used in their folio Bible of 1549. The O. T. Epistles and the table at the end are 'after the use of Salisbury.'

DESCRIPTION. The order of the preliminary leaves is somewhat uncertain. The following order is suggested: [...?] + twenty-six preliminary leaves: [a first title—perhaps with an almanack on verso, and other matter, now lost] *An Exhortacion to the diligent studye of scripture, made by Erasmus Roterodamus*—10 ff.; second title (in black and red, within woodcut border), on verso begins the Kalendar (with a mnemonic couplet at the foot of each page)—12 pp. *The office of all estates*—2 pp., list of books—1 p. (with catchword *Willam*), *Uvilliam Tindale vnto the Christian Reader*—8 ff. The text, B 1 to z 6 a; followed on the same page by the O. T. Epistles *after the vse of Salsburye*, which end on Bb 5 a; *This is the Ta-Table* .... *after the vse of Salsbury*—Bb 5 b to Cc 6 a, verso blank.

Signatures: [first title, etc.?] ✶¹⁰ ✠⁸ A–Z⁸ a–z⁸ Aa⁸ Bb⁶ Cc⁶; [...?] + 408 ff. Leaves not numbered. A full page contains 35 lines. Prologues to nearly all the books. References, subject-headings, and notes in the margins. There is no *Table necessary* ..., as mentioned in title; but contents are given before the chapters in the Gospels and Acts. Two leaves (h 1 and 8) are printed in a different type (like that used in Day and Seres' Bible of 1549), with 34 lines to the page. The book abounds in errors and omissions (e.g. 2 Cor. x. 11, 1 Pet. ii. 13, Rev. xix. 15, etc.)

The title-border has above—a small medallion with a man's head, and below—Venus in her car drawn by two peacocks. There are 21 cuts in Revelation.

¶ 156 × 94 mm. Imperfect: wanting title, ✠ 2 and 3, and Cc 5 and 6;—5 ff., supplied in facsimile. Perhaps another title is wanting (*cf.* Description). A quasi-facsimile title (from the collection of G. Offor) is inserted, with an almanack (1550–71) on verso, for which Fry could find no authority. [F. F.]

—— Another copy.

154 × 90 mm. Very imperfect: wanting all before L 4 (St. Luke iii), h 4 and 5, and all after s 8 (Heb. vii). One leaf V 7 is mutilated.

The Grenville copy (G. 12170) in the B. M. has the *Exhortacion* placed after the list of books; this arrangement ignores the catchword on ✠ 8 b, as Fry points out.

51.

1549. [The Newe Testament. Diligently Translated by Myles Couerdale and conferred with the translacion of Willyam Tyndale, with the necessary Concordances truly alleged. An. M.D.XLIX.]

Reynolde Wolfe: London. 8°. 𝕭.𝕷.

A revised edition of Coverdale's New Testament.

In the Address *To the Reader* on verso of the second title the editor writes: *Marke good gentle Reader, that we, besydes all other diligence vsed in this New Testamēt, haue conferred W. Tyndalles translacion with this M. Myles Couerdales. And whereas we haue founde any woordes or sentence in Tyndalles translacion, not, fully agreeyng with this translacion, but rather makyng diuersitee of vnderstandyng, or the sentence more plainer we haue sette it into the mergent of this booke, inclosed with these markes [ ], so that ye may reade the same, in steade of that, which is in lyke maner inclosed in the text of this booke* ... (he then goes on to explain the *Concordaunces* and *Tables or Cartes*). Thus in Matt. xix. 28 the text reads *in the* [*newe byrthe*] (Cov.), and the margin [*second generacion*] (Tin.).

DESCRIPTION. Sixteen preliminary leaves: first title (in black and red, within woodcut border), on verso *An Almanake for . ix . yeares* (1549–57), above which is the well-known rhyme *Thirtie dayes hath Nouember*, etc. (so Lea Wilson, p. 169, from whose description is taken the wording of the title), Kalendar (with a small cut at the head of each month)—6 ff., *For to knovve . vvhat . Signe the Sonne is*, etc.—1 p., verso blank; second title: *The Newe | Testament.| Translated by Myles Couerdale, | and conferred with W. Tynda | les translation. | An. M.D.XLIX. | Iesus Christvs. | The tyme is fulfylled, the kyngdome of | God is at hande: Amende your | lyues, and beleue the | Gospel. | Mar. 1*, on verso *To the Reader*, prologue: *The grace of the Lorde Jesus Christe* ...

5 pp., *The Description of the Lande of Promes* . . .—map filling 2 pp., *A true and perfect rekeninge* . . . (mentioning at the end . . . *this present 1549 yeare* . . .)— 5 pp., *A Godly prayer for all suche as doo studye and reade the Newe testament*— 1 p., 1 p. blank. The text, divided into two sections :—(1) Gospels and Acts, (2) Rom. to end—Aj to Yiij *b*; followed by the table: *By this table, shall ye fynde the Epistles and Gospels, for the Sondaies, and other feastiuall dayes*—7 pp., ending on Y 7 *a*, on verso a device of the brazen serpent *NVM. XXI.*, and the colophon: *Imprinted in London, at the signe of the Brasen Serpent in Paules churcheyarde, by Reynolde Wolfe. Anno. 1549. In June*, 1 f. (probably blank).

Signatures: [unsigned]⁸ ✠⁸, A–Z⁸ Aa–Gg⁸, A–Y⁸; 432 ff. Leaves not numbered. A full page contains 31 lines. References and alternative renderings in margins. Head-lines contain names of books in roman capitals, and chapter-numbers in black-letter. *The Order of Times* is printed at the end of Acts, to fill the last two leaves of sheet Gg (*cf.* note at foot of Gg 6 *b*).

Copies vary slightly in some of the preliminary leaves, e.g. in the Kalendar.

Border to first title: 'at the top of this border is a figure with outstretched hands, intended to represent the Almighty. At foot, on a base or plynth, is Reinold Wolf's device, the brazen serpent, in an oval shield, supported by a fox and a wolf, between the words REIN . WOLF, in Roman capitals' (Lea Wilson, p. 169). Second title page: the first three words are within a woodcut frame; below is a tailpiece. A small cut of the creation of Eve, before *A true and perfect rekeninge.* . . . The cuts in the text include small cuts of the Evangelists, and SS. Paul, James, Peter and Jude; larger cuts of the Day of Pentecost, and St. John (before Revelation); four illustrations in the Gospels (at Matt. xxvii, Luke i and xxii, and John xx) and over 20 in Revelation. (The cuts in Revelation and the device of the brazen serpent occur again in Lucas Harison's folio Bible of 1575.) The initials at the head of most of St. Paul's Epistles represent the Apostle delivering his letter to a messenger, sometimes through the bars of a prison; or he is chained in a dungeon, or confined in the stocks, etc. Besides the map in the preliminary matter there is another, *The Iovrney of Sainct Pavle the Apostle*, which fills 2 pp. before Acts.

¶ 140 × 90 mm.; printed on yellow paper. Imperfect: wanting first title, and first leaf of prologue; also Aa 1, Bb 8, Cc 1, ²I 8, and all ²Y; — 14 ff. Some of these are supplied in facsimile.

According to a letter inserted in the book, this copy was found on a beam in a hayloft.

[F. F.]

—— Another copy.

133 × 90 mm. Very imperfect: wanting all preliminary matter except the third, fourth and last leaves of Kalendar; all sheets A, B, C and D; and many other leaves. Facsimiles are inserted of the second titlepage, and the page containing the device and colophon.

The three Kalendar leaves, which appear to have been taken from another book, slightly differ from those found in the first copy. [F. F.]

—— Another copy.

153 × 102 mm. A fragment only; containing the sheet V—uncut. [F. F.]

52.

[R. Wolf printed a very similar edition in 1550. A copy is in Lambeth Palace Library.]

1549. The second parte of | the Byble, containyng | these Bookes fo-| lowyng | The boke of Josua. . . . The boke of Hiob.

J. Day and W. Seres: London. 1549. 8°. 𝔅.𝔏.

Taverner's version.

The second part of an edition of the Old Testament with Apocrypha, issued in separate volumes by Day and Seres (*cf.* note after No. 65). The text agrees with Taverner's version printed in the folio Bible, edited by Edmund Becke and published by Day in 1551.

DESCRIPTION. One preliminary leaf: title (within woodcut border), on verso a full-page woodcut; the text, A ii to SS ii *a*; on verso the colophon: *Imprinted at London by John Day dwellynge ouer Aldersgate, and Wylliam Seres, dwellyng in Peter Colledge. Cum priuilegio ad imprimendum solum.*

Signatures: A–Y⁸ Aa–Yy⁸ AA–RR⁸ SS²; 490 ff. Leaves not numbered. A full page contains 33 lines. No prologues. Contents before each chapter; references and notes in the margins; notes at the end of some chapters in Job.

The title-border is composed of four ornamental blocks (flowered design); that below contains the date 1549. The woodcut on verso of title is the same as that used in a similar place in the octavo New Testament printed by Day and Seres in Oct. 1548.

¶ 143 × 93 mm. [F. F.]

——— Another copy.

143 × 93 mm. A fragment: 8 ff. only—sheet B. [F. F.]

53.

1549. The volume of the | bokes called Apocripha : Cō-| teining these bokes folowing.| The thyrd boke of Esdras. . . . The . iii . boke of Machabees.
$\qquad$ *J. Day and W. Seres: London.* 1549. 8°. 𝔅. 𝔏.

Taverner's version.

The fifth part of an edition of the Old Testament with Apocrypha, issued in separate volumes by Day and Seres (*cf.* note after No. 65).

The text agrees with Taverner's version, as revised by Becke, and published by Day in his folio Bible of 1551. According to Lea Wilson, the books 3 Esdras, Tobit, and Judith are an entirely new translation. 3 Maccabees appears here for the first time in English. (For a separate edition [1550] of 3 Maccabees *cf.* Lea Wilson, pp. 291-2, and Cotton, p. 25 *n.*) According to the preface *To the Reader*, the editors in preparing this edition of the Apocryphal books took *the laboures to cōfer them with the translacion of Leo Iuda*; and as they found *therin more thē is conteined in our cōmon Bibles, it was thought good to learned men to supply our want by their exāples.*

DESCRIPTION. Two preliminary leaves: title (within woodcut border), on verso a full-page woodcut, *To the Reader*—1 f.; the text, A iii to Yy 3 *a*; on verso the colophon: *Imprinted at London by Jhon Day dwellynge ouer Aldersgate, and Wylliam Seres dwellinge in Peter Colledge. Cum priuilegio . . .*, 1 f. blank.

Signatures: A–Y⁸ Aa–Xx⁸ Yy⁴; 348 ff. Leaves not numbered. A full page contains 32 or 33 lines. No prologues. Contents before chapters; references and some notes in the margins.

The title-border and woodcut on verso are the same as in *The second parte . . .* printed in the same year.

¶ 146 × 100 mm. Imperfect: wanting titleleaf, A 8, and VV 7 and 8; which are supplied in facsimile. The last leaf (blank) is also missing. [F. F.]

54.

1550. The whole | Byble. | that is the holy scripture | of the Olde and Newe testament | faythfully translated into | Englyshe by Myles | Couerdale, and | newly ouer | sene and correcte. | M. D. L. | Pray for vs that the worde of God maye | haue free passage & be glorified. ii. Tess. iii. | Prynted for Andrewe Hester, dwellynge | in Paules churchyard at the sygne | of the whyte horse, and are | there to be solde.
$\qquad$ [*C. Froschover : Zurich.*] 4°. 𝔅. 𝔏.

Coverdale's version.

The latest reprint of the Bible of 1535 issued during the translator's lifetime. In an additional paragraph at the end of the Dedication in this edition Coverdale refers to his earliest Bible translation-work *sixtene yeares agoo*—i.e. in 1534; and he mentions the same date in his Prologue.

This edition seems to have been printed by Christopher Froschover of Zurich, who issued it with a title bearing his name and device, and eighteen leaves of preliminary matter (see below); but it was also published at London by Andrew Hester with another title and new preliminary leaves. A third issue, with yet another title and fresh preliminary leaves, appeared in 1553, bearing the name of Richard Jugge.

ENGLISH 45

DESCRIPTION. Eight preliminary leaves: title (in black and red, within woodcut border), verso blank, *The bokes of the hole Byble* . . . (divided into parts)—1 p., Dedication *Unto the moost victorious Prince and our moost gracious soueraigne lorde, kynge Edwarde the syxte* . . . (signed . . . *Myles Couerdale*)—4 pp., *Myles Couerdale, to the Christen Reader*—5 pp., *The kalender* (with table of Epistles and Gospels)—2 ff. The text: O. T. with Apocrypha—ff. I to CCCCXCIIII (really 492, QQ 4)*a*, verso blank; N. T.— ff. I to CXXI (qq 1) *b*; the table of Epistles and Gospels *after the vse of Salisbury*— 5 pp., ending on qq 4 *a* with the colophon: *To the honoure and prayse of God, was this Byble prynted and fynished in the yeare of oure Sauoure Jesu Christ M.D.L. the xvj. daye in the moneth of August,* verso blank.

Signatures: ✠⁸, A–Z⁶ a–z⁸ AA–PP⁸ QQ⁴, aa–pp⁸ qq⁴; 624 ff. Text printed in an angular foreign type; double columns, with 50 lines to the full column. The Apocrypha title and preface are printed on fo. CCCC (really 398, DD 6) *a*. The N. T. has no separate titlepage. References in margins, but no contents before chapters, and no notes.

The title-border is like that used in the quarto New Testament printed by W. Tylle in 1549,48; beneath are the words *Set forth with the Kynges mooste gracious licence.* A woodcut (with ornamental side-blocks) of the creation of Eve occurs before Genesis. Many initials represent scenes from the Dance of Death.

¶ 229 × 184 mm. Imperfect: wanting the title, and the last three leaves,—supplied in facsimile. Bound in the original boards. [F. F.]

—— Another copy.

Made up to represent the original state of this Bible, as first issued by the printer C. Froschover of Zurich. In place of the usual preliminary leaves are inserted facsimiles of the title (bearing, curiously; the name of *Thomas Mathewe*) and eighteen following leaves found in the remarkable copy in the Public Library at Zurich, which contains Froschover's autograph.

Nineteen preliminary leaves: title: *The whole Byble, | that is, the Olde and Newe | Testamente, truly and purely | transslated into Englische, by | Mayst. Thomas Mathewe. | Esaie.j. | Hearcken to ye heauens: and thou earth | geaue eare: for the Lord | speaketh. | Imprinted in Zürych by Chrystoffer Froschower* (bearing the printer's device, and enclosed within an ornamental frame), verso blank, *To the gentle Reader*—one column, followed (in the second column) by *Here after foloweth all the argumentes vpon the olde and newe Testament, euery boke by sonder hys Argumentes, and how muche and many Chapters they cōtayneth.* This matter (printed in angular type, with double columns) fills the remainder of the preliminary leaves. Signatures: [title], ⋆⁴ ⋆ ⋆ ⋆⁴ ⋆ ⋆ ⋆⁴ ⋆ ⋆ ⋆ ⋆⁶; 19 ff.

221 × 178 mm. Imperfect: wanting title and preliminary matter (see above); the rest of the book is perfect, with the exception of the last four leaves, which are supplied in facsimile. Inserted at the beginning is a 'Facsimile of the Autographs of Christopher Froschover, Zurich. Copied from Coverdale's Bible, and from the New Testament by Tindale, in the Public Library, of Zurich, both printed by C. Froschover, in the year 1550.' [F. F.]

—— Another copy (facsimile) of Froschover's preliminary leaves.

The original title and eighteen following leaves, with a copy of Froschover's autograph, reproduced in facsimile for Fry from the copy in the Public Library at Zurich. With a short MS. note on the three issues of this Bible.

Bound up with many blank leaves. Presented by Mr. Fry in 1871.

55.

1550. The Bible in Englishe, | that is to saye. The content of al the holy | scripture, both of the olde, and nevve | Testament, accordinge to the | translacion that is ap- | pointed to be rede | in the | Churches. | Prynted by Edvvard vvhytchurche. | Cum priuilegio ad imprimendum solum. | M.D.L.

4°. 𝕭.𝕴.

Great Bible version.

According to a MS. note by Fry, this edition 'is said to have been printed for circulation in Ireland.'

DESCRIPTION. Six preliminary leaves: title (without border), verso blank, *The Prologue to the reader*—7 pp., *The summe and cōtent* . . . —2 pp., *The names of all the bookes* . . . —1 p. The text, divided into five parts: (1) Pentateuch—ff. i to lxxxvij (L 7) *b*, 1 f. blank; (2) Joshua–Job, with title, verso blank, text—ff. ij to cxxxij (RR 4) *a*, verso blank; (3) Psalms–Malachi, with title, on verso begins the text—ff. 1 (not numbered) *b* to cl (T 6) *b*; (4) Apocrypha, with title: *The volume of the bookes called Hagiographa* . . . , on verso *To the reader*, text—ff. ij to lxxxviij (LL 8) *a*, verso blank; (5) N. T., with title: *The newe testament in english* . . . , on verso begins the text—ff. 1 (not numbered) *b* to cxi (Oo 7) *b*; on the same page begins *A Table to finde the Epistles and Gospels vsually reade in the Churche, accordyng vnto the booke of Cōmon prayer* . . . , which ends on Oo 8 *b*.

Signatures: ✠⁶, A–L⁸, AA–QQ⁸ RR⁴, A–S⁸ T⁶, AA–LL⁸, Aa–Oo⁸; 576 ff. A full column contains 61 or 62 lines. Marginal references, contents before chapters, etc. The letter W, wherever it occurs in the preliminary matter, has been taken from another fount of larger type.

Cranmer's Prologue contains the error *nede not the spurre* for *nede the spurre*.

No title-borders, and no illustrations. Many woodcut initials. A curious initial P, representing a schoolmaster wielding a birch rod, occurs before Galatians and elsewhere.

¶ 222 × 159 mm. Imperfect: wanting fo. 16 in pt. 3, and the last two leaves in pt. 5;—supplied in facsimile. Some leaves have evidently been taken from another copy. [F. F.]

56.

1550. The newe | Testament faythfully trans- | lated by Miles Couerdal. | Anno. 1550. | Roma . xv . a . | Whatsoeuer thinges are wrytten afore tyme, are wrytten for | oure learnynge.

[*C. Froschover : Zurich.*]   16°.   B. L.

Tindale's version.

The text of this edition is Tindale's, and not Coverdale's, as curiously stated on the title; it generally agrees closely with the G. H. edition.

Fry's No. 25. Printed at Zurich and issued in England. The first two sheets were evidently added by an English printer. Perhaps Day and Seres were the English publishers, as the contents of St. Matthew (see Description below) are printed in the peculiar type used by them in their folio Bible of 1549. The second title and the text are printed in C. Froschover's angular type. The copy in the Public Library at Zurich which bears Froschover's autograph and imprint has practically settled the question of printer and place (*cf.* Lea Wilson, p. 174).

DESCRIPTION. Seventeen preliminary leaves: first title (in black and red, with a medallion), verso blank, Kalendar—6 ff., 1 f. blank, *A Table to fynde the Epistles and Gospels newly set forth by the kynges commaundement, after the copy, called the Seruyce boke or communion* . . . —9 pp., *God speaketh* . . . (six texts taken from the New Testament)—1 p., . . . *What S. Mathew conteyneth*—3 ff.; second title: *The | Newe Testa- | mēt, of our saviour Jesu Christ, Newly | & faythfully ouer- | sene & corrected. | S. Paul . Colloss. iij. | Let* . . . (within woodcut border), verso blank. The text—ff. II to CCCCXLVI (Kk 6) *b* [ending, in the original issue, with Froschover's device and the colophon: *Imprynted at Zürich, by Christoffel Froschouer, in the yeare after the creacion of the worlde .5.5.25. And after the byrth of our Saviour .1.5.50*].

Signatures: [unsigned]⁸ ✠⁸, A–Z⁸ a–z⁸ Aa–Ii⁸, Kk⁶; 462 ff. A full page contains 26 lines. References, and a few subject-headings and notes in the margins. No prologues and no chapter-contents.

The words *and said this cup is the new testament in my bloude* are omitted from the text (1 Cor. xi. 25); but in some copies they are added in the margin, in type like that used by Day and Seres. In the headline on Kk 6 *a Judas* is printed for *John*.

The medallion (containing the Head of our Saviour) on the first title is like that in the 16° Testament printed by Jugge in 1548 (Fry's No. 20). The border to the second title represents : above—the creation of Eve, and the Nativity of our Lord ; at the sides—emblems of the Evangelists; below—Adam and Eve, and the Crucifixion. According to Fry, this border had been used by Froschover for the title in the first volume of his 16° German Bible 1527-29. Lea Wilson possessed a copy (No. 26, pp. 173-5, in his Catalogue) 'in the most immaculate condition,' with many leaves unopened, and in the original binding. It contained the first sheet of preliminary matter, but not the second; and the second title was cut away. Lea Wilson considered this to be the exact condition of the book when first issued. But since the first sheet, as well as the second, is printed in English black-letter, it seems more likely that the book as originally issued by Froschover contained only one preliminary leaf (the second title) and the text, which are printed in his well-known type, with the device and colophon on Kk 6 *b*. The Zurich copy has no more. Apparently Lea Wilson's copy lacked the device and the colophon, which he quotes somewhat differently. The B. M. copy (C.18.a.6) probably represents the book as published in England, with Froschover's title cancelled, and no device or colophon at the end. It contains everything else, except the blank leaves.

¶ 111 × 71 mm. Very imperfect: wanting all before Luke v (fo. 107, O 3); also ff. 111–113, 138–155, 265–272, 408, 409, 425, 432; and all after Rev. xviii (fo. 439, Ii 7). All the preliminary leaves (except five of Kalendar) and the last leaf (as in the Zurich copy) are supplied in facsimile. Some of the leaves have been damaged by fire. [F. F.]

57.

1550. The new | Testament in Englishe after | the greeke translation anne | xed wyth the translation of | Erasmus in Latin. | Wherunto is added a Kalendar, and | an exhortation to the readyng of the | holy scriptures made by the same | Erasmus wyth the Epistles taken | out of the olde testamēt both in Latin | and Englyshe, whereūto is added a ta- | ble necessary to finde the Epistles and | Gospels for euery sonday & holyday | throughout the yere after the vse of | the churche of England nowe. | Excusum Londini in officina | Thomæ Gaultier pro I. C. | Pridie Kalendas Decembris anno | Domini. M. D. L.

8°. Partly B. L.

The fourth edition of Tindale's English version with the translation of Erasmus in Latin.

Fry's No. 27: The English text closely agrees with the G. H. edition.
The initials *I. C.* (i.e. J. C.) stand for the name of the publisher, who, according to his preface, was also editor. They may indicate John Cawood, the London printer. That these initials point to some printer is assumed in the *Advertisement to the Reader* at the beginning of a Latin-English Testament printed by E. Tyler, London, 1659: *The Printers Undertaking in this Work is warranted by a former Example of J. C. 1550. being carried on with a like zeal to the publique good. For as J. C. that he might forward the Reformation intended by K. Edw. the sixth, set out the New Testament in English, together with Erasmus Translation in Latine; so E. T.* . . . etc. There appears to be no adequate reason for connecting this edition with the name of Sir John Cheke. (But see Herbert, p. 765; also p. 1673.)

DESCRIPTION. Fourteen preliminary leaves: title (in black and red, within woodcut border), on verso *An almanacke for . xxii . yeares* (1550-71), *J. C. vnto the Christen reders*—1 p., 1 p. blank, Kalendar—6 ff.; *An exhortacion . . . by Erasmus Roterodamus*—9 pp.; *The summe and content* . . . —2 pp., 1 p. blank. The text, A i to Hh 5 b; *The Epistles of the old testament* . . . —5 pp., 1 p. blank, table of Epistles and Gospels *accordynge vnto the booke of Common prayer*—3 pp., ending on Ii 2 a, verso blank.
Signatures: ✶⁸, ✠⁶, A–Z⁸ Aa–Hh⁸ Ii²; 264 ff. Leaves not numbered. The Latin and English texts are printed in parallel columns: the former inside, in roman type; the latter outside, in black-letter. A full column of the English contains 54 lines. References in margins. Contents before chapters. These occur only in the Gospels and Acts in the English text; in the case of the Latin, they are elegiac couplets, and are found throughout the book. No prologues, and no notes.
The title-border is an architectural design: at the top is the sun; below is a tablet, supported by two cupids, and bearing the monogram of the printer E. Whitchurch.

¶ 169 × 110 mm. Inserted is a variant leaf (C 7), which has the first few lines of Matt. xxii (Latin text) omitted; it is corrected by a pasted slip. [F. F.]

—— Another copy.

171 × 111 mm. Imperfect: wanting title and last leaf of Kalendar. The leaf C 7 has the pasted slip. At the bottom of D 8 a are printed by mistake a few lines of text from another part of the book.
On a blank page at the end of the book are written by an early hand two verses of the old song *From Oberon in fairy-land*, signed *William Penn* (possibly Admiral Sir W. Penn, 1621-70, the friend of Samuel Pepys and father of the founder of Pennsylvania).

58.

1550. The new te- | stament in Englishe | faythfully trāslated ac- | cordyng to the texte | of Erasmus, per- | mitted and au- | thorised by yᵉ | kynges ma- | iestie & his | counsaile. | Imprinted ad | London in Flete- | strete at the Si- | gne of yᵉ Rose | garland by | Wyllyam Copland. | for John Wayly. | 1550.

8°. 𝕭. 𝕷.

Great Bible version.

This edition, though the wording of the title is altered, appears to be a simple reprint of that issued by E. Whitchurch in 1547, with which it reads generally page for page. The two serious typographical errors are corrected, but many minor peculiarities reappear, e.g. in 1 Cor. xv. F. the words *and afterward that which is spiritual* (v. 46) are again omitted.

DESCRIPTION. Sixteen preliminary leaves: title (in black and red within woodcut border), on verso *An almanack for . xxviii . yeares* (1550-77), *The kalender*—3 ff., *A Table* ... —11 ff., *A compendious and brief rehersall* ... 1 f. The text—a i to R 4 a, verso blank. Signatures: *⁸ ‡⁸, a-z⁸ A-Q⁸ R⁴; 332 ff. Leaves not numbered. The text reads generally page for page with that of 1547, except in sheet O where the typographical errors are corrected. The headlines in this edition are printed in smaller type, the same size as the text. The Kalendar refers to the Epistles and Gospels on certain holy days. Apparently no table at the end, and no colophon.

The title-border is like that in E. Whitchurch's edition of 1547; but the tablet bears the date 1550, instead of the initials N. H.

¶ 134 × 86 mm. [F. F.]

59.

1550. The Boke of | the Prophetes. | Esaye ... Malachi.

J. Daye and W. Seres: London. 1550. 8°. 𝕭. 𝕷.

Taverner's version.

The fourth part of an edition of the Old Testament with Apocrypha issued in separate volumes by Day and Seres. (*Cf.* note after No. 65.)

The text agrees with Taverner's version, as revised by Becke, and published in Day's folio Bible of 1551.

DESCRIPTION. One preliminary leaf: title (within woodcut border), verso blank; the text, a ii to GG 3 a, ending with the colophon: *Imprinted at London by Jhon Daye, dwellynge ouer Aldersgate, and Wylliam Seres dwellinge in Peter Colledge. The yere of our Lord God M.D.L. the twēty, day of Auguste. Cum priuilegio ad imprimendum solum*, 1 f. blank.

Signatures: a-y⁸ A-Y⁸ AA-FF⁸ GG⁴; 404 ff. Leaves not numbered. A full page contains 32 or 33 lines. No prologues, except Tindale's before Jonah. Contents before each chapter; references in the margins; notes at the end of many chapters.

The title-border resembles that used in the second and fifth parts printed in 1549; but some of the dividing lines have disappeared, and the date is altered to 1550. The words *Cum priuilegio ad imprimendum solum* are printed below the border. No woodcut on verso of title.

¶ 143 × 92 mm. [F. F.]

60.

1550? (The New Testament.)

[Qu. *J. Day and W. Seres: London.* 1550?] 16°. 𝕭. 𝕷.

Tindale's version.

Fry's No. 24. The printer, place and date are uncertain. In most particulars the book agrees closely with Day and Seres' octavo edition of Oct. 1548. The wording of the titles to the table at the end of the volume is like that in the 16° Zurich Testament of 1550.

DESCRIPTION. There should probably be twelve preliminary leaves: [title unknown,] Kalendar—6 ff., *Uvillia Tindal vnto the Chrystyan Reader*—9 pp., list of books—1 p. The text—A 1 to Dd 1 a; the O. T. Epistles, *according as they be nowe read in the churche vpon certayne dayes*—6 pp., *A table to fynde the Epistles and Gospels newly set forth by the kynges commaundement, after the copye, called the Seruyce boke or communion.* . . .—8 pp., *An exhortation.* . . .—2 pp., *The summe and content of all the holye scripture* . . . ending probably on Dd 12 (Dd 9 is the last leaf known).

Signatures: [signature unknown]¹², A–Y¹² Aa–Dd¹²; (probably) 324 ff. Leaves not numbered. A full page contains 45 lines. References and subject-headings in margins. Contents before chapters, and generally notes at the end. Prologues to many of the books.

Cuts of SS. Matthew and Mark, the Day of Pentecost, and 20 cuts in Revelation (like those in Day and Seres' folio Bible of 1549).

¶ 128 × 66 mm. Imperfect: wanting apparently nineteen leaves:—title, first five leaves of Kalendar, and fourth leaf of prologue; also A 1, Cc 4 and 9, and Dd 4 to the end. Of these, Cc 4 and 9, Dd 4, 6 and 7 are supplied in facsimile; and photographs (taken from the copy in the Lenox Library) of the fourth leaf of prologue, A 1, Dd 5, 8 and 9 are added in an envelope. [F. F.]

61.

1551. The newe | Testament of oure Sa- | uioure Jesu Christe. | Wyth the notes and expo- | sitions of the darke | places there | in. | Cum Priuilegio ad imprimendum solum.

Jhon Oswen: Worceter. '12 Jan. 1550' [=1551]. 4°. 𝔅. 𝔏.

Great Bible version.

DESCRIPTION. Eighteen preliminary leaves: title (in black and red, within border), on verso *The bokes conteyned in the newe Testament, The prynter to the Reader*—1 p., *An Almanake for . xxv . yeares* (1550–74), Kalendar (with table of second lessons)—6 ff., *A Table of the feastes that haue their second proper lessons oute of the new testament* . . .—1 p., *A table to fynde the Epistles and Gospels read in the churche of Englande* . . . (with a note at the end *The order how* . . .)— 6 pp., *A Table for the foure Euangelistes* (and Acts) . . .—13 pp. The text, A i to Rr v *b*; followed on the same page by the O. T. Epistles, which end on Rr 8 *b*; *The Notes and expositions of the darke places throughe all the bokes of the newe Testamente* . . .—63 pp., ending on Xx 8 *a*; on verso is the colophon: *Imprinted the, xij, Daye of January. Anno Do. M.CCCCC.L. At Worceter by Jhon Oswen. Cum Gratia & Priuilegio ad imprimendum solum.*

Signatures: ✱⁸ ✱✱⁸ ✱✱✱², A⁴ B–Z⁸ Aa–Xx⁸; 366 ff. Leaves not numbered. A full page contains 32 lines. References, but no notes, in margins. No prologues, contents before chapters, etc.

A few words are omitted at the bottom of C v *a*.

The title is within a border of blocks arranged as follows:—above the letterpress is a cut of the royal arms (having lion and dragon as supporters) with the words *Dieu et mon droit;* below is a cut of the king seated on his throne, above which are the initials E. R., and below the words *Feare God. Honoure the Kynge, 1. Pet, 2*.; at the sides are arranged 8 ornamental slips, through which runs the legend *Go into yᵉ wholl world & preche the Gospel to all creaturs: he yᵗ beleueth | and is baptised, shalbe saued: he yᵗ beleueth not, shalbe damned. Mark . 16.* No other woodcuts except a few initials, one of which (before Hebrews) represents St. Veronica.

¶ 183 × 132 mm. Imperfect: wanting title and seven following leaves; ✱✱ 6, ✱✱✱ 1 and 2; Tt 8, Vv 3, and Xx 8;—14 leaves, all of which, except the title, are supplied in facsimile (taken from the copy in Balliol College Library, Oxford). [F. F.]

There is a perfect copy in the B. M.

62.

[Lewis (p. 191) describes an octavo edition of the New Testament, containing much the same supplementary matter as this quarto, and bearing J. Oswen's name as printer; it had no date, but the Almanack began with the year 1550. This copy, described as 'penes Tho. Rowe,' cannot now be traced. What appears to be a fragment of another quarto edition (styled *octavo* in the Cathedral Catalogue) is in St. Paul's Cathedral Library (38 C. 34). Herbert (p. 1459) mentions two editions, one in folio, and one in quarto, printed by Oswen in 1548.]

1551. [The new Testamēt of our sauiour Christ. . . .]

J. Day and W. Seres: London. '6 Feb. 1550' [=1551]. 8°. 𝔅. 𝔏.

Tindale's version.

VOL. I. E

Fry's No. 6. This edition agrees very closely—generally reading line for line—with the same printers' earlier edition of 1548. The Table by John Calvin, and the matter after the text, are new; and the cuts in Revelation differ.

DESCRIPTION. Forty preliminary leaves: title, on verso a woodcut, *The Printer to the Reader*—1 p., *An almanacke for . xxviii . yeares* (1550–77)—1 p., *The kalender* (with a table of Epistles and Gospels)—6 ff., *A Table of the principal matters conteyned in this new Testament. Gathered by J. C.*—45 pp., *A declaracion of the Table before goynge* (with colophon at end)—2 pp., 1 p. blank, *Uvilliam Tindale vnto the christian reader* (with list of books at end)—15 pp., prologue to St. Matthew—1 p. The text, C i to DD 6 b; followed by the O. T. Epistles *as they be now read in the churche*, which end on E ii (really EE 2) a; on the same page begins *A gatherynge of certayne harde wordes in the newe testament, wyth theyr expocission made by M. Jhon Caluin*, which ends on EE 7 a; on verso is the colophon: *Imprynted at London by Jhon Day, dwelling ouer Aldersgate and Wyllyam Seres dwellyng in Peter Colledge. These bokes are to be sold at the signe of the resurrection at the lytle counduyte in Chepside. Anno M.D.l. the .vi. day of February. Cum gratia* . . ., with a small cut of the Resurrection; 1 f. blank.

Signatures: ✱⁸ ‡⁸ B⁸ C⁸ B–Y⁸ Aa–Yy⁸ AA–EE⁸; 416 ff. Leaves not numbered. A full page contains 38 lines. J. C. mentioned in the title of the preliminary Table is apparently John Calvin.

No copy is now known with the titleleaf, which Herbert (p. 625) describes as follows: 'This title, printed in red and black, is within a compartment, with satyrs on the sides and the king's arms crowned, and supported by a lion and a dragon couchant at the bottom. On the back is the duchess of Suffolk's arms' (i.e. as in the very similar edition of 1548). There are cuts of the Evangelists, and 21 small cuts in Revelation.

¶ 143 × 98 mm. Imperfect: wanting title and three following leaves; also DD 8, EE 1 and 7. All these, except the title, are supplied in facsimile. The blank leaf is also missing.

[F. F.]
63.

1551. The Byble, | that is to saye, all the holye | Scripture : In whiche are contay-| ned the olde and new Testament, | truly and purely translated into | Englishe, & now lately with | great industry & diligence | recognysed. | Esay. i . | Herken to ye heauens, & thou earth | geue eare : For the Lorde | speaketh. | Imprynted at London by | Wyllyam Bonham, dwellynge in | Paules churche yarde, at the | sygne of the rede Lyon. | Cum gracia et Priuilegio ad Impri-| mendum solum | vi. day of Maye. M.D.LI.

Nicolas Hyll. f°. 𝕭. 𝕷.
Matthew's version.

This closely agrees with Raynalde and Hyll's Bible of 1549.
According to the colophon this edition was printed by Nicolas Hyll for *certayne honest menne of the occupacyon, whose names be vpon their bokes*. Differing copies show the names of William Bonham, John Whyte, Robert Toye, Thomas Petyt, and perhaps others.

DESCRIPTION. Twenty preliminary leaves: title (in black and red within woodcut border), on verso *An Almanake for . xxix . yeares* (1549–77); *A Table for the ordre of the Psalmes, to be sayed at Matyns and Euensonge* and *The order how the rest of the holy Scripture (besyde the Psalter) is appoynted to be redde*—1 p. ; *The Kalender* (with table of Psalms and Lessons) and *These thinges ensuynge* . . . —9 pp.; *An exhortacion, The summe and content* . . ., and *To the christian Readers.* . . . *As the Bees* . . . —1 f. ; *A description and successe* . . . —1 p.; *A table of the principall matters* . . ., *A perfit supputacion* . . ., and *A Prologue shewynge the vse of the Scripture*—23 pp. ; *The, names, of all the bokes* . . . —1 p. ; *A Register or a briefe rehearsall* . . . —1 p. The text, divided into five parts :—(1) Pentateuch, ff. j to cxii (O 8) b ; (2) Joshua–Job, with title (within border), verso blank, text—ff. ii to clv (v 3) a, verso blank, 1 f. blank ; (3) Psalter–Malachi, with title (within border), verso blank, text—ff. ii to cxc (& 6) b ; (4) Apocrypha, with title (within border), on verso *To the Reader*, text—ff. ij to Cii (NN 6) a, verso blank ; (5) N. T., with title : *The newe Testament . . . with Annotacions in the Mergēt, and other godlye Notes in the ende of the chapters . . . Imprynted at London in the yeare of our Lorde God. 1551* (within border), verso blank *william Tindale vnto the Christen Reader*—2 ff., text—ff. iiii to cxlix (TTt 5) *a*; on the same page begins *A table to find the Epistles and Gospels vsually reade in the Churche, accordinge vnto the booke of Common prayer* . . ., which ends on TTt 6 *b* with the colophon: *Here endeth the whole Byble after the translacion of Thomas Mathew, with all hys Prologues . . . And after euerye Chapter of the boke are there added many playne Annotacions . . . with other dyuers notable matters as ye shall fynde noted next vnto the Callender. Diligentlye perused and corrected. Imprynted at London, by Nicolas Hyll, dwelling in Saynct Johns streate, at the coste and charges of certayne honest menne of the occupacyon, whose names be vpon their bokes.*

Signatures: a⁶, ✱⁶ ❡⁶, A–O⁸, a–t⁸ v⁴, Aa–Zz⁸ &&⁶, AA–MM⁸ NN⁴, AAa–SSs⁸ TTt⁶ 730 ff. Printed in double columns, with 55 lines to the full column. Contents before the chapters, and notes at the end of many; references and notes in the margins; prologues before some books.

The border used for the general and N. T. titles is like that in Raynalde and Hyll's Bible of 1549. The borders to the titles of pts. 2, 3 and 4 are composed of four corner-blocks (like those in the Great Bibles) and six small side-blocks (representing New Testament subjects). An extra block is introduced below the letterpress of the titles to pts. 2 and 3. No illustrations.

¶ 308 × 194 mm. The titleleaf has been slightly mended, and mounted. The blank leaf at the end of pt. 2 is wanting.

On the last preliminary leaf is the autograph: *Wᵐ Herbert. 1778.* [F. F.]

—— Another copy.

The colophon on the last page in this copy ends: . . . *Imprynted at London by Nicolas Hyl, for John Wyghte, dwellynge in Paules churcheyarde at the sygne of the Rose. In the yere of our Lorde God. 1551. Cum priuilegio ad imprimendum solum.*

309 × 198 mm. Imperfect: wanting the general title; in place of which is inserted a N. T. title, with the words *The bokes of the Byble* on two printed slips, pasted over the first three lines.

64.

1551. The fyrste | parte of the Bible | called the . v . bookes of | Moses trans- | lated by . W | T . wyth all his prologes | before euery boke, and cer | teine learned notes vpon | many harde wordes. | Genesis. | Exodus. | Leuiticus. | Numeri. | Deuteronomium. | Anno Dom. M. | D.L.I.

J. Day: London. 8°. 𝔅. 𝔏.

Taverner's version.

The text agrees with Taverner's version as revised by Becke, and published in Day's folio Bible of 1551.

The first part of an edition of the Old Testament issued in four volumes, as appears from the following extract from the preface:—. . . *Consideringe also, that the bookes contaynynge the same* [i.e. Holy Scripture]: *beynge together in anye one volume, eyther are of so highe price that the pore . . . are not able to bye them . . . I (furthered by the honest request of diuers) haue to the cōmoditie of these pore, printed yᵉ whol old testament in . iiii . sundry partes, yᵗ they whiche ar not able to bie yᵉ hole, may bie a part . . .*

Probably this was intended to stand as a companion volume to the other parts of Day and Seres' edition of the Old Testament with Apocrypha, described above (Nos. 53, 54, and 60). It resembles that edition very closely in general appearance, though differing in the title-border, and bearing only Day's name in the colophon.

But why should the first part, which alone contains the preface explaining the object of this edition issued in separate volumes, appear latest of them all? Possibly this book is really the first volume of a *reissue* by Day alone of the five-volume edition which he had already brought out in conjunction with Seres. The other volumes may not have been reprinted; at any rate, no copies seem to have survived.

DESCRIPTION. Nine preliminary pages: title (within woodcut border), on verso *The Printer to the Reader, The Prologe shewinge the vse of the scripture made by William Tindal*—7 pp. Text, A 5 *b* to Vv 6 *b*; followed by 1 f. containing on recto the colophon: *Imprinted at London by Jhon Day dwellyng ouer Aldersgate. beneth Saint Martins. Anno Domi. M.D.L.I. Cum priuilegio ad imprimendum solum*, verso blank; 1 f. blank.

Signatures: A–Y⁸ Aa–Vv⁸; 336 ff. Leaves not numbered. A full page contains 33 lines. Tindale's Prologues. Contents before each chapter; references and notes in the margins.

The title-border contains at the sides—two supporting figures, above—a shield bearing crossed swords, and below—a tablet representing the story of Judith.

¶ 139 × 93 mm. Imperfect: wanting all before C 3, and all after Ss 8; also I 7 and 8 and T 7. Inserted are facsimiles of the titleleaf and the last leaf containing the colophon, taken from what appears to be the only other known copy in the B. M., which wants only the last leaf—probably blank. [F. F.]

65.

Note on the Parts of the Bible printed 1549-51.

Herbert (p. 622), Lea Wilson (p. 33 and p. 129*) and Cotton (p. 21 n.) are all inexact in their numbering of these parts. The true third part is a volume entitled *The thyrde parte . . .*, and containing Psalms to Song of Solomon, a copy of which is in the B. M. The following is a list of the parts, with printers and dates:—

(1) *The fyrste parte* . . . (Pentateuch). Day, 1551. 8° (perhaps a *reissue*).
(2) *The second parte* . . . (Joshua to Job). Day and Seres, 1549. 8°.
(3) *The thyrde parte* . . . (Psalms to Song of Solomon). Daie and Seres, 1550. 8°.
(4) *The Boke of the Prophetes* . . . (Isaiah to Malachi). Daye and Seres, 1550. 8°.
(5) *The volume of the bokes called Apocripha*. . . . Day and Seres, 1549. 8°.

Copies of all these parts are in the B. M.; and all except *The thyrde parte* are in this Library.

Perhaps the New Testament (Tindale's version) printed by Day and Seres in 1551 (Fry's No. 26)—or that issued by Day alone about the same date (Fry's No. 28)—though not quite uniform with the above, was meant for the supplementary volume, completing the Bible.

All these 'parts' were incorporated into the folio double-column Bible printed by John Day in 1551, which, in the O. T. and Apocrypha, is recognised as Taverner's version, revised by Edmund Becke. The type, initial letters, and matter are practically identical. The 'part' and the complete Bible often read together line for line through long passages of text. It seems probable that Becke was engaged for some time in this work of revision, and that instalments were published in octavo from 1549 to 1551. Finally these were united with Tindale's N. T. to form the folio complete Bible published by Day with Becke's preface in 1551. (See No. 66.)

1551. The Byble, | that is to say, al the holy | Scripture conteined in the olde | & new Testament, faythfully set | furth according to yᵉ Coppy of Thomas | Mathewes traūslaciō, wherunto are | added certaine learned Prologes, & | Annotaciōs for the better vnder | standing of many hard places | thorowout the whole | Byble. | Esay. i. | Hearken to ye heauens, & thou earth | geue eare : for the Lorde speaketh. | Imprinted at | London by Jhon Day | dwellyng ouer Al- | dersgate. | Cum gratia et priuilegio ad- | imprimendum solum. | Anno a. M.D.Li.

f°. 𝔅. 𝔏.

Taverner and Tindale's versions.

The title is misleading. The Old Testament and Apocrypha are a revised edition of Taverner's version, apparently prepared by Edmund Becke, the editor of this Bible (*cf.* No. 47), and previously published in separate octavo parts by Day and Seres. (See note above.) The New Testament closely agrees with Day and Seres' Tindale Testaments of 1548 and 1551; and is practically identical with that printed by Day alone, probably in 1551 (Fry's No. 28).

DESCRIPTION. Twenty-three preliminary leaves: title (in black and red, within woodcut border), on verso *An Almanacke for, xxvii yeares* (1551-77), Kalendar—3 pp., Dedication *To the most puisaunt and mightie Prince Edwarde the sixt* . . . signed : *Your graces faythfull obediente and humble subiecte Edmonde Becke*—3 pp., *To the Christen Readers* and *A table of the pryncipal matters* . . .—13 ff., *A gatheryng of certayne harde wordes in the newe Testament, with their exposicion* and *An exhortacion* . . .— 2 ff., *The summe and content* . . . and *A perfect supputation* . . .—3 pp., *The names of al the bookes* . . .—1 p., *A Regyster or a bryefe rehersall* . . .—1 p., *A descripcion and*

successe . . . 1 p., *The Prologe shewing the vse of the scripture, made by Wylliam Tyndall*—1 f. (numbered i, e 1). The text, divided into five parts:—(1) Pentateuch, ff. i (really 2) to xxxiiii (really 84, s 6) *a*, verso blank; (2) Joshua–Job, with title (within border), verso blank, text—ff. ii to cxvii (V 3) *b*, 1 f. blank; (3) Psalter–Malachi, with title (within border), on verso begins the text—ff. 1 (not numbered) to cxlii (BBB 4) *a*, verso blank; (4) Apocrypha, with title (within border), on verso *A Prologe* . . ., text—ff. ii to lxxxiiii (OOo 6) *a*, verso blank; (5) N. T., with title: *The Newe Testament* . . . *with certayne Notes folowynge the chapters* . . . *Anno.M.D.LI.* (within border), on verso begins *Uvyllyam Tyndall vnto the Christyan Reader*—4 pp., text—ff. iii (really 2) to xcviii (really 119, Vvvv 6) *a*, on verso begins *A Table to fynde the Epystles and Gospels vsually reade in the Churche, accordyng vnto the boke of Common praier* . . .—3 pp. ending on Vvvv 7 *b* with colophon: *The ende of the old and newe Testament. To the honour and prayse of God was thys Byble prynted, and fynyshed in the yeare of our Lord and sauiour Jesus Christ. M.D.LI. The .xxiii. daye of Maye. Imprinted at London by Jhon Daye, dwellyng ouer Aldersgate beneth Saynt Martyns. Cvm privilegio ad imprimendvm solvm*, 1 f. blank.
Signatures: ✱⁴ AA⁶ b(or B)⁶ c⁶, e–s⁶, A–T⁶ V⁴, AA–YY⁶ AAA⁶ BBB⁴, AAa–OOo⁶, Aaaa–Tttt⁶ Vvvv⁸; 572 ff. Printed in double columns, with 67 lines to the full column. Contents before each chapter, and notes at the end of many. References and notes in the margins. The Apocrypha include 3 Maccabees, and the new translation of 3 Esdras, Tobit, and Judith, which appeared for the first time in the separate volume published in 1549. The 'wife-beating' note (1 Pet. iii) occurs in this edition. Omitted lines at the bottom of QQ 6 *b* and RR 6 *b* are added by means of pasted slips.

The border used for the titles has supporting figures at the sides; above are the royal arms, and below Day's device and motto, *Arise, for it is Day*; at the top of the page are printed the initials E R. A cut of the Evangelist precedes each Gospel. At the beginning of the Dedication stands a woodcut initial, representing Becke offering his book to the King. A few copies (e.g. those in St. Paul's Cathedral, the University Library and St. John's College, Cambridge, and the John Rylands Library) contain an extra leaf bearing on one side an engraving with the arms of Edward VI, dated 1549; above are the words—*O Lord for thy mercyes sake, saue the Kyng*, and below—*Feare God, and honour the Kynge*. This leaf apparently does not belong to the book, but was inserted in a few copies as an embellishment, and placed opposite the first title.

¶ 275 × 181 mm. The general title is mounted. The last leaf (blank) is missing.
[F. F.]

—— Another copy.

262 × 178 mm. Imperfect: wanting first title and three following leaves. A made-up title is inserted, consisting of a facsimile centre enclosed within a genuine pt. 2 title-border; the initials at the top should be red, not black, on the first title, and the verso should contain the Almanack. Enclosed in the book are facsimile copies of the Almanack and the two leaves ✱ ii and iii. The blank leaf is also missing.

—— Another copy.

263 × 183 mm. Imperfect: wanting first title and two leaves of preliminary matter (B 4 and 5); and in pt. 5 the following leaves—Ffff 1, Qqqq 6, Ssss 3 and 4, the last leaf of print and the following blank leaf.

—— Another copy.

257 × 184 mm. Imperfect: wanting first title and ten following leaves; also in pt. 1, e 3 and 4; pt. 2, title; pt. 4, title and following leaf; pt. 5, title, Mmmm 2 to 4, Ssss 2 and 3, Vvvv 1 to 3, 6, 7, and the blank leaf. Some leaves mutilated. This copy contains duplicate copies of two leaves in pt. 1, m 3 and 4.

66.

1551? (The New Testament.)

J. Daye: London. 1551? 8°. 𝕭. 𝕷.

Tindale's version.

Fry's No. 28. This closely resembles in most particulars Day and Seres' editions of 1548 and 1551.

As all three extant copies of this edition are imperfect at the beginning and end, the date is uncertain. It was most probably issued in 1551, since it is practically identical with the New Testament of Day's Bible published in that year. Down to Feb. 1551 (see Fry's

No. 26) Day was printing Bibles and Testaments in conjunction with Seres; afterwards he printed independently. The colophon at the end of the preliminary table contains Day's name alone, as in his Bible of May 1551.

DESCRIPTION. — preliminary leaves: [title, etc., not known]; on a leaf signed ‡ ii (really ⋆ ii) begins *A Table of principall matters*...—43 pp., *A declaration of the Table* ...—2 pp. ending on ‡ 8 *a* with the colophon: *Imprinted at London By John Daye dwellynge ouer Aldersgate Cum priuilegio*..., verso blank; *Wyllyam Tyndale vnto the Christian Reader*—11 pp., the prologue to St. Matthew—1 p. The text, D 7 to CC 7 *b*; followed on the same page by the O. T. Epistles *as they be nowe read in the churche*, which end on D 2 *b*, and *A gatherynge of certaine harde wordes*... which ends probably on DD 8 *a* (DD 7 is the last leaf known), perhaps with colophon on verso, as in Fry's No. 26.

Signatures: [—], ⋆⁸ ✠⁸ ‡⁸, D–Y⁸ Z⁴, Aa–Yy⁸ AA–DD⁸; [—]+388 ff. Leaves not numbered. A full page contains 37 or 38 lines.

The woodcuts correspond generally to those in Fry's No. 26.

¶ 135 × 93 mm. Like the copies in the B. M. and the Lenox Library, imperfect. Wants all before I 8 (Matt. xxv), and all after CC 8; also three leaves, K 8, O 1 and 2—supplied in facsimile. Photographs (taken from the Lenox copy) of ‡ 8 *a* and Aa 1 *a* are inserted.
[F. F.]
67.

1552. The Byble | in Englishe, that is to say. The | content of al the ho- | ly Scripture, both of | the olde, and newe | Testament,| Accordynge to the translaci- | on that is appointed | to be redde in the | Churches. | N H | Printed at London by Nycolas Hyll. | Cum priuilegio ad imprimendum solum.

1552. 4°. 𝕭. 𝕷.

Great Bible version.

DESCRIPTION. Thirty-four preliminary leaves: title (in black and red, within woodcut border), on verso *An Almanacke for . xxvi . yeares* (1552–77), *A table for the ordre of the Psalmes*—1 p., *The order how the rest of the holy Scripture*...—1 p., Kalendar—6 ff.; *The order of Commen prayer*...—12 ff. (numbered i to xij), ending with colophon: *Imprinted at London by Nycholas Hyll, for Abraham Veale, dwelling in Pauls churcheyarde at the sygne of the Lambe*; *A table of the Princinal matters*...—14 ff. The text, divided into four parts:—(1) Genesis-Job, ff. i to cciiij (really 206, Cc 6) *b*; (2) with title: *The thyrd part of the Byble contaynynge these bookes. The Psalter . . . Malachy* (within border), on verso begins the text—ff. 1 (not numbered) *b* to Cxxxiij (really 137, s ii) *b*; (3) Apocrypha, with title: *The volume of the bokes called Hagiogropha*... (within border), on verso *To the reader*, text—ff. Cxxxv (really 139, s iii) to ccxiiij (really 218, cc 10) *a*, verso blank; (4) N. T., with title: *The newe Testament in Englyshe*... (in italics, within border), verso blank, text—ff. ij to 101 not numbered, NN 5) *a*, followed on the same page (in the second column) by *A Table to fynde the Epistles and Gospels vsually read in the church, according vnto the boke of comon prayer*... which ends on NN 6 *a* with the colophon: *Imprynted at London by Nycholas Hyll. Anno.M.D.L.II.*, verso blank.

According to the foliation and signatures the book is divided into three, not four parts; but the Apocrypha have a separate title and apparently form a distinct part. The title to pt. 2, *The thyrd part*..., is incorrect.

Signatures: [unsigned]⁸, A–C⁴, ⋆⁸ ℂ⁶, A–Z⁸ Aa⁸ Bb⁸ Cc⁶, a–z⁸ &⁸ aa⁸ bb⁸ cc¹⁰, AA–MM⁸ NN⁶; 560 ff. Printed in double columns, with 61 lines to the full column. No contents before chapters, and no notes; but marginal references. The headlines contain subject-headings only in the O. T. *The order of Commen prayer*, which is printed in larger type than the text, follows Edward VI's first Prayer Book.

The border to the four titles is like that first used in Nycolson's quarto Bible of 1537.

¶ 187 × 140 mm. Imperfect: wanting the general title and following leaf, the last leaf of Kalendar, and the last leaf of *The order of Commen prayer*; all of which, except the leaf after the title, are supplied in facsimile.
[F. F.]

There is a good copy in the University Library, Cambridge.

68.

1552. The newe Testament | of our Sauiour Jesu Christe. Faythfully tran- | slated out of the Greke. | Wyth the Notes and expositions of the darke pla- | ces therein. | Mathew. xiij f. | Vnio, quem præcepit emi servator Iesus, | Hic situs est, debet non aliunde peti. | The pearle, which Christ cōmaunded to be bought | Is here to be founde, not elles to be sought. *Rycharde Jugge : London.* [1552.] 4°. 𝔅. 𝔏.

Tindale's version ; Jugge's revision.

Fry's No. 29. The earliest of three illustrated quarto editions of Tindale's version, printed by Jugge, and ascribed to the dates 1552, 1553, and 1566. Here first appears Jugge's Dedication, explaining that the text was revised with the *aduise and helpe of godly learned men*. The book contains new introductions and notes.

The date, though not given on the title or in the colophon, was most likely 1552. The *perfecte supputation* mentions the year 1552 as *this presente yeare*. In some copies, on verso of the title is printed *The copy of the byll assigned by the kynges honorable counsell, for the Auctorisinge of this Testamente*, naming *twenty & two pens* as the limit-price for the unbound book, and dated *At Grenewiche the x. of June. M.D.Lij.* The Table of Epistles and Gospels allows for a second Communion on Easter Day, which was dropped from the service-book in August 1552.

DESCRIPTION. Sixteen preliminary leaves : title (in black and red, with woodcut), verso (in some copies) blank, Dedication *To the puysaunt and mightye Prince Edwarde the syxt* . . . 1 f., Kalendar (with table of second lessons)—6 ff., *An Almanacke for xxiiii. yeares* (1552-75)—1 p., *A Table of the principall matters* . . . —11 pp., *A perfecte supputation of the yeres and time* . . . —1 f., *An exhortation* . . . —1 p., *The lyfe of the blessed Euangelyste Saynte Mathew* . . . —1 p. The text, divided into two parts : (1) Matthew-Acts, A i to & i *b*, followed by *The descrjption of the Lande of promys* . . . (with a map and short note)—1 p., *The Order of tymes*—4 pp., and 1 p. containing Jugge's device and imprint ; (2) with title : *The epistles of Saint Paule . . . The Canonicall Epistles . . . The Reuelation of .S. Iohn* (within border), on verso *The Argumente . . . to the Romaynes*, text—Aa ii to Rr ii (really 3) *a* ; on verso begin *The Epistles of the olde Testament, according as they be now read*, which end on Rr 5 *b* ; on the same page begins *A table to fynde the Epystles and Gospels, reade in the churche of Englande* . . ., which ends on Rr 7 *a* ; on verso is Jugge's device and colophon : *Imprynted at London by Rycharde Jugge, dwellynge in Paules churche yarde at the signe of the byble. VVith the kynge his moost gratious lycence, and priuilege, forbyddynge all other men to print or cause to be printed, this, or any other Testament in Englyshe* ; 1 f. blank.

Signatures : ✥⁸ ❦⁸, A–Y⁸ z⁸ &⁴, Aa–Rr⁸ ; 340 ff. Leaves not numbered. A full page contains 37 lines. The margins give references and alternative renderings. Arguments or introductions before each book. Contents before, and generally notes at the end of, each chapter. All this matter is printed in italic type in this edition. Marginal notes in black-letter mark the Epistles and Gospels.

On Q 7 *b* the words *Beynge accused by their ovvne conscience* (John viii. 9) are printed in roman type, with the marginal note *This is read in the greke testamente of Stephanus prynte*. This seems to show that the revisers consulted the famous Paris edition of the Greek Testament printed in 1550.

The woodcut in the centre of the general title is a portrait of Edward VI, within an ornamental frame bearing the inscription *Edvardvs Sextvs Dei gracia, Anglie, Francie, et Hibernie Rex. etc. Ætatis sue. XV.* ; outside the frame are the words *Viuat Rex*. The second title has an ornamental frame formed of four blocks ; the bottom block contains the initials R I, within a circle inscribed *Omnia Desvper*. Jugge's device is that of the ' pelican in her piety,' within an oval frame inscribed *Pro lege rege, et grege*, and *Love kepyth the Lawe, obeyeth the kynge, and is good to the commen welthe* ; at the sides—figures of *Prvdencia* and *Ivsticia* ; and below—Jugge's monogram. The illustrations include cuts of the Evangelists and Apostles, many cuts in the Gospels (in one of which the Devil with a wooden leg appears as the Enemy sowing tares), and 21 cuts in Revelation. There are also ornamental blocks, initial letters (some flourished), etc. Over 100 blocks are employed, some of which occur in earlier editions of the Bible and New Testament.

¶ 215 × 155 mm. Wants only the last leaf (blank). The general title has verso blank. Two photographs are inserted of *The copy of the byll* . . . found in some copies. [F. F.]

1552. The newe Testamente | of our sauiour Jesu Christe. | Faythfully translated out of the greke, | and perused by the commaundemente of the | Kynges maiestie, and his honourable | counsell, and by them auctorised. | Math. xiii. f. | The pearle which Christ cōmaūnded to be bought | Is here to be founde, not elles to be sought.
R. Jugge: London. [1552.] 16°. 𝔅. 𝔏.

Tindale's version; Jugge's revision.

Fry's No. 30. Appears to be printed from Jugge's first quarto edition of 1552 (*q.v.*). It repeats certain misprints found in that book, but corrected in later issues; and the table allows for two Communions on Easter Day. The almanack begins at the year 1552, and *The copye of the byll* is dated 20 Oct. 1552. Hence that year may be assigned with great probability to the book. In many particulars this edition closely resembles three other 16° Testaments—Fry's Nos. 20, 31, and 39.
The copye of the byll . . . names *ix.d.* as the limit-price for the unbound book.

DESCRIPTION. [Ten] preliminary leaves: title (in black and red, with woodcut), on verso *An Almanacke for xvij. yeares* (1552–68), *The copye of the byll assigned by the Kynges honourable counsel, for the auctorising of this Testament* (dated *At Westm. the . xx . of October. 1552*)—1 p., Dedication—3 pp., Kalendar—6 ff., [1 f. blank?]. The text, A i to ℈ ℈ 5 b; followed by *A table to fynde the pistles and Gospels reade in the churche of Englande* . . .—5 pp., and 1 p. containing Jugge's device and colophon: *Imprinted at London by Rycharde Jugge, dwellynge in Paules churchyarde at the signe of the Byble* . . .
Signatures: [unsigned]¹⁰, A–Z⁸ &⁸ Aa–Zz⁸ &&⁸ ℈ ℈⁸; 402 ff. Leaves not numbered. A full page contains 34 lines. No prologues; and no contents before, or notes after, chapters. The margins contain a few subject-headings printed in italics. Headlines in italics. The O. T. Epistles are omitted.
The woodcut on the title is a portrait of Edward VI, resembling that in the quarto of 1552. Jugge's device is very similar to the larger device in the quarto Testament, but bears the words *Cogita mori* inscribed on the tablet at the top. The illustrations include cuts of SS. Luke and John, nearly 50 cuts in the Gospels, and 20 in Revelation.

¶ 106 × 71 mm. Imperfect: wanting title and following leaf, and the last leaf of Kalendar; also B 8, C 4, ℈ ℈ 1, and the last three leaves. All these are supplied in facsimile from the copy now in the Lenox Library, New York. [F. F.]
70.

1553. The whole | Byble, | That is the holye Scripture, | of the olde and new Testament, faith- | fullye translated into Englyshe by | Myles Couerdale, and newly | ouersene and correcte. | M.D.LIII. | ij. Tessa. iij. | Praye . . . glorifyed. | Prynted at London by Ry- | charde Jugge, dwellynge at the North | dore of Powles, at the sygne of | the Byble.
[*C. Froschover: Zurich.*] 1553,50. 4°. 𝔅. 𝔏.

Coverdale's version.

The body of this book is identical with the Bible printed by Froschover at Zurich, and published by A. Hester at London in 1550 (*q.v.*); the date 1550 appears in the colophon. The title and preliminary leaves, however, are new; the former bears R. Jugge's name, and the late 1553.

DESCRIPTION of the twelve preliminary leaves (printed in English black-letter): title (within woodcut border), verso blank, *The bokes of the whole Byble* . . . —1 p., Dedication—4 pp., Prologue—5 pp., *The Table and Kalender expressynge the ordre of the Psalmes and Lessons, to be sayde at the Morninge and Euenynge prayer throughout the yeare, excepte certayne propre feastes, as the Rules folowynge more playnly declare* (taken from Edward VI's second Prayer Book of 1552)—2 ff., *An Almanacke for xix. yeares* (1552–70)—1 p., *The kalender* (with table of Psalms and Lessons)—7 pp.
Signatures: ✠⁶, ‡‡⁴.
The rest of the book is identical with A. Hester's edition of 1550, described above.

ENGLISH

The title-border is composed of ornamental blocks; the bottom block contains the initials R I with the motto *Omnia Desvper*; and below are the words *Set forth with the Kinges moost gratious licence.*

¶ 233 × 183 mm. Imperfect: wanting the last three leaves, which are supplied in facsimile. The title is mounted. [F. F.]

71.

1553. The byble in | English, that is to say, the | contente of all the holy scrip- | ture, bothe of the olde and | new Testament, accor- | dyng to the transla- | ciō that is appoin- | ted to be read in | Churches. | Imprinted at Lon- | don by Edwarde | Whytchurche. | Cum priuilegio ad im- | primendum solum.

1553.   f°.   𝕭. 𝕷.

Great Bible version.

According to a MS. note in the B. M. copy, Queen Mary is said to have destroyed the greater part of this impression.

DESCRIPTION. Two preliminary leaves: title (within border), verso blank, *The names of al the bokes* . . . —1 f. The text, divided into five parts:—(1) Pentateuch, ff. i to lxxxviij (L 8) *a*, verso blank; (2) Joshua–Job, with title (within border), verso blank, text—ff. ii to cxxxiiii (Rr 6) *a*, verso blank; (3) Psalter–Malachi, with title (within border), verso blank, text—ff. ii to clii (really 150, T 6) *b* ; (4) *Hagiographa*, with title (within border), on verso begins the text—ff. 1 (not numbered) *b* to lxxxvii (really 86, L 6) *a*, verso blank: (5) N. T., with title: *The Newe Testament in englishe* . . . *Printed in the yeare of our Lorde God. M.D.LIII.* (within border), on verso begins: *A Table to finde the Epistles and Gospels vsuallye read in the Church, accordinge vnto the boke of Common prayer* . . . —3 pp., text—ff. i to cxvi (P 6) *b*.

Signatures: [unsigned]², A–L⁸, Aa–Qq⁸ Rr⁶, A–S⁸ T⁶, A–L⁸, A–N⁸ O⁶ P⁶; 578 ff. The leaves D 7 and 8 in pt. 3 are numbered respectively *Fol. xxxi. &. xxxii.* and *Fo. xxxiii. &. xxxiiii.* This makes the number of the last leaf 152 instead of 150. Double columns, with 58 lines to the full column.

The borders to the general title, and the titles of parts 2, 3 and 4, are formed of 10 or more woodblocks—4 corner-blocks (like those used in the Great Bibles) and 6 smaller side-blocks (representing New Testament subjects); one block is added under the letterpress in the case of the general and pt. 3 titles, and two blocks (of smaller size) in the case of the title to pt. 2. The N. T. title-border is formed of 6 blocks—4 corner blocks representing the Evangelists, and two ornamental side-blocks—boys blowing horns (first used in the Coverdale Bible of 1535).

¶ 316 × 213 mm. The general title has been mounted. [F. F.]

—— Another copy.

Very imperfect: beginning with fo. 67 in pt. 1, and ending with fo. 139 in pt. 3; many of the intervening leaves are missing. All the leaves are badly cropped; many are water-stained, and some show traces of damage by fire.

72.

1553. The Bi | ble in Englishe ac- | cording to the tran- | slation of the great | Byble | 1553.

R. Grafton: London.   4°.   𝕭. 𝕷.

Great Bible version.

A handy quarto edition, printed in very small type.

DESCRIPTION. Two preliminary leaves: title (within border), verso blank, *The names of all the bookes of the Byble* . . . —1 f. The text:—(1) Genesis–Malachi, ff. j to ccc.iiij (really 306, Q ij) *b*; *Hagiographa*, with title (within border), on verso *To the Reader*, text—ff. ccc.vi (really 308, Q iiij) to ccc.lxxxii (really 380, ℘ 4) *a*, ending with the words *The ende of the olde Testamente* (within narrow frame), verso blank; (2) N. T.

with title: *The newe Testamente in Englishe* . . . (within border), verso blank, text—ff. ii to xcii (really 93, M 5) *b*; followed by *A Table to fynde the Epystles and Gospels vsually read in the churche, after Salysbury vse* . . . —2 ff. (not numbered), ending on M 7 *b* with the colophon: *The ende* . . . *Imprinted at London by Richarde Grafton, printer to the Kinges highnes. An. M.D.LIII. Cum priuilegio ad imprimendum solum*; 1 f. blank.

Signatures: [unsigned]², a–z⁸ A–Z⁸ &⁸ ♉⁴, A–M⁸; 478 ff. The numbering of the leaves is most incorrect. Printed in an extremely small wiry type; double columns, with 62 lines to the full column. No contents before chapters; but references in the margins. In pt. 1 the daily lessons are marked in the margins, and the appropriate months in the headlines. Thus on H ij *a December* is printed in the headline, *The . xxx . daie Mattins* in the margin beside chap. lxiii (of Isaiah), and *Euensong* at the side of chap. lxiv.

The border used for the three titles is a narrow frame composed of four blocks, of architectural design.

Herbert (p. 536) and Cotton (p. 29) assert that some copies of this edition bear the names of R. Grafton and E. Whitchurch as the printers (cf. Lewis, p. 384).

¶ 186 × 132 mm. [F. F.]

—— Another copy.

174 × 124 mm. Imperfect: wanting general title and following leaf; a 1 to 5, 7 and 8, c 1; N. T. title, A 8, and the Table (2 ff.); —14 ff. The blank leaf (M 8) is also missing. Inserted at the beginning are 8 ff. taken from a Bible (1611 version), dated 1646. With Metrical Psalms (1642).

73.

1553. The newe Testament | of oure Sauiour Jesus Christe. Faythfully transla- | ted oute of the Greke. | With the notes and expositions of the darke pla- | ces therein. | Matthew xiii. f. | Vnio, quem præcepit emi seruator Iesus. | Hic situs est, debet non aliunde peti. | The pearle which Christ cōmaunded to be boughte | Ishere to be founde, not elles to be sought.

R. Jugge: London. [1553.] 4°. 𝕭. 𝕷.

Tindale's version; Jugge's revision.

Fry's No. 32. The second quarto edition of Jugge's revision.

The date is not given, but is generally believed to be 1553, the first year of the Almanack; it is undoubtedly subsequent to August 1552, since the Table at the end allows for only one Communion on Easter Day.

The copye of the bill . . . names *twentye & two pence* as the limit-price for the unbound book.

DESCRIPTION. Eighteen preliminary leaves: title (in black and red, with woodcut), on verso *The copye of the bill* . . . dated *At Grenewiche the x. of June. M.D.Lii*, Dedication —1 f. (signed ¶ ij), Kalendar (first leaf signed ✠ iii) - -6 ff., *An Almanacke for xviii. yeares* (1553–70)—1 p., *A Table of the principall matters* . . . —14 pp., *A true and perfect rekenynge* . . . —1 p., *An exhortation* . . . —1 f., *The description of the lande of promys* . . . (the map)—1 p., *The life of* . . . *Saynte Mathewe* . . . —1 p. Text: (1) A j to z iii *b*, followed by *The Carte Cosmographie of the Peregrination or Jorney of S. Paule, with the distaunce of the Myles* (a map and short note)—1 p., *The Order of tymes*—4 pp., and 1 p. with Jugge's device and imprint; (2) title (with argument on verso), text—Aa ij to Qq 8 *a*; on verso begin the O. T. Epistles, which end on Rr ii *b*; on the same page begins *A Table* . . ., which ends on Rr 4 *a* with the colophon: *Imprinted at London by Rycharde Jugge, dwellinge at the North dore of Paules, at the signe of the Byble* . . . and the block containing the initials R. I.; on verso is Jugge's device.

Signatures: ¶ (or ✠)⁸, ✠¹⁰, A–Y⁸ z⁶, Aa–Qq⁸ Rr⁴; 332 ff. In most particulars this edition closely resembles that of 1552; but, though the headlines are in italic type, the contents before chapters, notes, and marginal references are in black-letter.

Woodcuts generally as in the 1552 edition. A small cut of the creation of Eve occurs at the beginning of *A true and perfect rekenynge* . . .

¶ 211 × 155 mm. The title has been mounted. [F. F.]

74.

1553. The newe Testamente of | our Sauiour Jesu Christ. | Faythfully translated out of | the Greke. | and perused by the commaundement of the kyn- | ges maiestie and his honourable counsell, and | by them auctorised. | With the Notes and expositions of the darke | places therein. | Mathewe. xiii. f. | The pearle, whiche Christe commaunded to be | bought, | Is here to be founde, not elles to be sought.

R. Jugge : London. [1553.] 8°. 𝔅. 𝔏.

Tindale's version; Jugge's revision.

This edition reproduces many typographical errors from the 1552 quarto Testament, which it closely follows in most particulars.

The date most probably is 1553, as *The copy of the byll* is dated 29 March 1553, and the *Almanacke* begins with the same year. Partial allowance is made in the margins, but not in the table, for two Communions on Christmas Day and Easter Day. It was perhaps the last edition of the New Testament published in the reign of Edward VI. Fry had not seen this edition when he wrote *A Bibliographical Description* . . . It resembles in many points the octavo editions (1561 ?) described below (Nos. 80–83).

In *The copy of the byll* occur the words . . . *Forasmuche as the same bokes be nowe come forthe in printe in that kinde of volume which is called the octaue.* . . . The *pryce of . xii . pence* is named as the limit-price for the unbound book.

DESCRIPTION. Thirty-two preliminary leaves: title (in black and red, with woodcut), on verso *The copy of the byll* . . . (dated *At Westminster the . xxix . of Marche. 1553*), Dedication—1 f., Kalendar—6 ff., *An Almanacke for . xviij. yeares* (1553-70)—1 p., *A Table of the Principall matters* . . . —41 pp., *A true and perfect rekenynge* . . . —1 p., *An exhortation* . . . (ending with Jugge's device)—2 pp., *The description of the lande of promes* . . . (the map)—2 pp., *The lyfe of* . . . *Saynt Mathewe* . . . —1 p. The text, A j to Zz 8 a; followed on the same page by *The Epistles of the olde Testament, accordyng as they be nowe read*, which end on && ij b ; *A table to fynde the pistles and Gospels reade in the churche of Englande* . . . —2 ff., ending on && 4 b with the colophon : *Imprinted at London by Richarde Jugge, dwellynge at the North dore of Paules church at the sygne of the Byble.* (*With the kynge his most gratious lycence, and priuilege) forbyddynge all other men to prynt or cause to be prynted, this, or anye other Testament in Englysh.*

Signatures : [unsigned]⁸ ✠⁸ ✠✠⁸ ✠✠✠⁸, A-Z⁸ &⁸ Aa-Zz⁸ &&⁴ ; 412 ff. Leaves not numbered. A full page contains 35 lines. Life of the Evangelist before each Gospel; arguments before other books (except Revelation). References, and a few notes (especially in Revelation), in margins. Contents before each chapter, and notes generally at the end. *The Carte Cosmographic of the Peregrination and iourneye of Saynte Paule* . . . —a map filling 2 pp., and *The order of tymes* . . . —4 pp. (preceded by a note referring to both on Cc 7 a), come after Acts.

The woodcut on the titlepage is a portrait of Edward VI, within an ornamental frame, like that used for Jugge's quarto Testaments, and his later octavo editions. A small cut of the creation of Eve occurs at the head of *A true and perfect rekenynge* . . . There are also cuts of the Evangelists, and 20 cuts in Revelation; besides the two maps (mentioned above) and many woodcut initials representing Paul giving his Epistles to messengers. Jugge's device is that with the pelican, and the motto above *Cogita mori*.

¶ 129 × 81 mm. Wants only one leaf (Aa 1), which was probably lost in rebinding. Contains the book-plate of Lord Hampton.

For a descriptive and critical article on this copy, believed to be unique, see the *Athenæum*, June 1886. [F. F.]

75.

NOTE. DURING THE REIGN OF EDWARD VI (JANUARY 1547 TO JULY 1553) SOME FORTY EDITIONS APPEARED OF THE BIBLE OR THE NEW TESTAMENT IN ENGLISH. WITH THE ACCESSION OF QUEEN MARY, THE PUBLICATION OF ENGLISH SCRIPTURES SUDDENLY CEASED. HER REIGN WITNESSED THE ISSUE OF ONLY ONE EDITION—THE NEW TESTAMENT OF 1557, TRANSLATED BY AN EXILE, AND PRINTED AT GENEVA. QUEEN ELIZABETH SUCCEEDED TO THE THRONE IN NOVEMBER 1558 ; YET NO FRESH ENGLISH EDITION OF THE BIBLE APPEARED BEFORE 1561. NOT UNTIL SOME YEARS LATER DID THE ISSUE OF ENGLISH BIBLES REASSUME THE PROPORTIONS WHICH OBTAINED UNDER KING EDWARD.

ACCESSION OF QUEEN MARY: 6 JULY 1553.

1557. The | Nevve Testa- | ment of ovr Lord Ie- | sus Christ. , Conferred diligently with the Greke, and best ap- | proued translations. | VVith the arguments, as wel before the chapters, as for euery Boke | & Epistle, also diuersities of readings, and moste proffitable | annotations of all harde places : wherunto is added a copi- | ous Table. | At Geneva | Printed By Conrad Badius. | M.D.LVII.

8°.

This version of the New Testament is ascribed to William Whittingham, one of the band of English reformers who found an asylum at Geneva. The text is based upon Tindale's, compared with the Great Bible, and largely influenced by Beza's Latin translation.

Though this version forms the groundwork of the New Testament in the Geneva Bible of 1560, it is a distinct work, due to one translator, as the Address *To the reader* seems to show. Fry asserted that the text of this Testament was not reprinted in any of the numerous Geneva Bibles or separate Testaments, from 1560 to 1644, which he had examined. (*Cf. Standard Edition of the English New Testament of the Genevan Version*, 1864.)

This neat octavo is the earliest English Testament printed in roman type, and with verse divisions. With its elaborate apparatus of arguments, notes and tables, it forms the first critical edition of the New Testament in English.

Whittingham (1524?-1579) married Catherine Jaquemayne or Jaqueman, said to be the sister of Calvin's wife (*cf.* entry in Geneva archives, cited by Stoughton, *Our English Bible*, p. 190 *n.*), but see D. N. B. *s.v.* W. Whittingham.

DESCRIPTION. Twelve preliminary leaves: title (with engraving), on verso *The ordre of the bookes of the Newe testament, with the nomber of Chapters, The Epistle declaring that Christ is the end of the Lawe, By Iohn Caluin*—8 ff., *To the reader mercie and peace through Christ our Sauiour* and *The Argvment of the Gospel, writ by the foure Euangelists*—3 ff. The text, ff. 1 to 430 (really 431, Hh 7) *b*; followed by *The Table of the Nevve Testament* and *A perfecte svpputation of the yeres and time from Adam vnto Christ* . . . —49 pp., ending on 455 (really 456, Ll 8) *a* with the colophon: *Printed by Conrad Badivs M.D.LVII. this x. of Ivne,* verso blank; 1 f., containing on recto *Fautes committed in the printing*, verso blank. (In some copies the *Fautes* are printed on verso of Ll 8, and there is no extra leaf.)

Signatures: ★⁸ ★★⁴, a-z⁸ A-Z⁸ Aa-Ll⁸ ; 468 ff. (and one extra leaf). Leaves numbered from the beginning of the text to 455 ; the number 336 is repeated by error. The text is printed in a small, but beautifully clear, roman type; a full page contains 37 lines. Arguments to almost all the books, and contents before each chapter, printed in italics. Notes (in roman type) and some references (in italics) in the margins. The chapters are divided into verses, though the alphabetical divisions, A B C, etc., in the margins are retained. Words not in the Greek are marked by italics.

In the list of *Fautes* the error *fyue thousand* in Matt. xvi. 10 is miscorrected to *foure hundred*.

The symbolical engraving on the titlepage represents Time leading Truth up out of a cavern, with the legend: *God by Tyme restoreth Trvth | and maketh her victoriovs.* Many large initials and headpieces.

¶ 128 × 85 mm. With the extra leaf at the end. [F; F.]

—— Another copy.

This copy is possibly an earlier impression, since some mistakes occur in the foliation (e.g. 10 for 110, 306 for 321), which are corrected in the former copy.

121 by × 85 mm. Imperfect: wanting title and all preliminary matter except the last leaf; also 22 leaves of text, and most of the supplementary matter;—53 ff. Facsimiles are inserted of the title and Ll 7, and two copies of Ll 8, one with, and the other without, the *Fautes* on verso.

ACCESSION OF QUEEN ELIZABETH: 17 NOVEMBER 1558.

1560. The Bible | and | Holy Scriptvres | conteyned in | the Olde and Newe | Testament. | Translated accor- | ding to the Ebrue and Greke, and conferred With | the best translations in diuers langages. | With moste profitable annota- | tions vpon all the hard places, and other things of great | importance as may appeare in the Epistle to the Reader. | At Geneva. | Printed by Rouland Hall. | M.D.LX.

4°.

The first edition of the so-called 'Geneva version'; the earliest English Bible printed in roman type and with verse divisions. Translated by W. Whittingham (see No. 76), Anthony Gilby, Thomas Sampson, and perhaps others, at Geneva.

The New Testament is a careful revision of Whittingham's Testament of 1557 (*q.v.*), due to a further comparison with Beza's Latin translation. The Old Testament and Apocrypha are based mainly on the Great Bible, corrected from the original Hebrew and Greek, and compared with the Latin versions of Leo Juda and others; while the influence of the revisers of Olivetan's French Bible is also apparent.

The Geneva Bible showed a distinct advance on its predecessors, and appearing as it did in compact form, with roman type and verse divisions, obtained speedy and permanent popularity. Its arguments and numerous explanatory notes (often distinctly Calvinistic in tone), which amount to a running commentary, endeared it especially to the Puritans, and for three generations it maintained its supremacy as the Bible of the people. Its phrases find an echo in Scripture quotations from Shakespeare to Bunyan. Between 1560 and 1644 at least 140 editions appeared of the Geneva Bible or Testament—120 of which are represented in this Library. Examination of King James' Bible of 1611 shows that its translators in correcting the Bishops' Bible were influenced more by the Geneva than by any other English version.

The cost of the work was defrayed by members of the congregation at Geneva *whose heartes God . . . touched* to encourage the revisers *not to spare any charges for the fortherance of such a benefite and fauour of God*. Conspicuous amongst these was John Bodley (father of the founder of the Bodleian Library), who received from Elizabeth a patent, dated 8 Jan. 1561, for the exclusive right to print the version in England for seven years (Herbert, p. 1603).

The Geneva Bible of 1560 and its later editions are often called by the somewhat absurd title of 'Breeches' Bibles. The rendering *breeches* (for *aprons*) in Gen. iii. 7 had already occurred in Wycliffe's MS. Bible, as well as in Caxton's edition of the *Golden Legend* (1483). Such popular titles as 'Breeches Bible,' 'Bug Bible,' 'Treacle Bible,' etc., apart from any question of their vulgarity, are generally misleading, and convey no idea of the distinctive interest and importance of each edition.

DESCRIPTION. Four preliminary leaves: title (with woodcut), on verso *The names and order of all the bookes* . . ., Epistle: *To the moste Vertvovs and Noble Qvene Elisabet, Quene of England, France, ād Ireland, &c*. *Your humble subiects of the English Churche at Geneua, wish grace and peace from God the Father through Christ Iesus our Lord*—2 ff., Address: *To ovr Beloved in the Lord the Brethren of England, Scotland, Ireland, &c. Grace, mercie and peace, through Christ Iesus*—1 f. (Both the Epistle and the Address are dated *From Geneua. 10. April. 1560*.) The text: (1) O. T. and Apocrypha, ff. 1 to 474 (Bbbbb iiii) *a*, verso blank; (2) N. T., with title: *The Newe Testament of ovr Lord Iesvs Christ, Conferred diligently with the Greke, and best approued translacions in diuers languages. At Geneva. Printed by Rouland Hall. M.D.LX.* (with cut), verso blank, text—ff. 2 to 122 (HHh ii) *a*, verso blank; followed by *A brief table of the interpretation of the propre names* . . ., *A table of the principal things* . . ., *A perfite svppvtation* . . . (with a text at the end—*Ioshva Chap. 1. vers. 8. Let not this boke . . . good successe*), and *The order of the yeres from Pauls conuersion shewing the time of his peregrination, & of his Epistles writen to the Churches*,—27 pp., ending on LLl iiii *a*, verso blank.

Signatures: ✱✱⁴, a–z⁴ A–Z⁴ Aa–Zz⁴ &⁶ Aaa–Zzz⁴ Aaaa–Zzzz⁴ Aaaaa⁴ Bbbbb⁴, AA–ZZ⁴ AAa–LLl⁴; 614 ff. Printed in roman type; double columns, divided into verses. Marginal notes in very small roman type. References etc., and contents before chapters in italics. Subject headings in headlines. An argument is prefixed to each book. The Hebrew names are carefully spelt and accented, *e.g.* Iaakób, Izhák, Rebekáh, etc.

In Ecclus. xv. 13 occurs the following error (a negative omitted):—*The Lord hateth all abominacion [of errour :] and they that feare God, wil loue it.*

The cut on the titlepages represents the crossing of the Red Sea; above are the words *Feare ye not, stand stil, and beholde the saluacion of the Lord, which he will shewe to you this day. Exod. 14, 13*, below—*The Lord shal fight for you: therefore holde you your peace, Exod. 14, vers. 14*, and at the sides—*Great are the troubles of the righteous : | but the Lord deliuereth them out of all, Psal. 34, 19.*

The engravings in the text number 26, and include a plan *The sitvacion of the Garden of Eden*, and representations of the Flood, the crossing of the Red Sea, the Tabernacle and its furniture, the Temple and its furniture, Solomon's throne, the vision of Ezekiel, etc.; many of these are accompanied by descriptive notes.

The book contains five maps on separate leaves : (1) at Numbers xxxiii (to illustrate the wanderings of the Israelites), (2) at Joshua xv (the division of the land of Canaan), (3) at the end of Ezekiel (*The forme of the Temple and citie restored*), (4) in St. Matthew (*The description of the holie land . . .* with a list of *places specified . . . with their situation by the obseruation of the degrees concerning their length and breadth*), (5) in Acts (*The description of the covntreis and places mencioned in the Actes of the Apostles . . .* with list of names, etc.).

¶ 245 × 171 mm. The general title slightly mended. [F. F.]

The University Library, Cambridge, possesses an exceptionally fine copy on large paper.

77.

[The New Testament of this version was published separately in the same year. There is a copy in Lambeth Palace Library.]

1560 ? *Begins*: Here be- | gynneth the Pystles | and Gospels, of euerye Son- | day and holy day in the yere.

W. Powell: London. [1560 ?] 4°. 𝔅. 𝔏.

An edition of the Liturgical Epistles and Gospels.

DESCRIPTION. Begins on A j; *Here begynneth . . .*, ff. i to lxvi (R ii) *a*; on verso *Here endeth . . . This is the table wherin ye shall vnderstande in what lefe ye shal fynde the Pystels, and Gospels after the vse of Salysbury . . .* — 5 pp., ending on R 4 *b* with the colophon: *Imprynted at London in Fletestrete, by me Wyllyam Powell, dwelynge at the sygne of the George, nexte to saynt Dunstons Churche.*
Signatures: A–R⁴; 68 ff. Leaves numbered in the text. Double columns; 33 lines to the full column. The running title is *The Pystles and Gospels. in Englyshe.*

¶ 181 × 131 mm. Inserted is a quasi-facsimile title, for which there appears to be no authority. [F. F.]

78.

1560. B. 4°. See 1561.

1561. The Byble | in Englyshe, that is to say. | The contente of all the | holy Scripture, both of | the olde, and newe | Testamente. | Accordynge to the translation that is | appoynted to be red in the | Churches. | Anno.M.D.LX.

Jhon Cawoode : London. 1560,61. 4°. 𝔅. 𝔏.

Great Bible version.

The colophon is dated 1561.

DESCRIPTION. [Thirty-two] preliminary leaves : title (in black and red, within border), on verso *An Almanacke for . xxii . yeres* (1559–80), *A table for the order of the Psalmes . . .*—1 p., *The order howe the rest of the holy Scripture . . . is appoynted to be sayde*— 1 p., Kalendar (with table of lessons)—6 ff., *Proper Lessons . . .*—5 pp., *Proper Psalmes . . .* with a note *A breife declaration when euery Terme begynneth and endeth*—1 p.; *The Order vvhere Mornyng and Euenyng Prayer, shall be vsed and sayde*—20 ff. ; [1 f. blank]. The text, divided into four parts :—(1) Genesis–Job, ff. i to cciii (really 206, Cc 6) *b*; (2) Psalter-Malachi, with title (within frame), on verso begins the text—ff. 1 (not numbered) *b* to cxxxiij (really 137, s i) *b*; (3) *Hagiogropha* (with title within frame), on verso *To the Reader*, text—ff. cxxxv (really 139, s iii) to ccxiiij (really 218 cc 10) *a*, verso blank; (4) N. T., with title: *The Nevve Testament* . . . (within frame), verso blank, text—ff. ij to 101 (not numbered, NN 5) *a*; on the same page in the second column begins *A Table to fynde the Epystles and Ghospelles vsuallye reade in the churche, accordyng vnto the boke of common prayer* . . . which ends on NN 6 *a* with the colophon : *Imprinted at London in Povvles Churcheyarde, by Ihon Cawoode. Prynter to the Quenes Maiestie. Anno. M.D.LXJ. Cum priuilegio Regiæ Maiestatis*, verso blank.

Signatures: ¶⁸, A⁴ B⁸ C¹², A–Z⁸ Aaˢ Bb⁸ Cc⁶, a–z⁸ &⁸ aa⁸ bb⁸ cc¹⁰, AA–MM⁸ NN⁶; 558 ff. The numbering of the leaves in the text is most incorrect. The Apocrypha section may be called a distinct part, since it has a separate titlepage; pts. 2 and 3, however, have continuous foliation and register. Printed in double columns, with 61 lines to the full column. Marginal references in black-letter. Headlines in roman type; these include subject-headings (only in the earlier part of the volume), titles of books (generally in capitals in the O. T. and Apocrypha, but in minuscules in the N. T.), and folio numbers. No contents before chapters, except in 2 Maccabees.

The preliminary matter follows the Prayer Book of 1559.

The border to the general title is formed of five blocks; above the letterpress is a cut of the Crucifixion, and below another illustrating the parable of the labourers in the vineyard; at the sides are ornamental blocks—boys blowing horns (first used in the Coverdale Bible of 1535); at the bottom is a narrow ornamental slip. A similar border is used for the N. T. title, but the two cuts in this case represent the Last Supper and the Betrayal by Judas. The border to the titles of pt. 2 (incorrectly called *The thirde parte* . . .) and the Apocrypha is a frame of architectural design, containing at the bottom a shield bearing Cawood's monogram. Two cuts—representing John the Baptist preaching, and the Good Samaritan—occur at the end of 2 Maccabees. The Prayer-Book contains many curious initials, including two large blocks representing classical subjects, afterwards used in certain editions of the Bishops' Bible.

¶ 188 × 136 mm. Imperfect : wanting the general title and the second and third leaves of the Kalendar, which are supplied in facsimile. The facsimile of the title was made by Harris from the genuine title in the Holkham Library copy. A leaf (probably blank) before the text is also missing.

Inserted at the beginning is a supposed facsimile of a general title : *The Bi | ble in Englishe ac- | cording to the tran- | slation of the great | Byble | 1561* (within a frame like that described above, containing Cawood's monogram). According to a note by Fry this was a pure invention by G. Offor, and no such title exists. [F. F.]

79.

1561 ? The newe | Testament of our Sa | uiour Jesu Christ. | Faythfully translated out of the Greke, and | perused by the commaundement of the | Kynges Maiestie and his honou- | rable counsell, and by them | aucthorised. | With the Notes & expositions | of the darke places | therin. | Mathew. xiii. f. | The pearle which Christ commaunded to | be bought. | Is here to be found, not elles to be sought.

R. Jugge : London. [1561 ?] 8°. 𝔅. 𝕴.

Tindale's version ; Jugge's revision.

This closely follows the octavo edition (1553) by the same printer described above (No. 75). No date is given, and there is no ' Copy of the Bill ' printed on the verso of the title. The fact that partial allowance is made in the margins for two Communions on Christmas Day and Easter Day, though the table allows for only one, suggests that the book was printed in 1552–3. Yet the Almanack begins with the year 1561, and in the colophon Jugge calls himself *Printer to the Quenes Maiestie*. Possibly the sheets were printed in 1552–3, laid aside during Queen Mary's reign, and issued early in Queen Elizabeth's, about 1561. On this hypothesis one or two leaves—e.g. the Almanack and the last leaf containing the colophon—had to be reprinted ; but the cut containing the portrait of Edward VI was allowed to stand ; this cut occurs on the titlepages of Testaments as late as 1605.

There are three other editions, which so closely resemble the present, that the group of four may be conveniently described under one heading.

A. This edition is Fry's No. 36. (Lea Wilson, p. 185, No. 33.)

DESCRIPTION. Thirty-two preliminary leaves: title (in black and red, with woodcut), verso blank, Dedication *To . . . Prynce Edwarde the Syxt . . .* —1 f., Kalendar (with table of second lessons)—6 ff., *An Almanacke for . xx . yeares* (1561–80)—1 p., *A table of the principall matters . . .* —41 pp., *A true & perfect reckenyng . . .* —1 p., *An exhortacion . . .* (with Jugge's device at end)—2 pp., *The Description of the lands of promyse . . .* (the map)—2 pp., *The lyfe of . . . Saint Mathewe . . .* —1 p. Text, A i to Zz 8 a, followed on the same page by *The Epistles of the olde Testament, according as they be nowe read*, which end on && 2 b; *A table to fynde the Epystles and Gospelles read in the Churche of Englande . . .* —2 ff., ending on && 4 b with the colophon: *Imprinted at London in Poules Church yarde by Rychard Jugge, Printer to the Quenes Maiestie, forbyddynge all other men to prynt or cause to be printed, this, or any other Testament in Englyshe*.

Signatures: [unsigned]⁸ ✶⁸ ✶ ✶⁸ ✶ ✶ ✶⁸, A–Z⁸ &⁸ Aa–Zz⁸ &&⁴; 412 ff. Leaves not numbered. A full page contains 35 lines. Notes etc. as in the 1553 edition. *The Cart Cosmographie . . .* and *The order of tymes* follow Acts.

The initial letter to *A true & perfect reckenyng . . .* is E, instead of F. Heading to the Book of Acts: *. . . Saynt . . . doynges*. . . . The first line of the colophon is printed in italics.

The woodcut on the title contains the portrait of Edward VI. There are also cuts of the creation of Eve, the Evangelists (these differ from those in the 1553 edition), and 20 cuts in Revelation. Jugge's device is that with the pelican, and the motto above *Cogita mori*.

¶ 131 × 87 mm. Imperfect: wanting title and following leaf, Zz 6, and the last two leaves. These are supplied in facsimile taken from the Lenox Library copy. [F. F.]

80.

—— ANOTHER EDITION.

B. Fry's No. 35.

Title as before, with the following differences in spelling:—*Chryst* (twice), *founde, els*. The other preliminary leaves as before. Text A i to Zz 8 a; followed by the O. T. Epistles which end on && 2 b, [and probably a table ending on && 4 b with colophon].

Signatures etc. as before.

The initial at the beginning of *A true and perfect reckonyng . . .* is correct. Heading to Acts: *. . . Saint . . . doynges*. . . .

¶ 132 × 84 mm. Imperfect: wanting apparently three leaves—the sixth leaf of Kalendar, and two leaves at the end. The title is mounted. [F. F.]

81.

—— ANOTHER EDITION.

C. Fry's No. 38. (Lea Wilson, p. 187, No. 34.)

Title differs in spelling, e.g. *Newe, honorable, commañded*, and the second and third lines are printed in roman type. Preliminary leaves, text, etc. as before. The table ends on && 4 b with the word *Finis*, and the colophon: *Imprinted at London in Powles Churchyard by Richard Iugge, printer to the Queenes Maiestie. Forbyddyng all other men to prynt, or cause to be prynted, this, or any other Testament in Englyshe. Cum priuilegio Regiæ Maiestatis*.

Signatures, etc. as before.

The initial before *A true and perfect reckenyng . . .* is correct. Heading to Acts: first line printed in roman type, instead of black-letter. The first line of the colophon is printed in roman capitals, and the next two and the last in italics.

¶ 128 × 86 mm. Imperfect: wanting all before C 4, and all after Vv 8, besides other leaves;—113 ff. in all. Facsimiles are inserted of the title, the first page of Dedication, *A true and perfect reckenyng . . .*, the first page of Acts, and the last leaf. [F. F.]

There is a perfect copy in the Lenox Library.

82.

—— ANOTHER EDITION.

D. Fry's No. 37.

The two copies known are imperfect at the beginning and end, but probably this edition contained the same preliminary and final matter as A, B, and C. The text, signatures, etc.

correspond. The initial to *A true and perfect reckoning* . . . is correct. Heading to Acts: . . . *Saint . . . doinges* . . .

¶ 139 × 84 mm. Imperfect: wanting all before C 2 and all after Zz 5; also K 3 and Dd 1;—probably 58 ff. Two leaves are supplied in facsimile from a less imperfect copy:— (1) containing *A true and perfect reckoning* . . . and the first page of *An exhortation* . . ., and (2) the first leaf of text. Fry had not seen these leaves when he wrote his book *A Bibliographical Description* . . . A manuscript title agreeing with that in Fry's No. 36 has been inserted—probably by W. Herbert, whose autograph appears on the first page. [F. F.]
83.

1561. B. f°. See 1562.

1562. The Bible | and | Holy Scriptvres | conteyned in the Olde and | Newe Testament. | Translated according to the Ebrve | and Greke, and conferred With the best translations in diuers langages. | VVith moste profitable annotations | vpon all the hard places, and other things of great importance as | may appeare in the Epistle to the Reader. | This is the message vvhiche vve haue heard of him, and declare vnto you, | that God is the light, and in him is no darkenes. Iohn. 1. Ver. 5. | If vve vvalke in the light as he is in the light, vve haue fellovvship one | vvith another, and the blood of Iesus Christ clenseth vs from | all sinne. John. 1. Vers. 7. | Printed at Geneva. | M.D.LXII.
1562,61. f°.

Geneva version.

The second edition and the first in folio. Apparently produced by John Bodley (see above, No. 77, 1560). No printer's name is given. The N. T. title is dated 1561.

DESCRIPTION. Seven preliminary pages: title (wlth woodcut), on verso *The names and order of all the Bookes* . . ., Epistle—3 pp., Address—2 pp. (both dated: *From Geneua. 10. April. 1561*). The text:—(1) O. T. and Apocrypha, ff. 4 (not numbered) *b* to 432 (really 448, FFf iiij) *a*, verso blank; (2) N. T., with title: *The Newe Testament of ovr Lord Iesvs Christ. Conferred diligently vvith the Greke, and best approued translacions in diuers languages. This is the message . . . If vve vvalke . . . Printed at Geneva. M.D.LXI.* (with cut), on verso *The order of the yeres from Pauls conuersion* . . ., text—ff. 2 to 111 (really 112, TT iiij) *a*; followed by *A brief table of the interpretation of the propre names* . . ., *A table of the principal things* . . ., and *A perfite svppvtation* . . .—25 pp., ending with the text *Ioshua chap. 1. vers. 8* on XX iiij *b*.
Signatures: a–z⁶ aa–zz⁶ Aaa–Zzz⁶ AAa–EEe⁶ FFf⁴, AA–VV⁶ XX⁴; 572 ff. The leaves in the text are numbered—generally incorrectly. Marginal notes, etc., as in the 1560 edition. The letter w used in the marginal matter belongs to a larger fount than the rest of the type. Some copies have a variety of the leaf a ij with the last word on recto spelt *natural*, and a catchword *feare*. Words not in the original are enclosed within round brackets.
The woodcut on the two titlepages represents a seven-branched candlestick, with the following text: *No man lighteth a candell, for to pvt it vnder a bvshell, bvt vpon the candelsticke. Matthevv. V.* The book contains illustrations as in the 1560 edition, and five maps on separate leaves.
In Matthew v. 9 occurs the curious error *Blessed (are) the place makers*, which has given to this edition the name of the 'Whig Bible.' Another mistake is found in the contents of Luke xxi: *Christ condemneth the poore widdowe* (for *commendeth*); The error in Ecclus. xv. 13 is repeated in this edition.

¶ 308 × 217 mm. Last leaf supplied in facsimile. Title slightly mended. [F. F.]
84.

1562. The bible | in Englishe, that is to saye, | the contentes of al the holy Scrip- |ture, both of the olde and newe | Testament, according to the | translation that is apoin- | ted to be read in | Churches. | Imprinted at London in white | crosse strete by Richarde | Harrison. | Anno. Domi. 1 . 5 . 6 . 2 .
f°. 𝔅.𝔏.

Great Bible version.

DESCRIPTION. Eight preliminary leaves: title (within border), on verso *with what iudgemente the bokes of the olde Testament are to be read* and *A note to knowe what is meant by certaine diuersitie of letters and markes that we haue set in the Byble*, *The kalender*—2 ff., Cranmer's Prologue—3 ff., *A description and successe* ... —1 f., *The names of all bookes* ... —1 p., 1 p. containing engraving. The text, divided into five parts:—(1) Pentateuch, ff. j to xc (M ii) *a*; on verso title to (2) Joshua–Job, text—ff. j to cxxxviii (FF iiii) *a*; on verso title to (3) Psalter–Malachi, text—ff. 1 (not numbered) to clvi (really 154, BBB 6) *b*; on the same page title to (4) *Hagiographa*, text—ff. j to lxxxviij (NNN 8) *b*; (5) N. T., with title: *The nevve Testament* ... *Imprinted at London by Richarde Harrison. Anno. Do. M.VC.LXII.* (within border), on verso begins *A Table to finde the Epistles and Gospels vsually read in the Church according vnto the boke of Commō prayer* ... —3 pp., text—ff. j to cxvij (really 119, ✠P 9) *b*, ending with the colophon: *Imprinted at London in White Crosse strete by Richard Harrison, the yeare of our Lorde, a thousand fyue hundred three score and two. Cum priuilegio ad imprimendum solum*; 1 f. (probably blank).
Signatures: ✠⁸, A–Z⁸ AA–ZZ⁸ AAA⁸ BBB⁶ CCC–NNN⁸, ✠A–✠O⁸ ✠P¹⁰; 600 ff. Parts 1 to 4 have a continuous register, but separate foliation. In the Psalter the place of the folio numbers is occupied by headings: *The first day*, *The . ii . day*, etc. A full column of text contains 58 lines.

The border to the general and N. T. titles, and the engraving on the last preliminary page, are like those used in Matthew's Bible of 1537. The other titles are plain.

There are several engravings in pts. 2 to 4, many of which are identical with those in the Great Bible; also in the N. T. cuts of the Apostles, etc. and 20 small cuts in Revelation (like those in Day and Seres' 1549 folio Bible).

¶ 302 × 203 mm. The general title is slightly mended. The blank leaf (P 10) is missing.

[F. F.]

—— Another copy.

321 × 220 mm. Imperfect: wanting general title and last preliminary leaf. YY 3 is mutilated. On fo. cxiij, pt. 5, an initial A has been pasted over the incorrect L printed before chapter iii; in the former copy the correct initial appears. On the other hand, in this copy the last leaf is rightly numbered *Fo.cxix*. The blank leaf (P 10) is missing.

The B. M. copy 2. d. 7 contains a few maps and plans printed on separate leaves; these have been transferred from a copy of the folio Geneva Bible of 1562,61.

85.

1566. The Bible | In Englyshe of The | Largest and greatest volu- | me that is to saye: the contentes | of all the holye Scripture, booth of | the oulde and newe | Testament. | According to the translation apoyn- | ted by the Queenes Maiesties In- | iunctions to be read in all chur- | ches vvith in her Maiesties | Realme. | At Roven. | At the coste and charges of | Richard Carmarden. | Cum Priuilegio. | 1566.

C. Hamillon. f°. 𝔅. 𝔐.

Great Bible version.

DESCRIPTION. Twenty-two preliminary leaves: title (in black and red, within border), verso blank, *The order howe the rest of holy. Scripture ... is appoynted to be read*—1 p., *Proper Lessons* ... with *Proper Psalmes* ... and *A briefe declaration* ... —4 pp., *The Almanacke, For. xxx. years* (1561–90)—1 p., *To fynde Easter for euer* (with a list of holy dayes)—1 p., *A Table, for the order of the Psalmes* ... —1 p., Kalendar (with table of lessons, etc.)—6 ff., Tindale's Prologue: *Thoughe a man hadde a precyous Jewell* ... (with the words *At R. by C. Hamillon*, printed at the end, in some copies)—1 f.; Morning and Evening Prayer, Litany, and Collects—19 pp.; *The names of all the bookes* ... —1 p. The text, divided into five parts:— (1) Pentateuch, ff. j to lxxviii (L 8) *b*; (2) Joshua–Job, with title (within frame), verso blank, text—ff. ij to cxxxiiij (R 6) *a*, ending with the words: *At the cost and Charges of Rychard Carmarden. 1566*, verso blank; (3) Psalter–Malachi, with title (within frame), verso blank, text—ff. ij to cl (TT 6) *a*, verso blank; (4) Apocrypha, with title (within frame), on verso *A Prologe* ..., text—ff. ij to xc (Lll 10) *b*; (5) N. T., with title (within border), verso blank, text—ff. ii to cxiij (Mmm i) *b*, ending with the date *M.D.LXVI.*; *A Table to find the Epistles and Gospels vsually red in the Churche, accordyng vnto the Booke of Cōmon Prayer* ... —1 f.

Signatures: Aa¹², Bb¹⁰, A–L⁸, A–Q⁸ R⁶, AA–SS⁸ TT⁶, Aaa–Kkk⁸ Lll¹⁰, Aa–Oo⁸ Mmm²; 598 ff. Printed in double columns, with 58 lines to the full column.

The thyrd of the Machabees appears in the list of books, but is not printed in the text.

Some copies have no colophon at the end of the *Prologe*; and also exhibit variations in the setting-up of other leaves:—e.g. in pt. 1, the catchword on A j a is *so to* in some copies, and in others *sede*; A 8 *a*, 1st. col., 1st. line, *can do nothyng* . . ., other copies *can do nothynge* . . .; and slight variations occur in Aa ii and 7 in pt. 5.

The border used for the general and N. T. titles represents at the top the Sacred Name in Hebrew, Greek, Latin and English; at the sides—figures of Moses and Christ; and below—*Elisabetha Regina* enthroned beneath a canopy, and supported by two symbolical female figures; with four scrolls and a label bearing texts (printed in red in the case of the general title). The other title-borders are frames composed of twenty-four small blocks (some of which bear the initials I M, i.e. Iehan Mallart, according to Lea Wilson, p. 52), and two slips on either side of the letterpress.

¶ 397 × 260 mm. The general title, which was mutilated on one side, has been completed in facsimile and mounted. Contains both impressions of each of the five varying leaves mentioned above. The *Prologe* is misplaced. [F. F.]

—— Another copy.

387 × 256 mm. Imperfect: wanting general title and ten following leaves, fo. 56 in pt. 4, and in pt. 5 the last two leaves of text and the Table;—15 leaves in all. The N. T. title is slightly mutilated. The *Prologe* leaf in this copy has the colophon; in pt. 1, fo. 1 has catchword *sede*, and fo. 8 1st col. 1st line reads *can do nothynge*.

—— Another copy.

395 × 255 mm. Imperfect: wanting all preliminary matter; in pt. 1, ff. 1 and 2; in pt. 2, title, ff. 89, 128, and last leaf; in pt. 3, title, and last leaf; in pt. 4, title; in pt. 5, title, and last three leaves;—35 leaves in all. Fo. 8 in pt. 1 reads *can do nothyng*.

86.

[Herbert (p. 538) mentions an octavo Bible, printed by R. Grafton in 1566. This may be the edition which, according to Sir James Ware, had a large sale in Ireland (*cf. The Annals of Ireland of the reign of Queen Elizabeth*, under the date 1559). See Cotton, p. 33 *n*.]

1566? The Newe Testament of our Sauiour | Iesus Christe, faithfully transla- | ted out of the Greke, with | the Notes and Exposi- | tions of the darke | places therin. | Matthæwe. xiii. f. | Vnio, quem præcepit emi seruator Iesus, | Hic situs est, debet non aliunde peti. | The pearle which Christe commaunded to be bought, | Is here to be founde, not els to be sought.

R. Jugge: London. [1566?] 4°. 𝕭.𝕷.

Tindale's version; Jugge's revision.

Fry's No. 33. The third of Jugge's quarto editions. The date is not given, but the book is generally ascribed to 1566, the first year of the Almanack.

Apparently the last in the long series of over forty editions of Tindale's New Testament. Cotton (p. 57) under the date 1605 records an edition 'Tyndale's, as printed by R. Jugge . . . —St. Paul's'; and a similar entry occurs in the Cathedral Library Catalogue (p. 25). But the volume in question is merely a Testament of the Bishops' version. (See below, No. 216, 1605.)

DESCRIPTION. Eighteen preliminary leaves: title (in black and red, with woodcut), on verso *An Almanacke for . xxv . yeres* (1566–90), Dedication—1 f., Kalendar—6 ff., *A Table of the principall matters* . . . —15 pp., *A true and perfect reckoning* . . . —1 p., *An exhortation* . . . —1 f., *The description of the lande* . . . (map)—1 p., *The lyfe of . . . Saint Matthewe* . . . —1 p. Text: — (1) A i to Y 6 *b*, followed by *The Cart Cosmographic* . . . (map, with short note)—1 p., and *The order of times*—3 pp.; (2) with title and the argument of Romans—1 p., text—Aa i *b* to Q i (really Qq i) *a*; followed by the O. T. Epistles—4 pp., and the Table—3 pp., ending on Qq 4 *b* with the colophon: *Imprinted at London in Powles Churchyarde by Richard Iugge, printer to the Queenes Maiestie, Forbyddyng* . . .

Signatures: ❧⁸ ☙¹⁰, A–Y⁸, Aa–Pp⁸ Qq⁴; 318 ff. Leaves not numbered. A full page contains 37 lines.

In most particulars this edition agrees closely with that of 1552; but in this the headlines are in roman type.

The woodcut on title contains the portrait of Edward VI as in the 1552 and 1553 editions, but with touches of red ink; the words *Viuat Rex* have been removed. Many of the cuts are the same as in the earlier editions, but those of the Evangelists and St. Paul and the cuts in Revelation are new; most of these latter were used again in Jugge's folio edition of the Bishops' Bible, 1568.

¶ 211 × 150 mm. Imperfect: wanting title and following leaf, both supplied in facsimile. Inserted is a photographic copy of the titleleaf. [F. F.]

—— Another copy.

194 × 141 mm. Imperfect: wanting all before A 4, and all after Pp 6; also A 6, C 1, E 1, L 1, O 8, Y 2 and 7, and Ee 6.

87.

1568. The bible | in English, that is to | say : The content of | all the holy Scripture, | both of the olde and newe | Testament. According to | the translation that is | appointed to be read | in the Chur- | ches. | Anno. 1568.

R. *Jugge and J. Cawood : London.* 4°. 𝔅. 𝔏.

Great Bible version.

Possibly Cawood alone was responsible for the printing of the text. The colophon to the Prayer Book (see below) gives the names of Jugge and Cawood; but this large section (162 ff.) may have been printed separately. Cawood's similar editions, Nos. 90 to 92 (1569), contain only a short Order of Prayer (16 ff.). The discovery of a copy with the last leaf, which probably bore a colophon, might solve this question.

DESCRIPTION. One hundred and seventy preliminary leaves: title (in black and red, within border), on verso *An Almanacke for xiiij. yeares* (1567–80), Kalendar—6 ff., *A Table for the order of the Psalmes to be sayd at Morning and Euening prayer*—1 p., *The order how the rest of holy Scripture* (*beside the Psalter*) *is appointed to be read*— 1 p.; *The order where Morning and Euening prayer shal be vsed and saide*, etc.— 323 pp., 1 p. containing colophon : *Imprinted at London in Paules Churchyarde, by Richard Iugge and Iohn Cavvood Printers to the Queenes Maiestie. Cum priuilegio Regiæ Maiestatis.* Text, divided into five parts :—(1) Pentateuch, ff. 1 (not numbered) to 109 (O 5) *a*, verso blank ; (2) Joshua–Job, with title (within frame), text—ff. 1 (not numbered) *b* to 163 (really 162, XX 7) *b*, 1 f. blank ; (3) Psalter-Malachi, with title (within frame), ff. 164 (not numbered) *b* to 344 (really 343, Xxx 4) *a*, verso blank ; (4) Hagiographa, with title (within border), on verso *To the Reader*, text—ff. 345 to 438 (really 448, LLll 9) *b*, 1 f. blank ; (5) N. T., with title : *The Nevve Testament in English, translated after the Greke, contayning these bookes* . . . (within border), verso blank, text—ff. 1 (? really 2, A ij) to [132 (R 4) *a*, verso blank ?], *A Table to find the Epistles and Gospelles vsuallye read in the Churche, accordinge vnto the Booke of Common Prayer* . . .—2 ff. (?).

Signatures: [unsigned]⁴ B⁴, A–T⁸ V¹⁰, A–O⁸ BB–ZZ⁸ Aaa–Vvv⁸ Xxx⁴ Yyy⁸ Zzz⁸ AAaa–KKkk⁸ LLll¹⁰, A–Q⁸ R⁴, S⁷²; (probably) 862 ff. The numbering of the leaves is most incorrect. Printed in double columns, with 53 lines to a full column. Marginal references.

The first title-border is an architectural design with two cherubs in the upper part. The N. T. title-border is composed of ornamental blocks, and two blocks—one above and the other below the letterpress—representing the Last Supper and the Crucifixion. The title-border to pt. 2 is a simple narrow frame. That used for pts. 3 and 4 is an architectural design containing a head in a small medallion above, and Cawood's monogram on a shield below. The initial letter to Gen. i contains two birds.

Compare the very similar editions of the following year.

¶ 189 × 133 mm. Imperfect: wanting all preliminary matter; also Vvv 4 and 5, FFff N. T. titleleaf (A 1), R 4 and S 2. [F. F.]

The copy in the Library of Trinity College, Cambridge, contains the preliminary matter, but is imperfect towards the end.

88.

1568. The . holie . Bible . | conteynyng the olde | Testament and the newe.
R. Jugge : London. 1568. f°. 𝔅. 𝔏.

The first issue of the version known as the 'Bishops' Bible.' A revision of the Great Bible version, undertaken by Matthew Parker (1504–1575), Archbishop of Canterbury, with the assistance of many bishops and well-known Biblical scholars.

The work seems to have been carried out in separate sections, which vary considerably in value. In correcting the Great Bible, both the Hebrew and Greek originals were consulted. The influence of the Geneva version appears, especially in the prophetical books; while Castalio was also consulted. Westcott considers that the Greek attainments of the revisers were superior to their Hebrew, and that the alterations in the New Testament show original and vigorous scholarship.

The following are recognised as having shared in Parker's revision :—W. Alley (Bishop of Exeter), R. Davies (Bishop of St. David's), E. Sandys (Bishop of Worcester), A. Pearson (Canon of Canterbury), A. Perne (Canon of Ely), R. Horne (Bishop of Winchester), T. Bentham (Bishop of Lichfield and Coventry), E. Grindal (Bishop of London), J. Parkhurst (Bishop of Norwich), R. Coxe (Bishop of Ely), E. Guest (Bishop of Rochester), G. Goodman (Dean of Westminster), and Giles Lawrence. This last named was ' a man in those times of great fame for his knowledge in the Greek,' of whose labours Strype (*Parker*, II. App LXXXV) has preserved an interesting memorial in a series of 'notes of errors in the translation of the N. T.' (Westcott, *History*, pp. 247–8). See Arber, *Transcript*, vol. ii, pp. 740–5.

In April 1571 the Convocation of the Province of Canterbury ordered that copies of this edition should be placed in every cathedral, and as far as possible in every church; and enjoined every ecclesiastical dignitary to exhibit a copy in a prominent place in his house for the use of his servants and guests (Cardwell, *Synodalia*, p. 115 and p. 123).

In typography and illustration this is perhaps the most sumptuous in the long series of folio English Bibles. From the subjoined entry in an old account book of St. John's College, Cambridge, published by C. H. Hartshorne, in his *Book-rarities of Cambridge*, we learn the price at which this edition was then sold: ' 1571. For a new Bible in English, the last translation, 27*s*. 8*d*.' (equivalent to about £16 to-day).

DESCRIPTION. [Twenty-six] preliminary leaves : title (with engraving), verso blank, *The summe of the vvhole Scripture* . . . —1 f., *This Table setteth out to the eye the genealogie of Adam, so passing by the Patriarches, Judges, Kinges, Prophtees, and Priestes, and the fathers of their tyme, continuyng in lineal dissent to Christe our Sauiour*—11 pp., *The whole scripture of the Bible is deuided into two Testamentes* . . . with *Faultes escaped* and a note (pointing out that such passages in the text as are marked with *semy circles* (inverted commas), *may be left vnread in the publique reading to the people* . . . etc.)—2 pp., 1 p. blank, *Proper lessons* . . . —1 f., *Proper psalmes* . . . with *The order howe* . . . and *A briefe declaration* . . . —1 p., *An Almanacke* (1561–90)—1 p., *To fynde Easter for euer* (with a list of *holy dayes*)—1 p., *A Table for the order of the Psalmes* . . . —1 p., Kalendar (with table of lessons)—6 ff., *A Preface into the Byble folowyng* (by Archbishop Parker; ending with a prayer; in roman type)—3 ff., *A prologue or preface made by Thomas Cranmer, late Archbishop of Canterburie* (in black-letter)—5 pp., *A description of the yeres from the creation of the worlde, vntill this present yere of 1568* . . . —1 p., *The order of the bookes* . . . —1 p., 1 p. blank, [1 f. blank ?]. (The above order preserves the sequence of signatures, and therefore seems preferable to the order given by Lea Wilson, pp. 53–4.) The text, divided into five parts : (1) Pentateuch, ff. j to Cxxviij (Q 8) *b* ; (2) Joshua–Job, with title (with engraving), verso blank, text—ff. ij to clxxxv (Z 9) *b*, 1 f. blank ; (3) Psalter–Malachi, with title (with engraving), on verso *A Prologue of saint Basill the great vpon the Psalmes* (with a short passage from *Saint Austen*), text—ff. ii to CCiiij (really 202, Bb 12) *b* ; (4) Apocrypha, with title (with engraving), verso blank, text—ff. ij to cxviij (P 6) *a*, on verso *The description of the holy lande* . . . (a map, and a list of *The places specified* . . .) ; (5) N. T., with title : *The newe Testament of our sauiour Iesus Christe* (within border), on verso *A preface into the newe Testament* (by Archbishop Parker), text—ff. ii to clvj (V 4) *a* ; *A Table to fynde the Epistles and Gospels read in the Church of Englande* . . . —3 pp. ending on clix (really 157, V 5) *b* with the colophon : *Imprinted at London in povvles Churchyarde by Richarde Iugge, printer to the Queenes Maiestie. Cum priuilegio Regiæ Maiestatis*, and Jugge's device with an elegiac couplet beneath :

Matris vt hæc proprio stirps est saciata cruore :
Pascis item proprio Christe cruore tuos.

1 f. blank.

Signatures: [second leaf signed (ii), and fourth leaf (iiii)]⁸ ✱¹⁰ ✱⁷⁸, A–Q⁸, A–Y⁸ Z¹⁰, A–E⁶ F⁶ G–Z⁸ Aa⁸ Bb¹², A–O⁸ P⁶, A–T⁸ V⁶; 818 ff. The text is printed in double columns, with 57 lines to a full column. Headlines and marginal references in roman type; marginal notes and contents before chapters in black-letter. As in the Geneva Bible of 1560, each chapter is divided into verses; the numbers are printed at the side, though the old division-letters (A, B, C . . . .) are retained. Certain letters are placed at the end of some books; these appear to be the initials of the revisers to whom particular sections were entrusted.

Small variations are found in copies of this edition. A few are noticed below.

General titlepage: The first three words of the title are enclosed in an ornamental frame; the rest of the page is filled by a large engraving, containing in the centre a portrait of the Queen within an oval frame inscribed *Elisabeth Dei Gratia, Angliæ, Franciæ Et Hiberniæ Regina, Fidei Defensor, Etc.*; above, beneath a canopy, are the royal arms, and the arms of Ireland and of Wales; and on either side a symbolical female figure; beneath is a tablet, supported by a lion and a dragon, and inscribed *Non me pudet Euangelij Christi. Virtus enim Dei est ad salutem Omni credenti Rom. 1°.* The N. T. title is in the centre of a large engraving, containing above—the royal arms and the arms of Ireland and of Wales, with two symbolical female figures; and below—a tablet, supported by a lion and a dragon, and inscribed *I am not ashamed of the Gospel of Christe, because it is the power of God vnto saluation to all that beleue. Rom. i.* Pt. 2 titlepage contains a portrait of the Earl of Leicester, within an oval frame with the motto *Droit et Loyal.* Pt. 3 titlepage contains an engraving of King David, within a frame; and pt. 4 titlepage has a similar engraving representing the building of the walls of Jerusalem. At the beginning of the Psalter occurs an engraving of William Cecil, Lord Burghley; this contains a large B, the initial letter of Psalm i. The initial T before the Genealogical Table contains Archbishop Parker's arms quartered with those of Christchurch, Canterbury, the initials M P, and the date 1568; while the O before his Prologue contains his arms, with the motto *Mvndvs transit et concvpicentia eivs.* The initial C to Archbishop Cranmer's Prologue contains the arms of the see of Canterbury impaled with his own, and the letter T. The book is further embellished by 124 distinct blocks used to illustrate the text—of which all (except one) are enclosed within ornamental frames. There are also several maps, plans, and tables. In pt. 1: a small map (showing the position of Eden, with a note) on fo. ij *b*, a large full-page engraving of the Tabernacle, etc. on fo. liij *a*, tables of *Degrees of kinred . . . and . . . affinitie or aliaunce . . .* on lxxiiij *a*, and a *Charte* of the wanderings of the Israelites on Cv *a*; in pt. 2: a map (*The deuision of the lande . . .*) on xiiij *b*; in pt. 3: at the end of the Psalter a table: *Numerus secundum Hebreos* (omitted in some copies); in pt. 4: on the last page, the map mentioned in the Description; and in pt. 5: at the end of Acts, *The Cart Cosmographie . . .* and *The order of tymes*, together filling one leaf, fo. lxxxix. The maps are closely copied from those in the 1560 Geneva Bible, except *The Cart Cosmographie . . .* which is like that in Jugge's quarto Testaments of 1552, 1553, and 1566. In addition the book contains many large initial letters; some of which represent classical subjects (from Ovid's Metamorphoses), and others contain Parker's initials.

According to Archbishop Parker's *Observations respected of the translators* (see *Correspondence*, Parker Society Edition, pp. 336–7), 'the printer hath bestowed his thickest paper in the New Testament, because it shall be most occupied.'

This is sometimes called the 'Treacle Bible,' though the rendering *triacle* in Jer. viii. 22 is found in many Bibles of an earlier date, from 1535 downwards. A curious note occurs at Psalms xlv. 9:—

Ophir is thought to be the Ilande in the west coast, of late founde by Christopher Columbo: frō whence at this day is brought most fine golde.

¶ 394 × 264 mm. The general title is mounted. The last blank leaf (V 6), and also perhaps a blank leaf before the text, are missing. The order of the preliminary leaves is probably incorrect.

This copy has the table at the end of the Psalter. It contains two impressions of fo. lxij (H 6) in pt. 3—one with, and one without, the initials A. P. C. at the end of Proverbs. Mistakes in the Kalendar (Nov. 17 and 18), on the verso of the N. T. title, and on fo. cxxj *a* in pt. 5 are corrected by pasted slips.

At the beginning of the Psalter, opposite the portrait, is inserted an original document dated 1579, and signed by *W. Burghley* and *Wa. Mildmay.* [F. F.]

—— Another copy.

404 × 275 mm. Imperfect: wanting general title and one other preliminary leaf (beginning *The newe Testament in lyke maner . . .*); and fo. 143 in pt. 5. The last blank leaf (V 6) is also missing; and perhaps a blank leaf before the text. The preliminary leaves are arranged in the order given above in the Description.

This copy has the Table after the Psalter, no initials at the end of Proverbs, and the misprint on fo. 121 in pt. 5 corrected. At the foot of the first page in the Kalendar there is printed a short note: *An admonition to the Reader* (referring to the Saints' names given in the Kalendar); this note is lacking in the first copy.

—— Another copy.

397 × 267 mm. Very imperfect: wanting all preliminary matter, all pt. 1, and all after fo. 80 in pt. 5; also the blank leaf at the end of pt. 2. This copy has the Table after the Psalter, and no initials at the end of Proverbs. Ff. 43 and 44 in pt. 3 are set up differently from the corresponding leaves in the above copies.

89.

1568. B. 4°. See 1570.

1569. The bible | in English, that is to | say: The content of | all the holy Scripture, | both of the olde and newe | Testament. According to | the translation that is | appointed to be read | in the Chur- | ches. | Anno. 1569. J. Cawood: London. 4°. 𝕭.𝕷.

Great Bible version.

There are at least three editions printed by Cawood, and ascribed to this date, which, while generally agreeing so closely as to read together page for page, nevertheless differ in many small points, and are distinct issues. No doubt some copies are mixed.

A. This agrees with Lea Wilson's No. 31 (except in the last two leaves).

DESCRIPTION. Twenty-four preliminary leaves: title (in black and red, within border), on verso *An Almanacke for xiiii. yeares* (1567–80), Kalendar—6 ff., *A Table for the order of the Psalmes* . . .—1 p., *The order how the rest of holy Scripture . . . is appointed to be read*—1 p., Order of Morning and Evening Prayer—16 ff. The text, divided into five parts:—(1) ff. 1 (not numbered) to 109 (O 5) *a*, verso blank; (2) with title (within frame), text—ff. 1 (not numbered) *b* to 162 (Xx 7) *b*, 1 f. blank; (3) with title (within border), text—ff. 1 (not numbered) *b* to 178 (really 180, Xxx 4) *a*, verso blank; (4) with title (within border), on verso *To the Reader*, text—ff. 10 (really 2) to 104 (really 105, LLll 9) *b*, 1 f. blank; (5) with title: *The newe Testament . . . 1569* (within border), verso blank, text—ff. 1 (really 2?) to 132 (R 4) *a*, on verso is a cut; *A Table to find the Epistles and Gospelles vsuallye read in the Churche, according vnto the Booke of Common Prayer* . . .—2 ff., ending on S 2 *b* with colophon: *Imprinted at London in Powles Churchyard by Iohn Cawood, Printer to the Queenes Maiestie. Cum priuilegio Regiæ Maiestatis.*
Signatures: [unsigned]⁴ B⁴, A⁸ B⁸, A–O⁸, Bb–Zz⁸, Aaa–Vvv⁸ Xxx⁴, Yyy⁸ Zzz⁸ AAaa–KKkk⁸ LLll¹⁰, A–Q⁸ R⁴, S²; 716 ff. The numbering of the leaves is most incorrect. Double columns, with 53 lines to the full column. Headlines (in black-letter) include subject-headings only in the earlier part of the book. Marginal references, but no notes, and no contents before chapters.
The border used for the general and N. T. titles is an architectural design, with two cherubs at the top. Pt. 2 title has a simple narrow frame. The other two titles are within the border bearing Cawood's monogram. The cut at the end of the N. T. represents St. John in Patmos, and is like that used in Harrison's folio Bible of 1562. There is no vignette below the colophon, as described by Lea Wilson (p. 56), but only a small ornament.
The present edition (var. A) may be distinguished from those described below by (1) the separate foliation of each part, and (2) the N. T. titlepage. The first page of text is not numbered, and is headed: *The firste Booke of Moyses* . . .; the initial letter I contains two birds. Pt. 2 title runs: *The seconde parte of the Byble, conteyning these Bookes* . . .; pt. 3 title: *The thirde part of the Bible, conteyning these Bookes* . . .

¶ 199 × 144 mm. Imperfect: wanting all preliminary matter. A title is supplied, made up of a genuine N. T. title-border, with a facsimile centre. The two blank leaves are missing. Apparently identical with the B. M. copy, C. 36. c. 3, except in the last two leaves. [**F. F.**]

90.

HISTORICAL CATALOGUE

—— ANOTHER EDITION.

B. This appears to agree with Lea Wilson's No. 82.

DESCRIPTION. [Twenty-four] preliminary leaves: [title?] Kalendar—6 ff., *A Table for the order of the Psalmes* . . .—1 p., *The order howve the rest of the holie Scripture* . . . *is appoynted to be read*—1 p., *The Order where Mornynge and Euenyng Prayer, shall be vsed and sayd*—16 ff. Text: — (1) ff. 1 to 109 a, verso blank; (2) to (4), with titles as in var. A, ff. 1 (not numbered) to 438 (really 449, LLll 9) b, 1 f. blank; (5) with title (within border), text— ff. 1 (really 2) to 126 (really 132, R 4) a, on verso a cut; *A Table to fynd the Epistles and Gospels vsually readde in the Churche, accordynge vnto the Booke of Common Prayer* . . .—2 ff., ending on S 2 b with the colophon: *Imprinted at London in Powles Churchyarde by Jhon Cawood, Printer to the Quenes Maiestie* (within a frame), beneath which are the words *Cum priuilegio Regiæ Maiestatis*, and a narrow vignette.

Signatures: ¶⁸, A⁸ B⁸, A–O⁸ BB–ZZ⁸ Aaa–Vvv⁸ Xxx⁴, Yyy⁸ Zzz⁸ AAaa–KKkk⁸ LLll¹⁰, A–Q⁸ R⁴ S²; 716 ff. Type, etc. as in var. A.

No authentic first title is known (see below). The title-borders to pts. 2, 3 and 4 are like those in var. A. The N. T. title-border resembles that in Cawood's quarto Bible of 1560,61; but the two cuts represent above—the entombment of Christ, and below—Dives and Lazarus. The last words on R 4 a, *The ende of the new Testamente*, are within a narrow frame, which is also used for the colophon. The cut on R 4 b is like that in var. A. The small vignette on the last page contains the emblems of the Four Evangelists.

The first page of text is numbered *Fol. 1.*, and is headed: *The firste Boke of Moses* . . . ; the initial I contains a centaur. Pt. 2 title runs: *The seconde part of the Byble contayninge these bookes* . . . Pt. 3 title: *The thirde parte of the Byble contaynyng these bookes.*

¶ 186 × 136 mm. Imperfect: wanting the general title. The blank leaf after pt. 2 is also missing. Fry was unable to find a genuine title. Inserted in this copy is a manufactured title: *The Bible | in Englishe | according to the transl- | ation of the great | Byble. | 1569.* (enclosed within the border used for the titles of pts. 3 and 4). This, though printed on old paper (apparently the missing blank leaf), and having every appearance of antiquity, is nothing but an invention by G. Offor resembling the fictitious title made by him for Cawood's Bible of 1560,61 (No. 79). Another impression, taken on ordinary paper, is inserted with a MS. note by Fry.

Apparently identical with the B. M. copy, C. 36. c. 5, except in the preliminary leaves.

[F. F.]

——— Another copy.

Generally agreeing with var. B.

185 × 136 mm. Very imperfect: wanting all before F 2 in pt. 1, and many other leaves.

[F. F.]

91.

·—— ANOTHER EDITION.

C. This generally resembles var. B, yet differs in parts both from it and also from A.

The titles to pts. 2 and 5 are like those in var. B; pt. 3 title runs: *The thirde part of the Bible conteining these Bookes* . . .

¶ 186 × 138 mm. Imperfect: wanting all before H 1 in pt. 1, and all after N 7 in pt. 5, besides other leaves.

[F. F.]

——— Another copy.

This has been marked 'Wilson's No. 33'; but it is so imperfect that identification is impossible. It generally agrees with var. C, but in some parts resembles Jugge and Cawood's 1568 edition (No. 88).

186 × 135 mm. A fragment only, containing portions of pts. 2 and 3.

[F. F.]

92.

1569. The holi bible.

R. Jugge: London. 1569. 4°. 𝕭. 𝕷.

The second edition, now first printed in quarto, of the Bishops' version.

ENGLISH

The text of the Old Testament has received a certain amount of correction. A comparison of some representative chapters seems to show that, so far as the Old Testament is concerned, this quarto was adopted as the standard in all subsequent issues, except the folio editions of 1572, 74, and 78, which revert to the Bible of 1568. The New Testament also exhibits traces of revision. Westcott (*History*, pp. 252-4) gives 44 differences of reading in Ephesians between the first edition of 1568 and that of 1572 (*q. v.*). By comparison we find that in 22 instances this quarto reads with the former, and in the remaining 22 with the later edition. Thus it forms the connecting link between the two, as regards the New Testament section.

DESCRIPTION. [Twenty-two] preliminary leaves : [1 f. blank ?] title (within an engraving), verso blank, *The preface* . . . with *The prayer*—3 ff., *The whole scripture of the Bible is diuided* . . .—5 pp., 1 p. blank, Kalendar—6 ff., *The order howe* . . .—1 p., *Proper Lessons* . . . etc.—7 pp.; *The order of Mornyng prayer* . . . *Euenyng prayer* . . .— 4 ff. Text, divided into five parts, as usual: (1) ff. 1 to 105 (O j) *b*, followed by 1 f. containing Jugge's large device on recto, verso blank; (2) ff. 113 (really 106, P j) to 261 (really 255, Kk 5) *b*, 1 f. blank; (3) with title, on verso begins *A Prologue of saint Basil* . . .—2 pp., text—ff. 2 (not numbered) *b* to 172 (Y 4) *a*, verso blank; (4) with title, verso blank, text—ff. 2 to 101 (really 100, Nnn 4) *b*; *The description* . . . (map)—1 p., *A Table to make playne the difficultie that is founde in S. Matthewe and S. Luke, touching the generation of Iesus Christ* . . .—2 pp., 1 p. blank; (5) with title: *The newe Testament* . . . *1569. Cum priuilegio* (within border), verso blank, text—ff. 2 to 127 (Q 7) *a*; *A Table to fynde the Epistles and Gospels read in the Churche of Englande* . . .—3 pp., ending on Q 8 *b* with the colophon: *Imprinted at London in powles Churchyarde by Richarde Jugge, Printer to the Queenes Maiestie. Cum priuilegio Regiæ Maiestatis.* A leaf follows, containing on recto *Faultes escaped in the pryntyng*, verso blank, [1 f. blank ?].

[The foliation skips from 105 at the end of the text of pt. 1 to 113 at the beginning of pt. 2; yet nothing appears to be wanting; no intervening leaves are known to exist, except the one leaf containing the printer's device.]

Signatures : [—]² ¶⁶ ℂ¹⁰ (⁎⁎)⁴, A–N⁸ O² P–Z⁸ Aa–Ii⁸ Kk⁶, A–X⁸ Y⁴, Aaa–Mmm⁸ Nnn⁶, A–Q⁸, [—]²; 682 (?) ff. Double columns, with 61 lines to the full column ; arranged in paragraphs, the verse-numbers being intermingled with the text. The marginal notes (but not the references, etc.), contents of chapters, headlines, interpolations of the text, etc. are in roman type.

The large engraving on the first titlepage represents Queen Elizabeth seated on a throne, and crowned by *Ivstice* and *Mercie*; the throne is supported by *Fortitvde* and *Prvdence*; beneath the tablet bearing the title stands a man in a pulpit, with an hourglass at his side, preaching to a seated congregation ; at the base are printed the words *God save the Qveene.* The N. T. title is within a border with Jugge's cypher at the top, at the sides supporting figures, and below two lions.

An engraving (Adam naming the creatures) occurs before Genesis. The book contains maps and tables, as in the first edition of 1568, additional notes before 1 Esdras, 1 Maccabees, and before the N. T. title (see Description), and at Matthew xxvi. The initial letters at the beginning of Genesis, Joshua, and Psalms contain respectively Abp. Parker's arms with those of Christchurch, Canterbury (dated 1569), the Earl of Leicester's, and Lord Burghley's.

¶ 194 × 145 mm. The first title is mounted. Perhaps there should be a blank leaf before the general title, and another at the end. [F. F.]

—— Another copy.

184 × 133 mm. Imperfect : wanting all preliminary leaves, and the leaf of *errata* at the end of the book; of these, the title and the last leaf are supplied in facsimile. Perhaps two blank leaves are also missing (see above).

93.

1569. B. 4°. See 1570.

1570. The Bible . . . Translated according | to the Ebrue and Greke . . . With moste profitable anno | tations . . . There is added in this second edition certeine tables, one for the Explication of the degrees in ma- | riage in Leuiticus, with another for the Maccab. & a calender historical, with other things. | At Geneva. | Printed by Iohn Crispin. | M. D. LXX.

1570, 68, 69. 4°.

Geneva version.

The second quarto edition; a smaller book than the Bible of 1560. Some copies are said to be dated 1568, and others 1569, on the titlepage.

DESCRIPTION. Twelve preliminary leaves: *Calender Historical. Wherein is contained an easie declaration of the golden nombre. Of the Epacte. Of the indiction Romaine. Also of the Cycle of the sunne, and the cause why it was inuented. By Iohn Crispin. M.D.LXIX.*—title (with Crispin's device; enclosed within an ornamental frame), verso blank, *To the reader* ... —1 p., *Of the Golden Nombre* ... etc.—3 pp., *A svppvtation of the yeares world from the creacion thereof vnto this present year 1569, according as it is counted by D. M. Luther*—1 p., *A table of the Cycle of the Sunne* ... —1 p., Kalendar (with a small cut at the beginning of each month, the signs of the zodiac, and references to events—some contemporary)—3 ff., *Faires in Fraunce and elsevvhere*—1 p., 1 p. blank;—8 ff. in all, preceding the Bible title (which also bears Crispin's device), verso blank, Epistle (dated *From Geneva. 10. April. 1569*)—3 pp. Address (dated 1560)—2 pp., list of books (with *The prayer of Manasseth, apocryphe* placed after 2 Chronicles)—1 p. Text: O. T., ff. i to 410 (really 412, Gg 8) *b*; Apocrypha, ff. 1 to 94 (n 2) *b*, followed by *A brief table of the interpretation of the propre names* ... —9 pp., 1 p. blank, 1 f. blank; N. T., with title (with Crispin's device, and dated 1568), verso blank, text—ff. 2 to 129 (SS 1) *a*, verso blank; followed by *A table of the principal things* ... *A perfite svppvtation* ... and *The order of the yeres* ... —10 ff., 1 f. blank. The Metrical Psalms (evidently intended to form an essential part of the book), with title: *The Whole Booke of Psalmes, collected into Englishe metre by T. Sternhod I. Hopkins and others, conferred vvith the Ebrue, vvith apt Notes to synge them vvithall. Faithfully perused and allovved according to thorder appointed in the Quenes Maiesties Iniunctions* ... *At Geneva, Printed by Iohn Crespin. M.D.LXIX.* (with Crispin's device), verso blank, *A Treatise made by Athanasivs the Great* ... —2 ff., *Veni Creator* ... etc. ... —5 ff., the Psalms, ff. 1 to 58, *The x. Commavndementes* ... etc.—7 pp., *A table* ...—2 pp., Prayers—5 pp., *The Catechisme* ... *by* ... *Iohn Caluin*—17 ff., ending on fo. 82 (ZZZ 2) *b*.

Signatures in eights: ¶⁸; *‗*⁴, a–c⁴ d–z⁸ A–Z⁸ Aa–Gg⁸, a⁴ b–n⁸, AA⁴ BB⁴ CC–SS⁸ TT⁴; AAA–YYY⁴ ZZZ²; 754 ff.

Printed in roman type; double columns. With all the arguments, notes, etc.; also the illustrations and five maps (printed on separate leaves and inserted), as in the 1560 edition, and in addition a table of *Degrees of consanguinitie* ... etc. inserted at Leviticus xviii. Nothing appears to be known of the Table of Maccabees mentioned in the title.

According to a MS. note by Fry, the *Calender Historical* and the Metrical Psalms, etc., as described above, form essential parts of this edition. Exactly similar matter was included in Crispin's French Bible of 1567.

Crispin's device is the anchor and serpent, with the initials I. C.

¶ 212 × 131 mm. The 'Treatise of Athanasius' has been supplied from another copy.
[F. F.]

—— Another copy.

210 × 134 mm. Imperfect: wanting the *Calender Historical*, the general title, last leaf of table of Proper Names, and all the Metrical Psalms etc. at the end. The table of *Degrees of consanguinitie* ... is missing, as also the Joshua map, and the remaining four maps are mutilated.

—— Another copy.

209 × 136 mm. Imperfect: wanting all preliminary matter, and first 7 leaves of text; fo. 37 in the Apocrypha; and the last 22 leaves in the Metrical Psalms etc. The three maps in Ezekiel, St. Matthew, and Acts are missing and the other two are mutilated.

—— Another copy.

206 × 132 mm. Very imperfect: wanting all before fo. 7 of text, all the Apocrypha, and the Metrical Psalms etc. at the end; besides many other leaves.

94.

1571. The Gospels | of the fower Euangelistes | translated in the olde Saxons tyme | out of Latin into the vulgare toung | of the Saxons, newly collected out | of Aunciant Monumentes of | the sayd Saxons, and now | published for

testimonie | of the same. | At London. | Printed by Iohn Daye dwel- | ling ouer Aldersgate. | 1571. | Cum Priuilegio Regiæ Maiestatis | per Decennium.
4°. Partly 𝔅. 𝔏.

An edition of the Gospels in Anglo-Saxon (translated from the Vulgate) and English (the Bishops' version), published under the direction of Matthew Parker, Archbishop of Canterbury.

The preface by John Foxe (1516–1587), the martyrologist, includes a sketch of the early versions of the Scriptures, and the literary work of Bede, King Alfred, and others.

DESCRIPTION. Six preliminary leaves: title (within narrow frame), on verso *The Saxon Caracters or letters, that be most straunge, are here knowen by other common Caracters set ouer them. . . ., To the most vertuous, and noble Princesse, Queene Elizabeth* . . . (signed: *Your Maiesties most humble subiect, Iohn Foxe*) – 5 ff. The text, B i to HH iiij *b*, ending with the colophon: *At London. Printed by Iohn Daye dwelling ouer Aldersgate. 1571. These Bookes are to be solde at his shop vnder the gate.*
Signatures: A⁴ ¶², B–Y⁴ Aa–Yy⁴ AA–HH⁴; 210 ff. Leaves not numbered. The two texts are printed side by side,—the Saxon, occupying about two-thirds of the page, placed inside, and the English, printed in black-letter (apparently the same type as that used in the quarto Bishops' Bible of 1569), on the outside of each page. Directions are given for the reading of passages on certain days, e.g. *This Gospell belongeth on the thirde Sondaye after Pentecost, This shall be on Wednesdaye for the Imber within Haruest.*

The Spencer copy (now in the John Rylands Library) contains the following note in an old hand: *This is a rare and very excellent vsefull booke, and very harde to be mett with and deare. I was twenty yeares looking for to buy one of these bookes, before I could buy one under a Marke. I offer'd many times an Angel for suche a booke as this.* (Cotton, p. 37, *n.*)

¶ 190 × 132 mm.

95.

1572. The . holie . Bible.
R. Jugge: London. 1572. f°. 𝔅. 𝔏.

Bishops' version: the second folio edition.

A reprint of the 1568 Bible, so far as the Old Testament is concerned; but the New Testament has undergone further careful revision since the quarto edition of 1569 (*q. v.*). All later issues, with two exceptions, appear to follow the quarto of 1569 in the Old Testament, but generally adopt the text of this Bible of 1572 in the New Testament.

A remarkable feature of this edition is its two-version Psalter, which exhibits, printed side by side, (1) *The translation vsed in common prayer* (taken originally from the Great Bible, and still retained in the Prayer Book), in black-letter, and (2) *The translation after the Hebrewes* (i.e. the Bishops' version) in roman type.

DESCRIPTION. The order of the preliminary leaves is somewhat uncertain. According to the signatures, the six leaves (★ 2 to 7) containing the Preface, the Prologue, and *A discription of the yeeres*, apparently should precede the ten leaves (sig. ☾) containing *Proper lessons* . . . . etc. to the end. (This is the arrangement adopted by Lea Wilson for the order of the preliminary leaves in the first edition of 1568, as well as in this edition; but in the former case the signatures make this order improbable.) These leaves correspond to those in the first edition, but differ in many small points; e.g. the title is shorter, the date in the initial T of the Genealogical Table is altered, the *Faultes escaped* are omitted, the *Almanacke* is for 1572–1610, the signs of the Zodiac are inserted in the margins of the Kalendar, and *A discription of the yeeres* . . . . is carried down to 1572. Text :—pts. 1 and 2, ff. j to CClxx (Ll 6) *b*; pt. 3, text—ff. ii to Clxxxix (really 190, &&& 6) *b*; pt. 4, text—ff. ii to Cv (Nnnn 9) *a*; pt. 5, text—ff. ii to Cxxxviii (S ij) *b*. Table—3 pp., ending on S 4 *a* with the colophon: *Imprinted at London in Powles Chvrcheyarde by Richarde Iugge, Printer to the Queenes Maiestie. 1572. Cvm privilegio Regiæ Maiestatis,* and Jugge's device and elegiac couplet.
Signatures: (sigs. of preliminary leaves somewhat uncertain, perhaps—) [leaves signed (ij), (iii)]⁸ ★⁸ (last leaf blank) ☾¹⁰, A–Z⁸ Aa–Kk⁸ Ll⁶, Aaa–Zzz⁸ &&&⁶, Aaaa–Mmmm⁸ Nnnn¹⁰, A–R⁸ S⁴; 732 ff.

The general titlepage and those to pts. 2 and 5 are like the corresponding titlepages in the first edition. That to pt. 3 bears the portrait of Lord Burghley, taken from the beginning of the Psalter, but with the initial B removed from the plate; and that to pt. 4 has a composite engraving representing incidents in the Apocrypha.

Three Tables (as in the quarto Bible of 1569) are placed before 1 Esdras and 1 Maccabees, and before the N. T. title (on Nnnn 10 b). In Joshua is inserted a large map of Canaan, a fine two-page engraving, bearing the inscription: *Graven by Hvmfray Cole goldsmith a English man born in ye north and pertayning to ye mint in the Tower, 1572*, and containing Lord Burghley's arms and motto, and one of Jugge's devices (nightingale in tree) and his name. All the engravings are removed from the chapters. But before Isaiah there is a large cut of the prophet's vision, and at the beginning of certain books (Genesis, Exodus, Leviticus, Joshua, Judges, 1 Samuel, 1 Kings, and Jeremiah) and on pt. 4 titlepage appear large composite engravings illustrating many separate subjects. In the N. T. cuts are given before each Gospel, and Romans, James, and 1 Peter; while 18 small cuts are arranged together on one page opposite Rev. i. The large initial letters before Josh. i, Ps. i, and Jer. i contain respectively the arms of the Earl of Leicester, Lord Burghley, and the Earl of Bedford. Many of the initial letters (as in the 1568 edition) represent scenes from Ovid's Metamorphoses.

¶ 400 × 265 mm. The general title is mounted. [F. F.]

—— Another copy.

395 × 259 mm. Imperfect: wanting general title and seven following leaves, and the last two leaves in the volume; also the large map in Joshua. The initial letter at the beginning of Hebrews (representing Leda) has been partially erased.

96.

After 1572. [The Newe Testament of our Sauiour Iesus Christ. Diligently ouerseene, and faithfully translated out of the Greeke. The pearle which Christ commaunded to be bought: Is here to be found, not els to be sought. Imprinted ... Cum priuilegio ... solum.]

Richard Watkins: London. [After 1572.] 4°. 𝕭. 𝕷.

Bishops' version.

The text agrees with the Bible of 1572, rather than with the first edition of 1568. Taking Westcott's collation of Ephesians (*History*, pp. 252-4), we find that in every case this Testament reads exactly with the later edition; though a strange misprint occurs in chap. iv. 14, *wildernesse* (for *wiliness*) *of men*.

The date is doubtful. The Almanack begins with the year 1565 and ends with 1580. Hence Herbert's suggested date (p. 1029) of 1600 seems improbable. Cotton (p. 33) proposes 1565, which is impossible. Anderson (vol. ii., Index-List, p. xvi) gives 1577, 'between the privilege of Jugge, and the patent of Barker.' R. Jugge apparently ceased to print in 1577, and C. Barker received a very extensive patent in September of the same year (Herbert, p. 1075). The colophon to this edition includes the words *Cum priuilegio ad imprimendum solum*; hence Anderson's suggestion. But possibly Watkins printed this book under one of the special licences granted to him and certain other stationers (see note on No. 103).

DESCRIPTION. Eight preliminary leaves: [title, as above, according to Herbert (p. 1029), in black and red.] Kalendar (with table of lessons)—6 ff., *An Almancke for xvi. yeeres* (1565-80)—1 p., 1 p. blank. The text, A j to Fff v b; *A Table to finde the Epistles and Gospels read in the Church of England* ... —2 ff., ending on Fff 7 b with the colophon: *Imprinted at London by Richard VVatkins. Cum priuilegio ad imprimendum solum*, 1 f. (probably blank).

Signatures: A⁸, A–Z⁸ Aa–Zz⁸ Aaa–Fff⁸; 424 ff. Leaves not numbered. A full page contains 32 lines. The text is divided into verses. Marginal references and notes in roman type; contents of chapters and headlines in italics.

No woodcuts in the text. Some of the initials resemble those used by R. Jugge and J. Cawood, and subsequently by C. Barker.

'The only known title was in an imperfect copy burnt at Sotheby's fire in 1865' (MS. note by Fry).

¶ 174 × 126 mm. Imperfect: wanting title, and two leaves of text (A 4 and 5); also, probably, a blank leaf at the end. [F. F.]

Anderson mentions in his Index-List a copy in the University Library, Cambridge, but this cannot now be found.

97.

After 1572. The newe | Testament of our Sauiour | Iesu Christe. | Faythfully translated out of the | Greke, with the Notes & exposi- | tions of the darke | places therein. | Mat. 13. | The pearle whiche Christe commaunded to be bought, | Is here to be founde, not els to be sought.

R. Jugge : London. [After 1572.] 8°. 𝔅. 𝔏.

Bishops' version.

The text of this undated edition closely follows the Bishops' Bible of 1572. For this reason, it is placed here, though possibly not published till later.
It is fully described in Fry's *Bibliographical Description* (pp. 173–4). Owing to their close resemblance in form to certain Tindale Testaments issued by R. Jugge, this and a kindred edition have been erroneously entered in some catalogues as Tindale's. J. R. Dore (*Old Bibles*, pp. 275–6) fixes the date of these two editions as late as 1577, on the assumption that R. Jugge did not adopt the motto *Cogita mori* in his device until that year, 'having a premonition of his own death.' But that motto is found in the folio Bible of 1575 (No. 103) and in the quarto Bible of 1576, while it does not occur in the small quarto of 1577. It also occurs in some books which are almost certainly earlier still, e.g. the 16° Testament (Fry's No. 30), which has been assigned to 1552.

DESCRIPTION. Thirty-two preliminary leaves: title (in black and red, with cut), verso blank, *A Preface into the newe Testament* (printed in small roman type)—1 f., Kalendar—6 ff., *An Almanacke for . xxiiii . yeres* (1561–84)—1 p., *A Table of the principall matters* . . .—41 pp., *A true and perfect reckenyng* . . .—1 p., *An exhortation* . . .—2 pp., *The description of the lande* . . . (map)—2 pp., *The lyfe of . . . Saint Matthewe* . . .— 1 p. The text, A 1 to Tt 2 a ; the O.T. Epistles—5 pp. ; the table of Epistles and Gospels—2 ff. ; 1 f., on the recto of which is the colophon: *Imprinted at London in Powles Churchyarde by Richarde Iugge, Printer to the Queenes Maiestie. Forbidding all other men to print, or cause to be printed, this, or any other Testament in Englishe. Cum priuilegio Regiæ Maiestatis,* with Jugge's device, verso blank ; 1 f. (probably blank).
Signatures : ⋆⁸ ⋆⁸ ⋆⋆⁸ ⋆⋆⋆⁸, A–Z⁸ &⁸ Aa–Tt⁸ ; 376 ff. Leaves not numbered. A full page contains 36 lines. No verse-divisions. The book contains Lives of the four Evangelists and arguments ; notes at the end of chapters ; chapter-contents ; references and alternative readings in the margins, where also the Epistles and Gospels are noted. Words not in the Greek original are printed in roman type. After Acts follow *The Cart Cosmographie . . .* and *The order of tymes.*
The Preface is taken from the folio Bibles of 1568 and 1572, omitting the last paragraph. This edition generally follows the quarto issues of Jugge's revision of Tindale's Testament in the arguments, chapter-contents, notes, and other matter.
The cut on the titlepage is a portrait of Edward VI within a frame. Jugge's device is the pelican, with the motto above *Cogita mori.* There are 20 cuts in Revelation like those used in the folio Bible of 1572.

¶ 134 × 86 mm. Imperfect: wanting all the preliminary matter, except the last three leaves. The last blank leaf is also missing. There are inserted facsimiles of the title, first leaf of Kalendar, Almanack and first page of Table, and a photograph of the Preface leaf ;— taken from the only known perfect copy in the Library of All Souls' College, Oxford.
Bound in brocade, with modern brass corners. [F. F.]

98.

[Copies of the kindred edition mentioned above are in Lambeth Palace Library and the Chetham Library, Manchester. From the evidence of the text, which closely follows the 1569 quarto Bible, Fry dates this before 1572.]

See Appendix for another edition without verse-divisions, 1568 or 1569.

—— ANOTHER EDITION.

This somewhat resembles the preceding ; and the text follows the Bishops' Bible of 1572.

Fry failed to find another copy either in the British Museum or at Oxford. In the Library of St. John's College, Cambridge, however, he discovered an edition identical with this in some parts, but slightly differing in others.
Probably printed between 1572 and 1577. The colophon, if the words *Forbiddyng Englishe* are omitted, resembles that of Jugge's folio Bible of 1574.

DESCRIPTION. Sixteen preliminary leaves: [title,] *A Preface into the newe Testament*—
1 f., Kalendar—6 ff., *The pythe or contentes of the newe Testament*—7 pp., *By the
bookes of the newe Testament* . . .—3 pp., *A true and perfect reckonyng* . . .—1 p.,
An exhortation . . .—2 pp., *The discription of the lande* . . . (map)—2 pp., 1 p. blank.
The text, A i to && iii *b*; the O. T. Epistles—5 pp.; the table of Epistles and Gospels—
4 pp.; 1 p. containing the colophon: *Imprinted at London by Newegate Market,
next vnto Christes Churche, by Richarde Iugge, Printer to the Queenes Maiestie.
Forbiddyng all other men to print, or cause to be prynted, this, or any other Testament
in Englishe. Cum priuilegio Regiæ Maiestatis*, and Jugge's device.
Signatures: ✱⁸ ✶⁸, A–Z⁸ &⁸ Aa–Zz⁸ &&⁸; 400 ff. Leaves not numbered. The
text is divided into verses, with numbers in margin. A full page contains 37 lines.
Lives, arguments, and chapter-contents in roman type; notes at end of chapters, in
black-letter. References and alternative renderings in margins, where also the Epistles
and Gospels are noted. After Acts follow *The Cart Cosmographie* . . . and *The order
of tymes.*
No title is known. Jugge's device and the cuts in Revelation resemble those in the
preceding edition.

¶ 138 × 87 mm. Imperfect: wanting the title and last leaf of Kalendar. Inserted are
facsimiles of the two corresponding leaves in the almost identical edition in the Library of
St. John's College, Cambridge. A photograph of the first leaf of text in that copy, with
tracings etc., is also included for comparison. The title runs: *The nevve | Testament of our
Sa- | uiour Iesu Christe. | Faythfully translated out of | the Greeke, with the Notes | and
Expositions of the darke | places therein. | Math. 13. | The pearle* . . . etc.; on verso, *An
Almanacke for . xxiiii . yeres* (1562–84). [F. F.]
99.

1573. The holie Byble.

R. Jugge : London. 1573. 4°. 𝔅. 𝔏.

Bishops' version.

The second quarto edition.
This resembles in most particulars the quarto Bible of 1569; but the text in the New
Testament appears to be a close reprint of the folio of 1572.
In this and all succeeding editions of the Bishops' Bible (except the folio of 1585) the
Prayer Book version of the Psalter is substituted for the translation given in the folio of
1568.

DESCRIPTION. Forty preliminary leaves: title (with engraving), verso blank, Preface (in
small black-letter) with the prayer— 5 pp., *The whole Scripture* . . .—5 pp., Kalendar—
6 ff., *The order how . . . Proper Lessons . . . etc.*—4 ff.; *The booke of common prayer,
and administration of the Sacramentes*—24 ff. Text:—pt. 1, ff. 1 to 103, 1 f. blank;
pt. 2, with title (within border), text—ff. 106 to 252; pt. 3, with title (within border), text
— ff. 2 to 159, 1 f. blank; pt. 4, with title (within border), text—ff. 2 to 99, 1 f. containing map and table; pt. 5, with title dated 1573 (within border), on verso *A
Preface* . . ., text—ff. 2 to 126, ending on Q 6 *b* with the colophon: *Imprinted at
London in Powles Churchyarde by Richard Iugge, Printer to the Queenes Maiestie.
Cum priuilegio Regiæ Maiestatis*, and Jugge's device.
Signatures: ✱⁶ ℭ⁶ ℭℭ⁴, A–C⁸, A–Z⁸ Aa–Hh⁸ Ii⁴, A–V⁸, Aaa–Mmm⁸ Nnn⁴, A–P⁸ Q⁶;
678 ff. Pts. 1 and 2 have continuous foliation and register. A full column contains 60
lines.
The engraving on the general titlepage resembles that in the quarto edition of 1569;
but the title is here printed above the engraving, and the tablet contains a text: *Searche
the Scriptures . . . Iohn. v.* The border used for the part titles is an ornamental frame
containing above—the royal arms, and below—three of Jugge's small devices: (1) a
Cupid holding the letter R and an arrow, (2) a pelican, and (3) a nightingale in a tree,
with the printer's name on a scroll. The device below the colophon is the large device
of the pelican.

¶ 215 × 156 mm. Wants the second leaf of Kalendar (supplied in facsimile). The general
title is slightly mended. The blank leaf at the end of pt. 1 is missing. Bound in original
boards, covered with leather, stamped with the date 1574. [F. F.]

—— Another copy.

205 × 151 mm. Imperfect: wanting general title and seven following leaves, and two leaves
after the Kalendar; also pt. 4 ff. 10 to 12, and pt. 5 fo. 116. The last two Kalendar leaves
are badly mutilated.
With Metrical Psalms (? date).

—— Another copy.

203 × 142 mm. Imperfect: wanting all preliminary matter; in pt. 1, ff. 2 and 3 and last leaf (blank); pt. 2, title; pt. 3, title, and ff. 49, 88, and 112; pt. 5, title, and last leaf. Some leaves are mutilated.
With Prayer Book (? date); and Metrical Psalms (1573).
In seventeenth-century binding with brass clasps. [F. F.]

—— Another copy.

212 × 149 mm. Imperfect: wanting all preliminary matter; in pt. 1, ff. 76 and 77, and last leaf (blank); pt. 3, title and fo. 26; pt. 5, title, ff. 2 and 3, and last two leaves. Some leaves are mutilated. In place of the general title is inserted a leaf made up of a pt. 3 title and a pt. 5 title, with letterpress (taken from the title of an edition of King James' version) pasted on. Some of the missing text is supplied by leaves taken from other Bibles.

100.

1574. The holy | Byble, | conteynyng the olde | Testament and the | newe. | Set foorth by aucthoritie.

R. *Jugge : London.* 1574. f°. 𝔅. 𝔏.

Bishops' version.

The third folio edition.

DESCRIPTION. Twenty-eight preliminary leaves: title (within border), verso blank, *The summe of the vvhole Scripture* . . .—1 f., *The whole Scripture of the Byble is diuided* . . .—1 f., Preface—7 pp., Prologue—4 pp., *A description of the yeeres* . . .—1 p., *The order of the bookes* . . .—1 p., 1 p. blank, *Proper lessons* . . . etc.—3 pp., *An Almanacke* (1572–1610)—1 p., *To finde Easter* . . . etc.—1 p., *A Table for the order of the Psalmes* . . .—1 p. Kalendar—6 ff., 1 f. blank; *The order vvhere Morning and Euening prayer* . . .—8 ff. Text:—pt. 1, ff. 1 to 102; pt. 2, with title (with engraving), text—ff. 2 to 142 (really 150); pt. 3, with title (with engraving), on verso Prologue, text—ff. 2 to 156; pt. 4, with title (with engraving), text—ff. 2 to 102 a, on verso Table; pt. 5, with title (within border), on verso Preface, text—ff. 2 to 132; Table—3 pp. ending with the colophon: *Imprinted at London by Newgate market, next vnto Christes Churche, by Richard Iugge, Printer to the Queenes Maiestie. The fifth of Iuly. Anno. 1574. Cum priuilegio Regiæ Maiestatis,* and Jugge's large device, 1 p. blank.

Signatures in eights: ★¹⁰ ✱✱¹⁰ ☞⁸, A–M⁸ N⁴, Aa–Ss⁸ Tt⁶, Aaa–Sss⁸ Ttt⁶ Vvv⁶, Aaaa–Mmmm⁸ Nnnn⁶, A–Q⁸ R⁶; 672 ff. Printed in smaller type than the folio of 1572; with 63 lines to the full column. In most particulars this edition closely follows the folio of 1572.

The border used for the general and N. T. titles is like that employed for the N. T. title in the edition of 1568. The text on the tablet in the general title is *Searche the scriptures* . . . *Iohn. 5. verse. 39,* and in the N. T. title *I am not ashamed* . . . *Rom. j.* Pt. 2 titlepage has a composite engraving. Pt. 3 titlepage contains an ornamental block at the top, and below the letterpress a cut of David and Uriah. Pt. 4 titlepage has the same ornamental block, and a composite engraving. The composite engraving which stood before Leviticus is now rightly placed before Numbers; and that belonging to Joshua adorns the titlepage of pt. 2. The most notable alterations are (1) the insertion at Exod. xxvii of a large two-page engraving of the Tabernacle, and (2) the addition in Joshua of a two-page map from the same block as that used for the Coverdale Bible of 1535 (but with different letterpress in the scroll, and Parker's arms in the tablet, dated 1574); these replace the corresponding engravings found in the earlier edition.

¶ 350 × 223 mm. Wanting only the letterpress of the general title, which is supplied in facsimile. In the original binding. [F. F.]

101.

1574. Sermons | of M. Iohn Cal- | uine vpon the Epistle | of Saincte Paule | to the Gala- | thians. | Imprinted at Lon- | don, by Lucas Harison and | George Bishop. | 1574.

Henrie Bynneman, for Lucas Haryson and George Byshop. 4°.

Contains the greater part of the Epistle in English, which differs from any of the familiar versions of this date. Perhaps the translator of the sermons gave his own rendering of the version on which Calvin was commenting.

DESCRIPTION. Twenty preliminary leaves: title (within border), verso blank, *The Epistle Dedicatorie* (to . . . *Sir William Cecill knight, Baron of Burleygh* . . . signed: *Written at my lodging in the forestreete without Cripplegate the . 14 . of Nouember. 1574* . . . *Arthur Golding*)—3 ff., *The Argument* . . . —7 pp., 1 p. blank, *A necessarie Table* . . . —12 ff. The Sermons, ff. 1 to 329 b; followed by two prayers, which end on Tt 2 b with the colophon: *Imprinted at London by Henrie Bynneman, for Lucas Haryson and George Byshop.*

Signatures: ¶⁴ ‡⁴ ★⁴ ★★⁴ ★★★⁴, A–Z⁸ Aa–Ss⁸ Tt²; 350 ff. Printed in roman type; with 36 lines to the page. A few verses of the text are printed in larger type before each of the forty-three Sermons.

The title-border is an ornamental arch, with device, and motto *Non Vi sed Virtute*.

¶ 198 × 146 mm.

102.

1575. The holy | Byble, | conteynyng the olde | Testament and | the newe. | Set foorth by aucthoritie. | Search the scriptures . . . Iohn. 5. verse. 39. | Imprinted at London, | by Lucas Harison.

R. Jugge. 1575. f°. 𝔅.𝔏.

Bishops' version.

In this first small folio edition various printers' names are given on the titlepage in different copies. Anderson (vol. ii. p. 335) mentions Richard Jugge, Richard Kele, John Walley, Lucas Harrison, John Judson, and William Norton; and Cotton (p. 39) adds Francis Coldock. But the edition in each case is the same. Possibly R. Jugge, whose imprint appears at the end of the Order of Morning and Evening Prayer (see below), was the actual printer of the book. It appears, however, that the Master and Wardens of the Stationers' Company had issued special licences to certain stationers—including five of the above-named, and also R. Watkins—to print a folio Bible in pica (? this edition), and a quarto New Testament in ' the English or pica letter ' (? No. 97). See Arber, *Transcript*, vol. v, p. xlviii.

DESCRIPTION. Thirty preliminary leaves: title (within border), verso blank, Preface (in black-letter)—7 pp., Prologue (in roman type)—5 pp., *The summe of the whole Scripture* . . .—1 f., *The whole Scripture . . . is diuided* . . .—2 ff., *A description of the yeeres* . . . and *The order of the bookes* . . . — 1 f., *Proper lessons* . . . etc.— 3 pp., *An Almanacke* (1572-1610)—1 p., *To finde Easter* . . . etc.—1 p., *A Table for the order of the Psalmes* . . . —1 p., Kalendar (with a small cut at the head of each month)—6 ff.; *The order where Morning and Euening prayer shalbe vsed and sayde*—19 pp., ending with Jugge's device and the colophon: *Imprinted at London by Richarde Iugge* . . ., 1 p. blank. Text :—pt. 1, ff. 1 (not numbered) to 102 a, verso blank; pt. 2, with title (within border), verso blank, text—ff. 2 to 151 b, 1 f. blank; pt. 3, with title (within border), on verso *A Prologue* . . ., text—ff. 2 (not numbered) to 156 b; pt. 4, with title (within border), verso blank, text—ff. 2 to 103 a, on verso *A Table to make plaine* . . ., 1 f. blank; pt. 5, with title (within border), on verso *A Preface* . . ., text—ff. 2 to 136 b; *A Table to finde* . . . —3 pp., ending with the colophon: *Imprinted at London in the yere of our redemption, M.D.LXXV. and finished the XXIIII. day of Nouember. God saue the Queene*, beneath which is a device, verso blank.

Signatures: ★⁶ ★★⁶ ★★★⁸, ★¹⁰, A–M⁸ N⁶, Aa–Tt⁸, Aaa–Sss⁸ Ttt⁴ Vvv⁶, Aaaa–Nnnn⁸, A–Q⁸ R¹⁰; 682 ff. Printed in double columns, with 58 or 59 lines to the full column. In the margins, the notes are in roman type, but other matter in black-letter. Headlines and contents of chapters in roman type.

The border used for the titles contains at the top the date 1575, and below the words *God saue the Queene*; immediately beneath the letterpress is a mermaid holding a mirror. In the N. T. title the emblems of the Evangelists are added in the corners of the central compartment. A very small cut of the author appears before each of the following books:—Romans, James, 1 Peter, Jude, and Revelation; and in the last book there are 17 small illustrations. Jugge's device is the pelican, with the motto *Cogita mori*. The device on R 10 b is the brazen serpent.

¶ 279 × 187 mm. The centre of the first title and part of the following leaf are supplied in facsimile. The two blank leaves are missing; that at the end of pt. 4 appears to have been purposely cut out, so that the Table on Nnnn 7 b might face the N. T. title.

103.

1575. The holy | Byble, con- | teynyng the | olde and | newe | Testament. Set foorth by | aucthoritie. | 1575.

R. Jugge : London. 4°. 𝔅. 𝔏.

Bishops' version.

This edition generally agrees with the quarto Bible of 1573. The figure of Elizabeth on her throne has been cut from the block of the general titlepage, leaving a space in which appears the letterpress; the text as before in the label beneath. The other titlepages are the same as in the edition of 1573, except that to pt. 2, which has a different woodcut border, containing at the base a different device of the nightingale in tree, and the motto *Omne. Bonü. Svpernæ*; the N. T. title is dated 1575. The colophon runs: *Imprinted at London by Newgate Market, next vnto Christes Churche, by Richarde Iugge* . . .

Foliation and signatures as before. The 13th preliminary leaf (*The order howe* . . .) is signed ☙ iii.

¶ 210 × 150 mm. The blank leaf at the end of pt. 3 is missing. [F. F.]

104.

1575. The | Newe Te-|stament of | ovr Lord Iesvs | Christ. | Conferred with the Greke, | and best approued | translations. | VVith the arguments, asvvel before the | chapters, as for euery Boke and Epistle, | Also diuersities of readings, and | most profitable annotations of | all harde places : vvhere-| unto is added a co- | pious Table. | Imprinted at | London by T. V. for | Christopher Barker. | 1575.

Tho. Vautroullier. 8°.

Geneva version.

The text agrees generally with that of the 1560 Bible, though it shows traces of revision, e.g., the use of the word *child* for *babe* (1 Pet. ii. 2, *As newe borne children* . . . , etc.).

The first edition of the Geneva version printed in England. Thomas Vautrollier, a Frenchman, printed at London and at Edinburgh. He obtained in June 1574 a royal licence to print Beza's Latin New Testament (Herbert, pp. 1065–7).

The size of this edition is given as 12° by Lea Wilson (No. 37, p. 190), and in the B. M. Catalogue. The wire-marks are perpendicular, and the signatures are in eights.

DESCRIPTION. Twelve preliminary leaves : title (within border), on verso *The ordre of the bookes* . . . , *The Epistle* . . . *By Iohn Caluin*—8 ff., *To the reader* . . . —5 pp., *The Argvment of the Gospell* . . . —1 p. The text, pp. 1 to 813 (EEe 7 a), ending with a vignette and the colophon: *Imprinted at London by Tho. Vautroullier, for Christopher Barker*; *A Declaration of the Table* . . . —1 p., *A Table of the Principall things* . . . —pp. 815 to 850, *A perfect svppvtation* . . . —3 pp., ending on 855 (really 853, HHh 3 a), 1 p. blank, 1 f. blank.

Signatures : ★⁸ ¶⁴, A–Z⁸ Aa- Zz⁸ AAa–GGg⁸ HHh⁴; 440 ff. The pages are numbered from the beginning of the text to the end of the book. Arguments, marginal notes, references, etc.

The title-border is a frame containing above—the royal arms, at the sides—the crest and the arms of Sir F. Walsingham, and below—a tablet bearing the words *Cum priuilegio*. The only illustration is a small cut of the Holy City before Rev. i. The vignette on p. 813 is a female head between two cornucopiæ, below which are the initials T. V.

¶ 141 × 91 mm. The blank leaf (HHh 4) is missing. [F. F.]

105.

[The B. M. has a very similar octavo edition, printed by C. Barker, dated 1575 on the title, but 1576 in the colophon.]

1576. The Bible | and | Holy Scriptvres | conteined in | the Olde and Nevve | Testament. | Translated accor-|ding to the Ebrewe and Greeke, and confer-| red with the best translations in diuers | languages. | VVith most profitable anno-|tations . . . Imprinted at London | by Christopher Barkar, dwelling in | Povvles Churchyard at the signe | of the Tygers Head. 1576. | Cum priuilegio.

f°.

Geneva version.

There are two small folio editions of this date, which, while closely resembling one another, are yet quite distinct.

A. The first folio edition of this version printed in England.

DESCRIPTION. Four preliminary leaves: title (with cut), verso blank, Epistle—3 pp., 1 p. blank, Address—1 p., list of books—1 p. Text:—O. T., ff. 1 to 365 b, 1 f. blank; Apocrypha, ff. 1 to 84 a, verso blank; N. T., with title (with cut), on verso Barker's device, *The Description of the Holy Lande* . . . (map)—1 p., 1 p. blank, text —ff. 1 to 115 b (with device), *The order of the yeres* . . . —1 p., verso blank, *A briefe table* . . . and *A table of the principal things* . . . —19 pp., *A perfite svppvtation* . . . —1 p.
Signatures: *⁎*⁎⁴, A–Z⁶ Aa–Zz⁶ Aaa–Ppp⁶, Aaaa–Oooo⁶, [unsigned]², Aaaaa–Sssss⁶ Ttttt⁸, A⁶ B⁴; 582 ff.
The cut on the two titles is the same as that in the first edition of 1560, with the texts. Barker's large device represents above—a tiger's head (the crest of his patron, Sir F. Walsingham), and below—a lamb, with the legend *Tigre Reo Animale Del Adam Vecchio Figlivolo Merce L'Evangelio Fatto N'Estat Agnolo*; enclosed within a frame. This device occurs repeatedly in Barker's editions.
The mistake in Ecclus. xv. 13 (see the edition of 1560) is corrected.

¶ 278 × 179 mm. The blank leaf (Ppp 6) is missing. Contains a two-page plan in Ezekiel and a map in Acts, probably both taken from a copy of edition B (see below). With Metrical Psalms (1609). [F. F.]

106.

—— ANOTHER EDITION.

B. Lea Wilson's No. 44 (p. 72).

DESCRIPTION. Six preliminary leaves: title: *The Bible* (within narrow frame) | *that is, the Holy* | *Scriptvres con-|teined in the Olde* | *and Newe Testament.* | *Translated* . . . , verso blank, Epistle—3 pp., Address—1 p., *A table conteining the cycle of the svnne* . . . etc.—1 f., Kalendar—3 pp., list of books—1 p. Text:—O. T., ff. 1 to 366 a, verso blank; Apocrypha, ff. 1 to 84 a, verso blank; N. T., with title, verso blank, the map—1 p., 1 p. blank, text—ff. 1 to 115 b; *The order of the yeres* . . . —1 p., tables—19 pp., *A Perfite Svppvtation* . . . (mentioning date 1576 instead of 1560)—1 p., 1 p. blank.
Signatures: ¶⁶, A–Z⁶ Aa–Zz⁶ Aaa–Ppp⁶, Aaaa-Oooo⁶, [unsigned]², Aaaaa-Xxxxx⁶; 584 ff.
A large two-page plan *The forme of the Temple and citie restored* is inserted at Ezekiel; and a map *The description of the covntreis and places mencioned in the Actes* . . . in the N. T. There are woodcuts in Ezekiel. Some of the initials contain Walsingham's arms and crest, or the crest alone. A vignette at the end of the preliminary Epistle is a head between two cornucopiæ, with the initials C. B.
Ecclus. xv. 13 is incorrect.

¶ 275 × 187 mm. The general title is mounted. [F. F.]

107.

1576. The | Holy Byble, | conteynyng | the Old Testa- | ment, and | the Nevv | Set foorth by aucthoritie | Wherevnto is ioyned the whole seruice | vsed in the Churche of Englande. | 1576. | Iohn. 5. | Searche ye the Scriptures . . .

R. Jugge: London. 4°. 𝕭. 𝕷.

Bishops' version.

This agrees generally with the quarto editions of 1573 and 1575.

DESCRIPTION. Forty-two preliminary leaves: title (within border), verso blank, Preface (in italics) with the prayer (in roman type)—4 ff., *The whole Scripture* . . . —5 pp., 1 p. blank, Kalendar (with a small cut at the head of each month)—6 ff., *The order howe*

ENGLISH

..., etc.—7 pp., 1 p. blank: *The Booke of Common Prayer* ...—24 ff. Signatures of these leaves : ★⁸ ₓ★ₓ⁶ ★⁴, A–C⁸.

The text has foliation, signatures, etc., as before. It is printed in a smaller type, but it reads with the editions of 1573 and 1575 leaf for leaf throughout, though some of the marginal references etc. are omitted. A full column contains 60 lines.

The text ends on Q 6 b with Jugge's device and the colophon : *Imprinted at London, by Richard Iugge* ...

The general title is enclosed within the border used for the title of pt. 2 in the edition of 1575. The other titles have the same border as in the Bible of 1573. Jugge's device contains the motto *Cogita mori.*

¶ 186 × 134 mm. Wants general title; supplied in facsimile. [F. F.]

—— Another copy.

178 × 133 mm. Imperfect: wanting all preliminary leaves; and pt. 1, ff. 1 to 5, 7, 8, 41; pt. 2, fo. 113; pt. 3, title, ff. 2 and 17; all pt. 4; pt. 5, ff. 105, 112, and 126 (last leaf). The blank leaves at the end of pts. 1 and 3 are also missing. According to a MS. note this copy was rescued from a waste-paper heap at Bungay in 1782.

—— Another copy.

187 × 139 mm. Imperfect: wanting general title and some preliminary leaves, and many leaves throughout the book; other leaves are loose, some of them apparently having been taken from other copies. In original covers with brass corners and clasps. [F. F.]

108.

1576. The | Nevv Testa- | ment of ovr Lord | Iesvs Christ transla- | ted Out Of Greeke | By Theod. Beza : | Whereunto are adioyned brief Summaries of doctrine vpon | the Euangelistes and Actes of the Apostles, together | with the methode of the Epistles of the Apo- | stles by the said Theod. Beza : | And also short expositions on the phrases and hard places taken | out of the large annotations cf the foresaid Authour and | Ioach. Camerarius, By P. Loseler . Villerius . | Englished by L . Tomson . | Imprinted at London by Christopher Barkar | dwelling in Poules Churchyeard at the | signe of the Tigres head. | 1576. | Cum priuilegio.

8°.

The first edition of Tomson's revision of the Geneva New Testament.

The alterations are mainly due to a comparison with Beza's Latin version of 1565. Tomson's emphatic rendering of the Greek article, e.g. in John i. 1 : *In the beginning was that Word, and that Word was with God, and that Word was God,* exaggerates a tendency which Beza also displays. The notes are generally based on Beza's.

Laurence Tomson (1539–1608) was secretary to Sir F. Walsingham, to whom he dedicated the book. *Loseler Villerius* is M. L'Oyseleur, Seigneur de Villers (Cotton, p. 41).

This became the final and popular form of the Geneva Testament.

DESCRIPTION. Twenty-six preliminary leaves: 1 f. blank (✠ 1), title (with cut), on verso *The order of the bookes,* the Epistle *To the Right Honorable M. Francis VValsingham Esquier, one of the principall Secretaries to hyr Excellent Maiestie, and of hir Highnesse priuie Councell : And to the Right worshipfull M. Francis Hastings. L. T. wysheth prosperitie in this lyfe and lyfe euerlasting, in Christ oure Sauiour*—6 ff., an Address *To the most famous Prince Lewys of Bourbon, Prince of Conde, &c. And to the rest most famous and noble Dukes, Marquises, Earles, Barons, and Gentlemen, which haue embraced the true Gospell of Christ, in the Kingdome of Fraunce. Theodorus Beza of Vezels, Minister of the Chruch of Geneua, grace & peace from God the Father, and from our Lord Iesus Christ* ... (dated *At Geneua* ... *1565*)—29 pp., 1 p. blank, *The Printer to the Diligent Reader*—1 f., 1 p. blank, *The Description of the Holy Lande . . . The places specified* ...—1 p., the map—1 p., 1 p. blank. The text—ff. 1 to 460, ending on Mmm 4 a with the colophon : *Imprinted at London By Christopher Barkar dwelling in Powles Churchycard at the signe of the Tygres head. Cum priuilegio*; on verso is Barker's device.

Signatures: ✠² †⁸ ‡⁸ ★⁸, A–Z⁸ Aa–Zz⁸ Aaa–Lll⁸ Mmm⁴; 486 ff. The leaves in the text are numbered. Chapter-contents, verse-divisions, and marginal notes. A running commentary is added, except in the book of Revelation, which has a separate note at the beginning, filling six pages.

The cut on the titlepage represents the Angels appearing to the Shepherds, with the text *Beholde I bring you glad tidings of greate ioy that shalbe to all the people. Luk. 2. 10.* The only illustration is a small cut representing the Holy City before Rev. i. Some of the ornaments contain Walsingham's crest.

¶ 147 × 96 mm. The title has been mounted. The preliminary blank leaf is missing. Every leaf (according to a MS. note by Fry, who collated several copies) belongs to the correct edition; copies of this and the edition of 1577 are sometimes mixed. Bound up at the end of this copy are 16 pp. of tables, which belong to the 1577 edition; this edition has no tables after the text. [F. F.]

—— Another copy.

157 × 103 mm. Imperfect: wanting all preliminary matter, except the last three leaves, and the last four leaves of text (ff. 457 to 460); the blank leaf before the title is also missing.

Two leaves from an edition of the 1611 version are inserted at the end to complete Revelation.

—— Another copy.

155 × 106 mm. Imperfect: wanting title, all sheet †, and the last leaf (the map) in the preliminary matter; and in the text, ff. 1 to 17, 43 to 46, 113 to 120, 145, 152, 284, 285, 305, 312, and the last four leaves (457 to 460); the blank leaf before the title is also missing, and ★ 7 is mutilated. A facsimile copy of the title is supplied.

Enclosed are fragments of other copies, containing some of the missing leaves. [F. F.]

109.

1576. B. f°. See 1579.

1577. The Bible | that is, the Holy | Scriptvres con- | teined in the Olde | and Newe Testament. | Translated accor- | ding to the Ebrewe and Greeke, and conferred with the | best translations in diuers languages. | With . . annotations . . . Imprinted at London by | Christopher Barkar, dwelling | in Pater noster Rowe at the signe | of the Tygres head. | 1577. | Cum priuilegio.

f°.

Geneva version.

DESCRIPTION. Six preliminary leaves containing the same matter arranged in the same order as in the folio edition B of 1576. Text: O. T., ff. (1) to 360 a, verso blank; Apocrypha, ff. 1 to 76 b; N. T., with title, verso blank, map—1 p., 1 p. blank, text—ff. 1 to 115 b; tables, etc.—21 pp., 1 p. blank.

Signatures: ¶⁶, A–Z⁶ Aa–Zz⁶ Aaa–Ooo⁶, Aaaa–Mmmm⁶ Nnnn⁴, [unsigned]², Aaaaa–Xxxxx⁶; 570 ff.

In most particulars this Bible closely resembles the edition B of 1576. An ornament after the Address contains Walsingham's crest.

¶ 263 × 174 mm. The general title and following leaf are mended.
With Metrical Psalms (1576). [F. F.]

110.

1577. The Bible : | that is, the Holy Scrip- | tvres conteyned in | the Olde and New | Testament. | Translated according | to the Ebrewe and Greeke, and conferred | with the best translations in di- | uers languages . . . Imprinted at London | by Christopher Barkar, dwelling | in Pater noster Rowe at the | signe of the Tygres | head. 1577. | Cum priuilegio.

8°.

Geneva-version.

The edition of 1581 has been generally considered the first issue printed in this size. But there were certainly two earlier editions—this of 1577, and another of 1579.

DESCRIPTION. [Four] preliminary leaves: [1 f. blank,] title (with cut), verso blank, Epistle (first leaf signed ¶ iii,—so apparently a blank leaf should precede title)—3 pp., *The names and order of al the bookes* . . .—1 p. Text: O. T., ff. 1 to — . . . ; *A brief table* . . .—7 pp., *A table of the principall things* . . . (ending with Barker's device)—19 pp., *A perfite svppvtation* . . . (1577)—1 f., ending with colophon: *Imprinted at London by Christopher Barkar, dwelling in Pater noster row at the signe of the Tygres. heade. 1577* (beneath which is a small tailpiece dated 1576).
Signatures: ¶⁴, A–Z⁸ Aa— . . ., ⋆⁸ ⋆⋆⁶; —ff. A full column contains 68 lines. Arguments before books; contents before chapters: subject-headings in headlines; a few references, alternative renderings, etc. in margins.
The first two words of the title are enclosed in a frame. The cut represents the crossing of the Red Sea.

¶ 169 × 103 mm. Very imperfect: containing the preliminary leaves and the appended matter, but only 265 leaves of text, A 1 to Ll 1. [F. F.]

111.

1577. The Holy | Byble, contey- | ning the Olde | and Nevve | Testa- | ment. | Wherevnto is ioyned the | whole seruice, vsed in | the Church of | England. | 1577. | Set foorth by auc- | thoritie.
R. Jugge: London. 4°. 𝔅. 𝔏.
Bishops' version.

DESCRIPTION. Forty preliminary leaves: title (within border), verso blank, [Preface] with the prayer—5 pp., *The whole Scripture* . . . —5 pp., Kalendar—6 ff., *The order howe* . . . —1 p., *Proper Lessons* . . . —2 pp., 1 p. blank; *Certayne godly and comfortable Prayers, for all tymes, and for al persons*—3 pp., 1 p. blank; *The Booke of common Prayer* . . .—24 ff. Text: pts. 1 to 4, with separate titles, but continuous register and foliation, ff. 1 to 591 (really 511) b, followed by 1 f. (592, really 512) containing the map and table; N. T., with title, verso blank, text—ff. 2 to 126 b, ending with Jugge's device and the colophon: *Imprinted at London by Richard Iugge* . . .
Signatures: [—]⁶ ⋆ₓ⋆⁶ ✠⁴, A–C⁸, A–Z⁸ Aa–Hh⁸ Ii⁴ Kk–Zz⁸ Aaa–Sss⁸ Ttt⁴, A–P⁸ Q⁶; 678 ff.
A full column contains 60 lines. In most particulars this Bible agrees closely with the quarto editions of 1573 and 1575, reading generally with them, and with the rather smaller edition of 1576, leaf for leaf throughout the text; but it differs in places, e.g. the table after the Psalter (*Numerus secundum Hebreos*) is omitted.
The borders to the titles are like those used in the quarto Bible of 1575; but the letterpress of the general title is also framed within rules. Jugge's device contains the motto *Cogita Mori*.

¶ 212 × 150 mm. Imperfect: wanting two preliminary leaves after the title, containing, apparently, the Preface. The general title is mounted.
With Metrical Psalms (1574). [F. F.]

112.

1577. [The Holy Byble, conteyning the Olde Testament, and the Newe. Set foorth by aucthoritie. Whereunto is ioyned the whole seruice vsed in the Churche of Englande. 1577. John 5. Searche ye the Scriptures . . .]
R. Jugge: London. 4°. 𝔅. 𝔏.
Bishops' version.

Sometimes erroneously described as an octavo; it is really a small quarto.

DESCRIPTION. Thirty-six preliminary leaves: [Title, verso blank]. Preface (without the prayer)—5 pp., *The whole Scripture* . . . —5 pp., Kalendar—6 ff., *Proper Lessons* . . .—2 ff.; *The Booke of common prayer* . . . —21 ff., *Certayne godly and comfortable prayers* . . . —1 f. Text: O. T. and Apocrypha, ff. 1 to 400 b; N. T., with title (within border), verso blank, text—ff. 2 to 103 b; 1 f., containing on recto Jugge's device and the colophon: *Imprinted at London by Richarde Iugge, Printer to the Queenes Maiestie. Cum priuilegio Regiæ Maiestatis*, verso blank.

Signatures: [(✱ii.), etc.]⁶ [(i), etc.]⁶ ✱², A⁸ B⁸ C⁶, A–Z⁸ Aa–Zz⁸ Aaa–Ddd⁸, A–N⁸ 540 ff. Printed in minute black-letter, somewhat like the type used in Grafton's small quarto Bible of 1553; with 71 lines to the full column. Many of the usual marginal notes and references are omitted.

No copy containing the general title can now be traced; but Herbert (p. 725) quotes it as above, and describes it as having the same border as the N. T. title. This border, containing at the bottom the device with the motto *Omne bonū supernæ*, was first used for pt. 2 title in the quarto edition of 1575. No separate titles to pts. 2, 3 and 4. The large cut of Adam precedes Genesis; but all the maps and tables found in the preceding quarto editions are here omitted. Jugge's device is his larger device, without the motto *Cogita Mori*.

¶ 185 × 130 mm. Wanting only the general title. Inserted are (1) a genuine pt. 2 title from a copy of the other edition of 1577, and (2) a facsimile of the general title in the 1576 edition; both have the woodcut border mentioned above as belonging to the missing title of this edition.
With Metrical Psalms (1578).
Original binding, with brass corners and clasps.

[F. F.]

—— Another copy.

178 × 122 mm. Imperfect: wanting general title and 13 ff. before the Prayer Book, and the last preliminary leaf; also N. T. title and 10 ff. of text.
With Metrical Psalms (? date).

113.

1577. The | New Testa | ment of ovr Lord | Iesus Christ, Translated out of | Greeke by Theod. | Beza. | Whereunto are adioyned brief Summaries . . . And . . . expositions . . . Englished by L. Tomson. | Imprinted at London by Christopher Barkar | dwelling in Powles Churchyeard at the signe | of the Tygres Head. | 1577. | Cum priuilegio.

8°.

Geneva version; Tomson's revision.

Agrees closely with the octavo of 1576, but exhibits slight differences, even in the text (e.g. Matt. iii. 9: *And thinke not* . . . for *And presume not* . . .).

DESCRIPTION. Sixteen preliminary leaves: title (with cut), verso blank, Epistle—6 ff., Address (in very small type)—6 ff., *The Printer to the diligent Reader*—1 f., 1 p. bearing Barker's device, *The Description* . . . —1 p., map—1 p., list of books—1 p. Text, ff. 1 to 460 a, ending with colophon, on verso Barker's device; *A table of the principall things* . . . —16 ff.
Signatures: aᵇ bᵛ, A–Z⁸ Aa–Zz⁸ Aaa–Lllˣ Mmm⁴, Nnn⁸ Ooo⁸; 492 ff.

The last page of the table bears a catchword *A Per-*; but no copy examined by Fry contained *A perfect supputation*, and it seems quite possible that the book was issued without it; the table exactly fills two sheets, and the Supputation would make an odd leaf. (In the copy described by Lea Wilson [p. 193] the table fills 15 ff., and the Supputation 1 f., i.e. together 16 ff., or two sheets.)

¶ 156 × 100 mm. A note by Fry pronounces every leaf of this copy 'correct,' i.e. belonging to the edition of 1577.
Bound up at the end is a MS. sermon (14 ff.), entitled *A goode & a nedefull admonition* . . .

[F. F.]

—— Another copy.

147 × 97 mm. Imperfect: wanting title and five leaves of the Address (b 1 to 5), ff. 244 and 245 in the text, and the last leaf of the table;—9 ff.
Some leaves appear to belong to the edition of 1576. [F. F.]

—— Another copy.

143 × 87 mm. Imperfect: wanting title (supplied in facsimile) and four following leaves, the last leaf (460) of text, and Nnn 8 and Ooo 2 to 8 in the table;—14 ff. [F. F.]

114.

1578. The Bible. | Translated according to the Ebrew | and Greeke, and conferred with the | best translations in diuers | languages. | With most profitable Annotations . . . Whereunto is added the Psalter of the common translation | agreeing with the booke of Common prayer. | Ioshua . 1 . 8 . | Let not this booke . . . good successe. | Imprinted at London | by Christopher Barker, Prin- | ter to the Queenes Maiestie. | Cum gratia & priuilegio Regiæ Maiestatis.

1578. f°. 𝕭. 𝕷.

Geneva version.

The first large folio edition.

DESCRIPTION. Thirty-four preliminary leaves: a leaf before the title containing on verso *Of the incomparable treasure of the holy Scriptures, with a prayer for the true vse of the same* (verses and prayer, within narrow frame), title (within border), verso blank, Epistle—1 f., *To the diligent and Christian Reader* . . . —1 p., 1 p. blank, *A Prologue or preface* . . . (by Cranmer, with a short note explaining why it was inserted)—2 ff., *Proper Lessons* . . . etc.—2 ff., *An Almanacke* (1578–1610)—1 p., Kalendar (with notes below, containing some allusions to contemporary events)—12 pp., 1 p. blank; *The booke of Common prayer* . . . —19 ff. Text: O. T., ff. 1 to 376 b; Apocrypha, ff. 1 to 78 a, verso blank; N. T., with title, verso blank, *The names & order of all the bookes* . . . —1 p., *The description* . . . (with map)—1 p., text—ff. 1 to 118 a, *The summe of the vvhole Scripture* . . . —2 pp., ending with Barker's device and colophon, 1 p. blank; tables—9 ff., *A perfite Supputation* . . . (1578)—1 p., 1 p. blank.

Signatures: ⁎⁎⁎⁶ a–d⁶ e⁴, A–Z⁶ Aa–Zz⁶ Aaa–Qqq⁶ Rrr⁴, A–N⁶, [unsigned]², Aa–Tt⁶, ⋆⁶ ⋆ ⋆⁴; 614 ff. Double columns, with 66 lines to the full column. With the usual notes, etc.

In this edition the Geneva and the Prayer Book versions of the Psalter appear side by side, the former in roman type and the latter in black-letter.

This is the earliest Bible which contains the introductory verses, afterwards occurring so often:

> Here is the spring where waters flowe,
> to quenche our heate of sinne:
> Here is the tree where trueth doth grow,
> to leade our liues therein: etc.,

and the accompanying prayer.

The Prayer Book included in the preliminary matter exhibits many peculiarities; the word *Minister* is substituted throughout for *Priest*, and some of the Offices are omitted.

The title-border contains: above—the royal arms supported by two female figures, one carrying a sword and scales, the other a book and a sprig of heartsease; and below —a lion and a dragon on either side of a tablet containing the words *Imprinted* . . . *Maiestatis* (these words are on a slip pasted over the original imprint, which omits the words *Printer to the Queenes Maiestie* and *Regiæ Maiestatis*); the initials C B appear in the lower corners of the central space, and also at the base of the cut. The same border is used for the N. T. title; but the tablet in this case contains vv. 5 and 6 from Prov. xxx.

¶ 375 × 254 mm.

Fry states in a MS. note that the Prayer Book is generally missing from copies of this edition, as collectors of editions of the Book of Common Prayer are eager to acquire this peculiar variety, and often cut the leaves out of the Bible. [F. F.]

—— Another copy.

366 × 253 mm. Imperfect: wanting all preliminary leaves after Cranmer's Prologue; pt. 1, ff. 97 to 102, 133 to 138; and the last two leaves in the book. In place of ff. 133 to 138 in pt. 1 are inserted 6 ff. from another Bible. This copy has lost the pasted slip from the first title.

115.

1578. The | Holy Byble, | conteynyng the olde | Testament, and | the Newe. | Set foorth by aucthoritie. | Imprinted at London | by the assignement of Christopher | Barker, her Maiesties | Prynter. 1578.

f°. 𝕭. 𝕷.

Bishops' version.

This edition, though the book was entirely reset and issued by another printer, agrees so closely with that published by R. Jugge in 1574, that no further description is necessary beyond a few distinguishing marks. While type, signatures, and foliation are the same, the running titles of books are generally in roman type, instead of italics. In the preliminary leaves, the initial letters to the Preface and Prologue contain no coats of arms, and the leaf ✶✶✶ 1 (Proper Lessons) is printed all in black. The large two-page engraving in Exodus and the map in Joshua are omitted. The pt. 4 titlepage lacks the ornamental block above the letterpress. The N. T. title begins *The nevve Testament* . . . instead of *The newe Testament* . . . The cut of St. Matthew before his Gospel is displaced by a cut of St. Mark. There is no colophon on the last page (R 6 *a*); in its place stands the ornamental block used for pt. 3 titlepage.

¶ 362 × 240 mm. Perhaps there should be a blank leaf after the Kalendar, as in the edition of 1574. [F. F.]

116.

1578. The | Newe Testament of | ovr Lorde Iesvs Christ, | translated ovt of | Greeke by Theo. Beza, and Eng- | lished by L. T. | Whereunto is added a Kalender & a Table. | Beholde, I bring you glad tydings of great ioye | that shalbe to all the people, Luke.2.10. | Imprinted at London by Chri- | stopher Barker, Printer to the Queenes | Maiestie. | 1578. | Cum gratia & priuilegio.

16°.

Geneva version; Tomson's revision.

DESCRIPTION. Seventeen preliminary leaves: first title, on verso *An Almanacke for xxvi. yeeres* (1578 to 1603), Kalendar—6 ff., 1 f. blank; second title (very like the first), on verso *The order of the bookes* . . ., Epistle—8 ff. Text, ff. 1 (not numbered, B 2) to 279 *a*, verso blank; table—23 ff., ending on Rr 7 *b* with colophon; 1 f. blank.
Signatures: [unsigned]⁸, A–Y⁸ Aa–Rr⁸; 320 ff. No Arguments, or notes; but chapter-contents and marginal references.
The first word of each title is enclosed within a narrow frame; and below, under the text, is a small ornament occasionally used by Barker, with Walsingham's crest and the date 1576.

¶ 101 × 66 mm. Wants the two blank leaves. [F. F.]

117.

1578 ? (The New Testament.)
[Qu. *C. Barker: London.* 1578 ?] 8°. 𝔅. 𝔏.
Bishops' version.
Printer and date unknown. Probably printed by C. Barker, about 1578.

This differs entirely from Jugge's editions described above, and from the series printed by the Barkers, or their Deputies, from 1579 to 1617.

DESCRIPTION. No complete description is possible, since the imperfect copy in this library has not yet been identified. The text is divided into verses; 38 lines to the full page. The Lives of the Evangelists, Arguments, notes (at the end of chapters), and marginal references are in black-letter. The headlines (including titles of books and chapter-numbers), chapter-contents, interpolations, and marginal notices of Epistles and Gospels are in roman type.
Acts begins on Y ij *a*, and ends on Dd 8 *a*; and is followed on the next page by *The order of tymes.* Hebrews ends on Ss 5 *b*.
A few errors may be mentioned, as marks for identification:
Y 3 *a*, headline: *Apostls.*
Hb 7 *b*, note: γυνή.
Hb 8 *a* and Ii 8 *a*, headlines: *Corinthains.*

¶ 137 × 89 mm. Very imperfect: wanting all before M j (Luke ii) and all after Tt 8 (2 Peter i). [F. F.]

118.

1579. The Bible | and Holy Scriptvres | conteined in the | Olde and Newe | Testament. | Translated according to the | Ebrue & Greke, & conferred with the beste translations | in diuers languages. | With moste profitable annotations | vpon all the hard places of the Holy Scriptvre, | and other things of great importance, mete for | the godly Reader. | Printed in Edinbrvgh | Be Alexander Arbuthnot, Printer to the Kingis Maiestie, dwelling | at ye Kirk of feild. 1579. | Cvm gratia et privilegio regiar | maiestatis.

T. Bassandyne and A. Arbuthnot : Edinburgh. 1579,76. f°.

Geneva version.

The first Bible printed in Scotland, though Robert Lekpreuik had received a licence to print the Geneva Bible as early as 1568.

A reprint of the folio edition of 1562,61. The printing was begun by Bassandyne, whose name appears on the N. T. title dated 1576; and was finished by his coadjutor Arbuthnot in 1579. By order of the General Assembly every parish in Scotland subscribed the purchase price, £4 13s. 4d. (Scotch currency = about 7s. 6d. in contemporary English coin, or over £4 to-day), before the work was undertaken. An Act of the Scots Parliament passed in 1579 ordered every householder worth 300 merks of yearly rent, and every yeoman or burgess worth £500 stock, to have a Bible and Psalm Book, in the vulgar language, in his house, under the penalty of ten pounds. (*Cf.* J. Lee, *Memorial*, pp. 28–45, etc.; Eadie, vol. ii. chap. xxxvi.; Dobson, *History of the Bassandyne Bible*, 1887; and Dickson and Edmonds, *Annals of Scottish Printing*, 1890, pp. 202, 275 f., 320 f.

DESCRIPTION. [Ten] preliminary leaves: title (with cut), on verso *The names and order of all the bookes . . ., To the richt excellent richt heich and michtie prince Iames the Sext King of Scottis, zovr hvmble svbiectis the Commissionaris of the Kyrkis of your Realme, wisse grace and peace with a prosperous raigne, from God the Father, throuch our Sauiour Iesvs Christ* (dated *From Edinburgh in our general assemblie the tent day of Iulie, 1579*)—2 ff., *An dovble Calendare, to wit, the Romane and the Hebrew Calendare . . .* (with rules, etc., signed *R. Pont*) with the verses *Of the incomparable treasure . . .* and the prayer—9 pp., *A description and svccesse . . .* and *An exhortation . . .*—2 pp., *Howe to take profite in reading of the holie Scripture* (signed *T. Grasop*)—1 p. [Apparently there should be 1 f. blank after the Epistle, or at the end of the preliminary matter. Variations occur in these leaves (see below).] Text: O. T. and Apocrypha, ff. 1 to 503 b, 1 f. blank; N. T., with title: *The Newe Testament . . . At Edinbvrgh. Printed by Thomas Bassandyne . M . D . LXXVI. Cvm privilegio* (with cut), verso blank, text—ff. 1 to 125 b ; *A brief table . . ., A table of the principal things . . ., A perfite svppvtation . . .* (giving the date 1576) and *The order of the yeres . . .*—14 ff., 1 f. blank. Signatures: [(∴) ij, etc.]¹⁰, a–z⁶ aa–zz⁶ aaa–zzz⁶ aaaa–pppp⁶, A–Y⁶ Z⁸; 654 ff. Double columns, with 60 lines to a full column. At the bottom of the last page of 2 Macc. is printed a title: *The thirde boke of the Maccabees newlie translated out of the original Greke.* But the book itself apparently was not included.

The cut on the two titlepages displays the arms of *Jacob' Sextvs,* supported by two unicorns, with the motto *In Defens*; at the sides are the words *God save the King.* At the bottom of the last preliminary page occurs a small device, copied from Jugge's device of the pelican ; the shield at the base contains a coat of arms between the initials A A, and at the top appears the printer's name *Alexander Arbvthnet.* The book contains 26 engravings in the text; besides maps at Numbers xxxiii and Joshua xv, and a plan at the end of Ezekiel, printed on separate leaves.

¶ 328 × 210 mm. Wants the general title (supplied in facsimile) and the blank leaves. Inserted at the beginning are: (1) specimens of the last four preliminary leaves, which are differently set up from those in this copy; perhaps they are cancelled leaves. (2) A leaf containing a map, which does not seem properly to belong to this edition. [F. F.]

119.

1579. The Bible. | Translated according to the | Ebrew and Greeke, and conferred | with the best translations in | diuers languages. | With most profitable Annotations | vpon all the hard places, and other things | of great importance, as may appeare | in the Epistle to the Reader. | Ioshua.

1. 8. | Let not . . . successe. | Imprinted at London by Chri- | stopher Barker, Printer to the Queenes | most excellent Maiestie. | 1579. | Cum gratia & priuilegio Regiæ Maiestatis.

4°. 𝕭. 𝕷.

Geneva version.

Apparently the earliest in the long series of quarto Geneva Bibles printed in England.

There are two editions of this date, which while closely agreeing are yet distinct.

A.

DESCRIPTION. [Sixty] preliminary leaves: [1 f.], title (within border), verso blank, Epistle—1 f. (signed ¶ iii), Address *To the diligent and Christian Reader* . . . —1 p., *Proper Lessons* . . . etc.—4 pp., An Almanacke (1578-1610)—1 p., Kalendar (with chronological notes, containing references to some contemporary events)—6 ff. ; *The Booke of Common prayer* . . . —20 ff. ; the Psalter, with title *The Psalter or Psalmes of Dauid, of that translation which is vsed in Common prayer.* Imprinted at London by Christopher Barker . . . (within border), verso blank, —28 ff. [One leaf is required before or after the general title, since the Epistle leaf is signed ¶ iii. Probably it should precede the title, and have *Of the incomparable treasure* . . . printed on verso, as in B.] Text divided into three parts: (1) O. T., ff. 1 to 378 b ; (2) Apocrypha, ff. 1 to 86 a, verso blank; N. T., with title (within border), verso blank, *The summe of the whole Scripture* . . . —1 f., *Certaine questions & answers touching the doctrine of predestination, the vse of Gods worde and Sacraments*—3 pp., list of books—1 p., text— ff. 1 to 121 b, ending with the colophon: *Imprinted at London by Christopher Barker, Printer to the Queenes most excellent Maiestie, dwelling in Pater noster Rowe, at the signe of the Tygres head. Anno 1579*, 1 f. blank ; *A briefe Table of the interpretation of the proper names* . . . —7 pp., *A Table of the principall things* . . . —19 pp., *A perfite Supputation . . . vnto this present yeere . . . 1578* . . . —1 f., ending on ★ ★ 6 b with colophon.

Signatures: ¶⁴ ¶¶⁶, A⁸ B⁸ C⁴, A-C⁸ D⁴, A-Z⁸ Aa-Zz⁸ Aaa¹⁰, Aaa-Kkk⁸ Lll⁶, ★⁴, Aaaa-Oooo⁸ Pppp¹⁰ ★⁸ ★ ★⁶ ; 664 ff.

Double columns, with 70 lines to the full column. Arguments, marginal notes, etc. in roman type.

The border used for the general and N.T. titles resembles that in the folio edition of 1578 ; with two symbolical female figures, the royal arms, the lion and dragon, and the initials C B ; the tablet is blank. The title-border of the Prayer Book Psalter has at the sides—symbolical figures *Fides* and *Hvmilitas*, in the corners—emblems of the Evangelists, above—the royal arms, and below—Walsingham's crest.

Barker's device (*Tigre Reo* . . .) occurs at the end of the Prayer Book, and after the *Godly prayers* at the end of the Psalter. A small cut of the royal arms is placed above the colophon on Pppp 9 b.

¶ 234 × 158 mm. Imperfect: wanting the general title, and one other leaf. Inserted are:—(1) an incorrect quasi-facsimile title ; (2) a folding leaf, containing *Howe to take profite* . . . (signed *T. Grashop*).   [F. F.]

—— Another copy.

208 × 153 mm. Imperfect: wanting all before the second leaf of Kalendar, ¶¶ 8, and the first leaf of Prayer Book ; also a blank leaf (Pppp 10).

This copy is remarkable as containing five full-page engravings inserted at Exodus, Numbers, Joshua, Judges, and 1 Samuel (this last should come at 1 Kings). These appear to have been struck off the same wood-blocks as were used for the folio Bishops' Bibles of 1572, 1574 and 1578. They are printed on separate leaves, with verso blank.

With Metrical Psalms (1578).   [F. F.]

120.

—— ANOTHER EDITION.

B. Closely agreeing with A, but differing in some points.

A leaf precedes the title bearing the verses *Of the incomparable treasure* . . . and the prayer (within narrow frame) on verso. The general title differs very slightly from that of A ; in the text from Joshua i *and do* and *way* appear for *& do* and *waye*. The Prayer Book and Psalter have continuous register, A-F⁸ ; hence the Psalter titleleaf is C 5. Barker's device *Tigre Reo* . . . is absent from C iiij b. The Apocrypha contain 76 ff. In the colophon

on Pppp 9 b, the words *dwelling . . . head* are omitted. *A perfite Supputation . . .* reckons in the year 1579.
A double leaf containing *Howe to take profite . . .* is inserted before the text.

¶ 206 × 144 mm. [F. F.]
121.

1579. (The Bible.)
C. Barker : London. 1579. 8°.

Geneva version.

Apparently the second octavo edition.

DESCRIPTION. [Title and preliminary leaves.] Text: O.T., ff. 1 to 334 b (ending with a tailpiece dated 1576, and an ornament); Apocrypha, ff. 335 to 413 b (ending with ornament); N.T. (with title: *The Nevve Testament* in a small frame at the head of the first page) ends on fo. 520 a (with a tailpiece containing the initials C B), on verso *The order of the yeres* . . .; the two tables—13 ff. (ending with Barker's device), *A perfite svppvtation . . .* (1579)—1 f., ending with the colophon: *Imprinted at London by Christopher Barker, Printer to the Queenes Maiestie . 1579* (beneath which is the tailpiece, dated 1576).
Signatures: [—], A–Z⁸ Aa–Zz⁸ Aaa–Ttt⁸, ⋆⁸ ⋆ ⋆⁶; . . . + 534 ff. Type, etc. as in the octavo edition of 1577.

¶ 163 × 105 mm. Imperfect: wanting preliminary matter, and eight leaves of text— ff. 1 to 3, 6 to 8, 444 and 445; in place of the last two leaves are inserted two taken from an edition of the 1611 version. [F. F.]
122.

1580. (The Bible.)
C. Barker : London. 1580. 4°. B. L.

Geneva version.
There are two varieties of this date.

A. Lea Wilson's No. 51 (p. 80).

DESCRIPTION. [Fifty-eight] preliminary leaves: [1 f.], titleleaf, Epistle—1 f. (signed ¶ iii), Address—1 p., Proper Lessons, etc.—4 pp., Almanack—1 p., Kalendar—6 ff.; Prayer Book (with Psalter)—45 ff., *Howe to take profite . . .* —1 p., *Of the incomparable treasure . . .* —1 p. Text: O. T., ff. 1 to 358 b; Apocrypha end on fo. 435 (really 434) a, verso blank; N. T., with titleleaf, *The summe . . .* —1 f., *Certaine questions . . .* —3 pp., list of books—1 p., text ends on fo. 554 (really 552, Zzz 10) b. Concordances, with title: *Tvvo right profitable and fruitfull Concordances, or large and ample Tables Alphabeticall. The first contayning the interpretation of the Hebrue, Caldean, Greeke, and Latine wordes and names scateringly dispersed throughout the whole Bible, with their common places following euery of them : And the second comprehending all such other principall words and matters, as concerne the sense and meaning of the Scriptures, or direct vnto any necessarie and good instruction. The further contents and vse of both the which Tables, (for breuitie sake) is expressed more at large in the Preface to the Reader. Collected by R. F. H. . . .*, verso blank, *The Preface . . .* (dated 22 Dec. 1578, and signed: *Thine in the Lord, Robart F. Herrey*)—1 f.; tables—90 ff., ending on M 4 b with colophon.
Signatures: [—]⁴ ¶⁶, A–E⁸ F⁶, A–Z⁹ Aa–Zz⁸ Aaa–Hhh⁸ Iii², ⋆⁴, Kkk–Yyy⁸ Zzz¹⁰, A–L⁸ M⁴; 602 ff. Double columns, with 71 lines to the full column.
The Concordances, which form an essential part of the volume, were compiled by *Robart F. Herrey*, who is identified with Robert Harrison, the Norfolk Brownist (d. 1585 ?).
Title-border as in the edition of 1579.
Barker's device *Tigre Reo . . .* occurs at the end of *Godly prayers*, after Malachi, on the titlepage of the Concordances, and above the colophon on the last page. A small cut of the royal arms is found at the end of Revelation.

¶ 215 × 153 mm. Imperfect: wanting the first four leaves (the Epistle leaf signed ¶ iii appears to have been supplied from a copy of the 1579 B edition); and the last leaf of Kalendar.
With Metrical Psalms (1580). [F. F.]
123.

—— ANOTHER EDITION.

B. Lea Wilson's No. 51a (p. 182²).

It is possible that this should precede A, since this edition resembles one of 1579. while A is a new type of quarto Bible, which was frequently copied in later years.

DESCRIPTION. [Sixty] preliminary leaves: [Two leaves before title—the first page bears the signature A j, on the third printed longitudinally begins T. Grashop's *Howe to take profite* . . . which ends on the second page, the fourth page contains *Of the incomparable treasure* . . . ; titleleaf; (no Epistle;)—so Lea Wilson.] Address—1 p., Proper Lessons etc.—4 pp., Almanack—1 p., Kalendar—6 ff.; Prayer Book (with Psalter)—48 ff. Text: O. T., ff. 1 to 378 b; Apocrypha, ff. 1 to 78 b; N. T., with titleleaf, *The summe* . . . —1 f., *Certaine questions* . . . —3 pp., list of books—1 p., text—ff. 1 to 121 b, 1 f. blank. Concordances (with *A perfect Supputation* . . . dated 1580) end on V 8 a, with colophon, verso blank.

Signatures: A⁴ ¶¶⁸, A–F⁸, A–Z⁸ Aa–Zz⁸ Aaa¹⁰, Aaa–Iii⁸ Kkk⁶, ★⁴, Aaaa–Oooo⁸ Pppp¹⁰, A–C⁴ D–V⁸; 790 ff. Double columns, with 70 lines to the full column.

Title-border as before. The N. T. title has a double (instead of a single) ornament above the imprint. The Prayer Book Psalter has a separate title, as in edition A of 1579. The device *Tigre Reo* . . . does not occur after Malachi. The royal arms (above the colophon) show a dragon and a lion. The first page of the Preface to the Concordances has a headpiece, and an initial letter representing the Plague of Frogs.

¶ 211 × 152 mm. Imperfect: wanting apparently five leaves at the beginning. It has a double leaf before the title, containing *Howe to take profite* . . . (with Barker's imprint). With Metrical Psalms (1580).
Contemporary binding, with brass plates and corners. [F. F.]

124.

1580. The | Newe Testa- | ment of ovr Lord | Iesus Christ, translated out of | Greeke by Theod. | Beza . . . Englished by L. Tomson. | VVhereunto is adioyned a Concordance or Table made after the | order of the Alphabet, conteyning the principall both | wordes and matters, which are compre- | hended in the Newe Te- | stament. | Imprinted at London | by Christopher Barker, Prin- | ter to the Queenes | Maiestie. | 1580. | Cum priuilegio.

8°.
Geneva version; Tomson's revision.

DESCRIPTION. [Seventeen] preliminary leaves: [1 f. blank,] title, verso blank, Epistle— 6 ff., Address—6 ff., *The Printer to the diligent Reader*—1 f., 1 p. bearing Barker's device, *The Description* . . . —1 p., Map—1 p., *The order of the bookes* . . . —1 p. The text, ff. 2 to 403 b; *A table made after the order of the alphabet, conteyning the principall both wordes and matters* . . . —24 ff.; 1 f. containing on recto the colophon: *Imprinted at London, by Christopher Barker, Printer to the Queenes most excellent maiestie. Cum priuilegio Regiæ Maiestatis. 1580*, verso blank.

Signatures: a⁸ B⁸, A–Z⁸ Aa–Zz⁸, Aaa–Ggg⁸ Hhh⁴; 444 ff. Leaves numbered from A 1 to end of text.

No cut on titlepage, or before Revelation. Headpiece and vignette on the page containing colophon (Hhh 4 a).

¶ 156 × 98 mm. The title has been mounted. A blank leaf appears to be wanting before the title, since the first leaf of the Epistle is signed a iii. [F. F.]

125.

—— ANOTHER EDITION.

Printed by C. Barker, about the same date.

Fry states in a MS. note that he was unable to identify this edition. It agrees closely with that described above; yet small typographical differences throughout prove it to be quite distinct. The text begins on fo. 1 (A 1), instead of on fo. 2 (A 2); the type, however, is so arranged that before long this difference disappears, and from fo. 17 (C 1) onwards the two editions read together page for page.

DESCRIPTION. Probably sixteen preliminary leaves, arranged as in the above edition, except that the titleleaf would be a 1. The text, ff. 1 to 403 b; the table—24 ff., followed probably by 1 f. (Hhh 4) containing colophon on recto, verso blank.
Ornament dated 1576 after the Address; vignette with initials C B after *The Printer* . . .

¶ 150 × 95 mm. Imperfect: wanting apparently six leaves—the title and four following leaves, and one leaf at the end. Duplicates of ff. 115 and 118 are inserted. [F. F.]

—— Another copy.
Imperfect: wanting all before F 3, and other leaves. Unbound. [F. F.]

—— Another copy.
A fragment, containing 6 ff. of preliminary matter, and sheets A to Z in the text.
[F. F.]
126.

1580. The | Third Part of the | Bible, (after some | division) conteyning | fiue excellent bookes, most commodious for all | Christians: Faithfully translated . . . with . . . Annotations . . . Imprinted at London | by Christopher Barker, printer to | the Queenes Maiestie. | 1580. | Cum gratia & priuilegio.
16°.

Geneva version.

Contains Job, Psalms, Proverbs, Ecclesiastes and the Song of Solomon.

DESCRIPTION. [Eight] preliminary leaves: [1 f. blank,] title, on verso *The Contents, The Printer to the Reader*—1 f., *The Prayer of Manasseh, King of the Iewes*—1 f., *A Table for the order of the Psalmes*—1 f., *The Second Table concerning the chiefe pointes of our religion, contayned in the Psalmes*—3 ff. Text, A 1 to Ee 7 b; 1 f., containing on recto a cut (coat of arms) and colophon, verso blank.
Signatures: ¶⁸, A–Z⁸ Aa–Ee⁸; 232 ff.
In the Psalter, the morning and evening divisions of the Prayer Book version are noted throughout.
The first word of the title is within a small frame, and one of Barker's devices occurs above the imprint.

¶ 117 × 70 mm. Imperfect: wanting sheets H and K; a blank leaf also seems to be wanting before the title. [F. F.]
127.

1581. The Bible . . . With . . . Annotations . . . And also a most profitable Concordance . . . Imprinted at London by Chri- | stopher Barker, Printer to the Queenes | most excellent Maiestie. | 1581. | Cum gratia & priuilegio Regiæ Maiestatis.
4°. 𝔅. 𝔏.

Geneva version.

This closely resembles edition A of 1580, which became a favourite type for reprinting. The text ends on fo. 554 (really 552); and the tables on M 4.
Apparently the first sheet has only two leaves, the leaf before the title and that containing the Epistle being omitted in this edition. Fry compared five copies, which all agreed; and the quarto of 1582 and subsequent editions seem to have only two leaves in this sheet.

¶ 223 × 161 mm. Imperfect: wanting the first leaf of Prayer Book, in place of which is inserted a leaf from another edition.
With Metrical Psalms (1581).
Seventeenth-century binding. [F. F.]

—— Another copy.

210 × 154 mm. Imperfect: wanting all preliminary matter except the last leaf, and the tables.

128.

1581. The Bible : | that is, the Holy Scrip- | tvres . . . Imprinted at London | by Christopher Barker, Printer to | the Queenes Maiestie. | Anno. 1581. | Cum priuilegio.

8°.

Geneva version.

Sometimes described as the first octavo edition of the Geneva Bible; but see above, Nos. 111 and 122.

DESCRIPTION. Two preliminary leaves: title, verso blank, *To the diligent and Christian Reader* . . .—1 p., list of books—1 p. Text: O. T. and Apocrypha, ff. 1 to 413 b ; *A perfite svppvtation* . . . (1581)—1 f. (not included in the foliation); N. T. ends on fo. 520 a, on verso *The order of the yeres* . . .; tables—13 ff., ending on Xxx 8 b with Barker's device.
Signatures: A–Z⁸ Aa–Zz⁸ Aaa–Xxx⁸; 536 ff.
The titlepage resembles that in the edition of 1577. From Barker's small device, where it occurs, the date 1576 is now omitted; and the initials C B disappear from the vignette at the end of Revelation.

¶ 163 × 106 mm.
With Metrical Psalms (1581). [F. F.]

129.

1582. The Bible | that is, the Holy | Scriptvres con- | teined . . . With . . . annotations . . . Imprinted at London by | Christopher Barker, Printer | to the Queenes Maiestie. | 1582. | Cum priuilegio Regiæ Maiestatis.

f°.

Geneva version.

A close reprint of the folio edition of 1577.
Preliminary leaves, text, etc., as before.
Signatures, as before; 570 ff.

¶ 269 × 182 mm.
With Metrical Psalms (1583).
Silver corners to binding. [F. F.]

130.

1582. The Bible . . . With . . . Annotations . . . And . . . Concordance . . . Imprinted at London by Chri- | stopher Barker . . . 1582 . . .

4°. 𝔅. 𝔏.

Geneva version.

A close reprint of the quarto of 1581. The text ends on fo. 554 (really 552); and the tables on M 4.

¶ 221 × 157 mm.
With Metrical Psalms (1581).
Contemporary binding with brass corners. [F. F.]

—— Another copy.

213 × 157 mm. Imperfect: wanting the first thirteen leaves; also B 7.
With Metrical Psalms (1581).
Contemporary binding.

131.

ENGLISH

1582. [The New Testament . . .] Englished by L. Tomson. | VVhereunto is adioyned a Concordance . . . Imprinted at London | by Christopher Barker, Prin- | ter to the Queenes | Maiestie. | 1582. | Cum priuilegio.

8°.

Geneva version; Tomson's revision.

DESCRIPTION. Seventeen preliminary leaves: title, verso blank, Epistle—7 ff., Address—13 pp., *The Printer to the diligent Reader*—2 pp., *The description* . . .—1 p., the Map—1 p., *The order of the bookes* . . .—1 p. The text, ff. 2 to 403 *b*; the table—24 ff., 1 f. containing the colophon on recto, verso blank.

Signatures, etc. as in Nos. 125 and 126. The text begins on A 2. The map is smaller.

¶ 147 × 94 mm. Imperfect: wanting title. According to Fry's MS. note, no complete title is known to exist. Inserted is a tracing of a mutilated title, from which the lettering given above is copied. [F. F.]

—— Another copy.

151 × 91 mm. Imperfect: wanting title. The Epistle has been supplied from another copy. [F. F.]

132.

1582. The | Newe Testa- | ment of our Sa- | uiour Iesus | Christ. | Faithfully translated | out of the Greeke, with the | Notes and exposicions | of the darke pla- | ces therein. | Matth. 13. | The pearle which Christ commanded | to be bought, | Is here to be found, not els to be sought. | Imprinted at London, | by Christopher Barker, Prin- | ter to the Queenes Maiestie. | 1582.

8°. 𝕭.𝕷.

Bishops' version.

This generally resembles the editions of 1579 and 1581. A copy of the former is in the John Rylands Library (*cf.* R. Lovett, *The English Bible* . . ., p. 228); the latter is described by Lea Wilson (No. 45, p. 196).

DESCRIPTION. Sixteen preliminary leaves: title (within border), verso blank, Kalendar (giving the hours of sunrise and sunset each month)—6 ff., *An Almanacke for xxvi. yeeres* (1578-1603), verso blank, *A Preface into the newe Testament*—2 ff., *The pith or contentes of the newe Testament* . . .—7 pp., *By the bookes of ye new Testament* . . .—2 pp., *A true and perfect rekoning* and *An exhortation* . . .—2 pp., *The order of the bookes* . . .—1 p. Text, A 1 to Qq 8 *b*. [Probably the O. T. Epistles and the Table of Epistles and Gospels should follow, as in the similar editions of 1579 and 1581.]
Signatures: [unsigned]⁸ ★⁸, A–Z⁸ Aa–Qq⁸, [Rr¹]; 332 ff. Leaves not numbered. A full page contains 44 or 45 lines; with verse-divisions. Lives of the Evangelists and Arguments, chapter-contents, and notices of Epistles and Gospels, in italics. Headlines, notes at the end of chapters, interpolations, marginal references, etc., in roman type.

Acts ends on Z 7 *a*, and is followed on the next page by *The order of times*.

The title-border: above—the royal arms supported by a lion and a dragon; at the sides—female figures representing *Memoria* and *Inteligētia*, with the initials C B; and below—the arms of the Stationers' Company.

¶ 140 × 88 mm. Imperfect: wanting the first leaf of Kalendar, and probably four leaves after the text. The title is mounted. [F. F.]

—— Another copy.

132 × 81 mm. Imperfect: wanting preliminary matter, and other leaves. [F. F.]

133.

1582. The | Nevv Testament | of Iesvs Christ, trans- | lated faithfvlly into English, | out of the authentical Latin, according to the best cor- | rected copies of the same, diligently conferred vvith | the Greeke and other editions in diuers languages : Vvith | Argvments of bookes and chapters, Annota- | tions, and other necessarie helpes, for the better vnder- | standing of the text, and specially for the discouerie of the | Corrvptions of diuers late translations, and for | cleering the Controversies in religion, of these daies : | In the English College of Rhemes. | Psal. 118. | Da mihi intellectum . . . That is, | Giue me vnderstanding . . . S. Aug. tract . 2 . in Epist . Ioan. | Omnia quæ leguntur . . . That is, | Al things that are readde . . . Printed at Rhemes, | by Iohn Fogny. | 1582. | Cvm privilegio.

4°.

The *editio princeps* of the Roman Catholic version of the New Testament in English. Translated from the Vulgate by Gregory Martin, under the supervision of William Allen (afterwards Cardinal Allen), and of Richard Bristow.

The translation adheres very closely to the Latin, though it shows traces of careful comparison with the Greek. But its groundwork was practically supplied by the existing English versions, from which Martin did not hesitate to borrow freely. In particular there are many striking resemblances between Martin's renderings and those in Coverdale's diglot of 1538. Martin's own style is often disfigured by latinisms.

This Rheims New Testament exerted a very considerable influence on the version of 1611, transmitting to it not only an extensive vocabulary, but also numerous distinctive phrases and turns of expression. (See J. G. Carleton's exhaustive analysis, *The Part of Rheims in the making of the English Bible*, Oxford, 1902.)

Allen was the first President, and Bristow was Moderator (or Prefect of studies) of the English Roman Catholic College, established in 1568 in connection with the University of Douai, and removed temporarily to Rheims, 1578-93. Martin was one of the original scholars of St. John's College, Oxford, and is described in Wood's *Athenæ Oxonienses* as follows : 'He was a most excellent linguist, exactly read and vers'd in the Sacred Scriptures, and went beyond all of his time in humane literature, whether in poetry or prose.' In 1570 he joined the College at Douai, and became Lecturer in Hebrew and Holy Scripture. He died at Rheims, in October, 1582.

The translation was essentially Martin's work. The keenly controversial matter which accompanies the text is ascribed to Bristow. *The Censure and Approbation* is signed by four ecclesiastics of Rheims : *Petrus Remigius, Hubertus Morus, Ioannes le Besgue*, and *Gulielmus Balbus*. The Preface criticises certain renderings of the English Bibles, mentioning some editions by their dates.

For the English Roman Catholic Versions as a whole, see Cotton's *Rhemes and Doway* (Oxford, 1855).

DESCRIPTION. Fifteen preliminary leaves: title (within narrow frame), on verso *The Censvre and Approbation, The Preface to the Reader* . . . —11 ff., *The Signification or Meaning of the Nvmbers and Markes vsed in this Nevv Testament*—1 p., *The Bookes of the Nevv Testament, according to the counte of the Catholike Churche* . . . etc.— 3 pp., *The Svmme of the New Testament*—2 pp. (numbered 1 and 2). Text, pp. 3 to 745 ; *A Table of the Epistles and Gospels, after the Romane Vse* . . ., *An ample and particvlar Table directing the reader to al Catholike truthes* . . ., *The Explication of certaine vvordes in this translation* . . ., and *The faultes correcte thus* . . . —27 pp., ending on Eeeee ij *b* with the words *Lavs Deo*.

Signatures : a–c⁴ d², A–Z⁴ Aa–Zz⁴ Aaa–Zzz⁴ Aaaa–Zzzz⁴ Aaaaa–Ddddd⁴ Eeeee²; 400 ff. The pages are numbered from A 1 *a* to Bbbbb 1 *a*, the end of the text. The Annotations are placed at the end of each chapter, the shorter notes etc. in the outside margins, the references in the inside margins. The text is in paragraphs, with the verse-numbers on the inner side. Contents precede each chapter, and Arguments appear before most of the books. After St. John's Gospel is *The svmme, and the order of the Evangelical historie* . . . (pp. 281 to 285): and after Acts *The svmme of the Actes of the Apostles* . . . (pp. 374 to 376).

The list of words in the *Explication* at the end of the volume includes many which are now established in familiar use ; e.g., *acquisition, advent, calumniate, character, evangelize, resuscitate, victims*.

No illustrations ; but many vignettes, initial letters, etc.

¶ 222 × 151 mm. [F. F.]

ENGLISH

—— Another copy.

215 × 150 mm.

—— Another copy.

212 × 159 mm. The last leaf is supplied in manuscript.

—— Another copy,

215 × 153 mm. Imperfect: wanting Bbbbb 2 and the last three leaves; and a few sheets belong to the second edition (1600). [F. F.]
134.

1583. The Bible. | Translated according to the Ebrew | and Greeke . . . With most profitable Annotations . . . Imprinted at Lon- | don, by Christopher Barker, | Printer to the Queenes most excel- | lent Maiestie. | 1583. | Cum gratia & priuilegio.

f°. 𝔅. 𝔏.

Geneva version.

DESCRIPTION. [Twenty-two] preliminary leaves: [1 f. blank,] title (in black and red, within border), verso blank, Epistle (in roman type)—1 f. (signed A iii), Address—1 p., Cranmer's Prologue—4 pp., 1 p. blank; Genealogical Table—11 pp., *An Almanacke* (1578–1610)—1 p., Kalendar—6 ff., list of books—1 p., *Hovve to take profite* . . . —1 p., *The svmme of the whole Scripture* . . . —1 f., *Certaine questions and ansvveres* . . . —1 f., *Of the incomparable treasure* . . . (within frame)—1 p., 1 p. containing large engraving. Text: O. T. and Apocrypha, ff. 1 to 532 (Vvvv 6) *a*, verso blank; N. T., with title (within border), on verso *The Description* . . . (with map), text—ff. 1 to 137 (Z 6) *b*; tables—9 ff., *A perfite Suppvtation* . . . (1582) with colophon—1 f.
Signatures: A–C⁶ D⁴, A–Z⁶ Aa–Zz⁶ Aaa–Zzz⁶ Aaaa–Vvvv⁶, A–Z⁶, ⋆⁶ ⋆ ⋆⁴; 704 ff.
Job ends on fo. 262 *a*, verso blank, and is followed by a separate title to the Psalter (within border), verso blank. Malachi ends on fo. 437 *b*, and is followed by 1 f. blank, and a title to the Apocrypha (within border), verso blank; these two leaves are omitted from the foliation, although the Psalter title is included in the numbering of the leaves.
The general title-border: at the top—the Sacred Name surrounded by clouds whence issues a hand holding a book inscribed *Verbvm Dei Manet In Æternv̄*; at the sides—a Tudor rose and fleur-de-lys and the initials E R; and below—a tablet containing a text. The N. T. title has the same border. For the Psalter and Apocrypha titles a border is used like that found in many of Barker's Bibles: at the top—the royal arms supported by two female figures, one carrying a sword and balances, and the other holding a book and a sprig of heartsease. The full-page engraving represents Adam and Eve in Eden; within a frame. A cut of the royal arms occurs at the end of Malachi and above the colophon.

¶ 400 × 261 mm. Wants a blank leaf before the title.
Contemporary binding, with brass corners and clasps. [F. F.]
135.

1583. The Bible . . . With . . . Annotations . . . And . . . Concordance . . . Imprinted at London by Christo- | pher Barker . . . 1583 . . .

4°. 𝔅. 𝔏.

Geneva version.

A close reprint of the quarto of 1581. The text ends on fo. 554 (really 552); and the tables on M 4.

¶ 220 × 163 mm. [F. F.]
136.

1583. The | Newe Te- | stament . . . transla- | ted out of Greeke by | Theod. Beza. | Whereunto are adioyned . . . together with a | Table or Concord-

VOL. I. H

ance . . . Englished by L. Tomson. | Imprinted at London by | Christopher Barker, Printer to the | Queenes most excellent | Maiestie.

1583. 4°. 𝔅.𝔏.

Geneva version; Tomson's revision.

DESCRIPTION.—[Eight] preliminary leaves: [1 f. blank,] 1 f. (bearing only the signature ¶ ij), title (within border), verso blank, Epistle—7 pp., 1 p. blank, *The Printer to the diligent reader*—1 p., *The discription* . . . (with map)—1 p. Text, ff. 1 to 322 *b*; table—19 ff., ending on Vv 5 *b*, with colophon; 1 f. blank.
Signatures: ¶⁸, A–Z⁸ Aa–Tt⁸ Vv⁶; 350 ff.
The title-border contains at the sides—two female figures, and below—a bull's head, two masks, and two lions. Barker's device (*Tigre Reo* . . . etc.) occurs at the end of the Epistle; and the cut of the royal arms at the end of St. John, and on the last page of text.

¶ 254 × 189 mm. Wants the blank leaves. [F. F.]

137.

1583. The | Third Part of the | Bible, (after some | division) conteining | fiue excellent bookes . . . Imprinted at London | by Christopher Barker, Printer to | the Queenes Maiestie. | 1583. | Cum gratia & priuilegio.

16°.

Geneva version.

A close reprint of the edition of 1580, with the text ending on Ee 7.
Titlepage as before.

¶ 110 × 68 mm. Imperfect: wanting a leaf at the end, perhaps containing coat of arms and colophon as in the edition of 1580. [F. F.]

138.

1584. (The Bible.)

C. Barker: London. 1584. 4°. 𝔅.𝔏.

Geneva version.

A close reprint of the quarto of 1581. The text ends on fo. 554 (really 552); and the tables on M 4.

¶ 210 × 160 mm. Imperfect: wanting the first five leaves. [F. F.]

139.

1584. (The Bible.)

[C. Barker: London. 1584.] 8°.

Geneva version.

A perfite svppvtation gives the date 1584. No doubt C. Barker was the printer.
Closely resembles the octavo edition of 1581. The text ends on fo. 520; and the tables end on Xxx 8.

¶ 155 × 101 mm. Imperfect: wanting the first three leaves and fo. 400. With Metrical Psalms (1584). [F. F.]

140.

1584. The | Holy Bible, con- | teining the Olde Testament | and the Newe : | Of that Translation au- | thorised to be read in | Churches. | Imprinted at Lon- | don by Christopher Barker . . . Anno 1584.

f°. 𝔅.𝔏.

Bishops' version.

The immediate object of this edition, and of the larger folio Bible of the year after, is set forth in the following extract from a letter of Archbishop Whitgift to Bishop Wickham of Lincoln, dated 16 July 1587 (Cardwell, *Documentary Annals*, II, pp. 31–2): 'Whereas I am credibly informed that divers, as well parish Churches, as Chapels of Ease, are not sufficiently furnished with Bibles, but some have either none at all, or such as be torn and defaced, and yet not of the translation authorised by the Synods of Bishops: These are therefore to require you strictly in your visitations, or otherwise, to see that all and every the said Churches and Chapels in your diocese be provided of one Bible or more, at your discretion, of the translation allowed as aforesaid, and one book of Common prayer, as by the laws of this realm is appointed. And for the performance thereof, I have caused her Highness's Printer to imprint two volumes of the said translation of the Bible aforesaid, a bigger and a less: the largest for such Parishes as are of ability, and the lesser for Chapels and very small parishes, both which are now extant and ready . . .'

DESCRIPTION. Twenty-four preliminary leaves: title (in black and red, within border), verso blank, Kalendar—6 ff., *An Almanacke* (1580–1611)—1 p., *The order hovve* . . . —1 p., *Proper Lessons* . . .—1 f., *Morning and Euening praier with the Collectes*—11 ff., *The whole Scripture* . . .—5 pp., *A Prayer*—1 p., 1 f. containing on verso a full-page engraving. Text: O. T., ff. 1 to 368 *b*; Apocrypha, with title (within border), verso blank, end on fo. 459 *b*; N. T., with title (within border), verso blank, *The description* . . . (with map)—1 p., *A Table* . . .—1 p., text—ff. 462 to 560 (really 578, Dddd 4) *a*, with colophon, verso blank.

Signatures: *⁎*⁸ B⁸ C⁸, A–Z⁸ Aa–Zz⁸ Aaa–Zzz⁸ Aaaa⁸ Bbbb⁸ Cccc⁶ Dddd⁴; 602 ff. Double columns, with 61 lines to the full column. Marginal notes in black-letter; references, chapter-contents, headlines, etc. in roman type. The Psalter has a separate title: *The Psalter . . . after the translation of the great Bible, Appointed as it shall be sung or said in Churches . . . 1584* (within border), verso blank.

The border used for the general title, and the titles to the Apocrypha and N. T., contains at the top the royal arms supported by a lion and a dragon; its general design resembles that of the border in the folio of 1575. In the general title the border is touched with red, and contains below the words *Cum priuilegio*. The border to the Psalter title contains at the sides—two female figures, and below—a bull's head, two masks, and two lions. The full-page engraving is that used in the Geneva folio Bible of 1583, but has the greater part of the frame cut away. A cut of the royal arms occurs at the end of Job, and on the last page of text (above the colophon). A large ornament containing the Tudor rose and a crown within a wreath held by two cherubs is found at the end of *A Prayer*, Malachi, and the Apocrypha.

¶ 280 × 188 mm. Title mounted. [F. F.]

141.

1584. (The Bible.)

C. Barker: London. 1584. 4°. 𝕭. 𝕷.

Bishops' version.

Apparently the last quarto edition.

DESCRIPTION. Apparently thirty-six preliminary leaves: [titleleaf], Kalendar—6 ff., *An Almanacke for xxvj. yeeres* (1578–1603)—1 p., *The order howe* . . .—1 p., *Proper Lessons* . . .—1 f., *The Booke of Common prayer* . . .—24 ff., *The whole Scripture* . . . —5 pp., *A Prayer*—1 p. Text: O. T. and Apocrypha, ff. 1 to 438 *a*, verso blank; N. T. with title (dated *Anno 1584*, within border), verso blank, *The Description* . . . (with map)—1 p., *A Table to make plaine* . . .—1 p., text—ff. 1 to 111 *b*; 1 f., containing on recto a large cut of the royal arms and the colophon: *Imprinted at London by Christopher Barker, Printer to the Queenes Maiestie. 1584*, verso blank. [Lea Wilson's copy (No. 56, pp. 82–3) contained at the end of the text *A briefe Table* . . .—12 ff., 'concluding with a small cut of the Queen's arms, and the imprint as before but without date.' See below.]

Signatures: a–d⁸ e⁴, A–Z⁸ Aa–Zz⁸ Aaa–Hhh⁸ Iii⁶, Aaaa–Oooo⁸ Pppp²; 588 ff. A full column contains 70 lines. Headlines and marginal notes in roman type; marginal references etc. in italics. There is a special title before the Psalter (fo. 215): *The Psalter or Psalmes of Dauid, after the translation of the great Bible, Appoynted as it shall be sung or said in Churches. Anno Domini. 1584* (within border), verso blank. No general title is known. The titles to the N. T. and the Psalter are enclosed within a border like that used for the title of the Prayer Book Psalter in the quarto Geneva Bible of 1579.

The B. M. copy (337. b. 5.) has *A briefe Table of the interpretation of the proper names* . . .—12 ff., sigs. [§]⁸ [∵]⁴, inserted between the last leaf of text and the leaf containing the large cut of the royal arms and the colophon. The last page bears a small cut of the royal arms and colophon. (*Cf.* Lea Wilson, p. 83.) It is uncertain whether this table properly belongs to this edition.

¶ 213 × 151 mm. Imperfect: wanting the first two sheets of preliminary matter, containing title, Kalendar, etc., and perhaps 12 ff. (the table) at the end.
With Metrical Psalms (1584).
In seventeenth-century binding, with clasps. [F. F.]

—— Another copy.

212 × 155 mm. Imperfect: wanting nearly all preliminary matter and other leaves.
[F. F.]
142.

1585. The Bible ... With ... Annotations ... And ... Concordance ... Imprinted at London by Chri- | stopher Barker ... 1585 ...
4°. 𝔅. 𝔏.
Geneva version.

A close reprint of the quarto of 1581. The text ends on fo. 554 (really 552); and the tables on M 4. The Prayer Book and tables, however, are printed in smaller type.

¶ 210 × 156 mm.
With Metrical Psalms (1585). [F. F.]

—— Another copy.

207 × 151 mm. Imperfect: wanting all preliminary matter, except the last leaf; and fo. 400 in the text. A N. T. title dated 1636, with MS. title pasted over the letterpress, and a leaf containing Dedication to King James, are inserted at the beginning of the book.

—— Another copy.

218 × 158 mm. Imperfect: wanting all preliminary matter, except the last leaf; also M 2 and 3 in the tables.
143.

1585. The | Holy Byble, contei- | ning ... Authorised and appointed to be | read in Churches. | Imprinted at London | by Christopher Barker ... Anno. 1585. | Cum gratia & priuilegio.
f°. 𝔅. 𝔏.
Bishops' version.

The only edition after 1572 containing the Psalter of the Bishops' version (see No. 100).

DESCRIPTION. [Eighteen] preliminary leaves : [1 f. blank,] title (in black and red, within border), verso blank, Cranmer's Prologue—2 ff., Genealogical Table—11 pp., *An Almanacke* (1580–1611)—1 p., Kalendar—6 ff., *The whole Scripture* ...—3 pp., 1 p. containing a large engraving. (A blank leaf probably should precede the title, since the first leaf of the Prologue is signed A iii.) Text: O. T. and Apocrypha, ff. 1 to 536 *a*, verso blank; N. T., with title (within border), on verso *A preface* ..., *The Description* ... (with map)—1 p., *A Table* ...—1 p., text—ff. 3 to 137 (Z 5) *a*, on verso the colophon, 1 f. blank.
Signatures : A⁴ B⁶ ℂ⁶ ¶¶ ², A–Z⁶ Aa–Zz⁶ Aaa–Zzz⁶ Aaaa–Tttt⁶ Vvvv⁴, A–Z⁶; 692 ff.
The Psalter has a separate title (within border), with a list of the books from Psalms to Malachi; on verso the Prologue of St. Basil. Another separate title (within border) occurs before the Apocrypha.
The general title-border is like that used in the folio Geneva Bible of 1583; and the same border is used for the titles before the Psalter and the N. T. The border to the Apocrypha title resembles the corresponding border in the Geneva Bible of 1583. The full-page engraving is like that in the same Bible. A cut of the royal arms occurs above the colophon, and elsewhere.

¶ 409 × 269 mm. Apparently a blank leaf is wanting before the title, and another at the end of the book. [F. F.]
144.

ENGLISH

1585 ? (The New Testament.)

[*C. Barker : London.* 1585 ?] 16°.

Geneva version; Tomson's revision.

A reprint of the 16° edition of 1578.
The date is not known; but the Almanack begins with 1585. No doubt printed by C. Barker.

DESCRIPTION. Apparently eight preliminary leaves: [titleleaf], Kalendar—6 ff., *An Almanacke for xxiii. yeeres* (1585–1607)—1 p., *The order of the Bookes* ... —1 p. Text, A 1 to Ii 8 b. [There is nothing to show that a table followed; no catchword on the last page.]
Signatures: ★⁸, A–Z⁸ Aa–Ii⁸; 264 ff. This is rather more closely printed than the edition of 1578, and so contains fewer leaves.

¶ 97 × 62 mm. Imperfect: wanting title and following leaf, and a few leaves of text.

[F. F.]
145.

1586. The Bible ... With ... Annotations ... And ... Concordance ... Imprinted at London by Chri- | stopher Barker ... 1586 ...

4°. B. L.

Geneva version.

Apparently only two preliminary leaves: title, on verso *Of the incomparable treasure* ..., Address—1 p., *Howe to take profite* ... —1 p. In other respects this is a reprint of the edition of 1581. The text ends on fo. 554 (really 552); and the tables on M 4.

¶ 210 × 158 mm.
With Metrical Psalms (1584); and Speed's Genealogies and Map (1638).
On yellow paper.

[F. F.]
146.

1586. The | New Testament of | ovr Lord Iesvs | Christ, translated out of | Greeke by Theod. | Beza ... Englished by L. Tomson ... Imprinted at London by Chri- | stopher Barker, Printer, to the | Queenes most excel- | lent Maiestie. | 1586.

8°.

Geneva version; Tomson's revision.

DESCRIPTION. Eight preliminary leaves: title (within border), verso blank, Epistle— 11 pp., *The Printer to the diligent Reader*—1 p., *The order of the bookes* ...—1 p., *The Description* ... (with map)—1 p. Text, ff. 1 to 403 b; the table—49 pp., ending on Hhh 4 a, on verso colophon : *Imprinted at London by Christopher Barker, Printer to the Queenes most Excellent Maiestie. Cum priuilegio Regiæ Maiestatis. 1586.*
Signatures: a⁸, A–Z⁸ Aa–Zz⁸ Aaa–Ggg⁸ Hhh⁴; 436 ff.
The title-border resembles that used in the octavo Testament printed by T. Vautroullier in 1575.

¶ 155 × 96 mm. Wants title, which is supplied in facsimile from the B. M. copy.

[F. F.]
147.

1586. The | Newe Testament | of ovr Lorde Iesvs | Christ, translated | ovt of Greeke by Theo. | Beza, and Englished by L. T. | Whereunto is added a Table. | Luke . 2 . 10. | Beholde . . . people. | Imprinted at London | by Christopher Bar- | ker, Printer to the Queenes most | excellent Maiestie. | 1586. | Cum gratia & priuilegio.

16°.

Geneva version; Tomson's revision.

DESCRIPTION. One preliminary leaf: title, on verso *The order and names of the Bookes* . . . Text, A 2 to Dd 7 *b*; 1 f., containing on recto the colophon: *Imprinted at London by Christopher Barker, Printer to the Queenes most excellent Maiestie. 1586.* [In spite of the mention of a table on the titleleaf, it was probably omitted, as the last page of text bears no catchword.]
  Signatures: A–Z⁸ Aa–Dd⁸; 216 ff. The printed page is somewhat longer than in the two previous 16° editions of 1578 and 1585 (?).
  The first word of the title is within a narrow frame; above the imprint is an ornament which is repeated after the colophon on Dd 8 *a*.

¶ 113 × 70 mm.   [F. F.]
                                   148.

1587. The Bible : | that is, the Holy Scrip-| tvres conteined . . . With . . . annotations . . . Imprinted at London | by Christopher Barker, Printer to the | Qveenes Maiestie. | 1587. | Cum priuilegio.
                                        4°.

Geneva version; with Tomson's revised New Testament.

The earliest complete Bible which contains this revised New Testament. After this date the quarto Geneva Bibles printed in roman type as a rule contain Tomson's revision, while the black-letter quartos give the older version.

DESCRIPTION. [Four] preliminary leaves: [1 f. blank,] title, verso blank, Address—1 p., *Of the incomparable treasure* . . . —1 p., *Howe to take profite* . . . —1 p., list of books—1 p. [A leaf—probably blank—is required before the title, since the leaf after the title is signed ¶ iii.] Text: O. T. (1) Genesis–Job, ff. 1 to 190 *a*, verso blank; (2) Psalms–Malachi, with title, verso blank, text—ff. 2 to 127 *a*, verso blank, 1 f. blank; Apocrypha, ff. 129 to 197 *b*, 1 f. blank; N. T., with title: *The Newe Testament . . . translated ovt of Greeke by Theod. Beza. Wherevnto are adioyned briefe svmmaries . . . and . . . expositions . . . Englished by L. Tomson* . . . , verso blank, *The Printer to the diligent Reader*—1 p., *The description* . . . (with map)—1 p., text—ff. 3 to 116 *b*; tables—11 ff., ending on ¶¶ iij *b*, with colophon; 1 f. blank.
  Signatures: ¶⁴, A–Z⁸ &⁶, Aa–Zz⁸ &&⁸ ✶ ✶⁶, Aaa–Ooo⁸ Ppp⁴, ¶⁸ ¶¶⁴; 520 ff.
  The general titlepage bears a headpiece and a small cut of the crossing of the Red Sea. The pt. 2 and N. T. titlepages have the same headpiece with an ornament below.

¶ 217 × 160 mm. Wants the blank leaf before title, and that at the end.
Covers stamped with the royal arms.   [F. F.]
                                       149.

1587. (The Bible.)
                     [*C. Barker: London. 1587.*] 8°.
Geneva version.

A perfite svppvtation gives the date 1587. No doubt C. Barker was the printer.

This closely resembles an edition dated 1586, a copy of which is in the B. M. (335. a. 7). It corresponds generally to the former octavo editions, but differs in some points. A small cut of Adam and Eve stands at the beginning of Genesis. O. T. ends on fo. 306 (really 308, since the numbers 253, 254 are repeated) *b*; Apocrypha end on fo. 379 (really 381) *b*, followed by a leaf containing *A perfite svppvtation* . . . (1587); N. T. ends on fo. 479 (really 481) *a*, with *The order of the yeres* . . . on verso; the tables—23 pp., ending on Qqq 8 *a*, verso blank.
  Signatures: A–Z⁸ Aa–Zz⁸ Aaa–Qqq⁸; 496 ff.

¶ 155 × 108 mm. Imperfect: wanting the title.
With Metrical Psalms (1586).   [F. F.]
                                       150.

1588. The Bible . . . With . . . Annotations . . . And . . . Concordance . . . Imprinted at London by the | Deputies of Christopher Barker . . . 1588 . . .
                                    4°. 𝕭. 𝕷.
Geneva version.

A reprint of the quarto of 1586. The text ends on fo. 554 (really 552); but the table on L 2 (instead of M 4, as formerly).

¶ 214 × 157 mm. Imperfect: wanting the tables. [F. F.]

—— Another copy.

213 × 152 mm. Imperfect: wanting the first three leaves.

151.

1588. The | Holy Bible, contey- | ning ... Authorised and appointed to be | read in Churches. | Imprinted at London by the Depu- |ties of Christopher Barker ... Anno 1588. | Cum Priuilegio.

f°. 𝔅. 𝔏.

Bishops' version.

DESCRIPTION. Twelve preliminary leaves: title (in black and red, within border), verso blank, Prologue (in roman type)—5 pp., *An Almanacke* (1580–1611) – 1 p., Kalendar— 6 ff., *The whole Scripture* . . .—3 pp., 1 p. containing a large engraving. Text, with continuous register and foliation, ff. 1 to 562 a, with colophon, verso blank.
Signatures: A⁶ B⁶, A–Z⁶ Aa–Zz⁶ Aaa–Zzz⁶ Aaaa–Zzzz⁶ Aaaaa⁶ Bbbbb⁴; 574 ff.
There are no separate titles before the Psalter or the Apocrypha.
The general title-border is like that in the folio edition of 1585. The N.T. title has the border used for the Apocrypha title in that edition, but two blocks have been quaintly misplaced. The engraving before the text is also the same. The cut of the royal arms occurs at the end of Job.

¶ 370 × 251 mm. [F. F.]

—— Another copy.

382 × 252 mm. Imperfect: wanting the Prologue, Almanack, and Kalendar.
Original binding, with brass corners.

152.

1589. The Bible ... With ... Annotations ... And ... Concordance ... Imprinted at London by the | Deputies of Christopher Barker ... 1589 ...

4°. 𝔅. 𝔏.

Geneva version.

A close reprint of the quarto of 1588. The text ends on fo. 554 (really 552); and the tables on L 2.

There are three editions of this year, which while closely agreeing are yet distinct.

A.

As a test passage we may take a sentence from *Certaine questions and answeres . . .*,
✱ iii b, 2nd col. : *Yea verily : that by sight, taste & feeling, | as wel as by hearing, we might be instruc- | ted, assured, and brought to obedience.*

¶ 214 × 152 mm. [F. F.]

153.

—— ANOTHER EDITION.

B.

✱ iii b, 2nd col. : *Yea verily : that by sight, taste and fee- | ling, as well as by hearing we might bee | instructed, assured, and brought to obedi- | ence.*

¶ 216 × 167 mm.

154.

—— ANOTHER EDITION.

C.

✱ iii b, 2nd col. : *Yea verely : that by sight, taste and feeling, | as well as by hearing, we might be instruc- | ted, assured, and brought to obedience.*

¶ 208 × 153 mm.

The tables end on M 4 ; perhaps they belong to another edition. [F. F.]

155.

1589. The | Text of the New | Testament of Iesvs | Christ, translated ovt of | the vulgar Latine by the Papists of the traite- | rous Seminarie at Rhemes. With Arguments of | Bookes, Chapters, and Annotations, pretending to | discouer the corruptions of diuers transla- | tions, and to cleare the con- trouer- | sies of these dayes. | VVhereunto is added the Translation out | of the Original Greeke, commonly vsed in | the Church of England. | With | A Confvtation of all | svch Argvments, Glosses, and | Annotations, As Con- teine Manifest | impietie, of heresie, treason and slander, against the Catho- | like Church of God, and the true teachers thereof, or | the Translations vsed in the Church of England : | Both by auctoritie of the holy Scriptures, | and by the testimonie of the an- | cient fathers. | By William Fvlke, | Doctor in Diuinitie. | Imprinted at London by the Deputies of Chri- | stopher Barker, Printer to the Qveenes | most excellent Maiestie. | Anno 1589.

f°.

Bishops' version and Rheims New Testament in parallel columns.

The title given in full above, and the description below, sufficiently indicate the nature of this book. It was the first systematic and comprehensive attempt to refute the arguments and accusations contained in the Rheims New Testament of 1582. Many partial replies had been already published by T. Bilson, G. Wither, E. Bulkeley, and others, including W. Fulke himself.

Fulke (1538–89) became Master of Pembroke College, Cambridge, in 1578. He states in his Dedication to Queen Elizabeth that he was induced to bring forth his work owing to the delay in the publication of the *longer studied Commentaries* of others. No doubt he refers chiefly to Thomas Cartwright, whose work, undertaken at the suggestion of Walsingham, did not appear till 1618. Fulke was also the author of *A Defense of the sincere and true Trans- lations of the holie Scriptures into the English tong, against the manifolde cauils, friuolous quarels, and impudent slaunders of Gregorie Martin, one of the readers of Popish diuinitie in the trayterous Seminarie of Rhemes* . . . (1583), a copy of which is in this Library.

This 'counterblast' to Martin, by printing the Rheims Testament in full, side by side with the Bishops' version, secured for the former a publicity which it would not otherwise have obtained, and was indirectly responsible for the marked influence which Rheims exerted on the Bible of 1611. It was reprinted in 1601, 1617 and 1633.

Arber (*Transcript*, vol. ii, pp. 39, 40) prints a document (c. 1620), which shows that the printer G. Bishop, who defrayed Fulke's expenses during its production, owned the copyright till his death in 1610.

DESCRIPTION. Twenty-three preliminary leaves : Title (within border), verso blank, Dedi- cation : *To the most high and mightie prince Elizabeth, by the grace of God, Queene of England, Fraunce, and Ireland, Defender of the faith, &c.* (signed : *Your Maiesties most humble subiect William Fulke*)—3 pp., *The signification or meaning of the nvmbers and markes vsed in the New Testament of the Rhemes translation*—1 p., *The Explication of certaine vvordes* . . . —1 p., 1 p. containing three quotations in Latin and English (one from Ps. 118, the other two from St. Augustine) ; *The Preface to the Reader*, ending with the list of books, etc. (with *Confutations*)—19 ff. Text, ff. 1 to 496 a ; *A Table of Controversies*—10 pp., ending on Xxxx 4 a, verso blank.

Signatures : ✱⁴, A–Y⁶ Aa–Yy⁶ Aaa–Yyy⁶ Aaaa–Vvvv⁶ Xxxx⁴ ; 524 ff.

The text of the Rheims New Testament and the Bishops' version are printed in parallel columns, the former in roman type on the left, the latter in italics on the right side of each page; both are divided into verses. All the Arguments, marginal notes, and other annotations of the Rhemish New Testament of 1582 are reprinted, interspersed with the Confutations; the origin of each paragraph being indicated in the margin,—*Rhem. 1* being followed by *Fulke 1*, and so on.

The title-border is like that used in the quarto edition of the Geneva New Testament (Tomson's revision) printed in 1583.

¶ 279 × 189 mm. [F. F.]
156.

1590. The Bible: | that is ... With ... annotations ... Imprinted at London by | the Deputies of Christopher Barker ... 1590 ...

4°.

Geneva version; with Tomson's revised New Testament.

A reprint of the quarto of 1587. The N. T. ends on fo. 116; and the tables on ¶¶ 3. The Apocrypha, however, end on fo. 196 (★ ★ 4) *b*; the blank leaf after Malachi is omitted, and the first leaf of the Apocrypha is Qq 8.

¶ 207 × 150 mm. Wants the blank leaf before title. [F. F.]

—— Another copy.

196 × 144 mm. Imperfect: wanting preliminary matter, and first leaf of text. [F. F.]
157.

1590. The Bible: | that is, the Holy Scrip- | tvres ... Imprinted at London | by the Deputies of Christopher Barker, | Printer to the Queenes most excel- | lent Maiestie. | Anno 1590. | Cum priuilegio.

8°.

Geneva version.

Closely resembles the octavo edition of 1587. Text ends on fo. 479 (really 481), and tables on Qqq 8.

¶ 160 × 108 mm.
With Metrical Psalms (1590). [F. F.]
158.

1591. The Bible : | that is, | the Holy | Scriptvres con- | teined in the Old and New | Testament. | Translated ac- | cording to the Hebrue and Greeke, | and conferred with the best transla- | tions in diuers languages. | Printed by Iohn | Legate, Printer to the Vni- | uersitie of Cambridge. | Anno Do. 1591. | May 29.

8°.

Geneva version.
Apparently the earliest edition of the English Bible printed at Cambridge.

DESCRIPTION. Title (within border), verso blank, Address—1 p., list of books—1 p. Text: O. T., A 3 to Pp 5 *b*; Apocrypha, Pp 6 to Aaa 4 *b*; *A perfite svppvtation* ... (1591)—1 f.; N. T., Aaa 6 to Nnn 6 *b*; *The order of the yeeres* ...—1 p., the tables—23 pp., ending on Ppp 2 *b*.

Signatures: A–Z⁸ Aa–ZZ⁸ Aaa–Ooo⁸ Ppp²; 482 ff. Leaves not numbered. Double columns. Subject-headings and titles of books in headlines printed in capitals.

The title-border contains 'at the top the royal arms; on each side, in small ovals, the crest and paternal coat of the Earl of Leicester; and at foot, in two small escutcheons, the other quarterings borne by him' (so Lea Wilson, p. 87); date on tablet at base.

¶ 164 × 102 mm. Imperfect: wanting the first three leaves; also A 6 and 7, and all the Apocrypha. Title supplied in facsimile.
With Metrical Psalms (1591?).
In seventeenth-century binding. [F. F.]

Cotton mentions only one copy of this edition, viz. Lea Wilson's, which is now in the B. M. Another copy is mentioned on p. 32 of *Katalog over Bibel-Udstillingen afholdt den 20. og 21 April 1901* (Den norske Bogtrykkerforening, Kristiania, 1901).

159.

1591. The | Holy Bible, contey- | ning . . . Authorised and appointed to be | read in Churches. | Imprinted at London by the Depu- | ties of Christopher Barker . . . Anno 1591. | Cum priuilegio.

f°. 𝔅. 𝔏.

Bishops' version.

Closely resembles the folio edition of 1588; with the same preliminary matter, though arranged in a different order:—title, verso blank, Prologue—5 pp., *The whole Scripture* . . . —3 pp., Almanack—1 p., Kalendar—12 pp., 1 p. containing large engraving. Text as before, ff. 1 to 562 (Bbbbb 4) *a*, with colophon, verso blank.

Two title-borders as in the edition of 1588, but the blocks in the N. T. title-border are here correctly arranged. The large engraving is touched with red. Another ornament has displaced the royal arms after Job.

¶ 378 × 251 mm. Imperfect: wanting six preliminary leaves containing Almanack and Jan.–Nov. in the Kalendar. [F. F.]

160.

1591. B. f°. See 1592.

1592. The | Bible, that | is, the Holy | Scriptures contained . . . With . . . Annotations . . . Imprinted at | London by the Deputies of | Christopher Barker, Printer to the | Queenes most excellent Maiestie. | Anno Dom. | 1592.

1592,91. f°. 𝔅. 𝔏.

Geneva version; with Tomson's revised New Testament.

The N. T. title is dated 1591, but the colophon 1592.

DESCRIPTION. Four preliminary leaves: title (within border), verso blank, *To the Christian Reader*—1 f., *Of the incomparable treasvre* . . .—1 p., *Howe to take profite* . . .—1 p., list of books—1 p., 1 p. containing large engraving. Text: O. T., ff. 1 to 396 (really 390) *a*, verso blank; Apocrypha end on fo. 486 (really 480) *b*; N. T., with title: *The Newe Testament . . . translated ovt of Greeke by Theod. Beza. Wherevnto are adioined briefe svmmaries . . . And . . . expositions . . . Englished by L. Tomson* . . . (within border), verso blank, *The Printer to the diligent Reader*—1 p., *The Description* . . . (with map)—1 p., text ends on fo. 626 (really 620, Mmmmm 2) *b*; tables—8 ff., ending on Nnnnn 4 *b*, with colophon.

Signatures: A⁴, A–Z⁶ Aa–Zz⁶ Aaa–Zzz⁶ Aaaa–Zzzz⁶ Aaaaa–Mmmmm⁶ Nnnnn⁴; 632 ff. The foliation is incorrect; the numbers 121–126 are omitted. Double columns, with 60 lines to the full column.

Four lines of text are omitted at the beginning of K 6 (numbered 61) *a*. In some copies this mistake is corrected.

The border to the general and N. T. titles is like that in Barker's folio edition of the Bishops' Bible, 1584. In the lower part of the border to the general title are printed the words *Cum priuilgeio*; in the corresponding space in the N. T. title-border appears the date *Anno Dom. 1591*. The full-page engraving is the same as in the folio Bishops' Bible of 1584. Before the Psalter is placed a separate title: *This Second Part of the Bible . . . Psalmes . . . Malachi*, within the border used in the quarto edition of Tomson's N. T. printed in 1583.

¶ 275 × 184 mm.
A duplicate of K 6 is inserted, which has the mistake corrected.
With Metrical Psalms (1592). [F. F.]

—— Another copy.

315 × 200 mm. Imperfect: wanting title, Address, fourth preliminary leaf, fo. 1 of text, and the last leaf in the book.
The leaf K 6 has the mistake. [F. F.]

ENGLISH 107

—— Another copy.

261 × 186 mm. Imperfect: wanting preliminary matter, the last two leaves, and a few other leaves.
K 6 is correct. Part of this copy seems to belong to the very similar edition of 1595.

161.

1592. The Bible ... With ... Annotations ... And ... Concordance ... Imprinted at London, by the | Deputies of Christopher Barker ... 1592 ...

4°. 𝕭. 𝕷.

Geneva version.

A close reprint of the quarto of 1588. The text ends on fo. 554 (really 552); and the tables on L 2.

¶ 207 × 157 mm.
With Prayer Book (? date); and Metrical Psalms (1592).   [F. F.]

—— Another copy.

199 × 151 mm. This differs in some sheets from the above; probably a mixed copy.
With Metrical Psalms (1592).   [F. F.]

162.

1592. The | New Testa- | ment of ovr | Lord Iesvs | Christ. | Faithfully translated out | of Greeke. | Imprinted at London by the | Deputies of Christopher Bar- | ker, printer to the Queenes | most excellent Ma- | iestie. | Anno 1592. Cum priuilegio.

32°.

Geneva version; Tomson's revision.

The smallest edition of this version.
Identical, except for the title, with an undated edition printed by John Legate of Cambridge, which Lea Wilson (p. 199) calls 48° and ascribes to 1590, while Cotton (p. 49) calls it 24° and ascribes it to 1589. The B. M. copy (C. 48. a. 4) of Legate's edition is described as 32°, and placed under the date 1590.

DESCRIPTION.   One preliminary leaf: title, verso blank. Text, A 2 to Tt 8 b.
  Signatures: A–Z⁸ Aa–Tt⁸; 336 ff. Leaves not numbered. No contents before chapters, or marginal references, etc. No verse-divisions, but the verse-numbers are given at the side.
  A full page contains 32 lines.

¶ 72 × 43 mm.
Seventeenth-century binding; with silver clasps.   [F. F.]

163.

1593. The Bible : | that is, the Holy Scrip- | tvres ... Imprinted at London | by the Deputies of Christopher Barker, | Printer to the Queenes most | excellent Maiestie : | Anno 1593. | Cum priuilegio.

8°.

Geneva version.

This resembles generally the former octavo editions, but has a rather smaller page of type. Two preliminary leaves as before. Text: O. T., ff. 1 to 317 b; Apocrypha (with Supputation at end) ff. 318 to 393 b; N. T. (with ornamental headpiece on first page) ends on fo. 495 (really 496) b; *The order of the yeeres* ...—1 p., tables—25 pp., ending on Sss 7 b, 1 f. blank.
  Signatures: A–Z⁸ Aa–Zz⁸ Aaa–Sss⁸; 512 ff.

¶ 148 × 100 mm. Imperfect: wanting ff. 318 to 393, containing the Apocrypha with Supputation, as in the similar edition of 1594. The last blank leaf is also missing. [F. F.]

164.

1593. The | Newe Testa- | ment of ovr | Lord Iesvs | Christ. | Faithfully translated out | of Greeke. | Imprinted at London | by the Deputies of Christopher Barker, | Printer to the Queenes most | excellent Maiestie. | Anno 1593.

32°.

Geneva version; Tomson's revision.

DESCRIPTION. One preliminary leaf: title, verso blank. Text, A 2 to Xx 8 b.
Signatures: A–Z⁸ Aa–Xx⁸; 352 ff. Leaves not numbered. A full page contains 31 lines. This edition has short chapter-contents and marginal references, in italics.
Catchword on Mm 1 a: *Christ.*

¶ 71 × 45 mm. Imperfect: wanting title, Cc 8, Hh 2 and 8, and Xx 8.
Seventeenth-century binding; with silver clasp. [F. F.]

—— Another copy.

76 × 47 mm. Very imperfect: wanting all sheets X, Y and Aa; Bb 1 and 8, Cc 1 and 8; and all after Ee 8;—80 ff. It contains, however, the title.
Contemporary binding; with brass clasps. [F. F.]
165.

—— ANOTHER EDITION.

Date not known.
Agrees very closely with the preceding edition. Catchword on Mm 1 a: *thren.*

¶ 75 × 51 mm. Imperfect: wanting title and 15 ff. of text. [F. F.]

—— Another copy.

Agrees generally with the latter of the two above editions; but in parts (e.g. in sheet Mm) is identical with the former.

75 × 52 mm. Imperfect: wanting title and 22 ff. of text.
Contemporary stamped leather binding, lined with silk; imperfect. [F. F.]
166.

1593. B. 4°. See 1594.

1594. The Bible: | that is ... With ... Annotations ... Imprinted at London | by the Deputies of Christopher Barker ... 1594 ...

1594,93. 4°.

Geneva version: with Tomson's revised New Testament.

The N. T. title is dated 1593, but the colophon 1594.
A close reprint of the quarto of 1590. The N. T. ends on fo. 116; and the tables on ¶¶ 3. The last leaf of Apocrypha is numbered 197, instead of 196.

¶ 212 × 147 mm. Wants the blank leaf before the title and that at the end.
Contemporary binding; with brass plates and corners. [F. F.]
167.

1594. The Bible ... With ... Annotations ... And ... Concordance ... Imprinted at London by the | Deputies of Christopher Barker ... 1594 ...

4°. 𝕭. 𝕷.

Geneva version.

A close reprint of the quarto of 1588. The text ends on fo. 554 (really 552), and the ables on L 2.

Of this edition at least three varieties occur.

A. N. T. title dated by error 1495.
Gen. i. 3. *Then God sayde ...*

¶ 214 × 150 mm. [F. F.]
168.

—— ANOTHER EDITION.

B. N. T. title dated 1495.

Quite distinct from the preceding, though both have the same error on the N. T. title. Gen. i. 3, *Then God sayd* . . .

¶ 212 × 155 mm.
Imperfect: wanting preliminary leaves, ff. 76 and 77 in the text, and all the tables except the titleleaf.
It is assumed that the general title, which is wanting, was dated 1594, and that the date 1495 on the N. T. titlepage is a misprint for 1594.
With Metrical Psalms (1597). [F. F.]
169.

—— ANOTHER EDITION.

C. N. T. title dated 1594.

Gen. i. 3. *Then God saide* . . .

¶ 221 × 153 mm. [F. F.]

—— Another copy.

206 × 152 mm. Imperfect: wanting the last leaf.

—— Another copy.

Containing the Apocrypha only. [F. F.]
170.

1594. (The Bible.)
[*Deputies of C. Barker : London.* 1594.] 8°.
Geneva version.

A perfit svppvtation . . . gives the date 1594. No doubt printed by the Deputies of C. Barker.
Resembles the octavo edition of 1593. O. T. ends on fo. 317 *b*; Apocrypha (with title *Apocrypha* within small woodcut frame at head of first page) end on fo. 393 *a*, followed on the same page by *A perfit svppvtation* . . . (1594), which ends on verso; N. T. ends on fo. 496 *b*; *The order of the yeeres* . . .—1 p., tables—25 pp., ending on Sss 7 *b*; 1 f. blank. Signatures as before.

¶ 153 × 98 mm. Imperfect: wanting title, A 7 and 8, and the last blank leaf.
With Metrical Psalms (1593). [F. F.]

—— Another copy.

Very imperfect: beginning with D 1, and wanting all the N. T., and many leaves elsewhere. Part of the missing matter is supplied from an edition of the 1611 version. [F. F.]
171.

1594. The Revelation | of Saint Iohn the Apostle | and Evangelist, vvith a | briefe and learned Commentarie, | Written by Franc. Iunius, &c.
Richard Field, for Robert Dexter : London. 1594. 4°.

According to a MS. note by N. Pocock, this work was published in Latin in 1589; but Le Long (*Bibliotheca Sacra*, 1723 ed., p. 810) gives the date 1591. It was translated into English in 1592. The rendering of the text differs widely from the current English versions.

Franciscus Junius (1545–1602), in French Francois du Jon, Huguenot divine, is best known as the joint author with Emmanuel Tremellius of a Latin version of the Old Testament first published in 1579.

This work was, no doubt, intended to accompany quarto editions of the Geneva Bible (see two copies below); but it was produced as an independent publication.

It supplanted the normal version of Revelation in some editions of the Geneva New Testament (Tomson's revision). See below, No. 207 (1602).

DESCRIPTION. Apparently no titleleaf. The text begins (after the title given above) on p. 1, and ends with the words *To God onely be honour and glorie* on p. 22; one leaf, bearing on recto a printer's device with the initials R D and the legend *Devs imperat astris*, and the colophon: *Imprinted at London by Richard Field for Robert Dexter, dwelling in Paules Church-yard at the signe of the Brasen serpent.* 1594. Signatures: A–C⁴; 12 ff.

¶ 214 × 149 mm. [F. F.]

—— Another copy.

Bound up with a copy of the quarto Geneva Bible (Tomson's revision) dated 1595. (See below, No. 174.)

—— Another copy.

Bound up with a quarto Geneva Bible of 1598,97. (See below, No. 185.)

172.

1595. The | Bible: that | is, the Holy | Scriptures, contained . . . Imprinted at London by the | Deputies of Christopher Barker, Prin- | ter to the Qveenes most excel- | lent Maiestie. | Anno Dom. | 1595.

f°. 𝕭. 𝕷.

Geneva version; with Tomson's revised New Testament.

A close reprint of the folio edition of 1592,91.
Four preliminary leaves, as before. Text ends on fo. 626 (really 620); and the tables on Nnnnn 4.
Signatures, as before; 632 ff.
Title-borders, as before. The initial B before the Address represents Hercules and the Lernæan Hydra.

¶ 283 × 181 mm. [F. F.]

—— Another copy.

¶ 359 × 228 mm. Large paper copy.

—— Another copy.

283 × 191 mm.
With Metrical Psalms (1595).

173.

1595. The Bible: | that is . . . With . . . Annotations . . . Imprinted at London by | the Deputies of Christopher Barker . . . Anno 1595 . . .

4°.

Geneva version; with Tomson's revised New Testament.

A reprint of the quarto of 1590. The N. T. ends on fo. 116, and the tables on ¶¶ 3. The last leaf of Apocrypha is numbered 197.
The two titlepages have a new headpiece, and a printer's device—an open book, within an oval frame, inscribed *Dat esse manvs: svperesse Minerva*, and supported by figures of Minerva and Mercury.

¶ 205 × 152 mm.
This copy has the leaf before the title, signed A j.
With Metrical Psalms (1594).
The N. T. titlepage is inscribed *Marye ffayrefax*, and the first title bears the initials *M. ff.* —possibly Mary Fairfax, the daughter of Sir T. Fairfax, who was born in 1638, and married in 1657 the second Duke of Buckingham. [F. F.]

—— Another copy.

204 × 149 mm.
With a copy of Junius' Revelation (see above, No. 172) inserted after the text.

174.

1595. The | Holy Bible, contey- | ning . . . Authorised and appoynted to be | read in Churches. | Imprinted at London by the Depu- | ties of Christopher Barker . . . Anno 1595. | Cum priuilegio.

f°. 𝔅.𝔏.

Bishops' version.

A close reprint of the folio edition of 1591, with the preliminary matter arranged in the same order. The text ends on fo. 562 (Bbbbb 4) *a*, verso blank; and is followed by 2 ff. containing *A Table to finde the Epistles and Gospels* . . . —3 pp., 1 p. blank.
Two title-borders, and large engraving before text, as before.

¶ 398 × 257 mm.
Original binding, with brass corners and clasps. [F. F.]

175.

1595. The | New Testament of our Sauiour | Iesus Christ, | Faithfully translated out of the Greeke, with | the Notes and Expositions of the darke | places therein. | Matthew 13. | The pearle which Christ commaunded to be bought, | Is here to be found, not else to be sought. | Imprinted by the Deputy of Christopher Barker | Printer to the Queenes most excellent Maiestie.

1595. 8°. 𝔅.𝔏.

Bishops' version.

DESCRIPTION. Sixteen preliminary leaves: title (in black and red, with cut), verso blank, Kalendar—6 ff., *An Almanacke for xxvi. yeeres* (1578–1603)—1 p., verso blank, *A Preface into the new Testament*—2 ff., *The pith or contents of the new Testament*—7 pp., *By the books of the new Testament* . . . —2 pp., *A true and perfect reckoning* . . . and *An exhortation* . . . —2 pp., *The order of the bookes* . . . —1 p. Text, A 1 to Oo 4 *b*; *The Epistles of the old Testament, according as they be now read*—2 ff., *A Table to find the Epistles and Gospels read in the Church of England* . . . —2 ff., ending with a cut and the colophon: *Imprinted at London by the deputie of Christopher Barker, Printer to the Queenes most excellent Maiestie. 1595.*

Signatures: [unsigned]⁸ ★⁸, A–Z⁸ Aa–Oo⁸; 392 ff. Leaves not numbered. A full page contains 45 lines. The book generally agrees with the earlier edition of 1582. The chapter-numbers at the head of each leaf are given in *arabic* numerals.

The cut on the titlepage is a portrait of Edward VI within an oval frame inscribed *Edvardvs Sextvs*. . . . The cut on the last page represents three storks before a vine laden with fruit.

I 3 *a*, Life of St. Luke: *Lvke being a Physition of Antiochia (as his owne writings do testifie)* . . .

Y 5 *a*, Rom. i, contents: *Paul sheweth by whom, and to what purpose hee is called* . . .

¶ 142 × 91 mm. Wants only the last leaf of Kalendar, which is supplied in facsimile copied from the corresponding leaf in the edition of 1600. The sheets from P to X are misplaced in the following order—P, T, R, S, V, Q, X. [F. F.]

176.

1596. (The Bible.)

[*Deputies of C. Barker: London.* 1596.] 8°.

Geneva version.

A perfit svppvtation gives the date 1596. No doubt printed by the Deputies of C. Barker. In somewhat larger type than the preceding octavo editions. [Title, etc.] Text: O. T., ff. 1 to 327 *a*; Apocrypha begin on verso (with ornamental headpiece) and end on fo. 405 *a*;

on the same page begins *A perfit svppvtation* . . . (1596), which ends on verso; N. T. (with headpiece on first page) ends on fo. 513 a, on verso *The order of the yeeres* . . .; tables—12 ff., ending on Vvv 7 b; 1 f. blank.

Signatures: A–Z⁸ Aa–Zz⁸ Aaa–Vvv⁸; 528 ff.

¶ 164 × 105 mm. Imperfect; wanting the first four leaves, containing apparently the usual preliminary matter, and two leaves of text. [F. F.]

—— Another copy.

A fragment (pp. 420 to end) bound with part of an octavo Bible of 1632 (No. 362).

177.

1596. The Newe | Testament . . . translated out of Greeke, by | Theod. Beza. . . . Englished by L. Tomson. | Imprinted at London by the | Deputies of Christopher Barker, | Printer to the Queenes most | excellent Maiestie, | 1596.

4°. 𝔅. 𝔏.

Geneva version; Tomson's revision.

A reprint of the quarto edition of 1583.

DESCRIPTION. Four preliminary leaves; title, verso blank, Epistle—2 ff., *The Printer to the diligent Reader*—1 p., *The description* . . . (with map)—1 p. Text, ff. 1 to 322 b; table—23 pp., ending on Tt 6 a, with colophon, verso blank.
Signatures: ¶⁴, A–Z⁸ Aa–Ss⁸ Tt⁶; 338 ff.
The first two words of the title are enclosed within a frame. Above the imprint is the printer's device *Dat esse manvs: svperesse Minerva*.

¶ 235 × 170 mm. [F. F.]

178.

1596? (The New Testament.)

[Qu. *Deputies of C. Barker : London.* 1596?] 8°.

Geneva version; Tomson's revision.

Printed probably by the Deputies of C. Barker, about 1596.

DESCRIPTION. Eight preliminary leaves: [titleleaf], Epistle—11 pp., *The Printer to diligent Reader*—1 p., *The Description* . . . (with map)—1 p., *The order of the Bookes* . . .—1 p. Text, ff. 1 to 266 a, verso blank; table—22 ff., ending on Nn 8 b.
Signatures: a⁸, A–Z⁸ Aa–Nn⁸; 296 ff. Printed in smaller type than previous editions.

¶ 156 × 100 mm. Imperfect: wanting the title; also D 4 and 5, and M 8. A fictitious title is inserted.
With Metrical Psalms (1596).
Seventeenth-century binding. [F. F.]

179.

—— ANOTHER EDITION.

Very closely resembles the preceding in every particular. Date not known.

Gg 5 is incorrectly numbered 236.
1 Pet. iii, contents: *General extortations*.

¶ 154 × 99 mm. Imperfect: wanting general title.

—— Another copy.

155 × 100 mm. Imperfect: wanting general title and two following leaves, and the last sheet Nn. Some leaves have been taken from another copy. [F. F.]

180.

1596. B. 4°. See 1597.

1597. The Bible ... With .. Annotations ... And ... Concordance ... Imprinted at London, by the | Deputies of Christopher Barker ... 1597 ...
1597,96. 4°. 𝕭. 𝕷.

Geneva version.

The N. T. title is dated 1596.
A close reprint of the quarto of 1588. The text ends on fo. 554 (really 552); and the tables on L 2.

¶ 226 × 156 mm.
Contemporary binding; with brass plates and corners. [F. F.]
181.

1597. The Bible. | That is, the Holy | Scriptvres con- | teined ... With ... anno- | tations ... Imprinted at London by the De- | puties of Christopher Barker, | Printer to the Queenes most excel- | lent Maiestie. | Anno 1597. | Cum priuilegio.
f°.

Geneva version; with Tomson's revised New Testament.

DESCRIPTION. Six preliminary leaves, as in the folio Geneva Bible of 1582. Text: O. T., ff. 1 to 360 *a*, verso blank; Apocrypha end on fo. 77 *a*, verso blank; N. T., with title, verso blank, *The Printer to the diligent Reader*—1 p., *The description* ... (with map)— 1 p., text—ff. 2 to 129 *b*; tables—17 pp., ending on Zzzzz 6 *a*, with colophon, verso blank.
Signatures: ¶⁶, A–Z⁶ Aa–Zz⁶ Aaa–Ooo⁶, Aaaa Nnnn⁶, Aaaaa–Zzzzz⁶; 582 ff.
The cut (representing the crossing of the Red Sea), used on the two titlepages in the folio Bible of 1582 and earlier editions, is now replaced by the device *Dat esse manvs: svperesse Minerva*. The first two words of the general title, and the first word of the N. T. title, are enclosed within a frame.

¶ 309 × 208 mm.
Large paper copy. The title is mounted. [F. F.]

—— Another copy.

264 × 180 mm. Wants fo. 128 in the N. T.
With Metrical Psalms (1597).
Contemporary binding; with goffered edges. [F. F.]
182.

1597. (The Bible.)
[*Deputies of C. Barker : London.* 1597.] 8°.

Geneva version.

A perfit supputation gives the date 1597. No doubt printed by the Deputies of C. Barker.
Resembles the octavo edition of 1596, with the text ending on fo. 513 *a*, and the tables on Vvv 7 *b*. Signatures, etc. as before.

¶ 159 × 103 mm. Imperfect: wanting all before G 2 and many other leaves. At the beginning several leaves, including part of Speed's Genealogies, are supplied from an edition of the 1611 version.
With Metrical Psalms (? date). [F. F.]
183.

1597. B. 4°. See 1598.

1598. The Bible ... With ... Annotations ... And ... Concordance ... Imprinted at London by the | Deputies of Christopher Barker ... 1598 ...
1598,97. 4°. 𝕭. 𝕷.

Geneva version.

The N. T. title is dated 1597.
A close reprint of the edition of 1588. The text ends on fo. 554 (really 552); and the tables on L 2.
A misprint occurs in 1 John v. 20: . . . *his Sonne Jesus Church.*

¶ 227 × 161 mm.
With Prayer Book (1596); and Metrical Psalms (1598).
Contemporary binding; with brass plates and corners. [F. F.]
184.

1598. The Bible : | that is . . . With . . . Annotations . . . Imprinted at London by | the Deputies of Christopher Barker . . . Anno 1598 . . .
1598,97. 4°.
Geneva version; with Tomson's revised New Testament.

The N. T. title is dated 1597, but the colophon 1598.
A close reprint of the quarto of 1595. The N. T. ends on fo. 116, and the tables on ¶¶ 3. The last leaf of Apocrypha is numbered 197. The headpiece on the N. T. titlepage differs.

¶ 218 × 147 mm. Wants the leaf before title.
With Junius' Revelation (1594) inserted after the text.
Contemporary binding. [F. F.]
185.

1598. (The New Testament.)
Deputy of C. Barker : London. 1598. 8°. 𝕭. 𝕷.
Bishops' version.

The arrangement of the matter in this volume appears to be exactly the same as in the previous edition of 1595. The colophon below the ornamental cut on the last page runs: *Imprinted at London by the deputie of Christopher Barker, printer to the Queenes most excellent Maiestie. 1598.*
I 3 a, Life of St. Luke: *Lvke being a phisition of Antiochia (as his own writings do testifie)* . . .
Y 5 a, Rom. i, contents: *Paul sheweth by whom, and to what purpose he is called* . . .

¶ 129 × 81 mm. Imperfect: wanting apparently the first sheet, and 12 other leaves.
[F. F.]
186.

1599. The Bible . . . With . . . Annotations . . . And . . . Concordance . . . Imprinted at London by the | Deputies of Christopher Barker . . . 1599 . . .
4°. 𝕭. 𝕷.
Geneva version.

A close reprint of the quarto of 1588. The text ends on fo. 554 (really 552); and the tables on L 2.
1 John v. 20 is correct.

¶ 211 × 149 mm. [F. F.]
187.

1599. The | Bible, | that is . . . With . . . Annotations . . . Imprinted at London | by the Deputies of Christopher Barker . . . 1599 . . .
4°.
Geneva version; with Tomson's revised New Testament, but with Junius' Revelation.

This is in most respects a reprint of the previous quarto Geneva Bibles in roman type. But the titlepages are new, and Junius' Revelation here displaces Tomson's version of that book.

The Metrical Psalms (n.d.), which are almost invariably found in copies of the Bible dated 1599, may perhaps be considered an essential part of the book, though they have a separate title and distinct register; no imprint is given.

DESCRIPTION. Four preliminary leaves: first title (within border), verso blank; second title (with cut), verso blank, Address—1 p., *Of the incomparable treasure* . . .—1 p., *How to take profite* . . .—1 p., list of books—1 p. Text: O. T. (1) Genesis–Job, ff. 1 to 190 a, verso blank; (2) Psalms–Malachi, with title, verso blank, text, ff. 2 to 127 a, verso blank, 1 f. blank; [Apocrypha (apparently omitted);] (4) N. T., with title (within border), verso blank, *The Printer to the diligent Reader*—1 p., *The description* . . . (with map)—1 p., text—ff. 3 to 121 a, verso blank; tables—11 ff., ending on Rrr 4 b, with colophon.

Signatures: ¶⁴, A–Z⁸ &⁶, Aa–Qq⁸, Aaa–Qqq⁸ Rrr⁴; 454 ff.

The section containing the Apocrypha, though included in the list of books, was apparently omitted from all except a few copies. These Bibles were printed probably for English use in the Low Countries.

A note *The Order of Time* precedes Revelation.

The woodcut border to the first general title is a frame having twenty-four small compartments, showing on the left—the tents of the twelve tribes; on the right—figures of the twelve Apostles; the inner part exhibits the four Evangelists, with the symbols of the Dove and the Agnus Dei, and a lamp, and two open books inscribed *Verbum Dej Manet in Æternum*; the letterpress of the title is enclosed within a heart-shaped frame in the centre; at the base of the cut is a line of music. The same border is used for the N. T. title. The second general titlepage bears a cut of the crossing of the Red Sea. And the title to pt. 2 has a headpiece.

There are many editions bearing this date, which while agreeing closely are yet distinct. No doubt a certain number of copies were originally issued in a mixed state. The nominal date, 1599, is probably untrue in almost every case. See note *ad fin.*

The phenomena of the various editions described under the year 1599, and the very similar edition of 1633, constitute one of the most curious problems in the bibliography of the English Bible. See Lea Wilson, pp. 90–2. N. Pocock investigated the matter with great care, and published the results of his research in the *Bibliographer*, vol. iii. The following notes are based chiefly on his article.

A. Lea Wilson's No. 6 of this series.

Esther i. 1: . . . *seuen and twen- | ty prouinces.*).
This, according to Pocock, is probably the earliest of these editions, as it abounds more than any others in gross errors: e.g. Song of Solomon v. 3, *defile* for *put*; Isaiah xxx. 32, *beards* for *harps*, xxxvi. 12, *thing* for *dung*; Matt. xxiv. 50, line repeated.
Perhaps printed at Amsterdam about 1599.

¶ 209 × 162 mm.
With Metrical Psalms (n. d.). [F. F.]

—— Another copy.

¶ 213 × 156 mm.
With Metrical Psalms (n. d.).

—— Another copy.

This contains some variant leaves.
With Metrical Psalms (n. d.). [F. F.]

188.

—— ANOTHER EDITION.

B. Lea Wilson's No. 5 of this series.

Esther i. 1: . . . *seven and twen- | ty provinces.*).
Apparently printed from A at a somewhat later date. Many of the errors are corrected, e.g. S. of S. v. 3, Isa. xxxvi. 12, and Matt. xxiv. 50. Headline Ee 3 b, *Proverbers*.

¶ 222 × 162 mm.
The Apocrypha section in this copy has been supplied from an edition of the 1611 version.
With Metrical Psalms (n. d.). [F. F.]

—— Another copy.

Lea Wilson's No. 4; Esther i. 1: . . . *seven and twenty pro- | vinces*.). But, according to Fry, it is identical with his No. 5, with the exception of a few leaves in sheets I and Z—apparently reprinted (Esther begins on Z 1).

¶ 210 × 165 mm. Imperfect: wanting first title and two preliminary leaves.
With Metrical Psalms (n. d.). [F. F.]

189.

—— ANOTHER EDITION.

C. Lea Wilson's No. 1 of this series.

Esther i. 1: . . . *seven and | twenty provinces*.).
Probably printed after B, and generally more correct, e.g. in Isa. xxx. 32. Nearly all the marginal notes are in roman type.
A, B, and C all omit a line in Eccles. iv. 9: *Two are better* [than one: for they have better] *wages for their labour*.

¶ 230 × 170 mm.
With Metrical Psalms (n. d.). [F. F.]

190.

These three editions—marked A, B, and C—closely resemble one another in arrangement of type; and also in their peculiar spelling (e.g. confusion of d, t, and th), and needless insertion of vowels (*hoaste* for *host*, etc.). They differ much in these respects from the ordinary English editions. These three and the two following editions were probably printed at Amsterdam for the use of English Puritans in the Low Countries.

—— ANOTHER EDITION.

D. Unlike any of Lea Wilson's editions.

As in Lea Wilson's No. 3, the figure 7 is omitted on fo. 7 in the N. T.; that omission, however, may have been accidental, as in the second copy of E, described below. Lea Wilson's No. 3 appears to be a mixed copy; e.g. the title evidently belongs to the so-called 'Dort' edition (see below), and the verse in Esther i is arranged as in his No. 2.
The copy below seems to represent a distinct edition.
Esther i. 1: . . . *and | seuen and twenty prouinces*.).
N. Pocock considered it to have been printed from A by a compositor who knew enough English to correct a large number of the errors.
This is printed from identically the same setting of type as an edition issued with the date 1633; the latter, however, has a new imprint on the three titlepages and at the end of the book: *Imprinted at Amsterdam, for Thomas Crafoorth. By Iohn Fredericksz Stam* . . . Probably 1633 is the correct date, and copies were issued simultaneously, some with Barker's imprint and the date 1599, others with Stam's imprint dated 1633. Some copies, indeed, bear both imprints and dates. (See No. 364, 1633.)

¶ 212 × 155 mm.
With Metrical Psalms (n. d.). [F. F.]

—— Another copy.

215 × 166 mm. Imperfect: wanting first title and two preliminary leaves.
With Metrical Psalms (n. d.).

191.

—— ANOTHER EDITION.

E. Lea Wilson's No. 2 of this series.

Esther i. 1: . . . *seuen | and twenty prouinces*.).
Probably printed after D, which it closely follows. The mistake in Ps. lxxiii. 27, *that they* for *they that*, which occurs in A, B, C, and D, is corrected in this edition.

¶ 218 × 164 mm.
With Metrical Psalms (n. d.). [F. F.]

—— Another copy.

The number on fo. 7 in the N. T. is accidentally omitted.
With Metrical Psalms (n. d.). [F. F.]
192.

—— ANOTHER EDITION.

F. Lea Wilson's No. 78 (p. 90).

Easily distinguishable from the other editions; since every page is surrounded, and the columns are separated, by black lines. As in C, the marginal notes are almost entirely in roman type.
Esther i. 1: . . . *seven | and twenty prouinces.*). Ps. lxxiii. 27 is correct.

¶ 227 × 174 mm. [F. F.]
193.

—— ANOTHER EDITION.

G. Sometimes known as the 'Goose Bible,' from the bird in the device with the motto *God is my Helper*, which appears on the titlepage of the Metrical Psalms. Supposed to have been printed at Dort.

The printed titlepage has a coarser cut of the passage of the Red Sea and an ornament at the top, while the woodcut titlepages omit the imprint and date.
Esther i. 1: *seuē | and twentie prouinces.*).
This edition, which seems more correctly printed than any of the above, adopts generally the spelling of the first Geneva Bible of 1560 (e.g. *wil* for *will*, etc.).
Fry possessed four copies of this edition, which, though printed for the most part from the same setting of type, yet differ slightly in certain places. Probably some leaves are reprints. At B 1 *a* they all exhibit the same sudden enlargement of the type in the chapter contents, and all have *Quicuuque vult* in the headline on A 4 *b* in the Metrical Psalms.

¶ (i.) The first of Fry's four varieties.

218 × 160 mm.
With Metrical Psalms (n. d.). [F. F.]

—— Another copy.

(ii.) This differs slightly from the others in some places.

222 × 154 mm. Imperfect: wanting the second title (supplied in facsimile).
With Metrical Psalms (n. d.). [F. F.]

—— Another copy.

(iii.) Differing slightly in some places.

¶ 208 × 154 mm. Wanting the second title (supplied in facsimile).
With Metrical Psalms (n. d.). [F. F.]

—— Another copy.

(iv.) Differing slightly in some places.
It is remarkable in having a colophon on the last page of tables (beneath an ornament like that used on the printed titlepage): *Imprinted at London by the Deputies of Christopher Barker . . . 1599 . . .*

213 × 157 mm.
With Metrical Psalms (n. d.). [F. F.]
194.

'The whole investigation seems to show that these editions of the Geneva-Tomson were published at different times at Amsterdam and Dort, and adopted afterwards by Barker, who affixed the date 1599, probably because this was a well-known and popular edition' (Pocock).

See *Appendix for an edition of the N. T. (Geneva version) printed in Hutter's Polyglot N. T. 1599.*

1600. The Bible, | that is, the Holy | Scriptvres . . . Imprinted at London, by the Deputies of | Christopher Barker, Printer to the Queenes | most excellent Maiestie. | Anno Dom . 1600. | Cum priuilegio.

8°.

Geneva version.

Differs from former octavo editions.

DESCRIPTION. Title (with ornamental headpiece, and printer's device), verso blank, Address—1 p., list of books—1 p. Text: O. T. (with cut of Adam and Eve on first page), ff. 1 to 287 a; on verso begin Apocrypha (with ornamental headpiece), which end on fo. 355 a, followed on the same page by *A perfite supputation* . . . (1600), which ends on verso; N. T. (with ornamental headpiece on first page), ff. 356 to 448 b; *The Order Of The Yeeres* . . . —1 f., tables—12 ff., ending on Mmm 7 b; 1 f. blank.
Signatures: A–Z⁸ Aa–Zz⁸ Aaa–Mmm⁸; 464 ff.
The printer's device on the titlepage is *Dat esse manus : superesse Minerva.*

¶ 156 × 102 mm.
Original binding, stamped with the royal arms. [F. F.]

195.

1600. The | New Testament of our Sauiour | Iesus Christ, | Faithfully translated out of the Greeke, with | the Notes and expositions of the darke | places therein. | Matthew . 13. | The pearle . . . Imprinted by the Deputy of Christopher Barker | Printer to the Queenes most excellent Maiestie.

1600. 8°. 𝕭. 𝕷.

Bishops' version.

The colophon gives R. Barker's Deputy as printer.

DESCRIPTION. Sixteen preliminary leaves: title (in black and red, with cut), verso blank, Kalendar—6 ff., *An Almanacke for xxvi. yeeres* (1578–1603)—1 p., 1 p. blank, *A Preface into the new Testament*—2 ff., *The pith or contents of the new Testament*—7 pp., *By the books of the new Testament* . . . —2 pp., *A true and perfect rekoning* . . . and *An exhortation* . . . —2 pp., *The order of the bookes* . . . —1 p. Text, A 1 to Oo 4 b; the O. T. Epistles—2 ff., the table—2 ff., ending on Oo 8 b with a cut and the colophon : *Imprinted at London by the Deputie of Robert Barker, Printer to the Queenes most excellent Maiestie. 1600.*
Signatures: [unsigned]⁸ ★⁸, A–Z⁸ Aa–Oo⁸; 392 ff. Agrees very closely in all particulars with the editions of 1595 and 1598.
I 3 a, Life of St. Luke: *Lvke being a Phisition of Antiochia (as his owne writings doe testifie)* . . .
Y 5 a, Rom. i, contents : *Paul sheweth by whom, and to what purpose he is called* . . .

¶ 140 × 90 mm.
With Order of Morning and Evening Prayer and Psalter (1599); and Metrical Psalms (1600). [F. F.]

196.

1600. The Bible . . . With . . . Annotations . . . And . . . Concordance . . . Imprinted at London by | Robert Barker . . . 1600 . . .

4°. 𝕭. 𝕷.

Geneva version.

The earliest edition printed by R. Barker.
A close reprint of the quarto of 1588. The text ends on fo. 554 (really 552); and the tables on L 2.

¶ 210 × 152 mm. [F. F.]

ENGLISH

—— Another copy.

212 × 153 mm. This differs from the preceding in many places, and has been marked by Fry 'Variation'; but apparently it is merely a mixed copy.
With Junius' Revelation (1600) inserted after the text.
Contemporary binding; with brass plates and corners. [F. F.]

197.

1600. The | Nevv Testament | of Iesvs Christ faith- | fvlly translated into English . . . By the English | College then Resident in Rhemes. | Set forth the second time, by the same College novv | returned to Dovvay. | VVith addition of one nevv Table of Heretical Cor- | rvptions, the other Tables and Annotations somevvhat | augmented. | Search the Scriptures. Ioan . 5. | Geue me vnderstanding . . . Psalm . 118 . v. 34. . . . Printed at Antvverp | by Daniel Vervliet. | 1600. | VVith privilege.

4°.

The second edition of the Roman Catholic version of the New Testament in English, first published at Rheims in 1582.

A reprint of the earlier edition, with certain changes, such as the addition of *A Table of Heretical Corrvptions*.
A fresh *Approbation* is appended to that of 1582. It is dated 2 Nov. 1599, and is signed by three Professors at Douai: *Guilielmus Estius, Bartholomæus Petrus*, and *Iudocus Heylens*.

DESCRIPTION. Nineteen preliminary leaves, containing the same matter as in the first issue, with the addition of *A Table of Heretical Corrvptions*—3 ff., and *The Explication of certaine vvordes* . . .—1 f. Text, pp. 3 to 745; followed on the same page by *A Table of the Epistles and Gospels* . . ., which ends on Bbbbb iij *a* ; *A Table of Controversies*— 23 pp., ending on Eeeee 2 *b*, with the words *Lavs Deo*.
Signatures: a–d⁴ e², A–Z⁴, etc. as before; 404 ff.
The full title of the new table is: *A Table of certaine places of the Nevv Testament corrvptly translated in favovr of heresies of these dayes in the English Editions: especially of the yeares 1562 . 77 . 79 . and 80 . by order of the Bookes, Chapters, and Verses of the same.* It ends with a note: *The blessed Confessour, Bishop Tonstal noted no lesse then tvvo thousand corruptions in Tindals translation, in the Nevv Testament only. VVherby, as by these fevv here cited for examples, the indifferent reader may see, hovv vntruly the English Bibles are commended to the people, for the pure vvord of God.* The table condemns such renderings as *repent* for *do penance, Congregation* for *Church, elder* for *priest, images* for *idols*, etc.

¶ 215 × 156 mm.

—— Another copy.

211 × 162 mm. [F. F.]

198.

1600. The Revelation | of Saint Iohn the Apostle | and Evangelist, with a | briefe and learned Commentarie, | Written by Franc. Iunius, &c.
R. Field, for R. Dexter : London. 1600. 4°.

A close reprint of the edition of 1594.
Twelve leaves: text, pp. 1 to 22; 1 f. containing on recto device and colophon, verso blank.

¶ 209 × 150 mm.
Bound up with a quarto Bible of 1601, No. 200. [F. F.]

—— Another copy.

Wanting last leaf with colophon.
Bound up with a quarto Bible of 1600, No. 197. [F. F.]

199.

1601. The Bible: | that is . . . With . . . Annotations . . . Imprinted at London by | Robert Barker . . . Anno. 1601 . . .

4°.

Geneva version; with Tomson's revised New Testament.

A close reprint of the quarto of 1595.
The N. T. ends on fo. 116; and the tables on ¶¶ 3. The last leaf of Apocrypha is numbered 187. The general and N. T. titlepages have the same headpiece as the N. T. titlepage in the edition of 1598,97.

¶ 209 × 150 mm. Wants the leaf before title, and the last blank leaf.
With Junius' Revelation (1600) inserted after the text. [F. F.]

200.

1601. The | Bible, | That Is, | the Holy Scrip- | tures . . . Imprinted At London, | by Robert Barker, Printer to | the Queenes most excellent | Maiestie. | Anno 1601.

8°.

Geneva version.

Resembles the octavo edition of 1600, with the text ending on fo. 448, and the tables on Mmm 7. The title, however, is enclosed within a woodcut like that in the quarto editions of 1599, representing the twelve tribes, the twelve apostles, etc.; the central space, containing the title, is heart-shaped; and the words *Cum priuilegio* appear at the base of the cut. A *perfite supputation* . . . gives the date 1600.

¶ 164 × 110 mm.
With Metrical Psalms (1601). [F. F.]

201.

1601. The | Text of the | New Testament | of Iesvs Christ, | Translated out of the vulgar Latine by | the Papists of the traiterous Semi- | narie at Rhemes. | With Arguments . . . Wherevnto Is Added | the Translation out of the Original | Greeke, commonly vsed in the | Church of England, | with | A Confvtation . . . The Whole Worke, | perused and enlarged in diuers places by | the Authors owne hand before his death, with | sundry Quotations, and Authorities out of Holy | Scriptures, Counsels, Fathers, and History. | More amply then in the for- | mer Edition. | By W. Fulke D. in Diuinitie. | Imprinted At London | by Robert Barker, Printer to the | Queenes most excellent Maiestie. | Anno 1601.

f°.

The second edition of Fulke's work, first published in 1589 (see No. 156).

DESCRIPTION. Twenty-one preliminary leaves: title (within border), verso blank, followed by 20 ff. containing matter similar to that in the former edition. Text, pp. 1 to 914 (really 912); *A Table of Controversies*—9 pp., ending on Llll 8 a, verso blank.
Signatures: A–Z⁶ Aa–Zz⁶ Aaa–Zzz⁶ Aaaa–Kkkk⁶ Llll⁸; 482 ff. Two numbers (379 and 380) are omitted in the pagination. The arrangement of the matter is exactly the same as in the first edition.
The title-border: at the top is a lamb bound on an altar, with the legend *Possidete animas vestras*, and the initials N H and C T; at the bottom is a cup, whence springs a vine, which twines round the columns on either side; this design is dated 1574.

¶ 320 × 200 mm.

202.

1602. The | Bible, | That Is, | The holy Scriptures | contained ... Imprinted at London by | Robert Barker, Printer to | the Queenes most excellent | Maiestie. | Anno 1602.

f°. 𝕭. 𝕷.

Geneva version; with Tomson's revised New Testament.

A close reprint of the folio of 1592,91. With the text ending on fo. 626 (really 620), and the tables on Nnnnn 4.
Signatures, etc. as before.

¶ 285 × 190 mm. [F. F.]

203.

1602. The | Bible ... With ... annotations ... And ... Concordance ... Imprinted at London by | Robert Barker ... 1602.

4°. 𝕭. 𝕷.

Geneva version.

A reprint of the quarto of 1588. The text ends on fo. 554 (really 552); and the tables on L 2. The border to both titles, however, resembles that used for the first titlepage found in the quarto editions (roman type) dated 1599. But this block differs in many small points: e.g. in place of the musical notes at the base appear the words *Cum Priuilegio* with the initials E R.

¶ 214 × 159 mm. [F. F.]

—— Another copy.

Imperfect: wanting all before sheet B.
With Metrical Psalms (1602).

204.

1602. (The Bible.)

[*R. Barker: London.* 1602.] 8°.

Geneva version.

A perfect svppvtation gives the date 1602. No doubt printed by R. Barker.
Resembles the octavo of 1601. O. T. ends on fo. 287 a; Apocrypha, on fo. 355 (Yy 5) a, followed on the same page by *A perfect svppvtation* ..., which ends on verso.

¶ 157 × 105 mm. Imperfect: wanting title, and all N. T. etc. (Yy 6 to the end). [F. F.]

205.

1602. The | Holy Bible, | containing ... Authorised and appointed to be | read in Churches. | Imprinted at London | by Robert Barker ... Anno 1602.

f°. 𝕭. 𝕷.

Bishops' version.

The last edition of the Bishops' Bible. Cotton (p. 57) alludes to a folio edition of 1606, of which the Duke of Sussex was supposed to possess a copy. But no such book can now be traced, and no mention of it occurs in the Sale Catalogue of the Sussex Library (1844). It seems probable that the entry in Pettigrew's *Bibliotheca Sussexiana* (vol. ii. p. 327) was an error, due to some confusion between the preceding entry and the folio Geneva Bible of 1606. It is moreover unlikely that Barker would print another folio edition, after preparations for a new version—which he himself printed in 1611—had already been begun by royal command.

This edition of the Bishops' Bible was presumably used by King James' translators as the basis of their new version. The Bodleian Library possesses a copy, which contains many MS. corrections, and has been considered an actual relic of their work. But see Westcott, *History*, p. 122 n. An article by N. Pocock in the *Athenæum*, 25 Feb. 1888, pp. 243–5, deals with this Bodleian copy. As to the original MS. of King James' version, see below, No. 240.

DESCRIPTION. Eighteen preliminary leaves: title (within border), verso blank, Kalendar — 6 ff., *An Almanacke* (1601-33) — 1 p., Prologue (in black-letter) — 6 pp., *The whole Scripture* . . . — 3 pp., Genealogical Table — 11 pp., 1 p. containing large engraving. The text, with continuous register and foliation, ff. 1 to 496 (Oooo 4) *a*, with colophon, verso blank.

Signatures: A–C⁶, A–Z⁶ Aa–Zz⁶ Aaa–Zzz⁶ Aaaa–Nnnn⁶ Oooo⁴; 514 ff. Each page of print is enclosed within black lines.

There are two varieties of the general title. Some copies have the title as printed above within a woodcut border (like that subsequently used in the folio edition of King James' Bible, 1611) representing the twelve tribes, the twelve Apostles, etc.; a small ornament is placed above the imprint. Others (e.g. B. M. copy, 339. c. 5) contain a different title: *The | Holy Bible, contey- | ning . . . Authorised and appoynted to be | read in Churches. | Imprinted at London by | Robert Barker . . . Anno 1602. | Cum priuilegio* (in black and red), within the border used in the folio Bible of 1595 and earlier editions. The borders to the N. T. and Apocrypha titles are the same as in the folio edition of 1585. The usual large engraving occurs before the text.

¶ 402 × 275 mm. Imperfect: wanting general title, and Apocrypha title. Facsimiles of both varieties of the general title are inserted; the first has a genuine border. The small cut in the Genealogical Table and the engraving before the text are illuminated. Original binding of brown leather; each cover bears the royal arms etc. within an elaborate frame, with corner ornaments (containing Tudor rose and crown), in gold. [F. F.]

—— Another copy.

401 × 262 mm. Imperfect: wanting general title and following leaf. A duplicate of Eee 2 has been inserted by mistake instead of Ccc 2.

206.

1602. The | New Testament | of ovr Lord Iesvs | Christ, Translated out of | Greeke by Theod. Beza: | With briefe Summaries . . . Englished by L. Tomson. | Together with the Annotations of Fr. Junius | vpon the Reuelation of S. | John. | Imprinted at Lon- | don by Robert Barker, | Printer to the Queenes most Ex- | cellent Maiestie. | Anno 1602.

8°.

Geneva version; Tomson's revision, but with Junius' Revelation (see above, 1594).

Apparently the earliest issue of the Geneva New Testament in which Junius' Revelation displaces Tomson's version of that book. Nos. 188–194 (*q.v.*) were probably printed later.

DESCRIPTION. Two preliminary leaves: title (within border), on verso *The Printer to the Reader*, *The Description* (with map) — 1 p., *The order of the Bookes* . . . — 1 p. Text, ff. 1 to 274 (Mm 2) *b*.

Signatures: [unsigned]², A–Z⁸ Aa–Ll⁸ Mm²; 276 ff. Before Revelation is placed a table *The order of time whereunto the contents of this booke are to be referred* (on Ii 3 *a*). The border resembles that used in the octavo Geneva Bible of 1601.

¶ 161 × 104 mm. [F. F.]

207.

ACCESSION OF KING JAMES I: 24 MARCH 1603.

1603. The | Bible . . . With . . . anno- | tations . . . And . . . Concordance . . . Imprinted at Lon- | don by Robert Bar- | ker . . . 1603.

4°. 𝕭. 𝕷.

Geneva version.

This edition, though both titles and colophon bear the words *Printer to the Queenes . . . Maiestie*, must have been published after King James I's accession; otherwise it would be dated 1602, since the year began on 25 March.

A close reprint of the edition of 1602. The text ends on fo. 554 (really 552); and the tables on L 2. The leaf after the general title is signed ¶ iij, though there appear to be only two preliminary leaves. So in some later editions.

¶ 217 × 155 mm.
With Prayer Book (1603); and Metrical Psalms (1603).
Contemporary binding; with brass corners and clasps. [F. F.]
208.

1603. The | Bible: | that is ... With ... Annotations ... Imprinted At Lon- | don by Robert Barker ... Anno. | 1603.

4°.

Geneva version; with Tomson's revised New Testament, and Junius' Revelation.

Printer to the Queenes ... Maiestie on titles, but ... *Kings ... Maiestie* in colophon. This agrees generally with the quarto editions in roman type described under the date 1599.
The N. T. ends on fo. 121 *a*; and the tables on Rrr 4 *b*. Malachi ends on fo. 117 (really 127, Qq 7) *a*, verso blank; Apocrypha, ff. 128 (Qq 8) to 187 (really 196, ★ ★4) *b*. Signatures of the section containing Psalms–2 Macc.: Aa–Zz⁸ &&⁸ ★ ★⁴; 196 ff.

Fry specifies two varieties of this date.

A. On ★ ★ 4 *b*: *The end of the Apocrypha* (in italics). The headpiece (with head in centre) on the pt. 2 titlepage is the same as that in the edition of 1601. A note *The Order of Time* (on Ooo 6 *b*) precedes Revelation.

¶ 223 × 162 mm. With the leaf signed A j before the title. [F. F.]
209.

—— ANOTHER EDITION.

B. On ★ ★ 4 *b*: *The ende of the Apocrypha* (roman type). The headpiece on pt. 2 titlepage represents a vase with flowers. Ooo 6 *b* contains part of the preface *I have not thovght good* ..., though the next page begins with Junius' Revelation.

¶ 208 × 150 mm. Possibly to some extent a mixed copy. Wants the leaf before the title.
[F. F.]
210.

1603. The | Bible, | That Is, | the Holy Scrip- | tures ... Imprinted at Lon- | don by Robert Barker, Printer | to the Queenes most Excellent | Maiestie. | Anno 1603.

8°.

Geneva version.

DESCRIPTION. Title and following leaf as in the edition of 1601. O. T. ends on fo. 287 *b*; Apocrypha, ff. 290 (really 288) to 355 *a*, followed on the same page by *A perfit svppvtation* ... (1603), which ends on verso; N. T., with title: *The | New Testa- | ment ... Imprinted at London by | Robert Barker, | Printer to the Kings most | excellent Maiestie. | Anno 1603* (within same border as general title), verso blank; text—ff. 357 to 449 *b*; *The Order Of The Yeeres ...*—1 f., tables—12 ff., ending on Mmm 8 *b*.
Signatures, &c., as before; 464 ff.

There are two octavo editions of this date.

A. General title, as above; N. T. title: ... *Printer to the Kings ... Maiestie.*

¶ 164 × 102 mm.
With Metrical Psalms (1604).
Original binding, stamped with the royal arms; with brass corners and clasps; goffered edges. [F. F.]
211.

—— ANOTHER EDITION.

B. Both titles: . . . *Printer to the Kings* . . . *Maiestie*.
Differs from A in many small points throughout the volume. General title has on verso a cut of the royal arms. A colophon occurs at the end of the tables, on Mmm 8 *b*; which, like the titles, has the words . . . *Kings* . . . *Maiestie*.

¶ 163 × 112 mm.
With Metrical Psalms (1604).
Bound in 'silver tapestry'; floral design in coloured silks woven on silver thread; lined inside with stamped red satin; goffered edges. [F. F.]
212.

1603. The | Nevv Testament of | our Lord Iesus Christ, tran- | slated out of Greeke by | Theod. Beza . . . Englished by L. Tomson. | At Dort | Printed by Isaac Canin. | 1603.

8°.

Geneva version; Tomson's revision.

This edition, printed apparently for use in Scotland, closely resembles the London editions described above under the date 1596 (?), Nos. 179 and 180.

DESCRIPTION. Eight preliminary leaves: title (within narrow frame, with cut), verso blank, Epistle—5 ff., *The Printer to diligent Reader*—1 f., *A prayer for the King and Queenes Majestie of Scotland*— 1 p., *The Order of the Bookes* . . .—1 p. The text, ff. 1 to 266 (Ll 2) *a*, verso blank; table (three columns on a page)—13 ff., ending on Mm 7 *b*; 1 f. blank.
Signatures: ✱⁸, A–Z⁸ Aa–Mm⁸; 288 ff.
The headlines are not printed in capitals as in the corresponding London editions. Title enclosed within a narrow ornamental frame. The cut represents Faith trampling upon Death. The initial T before St. Matthew contains a dog.

¶ 154 × 97 mm. Imperfect: wanting preliminary leaves, fo. 82, and the last three leaves.
[F. F.]
The Euing Collection in the University Library, Glasgow, possesses a perfect copy.
213.

[The B. M. has a copy (C. 38. b. 39) of a very small New Testament printed by I. Canin at Dort in 1601 *at the expensis of the aires of Henrie Charteris, and Andrew Hart, in Edinburgh*.]

1605. The | Bible . . . With . . . anno- | tations . . . And . . . Concordance . . . Imprinted At London | by Robert Barker . . . 1605.

4°. 𝔅. 𝔏.

Geneva version.

A close reprint of the quarto of 1602. The text ends on fo. 554 (really 552); and the tables on L 2.
In the title-border the initials I R displace E R.

¶ 213 × 159 mm. [F. F.]
214.

1605. (The Bible.)

R. Barker: London. 1605. 8°.

Geneva version.

The name of printer and date appear both on the N. T. title, and in the colophon on the last page; and the date 1605 is also given in *A perfit supputation*.
Resembles the edition B of 1603; with the text ending on fo. 449, and the tables on Mmm 8.
An error occurs in Gen. ii. 13, *third Riuer* for *second Riuer*.

¶ 159 × 102 mm. Imperfect: wanting general title and Nn 1. [F. F.]
215.

1605. The | New Testament of our Sauiour | Iesus Christ, | Faithfully translated out of the Greeke, with | the Notes and expositions of the darke | places therein. | Matthew . 13. | The pearle . . . Imprinted by the deputie of Robert Barker | Printer to the Kings most excellent Maiestie. | 1605.

8°. 𝔅. 𝔏.

Bishops' version.

DESCRIPTION. Sixteen preliminary leaves: title (in black and red, with cut), verso blank, Kalendar—6 ff., *An Almanacke for xxvi. yeeres* (1602-27)—1 p., 1 p. blank, *A Preface into the new Testament*—2 ff., *The pith or contents of the new Testament*—7 pp., *By the books of the new Testament* . . . —2 pp., *A true and perfect reckening* . . . and *An exhortation* . . . —2 pp., *The order of the bookes* . . . —1 p. Text, A 1 to Oo 4 *b*; The O. T. Epistles—2 ff., the table—2 ff., ending on Oo 8 *b* with cut and colophon: *Imprinted at London by the assignes of Robert Barker. 1605.*

Signatures: [unsigned]⁸ *⁸, A–Z⁸ Aa–Oo⁸; 392 ff. The cuts on the titlepage and on the last page are the same as in the edition of 1600.

I 3 *a*, Life of St. Luke: *Lvke being a Phisitiō of Antiochia (as his owne writings do testifie)* . . .

Y 5 *a*, Rom. i, contents: *Paul sheweth by whome, and to what purpose he is called* . . .

¶ 140 × 93 mm. Imperfect: wanting all preliminary leaves but two, and other leaves.

[F. F.]

A copy of this edition in St. Paul's Cathedral Library, 38 C 20, is wrongly described in the Catalogue (1893) of that Library as 'Tyndale's, as printed by R. Jugge' (so Cotton, p. 57).

216.

—— ANOTHER EDITION.

Date not known. No doubt printed by Barker's Deputy.

I 3 *a*, Life of St. Luke: *Luke being a Phisition of Antiochia (as his owne writinges doe testifie)* . . .

Y 5 *a*, Rom. i, contents: *Haul sheweth by whome, and to what purpose he is called* . . .

¶ 139 × 94 mm. Imperfect: wanting all before B 2, and after Nn 7; besides other leaves. [F. F.]

217.

—— ANOTHER EDITION.

Date not known. No doubt printed by Barker's Deputy.

I 3 *a*, Life of St. Luke: *Lvke being a Phisition of Antiochia (as his own writings do testifie)* . . .

¶ 134 × 85 mm. Imperfect: wanting all preliminary and appended leaves, and many leaves of text. [F. F.]

218.

1605. B. 4°. See 1606.

1606. The | Bible : | that is . . . With . . . Annotations . . . Imprinted at | London by Robert Bar- | ker . . . 1606.

1606,05. 4°.

Geneva version; with Tomson's revised New Testament, and Junius' Revelation.

The colophon is dated 1605.

A close reprint of the edition A of 1603. The N. T. ends on fo. 121; and the tables on Rrr 4. The leaf before the title bears the signature A within an ornament.

¶ 207 × 150 mm. [F. F.]

—— Another copy.

209 × 155 mm. Imperfect: wanting the N. T. title.
With Prayer Book (1606); and Metrical Psalms (? 1605).

219.

1606. The | Bible . . . With . . . anno- | tations . . . And . . . Concordance . . . Imprinted At London | by Robert Barker . . . 1606.

4°. 𝕭. 𝕷.

Geneva version.

A close reprint of the quarto of 1605. The text ends on fo. 554 (really 552); and the tables on L 2.

¶ 219 × 153 mm.
With Prayer Book (1606); and Metrical Psalms (1605).
In two volumes.
[F. F.]
220.

1606. The | New Testament of | our Sauiour Iesvs | Christ, | Faithfully translated out | of the Greeke, with the | Notes and expositions of the | darke places therein. | Matth. XIII. | The pearle . . . Imprinted At | London by Robert Barker, | Printer to the Kings most | Excellent Maiestie. | Anno 1606. |

8°. 𝕭. 𝕷.

Bishops' version.

DESCRIPTION. Sixteen preliminary leaves: title (within border), verso blank, Kalendar — 6 ff., *An Almanacke for xxxij. yeeres* (1603-34) — 1 p., 1 p. blank; *A Preface* . . . — 2 ff., *The pith* . . . — 7 pp., *By the books* . . . — 2 pp., *A true and perfect reckening* . . . with *An exhortation* . . . — 2 pp., *The order of the bookes* . . . — 1 p. Text, A 1 to Nn 1 a; the O. T. Epistles and the table of Epistles and Gospels — 7 pp., ending on Nn 4 b with the colophon: *Imprinted at London by Robert Rarker, Printer to the Kings most excellent Maiestie. 1606.*
Signatures: [unsigned]⁸ *⁸, A–Z⁸ Aa–Mm⁸ Nn⁴; 300 ff. Leaves not numbered.
The title-border: at the top — the Sacred Name, below — the royal arms, at the sides — two symbolical female figures, and in the corners — the Evangelists.
X 5 a, 1st line: *worthinesse . . . vprightly*; 6th line ends: . . . *vpon the same.*

¶ 133 × 87 mm. Imperfect: wanting sheets D and E, and S 6; —17 ff. [F. F.]
221.

1607. The | Bible | that is, | The holy Scriptures | contained . . . Imprinted at London by | Robert Barker, Printer to the | Kinges most excellent | Maiestie | Cum privilegio.

1607. f°.

Geneva version; with Tomson's revised New Testament, and Junius' Revelation.

DESCRIPTION. Four preliminary leaves: title (within border, engraved), verso blank, Address — 1 f., *Of the incomparable Treasure* . . . — 1 p., *How to take profit* . . . — 1 p., list of books — 1 p., 1 p. containing large engraving. Text: O. T. and Apocrypha, ff. 1 to 444 b; N. T., with title: *The New Testament . . . Translated out of Greeke by Theod. Beza . . . Englished by L. Tomson. Together with the Annotations of Fr. Ivnivs vpon the Reuelation of S. Iohn* . . ., verso blank, *The Printer to the diligent Reader* — 1 p., *The description* . . . (with map) — 1 p., text — ff. 3 to 135 b; tables — 7 ff., ending on Fffff 4 b, with colophon.
Signatures: ¶⁴, A–Z⁶ Aa–Zz⁶ Aaa–Zzz⁶ Aaaa–Zzzz⁶ Aaaaa–Eeeee⁶ Fffff⁴; 590 ff.
The whole of the titlepage is engraved. The letterpress is enclosed within an architectural design in the form of an arch; round its two pillars twine the branches of

a vine; on the left are represented the tents of the twelve tribes, above—Moses receiving the Law, below—the Fall; on the right—the twelve apostles, above—the Transfiguration, below—the Resurrection; in the middle representing the letterpress the emblems of the four Evangelists, above—the Sacred Name, Christ seated in judgment, and Abraham and Isaac, below—Christ treading the wine-press with the legend from Is. lxiii, *Ego torcvlar calcavi solvs.* At the base are the words *Guilielmus Hole fecit.* The N. T. titlepage has a headpiece and another small ornament.

¶ 310 × 205 mm. [F. F.]

—— Another copy.

330 × 215 mm. Imperfect: wanting title.
With Metrical Psalms (1609).
Contemporary brown leather binding, executed for Henry, Prince of Wales (son of James I), who died in 1612. It bears the Prince of Wales' plumes and motto, and the initials H P, on the covers.

222.

1607. The | Bible ... With ... anno- | tations ... And ... Concordance ... Imprinted At London | by Robert Bakker ... 1607.

4°. 𝕭. 𝕷.

Geneva version.

A close reprint of the quarto of 1605. Text ends on fo. 554 (really 552); and the tables on L 2.

There are two varieties of this date, which differ throughout.

A. With misprint *Bakker* in general title; N. T. title dated 1607; colophon not dated. Gen. i. 2: *fourme.*

¶ 220 × 156 mm. [F. F.]

223.

—— ANOTHER EDITION.

B. Printer's name *Barker* correct in general title; N. T. title not dated; colophon dated 1607.
Gen. i. 2: *forme.*

¶ 221 × 159 mm. [F. F.]

—— Another copy.

205 × 150 mm.

224.

1608. The | Bible ... With ... Annota- | tions ... And ... Concordance ... Imprinted at | London by Robert Bar- | ker ... 1608.

4°. 𝕭. 𝕷.

Geneva version.

A close reprint of the quarto of 1605. Text ends on fo. 554 (really 552); and the tables on L 2.

There are two varieties of this date.

A. General title: ... *in the Epi- | stle to the Reader.*
Gen. i. 3: *Then God sayd ...*

¶ 217 × 156 mm.
Contemporary binding; with brass plates and corners. [F. F.]

—— Another copy.

210 × 153 mm. Imperfect: wanting both titles, and other leaves.
With Metrical Psalms (? date).

225.

—— ANOTHER EDITION.

B. General title: . . . *in the | Epistle to the Reader.*
Gen. i. 3: *Then sayd God . . .*

¶ 212 × 155 mm. [F. F.]

226.

1608. The | Bible.| That is . . . With . . . Annotations . . . Imprinted at | London by Robert Bar-| ker . . . 1608.

4°.

Geneva version, with Tomson's revised New Testament, and Junius' Revelation.

A close reprint of the quarto of 1606,05. N. T. ends on fo. 111 (really 121); and the tables on Rrr 4.
John vi. 67: *Judas* for *Jesus.*

¶ 212 × 150 mm. [F. F.]

—— Another copy.

210 × 152 mm. Wants leaf before title.

—— Another copy.

Differs in parts from the above, but is probably mixed.

208 × 149 mm. Imperfect: wanting preliminary matter and other leaves. The Apocrypha have been supplied from an edition of the 1611 version.
With Metrical Psalms (1608). [F. F.]

227.

1608. The | Bible, | That is, | the Holy Scriptvres . . . Imprinted at | London by Robert Barker, | Printer to the Kings most | Excellent Maiestie. | Anno 1608.

8°.

Geneva version.

Resembles the edition B of 1603; with the text ending on fo. 449, and the tables on Mmm 8.
Gen. ii. 13 correct.

¶ 162 × 103 mm. [F. F.]

228.

1608. The | New Testament | of our Sauiour Iesus | Christ . . . Imprinted at Lon- | don by Robert Barker, Prin- | ter to the Kings most Excel- | lent Maiestie. 1608.

8°. 𝕭. 𝕷.

Bishops' version.

Agrees very closely with the edition of 1606.
Title in black and red. The border is like that in the 1606 edition, but touched with red. The preliminary leaves, text, and appended matter are arranged precisely as in the earlier edition. The colophon on Nn 4 *b* is not dated. The second sheet is signed [A].
The ornament at the end of the text contains two fleurs-de-lys.
X 5 *a*, 1st line: *worthinesse* . . . *vprightly*; 6th line ends: . . . *vvō the same.*

¶ 139 × 83 mm. [F. F.]

229.

1609. The | Bible.| That is ... With ... Annotations ... Imprinted at | London by Robert Bar-| ker ... 1609.

4°.

Geneva version; with Tomson's revised New Testament, and Junius' Revelation.
A close reprint of the quarto of 1606,05.
N. T. ends on fo. 111 (really 121); and the tables on Rrr 4.
John vi. 67 : *Judas* for *Jesus*.

¶ 220 × 160 mm.
With Metrical Psalms (1610). [F. F.]

—— Another copy.

Last leaf of N. T. correctly numbered 121.

207 × 152 mm. Imperfect: wanting leaf before title, and all Apocrypha.
With Metrical Psalms (1608).

230.

1609. B. 4°. See 1610.

1610. The | Holie Bible | faithfvlly trans- | lated into English, | ovt of the avthentical | Latin. | Diligently conferred with the Hebrew, Greeke, | and other Editions in diuers languages. | With Argvments of the Bookes, and Chapters : | Annotations : Tables : and other helpes, | for better vnderstanding of the text : for discouerie of | Corrvptions in some late translations : and | for clearing Controversies in Religion. | By the English College of Doway. | Haurietis aquas in gaudio de fontibus Saluatoris. Isaiæ. 12. | You shal draw waters in ioy out of the Sauiours fountaines. | Printed at Doway by Lavrence Kellam, | at the signe of the holie Lambe. | M. DC. IX.

1609,10. 4°. 2 vols.

The *editio princeps* of the Roman Catholic version of the Old Testament in English.

This version of the Old Testament was based on the same lines, and came from the same hands, as the Rheims New Testament of 1582 (*q.v.*). The complete work is commonly known as the 'Douai-Rheims version,' or briefly the 'Douai Bible.'

The Preface to the Rheims New Testament speaks of *the holy Bible long since translated by vs into English, and the old Testament lying by vs for lacke of good meanes to publish the vvhole in such sort as a vvorke of so great charge and importance requireth.* Twenty-seven years later the Preface to this Old Testament expressly ascribes the long delay in its publication to *one general cause, our poore estate in banishment*. After referring to *those that trāslated it about thirtie years since* (clearly Martin and his coadjutors), the editor explains *only one thing we haue donne touching the text, whereof we are especially to geue notice ... we haue againe conferred this English translation, and conformed it to the most perfect Latin Edition,* i.e. the authorised recension of the Vulgate published under the authority of Clement VIII in 1592. Cardinal Allen (1532-94) had assisted in this revision of the Latin text.

The annotations (which are far less copious than in the New Testament, and also less vehement) and the tables, etc. are ascribed to Thomas Worthington, who became President of the College at Douai in 1599.

The *Approbatio* is signed by three Professors at Douai : *Guilielmus Estius, Bartholomæus Petrus,* and *Georgius Colvenerius*; and the *Censura trium Theologorum Anglorum, extra collegium commorantium* by *Ioannes Wrightus, Matthæus Kellisonus,* and *Guilielmus Harisonus*. The Preface criticises certain renderings of current English Bibles, mentioning the editions of 1552, 1577, 1579, and 1603.

DESCRIPTION. Vol. 1: Ten preliminary leaves: title (within narrow frame), on verso *Approbatio*, Preface *To the right vvelbeloved English Reader* . . . (dated *From the English College in Doway, the Octaues of al Sainctes. 1609*)—6 ff.; *The svmme and partition of the Holie Bible. With a brife note of the Canonical and Apochryphal Bookes, The svmme of the Old Testament . . .*, and *Of Moyses . . .*—2 ff.; *The argvment of the booke of Genesis*, and *The signification of the markes here vsed . . .*—1 f. Text, Genesis–Job, pp. 1 to 1114; on p. 1115 is a short note *To the Cvrteovs Reader*, 1 p. blank.

Vol 2: title: *The second tome of the Holie Bible* . . . etc. (as in vol. 1, but with a different text: *Spiritu Sancto inspirati, locuti sunt sancti Dei homines. 2. Pet. 1. The holie men of God spake, inspired with the Holie Ghost*, and dated M.DC.X.; within narrow frame), on verso the *Approbatio*, on the next page (p. 3) begin *Proemial annotations vpon the Booke of Psalmes*, which end on p. 14 with a short note *Concerning interpretation of holie Scriptvres*. Text, Psalms–4 Esdras, pp. 15 to 1071; *A table of the Epistles, taken forth of the old Testament* . . .—1 p., *An historical table of the times . . . of the Old Testament*—24 pp., *A particvlar table of the most principal thinges* . . .—27 pp., *Censura*—1 p., list of *errata*—1 p., 1 p. blank, 1 f. blank.

Signatures: vol. 1: †⁶ ††¹, A–Z⁴ Aa–Zz⁴ Aaa–Zzz⁴ Aaaa–Zzzz⁴ Aaaaa–Zzzzz⁴ Aaaaaa–Ssssss⁴ Tttttt⁶; vol. 2: A–Z⁴ Aa–Zz⁴ Aaa–Zzz⁴ Aaaa–Zzzz⁴ Aaaaa–Zzzzz⁴ Aaaaaa–Wwwwww⁴; 1132 ff. (The signature-alphabets include the letter w.)

The general arrangement of the matter resembles that employed in the Rheims New Testament. Besides the ordinary annotations there are longer notes on special subjects, styled *Recapitulations*, etc., in various parts of the book.

¶ 214 × 155 mm. [F. F.]

—— Another copy.

214 × 151 mm. Wants the title in vol. 1.

—— Another copy.

208 × 157 mm. Imperfect: wanting in vol. 1—three preliminary leaves and the last two leaves; and in vol. 2—title and following leaf, and the last two leaves;—6 ff. The title of vol. 1 is mounted.

231.

1610. The | Bible, | That Is, | The holy Scriptures con- | tained . . . Imprinted at | London by Robert Barker, | Printer to the Kings most Excel- | lent Maiestie. | 1610.

f°. 𝔅. 𝔏.

Geneva version; with Tomson's revised New Testament.

A reprint of the folio of 1592,91. The leaves are not numbered, but the signatures are the same as before, and the book ends on Nnnnn 4 b. The titles of books and chapter-numbers in the headlines are in italics.

The title-border to the general and N. T. titles is slightly altered. A small portion of the woodblock has been cut away, and a fresh piece inserted, which gives the new royal arms and the unicorn in place of the dragon.

¶ 292 × 186 mm. [F. F.]

—— Another copy.

277 × 188 mm.
With Prayer Book (1607), and Metrical Psalms (1611).

232.

1610. The Bible | that is, | the Holy Scrip- | tvres contained . . . At Edin- bvrgh, | Printed by Andro Hart, and are to be sold | at his Buith, on the North-side of the gate, | a little beneath the Crosse. | Anno Dom. 1610. | Cum Privilegio Regiæ Maiestatis.

f°.

Geneva version; with Tomson's revised New Testament, and Junius' Revelation.

The second edition printed in Scotland. Lee (*Memorial*, p. 53, and *Additional Memorial*, p. 69) mentions an edition of the Bible (Geneva version) printed at Dort in 1601 for Hart and the heirs of Henry Charteris. And certainly two editions of the New Testament were printed at Dort at that period for use in Scotland (*cf.* No. 213).

A revision of the Geneva Bible had been proposed in the Assembly at Burntisland, May, 1601; but evidently the project came to nothing (Lee, *Memorial*, p. 60 *n.*). The provincial assemblies appear to have ordered every kirk to be provided with a copy of Hart's Bible. Lee (p. 56) cites the following minute from the records of the diocesan synod of St. Andrew's, April, 1611 : ' Forasmeikle as it was thought expedient that there be in every kirk ane commoune Bible, it was concludit that every brother sall urge his parochiners to buy ane of the Bybles laitlie printed be Andro Hart, and the brother failzing either to caus buy ane as said is, or ellis to gif in his exact diligens sall pay at the next synod 6 lib. money ' (i.e. 10 shillings sterling, equivalent to about £3 to-day). This Bible of 1610 appears to have been regarded for many years as a standard edition. See the note on the titlepages of the Amsterdam editions of 1640 and 1644 (Nos. 424 and 449). (*Cf.* Lea Wilson, p. 96.)

DESCRIPTION. Six preliminary leaves : title, verso blank, *To the Christian Reader*—1 f., *An Almanacke and Table for 50 . yeeres to come* (1610-59)—1 p., *A declaration of the conformitie betwixt the Hebrew Calender, and our Romane Callender, and Iulian yeeres* with . . . *an exact Callender* . . .—4 pp., *How to take profit* . . .—1 p., *Of the incomparable Treasure* . . .—1 p., list of books—1 p. Text: O. T. and Apocrypha, ff. 1 to 513 (really 506) *b*; N. T., with title, verso blank, *The Printer to the diligent Reader*—1 p., *The description* . . . (with map)—1 p., text—ff. 5 (really 3) to 143 (really 148) *b*; tables—15 pp., ending on Cc 6 *a*, with the colophon, verso blank.

Signatures : ¶⁶, A-Z⁶ Aa⁶ Bb⁶ Cc⁴ Dd-Zz⁶ Aaa-Zzz⁶ Aaaa-Pppp⁶ Qqqq⁴, A-Z⁶ Aa-Cc⁶; 668 ff. The numbering of the leaves is most incorrect.

A line of text omitted at the bottom of G 4 *a* (Exod. xxx) is supplied by a pasted slip ; and an omission on P 5 *a* (Deut. xiii) is corrected in the same way.

The general title has an ornamental headpiece, with a cut (the crossing of the Red Sea) above the imprint. The N. T. title has the same headpiece, with a small device representing Faith trampling on Death (as in No. 213).

One of the maps in the text is a metal engraving; it is placed at Gen. ii. Two full-page engravings on separate leaves are inserted in Exodus.

Many of the initial letters and ornaments resemble Barker's. One vignette—a female head between two cornucopiæ—has the initials A H.

¶ 332 × 217 mm. [F. F.]

—— Another copy.

326 × 210 mm. Imperfect: wanting general title and four following leaves; also the last three leaves of tables. Inserted are a facsimile of the title, and three duplicate leaves. One of the large engravings is missing. The section containing the Apocrypha is wrongly placed after the tables. [F. F.]

233.

1610. (The Bible.)

R. Barker : London. 1610. 4°. 𝕭. 𝕷.

Geneva version.

A close reprint of the quarto of 1605. Text ends on fo. 554 (really 552).

¶ 210 × 158 mm. Imperfect: wanting general title. The tables are dated 1608, and have perhaps been supplied from a Bible of that year.
With Metrical Psalms (1609). [F. F.]

—— Another copy.

215 × 157 mm. Imperfect : wanting all the O. T., and the tables.

234.

1610. The | Bible, | That is, | the Holy Scriptvres . . . Imprinted at Lon- | don by Robert Barker | Printer to the Kings most Ex- | cellent Maiestie. | Anno 1610.

8°.

Geneva version.

Resembles the octavo B of 1603; with the text ending on fo. 449, and the tables on Mmm 8.

¶ 162 × 110 mm. Imperfect: wanting general title.
With Metrical Psalms (? date). [F. F.]
235.

1610. The | New Testament | of ovr Lord Iesvs | Christ, Translated out of | Greeke by Theod. Beza: | With briefe Summaries . . . Englished by L. Tomson. | Together with the Annotations of Fr. Iunius | vpon the Reuelation of S. | Iohn. | Imprinted at Lon- | don by Robert Barker | Printer to the King's most Ex- | cellent Maiestie. | Anno 1610.
8°.

Geneva version; Tomson's revision, with Junius' Revelation.

A close reprint of the edition of 1602, with the text ending on Mm 2. But from Hh 1 onwards the type is rearranged, so as to avoid the undue compression on the last page.

¶ 154 × 97 mm.
With Metrical Psalms (1614). [F. F.]
236.

1610. B. 4°. See 1611.

1611. The | Bible: | that is . . . With . . . Annotations . . . Imprinted at | London by Robert Barker . . . 1610.
1610,11. 4°.

Geneva version; with Tomson's revised New Testament, and Junius' Revelation.

The date 1611 appears in the colophon, though both titles are dated 1610.
A close reprint of the quarto of 1606,05. N. T. ends on fo. 121, and the tables on Rrr 4.
John vi. 67: *Judas* for *Jesus*.

¶ 216 × 153 mm.
With Speed's Genealogies and Map.
Seventeenth-century binding. [F. F.]

—— Another copy.
The misprint is corrected by a pasted slip.
209 × 154 mm. Wants leaf before title. [F. F.]

—— Another copy.
John vi. 67 correct.
This and the following copies contain some variant leaves.

220 × 156 mm.
Seventeenth-century binding.

—— Another copy.
John vi. 67 correct.
212 × 153 mm. [F. F.]

—— Another copy.
John vi. 67 correct.

199 × 147 mm. Imperfect: wanting N. T. title, and leaf before general title.
With Metrical Psalms (? date).

—— Another copy.
John vi. 67 correct.
207 × 149 mm. Imperfect: wanting 13 ff. at the beginning, and the tables at the end.

237.

1611. The | Bible . . . With . . . Annota- | tions . . . And . . . Concordance . . . Imprinted at | London by Robert Barker . . . 1611.
1611,10. 4°. 𝔅. 𝔏.

Geneva version.

The N. T. title is dated 1610 (though the tables are dated 1611), but differs from the N. T. title in the 1610 edition (No. 234), e.g. *Translations in diuers* printed in roman type, instead of italics, and *printer* for *Printer*.

A close reprint of the quarto of 1605. Text ends on fo. 554 (really 552); and tables on L 2.

Certaine questions and answeres . . ., ★ 3 *b*, second col.: *Yea verily : that by sight, tast and feeling,* | *as well as* . . .

¶ 214 × 154 mm. [F. F.]

—— Another copy.
216 × 157 mm. Imperfect: wanting the second preliminary leaf, and the N. T. title and three following leaves.

238.

—— ANOTHER EDITION.
Closely resembles the above; but the N. T. title is dated 1611.
★ 3 *b*, second col.: *Yea verily : that by sight, taste and fee-* | *ling, as well as* . . .

¶ 220 × 159 mm. [F. F.]

239.

1611. The | Holy | Bible, | Conteyning the Old Testament, | and the New : | Newly Translated out of the Originall | tongues : & with the former Translations | diligently compared and reuised, by his | Maiesties speciall Cōmandement. | Appointed to be read in Churches. | Imprinted at London by Robert | Barker, Printer to the Kings | most Excellent Maiestie. | Anno Dom. 1611.
f°. 𝔅. 𝔏.

The *editio princeps* of King James' Bible, commonly known as the 'Authorised' version.

The idea of this new translation was first mooted by John Rainolds or Reynolds (1549–1607), President of Corpus Christi College, Oxford, the Puritan leader at the Hampton Court Conference, Jan. 1604. The King took up the proposal warmly, and its achievement was due to his royal interest and influence. The preliminary work was accomplished in about four years. [We need not construe literally the *twise seuen times seuentie two dayes and more*—roughly two years and nine months—of the preface to the Bible.] The translators, who numbered about fifty, were divided into six companies, each company being responsible for a certain section of the Scriptures. Two companies met at Westminster, two at Cambridge, and two at Oxford ; and at these centres the directors of the work were Lancelot Andrewes (1555–1626), then Dean of Westminster, Edward Lively (1545 ?–1605), Regius Professor of Hebrew at Cambridge, and John Harding, Regius Professor of Hebrew at Oxford. The results of their several labours were subjected to mutual criticism, and then underwent nine months' final revision by a representative committee of six members, sitting in

London. The editors who passed the book through the press were Miles Smith, afterwards Bishop of Gloucester (d. 1624), and Thomas Bilson (1547–1616), Bishop of Winchester. The latter, perhaps, composed the headings to the chapters. To the former is ascribed the noble preface entitled *The Translators to the Reader*.

The translators were directed to take the rendering of the Bishops' Bible as their basis, and were advised also to consult the following versions : Tindale's, Matthew's, Coverdale's, Whitchurch's (i.e. the Great Bible), and the Geneva. The last exerted very considerable influence on their work ; and next to it the Rheims New Testament—though not mentioned—contributed appreciably to the changes introduced (see No. 134). (The Douai Old Testament appeared too late to be used.) But we must recognise that this Bible, like all the great English versions from 1537 down to 1885, was built on the sure foundations laid for all time by Tindale and Coverdale. Besides the Hebrew and Greek originals, reference was made to Tremellius, Beza, and earlier Latin versions, and also to the vernacular translations of Spain, France, and Italy. According to Westcott (p. 279), the revision of the New Testament was a simpler work than that of the Old, and may be generally described as a careful correction of the Bishops' version by the Greek text, with the aid of Beza's, the Geneva, and the Rheims versions.

No evidence exists that King James' version received any definite ecclesiastical or legislative sanction. But it won its way by sheer merit, until gradually it displaced even the Geneva Bible in popular affection, and established itself as the sole recognised version of the Scriptures in English. Under the Commonwealth some steps were taken in 1653, and again in 1657, towards a fresh translation, but without result (*cf.* Westcott, *History*, p. 124). From about the middle of the seventeenth century on to the appearance of the Revised Bible of 1881–5, King James' version reigned without a rival.

From the scanty data which survive it appears that most of the translators gave their services gratuitously, although the final committee received an allowance while at work in London, and some were perhaps rewarded, as the King had originally suggested, by preferment. The completed work was published by Robert Barker, the King's printer. (See below.)

Cardwell (*Documentary Annals*, vol. ii, pp. 84–8 and 140–6) prints three important documents dealing with the genesis of this version. For other details see Anthony Walker's *Life of John Bois* (1561–1644), one of the translators, in Harl. MSS. 7053, cited by Arber (*Transcript*, vol. iv, pp. 11–2), and Anderson (vol. ii, p. 381) ; and compare Peck's *Desiderata Curiosa*, 1779, pp. 325–342.

Walker states that during the final revision Bois and Downes, the Cambridge representatives, with their 'four fellow labourers,' 'went daily to Stationers' Hall, and in three quarters of a year fulfilled their task. All which time they received daily 30$^{s.}$ each of them by the week from the Company of Stationers, though before they had nothing.'

A reference to the original manuscript of this version occurs in the anonymous and undated tract (printed about June 1660), entitled *The London Printers Lamentacon, or, the Press opprest, and ouerprest*, which contains a vehement attack on the three Republican printers, Newcomb, Field, and Hills. The following passage is cited from Arber's *Transcript*, vol. iii, pp. 27–8 : '. . . But we cannot as yet pass ouer his Maiesties good friends, Hills and Feild (take them *coniunctim* or *divisim* :) . . . Have they not invaded and still do intrude upon his Maiesties Royall Priviledge, Prærogatiue and Præeminence ; And by the pusillanimous Cowardize and insignificant Compact of Master Christopher Barker, and another of his name, and (not without probable suspicion,) by the consent and connivance of Master John Bill (though he was artificially defeated in his expectations of profit;) Have they not obtained, (and now keep in their actuall possession) the Manuscript Copy of the last Translation of the *holy Bible* in English (attested with the hands of the Venerable and learned Translators in King *James* his time) ever since 6 March 1655. And thereupon by colour of an unlawfull and enforced entrance in the *Stationers* Registry, printed and published ever since for the most part in severall Editions of *Bibles* (consisting of great numbers) such egregious Blasphemies and damnable Errata's, as have corrupted the pure Fountain, and rendred Gods holy Word contemptible to multitudes of the people at home, and a *Ludibrium* to all the Adversaries of our Religion.' (*Cf.* W. Kilburne's tract, *Dangerous Errors* . . ., 1659, *ad fin.*)

This manuscript perhaps perished in the Great Fire of 1666. Two more allusions to the same manuscript are quoted by H. R. Plomer in a paper entitled ' The King's Printing House under the Stuarts' (*Library*, new series, vol. 2, 1901, pp. 353-375) :—(1) during a quarrel about the copyright 'a certain William Ball in a pamphlet of 1651 declared that the sole right of printing of the Bible was Matthew Barker's, in regard that his father [R. Barker] paid for the amended or corrected translation £3,500 " by reason whereof the translated copy did of right belong to him " ' ; (2) another quarrel between Roger Norton and C. Barker the third concerned '. . . the moiety of a manuscript of a Bible in English called the Bible of K. James his translation.'

By tracing the protracted law-suits between the Barkers and their rivals, H. R. Plomer (see above) has explained the extraordinary variations in the imprints of Bibles during the seventeenth century, and has shown who in each successive period actually held the office of King's Printer. Many editions which bear the name 'Barker' must have been produced by other printers.

DESCRIPTION. Eighteen preliminary leaves: title (in the centre of an engraving), verso blank, Dedication : *To the most high and mightie Prince, Iames* . . . —3 pp., *The Translators to the Reader*—11 pp., Kalendar—6 ff., *An Almanacke for xxxix. yeeres* (1603–41) with notes *Of the Golden number* etc.—1 p., *To finde Easter for euer*—1 p., *The Table and Kalender, expressing the order of Psalmes and Lessons to be said at Morning and Euening prayer throughout the yeere, except certaine proper feasts, as the rules following more plainely declare* (with tables of Proper Lessons etc.)—5 pp., *The names and order of all the Bookes* . . . —1 p. The text, divided into two parts : (1) O. T. and Apocrypha, A 1 to Ccccc 6 *b* (two pages, Bbb 3 *b* and Lll 6 *b*, are blank); (2) N. T., with title : *The | Newe | Testament of | our Lord and Sauiour | Iesvs Christ. | Newly Translated out of | the Originall Greeke : and with | the former Translations diligently | compared and reuised, by his | Maiesties speciall Com- | mandement. | Imprinted | at London by Robert | Barker, Printer to the | Kings most Excellent | Maiestie. | Anno Dom. 1611* (within woodcut border), verso blank, text—A 2 to Aa 6 *b*.

Signatures : A⁶ B² C⁶ D⁴, A-Z⁶ Aa-Zz⁶ Aaa-Zzz⁶ Aaaa-Zzzz⁶ Aaaaa-Ccccc⁶, A-Z⁶ Aa⁶; 732 ff. Leaves not numbered. Double columns, with 59 lines to the full column. Head-lines, chapter-contents, marginal references, and words not in the original, are printed in roman type ; alternative and other renderings, and a very few notes, in the margins, are in italics. The whole printed page is enclosed within rules. No Prologues, or expository notes.

The *Genealogies of Holy Scriptvres* and a Map are inserted before Genesis. In one variety of the former, the first page contains a large cut of the royal arms and the words *Cum Priuilegio Regiæ Maiestatis*, on verso is a preface *To the Christian Reader*, the Genealogies—pp. 1 to 34. Signatures : A–C⁶. The Map, *Begun by Mr. John More continued and finished by John Speede Anno Domini 1611*, fills two pages, on verso of which is printed *An Alphabeticall Table of the Land of Canaan, and the borders adioyning : the diuersitie of names obserued ; the texts of Scriptures quoted ; and the Tribes, Cities, Townes, and places set in their receiued graduations*. These Genealogies and Map were compiled by John Speed (1552?–1629), the historian, apparently at the suggestion, and with the assistance, of Hugh Broughton (1549-1612), the eminent Hebraist. Speed obtained a patent for ten years, dated 31 Oct. 1610, giving him the right to print and insert them in every edition of the new version of the Bible. Speed's prices were fixed : large folio, two shillings ; small folio, eighteen pence ; quarto, twelve pence ; octavo, six pence. (*Cf.* Fry, *A Description* . . ., p. 32, and pp. 40-1.) Thus, though they really formed no part of the book, the Genealogies and Map are generally found in copies of the early editions of King James' Bible. Several varieties of both are enumerated by Fry.

The general title is a fine copper-plate engraving, inscribed *C. Boel fecit in Richmont*, and representing : above—the Sacred Name יהוה, the Holy Dove, and the Agnus Dei, and a group of Apostles, with St. Matthew seated on the extreme left, and St. Mark on the extreme right ; on the left side—Moses, and on the right side—Aaron ; below, in the centre—the pelican in her piety, on the left—St. Luke, and on the right—St. John. The N. T. title-border is a wood-engraving, representing : above—the Sacred Name, the Agnus Dei and the Holy Dove, and SS. Matthew and Mark ; on the left side—the tents of the twelve tribes ; on the right side—the twelve Apostles ; and below—the Lamb slain, and SS. Luke and John ; at the bottom is a tablet bearing the words *Cum Priuilegio*. (This border was used for the general title in a few copies of the folio Bishops' Bible of 1602, No. 206.) A few copies have a general title with this woodcut border.

No illustrations (except a few cuts in the Genealogies) ; but many head-pieces, vignettes etc. and ornamental initials, some of the latter (e.g. that before Romans) resembling those used in folio editions of the Bishops' Bible.

THE 'HE' AND 'SHE' BIBLES.—The intricate typographical problems connected with the early editions of King James' version are discussed at length in the following : F. Fry's *A Description of . . . the Editions, in large folio, of the Authorized Version* . . (1865), F. H. A. Scrivener's *The Authorized Edition of the English Bible* . . .

(1884), an article in the *Athenæum* (20 Sep. 1884), a pamphlet by W. E. Smith entitled *A Study of the Great 'She' Bible* (reprinted from the *Library*, 1890), and R. Lovett's *The English Bible in the John Rylands Library* (pp. 246-253).

It is recognised that from 1611 to 1614 there are two distinct series of editions in various sizes, which differ throughout in many minor points of typography, and are generally distinguished by the names 'He' Bibles and 'She' Bibles, from their respective readings in Ruth iii. 15 . . . *he went into the city*, and . . . *she went into the city*. The suggested explanation of this dualism is that the printing was at first carried on in two separate offices, in order to facilitate rapid production; and that two standard copies were used, one of which had received a certain amount of additional correction from the press editors.

Bibliographers generally agree that the folio 'He' Bible of 1611 is the first impression of this version. Scrivener argues keenly for the priority in printing (though not necessarily in publication) of the folio 'She' Bible of 1613,11. But Smith shows that inferences drawn from apparent corrections or corruptions of the text are too precarious to be conclusive. He makes a minute comparison of the varieties in the sizes of the ornamental initials, and in the spaces between the chapters, throughout the first half of the volume, and proves by this method that the 'He' Bible was undoubtedly the earlier of the two.

For the variations in copies of the 'She' Bible of 1613,11, see below, No. 246.

The following large type folio editions of this Bible closely resemble one another:—
(1) 1611 (No. 240); (2) 1613,11 (No. 246); (3) 1617 (No. 273); (4) 1634 (No. 376); (5) 1640,39 (No. 421). These agree so closely that the corresponding leaves practically always end with the same word, and are thus interchangeable. Hence many copies of these large editions are mixed.

This is a 'He' Bible; with the text styled 'A' by Smith in his pamphlet cited above. In Exodus xiv. 10 three lines are repeated: this passage is correctly printed in the 'She' Bible of 1613,11. Other special readings of this edition are: Gen. x. 16, *Emorite* for *Amorite*; Exod. xxxviii. 11, *hoopes* for *hookes*; Lev. xiii. 56, *plaine* for *plague*; headline on Iiii 6 a, *Anocrynha* for *Apocrypha*; etc.

A verbatim reprint of this folio was issued by the Oxford University Press in 1833.

¶ 428 × 279 mm. A large copy, with original rough edges to some of the leaves; printed on unusually thick paper. Fry's 'Standard Copy of the first issue, 1611.'
The Genealogies represent the variety distinguished by Fry as No. 2. The Map has the sea unshaded, and does not bear R. Elstrack's name as engraver. [F. F.]

—— Another copy.

403 × 260 mm. Imperfect: wanting the general title, and five following leaves. A facsimile of Boel's title is inserted.
The Genealogies—Fry's No. 3. No Map.

240.

1611. B. f°. See 1612 and 1613.

NOTE. ALL BOOKS AFTER THIS DATE ARE EDITIONS OF KING JAMES' VERSION, EXCEPT SUCH AS ARE OTHERWISE DESCRIBED.

1612. The | Bible | that is, | The holy Scriptures | contained . . . Imprinted at London by | Robert Barker, Printer to the | Kinges most excellent | Maiestie. | Cum privilegio.

1611,12. f°.

Geneva version; with Tomson's revised New Testament, and Junius' Revelation.

N. T. title dated 1611, and colophon 1612.
A close reprint of the folio edition of 1607; with the tables ending on Fffff 4 b.
Signatures etc., as before; 590 ff.

¶ 328 × 206 mm. Imperfect: wanting ff. 93 and 94 in the O. T.
With Speed's Genealogies and Map; and Metrical Psalms (1618).
Contemporary binding of brown leather, stamped G. H.; with central and corner o
ments in gold, and goffered edges.

—— Another copy.

294 × 193 mm. Imperfect: wanting preliminary leaves.
With Speed's Genealogies and Map; Prayer Book (1611); and Metrical Psalms (1612).

241.

1612. The | Holy | Bible, | Conteyning the Old Testament | and the New : | Newly Translated out of the Originall | tongues : & with the former Translations | diligently compared and reuised by his | Maiesties speciall Comandement. | Appointed to be read in Churches. | Imprinted at London by Robert | Barker Printer to the Kings | most Excellent Maiestie. | Anno Dom. 1612.

4°.

The first quarto edition of King James' version; printed in roman type.

The N. T. title omits the words *Appointed* . . .
According to Scrivener, this edition closely follows the text of the folio Bible of 1611; e.g. Gen. x. 16, *Emorite*; Ruth iii. 15, *hee*. It corrects, however, some mistakes of the first edition: e.g. Exod. xiv. 10 and Mark vii. 4, *marg*.
The three quarto editions of 1612, 1613,12, and 1613, although quite distinct, generally read together page for page.

DESCRIPTION. Eight preliminary leaves: title (engraved), verso blank, *The Epistle Dedicatorie*—3 pp., *To the Reader*—9 pp., *The names and order of all the Bookes* . . . —1 p., 1 p. blank. The text: O. T. ends on Ggg 4 *b* (Job ends on Kk 4 *a*, verso blank); Apocrypha end on Ttt 6 *b*; N. T. (with title dated 1612, within woodcut border, verso blank) ends on [M 8] *a*, with colophon dated 1612, verso blank.
Signatures: A⁸, A–Z⁸ Aa–Zz⁸ Aaa–Zzz⁸ [A]–[M]⁸; 656 ff. Leaves not numbered.
Text printed in double columns; each page enclosed within rules.
The engraved general title (signed *Iaspar. Isac. fecit.*) is an adaptation of C. Boel's design of 1611. The N. T. title is enclosed within the woodcut border with heart-shaped centre used in so many quarto editions of the Geneva Bible.
Heading on [H 5]*b* : *To the Galaitans.*

¶ 225 × 168 mm.
With Genealogies and Map.

[F. F.]

—— Another copy.

215 × 158 mm.
With Genealogies and Map.

242.

1612. The | Holy Bible, | Conteining the | Olde Testament, | and the New. | Newly Translated out of the Originall | Tongues : and with the former Translations dili- | gently compared and reuised, by his Maie- | sties speciall Commandement. | Imprinted at Lon- | don by Robert Barker | Printer to the Kings most Ex- | cellent Maiestie. | Anno 1612.

8°.

The first octavo edition of King James' version; printed in roman type.
In general appearance this and subsequent issues resemble the octavo editions of the Geneva Bible. (*Cf.* No. 250.)

A close reprint of the folio of 1611, reproducing its special readings, e.g. Gen. x. 16 *Emorite*, Ruth iii. 15 *he*, and even the mistake in Exod. xiv. 10; though some errors are corrected, e.g. Mark vii. 4 *marg*.
The words *Appointed* . . . are regularly omitted from both titles in the early octavo editions, down to 1630.

DESCRIPTION. Two preliminary leaves: Title (within woodcut border), on verso a cut of the royal arms, Dedication—1 p., list of books—1 p. The text: O. T., A 3 to Qq 5 *b*;

Apocrypha end on Bbb 5 *b*; N. T. (with title dated 1612, within border, verso blank) ends on Ooo 4 *b* with colophon dated 1612.

Signatures: A–Z⁸ Aa–Zz⁸ Aaa–Nnn⁸ Ooo⁴; 476 ff. Leaves not numbered. Each page is enclosed within rules.

Both titles have the common border representing the four Evangelists, the twelve Tribes, the twelve Apostles, etc. The cut of the royal arms has a crown at the top with roses on one side and thistles on the other. A small cut of Adam and Eve occurs before Genesis.

Gen. i. 2 *voide*; Rev. xxii. 15 *scorners* for *sorcerers*. A 4 is signed A 2.

¶ 167 × 109 mm. General title repaired.
With Genealogies and Map (supplied from another copy).
In original binding with brass corners, etc. [F. F.]

243.

—— ANOTHER EDITION.

This differs throughout from the preceding, e.g. Ruth iii. 15 *she*, and the mistake in Exod. xiv. 10 does not occur. It was apparently printed from the folio of 1613,11 (No. 246). The titleleaves appear to be the same, though their followers differ.

The mistake *scorners* for *sorcerers* occurs in Rev. xxii. 15. Gen. i. 2 *voyde*. A 4 is correctly signed.

¶ 162 × 107 mm. Wants general title. The title supplied consists of a genuine border taken from a copy of another edition, with a facsimile centre. [F. F.]

244.

1612. The | New Testament | of our Lord and Sauiour | Iesvs Christ. | Newly Translated out of the Origi- | nall Greeke : And with the former | Translations diligently com- | pared and reuised, | By his Maiesties speciall commandement. | Imprinted at London by | Robert Barker, Printer to | the Kings most Excel- | lent Maiestie. | 1612.

4°. 𝔅. 𝔏.

The first quarto New Testament of King James' version.

A close reprint of the text of the folio of 1611, though obvious mistakes like Mark vii. 4 *marg.* are corrected. Taking the passages quoted by Scrivener on p. 206 and p. 213 of his book *The Authorized Edition* . . ., we find that in every case except one (Luke x. 36) this New Testament agrees with the 1611 edition against that of 1613,11.

DESCRIPTION. One preliminary leaf: title (within border), on verso the list of books. The text, pp. 1 to 686, ending on Vv 8 *b*, with colophon dated 1612.

Signatures: A–Z⁸ Aa–Vv⁸; 344 ff. The pages are numbered throughout the text, which is printed in a black-letter type like that used in the folio Bible of 1613 (No. 249), with long lines. The headings, chapter-contents, marginal references, etc. are in roman type.

The woodcut title-border resembles that used in certain editions of the Geneva and Bishops' Bibles, with the emblems of the Evangelists and figures of *Fides* and *Hvmilitas*; a new block of the royal arms has been inserted at the top.

John xix. 19: *tile* for *title*; but generally the edition is correctly printed.

¶ 183 × 136 mm.
With Prayer Book (1620), Great Bible Psalter (1622), and Metrical Psalms (1621).
[F. F.]

245.

[The earliest separate New Testament of King James' version was a duodecimo edition printed in 1611. See Lea Wilson, pp. 201-2.]

1612. B. 4°. See 1613.

B. 8°. See 1613.

1613. The | Holy | Bible,| Conteyning the Old Testa-| ment, and the New : | Newly Translated out of | the Originall Tongues : and with | the former Translations diligently | compared and reuised, by his | Maiesties speciall Com- | mandement. | Appointed to be read in Churches. | Imprinted | at London by Robert | Barker, Printer to the | Kings most Excellent | Maiestie. | Anno Dom. 1611.

1613,11. f°. 𝕭. 𝕷.

Fry's ' first edition, second issue, without reprints,' of King James' Bible. Others more correctly style it the ' second folio edition, 1613,11,' inasmuch as it deserves to be reckoned a distinct edition.

Commonly known as the ' Great She Bible.' The general title is usually dated 1613, though the N. T. title bears the date 1611. Probably the greater part of the book was printed in 1611, but the publication, for some reason or other, was delayed till 1613. Scrivener supposes that this delay was due to the incorrectness of the edition ; Smith suggests an accident in the printing-office, which destroyed a large number of sheets (see below).

The words *Appointed to be read in Churches* appear on the N. T. title, as well as on the general title.

DESCRIPTION. Eighteen preliminary leaves, containing the same matter arranged in the same order as in the first edition. Text as before. The general title is enclosed within the woodcut border used for the N. T. title in the first edition. The N. T. title reads : The | Newe | Testament of | our Lord and Sauiour | Iesvs Christ.| Newly Translated out of | the Originall Greeke : And with | the former Translations diligently | compared and reuised, By his | Maiesties speciall Com- | mandement. | Appointed to be read in Churches. | Imprinted | at London by Robert | Barker, Printer to the | Kings most Excellent | Maiestie | Anno Dom. *1611* ; it is enclosed within the same woodcut border.

Signatures : A⁴ B⁴ C⁶ D⁴, A–Z⁶ . . . etc. ; 732 ff., as in No. 240.

This edition contains a general title with a woodcut border (like that occurring in a very few copies of No. 240), which as a rule is dated 1613. This date, however, has been ingeniously altered by pen into 1611 in very many copies. J. Lenox even doubted whether any copies of this Bible existed, having a general title which had been originally dated 1611. But Fry mentions, besides the copy in this Library, two others – at St. John's College, Cambridge, and in the B. M.— both with this rare title. Scrivener (*The Authorized Edition* . . ., pp. 9, 10) argues for the priority of this ' She ' Bible from the apparent fact that it adopts a woodcut title-border previously used in some copies of the Bishops' Bible of 1602 (No. 206), and never has Boel's engraved title, which almost invariably appears in the ' He ' Bible of 1611. But his suggestion that this woodcut border was employed as a makeshift, while the engraving was being finished, loses its force when we find the same woodcut a favourite in later editions.

Ruth iii. 15, *she.* A remarkable error occurs in Matt. xxvi. 36, *Judas* appearing for *Jesus*; sometimes a pasted slip corrects the mistake. The initial P at Ps. cxii. contains Walsingham's crest. In the list of books three lines are printed in red ink in this edition ; and *1. Corinthians* and *2. Corinthians* occur for *1. Chronicles* and *2. Chronicles.*

FRY'S REPRINTS.—We must notice here the curious phenomenon, first investigated by Fry, which characterises this particular edition. About one third of the sheets exist in two different forms. ' Every copy . . . is made up of its own individual combination from these two sets of sheets. It is hard to find two exactly identical throughout, though a large group are very nearly so.' (Smith, *A Study* . . ., p. 13.) On some obscure ground, Fry selected one of his own copies as a ' standard,' and classed as ' reprints ' all leaves found in other copies which varied from the corresponding leaves in his ' standard.' But, since hardly one of the many copies which he describes agrees with his ' standard ' at all closely, this classification appears quite arbitrary. Smith has discovered a more satisfactory ' standard ' in a certain type to which thirteen of the copies examined by himself, and seventeen in Fry's No. 2 Table, closely conform. This he styles the ' B ' text, and all the variants from this text he calls ' C.' A table at the end of his pamphlet gives tests for distinguishing the different mixed leaves, and indicates those which are styled by Fry ' reprints,' and those which the writer himself judges to be ' posterior.' In conclusion, Smith considers ' that (on account of a fire or for other unexplained reason) a large reprint took place before any copies were completed, and that then the prior and posterior sheets were so mixed that no copies were made up with all the sheets prior.'

¶ 402 × 274 mm.
The general title is dated 1611. Fry's MS. note reads: 'This is my Standard Copy of the second issue without reprints . . . This copy is perfect, every leaf correct and genuine.' Smith styles the text 'a mixture of B and C.'
The Genealogies—Fry's No. 6. The Map is unshaded, and does not bear R. Elstrack's name. [F. F.]

—— Another copy.

Fry's 'second issue, with reprints.' For a full description of these 'reprints' or variant leaves, see Fry's *A Description* . . . But compare the note above.
Fry's MS. note reads: 'This is No. 5 in Table No. 2 in my work on these Bibles. This is a very valuable standard copy, the one I have used in all my comparisons.' Smith describes the text as 'purely C.'

406 × 264 mm. Imperfect: wanting the general title, which is supplied in facsimile (with genuine border), dated 1611. The follower to the title is that distinguished by Smith as No. 2.
The Genealogies—Fry's No. 23. The Map has the sea unshaded, and does not bear R. Elstrack's name. [F. F.]

—— Another copy.

The general title is dated 1613, and differs very slightly in the letterpress from that dated 1611, e.g. no comma after *reuised, excellent* for *Excellent*, etc.
Fry's MS. note reads: 'This is a copy of the first edition, second issue with reprints, published with the 1613 title and follower. This copy is No. 3 in Table No. 2 in my work on these Bibles. Nos. 3 and 5 contain all the reprints I have found, except eight leaves in other copies; these I have placed [with two others] in front of this copy . . . This is one of my standard volumes—what I use for all my comparisons, and very valuable;' adding that he was probably mistaken in stating in his book that Eee 2 and 5 were reprints. The follower to the title is Smith's No. 3. Smith describes the text as 'purely C.'
The Genealogies—Fry's No. 7. The Map has the sea shaded, and the words *Renold Elstrack sculpsit* added at the bottom near the circle bearing J. Speed's name.

409 × 265 mm. The reprints inserted at the beginning are: L 1 and 6, Ii 3 and 4, Bbb 1 and 6, Qqq 2 and 5, Xxxx 2 and 5. [F. F.]

—— Another copy.

The first title is dated 1613; with follower No. 3.
According to Smith's tests, the text is C with a slight admixture of B.
The Genealogies—Fry's No. 14. The Map has the sea shaded, and bears the inscription *Renold Elstrack sculpsit.*

410 × 275 mm.
In red leather binding, stamped on the covers with the initials C S, surmounted by a ducal coronet. According to a MS. note by a former owner, Granville Sharp, the book is supposed to have belonged to Charles Seymour, Duke of Somerset (1662–1748).

—— Another copy.

No. 29 in Fry's List. Title dated 1613, with follower Smith's No. 2.
Smith styles it 'a C Bible.'
Genealogies— Fry's No. 7. No Map.

406 × 268 mm. Contains some leaves from the 'He' edition of 1611; including G 1, with the repetition in Exod. xiv. 10. The title and its follower are kept in an envelope inside the cover, to show that they are genuinely joined together.
In seventeenth-century binding. [F. F.]

246.

1613. The Holy Bible . . .

R. Barker : London. 1613,12. 4°.

Closely resembles the first quarto of 1612.

Dated 1613 on the general title, but 1612 on the N. T. title, and in the colophon. A MS. note by Fry gives the results of his collation of 23 copies of this edition, with those dated 1612

and those dated 1613 on both titles. This is a distinct edition, differing in nearly every leaf from the other two.
Both titles omit the words *Appointed* . . .
Eight preliminary leaves; text, ending on [M 8] *a*; etc. as before.
The titles have the woodcut border with heart-shaped centre.
Ruth iii. 15, *she.* Gen. i. 11, *bring foorth.*

¶ 214 × 155 mm.
With Genealogies and Map. [F. F.]

247.

1613. The Holy Bible . . .
R. Barker: London. 1612,13. 8°.

The general title is dated 1612, but the N. T. title and colophon 1613.
Distinct from the octavos of 1612 (Nos. 243 and 244). According to Fry's collation, it agrees in very few sheets with the edition of 1613 (No. 252).

DESCRIPTION. Two preliminary leaves, as before. Text: O. T., A 3 to Nn 7 *b*; Apocrypha end on Yy 3 *b*; N. T. ends on Kkk 8 *a*, with colophon, verso blank.
Signatures: A–Z⁸ Aa–Zz⁸ Aaa–Kkk⁸; 448 ff. Leaves not numbered. No rules round each page.
Title-borders, and cut before Genesis, as in the 1612 editions.
Gen. i. 2, *void, darknesse*; Ruth, iii. 15, *she*; Matt. i. 23, *foorth.* Rev. xxii. 15 is correct.

¶ 160 × 104 mm. In two volumes.
With Metrical Psalms (1613). [F. F.]

—— Another copy.

158 × 109 mm. General title repaired.
Inserted are some MS. notes by Fry, giving the results of his collations, which show that this copy contains some variant leaves. These may be reprinted leaves; or possibly they belong to another issue, making this a mixed copy. [F. F.]

248.

1613. The | Holy | Bible, | Conteyning the Old Testa- | ment, and the New: | Newly translated out of | the Originall Tongues: and with | the former Translations diligently | compared and reuised by his | Maiesties speciall Com-|mandemente, | Appointed to be read in Churches. | Imprinted | at London by Robert⌋ Barker, Printer to the | Kings most excellent | Maiestie. | Anno Dom: 1613.

f°. 𝕭. 𝕷.

The true 1613 folio edition of King James' Bible; easily distinguishable from the other large folio editions by its smaller type.

A very few copies are found with Boel's engraved title of 1611 (see below).

DESCRIPTION. Eighteen preliminary leaves: title (within woodcut border), verso blank, Dedication—3 pp., Preface—11 pp., Kalendar etc.—10 ff. The text: O. T., A 1–Ggg 2 *b*; Apocrypha end on Ttt 5 *a*, verso blank; N. T., with title: *The Newe Testament . . . Appointed to be read in Churches . . . 1613* (within woodcut border), verso blank, text—Vvv 1 to Nnnn 4 *a*, verso blank.
Signatures: A⁴ B⁴ C⁶ D⁴, A–Z⁶ Aa–Zz⁶ Aaa–Zzz⁶ Aaaa–Mmmm⁶ Nnnn⁴; 508 ff. Leaves not numbered. The preliminary leaves are set up as in the other large folio editions, but the text is printed in smaller type with 72 instead of 59 lines to the full column.
Title-border—the woodcut representing the twelve tribes, etc.
For a collation of the text of this edition with the folio of 1611, see the Oxford reprint (1833) of the latter book. Variations occur in about 400 places, and involve many serious mistakes, e.g. vv. 13 and 14 omitted in Ecclus. xvi; 1 Cor. xi. 17: *I praise you* (*not* omitted), etc.

¶ 407 × 274 mm.
Genealogies—Fry's No. 13. No Map.
Bound in seventeenth-century covers. An iron chain is attached, which apparently had served to fasten a copy of the Great Bible to a pillar or lectern in some church.　　　[F. F.]

—— Another copy.

A remarkable copy, containing Boel's engraved title, dated 1611, with Smith's follower No. 3. These two leaves still joined together are kept separate in a pocket inside the cover to show that they were originally thus issued. (See Fry's *Description* . . ., p. 27.)

409 × 270 mm.
Genealogies—Fry's No. 17. Map—with unshaded sea.　　　[F. F.]

249.

1613.　The Holy Bible . . .
　　　　　　　　　　　　　R. Barker: London. 1613. 4°. 𝕭.𝕷.

The first black-letter quarto edition of King James' version.
This and many subsequent issues were produced in close imitation of those black-letter quarto editions of the Geneva Bible which had proved so popular.

Apparently a close reprint of the folio of 1611. Gen. x. 16, *Emorite*, Ruth iii. 15 *he*, etc. Both titles omit the words *Appointed* . . .

DESCRIPTION. Eight preliminary leaves (in roman type): title (within border), verso blank, Dedication—3 pp., Preface—9 pp., list of books—1 p., 1 p. blank. Text: O. T. ends on Ss 6 *a*, verso blank; Apocrypha end on Eee 2 *b*; N. T. (with title within border, verso blank) ends on Sss 8 *a*, with colophon dated 1613, verso blank.
　　Signatures: A⁸, A–Z⁸ Aa–Zz⁸ Aaa–Sss (no Hhh)⁸; 512 ff. Leaves not numbered. Headlines and marginal references in roman type; chapter-contents and marginal readings in italics.
　　Both titles have the border with heart-shaped centre.

¶ 218 × 161 mm.
With Genealogies and Map; and R. F. H.'s *Two right profitable and fruitfull Concordances* . . . (1611,13), so often issued with quarto Geneva Bibles.　　　[F. F.]

—— Another copy.

215 × 159 mm.
A second copy of the leaf containing the list of books is bound in at the end.

250.

1613.　The Holy Bible . . .
　　　　　　　　　　　　　R. Barker: London. 1613. 4°.

Closely resembles the quartos of 1612 and 1613,12 (*q.v.*), but a distinct edition.

Dated 1613 on both titles and in the colophon.
Preliminary leaves, text, etc., as before.
Both titles have the woodcut border with the heart-shaped centre. The N. T. title omits the words *Appointed* . . .
　　Heading on [A 2] *b*: *S. Suke.*
　　Ruth iii. 15 *she.* Gen. i. 11 *bring forth.*

¶ 225 × 165 mm.
According to Fry's MS. note this is a 'standard' copy of the 1613 quarto edition. Four leaves only belong to the 1612 edition, but four 'correct' 1613 leaves are inserted.
With Genealogies and Map.　　　[F. F.]

—— Another copy.

This, like the above, has the four leaves which, according to Fry, really belong to the 1612 edition.

208 × 153 mm. Imperfect: wanting general title and following leaf.
With Genealogies and Map.
With Prayer Book (1615), and Metrical Psalms (1615).

ENGLISH 143

—— Another copy.

208 × 148 mm.
According to Fry's note, this is a strangely mixed copy. The bulk of the book belongs to this edition of 1613. The general title is dated 1614, but differs from that in the 1614,15 quarto (No. 263), which begins *The Bible* . . . Six of the preliminary leaves belong to the 1612 edition. And the N. T. title and following leaf are the same as in the quarto of 1613,12.
With Genealogies and Map.
With Prayer Book (1613), and Metrical Psalms (1615). [F. F.]
251.

1613. The Holy Bible . . .
R. Barker: London. 1613. 8°.

Closely resembles the edition of 1612,13 (No. 248), with the text ending on Kkk 8 a. A MS. note by Fry states that this is the true 1613 octavo edition, and differs from that of 1612,13 in every part except in the sheets Z, BB, Iii and Kkk.
Gen. i. 2 *void, darknesse*; Ruth iii. 15 *she*; Matt. i. 23 *forth*.

¶ 163 × 103 mm.
With Genealogies and Map. [F. F.]
252.

1613. The New Testament . . . Translated out of the Greeke by Theod. Beza, And Englished by L. T. . . .
R. Barker: London. 1613. 16°.
Geneva version; Tomson's revision.

DESCRIPTION. Title (within border), on verso list of books. The text, A 2 to Gg 8 b.
Signatures: A–Z⁸ Aa–Gg⁸; 240 ff.
John i. 1: *In the beginning was the Word, and that Word* . . .
The title-border resembles that used in certain of Barker's editions; containing at the top the royal arms and two symbolical female figures; and below, a lion and a dragon. An ornament at the head of the first page of text contains roses and thistles, Another at the end contains two fleurs-de-lys.

¶ 106 × 72 mm.
Elaborately embroidered binding; central panels of very fine needlework in coloured silks, representing (1) The Virgin and Child, (2) St. John the Baptist; the borders worked in purl and silver thread; all on a ground of purple velvet; goffered edges.
With *The Whole Booke of Davids Psalmes, Both in Prose and Meetre* . . . (1617). (See No. 279.) [F. F.]

—— Another copy.

102 × 67 mm. Imperfect: wanting title and 8 ff. of text. A fictitious title, dated 1598, has been inserted. [F. F.]
253.

1613. The | New Testament | of our Sauiour Iesus | Christ . . . Imprinted at Lon- | don by Robert Barker, Prin- | ter to the Kings most Excel- | lent Maiestie. 1613.
8°. 𝔅. 𝔏.
Bishops' version.

A close reprint of the edition of 1606.
Title in black and red; within the same border as before, not touched with red. The colophon on Nn 4 b is dated 1613. The second sheet is signed [A].
X 5 a, 1st line: *worthinesse* . . . *in*.

¶ 140 × 87 mm. Imperfect: wanting the eighth preliminary leaf, and 18 ff. of text.
[F. F.]
254.

1613. B. 4°. See 1614.

1613? (The New Testament.)

Qu. *R. Barker : London.* 1618? 12°.

Geneva version ; Tomson's revision.

This small 12° New Testament closely resembles an edition printed in 1609 (B. M. copy, 3053. aa. 4). It has the same reading in John i. 1 as the 16° edition of 1613, and may perhaps be placed under that date. Lea Wilson (p. 202) mentions an edition of 1613, described as 24°, which may correspond to this.

DESCRIPTION. [Title.] Text, A 2 to Y 6 *b*.
Signatures: A–X^{12} Y^6; 258 ff. Chapter-contents, but no marginal matter.

¶ 102 × 51 mm. Imperfect: wanting title.
With Prayer-Book (? date). [F. F.]

255.

1614. The Bible . . . With . . . Annotations . . . And . . . Concordance . . . Imprinted at London by Robert Barker . . . 1614.

1614,13. 4°. 𝔅. 𝔏.

Geneva version.

The N. T. title and the Concordance are dated 1613.
A close reprint of the edition of 1605. Text ends on fo. 554 (really 552); and Concordance on L 2.

¶ 212 × 156 mm.
With Speed's Genealogies and Map. [F. F.]

—— Another copy.

220 × 163 mm.
With Prayer Book (? date), and Metrical Psalms (1614).

256.

1614. The Holy Bible . . .

R. Barker : London. 1613,14. 4°. 𝔅. 𝔏.

Closely resembles, but is quite distinct from, the quarto of 1613 (No. 250). General title dated 1613 ; N. T. dated 1614 on title, and in colophon.
Both titles omit the words *Appointed* . . .
Text ends on Sss 8 *a*.
Ruth iii. 15 *she*, Is. xxviii. 9 *beasts* for *breasts*.

¶ 213 × 159 mm.
With Concordance (1615). [F. F.]

—— Another copy.

The N. T. only. Bound up with an O. T. of 1619 (No. 283).

257.

1614. The Holy Bible . . .

R. Barker : London. 1614. 8°.

Text ends on Kkk 8 *a*.
Ruth iii. 15 *she*.
Three issues of this date are found, which differ slightly in various parts. No doubt, as in the case of the quartos, many of these octavos were issued in a mixed state, so that it is practically impossible to distinguish between all the varying editions. (See note on No. 333.)

A.
Prov. xxx. 4, *winde, the waters*.

¶ 161 × 102 mm.
With Genealogies and Map.
With Metrical Psalms (1615). [F. F.]

258.

ENGLISH

—— ANOTHER EDITION.

B.
Prov. xxx. 4, *wind, the waters.*

¶ 163 × 110 mm.
With Genealogies and Map.
With Prayer Book (1615), and Metrical Psalms (1617). [F. F.]

—— Another copy.

The N. T. is dated 1615; the rest of the book is the B variety of 1614.
160 × 102 mm. Wants one leaf (Hhh 1). [F. F.]
259.

—— ANOTHER EDITION.

C.
Prov. xxx. 4, *wind, ye waters.*

¶ 160 × 105 mm. [F. F.]
260.

1614. (The New Testament.)
R. Barker: London. 1614. 8°. 𝕭. 𝕷.

Bishops' version.

A close reprint of the edition of 1606.
The colophon on Nn 4 b reads: *Imprinted at London by Robert Barker, Printer to the Kings most Excellent Maiestie. 1614.* The second sheet is signed [A].
X 5 a, 1st line: *fession . . . that*; 5th line: *. . . shalbe . . .*

¶ 143 × 89 mm. Imperfect: wanting the first sheet. [F. F.]
261.

1614. The Third Part of the Bible, (after some division) conteining fiue excellent Bookes . . .
R. Barker: London. 1614. 16°.

Geneva version.

A reprint of the little book printed in 1580, and again in 1583.

DESCRIPTION. Title, on verso *The Contents, The Printer to the Reader*—1 f., *The Prayer of Manasseh* . . . —1 f., the tables—9 pp. The Argument of Job begins on A 8 b. The text ends on Z 8 a.
Signatures: A–Z⁸; 184 ff. Printed in smaller type than the editions of 1580 and 1583.
The titlepage has two ornaments, one being a headpiece of roses and thistles.

¶ 108 × 73 mm. [F. F.]
262.

1614. B. f°. See 1617.
B. 4°. See 1615 and 1619.

1615. The Bible . . .
R. Barker: London. 1614,15. 4°. 𝕭. 𝕷.

General title dated 1614; N. T. dated 1615 on title and in colophon.
Remarkable for the omission of the word *Holy* in the general title. (For a different title, dated 1614, see above, No. 251.)
Both titles omit the words *Appointed* . . .
Text ends on Sss 8 a.
Ruth iii. 15 *she.*

VOL. I.   L

¶ 212 × 159 mm.
With Genealogies and Map, and Concordance (1615). [F. F.]

—— Another copy.

209 × 159 mm.
With Genealogies, and Concordance (1615).
With Prayer Book (? date), and Metrical Psalms (1618).

263.

1615. The Bible . . . With . . . Annotations . . . And . . . Concordance . . . Imprinted at London by Robert Barker . . . 1615.

4°. B. L.

Geneva version.

Apparently the last black-letter quarto edition of this version printed by Barker.
A close reprint of the quarto of 1605. Text ends on fo. 554 (really 552); and Concordance on L 2.
There are two varieties of this date.

A.
General title : . . . rea- | die finding . . ., Certaine questions and answeres . . ., ★ 3 b, 2nd col. : . . . be instruc- | ted, assured . . .

¶ 215 × 155 mm.
With Speed's Genealogies and Map; and Metrical Psalms (1616,17).
In contemporary binding; with brass plates and corners. [F. F.]

264.

—— ANOTHER EDITION.

B.
General title : . . . rea- | dy finding . . ., ★ 3 b, 2nd col. : . . . be instructed | assured . . .

¶ 208 × 156 mm.
With Speed's Genealogies. [F. F.]

—— Another copy.

218 × 159 mm.
The Concordance is dated 1613 (probably supplied from a copy of the 1613 edition) and lacks 18 ff. at the end.
With Speed's Genealogies; and Prayer Book (1614).

—— Another copy.

204 × 157 mm. Imperfect : wanting general title and many leaves at the end.

265.

1615. The Bible: that is . . . With . . . Annotations . . . Imprinted at London by Robert Barker . . . 1615.

4°.

Geneva version; with Tomson's revised New Testament, and Junius' Revelation.

Apparently the last roman type quarto edition of this version printed by Barker.
A reprint of the quarto of 1606,05. N. T. ends on fo. 121, and the tables on Rrr 4.
The list of books is printed on verso of general title.

¶ 218 × 154 mm.
With Speed's Genealogies and Map. [F. F.]

—— Another copy.

Differs slightly from the above; but the titles are identical.

ENGLISH

218 × 152 mm. Imperfect: wanting Apocrypha.
With Speed's Genealogies and Map; Prayer Book (1615); and Metrical Psalms (1615).
Seventeenth-century binding stamped with the royal arms. [F. F.]
266.

1615. The Holy Bible . . .
R. Barker: London. 1615. 8°.

Text ends on Kkk 8 *a*.

¶ 162 × 104 mm.
With Genealogies and Map.

—— Another copy.

According to Fry's notes, this differs in a few leaves from the above copy.

164 × 105 mm. Imperfect: wanting general title, and Cc 1.
[F. F.]

—— Another copy.

A mixed copy, containing some sheets in the N. T. which belong to an edition of 1636; thus the colophon contains the names of R. Barker and the Assigns of John Bill, and is dated 1636. A very few leaves in the rest of the book differ from the first copy.

162 × 106 mm.
With Genealogies and Map. [F. F.]

—— Another copy.

The N. T. only, bound with part of an edition of 1614 (No. 259). It differs very slightly from the first copy mentioned above.
267.

1615. (The New Testament.)
R. Barker: London. 1615. 8°. 𝔅. 𝔏.

Bishops' version.

A close reprint of the edition of 1606.
The colophon on Nn 4 *b* reads: *Imprinted at London by Robert Barker, Printer to Kings most excellent Maiestie. 1615.* The first three years in the Almanack are misprinted 1605, 1603, 1604.
The second sheet is signed [A].
X 5 *a*, 1st line: *fession . . . that;* 5th line: *. . . shall be . . .*

¶ 137 × 85 mm. Imperfect: wanting the title and Ee 8. [F. F.]
268.

1615. B. 4°. See 1616.

1616. The Holy Bible.
R. Barker: London. 1616,15. 4°.

A new form of quarto in roman type. The titles are dated 1616, but the colophon 1615. This edition is remarkable for its two general titles, the engraved specimen being inserted as an additional embellishment. The words *Appointed . . .* occur only on the engraved title.

DESCRIPTION. Engraved title; eight preliminary leaves: title (within border), with list of books on verso, Dedication—3 pp., Preface—9 pp., 1 f. blank. Text: O. T. ends on Pp 7 *b*; Apocrypha end on && 8 *b*, 1 f. blank; N. T. (with title within border, verso blank) ends on Nnn 1 *b*, with colophon (dated 1615), 1 f. blank.
Signatures: [first title], A⁸, A–Z⁸ Aa–Zz⁸ &&⁸, Aaa–Mmm⁸ Nnn²; [1+] 482 ff.
The first title has the design engraved by *Iaspar Isac*, used in the first quarto edition of 1612. The second and N. T. titles have the usual border with the heart-shaped centre.

¶ 214 × 160 mm.
With Genealogies and Map. [F. F.]
269.

1616. The | Bible: | That Is, | The Holy Scrip- | tures contained . . . Imprinted at London by Robert | Barker, Printer to the Kings | most Excellent Maiestie. | Anno Dom. 1616.

f°. 𝕭. 𝕷.

Geneva version; with Tomson's revised New Testament, and Junius' Revelation.

This somewhat resembles the black-letter folio editions of 1592,91, etc.; but the columns of print are four lines longer.

DESCRIPTION. Four preliminary leaves: title (within border), verso blank, Address—1 f., *Of the incomparable treasure* . . .—1 p., *How to take profit* . . .—1 p., list of books —1 p., 1 p. containing large engraving. Text: O. T. and Apocrypha, ff. 1 to 444 *b*; N. T., with title, verso blank, *The Printer to the diligent reader*—1 p., *The description* . . . (with map)—1 p., text—ff. 3 to 135 *b*; tables—7 ff., ending on Fffff 4 *b*, with colophon.
Signatures: A⁴, A–Z⁶ Aa–Zz⁶ Aaa–Zzz⁶ Aaaa–Zzzz⁶ Aaaaa–Eeeee⁶ Fffff¹; 590 ff.
A full column contains 64 lines.
The title-border resembles that used in the folio Geneva Bible of 1583 and other editions; with the book inscribed *Verbvm Dei* . . ., etc. The initials, however, are changed to I R. The tablet below bears the words *Cum Priuilegio Regiæ Maiestatis*. The N. T. titlepage bears a headpiece and a small ornament.

¶ 332 × 216 mm.
With Prayer Book (1616), and Metrical Psalms (1629). [F. F.]

270.

1616. The | Holy | Bible, | containing | the Old Testament, | and the New: | Newly translated out of the Original Tongues: | And with the former Translations diligently | compared and reuised, By his Maiesties spe | ciall commandement. | Imprinted at London by Robert | Barker, Printer to the Kings | most excellent Maiesty. 1616.

f°.

The first small folio edition of King James' version; printed in roman type.

According to Scrivener (*The Authorized Edition* . . ., p. 17) this was the earliest to receive any considerable revision.
The line *Appointed* . . . is omitted from both titles.

DESCRIPTION. Ten preliminary leaves: title (within woodcut border), verso blank; Dedication —1 f., Preface —7 ff., list of books —1 p., 1 p. containing a large engraving. The text: O. T., ff. 1 to 344 (Mmm 2) *a*, verso blank; Apocrypha end on fo. 425 (Bbbb 5) *b*, followed by 1 f. blank; N. T., with title (within border), ends on fo. 535 (Vvvv 7) *b*, with colophon dated 1616; 1 f. blank.
Signatures: a⁴ b⁶, A–Z⁶ Aa–Zz⁶ Aaa–Zzz⁶ Aaaa–Tttt⁶ Vvvv⁸; 546 ff.
The title-border resembles that used in some editions of the Bishops' Bible; at the top are the royal arms supported by figures representing Justice and Mercy; below is a tablet bearing the words *Cum Priuilegio Regiæ Majestatis*, supported by a lion and a unicorn; at the bottom are the initials C. B. The large engraving before the text represents Adam and Eve.

¶ 330 × 215 mm. Wants the last leaf (blank).
With Genealogies and Map.
With Prayer Book (1616). [F. F.]

—— Another copy.

318 × 201 mm. Wants blank leaf.
With Genealogies and Map.
With Prayer Book (1616), and Metrical Psalms (1624).

—— Another copy.

326 × 215 mm. Wants blank leaf.
With Genealogies.
With Prayer Book (? date), and Metrical Psalms (1618).

271.

1616. The | New Testament | of ovr Lord Iesvs | Christ, Translated out of | Greeke, by Theod. Beza. | With briefe Summaries . . . Englished by L. Tomson. | Together with the Annotations of Fr. Iunius | vpon the Reuelation of S. | Iohn. | Imprinted at Lon- | don by Robert Barker | Printer to the Kings most Ex- | cellent Maiestie. | Anno 1616.

8°.

Geneva version; Tomson's revision, with Junius' Revelation.

A close reprint of the edition of 1610; with the text ending on Mm 2.

¶ 165 × 106 mm. [F. F.]

272.

1617. The | Holy | Bible, | Containing | the Old Testa- | ment, and the New : | Newly translated out of the | Originall Tongues : and with | the former Translations diligently | compared and reuised by his Ma- | iesties speciall Commande- | ment. | Appointed to be read in | Churches. | Imprinted at | London by Robert Barker, | Printer to the Kings most | Excellent Maiestie. | Anno 1617.

f°. 𝕭. 𝕷.

The third distinct folio edition, printed in large black-letter, of King James' version.

Two copies have a title dated 1614 (see below).
This reads leaf for leaf with the two preceding editions of 1611 and 1613,11. A few distinguishing marks may be noted : there is a small cut of the Royal arms without initials at the head of the Dedication ; initial I before Psalm cxxii represents St. John ; Jer. xviii. 3 *whelles* for *wheels*.   For other details see Fry's *Description*.
Signatures : A⁴ B⁴ C⁶ D⁴ A–Z⁶ Aa–Zz⁶ Aaa–Zzz⁶ Aaaa–Zzzz⁶ Aaaaa–Zzzzz⁶ Aaaaaa–Dddddd⁶ ; 732 ff.

¶ 408 × 264 mm. Genealogies—Fry's No. 17.   Map with the sea shaded.
Three leaves are inserted at the beginning. T 3 and 4 (these are the usual impression ; those in the copy are variants) ; and Yyyy 1 (a variant). [F. F.]

—— Another copy.

384 × 259 mm. A remarkable copy, containing a title dated 1614 : *The | Holy | Bible, | Conteyning the Old Testa- | ment, and the New : | Newly translated out of | the Originall Tongues : and with | the former Translations diligently | compared and reuised, by his | Maiesties speciall Com- | mandement. | Appointed to be read in Churches. | Imprinted | at London, by Robert | Barker, Printer to the | Kings most Excellent | Maiestie. | Anno Dom. 1614.*   No distinct folio edition of 1614 is known to exist.
Fry acquired this curious titleleaf together with the Genealogies, Old Testament and Apocrypha found in this volume ; he added the New Testament, which was wanting, taking it from another copy.   Loftie (p. 65), who states that a duplicate was in G. Offor's Collection, considers that the title was probably experimental.   In letterpress it closely resembles the titles of 1611 and 1613, differing, however, in setting-up, as well as in date.   The border is the woodcut border.
Genealogies—Fry's No. 13 ; no Map.
Inserted at the beginning, for the purpose of comparison, is a leaf containing facsimiles of the letterpress of the general titles dated 1611, 1613, 1617, 1634 and 1640. [F. F.]

273.

1617. The Holy Bible . . .
R. Barker : London. 1617. 8°.

Text ends on Kkk 8 a.

¶ 161 × 107 mm. Imperfect: wanting the Apocrypha; the last leaf has been completed in facsimile. [F. F.]

274.

1617. (The New Testament.)
R. Barker : London. 1617. 8°. 𝕭. 𝕷.

Bishops' version.

A close reprint of the edition of 1606.
Cotton (p. 63) records two still later editions of 1618 and 1619,17, printed by Norton and Bill.
The colophon on Nn 4 b reads: *Imprinted at London by Robert Barker, Printer to the Kings most excellent Maiestie. 1617.*
X 5 a, 1st line: *vprightly . . . no.*

¶ 140 × 85 mm. Imperfect: wanting title. [F. F.]

—— Another copy.
142 × 85 mm. Imperfect: wanting title and two following leaves, and E 8. [F. F.]

—— Another copy.
139 × 81 mm. Imperfect; wanting all preliminary leaves, and X 4 and 5. [F. F.]

275.

—— ANOTHER EDITION.
Date not known. No doubt printed by Barker.

Corresponds to the editions printed in 1606, 1608, 1613, 1614, 1615, and 1617. In some parts it appears identical with that of 1613; e.g. X 5 a, 1st line: *worthinesse . . . in.* But elsewhere it differs. Probably some of these Testaments are mixed.

¶ 144 × 88 mm. Imperfect: wanting all before F 1, the last four leaves, and other leaves. [F. F.]

276.

—— ANOTHER EDITION.
Date not known. No doubt printed by Barker.

This in parts appears identical with the edition of 1615; e.g. X 5 a, 1st line: *fession . . . that*; 5th line: *. . . shall be . . .* But elsewhere it differs.

¶ 139 × 83 mm. Imperfect: wanting the first eleven leaves, the last four, and other leaves. [F. F.]

—— Another copy.
137 × 89 mm. Imperfect: wanting all the preliminary matter, and the last three leaves, and other leaves. [F. F.]

277.

1617. The Text of the New Testament . . . Translated. . . . by the Papists . . . at Rhemes. With Arguments . . . Wherevnto Is Added the Translation . . . vsed in the Church of England, With a Confvtation . . . By W. Fvke . . . London, Printed for Thomas Adams. Anno 1617.
f°.

The third edition of Dr. Fulke's work. See No. 156.

This closely agrees with the second edition of 1601.
The Bishops' version still appears as *The Translation of the Church of England*.
Preliminary matter, as before; filling 28 ff. Text, pp. 1 to 912; table—13 pp., ending on Mmmm 4 a, verso blank.
The title-border is the same as before.

¶ 301 × 200 mm.
Probably a blank leaf should precede the title, since the leaf after the title is signed ¶ 3.
[F. F.]
278.

1617. The Whole Booke of Davids Psalmes, Both in Prose and Meetre: With apt Notes to sing them withall.
Printed for the Company of the Stationers: London. 1617. 16°.

The Geneva version of the Psalter; printed with Sternhold and Hopkins' Metrical Psalms.

Lea Wilson's No. 63, p. 245.
Text of Psalter, A 2 to Aa 8 *b*; 384 pp.

¶ 106 × 72 mm.
Bound up with a 16° Geneva N. T. of 1613 (No. 253). [F. F.]
279.

1618. The Holy Bible . . .
R. Barker: London. 1618. 12°.

The earliest duodecimo edition of King James' version was probably that issued in 1617, of which this is a reprint.

Both titles, as is usual in these small editions, omit the words *Appointed* . . .

DESCRIPTION. Three preliminary leaves: one leaf bearing the signature A on recto, verso blank, title (within border), verso blank, Dedication and list of books—1 f. The text: O. T., A 2 to Ff 2 *b*; Apocrypha end on Mm 12 *a*, verso blank; N. T., with title (within border), ends on Xx 11 *b*, 1 f. blank.
Signatures: A² A–Z¹² Aa–Xx¹²; 530 ff. Double columns; short headlines; no chapter-contents.
The title-border is an architectural design; above are the Sacred Name, an altar and two kneeling figures; below is King David with his harp; under the title is the text *Cor mundum crea in me Deus. Psa. 51.*

¶ 144 × 80 mm.
With Genealogies and Map.
With Metrical Psalms (1618). [F. F.]
280.

1618. The Holy Bible . . .
Bonham Norton and John Bill, Deputies and Assigns of
R. Barker: London. 1618. 8°.

The names of Norton and Bill now begin to appear on the titlepages of Bibles.

Text ends on Kkk 8 *a*.

¶ 165 × 109 mm. Imperfect: wanting the N. T.
With Genealogies and Map.
With Prayer Book (? date), and Metrical Psalms (1614). [F. F.]
281.

1618. A Confutation of the Rhemists translation, glosses, and annotations on the New Testament, so farre as they containe manifest impieties, heresies, idolatries, superstitions, prophanenesse, treasons, slanders, absurdities, falsehoods and other evills . . . By . . . Thomas Cartwright . . . Printed in the yeare 1618.

[Qu. *Barker : London* ?] f°.

A 'Confutation' of the Rheims New Testament by Thomas Cartwright (1535–1603), the eminent Puritan, who was for a time Lady Margaret Professor of Divinity at Cambridge.

According to the title this work had been *written long since by order from the chiefe instruments of the late Queene and State, and at the speciall request and encouragement of many godly-learned Preachers of England*. The publisher's preface refers to the encouragement which the author received from Walsingham, members of the University of Cambridge, and many others, as early as 1583; and explains the subsequent delays, caused partly by the opposition of Archbishop Whitgift and others, which prevented the whole work from appearing till 1618, though a portion of it had been published at Edinburgh in 1602, the year before the author's death (*cf.* Lee, *Memorial*, p. 54 n.). The preface explains that the MS. stopped at Revelation ch. xv, and that the missing portion, *beside the small defects by Mice, through 30. yeares neglect*, was supplied from Dr. Fulke's work.

The place and printer are not given, but the headpieces, vignettes, etc. are like those of Barker, London.

Twenty-nine preliminary leaves : title, publisher's preface, *A copy of a letter written by sundry learned men unto Mr. Cartwright to provoke and encourage him to the answering of the Rhemists* (in Latin and English, signed by W. Fulke and others), the Preface etc. with Cartwright's answers. Text, etc. —pp. 1 to 761 ; table, —17 pp. ; list of *Errata* —1 p., 1 p. blank.

The full text of the Rhemish version is given only to the end of St. Matthew, after which, in accordance with the publisher's note on p. 137, it is omitted, those verses only being quoted to which the controversial notes refer.

¶ 287 × 185 mm.
Contemporary binding, with central and corner ornaments stamped in gilt on each cover.

282.

1618. B. 8°. See 1619.

1619. The Holy Bible . . .
Norton and Bill : London. 1619 ; *Barker : London.* 1614. 4°. 𝔅. 𝔏.

Both titles omit the words *Appointed* . . .
The N. T. section is the same as that in the 1613,14 black-letter quarto (No. 257), and bears the name of R. Barker as printer. No doubt many of these Bibles were issued in a mixed state. It is practically impossible to distinguish between all the various editions.
Apocrypha end on Eee 2 b.

¶ 214 × 161 mm.
With Genealogies and Map, and Concordance (1619,20).
With Prayer Book (1615), and Metrical Psalms (1619).
In original binding, with brass corners, etc.
[F. F.]
283.

1619. The Holy Bible . . .
Norton and Bill : London. 1619,18. 8°.

Norton and Bill are described as ' Deputy Printers for the King's most excellent Majesty.'
Text ends on Kkk 8 a.
The N. T. is dated 1619 on the title, but 1618 in the colophon. Distinct from the octavos of 1618 and 1619.
N. T. title : . . . *the Originall Tongues* . . .

¶ 165 × 106 mm.
[F. F.]
284.

1619. The Holy Bible . . .
                              Norton and Bill : London. 1619. 4°.

Another form of quarto in roman type. O. T. ends on Ccc 4 *b*; Apocrypha end on Ooo 8 *b*; N. T. ends on Gggg 2 *a*, with colophon.
Both titles omit the words *Appointed* . . .
The titles have the usual border with heart-shaped centre.
First page of Dedication : . . . *The Trancelators* . . .

¶ 224 × 162 mm.
With Genealogies and Map.
With Prayer Book (1619).
In seventeenth-century binding; with central and corner ornaments (the latter containing eagle and sun) on ground of flowers.   [F. F.]
                                                                                                         285.

1619. The Holy Bible . . .
                              Norton and Bill : London. 1619. 8°.
Text ends on Kkk 8 *a*.
The general title has a new cut of the royal arms on verso, with a cornucopia on each side of the crown, and a rose and a thistle in the lower corners.
N. T. title : . . . *the Originall Greeke* . . .

¶ 162 × 102 mm.
With Genealogies and Map.
With Prayer Book (1619), and Metrical Psalms (1619).
In seventeenth-century binding, with silver clasps and goffered edges, the stamps on which somewhat resemble those which characterise books bound at Little Gidding.

——— Another copy.
The N. T. only; bound with an O. T. etc. of 1620 (No. 291).   [F. F.]
                                                                                                         286.

1619. The Holy Bible . . .
                              Norton and Bill : London. 1619. 12°.

Another reprint of the 12° edition of 1617. Text ends on Xx 11 *b*.

¶ 150 × 81 mm. Imperfect: wanting the leaf before title, and the Apocrypha.
With Metrical Psalms (1620).   [F F.]
                                                                                                         287.

1619. The New Testament . . .
                              Norton and Bill : London. 1619. 12°.
A very small duodecimo.
Catalogues vary much in stating the size of this and similar small editions. The measurements given of each copy will best indicate the dimensions of the book.

DESCRIPTION. One preliminary leaf: title (within border) with list of books on verso.
   Text, A 2 to Y 12 *b*.
       Signatures : A–Y^{12}; 264 ff. A full page contains 44 lines. Contents before chapters.
       The title-border is an architectural design with figures of the Evangelists in the corners.
       John xiv. 3, *may ye* for *ye may*; Rom. viii. 18, *suffering* for *sufferings*; 1 Tim. iv. 16, *doing this* for *in doing this*.

¶ 104 × 48 mm.
With Metrical Psalms (1619).
Contemporary *dos-à-dos* binding, with goffered edges. The Psalms are bound side by side with the Testament, but turned the reverse way. Thus the book has three boards and two backs—a favourite style of binding in the case of these miniature books.   [F. F.]
                                                                                                         288.

1619. B. 4°. See 1620.

1620. The Holy Bible . . .
  Norton and Bill, etc. : London. 1619,20. 4°. 𝔅. 𝔏.

General title dated 1619; N. T. title and colophon dated 1620. The general title bears the names of Norton and Bill; the N. T. title has Barker and Bill; and the colophon, Barker only.
Both titles omit the words *Appointed* . . .
Text ends on Sss 8 a.
Ggg 6 b: heading, *S. Matthew* for *S. Mark*.

¶ 225 × 162 mm.
With Genealogies and Map, and Concordance (1619,20).
With Prayer Book (1615), and Metrical Psalms (1619).
In original binding, with brass corners, etc. [F. F.]
289.

1620. The Holy Bible . . .
  Norton and Bill : London. 1620. 8°.

Text ends on Kkk 8 a.
General title : . . . *Originall Greeke* . . . Jer. i. 1, *words*.

¶ 162 × 105 mm.
With Genealogies and Map. [F. F.]
290.

—— Another edition.

The N. T. is identical with that in the Bible of 1619, except in one sheet. The rest of the book generally differs from the above, though the title is the same. Jer. i. 1, *wordes*.

¶ 159 × 105 mm.
With Genealogies.
With Prayer Book (? date), and Metrical Psalms (1621); also *The VVay to Trve Happines* . . : *By Questions and Answers, opening briefly the meaning of euery seuerall Booke and Chapter of the Bible, from the beginning of Genesis, to the end of the Revelation* (n. d.).
[F. F.]
291.

1620. B. 4°. See 1621.

1621. The Holy Bible . . .
  Norton and Bill : London. 1620,21. 4°. 𝔅. 𝔏.

General title dated 1620; N. T. title and colophon dated 1621.
Both titles omit the words *Appointed* . . .
Text ends on Sss 8 a.
The signature D 4 is printed C 4; heading on Ppp 2 b, *II. Coainthians*; in Mark xiv. 46, *on* is omitted. In some copies, according to Loftie (p. 73), the Preface is headed *EHE* for *THE*.

¶ 212 × 159 mm.
With Genealogies and Map, and Concordance (1619,20). [F. F.]

——— Another copy.

217 × 157 mm.
Signature D 4 is correct.
With Genealogies and Map, and Concordance (1619,20).

——— Another copy.

209 × 159 mm.
Signature D 4 is correct.
With Genealogies, and Concordance (1619,20).
With Prayer Book (? date), and Metrical Psalms (? date).
292.

ENGLISH

1621. The Holy Bible . . .
Norton and Bill: London. 1621. 8°.

Text ends on Kkk 8 *a*, without colophon.
General title: . . . *Originall Greeke* . . . ; on verso occurs a new cut of the royal arms, with foliage on either side of the crown. The N. T. title omits the printers' names.

¶ 158 × 104 mm.
With Genealogies and Map. [F. F.]

293.

1621. The Nevv Testament . . . VVith Annotations, and other helpes . . . In the English College of Rhemes. Printed at Antvverp. By James Seldenslach. 1621.
12°.

The third edition of the Rheims New Testament.

This closely agrees with the second edition of 1600.
The first pocket edition of the Roman Catholic version.

DESCRIPTION. Twelve preliminary leaves: title, on verso, *The Censvre and Approbation* of the first two editions and the present issue (the last, dated 10 Apr. 1620, being signed: *Laur. Beyerlink Archipresbyter Eccl. Cathedr. Antuerp. Librorumque censor*), the preface—21 pp., *The signification* . . . and list of *The Favltes* . . .—1 p. The text, pp. 1 to 285, ending on M 11 *a*, verso blank, 1 f. blank. The *Annotations*, pp. 1 to 349, table—2 pp., and a list of *The Favltes* . . .—1 p.
Signatures: ★ ★¹², A–M¹², Aa–Oo¹² Pp⁸; 332 ff. The text is printed in double columns; the rest of the book in long lines. The type is small and very indistinct.

¶ 133 × 71 mm. [F. F.]

—— Another copy.
Bound in two volumes.

294.

1621. (The New Testament.)
Norton and Bill: London. 1621. 8°. 𝕭. 𝕷.

Similar to the edition of 1622 (No. 297).
Text ends on Ii 7 *b*.

¶ 149 × 91 mm. Imperfect: wanting first sheet A, and sheets I to V inclusive.
[F. F.]
295.

1622. The Holy Bible . . .
Norton and Bill: London. 1622. 8°.

Text ends on Kkk 8 *a*.
General title correct: . . . *Originall Tongues* . . . The cut of the royal arms is like hat in the earliest octavo editions.

¶ 166 × 105 mm.
With Genealogies. [F. F.]

296.

1622. The New Testament . . .
Norton and Bill: London. 1622. 8°. 𝕭. 𝕷.

DESCRIPTION. One preliminary leaf (within border), with list of books on verso. Text, A 2 to Ii 7 *b*, ending with colophon; 1 f. blank.
Signatures: A–Z⁸ Aa–Ii⁸; 256 ff. A full page contains 46 lines. Headlines, marginal references, and chapter-contents, in roman type.

The title-border contains: above—the Sacred Name; below—the royal arms; in the corners—the Evangelists, and at the sides—symbolical female figures.

¶ 135 × 86 mm. Imperfect: wanting 39 ff. of text, and the blank leaf. [F. F.]
297.

1622. B. 4°. See 1623.

1623. The Holy Bible . . .
Norton and Bill: London. 1622,23. 4°.

Both titles dated 1622, but colophon dated 1623.
The N. T. title omits the words *Appointed* . . .
Text ends on Gggg 2 a.

¶ 213 × 158 mm.
With Genealogies and Map. [F. F.]
298.

1623. The Holy Bible . . .
Norton and Bill: London. 1623. 8°.

Text ends on Kkk 8 a.

A new cut of the royal arms appears in this edition, with lion and unicorn as supporters, and the initials I R.

There are two distinct editions of this date.

A.
General title: . . . *Kings | most Excellent | Maiestie. | Anno 1623.* The ornament before Psalms contains Walsingham's crest.

¶ 164 × 106 mm.
With Genealogies and Map.
With Metrical Psalms (1623). [F. F.]
299.

—— ANOTHER EDITION.

B.
General title: . . . *Kings most | Excellent Maiestie | Anno 1623.* The ornament before Psalms contains cherubs with musical instruments.
Isa. liii. 10 *plased* for *pleased*; Luke ii. 2 *tazing* for *taxing*.

¶ 169 × 110 mm.
With Prayer Book (1623), and Metrical Psalms (1623).
In seventeenth-century binding, stamped with the royal arms. [F. F.]
300.

1624. The Holy Bible . . .
Norton and Bill: London. 1624. 8°.

Text ends on Kkk 8 a.
The ornament before Psalms represents King David; a small cut before Matthew contains the figures of the four Evangelists.

¶ 164 × 109 mm.
With Genealogies and Map.
With Metrical Psalms (1624).
In seventeenth-century binding, with silver corners and plates stamped T V. [F. F.]
301.

1624. The Holy Bible . . .
Norton and Bill: London. 1624. 12°.

Text ends on Xx 11 b.
The last leaf Xx 12 contains on recto a colophon between two ornaments.

¶ 150 × 84 mm. Wants leaf before title, and Apocrypha.
With Metrical Psalms (1623).
Covers embroidered with silk threads, silver wire, and purl, on white satin; showing a symbolical female figure under an arch on each cover; goffered edges. [**F. F.**]
302.

1624. B. 4°. See 1625.

ACCESSION OF KING CHARLES I: 27 MARCH 1625.

1625. The Holy Bible . . .
Norton and Bill: London. 1625,24. 4°. 𝕭. 𝕷.

Both titles dated 1625, but colophon dated 1624.
Both titles omit the words *Appointed* . . .
The text now ends on Rrr 8 *a*; in former editions of this type the signature Hhh was omitted.
The signature Lll 4 is printed Mmm 4.

¶ 222 × 163 mm.
With Genealogies and Map, and Concordance (1622,21).
In original binding, with brass corners etc. [**F. F.**]
303.

1625. The Holy Bible . . .
Norton and Bill: London. 1625. 4°. 𝕭. 𝕷.

Both titles omit the words *Appointed* . . .
Distinct from the similar edition dated 1625 on both titles, but 1624 in the colophon. *Cf.* the ornament (two squirrels) before Genesis; 2 Kings heading, *The first Booke* . . .; Hhh 4 *b* heading, *Luke* for *S. Luke.*
Colophon on Rrr 8 *a* is dated 1625.

¶ 216 × 157 mm. [**F. F.**]

—— Another copy.

Generally agrees with the above; yet the colophon is dated 1624. Probably a mixed copy.

206 × 154 mm.
With Genealogies and Map. [**F. F.**]

—— Another copy.

Apparently mixed.

209 × 159 mm. Wants the first five preliminary leaves, and the last leaf with colophon.
With Genealogies and Map.
304.

1625. The Holy Bible . . .
Norton and Bill: London. 1625. 8°.

Text ends on Kkk 8 *a*.
The initials C R appear with the royal arms on verso of the general title.
There are two distinct editions of this date.
A.
Num. xxvi. 3 : . . . *nere Iericho,* | *saying,*

¶ 161 × 103 mm. Slightly imperfect.
With *The VVay to Trve Happines* . . . (n. d.). [**F. F.**]
305.

—— ANOTHER EDITION.
B.
Num. xxvi. 3 : . . . *neere Ieri-* | *cho, saying,*

¶ 167 × 108 mm. Imperfect: wanting Apocrypha.
Apparently a mixed copy. The N. T. is dated 1628 on the title, and 1627 in the colophon. The rest of the book represents a variety of 1625.
With Genealogies and Map. [F. F.]

306.

1625. The Holy Bible . . .
[*Amsterdam* ?]   1625.   8°.

No name of printer or place is given on either title; nor is there a colophon on Kkk 8 a. Supposed to be a foreign, or a pirated edition. Closely resembles Norton and Bill's octavo Bibles.
The cut of the royal arms has the cornucopiæ.

¶ 169 × 108 mm. [F. F.]

307.

1625. The New Testament . . .
Norton and Bill: London.   1625.   16°.

Closely resembles in general appearance the 16° Geneva New Testament printed by Barker in 1613. Remarkable as containing the Old Testament Epistles.
Loftie (p. 76) gives the size of this edition as '8vo. very small: apparently 24mo.'

DESCRIPTION. One preliminary leaf: title (within border), with list of books on verso. Text, A 2 to Gg 5 *a*; on verso begin *The Epistles of the Old Testament, according as they bee now read*—4 pp., ending on Gg 7 *a* with colophon, verso blank, 1 f. blank.
    Signatures: A-Z⁸ Aa-Gg⁸; 240 ff. Marginal references, etc. Contents before chapters.
    Title-border as in 16° Geneva N. T. of 1613.
    Headline on F 4 *b*, *S. Mare*; 1 Cor. x. 13, *temptatatio*; 2 Pet. i. 8, *bound* for *abound*; 2 John 7, *is* repeated.

¶ 109 × 76 mm. Wants last leaf (blank).
With *The Whole Booke of Davids Psalmes, Both in Prose and Meetre* . . . (1628).
Seventeenth-century binding. [F. F.]

— — Another copy.

105 × 71 mm. Imperfect: wanting titleleaf (supplied in facsimile), and the last three leaves. [F. F.]

308.

1626. The Holy Bible . . .
Norton and Bill: London.   1626.   8°.

Text ends on Kkk 8 *a*.
The ornament representing King David appears before the Apocrypha.

Two distinct editions occur of this date.

A.
Ruth iii. 15: . . . *when shee held it* . . .

¶ 160 × 102 mm.
With Genealogies and Map. [F. F.]

309.

——— ANOTHER EDITION.

B.
Ruth iii. 15: . . . *when she held it* . . .

¶ 159 × 107 mm.
With Genealogies and Map.
With Metrical Psalms (1626). [F. F.]

ENGLISH 159

—— Another copy.

168 × 105 mm. Wants the Apocrypha.
With Genealogies and Map.
With Metrical Psalms (1626).
Illuminated in gold and colours. [F. F.]
310.

1626. The New Testament . . .
Norton and Bill: London. 1626. 12°.

A corrected reprint of the small duodecimo edition of 1619, with text ending on Y 1 *b*.

¶ 106 × 49 mm. [F. F.]

—— Another copy.

106 × 49 mm.
With Metrical Psalms (1622), and Prayer Book (1625).
Contemporary *dos-à-dos* binding, with goffered edges. [F. F.]
311.

1627. The Holy Bible . . .
Norton and Bill: London. 1627. 4°.

Text ends on Gggg 2 *a*.

¶ 213 × 155 mm.
With Genealogies and Map. [F. F.]

—— Another copy.

214 × 150 mm.
With Genealogies.
312.

1627. The Holy Bible . . .
Norton and Bill: London. 1627. 8°.

Text ends on Kkk 8 *a*.

¶ 165 × 108 mm.
With Genealogies and Map.
Contemporary binding, with the royal arms and corner ornaments, on ground of stars;
goffered edges. [F. F.]
313.

1627. The New Testament . . .
Norton and Bill: London. 1627. 8°. 𝕭. 𝕷.

Text ends on Ii 7 *b*.

¶ 137 × 86 mm. Wants blank leaf. [F. F
314.

1628. The Holy Bible . . .
Norton and Bill: London. 1628. 4°. 𝕭. 𝕷.

Text ends on Rrr 8 *a*.

¶ 218 × 160 mm.
With Genealogies and Map.
In original binding, with brass corners and clasps. [F. F.]
315.

1628. The Holy Bible . . .
Norton and Bill: London. 1628. 8°.

Text ends on Kkk 8 *a*.
Fry enumerates five distinct editions of this date. Some of his copies, however, may be mixed.

A.
Ornaments before Isaiah and Mark—grotesque animals.

¶ 169 × 110 mm. [F. F.]
316.

—— ANOTHER EDITION.
B.
Ornaments before Isaiah and Mark—dogs.

¶ 160 × 106 mm.
With Genealogies and Map. [F. F.]
317.

—— ANOTHER EDITION.
C.
Ornaments before Isaiah and Mark—foliage and flowers. Catchword on Nn 7 b: PO- for APO-.

¶ 167 × 106 mm.
With Genealogies and Map. [F. F.]

—— Another copy.
This agrees with C, except in the last leaf, which is taken from an edition of 1631.

154 × 103 mm.
With Genealogies and Map.
With Prayer Book (? date), and Metrical Psalms (1628).
318.

—— ANOTHER EDITION.
D.
Differs in parts from all the others: e.g. ornament before Mark—zigzag design.

¶ Represented by the N. T. bound with part of an edition of 1625 (No. 306). The last sheet, Kkk, with colophon, belongs to the edition of 1627. [F. F.]
319.

—— ANOTHER EDITION.
E.
Generally like B; but differs in places from all, e.g. ornament before Ezra—rose, thistle, etc.

¶ 159 × 102 mm.
With Genealogies and Map. [F. F.]
320.

1628. The New Testament ...
Norton and Bill: London. 1628. 8°. 𝔅. 𝔏.
Text ends on Ii 7 b.

¶ 140 × 84 mm. Titleleaf mutilated. Wants blank leaf. [F. F.]
321.

1628. The Whole Booke of Davids Psalmes, Both in Prose and Meetre. With Apt Notes to sing them withall.
Printed for the Company of Stationers: London. 1628. 16°.

The Geneva version of the Psalter; printed with Sternhold and Hopkins' Metrical Psalms.

ENGLISH 161

Lea Wilson's No. 75, p. 247.
Psalter ends on p. 384 (Aa 8 b). (See above, No. 279.)

¶ 109 × 76 mm.
Bound up with a 16° Geneva N. T. of 1625. [F. F.]
322.

1629. The Holy Bible . . .
Norton and Bill: London. 1629. f°.

DESCRIPTION. Six preliminary leaves: title (engraved), verso blank, Dedication—1 f., Preface—7 pp., list of books—1 p. The text: O. T., pp. 1 to 612; Apocrypha end on p. 759, 1 p. blank; N. T., with title (within border), ends on p. 951 (Llll 8 a) with colophon, 1 p. blank.
    The general title engraved by *Iaspar Isac*. The N. T. title has an ornamental woodcut border. A cut representing Adam occurs before Genesis.

¶ 309 × 207 mm.
With Genealogies and Map.
With Prayer Book (1629), and Metrical Psalms (1629,30). [F. F.]
323.

1629. The Holy Bible . . .
Tho. and John Buck, printers to the University of Cambridge. 1629. f°.

The first edition of King James' version printed at Cambridge.

The line *Appointed* . . . occurs on both titles.
Lea Wilson (p. 104) says: 'For this beautiful edition the text appears to have undergone a complete revision, although I can find no record of such having been done by authority. Yet the errors in the first and intermediate editions are here corrected, and considerable care appears to have been exercised as to the words printed in italics, punctuation, etc.'
    This seems to be the earliest edition in which occurs the error: 1 Tim. iv. 16. *Take heed unto thyself and unto thy doctrine* (for . . . *the doctrine*).

DESCRIPTION. [Eight] preliminary leaves: [1 f. blank?] title (engraved), verso blank, Dedication—1 f., Preface—4 ff., 1 p. blank, list of books—1 p. Text: O. T., pp. 1 to 540; Apocrypha end on p. 668; N. T.. with title (bearing device), verso blank, ends on p. 842 with device and colophon, 1 f. blank.
    Signatures: [—]² ¶⁶, A–Z⁶ Aa–Zz⁶ Aaa–Iii⁶ Kkk⁴, Lll–Zzz⁶ Aaaa⁶ Bbbb⁴; 430 ff.
    General title engraved, and signed *Jo. Payn sculp.*; it represents Moses and David, the four Evangelists, the Last Supper, the hart (Ps. xlii. 1), and other subjects. The device, which occurs on the N. T. titlepage, and above the colophon, is that of *Alma Mater Cantabrigia* with the legend *Hinc Lvcem Et Pocvla Sacra*.

¶ 309 × 216 mm.
With Prayer Book (1629), and Metrical Psalms (1629). [F. F.]

—— Another copy.

Marked by Fry as 'Variation Edition'; but apparently it differs only in the first sheet of text; e.g. the first page has a headline and a different ornament.
287 × 190 mm.
With Prayer Book (1629), and Metrical Psalms (1629). [F. F.]
324.

1629. The Holy Bible . . .
Norton and Bill: London. 1629. 4°.

Text ends on Gggg 2 a.
In many sheets there is a small asterisk on the verso of the sixth or the last leaf—or both.

¶ 222 × 165 mm.
With Genealogies and Map. [F. F.]
325.

VOL. I. M

1629. The Holy Bible . . .
       Norton and Bill : London. 1629. 8°.

Text ends on Kkk 8 *a*.

¶ 156 × 105 mm.
With Genealogies and Map.
With *The Way to Trve Happines* . . . (n. d.).   [F. F.]
                        326.

1629. The Holy Bible . . .
       Norton and Bill : London. 1629. 12°.

Colophon on Xx 12 *a*.

¶ 150 × 79 mm. Wants leaf before title and Apocrypha.
With Metrical Psalms (1628).
Goffered edges.   [F. F.]
                         327.

1630. The Holy Bible . . .
   Robert Barker and J. Bill, etc. : London. 1630. 4°. 𝔅. 𝔏.

The names Norton and Bill occur on the N. T. title and in the colophon. Distinct from the following edition.
Wisd. xix. 22 : *neither didst thou* . . .
Text ends on Rrr 8 *a*.

¶ 214 × 158 mm.
With Genealogies and Map.   [F. F.]

—— Another copy.

222 × 165 mm.
With Genealogies and Map.
With Prayer Book (? date), and Metrical Psalms (1630).
                        328.

—— ANOTHER EDITION.

The names Barker and Bill occur on both titles and in colophon. Distinct from the preceding edition.
Wisd. xix. 22 : *neither diddest thou* . . .

¶ 215 × 155 mm.
With Genealogies and Map.
In seventeenth-century binding, stamped with the royal arms. [F. F.]

—— Another copy.

212 × 163 mm.
With Genealogies and Map.
With Prayer Book (? date), and Metrical Psalms (1631).
                        329.

1630. The Holy Bible . . .
    R. Barker and Assigns of J. Bill : London. 1630. 4°.

Text ends on Gggg 2 *a*.
Scrivener (p. 20) mentions two readings as peculiar to this edition : 1 Macc. x. 20 *require of thee* for *require thee*, xii. 53 *amongst them* for *amongst men*.

¶ 221 × 161 mm.
With Genealogies and Map.
With Prayer Book (1629), and Metrical Psalms (1630).
In seventeenth-century binding.   [F. F.]
                        330.

ENGLISH

1630. The Holy Bible . . .
                              T. and J. Buck : Cambridge. 1630. 4°.

This and the black-letter issue of the same year are the first quarto editions of King James' version printed at Cambridge.

A reprint of the Cambridge folio of 1629. 1 Tim. iv. 16, *thy*.

DESCRIPTION. Eight preliminary leaves : title (engraved), verso blank, Dedication —1 f., Preface—11 pp., list of books—1 p. Text: O. T. pp. 1 to 744 ; Apocrypha end on p. 920 ; N. T. (with title bearing device, verso blank) ends on p. 1153 (Eeee 5 *a*) with colophon, verso blank, 1 f. blank.
Signatures: ¶⁸, A–H⁸ I⁴ K–X⁸ Y⁴ Z⁸ Aa–Zz⁸ Aaa⁸ Bbb⁴ Ccc–Zzz⁸ Aaaa–Dddd⁸ Eeee⁶ ; 586 ff.
The general title (not dated) is that engraved by *Jo. Payn*, and used in the folio of 1629 by the same printers. The device *Alma Mater Cantabrigia* occurs on the N. T. title.

¶ 225 × 162 mm.   [F. F.]
                                                                                  331.

1630. The Holy Bible . . .
                              T. and J. Buck : Cambridge. 4°. 𝕭. 𝕷.

DESCRIPTION. Eight preliminary leaves : title (engraved), verso blank, Dedication —1 f., Preface - 11 pp., list of books—1 p. Text: O. T., pp. 1 to 590 ; Apocrypha end on p. 730 ; N. T. ends on p. 918 (Mmm 3 *b*) without colophon, 1 f. blank.
Signatures: ¶⁸ A–Z⁸ Aa–Zz⁸ Aaa–Lll⁸ Mmm⁴ ; 468 ff.
Titles, as in the Bucks' quarto edition in roman type of the same year.
1 Tim. iv. 16, *thy*.

¶ 219 × 161 mm.   [F. F.]
                                                                                  332.

1630. The Holy Bible . . .
                              Barker and Assigns of Bill : London. 1630. 8°.

Text ends on Kkk 8 *a*.
Both titles now bear the words *Appointed* . . .
Fry possessed more than twenty octavo copies of 1630, 31, or 32. Nearly all differ in parts from one another, but probably the majority are mixed copies. Each copy contains MS. notes of his collations. All the London octavo editions from 1612,13 to 1631 read together ; and the publishers seem to have freely mixed the sheets printed at various dates.
H. R. Plomer (see above, No. 240) has unearthed a fact which accounts for the mixing of sheets in Bibles of this period. During one phase of R. Barker's law-suits, B. Norton presented a cross-petition (1622) in which he stated that his opponent 'very unadvisedly used (for present money) to sell his books . . . before they were half printed, at half the prices he might otherwise have sold the same.' Barker, who was living in a state of chronic debt, seems to have sold from time to time sheets of incomplete Bibles in order to realise money. His customers had to complete their copies as best they could. Hence the mixing of sheets.

Three distinct editions occur of this date.

A.
Headline on Qq 8 *b* : *Apocrppha*.

¶ 163 × 110 mm.
With Genealogies.
With Prayer Book (1630), and Metrical Psalms (1631).   [F. F.]
                                                                                  333.

—— ANOTHER EDITION.

B.
Headline on C 5 *b* : *The burning bush*.

¶ 165 × 108 mm.
With Genealogies and Map.   [F. F.]
                                                                                  M 2

—— Another copy. Very imperfect.
With Metrical Psalms (1630). [F. F.]
334.

—— ANOTHER EDITION.

C.
Ornament before Wisdom—cherub.

¶ 170 × 111 mm.
With Genealogies and Map.
With Prayer Book (1630), and Metrical Psalms (1631).
Covers embroidered in coloured silks and metal threads on a ground of red silk. The decoration of both covers is the same : ornamental circles, with quarter-circles in the corners, bordered on one side by a row of conventional flowers in compartments ; a similar row of flowers adorns the back. The general scheme and the stamps on the gilt edges suggest that the book was bound at Little Gidding. [F. F.]
335.

1630.   B.   4°.   See 1632.
B.   8°.   See 1631.

1631. The Holy Bible. . . .
Barker and Bill : London. 1631,30. 8°.

Text ends on Kkk 8 *a*.
The N. T. is dated 1630 on the title and in the colophon.
The words *Appointed* . . . occur only on the general title.
General title engraved (like that by Isac in the quarto Bible of 1612). N. T. title within woodcut architectural border like that used in many 12° editions, but with figures of *Fides* and *Religio* on either side of the altar.

¶ 163 × 105 mm. Wants the general title, which is supplied in facsimile.
With Genealogies and Map. [F. F.]
336.

1631. The Holy Bible . . .
Barker and Assigns of Bill : London. 1631,30. 8°.

Text ends on Kkk 8 *a*.
N. T. is dated 1630 on title and in colophon.
With the usual woodcut title-borders.

There appear to be three distinct editions.

A.
Gen. l. 26 . . . *hee was | put in a coffin in Egypt*; Deut. heading *The Fift* . . .

¶ 160 × 106 mm.
With Genealogies and Map. [F. F.]
337.

—— ANOTHER EDITION.

B.
Gen. l. 26 . . . *he was put | in a coffin in Egypt.*

¶ 158 × 105 mm. [F. F.]
338.

—— ANOTHER EDITION.

C.
No ornament before Exodus.

¶ 162 × 104 mm. [F. F.]

—— Another copy.
Evidently a mixed copy, agreeing now with one, and now with another, of the above editions.

ENGLISH 165

161 × 105 mm. Imperfect: wanting the N. T. title and some other leaves. The general title and the colophon are like those found in A B and C, and doubtless the N. T. title was similar and dated 1630.
With Genealogies (1631), and Downame's Concordance (? date).
With Prayer Book (? date). [F. F.]
339.

1631. The Holy Bible . . .
    Barker and Assigns of Bill: London. 1631,30. 8°.
Text ends on Kkk 8 *a.*
General and N. T. titles dated 1631; colophon dated 1630. This edition is distinct from those dated 1631 on the general title and 1630 on the N. T. title and in the colophon. There are lines above and below the words *Appointed* . . . . on the general title. A large cut of the royal arms, with lion and unicorn as supporters, occurs on verso.

¶ 166 × 110 mm.
With Genealogies (1631) and Map.
With Prayer Book (1631), and Metrical Psalms (1631). [F. F.]
340.

1631. The Holy Bible . . .
    Barker and Assigns of Bill: London. 1631. 8°.
Text ends on Kkk 8 *a.*
Dated 1631 on both titles and in colophon.

Fry distinguished several varieties of this date.

A.
This edition is known as the 'Wicked Bible' from the error in Exod. xx. 14, where the Seventh Commandment reads: *Thou shalt commit adultery.* The printers are said to have been fined £300 for the offence. Martin Lucas is sometimes named as Barker's partner in the production of this book. Kilburne mentions it in his *Dangerous Errors* . . .
Peter Heylyn in his *Cyprianus Anglicus*, London, 1668, p. 228, under the date 1632 gives the following account of this edition: 'His Majesties Printers, at or about this time, had committed a scandalous mistake in our *English* Bibles, by leaving out the word *Not* in the Seventh Commandment. His Majesty being made acquainted with it by the Bishop of *London*, Order was given for calling the Printers into the *High-Commission*, where upon Evidence of the Fact, the whole Impression was called in, and the Printers deeply fined, as they justly merited. With some part of this Fine *Laud* causeth a fair Greek Character to be provided, for publishing such Manuscripts as Time and Industry should make ready for the Publick view; of which sort were the *Catena* and *Theophylact* set out by *Lyndsell.*'
Addison refers to the same edition in the *Spectator* No. 579. According to Stevens (*Printed Bibles in the Caxton Exhibition*, pp. 114-5) a German Bible of 1731 in the Library at Wolfenbüttel contains the same error.

¶ 158 × 105 mm.
With Genealogies and Map. [F. F.]

As the edition of 1000 copies was ordered to be suppressed, specimens are very rare. Stevens mentions only four—in the B. M., Bodleian, Glasgow, and Lenox Libraries.
341.

—— ANOTHER EDITION.
B.
Sig. Z 1 *a*, heading: *His power in the creature*; Job xl. 8: . . . *iudgement* . . . *mee* . . . *bee* . . . This page Z 1 *a* will serve in distinguishing all the following editions.

¶ 166 × 105 mm.
With Genealogies (1636) and Map. [F. F.]
342.

—— ANOTHER EDITION.
C.
Z 1 *a*, heading: *His power in the creature*; Job xl. 8: . . . *Iudgement* . . . *me* . . . *be* . . .

¶ 170 × 110 mm.
With Genealogies (1631) and Map, and Downame's Concordance (1630).
With Metrical Psalms (1631). [F. F.]
343.

—— ANOTHER EDITION.

D.
Z 1 a, heading: *His power in the creature*; Job xl. 8: . . . *iudgement* . . . *me* . . . *be* . . .

¶ 162 × 108 mm. [F. F.]
344.

—— ANOTHER EDITION.

E.
Z 1 a, heading: *His power in his creatures*; Job xl. 8: . . . y^u . . . y^t . . .

¶ 167 × 110 mm.
With Genealogies (1638) and Map.
With Prayer Book (? date), Metrical Psalms (1638), and *The Way to True Happinesse* . . . (1633). [F. F.]
345.

—— ANOTHER EDITION.

F.
Z 1 a, heading: *His power in his creatures*; Job xl. 8: . . . *thou* . . . *that* . . . , v. 2 *Almightie*.

¶ 158 × 103 mm. Wants general title.
With Genealogies (1631) and Map, and Downame's Concordance (1652).
With Prayer Book (? date) and Metrical Psalms (1631). [F. F.]
346.

—— ANOTHER EDITION.

G.
Z 1 a, heading: *His power in his creatures*; Job. xl. 8: . . . *thou* . . . *that* . . . , but v. 2 *Almighty*.

¶ 164 × 112 mm. Wants all matter before E 1.
With Genealogies (1631).
With Prayer Book (? date), Metrical Psalms (1630), and *The Way to Trve Happines* . . . (n. d.). [F. F.]
347.

1631. The Holy Bible . . .
                    Barker and Assigns of Bill: London. 1631. 12°.

Colophon on Xx 12 a.
The signature A on the leaf before title is within an ornament.

¶ 151 × 80 mm. Wants Apocrypha.
With Metrical Psalms (1631). [F. F.]
348.

1631. The New Testament . . .
                    Barker and Assigns of Bill: London. 1631. 4°. B. L.

Closely resembles the quarto New Testament of 1612, No. 245 (q.v.). Text ends on p. 686 (not numbered, Vv 8 b), with colophon dated 1631.
Heading on p. 279: *S. Luke* for *S. Iohn*.

¶ 187 × 138 mm. [F. F.]
349.

1631. (The New Testament.)
                    Barker and Assigns of Bill: London. 1631. 8°. B. L.

Text ends on Ii 7 b.
1 Tim. iv. 16, *thy*.

¶ 148 × 94 mm. Imperfect: wanting first sheet. [F. F.]
350.

ENGLISH 167

—— ANOTHER EDITION.

Date not known. No doubt by the same printers.

Headline on Dd 3 a, *to Timohie.*

¶ 143 × 92 mm. Imperfect: wanting several leaves. [F. F.]
351.

1631. (The New Testament.)
　　　　　　Barker and Assigns of Bill: London. 1631. 12°. 𝔅. 𝔏.

A full page contains 42 lines.

¶ 130 × 73 mm. A fragment, containing only the last two leaves of text (with colophon).
[F. F.]
352.

1631. B. 4°. See 1632.
*　　B. 8°. See 1632.*

1632. The Holy Bible . . .
　　　　　　Barker and Assigns of Bill: London. 1632,30. 4°.

N. T. dated 1630, both on the title and in the colophon.
Text ends on Gggg 2 a.

¶ 227 × 163 mm. [F. F.]
353.

1632. The Holy Bible . . .
　　　　　　Barker and Assigns of Bill: London. 1632,31. 4°. 𝔅. 𝔏.

N. T. dated 1631 on title and in colophon.
Text ends on Rrr 8 a.

There are two varieties. Both have a misprint in Jer. viii. 22, *blame* for *balme.*

A.
Ruth iii. 15 *citie*; heading to Deut. *The fifth Booke . . .*

¶ 222 × 166 mm.
With Prayer Book (1630), and Metrical Psalms (1630). [F F.]
354.

—— ANOTHER EDITION.

B.
Ruth iii. 15 *city*; heading to Deut. *The fifth booke . . .*

¶ 204 × 158 mm.
With *A Concordance to the Bible of the Last Translation . . . Allowed by Authority to be printed, and bound with the Bible in all volumes* (1632). This Concordance, by John Downame, or Downham (d. 1652), was apparently first printed in 1631. [F. F.]
355.

1632. The Holy Bible . . .
　　　　　　Barker and Assigns of Bill: London. 1631,32. 8°.

Text ends on Kkk 8 a.
General and N. T. titles dated 1631; colophon dated 1632.

¶ 168 × 111 mm.
With Genealogies (1632) and Map.
With Prayer Book (1632), and Metrical Psalms (1632).
　In contemporary binding, stamped with the royal arms and corner ornaments; with goffered edges. [F. F.]
356.

1632. The Holy Bible . . .
  Barker and Assigns of Bill: London. 1631,82. 8°.

Text ends on Kkk 8 a.
General title dated 1631; N. T. dated 1632 on title and in colophon.
According to Fry, a distinct issue. Ornament to Proverbs—sun (unlike any editions dated 1631 on general title); ornament to Revelation—lion's head (different from the editions dated 1632 in the N. T.).

¶ 158 × 105 mm.
Possibly a mixed copy.
With *The Way to True Happinesse* . . . (1633). [F. F.]

—— Another copy.

164 × 108 mm. Imperfect: wanting both titles and other leaves, but apparently belonging to this edition.
In contemporary binding with brass corners. [F. F.]
357.

1632. The Holy Bible . . .
  Barker and Assigns of Bill: London. 1682,81. 12°.

The colophon on Xx 12 a is dated 1631.

¶ 148 × 84 mm. Wants Apocrypha (supplied from another edition).
With Genealogies and Map.
With Metrical Psalms (1632).
Binding stamped M W; goffered edges. [F. F.]

—— Another copy.

¶ 152 × 81 mm. Wants Apocrypha.
With Metrical Psalms (1634).
Bound in purple velvet, with silver corners and clasps, one of which bears the date 1717.
[F. F.]
358.

1632. The Holy Bible . . .
  Barker and Assigns of Bill: London. 1632. f°.

Perhaps published early in 1633; since in many copies the last figure 2 of the date on the general title has been altered by pen to 3; and possibly in others the date was actually thus printed.

DESCRIPTION. Ten preliminary leaves: title (engraved), verso blank, Dedication—1 f., Preface —7 ff., list of books —1 p., 1 p. containing a large engraving. Text: O. T., ff. 1 to 327 (really 323); Apocrypha end on fo. 404 (really 400) a; N. T. (with title within border) ends on fo. 507 (really 503, Pppp 5) a, with colophon, 1 f. blank.
  Signatures: A¹⁰, A–Z⁶ Aa–Zz⁶ Aaa–Zzz⁶ Aaaa–Pppp⁶; 514 ff. The incorrect foliation is due to mistakes in sheet Qq. At the top of each page are horizontal rules enclosing the headlines.
  The elaborate title-border is that engraved by Hole, and used before in the Geneva folio Bible of 1607 (No. 222). The N. T. title-border resembles that found in the folio edition of 1616 (No. 271), but the lower block has been altered.

¶ 346 × 217 mm.
With Genealogies and Map, supplied from another copy.
With Prayer Book (1632), and Metrical Psalms (1632).
In seventeenth-century binding. [F. F.]

—— Another copy.

327 × 216 mm. Wants the general title, last preliminary leaf, and first leaf of text.
With Prayer Book (? 1633,82), and Metrical Psalms (1632). [F. F.]

—— Another copy.

340 × 216 mm. Wants the general title, some preliminary matter, and other leaves. With Metrical Psalms (1632).

—— Another copy.

This differs from the above in lacking the horizontal rules at the top of each page; but in all other respects it is identical.

347 × 220 mm. The last figure of the date on the general title has been altered by pen to 3.
With Genealogies and Map, supplied from another copy.
With Prayer Book (1633,32), and Metrical Psalms (1632). [F. F.]
359.

1632. The Holy Bible . . .
Barker and Assigns of Bill: London. 1632. 8°.

Text ends on Kkk 8 *a*.

There are at least three varieties of this date.

A.
1 Chron. xxix. 30, last line begins: *all the kingdoms* . . .

¶ 165 × 105 mm. [F. F.]
360.

—— ANOTHER EDITION.

B.
1 Chron. xxix. 30, last line: *uer all the kingdomes* . . . ; ornament before 2 Chron.—face.

¶ 161 × 108 mm.
With Genealogies (1632) and Map.
With Prayer Book (1630), and Metrical Psalms (1632). [F. F.]
361.

—— ANOTHER EDITION.

C.
1 Chron. xxix. 30, last line: *uer all the kingdomes* . . . ; but ornament before 2 Chron.—crown.

¶ 157 × 106 mm. Imperfect: wanting general title and Apocrypha.
A mixed copy, since the colophon is dated 1631; probably it represents a distinct variety of 1632. [F. F.]

—— Another copy.

A mixed copy, the N. T. title and other leaves belonging to an edition of 1639. The test page agrees with var. C.

166 × 106 mm. Imperfect: wanting most of the N. T. (which is supplied from a Geneva Bible of 1596, No. 177), and the Apocrypha.
With Genealogies (1633) and Map. [F. F.]
362.

1632. B. 8°. See 1633.

1633. The Holy Bible . . .
Barker and Assigns of Bill: London. 1682,83. 8°.

Text ends on Kkk 8 *a*.
General title dated 1632; N. T. title and colophon, 1633. Apparently a distinct issue.

¶ 159 × 97 mm. Imperfect: wanting Apocrypha.
With Genealogies (1633) and Map. [F. F.]
363.

1633. The Bible, that is . . . With . . . Annotations . . . Imprinted at Amsterdam, for Thomas Crafoorth. By Iohn Fredericksz Stam, dwelling by the South-Church, at the signe of the Hope. 1633. Cum priuilegio.

4°.

Geneva version; with Tomson's revised New Testament, and Junius' Revelation.

C. Sayle in his *Early English Printed Books in the University Library, Cambridge,* vol. iii. p. 1433, quotes the following passage in illustration of Stam and Crafoorth's connection with the trade in English Bibles: 'On 29 March 1644 J. F. Stam and Thomas Craffurt sell to Hugo Fitz 6000 English Bibles, 12°, to be delivered in August 1644.'

Except for the imprints on the two general titles, on the N. T. title, and in the colophon, this edition is identical with D in the series of quartos in roman type described above under the date 1599 (see No. 191). Apocrypha apparently omitted, though included in list of books. A blank leaf (Qq 8) follows Malachi.

¶ 207 × 156 mm.
With Metrical Psalms (n. d.) [F. F.]

——. Another copy.

Exactly the same as the above, except for the imprints on the N. T. title and in the colophon, which mention *the Deputies of Christopher Barker* . . ., and give the date 1599.
With Metrical Psalms (n. d.) [F. F.]

364.

1633. The Holy Bible . . .

T. and J. Buck: Cambridge. 1633. 4°. 𝔅. 𝔏.

Reprint of the Cambridge edition of 1630.
Text ends on p. 918 (Mmm 3 *b*).
The preliminary leaves are the same as those in the Bucks' black-letter quarto of 1630.
1 Tim. iv. 16, *thy.*

¶ 221 × 158 mm.
With Genealogies and Map, and Downame's Concordance (1632).
With Prayer Book (1630), and Metrical Psalms (1633).
In original binding with brass clasps, etc. [F. F.]

—— Another copy.

Marked by Fry as a 'variation.' But the preliminary leaves which differ have been taken from a copy of the Bucks' quarto in roman type of 1630.

219 × 155 mm.
With Genealogies and Map. [F. F.]

365.

1633. The Holy Bible . . .

Barker and Assigns of Bill: London. 1633. 8°.

Text ends on Kkk 8 *a.*

¶ 165 × 105 mm.
With Genealogies (1633) and Map.
In original binding with brass corners, etc. [F. F.]

366.

1633. The | Holy Bible | Containing | the Old Testament | and the New. | Newly translated out of | the originall tongues, and | with the former diligently | compared and reuised, | by his Majesties speciall | commandement. | Appointed to be read | in Churches. | Edinbvrgh, | Printed by the printers to the | Kings most exellent Majestie. | Cum Privilegio. | Anno Dom 1633.

[*Robert Young.*] 8°.

The first edition of King James' Bible printed in Scotland.

Loftie (No. 66, p. 80) records an octavo edition of the New Testament of this version printed at Edinburgh by the heirs of Hart in 1628 (*cf.* Lee, *Memorial*, p. 82).

It has been supposed that this Bible was published in connection with the coronation of Charles I. at Edinburgh in June, 1633. Robert Young, a Londoner, is said to have become King's Printer for Scotland, 12 April 1632.

The New Testament of this Bible, and the separate New Testament in larger type issued from the same press (see below, No. 372), often contain a series of inserted plates. A contemporary letter, dated 11 July 1638, 'from a person in England to two confidents in Scotland' (printed by Lord Hailes in his *Memorials and Letters relating to the History of Britain in the reign of Charles the First* . . ., Glasgow, 1766, pp. 39–45), contains a manifest allusion to these illustrations : ' That you may taste a little of our condition, I have sent you two of your own Scots Bibles, your New Testament only, wherein they have placed such abominable pictures, that horrible impiety stares through them ; these come forth by public authority ; do you show them to such as you think meet ; I send to each of you one of them.'

The introduction of these plates is described in a pamphlet entitled 'A Second Beacon fired by *Scintilla* . . . Wherein is remembered the former Actings of the Papists in their secret Plots: And now discovering their wicked Designes to set up, advance, and cunningly to usher in *Popery*; By introducing *Pictures* to the *Holy Bible* . . .' (London, 4 Oct. 1652). [See B. M. copy, E. 675. (29).] The author, Michael Sparke (see note after 1640), asserts that a bookbinder of Worcester named Francis Ash, 'a strong and secret Papist,' developed a large business in procuring ' *Popish Books, Pictures*, and the like ' for Roman Catholics in the West of England. Ash 'found an extraordinary *Trade*, especially to join *pictures* to the English Bible in 8ᵛᵒ· which *pictures* he had from Mr. *Robert Peake*, (who after went to *Basing-house*) so that Mr. *Ash* after took a voyage to *France* for *Popish Books*, and *pictures* for the *Bible*, which the *Papists* so much extolled, so that now the *Papists* of late will have *Bibles* in English, and the *Pope* cannot avoid it, but so that all their sorts must have *pictures*, and I fear Popish notes: and by this means *Ash* grew into an extraordinary way to get *Trade* ; I am credibly informed there, that in *France* he dealt for the *pictures* of all the *Popish* sorts, and the most excellent, as of *Vandikes Draft*, and there bargained with an excellent workman Mr. *Hollard* to ingrave and cut them, and gave a piece of money in hand to begin withall, and they there were begun, and divers proffers made of them since.'

For Laud's connection with these illustrated editions called 'the Archbishop of Canterbury's Bibles,' see William Prynne's *Canterburies Doome* . . . (1646), pp. 109–10 : '. . . The Archbishop had in his own private Study a Book of Popish pictures of the Life, Passion, and Death of our Lord Jesus Christ, and of the Virgin *Mary*, printed by *Boetius à Bolswert* in forein parts, *Anno* 1623. [See below, No. 372.] These very Pictures were all licensed by the Archbishops own Chaplain Doctor *Bray*; printed by his own printer and Kinsman *Badger*, in the year 1638. for one *Peake* a *Stationer* (now in armes against the Parliament) and publickly sold and bound up in Bibles ; as was testified by Mr. *Walley* Clerk of Stationers Hall, and *Michael Sparke Senior*. Master *Willingham* likewise attested upon oath concerning these Pictures and Crucifixes put into the Bibles: that Captain *Peak* at Holborne Cundit, Bookseller, who printed these pictures for Bibles, did affirme, that he printed them *with the good liking, and by the speciall direction of the Archbishop, and his Chaplaine* Dr. *Bray*: which Dr. *Bray*, as he said, *carried him divers times to the Archbishop to shew him the prints thereof, as they were cut and finished, who liked them all well, and gave his consent for the binding them up in Bibles* ; saying, *That the Bibles wherein these pictures were bound up, they should be called* THE BISHOP OF CANTERBURIES BIBLES . . .' Prynne continues : '. . . he would corrupt, pollute all our Bibles and New Testaments with these Romish Images bound up in them, to which they are most repugnant. He would suffer no English Bibles to be printed or sold with marginal Notes [i.e. the Geneva version : see note after 1640] to instruct the people, all such must be seized and burnt, as we shall prove anone : but himself gives speciall approbation for the venting of Bibles with Popish pictures taken out of the very Masse book, to seduce the people to popery and idolatry.' *Cf.* pp. 471, 491, 497, and 515 ; and also *The History of the Troubles and Tryal of . William Laud* . . . (1695), pp. 335–6.

DESCRIPTION. Four preliminary leaves : 1 f. bearing on verso a cut of the royal arms, 1 f. bearing on verso a full-page engraving, title (engraved), verso blank, Dedication—1 p., list of books—1 p. Text : O. T., A 3 to Nn 8 *b* ; Apocrypha end on Yy 4 *b* ; N. T. (with title within frame, on verso cut of the royal arms) ends on Mmm 4 *a*, on verso cut of the royal arms.

Signatures : [unsigned]² A–Z⁸ Aa–Xx⁸ Yy⁴, Aaa–Lll⁸ Mmm⁴ ; 450 ff. Leaves not numbered.

The engraved titlepage represents Moses and Aaron, the twelve Tribes, the twelve Apostles, and the four Evangelists. At the top is a triangular symbol of the Trinity, surrounded by a glory, whence issues a hand holding a book, which bears all the letterpress except two lines inscribed on a scroll below. The engraved frontispiece pictures the Fall. The cut of the royal arms displays the shield within a garter. 1 Tim. iv. 16, *thy*.

There are two varieties of this Bible.

A.
Is. lxvi. 24 *carkases*; Ggg 1 *a* catchword: *37 But*; Kkk 3 *a* headline: *Of Widows*.

¶ 172 × 111 mm.
With Metrical Psalms (1633).
In two volumes, the Apocrypha being bound separately from the rest of the Bible.
[F. F.]

—— Another copy.

163 × 106 mm. Very imperfect. [F. F.]

—— Another copy.

165 × 102 mm. Imperfect: containing only the N. T.
This should not be called a distinct edition of the New Testament, though probably some copies were issued separately. It has no list of books, and is merely the N. T. extracted from the above Bible. There is a distinct octavo N. T. of this date printed by Young at Edinburgh (see No. 372).
Contains 50 plates. Many of these are copied from the designs of Boetius à Bolswert (see below, No. 372). The plate of St. Matthew is inscribed *Are to be sould by Robt. Peake at his shopp nere Holborne Conduit*; and others also bear Peake's name. The descriptions are in English. These are evidently some of the 'Popish Pictures' introduced by Ash (see note above). [F. F.]

367.

—— ANOTHER EDITION.

B.
This differs considerably from A in various parts of the book. Isa. lxvi. 24 *carcases*; Ggg 1 *a* catchword: *us*; Kkk 3 *a* headline: *Of widows and elders*.

¶ 161 × 106 mm. Wants the first preliminary leaf.
According to Fry's MS. note the N. T. in this copy was taken from a Bible, the rest of which belonged to the edition of 1637,36 (No. 395). This N. T. differs from that in No. 395.
With Genealogies (1633) and Map.
With *The Way to True Happinesse* . . . (1633). [F. F.]

368.

1633. The Holy Bible . . .
 Barker and Assigns of Bill: London. 1633. 12°.
Colophon on Xx 12 *a*.
Catchword on A 2 *a*: *rested*.

¶ 153 × 83 mm. Wants Apocrypha.
With Prayer Book (1634), and Metrical Psalms (1634).
Bound in vellum. [F. F.]

—— Another copy.

Marked by Fry as a variety, but evidently a mixed copy. Many sheets at the beginning are taken from a copy of the edition of 1632,31; catchword on A 2 *a*: *and*.

146 × 77 mm. Imperfect: wanting preliminary leaves, and Apocrypha.
With Metrical Psalms (1631). [F. F.]

—— Another copy.

The first two leaves belong to the edition of 1632,31; the rest of the book is the edition of 1633.

149 × 79 mm. Wants Apocrypha.
With Metrical Psalms (1632).

Covers embroidered with coloured silks, gold and silver threads, and purl, on a ground of white silk. In the centre of each cover is a pelican feeding her young. The ornaments include peasecods and rosettes. With a beautiful marker of contemporary work.

369.

1633. The New Testament . . . faithfvlly translated . . . By the English Colledge . . . in Rhemes . . . The fourth Edition, enriched with Pictures . . . By Iohn Covstvrier. 1633.

[Qu. *Rouen* ?].   4°.

The fourth edition of the Rheims New Testament.

This generally follows the second edition of 1600. Printed probably at Rouen (see No. 387, 1635).

DESCRIPTION. Fourteen preliminary leaves : first title (engraved), second title (as above), *The Censvre* . . ., Preface, *The Books of the New Testament* . . ., *The signification* . . ., and *The Svmme* . . . Text, pp. 3 to 693; followed by *The Explication* . . ., and tables, ending with a list of *errata* on Ccc 2.
Signatures : [first title,] ā⁴ ē⁴ ī⁴, A–Z⁸ Aa–Xx⁸ Yy⁴ Zz⁴ Aaa⁴ Bbb⁴ Ccc² ; [1 +] 382 ff.
The engravings include the first title, portraits of the four Evangelists, St. Paul, and St. John before Revelation, and a representation of the Day of Pentecost. They are signed *Picquet* and *Michel van Lochom*. The engraved title represents Christ on the Cross and two symbolical figures, *Ecclesia* and *Synagoga*.

¶ 237 × 173 mm.
Bound uniformly with the copy of the O. T. in 2 vols. printed by Coustourier in 1635. All three volumes bear on the titlepage and fly-leaf the following inscriptions : *Miss. Scot. Ord. S. Benedicti comparavit f. Jac. Blair, 1682. Herbipolensis P. P.—Ex Scotica Missione Herbipolim me misit R. P. Jacobus Blair.—Ex libris Monasterij S. Jacobi Scotorum Herbipoli.* [Herbipolis = Würzburg.]   [F. F.]

370.

1633. The Text of the New Testament . . . Translated . . . by the Papists . . . at Rhemes. With Arguments . . . Wherevnto Is Added the Translation . . . vsed in the Church of England : With A confutation . . . By W. Fvlke . . . The 4th Edition, wherein are many grosse absurdities Corrected. London Printed by Augustine Mathewes on of the assignes of Hester Ogden. Cum privilegio Regis. 1633.

f°.

The fourth edition of Dr. Fulke's work. See No. 156.

See Arber, *Transcript*, vol. iii, pp. 39, 40, for a dispute about the ownership of the copyright, between Hester Ogden, and J. Bill, B. Norton and T. Adams, who claimed to be the proprietors of the work after G. Bishop's death.
The Bishops' version still appears as *The Translation of the Church of England.*
A portrait of the author precedes the engraved title. The border of the title contains figures of the Evangelists, SS. Peter and Paul, a Jesuit (*Hinc Zizania*), and a Doctor of the Reformed Church (*Hinc Semen Bonvm*), etc. Both are engraved by W. Marshall. The Dedication to Charles I. is signed by the author's daughter, *Hester Ogden*. Then follow Fulke's Dedication to Elizabeth, etc., *A Catalogve of . . . books . . . written by William Fvlke* . . ., Preface, etc. Text, pp. 1–912 ; table—13 pp., 1 p. blank.

¶ 334 × 214 mm.
With *A Defense of the sincere and trve translation . . . By William Fvlke* . . . (1633). (See No. 156.)

371.

1633. The | New Testament . . . Edinburgh, | Printed by the Printers to the Kings | most excellent Majestie. | Cvm Privilegio. | Anno Dom. 1633.

[*R. Young.*]   8°.

This is usually styled the first edition of the New Testament of King James' version printed in Scotland; but there appears to have been an earlier issue of 1628 (see No. 367).

DESCRIPTION. One preliminary leaf: title (within frame), on verso list of books. Text, A 2 to Oo 4 *a* (?).
Signatures: A–Nn⁸ Oo¹; 108 ff. Printed in fairly large type, with long lines.
1 Tim. iv. 16, *thy*.
Some copies contain a series of plates. (See above, No. 367.)

¶ 159 × 95 mm. Imperfect: wanting I 8, and the last four leaves.
Contains a set of 76 plates. These are identical with those issued in a small devotional book, bearing the title *Vitæ Passionis et Mortis Jesu Christi Domini nostri Mysteria, Piis Meditationibus et Adspirationibus exposita per P. Joannem Bourghesium Malbodiensem é Societate Jesu, Figuris æneis expressa per Boetium a Bolswert* (Antwerp, 1622). The plates are numbered in the right-hand bottom corner. No. 1, *De Annuntiatione B. Virginis*, bears the words *Cum gratia et privilegio*. No. 76, *De Assumptione Deiparæ*, which is placed as a frontispiece before the title, certainly gives ground for the Protestant criticisms in Prynne's *Canterburies Doome* . . . , p. 515, where this particular picture is denounced. See also above, No. 367. The descriptions are in Latin. [F. F.]
372.

1633. The New Testament . . .
    Barker and Assigns of Bill : London. 1633. 12°.
Text ends on Y 12 *b*.

Two varieties occur with this date.

A.
First page of text contains 16 verses.

¶ 102 × 50 mm.
With Metrical Psalms (1633).
Dos-à-dos binding. Covers embroidered with silver threads and coloured silks, representing carnations and pansies, on a background of white silk; with goffered edges. [F. F.]

—— Another copy.

107 × 51 mm.
With Prayer Book (1633), and Metrical Psalms (1634).
Covers embroidered; silk network over canvas, with pattern worked in silver threads; goffered edges. [F. F.]
373.

—— ANOTHER EDITION.

B.
First page of text contains 15 verses.

¶ 102 × 50 mm. Slightly imperfect: wanting a few leaves towards the end. [F. F.]
374.

1633. B. 4°. See 1634.

1634. The Holy Bible . . .
    Barker and Assigns of Bill: London. 1633,34. 4°.

The colophon only is dated 1634.
Text ends on Gggg 2 *a*.

¶ 224 × 166 mm.
With Genealogies and Map, and Downame's Concordance (n. d.).
With Prayer Book (1633,32) and Metrical Psalms (1633). [F. F.]
375.

1634. The | Holy | Bible, | Containing | the Old Testa- | ment, and the New : | Newly Translated out of the | Originall Tongues : And with | the former Translations diligently | compared and reuised, By his | Maiesties speciall Com- | mandement. | Appointed to be read in Churches. | Imprinted at | London by Robert Barker, | Printer to the Kings most Excellent | Maiestie : and by the Assignes | of Iohn Bill. | Anno Dom. 1634.

f°. 𝕭. 𝕷.

The fourth distinct folio edition, printed in large black-letter, of King James' version.

This agrees very closely in all particulars with the folio of 1617. In the preliminary matter, however, a new cut of the royal arms with the initials C R precedes the Dedication, *These to bee obserued* . . . is printed on D 1 b, and *To finde Easter for euer* on D 4 a. Heb. xii. 1 : . . . *runne with patience the race* . . ., instead of *unto the race* as before.
Signatures, as in the 1617 edition.

¶ 423 × 276 mm. Printed on paper stained green.
In seventeenth-century binding, with fleurs-de-lys, etc. [F. F.]
376.

1634. The Holy Bible . . .
        Barker and Assigns of Bill : London. 1634. 4°. 𝕭. 𝕷.

A new form of quarto Bible in black-letter.

DESCRIPTION. Eight preliminary leaves : title, verso blank, Dedication—3 pp., 1 p. blank, Preface—9 pp., list of books—1 p. Text : O. T., pp. 1 to 582 ; Apocrypha end on p. 718 ; N. T. ends on p. 904 (Lll 4 b) with colophon.
    Signatures : A⁸, A–Z⁸ Aa–Zz⁸ Aaa–Kkk⁸ Lll⁴ ; 460 ff.
    1 Tim. iv. 16, *thy.*

There appear to be no less than three varieties.

A.
General title : . . . *revised,* | *by* . . .; Gen. i. 4, *darkenesse* ; N. T. title : . . . *of our* . . .

¶ 220 × 164 mm.
With Genealogies and Map. [F F.]
377.

—— ANOTHER EDITION.
B.
General title : . . . *re-* | *vised, By* . . .; Gen. i. 4, *darkenesse* ; N. T. title : . . . *Of our* . . .

¶ 217 × 160 mm.
With Genealogies and Map. [F. F.]

—— Another copy.

223 × 166 mm. Wanting general title.
With Genealogies, and Downame's Concordance (1632).
With Prayer Book (? date), and Metrical Psalms (1634).
378.

—— ANOTHER EDITION.
C.
General title as in B ; Gen. i. 4, *darknesse* ; N. T. title as in A ; p. 3 heading *Cains genealogie* for *Adams genealogie*.

¶ 229 × 165 mm.
With Genealogies and Map.
With Prayer Book (1634), and Metrical Psalms (1634).
In original binding, with brass corners, etc [F. F.]
379.

1634. The Holy Bible . . .
  Barker and Assigns of Bill: London. 1634. 8°.
Text ends on Kkk 8 *a*.

There are some varieties of this date.

A.
Small cut of royal arms with initials C R on verso of general title; N. T. title: *The | New Testament |* . . .

¶ 163 × 104 mm.
With Genealogies (1634) and Map. [F. F.]
380.

—— ANOTHER EDITION.

B.
Large cut on verso of general title (which has one line *Appointed . . . Churches* between black lines); N. T. title: *The | New Testa- | ment |* . . .

¶ 165 × 107 mm.
With Genealogies (1634) and Map.
With Prayer Book (1633), and Metrical Psalms (1634).
In seventeenth-century binding. [F. F.]

—— Another copy.

163 × 106 mm.
With Genealogies (1635).
With Prayer Book (? date), and Metrical Psalms (1636).

—— Another copy.

163 × 107 mm.

—— Another copy.

161 × 102 mm. Imperfect: wanting general title and all the N. T. In two volumes.
With Genealogies (1633) and Map.

—— Another copy.

The N. T. only; bound with an imperfect copy of an octavo of 1636 (No. 391).
381.

—— ANOTHER EDITION.

C.
Large cut on verso of title (which has no black lines); N. T. title as in A.

¶ 168 × 104 mm.
With Genealogies (1634) and Map. [F. F.]
382.

1634. The Holy | Bible | Containing . . . Newly translated . . . Appointed to be read in | churches. | Edinbvrgh, | Printed by the Printers to the | Kings most excellent | Majestie. | Cvm Privilegio. | Anno Dom. 1634.
  [*R. Young.*] 12°.

The first duodecimo edition of King James' version published in Scotland.

DESCRIPTION. Two preliminary leaves: title (within narrow frame), on verso the list of books, Dedication—1 f. Text: O. T., A 3 to Hh 6 *b*; [Apocrypha, ——;] N. T., with title (within frame, with list of books on verso), ends on K 6 *b*.
Signatures: A–Z¹² Aa–Gg¹² Hh⁶, [—,] A–I¹² K⁶; 480 [+—] ff. Double columns; short headlines; chapter-contents.

ENGLISH 177

It is possible that the Apocrypha, though given in the list of books, were not included in this edition. There is no catchword on the last page of Malachi. In the N. T. the signatures begin afresh, the title being A 1.
Headline to second page of Dedication: *The Epitsle Dedicatorie.* 1 Tim. iv. 16, *thy.*

¶ 145 × 83 mm.
Wants Apocrypha?
Title slightly mended. [F. F.]

383.

1634. B. 4°. *See 1636.*
B. 12°. *See 1635 and 1644.*

1635. The Holy Bible . . .
Barker and Assigns of Bill: London. 1684,85. 12°.

General title dated 1634; N. T. dated 1635 on title and in colophon.
A new style of duodecimo Bible. Text: O. T., A 3 to Gg 6 *b*; [Apocrypha—;] N. T., Pp 2 to Zz 12 *b*. Both titles have the architectural border (with figure of King David, etc.).

¶ 146 × 82 mm. Wants Apocrypha.
With Prayer Book (? date), and Metrical Psalms (1635). [F. F.]

—— Another copy.

146 × 79 mm. Imperfect: wanting N. T. title and other leaves, and all the Apocrypha.
With Genealogies.
With Prayer Book (? date), and Metrical Psalms (1635).

384.

1635. The Holy Bible . . .
Tho : Buck and Roger Daniel, printers to the University of Cambridge. 1635. 4°.

Reprint of the Cambridge quarto in roman type of 1630.
Text ends on Eeee 5 *a*.
1 Tim. iv. 16, *thy.*

¶ 226 × 168 mm.
With Genealogies (1638) and Map.
With Metrical Psalms (1634), and Prayer Book (1635). [F. F.]

385.

1635. The Holy Bible . . .
Barker and Assigns of Bill: London. 1635. 8°.

Text ends on Kkk 8 *a*.
Small cut of royal arms on verso of general title.

¶ 169 × 109 mm.
With Genealogies (1634) and Map.
With Prayer Book (1635), and Metrical Psalms (1636).
Seventeenth-century binding, with silver clasps.

—— Another copy.

162 × 108 mm.
With Genealogies (1634) and Map.
With Prayer Book (1634), and Metrical Psalms (1635). [F. F.]

—— Another copy.

Marked by Fry as a variety, but evidently a mixed copy. The general title belongs to an edition of 1636; the last figure of the date has been altered by pen to 5. The N. T. is dated 1635.

160 × 101 mm. Imperfect: wanting Apocrypha. F F⌋

386

VOL. I. N

1635. The Holy Bible faithfvlly translated ... By the English Colledge of Dovvay ... Printed by Iohn Covstvrier. Permissv svperiorvm. M.DC.XXXV.

[*Rouen.*]   4°.   2 vols.

The second edition of the Roman Catholic version of the Old Testament, first published in 1609,10 at Douai.

For a period of 115 years after this date (1635-1750), according to Cotton, not a single edition of the Douai-Rheims version of the Bible was published.

> The general arrangement of the matter in these volumes follows that of the earlier edition. An engraved title is found in some copies placed before the ordinary title. Each page is surrounded by rules.
> Signatures: vol. 1: [first title] A-Z⁴ Aa-Zz⁴ Aaa-Zzz⁴ Aaaa-Zzzz⁴ Aaaaa-Zzzzz⁴ Aaaaaa-Nnnnnn⁴ Oooooo²; vol. 2: [first title] A-Z⁴ Aa-Zz⁴ Aaa-Zzz⁴ Aaaa-Zzzz⁴ Aaaaa-Zzzzz⁴, Aaaaaa-Kkkkkk⁴ ā⁴ ē⁴ ī⁴ ō⁴ ū²; [2+] 1032 ff.
> The last page contains an extract from the royal license granted to *Iean le Covstvrier* of Rouen to print these Bibles in English, dated 3 August 1634.

231 × 178 mm.   Wanting the engraved title in each volume.   [F. F.]

387.

1635. The New Testament ...

Barker and Assigns of Bill: London.   1635.   8°.   𝕭. 𝕷.

A new style of black-letter octavo New Testament, with a rather longer page, containing 49 lines. Text ends on Ee 8 *b*; no colophon.
Signatures: A-Z⁸ Aa-Ee⁸; 224 ff.
Title-border as in the edition of 1622, No. 297.
1 Tim. iv. 16, *thy.*

¶ 141 × 86 mm.
With Metrical Psalms (1635,36).   [F. F.]

388.

1635. The New Testament ...

Robert Young, Printer to the Kings most excellent Majesty:
Edinburgh.   1635.   8°.   𝕭. 𝕷.

Corresponds generally to the London edition of the same date. One preliminary leaf: title (within narrow frame), with list of books on verso. Text, A 2 to Ee 8 *b*.
1 Tim. iv. 16, *thy.*

¶ 145 × 92 mm.   [F. F.]

389.

1636. The Holy Bible ...

Barker and Assigns of Bill: London.   1634,36.   4°.   𝕭. 𝕷.

General title dated 1634; N. T. dated 1636 on title, but 1634 in colophon.
Text ends on p. 904 (Lll 4 *b*).
The general title is like that in var. A of 1634; Gen. i. 4, *darknesse*; p. 3 headline *Adams genealogie.*

¶ 231 × 166 mm.
With Genealogies, and Downame's Concordance (n d.).   [F. F.]

--- Another copy.

220 × 163 mm.
With Downame's Concordance (n. d).

390.

1636. The Holy Bible . . .

     Barker and Assigns of Bill: London. 1636. 8°.

Text ends on Kkk 8 *a*.

Several varieties are found with this date.

A.
General title: . . . *the | Old Testament |* . . ., with small cut of royal arms on verso; N. T. title: . . . *Saviovr | Iesvs* . . .

¶ 169 × 109 mm.
With Genealogies (1636) and Map.
Original binding, with brass corners, etc.   [F. F.]

—— Another copy.

Evidently a mixed copy. The O. T. is partly like A; the N. T. belongs to var. B of 1634.

167 × 109 mm. Imperfect: wanting Apocrypha.
With Prayer Book (1635), Metrical Psalms (1636), and *The Way to True Happinesse* . . . (1633).
 Inserted in the N. T. are many plates. Some are like those occasionally found in the Edinburgh editions of 1633 and 1636 (Nos. 367, 368, 372, 395); and others bear the inscriptions *M. de Vos figuravit, Iac. de Weert sculp.*, and *Ioan. Baptista Vrints excud.* They include large portraits of the Apostles.   [F. F.]
                               391.

—— ANOTHER EDITION.

B.
General title: . . . *the Old | Testament |* . . . with large cut on verso. Ornament before Mark—man's head.

¶ 169 × 102 mm. Imperfect; wanting N. T. title and four other leaves. [F. F.]

—— Another copy.

Generally agrees with B, but differs in places. Probably a mixed copy.

161 × 103 mm.
With Genealogies (1636) and Map.   [F. F.]
                               392.

—— ANOTHER EDITION.

C.
General title as in B; N. T. title: . . . *Saviour | Jesus* . . . Ornament before Mark— open book.

¶ 164 × 102 mm.
With Metrical Psalms (1637), and *The Way to True Happinesse* . . . (1633).

—— Another copy.

Generally agrees with C, but differs in places. Probably a mixed copy.

160 × 105 mm.
With Genealogies (1636) and Map, and Downame's Concordance (1633).
With *The Way to True Happinesse* . . . (1633).   [F. F.]

—— Another copy.

Generally agrees with C; but a mixed copy.

160 × 104 mm. Imperfect: wanting general title and following leaf, and N. T. title; other leaves are supplied from another edition.
With Metrical Psalms (? date).   [F. F.]

—— Another copy.

A fragment only.   [F. F.]
                               393.

1636. (The New Testament.)
Barker and Assigns of Bill: London. 1636. 8°. B. L.

Text ends on Ee 8 b. A colophon is added in this edition.
1 Tim. iv. 16, *thy*.

¶ 144 × 85 mm. Imperfect: wanting title, and seven other leaves. [F. F.]
394.

1636. B. 8°. See 1637.

1637. The Holy Bible . . .
R. Young: Edinburgh. 1637,86. 8°.

The second octavo edition of King James' version printed in Scotland.
The N. T. title is dated 1636.
Closely resembles the edition of 1633, with the text ending on Mmm 4 a. The cut of the royal arms on verso of the first preliminary leaf is smaller than that on the last page. No cut on verso of N. T. title.

¶ 162 × 108 mm.
With Genealogies (1637) and Map. F. F.]

—— Another copy.

158 × 101 mm. Containing the N. T. only.
Inserted are many plates like those found in the edition of 1633 (No. 367). [F. F.]
395.

1637. The Holy Bible . . .
Buck and Daniel: Cambridge. 1637. 4°.

A new form of quarto in roman type.

DESCRIPTION. [Eight] preliminary leaves: [engraved title, or 1 f. blank?] title, verso blank, Dedication—1 f., Preface—9 pp., list of books—1 p. Text: O. T., 612 pp.; Apocrypha, 144 pp.; N. T., 191 pp., ending on M 8 a.
Signatures: F⁸, A–Z⁸ Aa–Oo⁸ Pp¹⁰, (A)–(I)⁸, A–M⁸; 482 ff.
Both titles enclosed in a narrow frame, with the device *Alma Mater Cantabrigia*.
Matt. i. 24 *he called his sonne Jesus* for *he called his name Jesus*, xii. 42 *shall up* for *shall rise up*; 1 Tim. iv. 16, *thy*.

¶ 233 × 162 mm. Wants one leaf before general title. [F. F.]
396.

1637. The Holy Bible . . .
The Printers to the University of Cambridge. 1637. 4°. B. L.

Text ends on p. 918 (Mmm 3 b). Each page enclosed within rules.
Both titles have a narrow frame, and device.
1 Tim. iv. 16, *thy*.

¶ 225 × 166 mm.
With Genealogies and Map. [F. F.]
397.

1637. The Holy Bible . . .
Barker and Assigns of Bill: London. 1637. 8°.

Text ends on Kkk 8 a.

At least three varieties occur with this date.

A.
General title, *Tongues*; N. T. title, *Greek*.

ENGLISH 181

Subject-headings in headlines in italics.

¶ 170 × 112 mm.
With Genealogies (1638) and Map. [F. F.]
398.

—— ANOTHER EDITION.

B.
General title, *Tongues*; N. T. title, *Greeke*.
Subject-headings in headlines in italics. A different cut before Genesis.

¶ 167 × 110 mm.
With Genealogies (1636) and Map. [F. F.]
399.

—— ANOTHER EDITION.

C.
General title, *tongues*; N. T. title, *Greeke*.
Subject-headings in headlines in roman type.

¶ 164 × 104 mm.
With Genealogies (1636) and Map. [F. F.]

—— Another copy.

158 × 101 mm. Imperfect: wanting Apocrypha; also some leaves in the N. T. (supplied from another edition). [F. F.]

—— Another copy.

A mixed copy. The first part of the volume belongs to var. B of 1639 (No. 420).
400.

1637. B. 4°. See 1638.

1638. The Holy Bible . . .
Barker and Assigns of Bill: London. 1637,38. 4°.

General title dated 1637; N. T. dated 1638 on title and in colophon.
Another new form of quarto in roman type.

DESCRIPTION. Eight preliminary leaves: title, etc. Text: O. T. ends on p. 744; Apocrypha end on p. 920; N. T. ends on p. 1152 (Cccc 8 *b*).
Signatures: ¶⁸, A–Z⁸ Aa–Zz⁸ Aaa–Zzz⁸ Aaaa–Cccc⁸; 584 ff.
Both titles are within the border with heart-shaped centre; the general title has a cut of the royal arms on verso. A cut of Adam and Eve occurs before Genesis.
1 Tim. iv. 16, *thy*.

¶ 229 × 165 mm. [F. F.]

—— Another copy.

Marked by Fry as a 'variation'; but apparently it differs only in the ornament before the Preface.

231 × 166 mm.
In seventeenth-century binding. [F. F.]
401.

1638. The Holy Bible . . .
Buck and Daniel: Cambridge. 1637,38. 4°.

General title not dated. N. T. dated 1637 on title, but 1638 in colophon
Text ends on p. 1153 (Eeee 5 *a*).
General title engraved. N. T. title in narrow frame, with device.
1 Tim. iv. 16, *thy*.

¶ 229 × 167 mm.
With Prayer Book (1638), and Metrical Psalms (1638).　　　　　　　[F. F.]

—— Another copy.

Marked by Fry 'variation'; but differs only in the ornament before the Preface. This leaf (¶ 3) is identical with that in the Cambridge black-letter quarto of 1637.

225 × 165 mm.
In seventeenth-century binding, stamped with the royal arms, etc.　　　[F. F.]
402.

1638. The Holy Bible . . .
Tho: Buck and Roger Daniel, Printers to the University of Cambridge. 1638. f°.

'The authentique corrected *Cambridge Bible*, revised *Mandato Regio*, by the learned Doctor *Ward*, Doctor *Goad* of *Hadley*, Mr. Boyse, Mr. Mead, &c., and printed by the elaborate industry of *Thomas Buck* Esquire and Mr. *Roger Daniel* in *folio* in 1638.' (William Kilburne's tract *Dangerous Errors in Several late printed Bibles* . . ., 1659, reprinted in the Introduction to Loftie's *A Century of Bibles*, 1872, p. 35.)

In this edition, thus favourably noticed by Kilburne, the work of correction begun in the folio Cambridge Bible of 1629 was carried further. The revisers took special pains to render uniform the use of italics; and they also introduced a certain number of new readings: e.g. Matt. xii. 23, *Is not this the sonne of David?* (for *Is this* . . .), and 1 John v. 12 . . . *hath not the Sonne of God (of God* added). Here first occurs the famous reading in Acts vi. 3, . . . *whom ye may appoint* (for . . . *whom we* . . .). This alteration has often been ascribed to the Puritans, and was reputed to have cost Cromwell a bribe of 1000*l.*; yet here it is found as early as 1638, in a Bible prepared under the royal sanction.
1 Tim. iv. 16, *thy.*

This remained the standard text until the publication of Dr. Paris' Cambridge edition of 1762.

DESCRIPTION. [Seven] preliminary leaves: [1 f. blank?] title (engraved), verso blank, Dedication—1 f., Preface—7 pp., list of books—1 p. Text: O. T. pp. 1 to 642 (Iii 4 *b*); Apocrypha, pp. 1 to 151 (Yyy 4 *a*), verso blank; N. T. (with title, bearing device and date 1638), pp. 1 to 202 (R 6 *b*).
Signatures: [—]² A–Z⁶ Aa–Zz⁶ Aaa–Ggg⁶ Hhh⁴ Iii⁴, Kkk–Xxx⁶ Yyy¹, A–R⁶; 506 ff. The text begins on A 6. There is no colophon.
The engraved title (*Will: Marshall. sculp:*) resembles in general design that in the 1629 edition, but it is redrawn and enlarged, and contains a small device *Alma Mater Cantabrigia* in the centre. The ordinary device occurs on the N. T. titlepage.

¶ 375 × 234 mm.
With Metrical Psalms (1638).　　　　　　　　　　　　　　　　　　[F. F.]

—— Another copy.

397 × 270 mm. Wants the Apocrypha. Printed on large thick paper.
In seventeenth-century binding.　　　　　　　　　　　　　　　　　[F. F.]
403.

1638. The Holy Bible . . .
Barker and Assigns of Bill: London. 1638. 8°.
Text ends on Kkk 8 *a.*

At least three varieties occur with this date.

A.
Ornament before Ezra—church; ornament before Hebrews—man's face.

¶ 163 × 103 mm.
With Genealogies (1637) and Map.　　　　　　　　　　　　　　　　[F. F.]

—— Another copy.

169 × 112 mm. Slightly imperfect.
With Genealogies (1638) and Map. [F. F.]
404.

—— ANOTHER EDITION.

B.
Ornament before Ezra—lion and unicorn; ornament before Hebrews—lion and unicorn (inverted).

¶ 166 × 107 mm.
With Genealogies (1638) and Map. [F. F.]
405.

—— ANOTHER EDITION.

C.
Ornament before Ezra—hare and dogs; ornament before Hebrews—foliage.

¶ 165 × 105 mm.
With Genealogies (1638) and Map.
With Prayer Book (? date), and Metrical Psalms (1638). [F. F.]
406.

1638. The Holy Bible . . .
Barker and Assigns of Bill : London. 1638. 12°.

Similar to the edition of 1634,35, with the text ending on Zz 12 b.
1 Tim. iv. 16, *the*.

¶ 146 × 82 mm. Wants Apocrypha.
With Genealogies (1638) and Map.
With Metrical Psalms (1638).
Covers embroidered with coloured silks, silver threads, and purl, on white satin; showing under arches figures of Faith and Hope. [F. F.]
407.

1638. The Holy Bible . . .
Barker and Assigns of Bill : London. 1638. 12°.

Possibly printed abroad; but quite distinct from the very incorrect Dutch editions described below under this same date. A full column contains 71 or 72 lines.

> One preliminary leaf: title, with list of books on verso. Text: O. T., A 2 to Ee 6 b; N. T. Ee 8 to Oo 4 a. The Apocrypha, though mentioned in the list of books, were perhaps omitted, as the signatures run continuously through the O. T. and N. T. Contents before chapters.
> Both titles are plain, with a small ornament above the imprint.
> 1 Tim. ii. 9, *shamefulnesse*; iv. 16, *thy*.

¶ 160 × 90 mm.
Wants Apocrypha?
With Metrical Psalms (1638).
On a blank leaf at the end an early hand has written out *Ane animadversion anent purgatorie.*
Seventeenth-century binding, with clasps. [F. F.]
408.

1638. The Holy Bible . . .
Barker and Assigns of Bill : London. 1638. 12°.

Considered to be a spurious edition, printed in Holland, and published some years after the date given on the title.

Kilburne, in his tract *Dangerous Errors* . . . (1659), evidently refers to this issue when he says: 'Moreover during the time of the late Parliament great numbers of Bibles in a large 12° volume, were imported from *Holland* in 1656 with this false Title (*Imprinted at London by Rob. Barker, &c. Anno* 1638.) wherein Mr. *Kiffin* and Mr. *Hills* cannot be excused, (if reports be true,) being contrary to the several Acts of Parliament of 20° *Sep.* 1649, and 7. *Janu*, 1652. for regulating of Printing. Wherein are so many notorious *Erratas*, false English, Nonsense, and Corruptions, that in reading part of *Genesis*, I found 30 grand faults . . . The very Importation of the Books being an offence contrary to the said Statutes, and ought deservedly to be suppressed; which notwithstanding are dispersed in the Country as aforesaid.'

A manifest reference to this same edition occurs in *Operis Historici et Chronologici Libri Duo* . . . Amsterdam, 1668, by Robert Baillie (1599-1662), Divinity Professor in Glasgow University. See Lib. 1. Cap. 6. Quæstio 12, p. 55 : 'An Samuel ex posteris Corhæ ? Queritur duodecimo, Quomodo Samuelis prosapia referatur ad Corham, nam 1 Paral. 6. v. 26. & 27. Samuel numeratur decimus septimus à Corhâ, & tamen tota Corhæ progenies cum patre destructa videtur; nam Num. 26. v. 10. bis mille quinquaginta ex posteris Corhæ cœlesti flammâ necati sunt? Resp. Sic quidem habent Biblia vernacula in octavo minori quæ dicuntur impressa Londini à Roberto Barkero, ann. 1638. sed monendi estis ad vestram & aliorum cautelam, editionem istam multis centuriis crassissimorum errorum scatere & in ipsa fronte putidissimum mendacium ferre, nequaquam enim vel Londini vel à Barkero vel anno 38. excusa est, sed nuper Amstelodami, Delphis, & alibi in Bataviâ ab Hollandis cupiditate quæstus (ut ab ipsis Typographis accepi) supra septies centena millia corruptissimorum istorum Bibliorum edita sunt, in magnum ecclesiarum nostrarum detrimentum.' The number given—700,000 copies—is almost incredible, but these pirated editions, printed abroad, certainly had an enormous circulation.

This edition agrees generally page for page with the Edinburgh edition of 1634, and with that of 1634,44. It abounds in gross misprints.

DESCRIPTION. Two preliminary leaves: title, with list of books on verso, Dedication—1 f. Text: O. T., A 3 to Gg 12 b; [Apocrypha—;] N. T. (with title, verso blank) A 2 to K 6 b. Each page is surrounded by rules. Contents before chapters. Apparently the Apocrypha, though included in the list of books, were generally omitted.

Both titles have the border with architectural design (King David, etc.).
1 Tim. iv. 16, *thy*.

There are some varieties. All abound in errors.

A.
This has all the errors in the specimen-list given by Lea Wilson (pp. 110-11)—e.g. Gen. xxxvii. 2, *Belial* for *Bilhah*; Isa. i. 6, *purifying* for *putrifying*; Luke xix. 29, *ten* for *two*— except those in Num. xxv. 18 and xxvi. 10 (on one leaf).

¶ 149 × 87 mm. Wants Apocrypha?
With Metrical Psalms (1638).
Bound in vellum. This copy came from a Bavarian monastery; the titlepage bears the inscription: *Est Stephani F. Tolnai Monrij S. Iacobi Scotorum Ratisbonæ Sub Abbate Placido*.
[F. F.]
409.

—— ANOTHER EDITION.

B.
Some of the words given in Lea Wilson's list of errors are here correct; e.g. Gen. i. 26, *man* not *men*; 2 Chron. xxxiv. 2, *right* not *evil*; Isa. xxix. 13, *precept* not *people*; 1 Cor. vii. 34, *please* not *praise*. But Num. xxv. 18 *wives* for *wiles*, etc.

¶ 152 × 88 mm. Wants Apocrypha?
With Metrical Psalms (1638).
[F. F.]
410.

—— ANOTHER EDITION.

C.
This has some of the errors in Lea Wilson's list; e.g. 2 Sam. xxiii. 20, *lions like men* for *lion-like men*; Ezek. v. 11, *piety* for *pity*; Luke vii. 47, *forgotten* for *forgiven*. Others are correct; e.g. Neh. iv. 9, *made* not *read*; John xviii. 29, *out* not *not*.

¶ 146 × 80 mm. Wants Apocrypha?
[F. F.]
411

ENGLISH 185

—— ANOTHER EDITION.

D.

This has some of the errors in Lea Wilson's list; e.g. Isa. xlix. 22, *their sons* for *thy sons*; 1 Tim. ii. 9, *shamefulnesse* for *shamefastnesse*. Others are correct; e.g. 2 Chron. xxxvi. 14, *hallowed* not *polluted*.

¶ 152 × 81 mm. Wants Apocrypha?
The N. T. title in this copy is dated 1669, and has evidently been inserted. Its border differs somewhat from that of the general title.
With Metrical Psalms (1638). [F. F.]
412.

1638. The New Testament . . .
    Barker and Assigns of Bill: London. 1638. 8°. 𝕭. 𝕷.

Text ends on Ee 8 *b*, without colophon.
1 Tim. iv. 16, *thy*.

¶ 138 × 85 mm. [F. F.]
413.

1638. The New Testament . . .
    Barker and Assigns of Bill: London. 1638. 12°.

Text ends on Y 12 *b*.
Matt. i. contents, *genealogie*; i. 1, *sonne*.

¶ 104 × 48 mm.
With Metrical Psalms (1640).
Covers embroidered with coloured silks, silver thread, and purl, on a ground of satin; each central panel contains a tulip; goffered edges. [F. F.]
414.

—— ANOTHER EDITION.

Date not known. No doubt by the same printers

Similar to the above.
Matt. i. contents, *genealogie*; i. 1, *son*.

¶ 109 × 51 mm. Imperfect: wanting title and Y 5.
With Prayer Book (1638), and Metrical Psalms (1640).
Contemporary *dos-à-dos* binding; with goffered edges.
415.

—— ANOTHER EDITION.

Date not known. No doubt by the same printers.

Similar to the above.
Matt. i. contents, *genealogy*; i. 1, *sonne*.

¶ 102 × 50 mm. Imperfect: wanting title and one or two other leaves. [F. F.]
416.

1639. The Holy Bible . . .
    Barker and Assigns of Bill: London. 1689. 4°. 𝕭. 𝕷.

Text ends on Lll 4 *b*. Leaves not numbered. Each page is enclosed within rules.
1 Tim. iv. 16, *thy*.

¶ 222 × 166 mm. [F. F.]
417.

1639. The Holy Bible . . .
     Buck and Daniel : Cambridge. 1639. 4°. 𝕭. 𝕷.

Text ends on p. 918 (Mmm 3 *b*).
1 Tim. iv. 16, *thy*.

¶ 230 × 163 mm.
With Genealogies (1638) and Map, and Downame's Concordance (n. d.).
With Metrical Psalms (1639), and Prayer Book (1640).
In contemporary binding, with brass clasps.   [F. F.]
                         418.

1639. The Holy Bible . . .
     Barker and Assigns of Bill : London. 1639. 8°.

Text ends on Kkk 8 *a*.

Varieties occur with this date.

A.
Gen. l. 10 : . . . *of Atad,* | *which* . . .; N. T. title, *Tetsament*.

¶ 166 × 107 mm.
With Genealogies (1638) and Map.   [F F.]

—— Another copy.

161 × 102 mm. Imperfect : wanting N. T. title, and other leaves. [F. F.]

—— Another copy.

169 × 107 mm.
With Genealogies (1638) and Map.
                         419.

—— ANOTHER EDITION.

B.
Gen. l. 10 : *of A-* | *tad, which* . . .; N. T. title, *Testament* (correct).

¶ 162 × 103 mm.   [F. F.]

—— Another copy.

165 × 103 mm. Imperfect : wanting the Apocrypha ; also the N. T. title, and part of the text (supplied from an edition of the Geneva version). In two volumes.

—— Another copy.

A mixed copy. Half the volume belongs to var. C of 1637 (No. 400).

163 × 103 mm.   [F. F.]
                         420.

1639. B. *f°.* *See 1640.*
    B. *4°.* *See 1640.*
    B. *8°.* *See 1640.*
    B. *12°.* *See 1641.*

1640. The Holy | Bible : | Containing | The Old | Testament | and | The New. | Newly Translated out of | the originall Tongues : | And with the former Translations | diligently compared and revised, | by His Majesties speciall | commandment. | Appointed to be read in Churches. | London : | Printed by Robert Barker, | Printer to the Kings most Excellent | Majestie : And by the Assignes of | John Bill. 1640.
                 1640,39. f°. 𝕭. 𝕷.

The last of the folio editions in large black-letter printed between 1611 and 1640.
The N. T. title is dated 1639.
It generally agrees very closely with the earlier editions; but the type is somewhat worn, and the rules round the pages do not meet at the corners. Marginal readings in roman type, instead of italics.
Signatures, etc., as before.

¶ 432 × 273 mm.
In the original binding with brass corners, clasps, etc. [F. F.]

421.

1640. The Holy Bible . . .
              Buck and Daniel : Cambridge.   1640,39.   4°.   𝕭. 𝕷.

The N. T. is dated 1639, according to Loftie p. 110.
Texts ends on p. 918 (Mmm 3 b).
1 Tim. iv. 16, *thy.*

¶ 217 × 163 mm. Wants N. T. title and other leaves.
With Prayer Book (? date), and Metrical Psalms (? date). [F. F.]

422.

1640. The Holy Bible . . .
              Barker and Assigns of Bill : London.   1640,39.   8°.

N. T. dated 1639 on the title, but 1640 in the colophon.
A new form of octavo Bible, in somewhat larger type, with 72 lines to the full page. O. T. begins on A 3 and ends on Pp 7 b; Apocrypha end on Aaa 7 b; N. T. ends on Nnn 8 a. Small cut of royal arms with initials C R on verso of general title. Cut of Adam and Eve before Genesis, similar to that used in var. B of 1637 (No. 399).

¶ 179 × 113 mm.
With Genealogies (1640) and Map. [F. F.]

—— Another copy.

180 × 114 mm. Imperfect : wanting Apocrypha.
Covers embroidered with coloured silks and silver threads, representing figures of Hope and Faith. Silver corners and clasps—perhaps of a later date. Contains record of successive owners, from the original possessor, who worked the covers.
With Metrical Psalms (1640). [F. F.]

—— Another copy.

184 × 119 mm. Imperfect : containing only the O. T., the title of which is wanting.
[F. F.]

—— Another copy.

178 × 111 mm. Imperfect: wanting all the Apocrypha, and many other leaves. Inserted at the beginning is the first sheet of an edition of 1644 (No. 450). [F. F.]

423.

1640. The Bible: | That is, | The Holy Scriptvres | contained . . . Amsterdam. | Printed by Thomas Stafford : And are to be sold at his house, at the | signe of the Flight of Brabant, upon the Milk-market, over against the | Deventer Wood-market. cIɔ Iɔ c xl. | According to the Copy printed at Edinburgh by Andro Hart, in the year 1610.

f°.

Geneva version ; with Tomson's revised New Testament, and Junius' Revelation.
The Apocryphal books, with the exception of the Prayer of Manasses, are omitted, for reasons specified in a note inserted after Malachi. This seems to be the earliest example of an English Bible which deliberately omits the Apocrypha from the list of books. See Preface to this volume.

DESCRIPTION. Four preliminary leaves: [1 f. blank], title, verso blank, *To the Christian Reader*—1 f. (signed ¶ 3), *Of the incomparable treasure* ...—1 p., list of books—1 p. Text: O. T. (1) Genesis–Job, pp. 1 to 469 (really 467), 1 p. blank; (2) Psalms–Malachi, pp. 1 to 316 (not numbered); *An Admonition to the Christian Reader : Concerning the Apocrypha-Books* ... ending with the words *Ordained at the Synode of Dort in the yeare 1618*. *Set out and annexed, by the Deputies, to the end of the Dutch Bible newly Translated*— 2 ff. N. T., with title, verso blank, *The Printer to the Diligent Reader*—1 p., *The description* ... (with map)—1 p., text – pp. 1 to 267; tables—13 pp., ending on Mm 4 b. Signatures: ¶^{4}, A–Z^6 Aa–Qq^6, A–Z^4 Aa–Pp^4 Qq^6, ¶^{2}, ¶^{2}, A–Z^4 Aa–Mm^4; 540 ff. The page-number is given only on the recto of each leaf.

The running title *Psalmes* in the Psalter is printed in italics.

The general titlepage bears a cut of the crossing of the Red Sea; the N. T. titlepage has an ornament—a female head between two cornucopiæ. Two full-page engravings, copied from those inserted in A. Hart's edition of 1610, occur in Exodus, on G 1 a and G 2 b.

Lea Wilson (p. 111–2) considers that there are two distinct impressions of this edition; and Fry alludes to a 'variation edition.' But probably these 'varieties' are merely mixed copies containing a certain number of leaves which correctly belong to the very similar edition of 1644; though perhaps a few sheets, of which the supply ran short, were reprinted before that date.

Christianus Ravius of Berlin refers, in the preface of his work *Prima tredecim partium Alcorani Arabico-Latini* (Amsterdam, 1646, 4°), to the large number of English Bibles printed in Amsterdam: '... Quod si forte non videatur credibile, sciendum, nullam nationem, ne ipsam quidem Germaniam, ut typographia longè anteriorem, tot editiones Bibliorum annumerare posse, quot sola Anglia : cum unus vir Anglus, hic Amstelodami intra 4. vel 5. annos ad 40000 exemplarium impresserit, ubi ultima editio erat 12500 exemplarium; & hic Amstelodami ultra centum quinquaginta millia exemplarium Bibliorum Anglicanorum sint impressa, præterquam quæ in Anglia ipsa ad duas myriadas exemplarium impressa sunt.'

¶ 357 × 225 mm. Wants apparently one blank leaf before title. A duplicate of *An Admonition* ... is inserted at the end. [F. F.]

—— Another copy.

339 × 217 mm.
Fry marked this copy 'variation edition,' but it is merely mixed. Where it differs from the preceding it seems to agree with the edition of 1644. The N. T. title is dated 1644.
With Speed's Genealogies and Map; and Downame's Concordance (1639). [F. F.]

424.

1640. The Holy Bible . . .
      Barker and Assigns of Bill : London. 1640. 8°.
Text ends on Kkk 8 a.
Two varieties occur with this date.

A.
N. T. title, *Commandment*; Matt. ix. 13 . . . *I not am come* . . . (for *I am not come*).

¶ 168 × 108 mm.
With Genealogies (1638) and Map.
With Prayer Book (1639), and Metrical Psalms (1640).
Seventeenth-century binding: with central and corner ornaments stamped in gilt. [F. F.]

—— Another copy.

169 × 111 mm.
With Genealogies (1638).
With Prayer Book (? date), Metrical Psalms (1640), and *The Way to True Happinesse* . . (? date). [F. F.]

425.

—— ANOTHER EDITION.

B.
N. T. title, *commandment*; Matt. ix. 13 correct.

¶ 163 × 104 mm.
With Genealogies (1640) and Map. [F. F.]

426.

1640. The New Testament . . .
                Barker and Assigns of Bill: London. 1640. 12°.
Text ends on Y 12 b.
1 Tim. iv. 16, thy.

¶ 109 × 52 mm.
With Metrical Psalms (1644). [F. F.]

—— Another copy.
107 × 51 mm. [F. F.]
                                                                              427.

1640. B. 4°. See 1642.

NOTE ON THE PRICES OF BIBLES IN THE EARLY SEVENTEENTH CENTURY.

A scarce tract entitled *Scintilla*, printed in 1641, which throws a flood of light on the prices of Bibles and the general bookselling trade in the early seventeenth century, is here printed *in extenso*. Prof. Arber included it in his *Transcript of the Registers of the Stationers' Company* (vol. iv., 1877, pp. 35–88); but from its bearing on the history of the English Bible it claims a place in this Catalogue. Arber sums up the value of *Scintilla* as follows: 'This tract is a remarkable testimony to the never-ending competition in the book trade; to the power of the King's Printers, partly as patentees, and partly as capitalists only; to the vast extent (proportionately to other books) of the production of Bibles, etc., and school books under the earlier Stuarts; and, lastly, to their steady rise in price, despite the much larger editions than formerly, owing in some degree to the increasing wealth of the country, but still more through monopolies and "rigging the market."' It will be seen that *Scintilla* also gives interesting details as to the importation of English Scriptures printed in Holland.

The author was a London bookseller named *Michael Sparke*, a native of Eynsham, near Oxford, who died at Hampstead 29 Dec. 1653. He is remembered chiefly as the publisher of William Prynne's works, including the famous *Histriomastix* (1633), for the publication of which Sparke was fined £500, and condemned to stand in the pillory. More than once he infringed copyrights, and dared even to attack the Bible-monopoly of Barker. 'The printing of Bibles and liturgies belonged by patent to Robert Barker, the King's printer and his assignees. In order to defeat this monopoly, Sparke imported large quantities of these books from Holland, and sold them at much cheaper rates than those printed in London. Barker obtained a warrant to search the ports and seize all the foreign printed Bibles he could find. Sparke retaliated by bringing an action for trespass against those who seized the books, and went on importing fresh supplies.' (*Cf.* D. N. B., art. *R. Barker*.)

For theological reasons, Archbishop Laud actively hindered the introduction of Geneva Bibles printed abroad. See *The History of the Troubles and Tryal of . . . William Laud* . . . (1695), pp. 349, 350; and W. Prynne's *Canterburies Doome* . . . (1646), pp. 181, 513, 515–6, and 529; in some of these passages Sparke is mentioned by name. In August, 1645, Parliament prohibited the sale of imported Bibles, until these had been examined, and sanctioned as correct, by the Assembly of Divines.

Besides *Scintilla*, Sparke was responsible for another pamphlet, *A Second Beacon, fired by Scintilla* . . . (1652), which is quoted above in connection with the 'Popish pictures' inserted in the Edinburgh Bibles of 1633 and other dates (see No. 367).

(For further details, see 'Michael Sparke, Puritan Bookseller,' by H. R. Plomer, in the *Bibliographer*, New York, Dec. 1902.)

The following is printed *verbatim et literatim* from the British Museum copy [E. 169 (8)] of the small quarto four-leaved tract. In the margin are added a few explanatory notes. It should be noted that the prices mentioned are in every case for the book 'in quires,' i.e. in sheets—unbound. These prices must be multiplied by five to obtain approximately their equivalent value to-day.

[Title, A 1 a.]
Scintilla, | or | a Light broken into | darke *Warehouses*. | With | Observations vpon the | Monopolists of Seaven severall *Patents*, | and Two *Charters*. | Practised and performed, By a Mistery of | some *Printers*, Sleeping *Stationers*, and | Combining *Book-sellers*. | Anatomised | And layd open in a *Breviat*, in which is only a | touch of their *forestalling* and *ingrossing* of | Books in *Pattents*, and Raysing them | to excessive *prices*. | *Left to the Consideration of the High and Honou-|nourable House of* Parliament *now assembled*. | Let not one Brother oppresse another. | *Doe as you would be done unto.* | At *London*, | Printed, not for *profit*, but for the Common Weles | good: and no where to be *sold*, but some where | to be given. 1641.

[A 1 b.]
The Epistle to the Reader.

Courteous Reader (or otherwise) if thou lookest for the Reason of writing this Book, here it is, and so *Anonimus* leaves thee.

Non nobis Solum, nati sumus, sed partim patriæ.

[p. (1), A 2 a.]
new Translation, i.e. King James' version.

Bibles for Churches new Translation
large Folio.

Church Bibles sold in former times in quires at 1¹ 10ˢ sold now (in quires) 2¹, so raysed in every Book 10ˢ. If they Print 3000. of an Impression, raised 1500¹. In former times these were bought in quires at 1¹ 5ˢ.

Kings Printers Patent of *London*.
1.

Church Bibles of a thinner sort have been sold at 1¹ in quires: Partners have bought them cheaper, buying a quantity, and those Partners sold them severally at 17ˢ 6ᵈ, not stocking or combining as now they doe, these Bibles were excellent for poore Parishes.

i.e. the Notes of the Geneva Bible.
Large Folio Bibles of a Roman Print, with the Notes, sold in former times in quires at 12ˢ 6ᵈ: The same sort now without the Notes be raysed 7ˢ 6ᵈ in a Book: 1500. of an Impression so raysed in every Book, amounts to 562¹ 10ˢ.

i.e. black-letter.
Large Folio English Letter with Notes, be sold at 13ˢ 4ᵈ in quires. And small Folio English, sold 12ˢ in quires: none of this sort Printed now.

In the yeare 1629, the want of these sorts of Folio Bibles caused *Cambridge* Printers to print it, and they sold it at 10ˢ in quires: upon which the then Kings Printers set six Printing-houses at worke, and on an instant Printed one Folio Bible in the same manner, and sold with it 500. Quarto Roman Bibles, and 500. Quarto English, at 5ˢ a Book, to overthrow the *Cambridge* Printing, and so to keep all in their own hands. It were well if they would alwayes sell at this price.

Cambridge Bibles Folio of long primer letter, *vide Cambridge* Charter.
2.
This Folio would not have bin sold under 12 or 14 *sh*. if it had not bin that *Cambridge* had Printed it: but now they sold

ENGLISH

[p. (2), A 2 b.]

In former times our Kings Printers did agree with Mr. *Andrew Hart*, and after with Mr. *John Hart* Book-sellers of *Edenburg* to serve them *London* Bibles at lower rates then they sold them at here: so that they would not Print whereby they might keep all the priviledges to themselves, since which *Robert Young* and *Miles Flesher*, most cunningly com-|bined with the Kings Printers here, and so sunke the Printing-house there, so that now *Scotland* is destitute; and by this means Books are raysed to greater rates here, and there likewise.

it at 5 sh, which would have bin 12 *sh* at least, and the 4*to* at 5 *sh*, which was before 9 *sh*.

Scots Printers.

i.e. of 11 July 1637: see Arber, *Transcript*, vol. iv. pp. 528–536.

The Kings Printers and others here being interested in the Irish stock, sold Mr. *William Bladon* of *Dublin* their Stock there, and Pattent, and have so Bound him, as he shall not Print but what they list of their priviledge, so that *Scotland* and *Ireland* must grind at their Mill. Observe in what a case these be: for Bibles, especially if the last Decree in Star-chamber had held, concerning Printing: for all must be bought at one place to serve three Kingdomes.

Ireland Patent, 2.

Cambridge Bible Folio.

Cambridge Large Folio Bible Roman, of the best paper, sold at 1¹ 10ˢ, in quires, or cheaper, they raysed it 10ˢ on a Book, and sold it at 2¹.

Cambridge Medyum Folio Bible Roman, sold at, or cheaper then 1¹ 2ˢ 6ᵈ in quires; the Monopolists raise 7ˢ, 6ᵈ and sell it at 1¹ 10ˢ.

Cambridge thinne paper Folio Roman, sold at, or cheaper then 16ˢ in quires; the Monopolists raised it 4ˢ, and so sell it at 1¹ in quires.

See the errors corrrected in the *Cambridge* Bibles, which were printed in the *London*.

Cambridge Quarto Roman Letter Bibles, with Psalms, sold at 7ˢ. They have raised on a Book 3ˢ, and so sell it with Psalmes at 10ˢ in quires, which if the Monopolists should buy but a 1000. it would be raised 150¹.

Cambridge Quarto English Letter, with Psalmes sold in quires at 6ˢ. raysed on a Book 2ˢ 4ᵈ. now the Monopolists sell it at 8ˢ 4ᵈ: if 3000 be ingrossed by them, it would raise 350¹.

Observe, they have not only bought in al those Bibles with Psalmes, and Grammers, and Schoole Books, but have for ever agreed for what shalbe printed both there and at *Oxford* Books Priviledge: and where they were there Printed bravely, true, and in good paper, now look for other.

It is judged that the price Raised in these three sorts, is not lesse in the totall sum then 200 *li*. And the Monopolists have compounded with them that they shall print no more Bibles, but for the Monopolists.

Oxford Charter. 2.

London Bibles in Quarto.

[p. (3), A 3 a.] i.e. the Geneva Bible, with R.F.H.'s Concordance.

London Bible Quarto English Letter, with the Notes and Concordance of the old Translation in times past was sold at 7 *sh*. in quires, and then it was 139. sheets, and now but 116 and no Notes, and sold at 9. *sh* 2ᵈ with Concordance: 3000. raysed makes 350¹.

London Quarto Roman with Notes, sold in times past at 7ˢ. The Quarto Roman now with no Notes sold at 10. *sh*. in quires, so raysed in an Impression of 3000 500¹.

There hath been at least 12000. of these Bibles Quarto with Notes

Printed in *Holland*, and sold very reasonable: and many brought from thence hither, and they have been seised by the Kings Printers, and the parties that Imported them, not only lost them, but were put in ★ *Purgatory*, and there glad to lose their Bibles and all cost to get off; and then the Monopolists sold them again, and so kept al others in awe. The High Commission.

Great pitty our Printing should be forced to be carryed to Strangers, in my judgement: better to have our own Nation set at work. More punishment for selling a 4^(to) Bible with Notes, then a 100. Masse Books in the High Commission. I have known divers punished for selling Bibles, but none for Masse Books

In former times Bibles in Octavo sold at 3. *sh.* 4^d in quires, are now sold at 4. *sh.* in quires, though then 9. sheets more then now. There have been 10000. printed in a year, which might have been afforded at 3 *sh.* a Book. So that there might have been saved to the Subject in an Impression 500^l. *London* Octavo Bibles.

[i.e. 3^d worth of paper.] Bibles 8^(to) of a Large paper, not 3^d in a Book more then the other, and sold at 6. *sh.* 2^d in quires: are raysed 2. *sh.* 2^d in a Book, which makes in that Impression of 6000. the summe of 650. *London* Bibles of a little Larger paper.

Scottish Bibles,

Printed of excellent paper and print at *Edenburg*, sold in *London* 26. to the quartern, and *London* Bibles but 25. to the quartern at our rates, notwithstanding the charg and hazard of importation. *London* Bible in 12 sold at 4. *sh.* in quires, stands not them in 1. *sh.* 8^d; there may be saved to the Subject in an Impression 500^l, and they great gainers. *Scots* Bibles Octavo, *Scots* Patent 3 *London.*

[i.e. a quarter of a hundred.]

Scottish Bible 12. sold 26 to the quartern, better paper, and better print then those here: now al *Scots* printing of Bibles is taken away by *Young* and *Fletcher*, two main projectors. *Scots* Bible *Edenburg.*

Holland Bible in 12 sold at 2. *sh.* in quires, better then the *London* one of 1639 sold at 4 *sh.* pitty the manufactory should be carried thither by deare selling here. *Holland* vide 1639.

[p. (4), A 3 b.] Latin Bibles 12 of *Amsterdam*, printed well, and sold at 2 *sh.* in quires, and good paper. *London* Latin Bible 12 printed with a popish Index, sold at 4 *sh.* in quires, and not under. Lattin Bibles.

Observe *London* Stationers that bought of the Lattin *Holland* Bibles, punished in the High Commission for buying Lattin Bibles from *Holland*, a yeare before ever any were printed in *London*; observe what a but of Sack might doe.

London Testament *octavo*, sold at 10^d in quires, raised to 1 *sh.* which 2^d upon a Book makes in 12000 impression a year 100^l.

Scots Testament at *Edenburg*, sold here in *London* at 10^d, better paper and print than ours here.

London Testaments in 12, at 7^d. raysed 3^d in a Book, sold now at 10^d, make in 6000. the over prise, rated 75^l.

Cambridge Testament 24. were sold at 6^d in quires. *London* Test. 24 sold at 8^d a Book, 2^d a Book raysed in 4000, is 80^l.

[i.e. a half-penny.] *London* Common prayers in 24. raised *ob* upon a Book 4000 of them is 8^l 6 *sh* 8^d.

London Common prayer Books in *folio*, sold at 3 *sh* in quires, raysed 1 *sh*. on a Book, now sold at 4 *sh*. comes to in 3000 an Impression 150¹.

Common prayers 4^(to) sold at 1 *sh* 6^d a Book : raysed 6^d on a Book, sold at 2 *sh* 3000. the Impression is raysed 57¹.

Common prayers for *quarto* Bibles raysed 2^d on a Book.

Common prayers in 16, raised 1^d on a Book, comes to 12 *li* 10 *sh* 3000 of the Impression.

Observe I pray now, I come to the Law Books, I had need to break two lights into the *Warehouse* : but I perceive then this would rise too bigge. I will only nominate 3 Books in 3 severall volumes, so by the 3 you may conceive the rest. Law Books. Law Pattent. 4.

The Monopolist have not only gotten all the *Gospel*, but also the *Law* as followes. Law Books.

Poltons Statutes sold at 1*l* 10 *sh* in quires, in former times, now raysed to 6 *sh* 8*d* a Book; the Impression of 1500 so raysed by the Monopolist amounts to 500 *li*. Folio,

Edward the 4^(th) sold at 13 *sh* 4*d*, now raysed 8 *sh* in a Book, comes to in a 1000 Books to 400 *li*. Quarto,

Compleat Iustice sold at 2 *sh* 2*d* a Book, I will sell every Impression cheaper by a 100 *li*. And here have they ingrossed the Schoole Books Patent. Octavo,

[p. (5), A 4 *a*.] 'qs' i.e. quires.

Grammer of *Oxford* and *Cambridge* sold at 5*d* a Booke; but these the Monopolists buy in, and sell them, and theirs at 8*d* a Book, qs which in an yearely Impression of 20000 is raysed 250 *li*. Schoole Books Patent 5, Lylies Grammer

Camdens Greek Grammer sold at 8*d*. a Book in quires alwayes, now sold at 1 *sh*. 2*d*. Raysed 6*d* on a Book. The same Printed in *France*, is sold here at 4*d*. ob. a Book, and so Raysed in 3000 to the summe of 75 *li*. Camden Greek Grammer,

i.e. 4½d.

Accedence, this Book by chance a yeare a goe broke loose from the Stake of the Monopolist, and was sold at six shillings in the pound cheaper then they sell them : but they have by Combination tyed him to the Stake again : for observe, if the old Partners cannot agree together, the *Young* will, though never so Indirect. Accedence,

The Monopolist keep all others from Printing Concordances by their Pattent, and these being printed in another Volume beyond Sea, and brought over, and sold at half their prise, they seise and take them from others, and sel them again themselves, although theirs be not to be had here : So have they likewise seised other Books Printed beyond the Seas, when not any Printed here were to be had. Concordance Pattent, 6,

But a touch of this : for it is too tart, and I verily beleeve picks the Subjects pockets, that eats brown bread to fill the *sleeping Stationers* belly with Venison and Sacke, and robs the Common-wealth in too still away; and when the Sellers by Retale get not a *ob*. these Monopolists get a shilling; for the Octavo *Geneologie*. and the twelve, of every 4 *li*. they make 15 *li*. and for the 12. what the Retalers give 4 *li*. for, they will not if they were to be returned again give six shillings for it. Geneology pattent, 7,

I hope when the Honourable Assembly of *Parliament* sees this, as I shall be ready to make proof of all; they will put an end to these crying grievances, and help the calamities of the poore pinshed subjects.

Here I could open another window, but I see many poore stand within to keep it shut, and I will not adde misery to their affliction.

[p. (6), A 4 b.]

Lastly, some few observations shall serve for the *Errata*, which the Honourable House of *Parliament* may correct in the Society of *Stationers*, by taking order that the Statute of 25 *H*. 8. *c*. 15. concerning the prises of Bookes may be duly exercised; that there may be at least 20 or 24 Assistants to the Company, and none of those to be above twice Master, for now six or 8 of the Eldest Combining, carry all to their own mark, and ayme alwayes at their own end: and that if they wil not Print such Coppies as are there entred to the Company, it may and shallbe free for any to imprint or Import them, untill such times they Print them here to furnish the Kingdome.

This may serve in part for should I make awhole *Errata*, it would be farre bigger then this Breviat, and here look but into a window of the Monopolists Law-Warehouse: and there behold a free discovery as here followes.

Bought of the Law Printers Bookes at the partners prises   Stocked, Ian. 1639 1879.Tables to Cookes Littleton at a 11d. a Book fol. 2s. 4d.
October 1630.
1500 Eliments of the Law at 12 *sh* 6 *d*. per reame which is 7 or 8 *d*. a Book Stocked at 1 *sh*. 6 *d*. Iuly 1631.   1500 English Lawers at 9*d*. a Book, Stocked at 2 *sh*   October 1630.   1334 Daltons Iustice, at 4 *sh*. a Booke Stocked at 6 *sh*. 25 to the quartern.   1200. Statuts at 22 *sh*. Stock 36 *sh*. 8 *d*. 26 to the quarter.   1200 Cookes Tables to reports, 2 *sh*. 2 *d*. a Booke, Stocked at 4 *sh*. 25 to the quartern. 1200 Cooks 11ᵗʰ Report at 1 *sh*. 10 *d*. a Booke, Stocked at 5 *sh*. 25 to the quartern. 1200 West 1 part at 2 *sh*. 2 *d*. a Booke, Stock 3 *sh*. 6*d*. 26 to the quarter. 700. Woemans Lawer at 22 *d*. a Booke, Stock at 3 *sh*. 26 to the quarter. 600. Kellowayes at 3 *sh*. 6 *d*. a Booke, Stock at 7 *sh*. 6 *d*. 26 to the puarter.   1200 Littleton

['6d.' is struck out by hand.]

['leet' is added by hand before 'Courte.']

fol. at 10 *sh*. a Booke, Stock, at 15 *sh*. 6 *d*., 26 to the quarter.   600. Regesters at 6 *sh*. 8 *d*. a Booke, Stock at 15 26 to the quarter.   600 Cooks 2 *d* report Stocked at 4 *sh*. 600 3 *d*. report at 4 *sh*.   600 4ᵗʰ report at 5 *sh*. bought at 1 *sh*. 8 *d*. a Booke. 600 Natura Brevium 80 at 1 *sh*. 8 *d*., Stock't at 3 *sh*. 8 *d*. 26 to the quarter. Aprill 1637.   1700 Courte at 12 *sh*. 6 *d*. a Reame, Stock at 3 *d*. 26 to the quarter. 1600 Tearmes of the Law, at 2 *sh*. a Booke, Stock at 3 *sh*. 8 *d*. 26 to the quarter. 700 Finches Lawe 80 at 1 *sh*. a Booke, Stock at 2 *sh*. 6 *d*. 26 to the quarter.   1000 Presidents 80 at 6 *d*. a Book, Stock at 10 *d*. 26 to the quarter.   600 Cooks 1 Report at 2 *sh*. 6 *d*. a Booke, Stock at 6 *sh*. 2 *d*. 26 to the quarter.   2000 Compleat Iustice, 80 at 1 *sh*. 3 *d*. a Booke, Stock at 2 *sh*. 2 *d*. 26 to the quarter.   500 Longe Quinto at 1 *sh*. Stock't at 6 *sh*.   1000 Doctor and Studient 13 *sh*. 4 *d*. a Reame be 6 *d*. a Booke Stock 1 *sh*.

But I know   *Obsequium amicos, Veritas odium parit.*

FINIS.

NOTE ON ENGLISH BIBLES PRINTED ABROAD.

It will be convenient to give here a list of all the editions of the English Bible, catalogued in this volume, between the dates 1599 and 1746, which are known, or conjectured, to have been printed in Holland, or elsewhere on the Continent. Many of these bear a false imprint, and some probably a false date. A few are well and correctly printed, but others abound in errors. Differences in typography and peculiarities of spelling afford the best criteria for distinguishing these Bibles from contemporary editions printed in England.

List of foreign editions: Nos. 188–194, 198, 213, 231, 294, 307, 364, 370, 387, 408–412, 424, 438, 444, 448, 449, 452, 453, 455, 456, 461, 465, 499, 500, 520–523, 541, 551, 552, 557, 574, 580, 583, 584, 592, 611–613, 616, 622, 626, 656, 672, 675, 688–691, 700, 731, 774, 776, 781, 784, 796, 814.

1641. The Holy Bible . . .
     Barker and Assigns of Bill : London. 1639,41. 12°.

General title dated 1639; N. T. dated 1641 on title and in colophon.
Text ends on Zz 12 *b*.

¶ 150 × 85 mm. Wants Apocrypha.
With Metrical Psalms (1641).
Covers embroidered with coloured silks and silver threads, on ground of white silk
[F. F.]
428.

1641. The Holy Bible . . .
     Barker and Assigns of Bill : London. 1641. 8°.

Text ends on Kkk 8 *a*.
Apparently three varieties occur.

A.
Small cut on verso of general title; Gen. xxxvii contents, last line: *phar in Egypt*;
Matt. i. 25 fills two lines.

¶ 168 × 108 mm. [F. F.]
429.

—— Another edition.
B.
Gen. xxxvii contents, last line: *Egypt*; Matt. i. 25, three lines.

¶ 162 × 103 mm. Imperfect: wanting all before B 7.
With *The Way to True Happinesse* . . . (? date). [F. F.]
430.

—— Another edition.
C.
Large cut on verso of title; Gen. xxxvii contents, last line: *Potiphar in Egypt.*

¶ 156 × 95 mm.
A fragment only (formerly bound up with a Geneva Bible), containing general title and
part of the O. T. [F. F.]
431.

1641. The New Testament . . .
     Barker and Assigns of Bill : London. 1641. 8°. 𝕭. 𝕷.

Text ends on Ee 8 *b*, without colophon.
1 Tim. iv. 16, *thy*.

¶ 148 × 90 mm.
With Metrical Psalms (1641,42). [F. F.]
432.

—— Another edition.
Date not known. No doubt by the same printers.

This and the two following editions closely resemble the above.
No colophon. Initial J before James—flowering letter.

¶ 143 × 91 mm. Imperfect: wanting title and eight other leaves. [F. F.]
433.

—— Another edition.
Date not known. No doubt by the same printers.

No colophon. Initial I before James has two cornucopiæ.

¶ 142 × 86 mm. Imperfect: wanting title and two other leaves. [F. F.]
434.

—— ANOTHER EDITION.

Date not known. No doubt by the same printers.

Initial J before James in factotum.

¶ 138 × 87 mm. Imperfect: wanting several leaves. [F. F.]
435.

1641. B. 4°. See 1642.
B. 8°. See 1642.

1642. The Holy Bible . . .
Barker and Assigns of Bill: London. 1640,41,42. 4°. 𝕭. 𝕷.

General title dated 1640; N. T. dated 1641 on title, and 1642 in colophon.
Text ends on Lll 4 b.
1 Tim. iv. 16, *thy*.

¶ 227 × 162 mm.
With Downame's Concordance. [F. F.]
436.

1642. The Holy Bible . . .
Barker and Assigns of Bill: London. 1642,41. 8°.

Titles dated 1642; colophon dated 1641.
Text ends on Kkk 8 a.

¶ 172 × 104 mm. [F. F.]
437.

1642. The Holy Bible . . . VVith most profitable Annotations . . . which notes have never before been set forth with this new translation; But are now placed in due order with great care and industrie.
Printed by Joost Broerss dwelling in the Pijl-Street, at the signe of the Printinghouse: Amsterdam. 1642. f°.

King James' version, with the notes of the Geneva Bible, and Junius' Annotations on Revelation. According to the New Testament title these were *placed in due order by I. C.* (? John Canne).

Apparently the first Bible of this version avowedly printed abroad.

DESCRIPTION. [Fourteen] preliminary leaves: title (within engraved border), verso blank, Dedication—1 f., Preface—3 ff., two tables and *Of the incomparable treasure* . . . —15 pp., list of books—1 p., [1 f. blank]. Text: O. T., pp. 1 to 730 (really 712); N. T., 248 pp. No Apocrypha.
    Engraved border to both titles represents figures of Adam and Noah, the Fall, the Sacred Name, the Lamb and Book, etc., with the text John i. 17. The N. T. title gives the imprint as *Amsterdam, Printed by Joost Broersz. dwelling in the Pijl-steegh, in the Druckerije, 1642.*
    1 Tim. iv. 16, *thy*.
    For an almost identical edition see below, No. 444.

¶ 352 × 224 mm. Wants blank leaf. [F. F.]
438.

1642. The Holy Bible . . .
Barker and Assigns of Bill: London. 1642. 8°.
Text ends on Kkk 8 a.
Three varieties occur.

A.
Small cut on verso of general title, enclosed within ornamental border.

¶ 166 × 107 mm. [F. F.]
439.

—— ANOTHER EDITION.
B.
Small cut, without border.

¶ 162 × 108 mm.
With Prayer Book (1642), Metrical Psalms (1645), and *The Way to True Happinesse* . . . (n. d.). [F. F.]
440.

—— ANOTHER EDITION.
C..
Has the small cut as B, but differs in most places from A and B, e.g. ornament before Proverbs—head of cherub.

¶ 168 × 111 mm. Imperfect: wanting Apocrypha.
With Metrical Psalms (1649).
Edges painted with flowers. With silver clasps. [F. F.]

—— Another copy.

Very imperfect : but contains Apocrypha. [F. F.]
441.

1642. The New Testament . . .
Evan Tyler : Edinburgh. 1642. 12°.

This, perhaps, is the N. T. belonging to an edition of the Bible of the same year. Lee (*Memorial*, p. 114) mentions a pocket Bible of this date printed by Tyler.
Signatures: A² F–O¹².
1 Tim. iv. 16, *thy.*

¶ 144 × 79 mm. [F. F.]
442.

1642. The Third Part of the Bible : (After some division.) Containing Five . . . Books . . . As they are part of the Bible newly translated . . .
E. Tyler : Edinburgh. 1642. 16°.

Editions of this little volume containing Job, Psalms, Proverbs, Ecclesiastes, and Song of Solomon, were published by Barker in 1616, and by Norton and Bill in 1626. The same section of the Bible had more than once been issued in the Geneva version (see Nos. 127, 138, and 262).
Title, with list of books on verso. Text, A 2 to Q 8 *b*, ending with colophon.

¶ 111 × 54 mm. [F. F.]
443.

1642. B. f°. See 1643.

1643. The Holy Bible . . . With most profitable Annotations . . .
Joost Broerss : Amsterdam. 1642,43. f°.

Almost identical with the folio of 1642 (No. 438); but it has a printed N. T. title, bearing a cut and legend *Sic itvr ad astra*, and dated 1643.

¶ 352 × 224 mm. [F. F.]
444.

1643. The Holy Bible . . .
    Barker and Assigns of Bill : London. 1643. 8°.

A new form of octavo Bible, with a longer page. Text: O. T. ends on Rr 6 *b* ; N. T., Ss 1 to Ggg 4 *b*. No Apocrypha. With rules surrounding each page.

¶ 186 × 114 mm.   [F. F.]
                           445.

—— ANOTHER EDITION.
Similar to the preceding edition; but O. T. ends on Rr 2 *b* ; N. T., A 2 to N 4 *a*. Without rules.

¶ 184 × 111 mm.   [F. F.]
                           446.

1643. FACSIMILE. The Souldiers Pocket Bible : Containing the most (if not all) those places contained in holy Scripture, which doe shew the qualifications of his inner man, that is a fit Souldier to fight the Lords Battels, both before the fight, in the fight, and after the fight; Which Scriptures are reduced to severall heads, and fitly applyed to the Souldiers severall occasions, and so may supply the want of the whole Bible, which a Souldier cannot conveniently carry about him : And may bee also usefull for any Christian to meditate upon, now in this miserable time of Warre. Imprimatur, Edm. Calamy. Jos. 18. This Book . . . good successe. *Printed at London by G. B. and R. W. for G. C.* 1643. 8°.

A selection of short passages (nearly all from the Geneva version), printed in pamphlet-form for the use of the Parliamentary soldiers in the Civil War.

Facsimile reproduction; with a preface by F. Fry. (Willis and Sotheran, London, 1862.)

A tradition has always existed that Cromwell's troops were supplied with pocket-Bibles, and some have confidently asserted that a very small complete Bible, like the 24° printed by Field in 1653, served this purpose. The discovery of the real *Souldiers Pocket Bible* was due to George Livermore of Massachusetts, who described his own copy in 1854. Another copy has come to light among the George Thomason collection in the British Museum ; this has *Aug. 3d.* (apparently the day of publication) written alongside the date on the titlepage. The pamphlet was duly licensed, and bears the *imprimatur* of Edmund Calamy, the eminent nonjuror. Another issue, somewhat altered, appeared in 1693 (see No. 655).

Mr. Livermore states that five distinct editions (amounting to about 50,000 copies) of a reprint of this pamphlet were circulated among the Federal troops in the American Civil War. His own reproduction appeared in 1861, just before the issue of Mr. Fry's facsimile. A later facsimile was published by E. Stock, London, in 1895.

Title (within narrow frame), on verso begins the text, which ends on p. 16 (A 8 *b*) with the words *This is Licensed according to order.*

The passages are chosen mainly from the Old Testament, and are grouped under suitable headings, with the references in the margins.

                           447.

1644. The Holy Bible . . .
  King's Printers : Edinburgh. 1634. *Barker and Assigns of*
                 Bill : London. 1644. 12°.

Agrees page for page with the Edinburgh edition of 1634 (No. 383), and also with the foreign duodecimo Bible (four varieties) catalogued under 1638 (Nos. 409-412) ; and is quite distinct from the London duodecimo of 1644 (No. 451).

The general title ends : . . . *Imprinted at Edinburgh, by the Printers to the Kings most Excellent Maiestie. Cum Privilegio. 1634.* The N. T. title gives other printers, and a date ten years later: *Imprinted at London by Robert Barker, printer to the Kings most Excellent Majesty: and by the Assignes of Iohn Bill. 1644.* It is difficult to account for this inconsistency. The O. T. and N. T. are quite uniform. The type is identical with that used for an edition of the Metrical Psalms, bearing the names of the London printers and dated 1644, which is appended to the copy described below. The whole book has a foreign appearance, and most probably is one of the many Bibles which were printed in Holland in close imitation of favourite English and Scotch editions, and imported or smuggled in large numbers into Great Britain. (See above, *Scintilla*, 1641.) Possibly this may be the identical duodecimo edition referred to as having been prepared by J. F. Stam and T. Crafoorth (or Craffurt) for delivery to Hugo Fitz in 1644 (see No. 364).

The general title alone bears the words *Appointed* . . . Both titles have as border the same architectural design (with the figure of King David, etc.) which is commonly used in London editions of this period. A rule is drawn across the end of each chapter.

The misprint *The Epitsle Dedicatorie* occurs, as in the 1634 edition; but 1 Tim. iv. 16, *the*.

¶ 147 × 87 mm. Apparently wants Apocrypha (included in list of books).
Interleaved; with MS. notes.
With Metrical Psalms (1644). [F. F.]

448.

1644. The Bible: | That is, | The Holy Scriptvres | contained . . . Amsterdam. | Printed by Thomas Stafford . . . cIɔIɔ cxliv. | According to the Copy printed at Edinburgh . . . in . . . 1610.

f°.

Geneva version, with Tomson's revised New Testament and Junius' Revelation.

A close reprint of the folio of 1640 (No. 424). Probably the latest seventeenth-century issue of the Geneva Bible.
Pagination and signatures as before. The running title in the Psalter is in roman type.

¶ 371 × 228 mm. Apparently wants *An Admonition* . . . (2 ff.) after Malachi; also one blank leaf before the title. [F. F.]

449.

1644. The Holy Bible . . .

London. 1644. 8°.

Printer's name not given.
Title, within ornamental border made up of roses, thistles, etc.; royal arms on verso; Dedication and list of books. The title has the words *Appointed* . . .

¶ 178 × 111 mm.
A fragment, containing only the first sheet A. Bound with an imperfect copy of No. 423. [F. F.]

450.

1644. The Holy Bible . . .

Barker and Assigns of Bill: London. 1644. 12°.

Text ends on Bbb 12 b with colophon.

¶ 146 × 81 mm. Wants Apocrypha. [F. F.]

451.

1644. The Holy Bible . . .

Printed for C. P.: Amsterdam. 1644. 24°.

Title (with architectural border), list of books; text: O. T., A 1 to Eee 4 b; N. T. (with plain titlepage), A 1 to Q 4 b. No Apocrypha. Each page is surrounded by rules. Short headings in headlines. Signatures in eights and fours.
Running title in Revelation: *Revelations*.

¶ 115 × 58 mm. A second copy of the general titleleaf is inserted before the N. T. title.
With Metrical Psalms (1644).
Original binding, with silver clasps. [F. F.]

452.

1645. The Holy Bible . . . According to the copie, Printed by Roger Daniel, printer to the Universitie of Cambridge.
[*Amsterdam?*] 1645. 4°.

Apparently printed in Holland. The words *According to the copie* are in very small type. General title engraved (with view of London, etc.). N. T. title gives the date, 1645. Text: O. T. ends on Ppp 6 b; N. T., Ooo 2 to Dddd 6 b (pp. 1 to 218). No Apocrypha. The N. T. is printed in somewhat smaller type than the O. T., and has the pages numbered.

¶ 237 × 173 mm.
With Metrical Psalms (1645).

453.

1645. The Holy Bible . . .
Roger Daniel, Printer to the Universitie of Cambridge. 1645. 12°.

A small duodecimo. General title engraved (architectural design, with a view of London below, showing Old St. Paul's, St. Saviour's Southwark, the Bridge, etc.), Dedication, list of books. Text: O. T., A 3 to Hh 1 b; . . . No Apocrypha.
Quite distinct from the edition of 1645,46 (No. 458).

¶ 124 × 68 mm. Imperfect: containing only the O. T. [F. F.]

454.

1645. The Holy Bible . . .
Joachim Nosche, dwelling upon the Sea-dijck: Amsterdam. 1645. 12°.

A small duodecimo. Title (with architectural border, containing a representation of the Last Supper, etc.), list of books, Dedication; text: O. T., A 3 to Gg 5 b; N. T. (with plain title) ends on Qq 4 b. No Apocrypha.

¶ 122 × 71 mm. [F. F.]

455.

1645. The Holy Bible . . .
Printed for C. P.: Amsterdam. 1645. 24°.

Printed from the same type as No. 452 (1644). The list of books is given on verso of the title, instead of on a separate leaf; and apparently there is no N. T. title.

¶ 120 × 60 mm. [F. F.]

456.

1645. An Exposition with practical observations continued upon the fourth, fifth, sixth and seventh chapters of . . . Job. Being the substance of xxxv. Lectures, delivered at Magnus neare the Bridge, London. By Joseph Caryl, Preacher to the Honourable Society of Lincolnes-Inne . . .
G. Miller for H. Overton, L. Fawne, I. Rothwell, and G. Calvert: London. 1645. 4°.

With the text. Preface (dated 28 Apr. 1645), Exposition, etc. (725 pp.), and tables.
J. Caryl (1602–1673) held for some time the office of preacher to Lincoln's Inn, and was frequently called to preach before the Long Parliament on solemn occasions. In 1643 he was appointed a member of the Westminster Assembly of Divines, and in 1645 he became incumbent of the Church of St. Magnus. Ejected in 1662 he continued to live in London, where he gathered round him a Nonconformist congregation. His great work was a commentary on Job, first published in its complete form in 12 quarto volumes, 1651–66; a second edition appeared in 2 folio volumes in 1676–7.

¶ 193 × 146 mm.
Bound with *An Exposition . . . upon the three first chapters of . . Job . . .* (by the same author, 1647). See No. 467.

457.

1645. B. 12°. See 1646.

1646. The Holy Bible . . .
R. Daniel: Cambridge. 1645,46. 12°.

General title engraved (with figures of Moses and Aaron, and a view of *London*), and dated 1645. N. T. title dated 1646. Text ends on Qq 8 *b*. No Apocrypha.

¶ 147 × 88 mm.
With Metrical Psalms (1646). [F. F.]
458.

1646. The Holy Bible . . .
William Bentley: London. 1646. 8°.

Each title within narrow frame. Text: O. T. ends on Nn 8 *a*; N. T. ends on Bbb 3 *b*. No Apocrypha.
Kilburne alludes to Bentley's editions in his tract *Dangerous Errors* . . . (1659): 'This Affair also occasioned the said [Westminster] Assembly [of Divines] by direction of the Parliament . . . to propose the Bible printing to several Stationers of *London*; who refusing that laudable work, the same was commended to Mr. *William Bentley* Printer in *Finsbury*, and his partners, who have so exactly, and commendably imprinted several volumes by Authority of Parliament in 8°. and 12°. in the years 1646. 48. 51, &c. (according to the authentique corrected *Cambridge Bible* . . . printed by . . . *Thomas Buck* . . . and . . . *Roger Daniel* in *folio* in 1638,) that some small remainders of them yet unsold are now daily exposed at 12*s. per* Book in quires unbound by the Stationers (for the fairness of the Print, and truth of the Editions) which Mr. *Bentley* afforded heretofore at 2*s. per* Book, or thereabouts, untill he hath been unjustly obstructed by Mr. *Hills* and Mr. *Field* . . .'
The reading in Matt. xii. 23, first introduced by the Cambridge Bible of 1638 (*q.v.*), is here corrected to the original, *Is this the Son of David?* Acts vi. 3 is correct; but the alterations in 1 Tim. iv. 16 and 1 John v. 12 are retained.
Fry mentions varieties of this edition and that of 1648, but the differences are due to the mixed state of two of his copies (see below).

¶ 163 × 108 mm. Imperfect: wanting the N. T., in place of which is inserted a Greek N. T. (see Greek section, 1633). [F. F.]

—— Another copy.
A large section of this copy belongs to the edition of 1648 (No. 471).
With Metrical Psalms (1646). [F. F.]

—— Another copy.
A large section of this copy belongs to the edition of 1648 (No. 471).
Seventeenth-century binding. [F. F.]
459.

1646. The Holy Bible . . .
London. 1646. 8°.

Resembles the edition of 1644, which also is without printer's name (No. 450).

¶ 174 × 124 mm.
A fragment, containing only the first sheet. Bound with a copy of Grafton's small quarto Bible of 1553 (No. 73). [F. F.]
460.

1646. (The Holy Bible.)
Barker and Assigns of Bill: London. 1646. 12°.

Perhaps printed abroad.
Text ends on Yy 6 *a*.

¶ 148 × 86 mm. Contains the N. T. only, which evidently belongs to an edition of the whole Bible.
With Metrical Psalms (1647).

461.
1647. The Holy Bible . . .
   Barker and Assigns of Bill :   London.   1647.   8°.

General title engraved (figures of Moses and Aaron; view of London at base). Text: O. T. ends on Rr 2 b; N. T., Ss 2 to Ggg 4 b. No Apocrypha.

¶ 186 × 113 mm. Wants N. T. title. [F. F.]

462.
1647. The Holy Bible . . .
   Assigns of J. Bill and Christopher Barker : London. 1647. 8°.

Text ends on Zz 7 b. No Apocrypha. Titles within the familiar border with heart-shaped centre. Names of books (in headlines) in italics.

¶ 171 × 107 mm.
With *The Way to True Happinesse* . . . (1642), Downame's Concordance (1646), and Metrical Psalms (1648). [F. F.]

—— Another copy.

With Apocrypha inserted. [F. F.]

— Another copy.

N. T. title mutilated. Wants some leaves.
With Apocrypha inserted. [F. F.]

463.
1647. The Holy Bible . . .
   Company of Stationers : London. 1647. 8°.

Perhaps the earliest English Bible which bears the imprint of the Company of Stationers.

Text ends on Zz 7 b. No Apocrypha. Titles within architectural border (King David, etc.). Names of books (in headlines) in roman type. Colophon on last page.

¶ 170 × 106 mm.
With Apocrypha inserted.
With Genealogies (1643) and Map.
With Prayer Book (1642), Downame's Concordance (1646), and Metrical Psalms (1647).
Seventeenth-century binding, with central and corner ornaments stamped in gilt; goffered edges. [F. F.]

464.
1647. The Holy Bible . . .
   R. Daniel : *Cambridge* ; *R. Barker* : *London*. 1647. 12°.

Closely resembles Nos. 409–412 (1638), which bear the imprint of *Barker and the Assigns of Bill*, but were probably printed abroad. The same type is used, with rules round each page. From the errors and strange spelling, e.g. *abroath* for *abroad*, it seems likely that this Bible also was printed in Holland.
The Cambridge imprint appears on the general title, and the London imprint on the N. T. title.   O. T. ends on Hh 6 b ; N. T. ends on K 6 b.   Apocrypha mentioned in list of books.
Isa. i. 6, *purrifying* ; 1 Tim. iv. 16, *the*.

¶ 152 × 83 mm.
Perhaps wants Apocrypha.
With Metrical Psalms (1638).
Bound in vellum; from a foreign Library. [F. F.]

465.

1647. The New Testament . . .
>Assigns of Bill and Barker : London. 1647. 12°. 𝔅. 𝔏.

A small duodecimo. Resembles the small edition of 1631 (No. 352).
Title, with list of books on verso. Text, A 2 to Bb 6 b.

¶ 121 × 71 mm. [F. F.]
466.

1647. An Exposition with practicall observations upon the three first chapters of . . . Job. Delivered in xxi. Lectures, at Magnus near the Bridge, London. By Joseph Caryl . . .
>For Henry Overton, Luke Fawne, and John Rothwell :
>London. 1647. 4°.

With the text. *Imprimatur,* signed by John White, and dated 11 May 1643, on verso of title. Preface (dated 8 Nov. 1643), Exposition etc. (479 pp.) and tables.
See No. 457.

¶ 193 × 146 mm.
Bound with *An Exposition . . . upon the fourth, fifth, sixth and seventh chapters of . . . Job . . .* (by the same author, 1645).
467.

1648. The Holy Bible . . .
>Company of Stationers : London. 1648. 4°.

Both titles have the woodcut border with heart-shaped centre used in so many of Barker's quarto Bibles. A small cut of Adam and Eve, with lion on one side and unicorn on the other, before Genesis. Text ends on Ppp 8 b with colophon (. . . *for the Company of Stationers*). Apocrypha mentioned in list of books, but not required by signatures.

¶ 213 × 162 mm.
Wants Apocrypha? [F. F.]
468.

1648. The Holy Bible . . .
>John Field : London. 1648. 4°.

General title engraved by *Jo. Payne.* Text: O. T., B 1 to Ppp 4 a ; Apocrypha, 200 pp. ; N. T., A 2 to T 4 a, ending with colophon.
Ps. cv. 29, *flesh* for *fish.* Kilburne mentions this error.

Two varieties occur of this Bible, differing in the engraved title and following leaf.

A.
Title signed *Jo. Payne sculp.,* . . . *Ioh⁻ Field* . . . ; A 2 a, catchword *veraign.*

¶ 233 × 177 mm.
The Apocrypha possibly do not belong to this edition.
With Prayer Book (1641), and Metrical Psalms (1655).

—— Another copy.

Wants Apocrypha.
With Prayer Book (1641), and Metrical Psalms (1647). [F. F.]
469.

—— ANOTHER EDITION.
B.
Title differs, not signed, . . . *Iohn Field* . . . ; A 2 a, catchword *and.*

¶ 224 × 163 mm.
With Metrical Psalms (1655). [F. F.]
470.

204   HISTORICAL CATALOGUE

1648. The Holy Bible . . .
        W. Bentley : London. 1648. 8°.

Resembles Bentley's edition of 1646 (No. 459).

¶ 168 × 110 mm.   [F. F.]

—— Another copy.
See above, No. 459.

—— Another copy.
See above, No. 459.
                      471.

1648. The Holy Bible . . .
     Company of Stationers : London. 1648. 8°.

Text ends on Zz 7 b, with colophon. No Apocrypha. Titles within architectural border (royal arms with lion and unicorn above, King David below).

¶ 165 × 106 mm.
Apocrypha inserted.
With Genealogies (1642) and Map.   [F. F.]

—— Another copy.
Slightly imperfect.   [F. F.]
                      472.

1648. The Holy Bible . . .
     Company of Stationers : London. 1648. 12°.

Text ends on Mm 12 b. No Apocrypha.

Two varieties occur.

A.
I 7 a, catchword *he*.

¶ 138 × 70 mm.   [F. F.]
                      473.

—— ANOTHER EDITION.

B.
I 7 a, catchword *Obed*.

¶ 138 × 71 mm.
With Metrical Psalms (1648).
Covers embroidered with coloured silks on a white ground, representing symbolical figures of Justice and Mercy, surrounded by flowers, etc., with a border of silver thread. [F. F.]
                      474.

1648. (The Holy Bible.)
         R. Daniel : Cambridge. 1648. 12°.

O. T. ends on Gg 5 b. No Apocrypha. Signatures in twelves.

¶ 145 × 83 mm. Wants general title and many other leaves. [F. F.]
                      475.

1648. The Holy Bible . . .
         R. Daniel : Cambridge. 1648. 18°.

A small 18°. General title engraved (figures of Moses and Aaron, view of London, etc.) No Apocrypha. Signatures generally in eighteens.

Varieties occur, differing slightly in the engraved title, and other details.

A.
The last three signatures are: Y¹⁸ Z⁶ Aa². Engraved title: . . . *originall* . . . *speciall* . . . Gen. xix. 4, *yᵉ men*.

¶ 136 × 72 mm.
With Scotch Metrical Psalms (1650). [F. F.]
476.

—— ANOTHER EDITION.
B.
Last two signatures: Y¹⁸ Z¹⁸. Isa. i. 6, *purifying* for *putrifying*. Gen. xix. 4, *the men*.

¶ 135 × 70 mm.
With Metrical Psalms (1648).
Contemporary binding, stamped T M; with silver clasps. [F. F.]
477.

—— ANOTHER EDITION.
C.
Text ends on Aa 18 *b*. Isa. i. 6, *purifying*. Rev. xxi. 20, *seveth* for *seventh*.

¶ 131 × 71 mm. [F. F.]
478.

—— ANOTHER EDITION.
D.
Signatures, etc. as in A; but . . . *original* . . . *special* . . . in engraved title.

¶ 135 × 72 mm. [F. F.]
479.

—— ANOTHER EDITION.
E.
Generally like A; but title differs slightly in the engraving.

¶ 131 × 68 mm. [F. F.]
480.

1648. (The New Testament.)
Robert White and Thomas Brudenell: London. 1648. 12°. 𝔅. 𝔏.

A small duodecimo.
Text ends on R 6 *a* with colophon.

¶ 116 × 63 mm. Wants title. [F. F.]
481.

1648. B. 8°. See 1649.

BEGINNING OF THE COMMONWEALTH: 30 JANUARY 1649.

1649. The Holy Bible . . .
E. Tyler: Edinburgh. 1649,48. 8°.

General title dated 1649; N. T. dated 1648 on title and in colophon. Text ends on Zz 7 *b*. No Apocrypha. Each title within an ornamental frame. The general title has on verso the royal arms within garter, with initials C. R.
Lee (*Memorial*, p. 114) states that this is the largest Bible printed by Tyler.

¶ 166 × 106 mm.
Apocrypha inserted.
With Prayer Book (1639), Downame's Concordance (1646), and Metrical Psalms (1649).
[F. F.]
482.

1649. The Holy Bible . . .
  Company of Stationers : London. 1649. 4°.

Title-border with heart-shaped centre. Text: O. T., B 1 to Ppp 4 a; N. T. ends on Kkkk 8 a. No Apocrypha.
This edition agrees generally with Field's quarto of 1648, but is more correctly printed.

¶ 221 × 164 mm. Imperfect: wanting five leaves (Ppp 4 to 8).
Apocrypha inserted.
With Prayer Book (1641), and Metrical Psalms (1649).

483.

1649. The Holy Bible . . . With most profitable Annotations . . . Which notes have never before been set forth with this new Translation : But are now placed in due order with great care and industrie.
  Company of Stationers : London. 1649. 4°.

King James' version, with Geneva notes, and Junius' Annotations on Revelation.
In general appearance this edition closely imitates the favourite quarto Geneva Bible.

DESCRIPTION. Five preliminary leaves: title, verso blank; Dedication —1 f.; Preface, list of books, and *Of the incomparable treasure* . . . — 3 ff. Text: O. T., A 6 to Ss 1 b; N. T., Aaa 1 to Ppp 7 a; followed by tables, ending on Qqq 8 b with colophon. No Apocrypha.
Both titles have the woodcut border with heart-shaped centre. On verso of the N. T. title occurs a short note *The Printer to the diligent Reader*.
John vii. 32, *fathers* for *Pharisees*.

¶ 216 × 155 mm.
With Metrical Psalms (1649). [F. F.]

484.

1649. The Holy Bible . . .
  Company of Stationers : London. 1649. 12°.

Text ends on Mm 12 b. No Apocrypha.

¶ 136 × 73 mm.
With Metrical Psalms (1648). [F. F.]

485.

1650. The Holy Bible . . .
  Company of Stationers : London. 1650. 8°.

Like the same printers' octavo of 1648 (No. 472). Sometimes mixed with No. 488.
Text ends on Zz 7 b with colophon. No Apocrypha.

¶ 164 × 103 mm.

486.

1650. B. 12°. See 1651.

1651. The Holy Bible . . .
  Company of Stationers : London. 1651,50. 12°.

General title dated 1651; N. T. dated 1650 on title, but 1651 in colophon. General title has an open book inscribed *Verbum Dei* in the arch; the N. T. title bears the royal arms in the same place. Text ends on Qq 12 b. No Apocrypha.

¶ 143 × 78 mm.
With Metrical Psalms (1651). [F. F.]

487.

1651. The Holy Bible . . .
Company of Stationers: London. 1651. 8°.

Text ends on Zz 7 b. General title within narrow frame. No Apocrypha.
Loftie calls this 'a mixed and irregular edition.'

¶ 164 × 106 mm.
A mixed copy. The N. T. title is dated 1650; while the colophon runs: *London: Printed by E. T.* [Evan Tyler] *for a Society of Stationers, 1655.*
With Metrical Psalms (1653). [**F. F.**]

—— Another copy.

Imperfect: wanting a few leaves at the beginning. N. T. title dated 1650, and colophon dated 1655, as in the copy above. The missing matter is supplied by 8 ff. of an Edinburgh edition of 1789 (No. 944). [**F. F.**]
488.

1651. The Holy Bible . . .
Company of Stationers: London. 1651. 12°.

Text ends on Qq 12 b. No Apocrypha.
Distinct from the similar edition with N. T. title dated 1650 (No. 487). The open book, *Verbum Dei*, occurs in both title-borders. Headline on Ii 7 b, *S. Luke* for *S. Mark*.

¶ 147 × 78 mm.
With Metrical Psalms (1652).
Contemporary binding; with silver corners, clasps, and plates (inscribed K M). [**F. F.**]
489.

1651. The Holy Bible . . .
Company of Stationers: London. 1651. 12°.

Text ends on Mm 12 b. No Apocrypha. Title-border has in the arch an open book inscribed *Verbum Dei*.

¶ 138 × 70 mm. [**F. F.**]
490.

1652. The Holy Bible . . .
Company of Stationers: London. 1652. 12°.

Text ends on Mm 12 b. No Apocrypha.

¶ 139 × 67 mm.
With Metrical Psalms (1654). [**F. F.**]
491.

1652. The Holy Bible . . .
John Field, Printer to the Parliament of England: London. 1652. 12°.

The earliest edition in which the Parliament is mentioned on the titlepage. The Dedication is omitted.

Text ends on Qq 12 b, with colophon. No Apocrypha.
Woodcut border to both titles: above—an open Bible, and two shields, one bearing a cross, the other a harp; below—a view of London, the river bearing the name *Thames*.

¶ 143 × 79 mm.
With Metrical Psalms (1652). [**F. F.**]
492.

1652. B. 12°. See 1653.

1653. The Holy Bible . . .
Company of Stationers: *London.* 1652,53. 12°.

General title dated 1652; N. T. dated 1653 on title and in colophon.
Quite distinct from the same printers' edition of 1652 (No. 491). Text ends on Kk 12 b.
No Apocrypha.

¶ 145 × 82 mm.
With Downame's Concordance (1652). [F. F.]
493.

1653. The Holy Bible . . .
J. Field: *London.* 1653. 12°.

Text ends on Qq 12 b. No Apocrypha.
Rom. vi. 13, *unto righteousness* for *of unrighteousness*.

¶ 145 × 81 mm.
With Metrical Psalms (1653).
Silver clasps. [F. F.]
494.

1653. The Holy Bible . . .
Printed for Giles Calvert, and are to be sold at the Sign of the
Black-spread-Eagle, near the west end of Pauls: *London.* 1653. 12°.

This small edition has been called the 'Quakers' Bible,' as Calvert printed for many members of the Society of Friends.

Title (within narrow frame); list of books on verso. Text ends on Mm 10 b. Apocrypha mentioned in list of books, but not required by signatures. The line *Appointed* . . . occurs only on the N. T. title. With full marginal references, similar to those in Canne's Bibles (see below, No. 541).

¶ 136 × 75 mm. Wants the general title (supplied in facsimile), and also perhaps the Apocrypha.
With Downame's Concordance (1654). [F. F.]
495.

1653. The Holy Bible . . .
J. Field: *London.* 1653. 24°.

General title engraved; with figures of Moses and David, the Evangelists, etc. Text ends on Ddd 11 a, with colophon. No Apocrypha. The first four Psalms fill one page, Aa 8 a. A full column contains 62 lines.

This small Bible is very incorrectly printed, and was singled out by Kilburne for special condemnation: 'In a Pearl Bible printed by *John Field* at *London* in 1653. in volume 24°. (very small to carry in pockets) whereof there have been neer 20000 dispersed, are these egregious faults, viz.:—All the Dedications and Titles of *David's* Psalms are wholly left out, being part of the original Text in *Hebrew*, and intimating the cause, and occasion of the writing and composing those Psalms, whereby the matter may be better illustrated. John 9. 21. *Or who hath opened his eyes we know not.* These words are wholly omitted. Rom. 6. 13. *Neither yield ye your members as instruments of righteousness unto sin.* for *unrighteousness.* 1 Cor. 6. 9. *Know ye not that the unrighteous shall inherit the Kingdom of God?* for *Shall not inherit.* This is the foundation of a damnable Doctrine for it hath been averred by a reverend Doctor of Divinity to several worthy persons, that many Libertines and licentious people did produce, and urge this Text from the authority of this corrupt Bible against his mild Reproofs, in Justification of their vicious and inordinate Conversations.' (*Cf.* a pamphlet of 1660, cited above, on p. 134.)

Lea Wilson mentions three other misprints: Matt. vi. 24, *Ye cannot serve and mammon* (*God* omitted); John ii. 10, *when they have* for *when men have*, and iii. 21 *might be manifest* for *may be made manifest*.

Varieties occur, differing in the engraved title, the number of errors, and other details. Many copies, probably, were corrected by cancel-leaves.

A.
General title: . . . y^e : Old . . . Contains all the six errors mentioned above.

¶ 110 × 53 mm. [F. F.]

—— Another copy.
Wants general title.
Silver corners and clasp.
496.

—— ANOTHER EDITION.
B.
General title: . . . the Old . . . ; engraving signed W V at the bottom. Rom. vi. 13 is correct.

¶ 108 × 52 mm. [F. F.]
497.

—— ANOTHER EDITION.
C.
General title differs slightly from B; signed W V. The first three errors are corrected.

¶ 111 × 53 mm.
Contemporary binding; with silver corners and clasp.
498.

1653. The Holy Bible . . .
J. Field : London. 1653. 24°.

An edition similar to, but quite distinct from, the preceding Bible. It is far less incorrect, and is printed on thicker paper. Some conjecture that it was produced abroad, and call it the 'spurious' edition of 1653.
Engraved title as in No. 497. Text ends on Zz 12 b. No Apocrypha. The first three Psalms are printed on Y 10 a. A full column contains 66 lines in the O. T., and 65 lines in the N. T.
This has only one of the six errors mentioned above, viz. that in John iii. 21.

¶ 113 × 62 mm.
With Metrical Psalms (1654). [F. F.]
499.

1653. The Holy Bible . . .
J. Field : London. 1653. 24°.

Marked by Fry as a variety of the edition immediately preceding (No. 499); but it is quite a different book. The B. M. Catalogue calls it 'a spurious edition, not printed by Field.'
The engraved title is signed in the left hand bottom corner: *L. Lucas fecit*, and has a list of books on verso. The N. T. title is undated; it bears the words *Appointed* . . ., and designates Field *one of His Highness's Printers*. (Oliver Cromwell became Protector 16 Dec. 1653; succeeded by his son Richard, 3 Sept. 1658.) The text ends on Ddd 7 a. No Apocrypha. Only two verses of Ps. i are printed on Aa 4 a, the first page of the Psalter. A full column contains 67 lines.
John iii. 21 is correct.

¶ 121 × 61 mm.
With Scotch Metrical Psalms (1698). [F. F.]

—— Another copy.

—— Another copy.
Slightly imperfect. In two volumes. [F. F.]
500.

1653. A Paraphrase, and Annotations Upon all the Books of the New Testament: Briefly explaining all the difficult places thereof. By H. Hammond, D.D.

J. Flesher, for Richard Royston, at the Angel in Ivie-lane:
London. 1653. f°.

Henry Hammond (1605–1660) was appointed President of Magdalen College, Oxford, in 1645, and in 1647 was allowed to attend Charles I. as his chaplain. A voluminous writer, he is chiefly known by his 'Practical Catechism' (Oxford, 1644), and this 'Paraphrase.' The latter 'is a great work, though largely superseded now, and gives Hammond a claim to the title of father of English Biblical criticism.' He also assisted Brian Walton in his famous London Polyglot, 1657.

DESCRIPTION. Ten preliminary leaves: 1 f. blank, title (with engraving), verso blank *A necessary Advertisement to the Reader*—2 ff., *A Postscript concerning New Light* ...—pp. I to XII. Text with Annotations, pp. 1 to 1008; followed by two indexes, list of *Errata*, and catalogue of Royston's publications. The *Paraphrase* is given side by side with the text of King James' version.
Symbolical engraving on title by *W. Hollar.*
Later editions of this work appeared in 1659, 1671, 1675, 1681, 1689, and 1702.

¶ 326 × 206 mm.

501.

1653. The New Testament . . .
R. Daniel: London. 1653. 8°.

Title (within narrow frame), with list of books on verso. Text, G 1 to Gg 4 a, pp. 1 to 375. Double columns.

¶ 191 × 126 mm.
Contains 46 plates (many double) signed *P. V. Borcht.* One gives the title of the series: *Testamentum Novum hoc est, Historiæ, Miracula, et Passio domini nostri Iesu Christi Iconibus expressa operâ et studio Petri vander Burght excudente Nicolao Iohannis Piscatore.*
[F. F.]

502.

1653. B. *4°.* See *1654.*

1654. The Holy Bible . . .
R. Daniel: London. 1654, 53. 4°.

General title engraved (as in Field's quarto Bible of 1648), and dated 1654; N. T. title dated 1653.
Text: O. T. ends on Fff 5 b; N. T., Aaa 2 to Qqq 8 b. Apocrypha mentioned in list of books.

¶ 222 × 167 mm.
Wants Apocrypha?
With Downame's Concordance (1652), and Metrical Psalms (1653). [F. F.]

—— Another copy.
Wants general title and other leaves.
Apocrypha apparently supplied from another edition. [F. F.]

503.

1654. The Holy Bible . . .
Evan Tyler, for a Society of Stationers: London. 1654. 24°.

Title in woodcut border. Text ends on Ddd 12 b. No Apocrypha
Acts vi. 3 and 1 Tim. iv. 16 correct. (So in other editions by Tyler.)

¶ 111 × 54 mm. Wants four leaves, including N. T. title. [F. F.]

—— Another copy.
Imperfect : containing the text only as far as end of Job. [F. F.]
504.

1655. The Holy Bible . . .
E. T. for a Society of Stationers : London. 1655. 4°.

Both titles have the woodcut border with heart-shaped centre. Text ends on Kkkk 8 *a*. No Apocrypha.

¶ 226 × 163 mm. [F. F.]
505.

1655. The Holy Bible . . .
E. T. for a Society of Stationers : London. 1655. 8°.

This edition is sometimes mixed with No. 488.
Text ends on Zz 7 *b*, with colophon. No Apocrypha.

¶ 174 × 111 mm.
Apocrypha inserted.
With Genealogies (1642) and Map.
With Prayer Book (1642), and Metrical Psalms (1648). [F. F.]

—— Another copy.

Imperfect: wanting general title and other leaves. Apocrypha inserted.
Contains many plates in Genesis and in the N. T.; one page bears two Latin dedications to King Charles, signed by *Guliel. Slatyer*, and *Iacob' Fl : van Langeren*. Some of the plates are like the 'Popish pictures' referred to above (see Nos. 367 and 372). [F. F.]

—— Another copy.
Contains the N. T. only. [F. F.]
506.

1655. The Holy Bible . . .
Evan Tyler for a Society of Stationers : London. 1655. 12 .

General title engraved by *R. Gaywood*. Text ends on Qq 12 *b*. No Apocrypha.

¶ 147 × 80 mm.
With Metrical Psalms (1655). [F. F.]
507.

1655. The Holy Bible . . .
J. Field, one of his Highnes's Printers : London. 1655. 12°.

Another of Field's editions condemned by Kilburne ; in 2 Cor. xiii v. 6 is omitted.
For Field's designation see No. 500.
General title engraved. Text ends on Tt 12 *b*. No Apocrypha.

Two varieties occur.
A.
General title : . . . *the Old* . . . Colophon on last page.

¶ 138 × 70 mm.
With Metrical Psalms (n. d.). [F. F.]
508.

—— ANOTHER EDITION.
B.
General title : . . . *y*ᵉ *Old* . . . No colophon.

¶ 138 × 72 mm. Wants four leaves.
With Metrical Psalms (n. d.). [F. F.]
509.

1655. The New Testament . . .
R. Daniel: London. 1655. 8°. 𝔅. 𝔏.

The titlepage bears a device with the motto *Ad ardua per aspera tendo*; list of books on verso. Text, A 2 to X 8.
Signatures: A–H⁸ I⁴ K⁴ L–X⁸; 160 ff. Double columns; no chapter-contents.
1 Tim. iv. 16, *thy*.

¶ 155 × 97 mm. Wants the last leaf.
Seventeenth-century binding.
510.

1655. B. 12°. See 1656.

1656. The Holy Bible . . .
J. Field: London. 1656,55. 12°.

General title engraved, and dated 1656; N. T. dated 1655 on title and in colophon.
Text ends on Mm 12 b. No Apocrypha.

¶ 133 × 72 mm. Wants one leaf of text, X 11.
With Metrical Psalms (n. d.). [F. F.]
511.

1656. The Holy Bible . . .
J. Field: London. 1656. 12°.

Another edition condemned by Kilburne, who cites many of its errors; e.g. Isa. xxviii. 17, *overthrow* for *overflow*; John v. 2, *Bethsaida* for *Bethesda*.
General title engraved, verso blank; list of books on B 2 a, verso blank. Text: O. T., B 3 to Ff 12; N. T. ends on Pp 8 b, with colophon. No Apocrypha.

¶ 150 × 80 mm.
With Metrical Psalms (1656). [F. F.]

—— Another copy.
A general title dated 1657 (like that in No. 514) has been substituted for the ordinary title.
With Metrical Psalms (1656). [F. F.]
512.

1656. The New Testament . . .
John Streater: London. 1656. 8°. 𝔅. 𝔏.

Title, with list of books on verso. Text, A 2 to X 8 b; printed in double columns; no chapter-contents.

¶ 143 × 90 mm. Wants sheets S and T. [F. F.]
513.

1656. B. 12°. See 1657.

1657. The Holy Bible . . .
J. Field: London. 1657,56. 12°.

General title engraved by *Guli. Vaughan*, and dated 1657; N. T. dated 1656 on title and in colophon.
Text, A 3 to Tt 12 b. No Apocrypha.
Isa. xxviii. 17, *overthrow*; but John v. 2 is correct.

¶ 150 × 80 mm. [F. F.]
514.

1657. (The Holy Bible.)

R. Daniel: London. 1657. 8°.

O. T. ends on Tt 6 *b*. No Apocrypha.
Loftie states that this edition usually contains a series of engravings on copper.
Matt. xiii. 4, *wayes said* for *wayside*.

¶ 180 × 104 mm. Wants general title, and leaves at beginning and end. [F. F.]
515.

1657. The Holy Bible . . .

J. Field, Printer to ye Universitie: Cambridge. 1657. 8°.

General title engraved with architectural design and device *Alma Mater Cantabrigia*; signed *Rob: Vaughan Sculp:*. Device on N. T. title, and at end of text.
Text: O. T. ends on Ppp 4 *a*; N. T. ends on Llll 3 *a*. The Metrical Psalms follow with continuous register, ending on Rrrr 4 *b*. No Apocrypha.
Kilburne mentions this edition: 'In another Minion Bible in 8° volume, printed by *John Field* at *Cambridge* in 1657. Which sels very much, and very dear, at least for 8*s*. 6*d*. *per book*. *Psal.* 143. 4. *Therefore is my Spirit over*, is wholly omitted in many that I have seen. And there are many other faults as I am well informed of very great notoriety.'
Acts vi. 3, *ye*; 1 Tim. iv. 16, *thy*.

¶ 167 × 111 mm.
Apocrypha inserted.
With Metrical Psalms (1657)—see above. Wanting last leaf. [F. F.]

—— Another copy.

Ps. cxliii. 4 correct.
With Metrical Psalms (1657), as above.
Edges painted with flowers. [F. F.]

—— Another copy.

Ps. cxliii. 4 correct.
Contains engravings of King David, and the Evangelists. These, with the general title, are illuminated.
With Metrical Psalms (1657), as above.

—— Another copy.

A fragment, containing only the first four sheets. With many plates inserted, like some of those in the second copy of No. 506.
Bound up with this are: the Apocrypha, *The Way to True Happiness* (? date), Downame's Concordance (1652), and the Metrical Psalms (1661). Between the last two is inserted the titleleaf of an edition of the Metrical Psalms (1656). [F. F.]
516.

—— ANOTHER EDITION.

Similar to the above, but differently set up. O. T. ends on Ppp 2 *b*, and N. T. on Kkkk 8 *b* without device.

¶ 170 × 112 mm.
The general title in this copy is the same as that of Field's octavo of 1661 (No. 534), the date being altered by hand; the body of the book is quite distinct from the edition of 1661 (which has the pages numbered). The volume not improbably was issued by Field in this state. [F. F.]
517.

1657. The Dutch Annotations upon the whole Bible: or, all the Holy Canonical Scriptures of the Old and New Testament, together with, and according to their own Translation of all the Text: as both the one and the other were ordered and appointed by the Synod of Dort, 1618. and published by Authority, 1637. Now faithfully communicated to the use of

Great Britain, in English. Whereunto is prefixed an exact Narrative touching the whole Work, and this Translation. By Theodore Haak Esq.
Henry Hills, for John Rothwell, Joshua Kirton, and
Richard Tomlins: London. 1657. f°. 2 vols.

An English translation of both text and notes of the famous Dutch Bible of 1637, whose preparation had been ordered by the Synod of Dort.

In the 'Attestation' the translator, Theodore Haak (1605-1690), is described as 'a learned Gentleman . . . every way fitted for such a Task, he being by Birth and Breeding a German, about twenty years [Anno 1645] conversant in England, where not only his faithfulness is known in divers publick Employments, but his Dexterity also in Translating divers English Books of Practical Divinity into the German Tongue . . .' Haak executed this work at the request of the Westminster Assembly of Divines. On 30 March 1648 Parliament granted him the sole right in the translation for fourteen years from the time of publication; and in the following year settled on him a pension of £100 a year. During the Commonwealth he was frequently rewarded by the Council of State for procuring foreign intelligence and translating documents.

The Annotations are enclosed within brackets, and mingled with the text, which is printed in italics. With Arguments, Prefaces, etc. The book is divided into two volumes at the end of the Song of Solomon; but the N. T. has a separate titleleaf and register. No Apocrypha. The preliminary leaves include a Dedication to the Lord Protector—1 f., *A Plain and True Narrative touching the late Version of the Bible . . . into the Belgick or Netherlandish . . . 1637* . . .—3 ff., *A Copy of the Certificate or Attestation, about the General desire . . . to have the . . . Dutch Annotations upon the Bible . . . Translated into English*, by Theodore Haak (dated 1645, and signed by thirty-five names—including *Stephen Marshall, Thomas Goodwin, Sydrack Simson, Adoniram Byfield, Alexander Henderson*, and *Samuel Rutherford*)—1 f., and a declaration by the States General of the United Netherlands (dated 1637)—3 pp.

¶ 283 × 113 mm. Wants the last leaf of the N. T.
Bound in one volume.

518.

1657. B. 12°. See 1658.

1658. The Holy Bible . . .
Henry Hills and John Field, Printers to his Highnes:
London. 1657,58. 12°.

Kilburne states that Hills and Field had to pay for their privilege of Bible-printing an annual sum of £500 to certain men in power, 'whose names out of respect to them I forbear to mention.'

These printers produced a duodecimo Bible in 1656, which is severely condemned by Kilburne for its inaccuracy.

General title engraved by *P. Lombart*, and dated 1657; N. T. dated 1657 on title, but 1658 in colophon. Text, B 3 to Pp 8 *b*. No Apocrypha.

¶ 151 × 78 mm. Wants two leaves of text. [F. F.]

519.

1658. The Holy Bible . . .
J. Field: London. 1658. 24°.

There are two distinct 24° Bibles of 1658, which both bear J. Field's imprint. It is possible that, while one of these is really Field's production, the other is a foreign or pirated edition. But it is not easy to determine which is the 'genuine,' and which the 'spurious' Bible.'

According to the B. M. Catalogue this is the 'genuine' Bible; Fry and Lenox call it 'spurious,' though Fry confesses that it is difficult to see why such an epithet should be applied to it or to the other 24° Bible. Very incorrectly printed, e.g. John vii. 31, *no miracles*; 2 Thess. ii. 15, *Paul fast* for *stand fast*.

General title engraved (with view of London, etc.). Text ends on Zz 12 *b*. No Apocrypha.

ENGLISH

Two varieties occur.

A.
With the words *Appointed* . . . on the general title.

¶ 115 × 63 mm.
With Metrical Psalms (1658). [F. F.]
520.

—— Another edition.

B.
This differs only in the title, which lacks the words *Appointed* . . .

¶ 116 × 62 mm.
With Metrical Psalms (1658). [F. F.]

—— Another copy.

With Metrical Psalms (1658).
Silver corners and clasps.

—— Another copy.
521.

1658. The Holy Bible . . .
J. Field: London. 1658. 24°.

General title engraved (with view of London, etc.). Text ends on Ddd 12 b. No Apocrypha.
This is the Bible called 'spurious' in the B. M. Catalogue; though Fry and Lenox call it 'genuine.' It is more correctly printed than Nos. 520 and 521 (*q.v.*); yet it has some of the same mistakes, e.g. Jer. ii. 26, *chief* for *thief*. Headline Hh 2 b, *Jesaiah*.

Two varieties occur.

A.
With the words *Appointed* . . . on the general title.

¶ 111 × 61 mm. [F. F.]
522.

—— Another edition.

B.
This differs from A only in the title, which lacks the words *Appointed* . . .

¶ 108 × 59 mm.
With Metrical Psalms (1658).
In two volumes. [F. F.]
523.

1659. The New Testament . . . Heretofore Translated out of the Originall Greek, By K. James's Command.
E. Tyler: London. 1659. 12°.

Diglot; the English version and Beza's Latin Testament (see Latin section).
The Preface contains an allusion to the diglot printed *pro I. C.* in 1550 (see No. 58).
Latin title, English title, *An Advertisement to the Reader* . . . (signed *Charles Hoole*)— 4 ff. Text, A 1 to Gg 10 a.
Printed in parallel columns, the Latin inside in roman type, the English outside in italics.

¶ 147 × 81 mm. [F. F.]
524.

1659. B. f°. See 1660.

RESTORATION OF KING CHARLES II: 29 MAY 1660.

1660. The Holy Bible . . .
  John Field, Printer to the Vniversitie:
    Cambridge. 1660,59. f°. 2 vols.

A reissue of Field's large folio of 1659, with a new general title, dated 1660, and 'illustrated wth Chorographical Sculps. by J. Ogilby.'

The Bible is divided at the end of Job. Vol. 2 has a separate titlepage, dated 1660. The N. T. title is dated 1659.

Pepys alludes to this Bible in his *Diary* under the date 27 May 1667: 'There come Richardson, the bookbinder, with one of Ogilby's Bibles in quires for me to see and buy, it being Mr. Cade's, my stationer's; but it is like to be so big that I shall not use it.'

Text: O. T., 1103 pp.; Apocrypha, 258 pp.; N. T. ends on p. 338 with colophon dated 1659. General title representing Solomon on his throne, designed by *Diepenbeck*, engraved by *Lombart*. The large two-page plates are generally signed with the names of the various artists (*P. P. Rubens, T. Tintoret, M. de Vos, N. de Bruyn*, etc.), and with that of the engraver *Visscher*.

¶ 452 × 292 mm.
With Prayer Book (1660), preceded by a full-page engraving of the royal arms (by *W. Hollar*), and dedication of the whole volume to King Charles II (signed by *John Ogilby*).
[F. F.]
525.

1660. The Holy Bible . . .
  H. Hills and J. Field: London. 1660. 8°.

On 7 July 1660 the University of Oxford farmed out to Hills and Field for four years its privilege of printing Bibles, in consideration of an annual payment of £80. (D.N.B., art. *Henry Hills*.)

Text ends on Aaa 3 *b*. No Apocrypha. Each title printed, within narrow frame.

¶ 167 × 105 mm. [F. F.]

—— Another copy.

Wants last leaf.
Interleaved, and bound in four volumes.
526.

—— ANOTHER EDITION.

Apparently the same as the above, with the exception of the general title, which is engraved (architectural design, with royal arms above, and King David below), and bears the name of *Henry Hills* only.

¶ 170 × 110 mm.
Apocrypha inserted.
With Metrical Psalms (1661), and Prayer Book (1662).
Morocco binding, decorated with inlaid work. A flyleaf bears the inscription: *For the Excellent and Vertuous Madame Dugdale ex dono Doct: South.* [F. F.]
527.

1660. The Holy Bible . . .
  J. Field: London. 1660. 12°.

General title engraved by *Guli. Vaughan*. Text ends on Vv 11 *b* with colophon. No Apocrypha.

¶ 149 × 79 mm. [F. F.]
528.

1660 ? (The New Testament in short-hand.)
Printed for the Authour And are to be sold by Henry Eversden under the Crown Tavern in West-Smithfeild :
London. [1660 ?] 64°.

The New Testament written in short-hand by Jeremiah Rich ; engraved apparently by T. Cross.

First published in 1659.
J. Rich (d. 1660 ?) learnt his short-hand from an uncle, William Cartwright. He published 'Semography' in 1642, 'Charactery' in 1646, and other works on his system in 1654 and 1659. His Metrical Psalms in short-hand, first published in 1659, are often bound up with his N. T. Thomas Shelton, another stenographer, also published an edition of the Metrical Psalms, about 1670. For Rich, Shelton, and Addy (see below, No. 638), consult J. H. Lewis' History of Short-hand.

DESCRIPTION. Frontispiece; title (in short-hand, except *Ieremiah Rich* and imprint), verso blank. Text, with pages not numbered; followed by *The Names of the Subscribers to this Incomparable Worke*—2 ff.
Distinguishable from the edition of 1659, which it closely resembles, by four new names inserted in the list of subscribers.
A portrait of Rich stands as frontispiece. The title bears the inscription : *T. Cross sculpsit.*
For another edition see No. 676.

¶ 65 × 42 mm. Wants title.
Agrees with the B. M. copy C. 18. a. 33 (1).

529.

1660. B. 12°. See 1661.

1661. The Holy Bible . . .
J. Field : London. 1661,60. 12°.

General title engraved by *Guli. Vaughan*, and dated 1661 ; N. T. dated 1660 on title, and in colophon.
Text ends on Vv 11 b. No Apocrypha.
Apparently identical with No. 528, except for the general title.

¶ 148 × 78 mm.
Two or three plates are inserted. [F. F.]

530.

—— ANOTHER EDITION.

Identical with the above, except for the general title (which is not engraved, and bears the names of *John Bill and Christopher Barker, Printers to the Kings most excellent Majesty*), and a few other leaves.

¶ 152 × 84 mm. Slightly imperfect. [F. F.]

531.

1661. The Holy Bible . . .
C. Barker ; H. Hills : London. 1661. 4°.

General title, engraved by *P. Williamson* (architectural design, with royal arms above, and King David below), mentions *Christopher Barker* as printer. N. T. title (with cut of royal arms) and colophon give the name of *Henry Hills.*
Text : O. T., B 1 to Ppp 4 b ; Apocrypha, Qqq 1 to Gggg 2 b ; N. T., A 2 to T 4 b.

¶ 235 × 168 mm.
With Metrical Psalms (1661), and Prayer Book (1664). [F. F.]

532.

—— Another edition.

General title (with cut of royal arms) gives the names *John Bill and Christopher Barker*. The following leaf also differs; but the rest of the book appears to be identical with the preceding edition.

¶ 232 × 168 mm.
Wants Apocrypha.
With *Index Biblicus: or an Exact Concordance to the Holy Bible . . . by John Jackson . . .* (1668). [F. F.]
533.

1661. The Holy Bible . . .
         J. Field : Cambridge. **1661.** 8 .

Text: O. T., 965 pp.: N. T., 299 pp. (ending on Llll 3 *a*). No Apocrypha.
General title engraved by *Guli: Vaughan*.

¶ 172 × 110 mm.
With Metrical Psalms (1661). [F. F.]
534.

1661. The Holy Bible . . .
      C. Barker ; J. Field : London. **1661.** 12°.

General title, engraved by *Vaughan*, gives *Christopher Barker* as the printer. N. T. title bears the name of *John Field*. Text ends on Qq 10 *b*. No Apocrypha.

¶ 149 × 79 mm.
With Metrical Psalms (1661).
Silver clasps. [F. F.]
535.

1661. B. 8°. See 1662.

1662. The Holy Bible . . .
         J. Field : Cambridge. **1661,62.** 8°.

Engraved general title dated 1661; N. T. title dated 1662. Last page of O. T. numbered 985 (for 965); N. T. ends on p. 299. No Apocrypha.

¶ 173 × 110 mm.
With Metrical Psalms (1661). [F. F.]
536.

1662. B. 8°. See 1663.
* B. 12°. See 1665.*

1663. The Holy Bible . . .
         J. Field : Cambridge. **1663,62.** 8°.

Apparently identical with No. 536, except for the engraved title, which is dated 1663 and is unsigned.

¶ 172 × 105 mm.
With Metrical Psalms (1661), and Prayer Book (1665). [F. F.]
537.

1663. The Holy Bible . . .
         J. Field : Cambridge. **1663.** 4°.

General title engraved by *Iohn Chantry*.
Text: O. T. ends on Ppp 4 *a*; Apocrypha end on P 4 *a*; N. T. ends on T 4 *a*.

¶ 221 × 164 mm. [F. F.]
538.

1663. The Holy Bible . . .

                        J. Bill and C. Barker : London. 1663. 8°.

General title engraved. Text: O. T. ends on Ppp 2 *b*; N. T. ends on Kkkk 8 *b*. Pages not numbered. No Apocrypha.

¶ 163 × 107 mm.

                                                                                  539.

1663. B. 8°. *See 1665.*

1664. The Holy Bible . . .

                        J. Field : Cambridge. 1664. 12°.

General title engraved (with view of London, etc.). Text: O. T., A 2 to Z 7 *b*; Apocrypha, a 1 to f 6 *a*; N. T., A 2 to G 12 *b*.
Field is described on the general title *Printer to the Uneversete of Cambrig.*

¶ 152 × 83 mm.
With Metrical Psalms (1664), and Prayer Book (1671).   [F. F.]

                                                                                   540.

1664. The Holy Bible . . .

                                    [*Amsterdam?*] 1664. 12°.

No doubt printed abroad, perhaps at Amsterdam. With Canne's marginal matter.

John Canne (d. 1667 ?) lived for many years abroad, and in 1642 was styled by John Ball ' the leader of the English Brownists in Amsterdam.' His edition of the English Bible was the first to contain a full apparatus of carefully selected marginal references. Anderson (vol. ii, p. 559) mentions a quarto edition of his Bible printed at Amsterdam in 1644 ; but the D. N. B. gives 1647 as the date of the first authenticated edition. In 1653 he received an exclusive licence for seven years ' to print a Bible with annotations, being his own work, and that no man, unless appointed by him, may print his said notes, either already printed, or to be printed ' (*Calendar of State Papers,* 9 June 1653). Anderson enumerates other editions of 1662, 1664, 1671, 1682, 1698, 1700, 1720, 1727, and 1754. Canne's Bible ' was used in the preparation of Bagster's " Comprehensive Bible," of which it is indeed the basis.'
Text ends on Yy 4 *b*. No Apocrypha.
The woodcut title-border represents : above, the giving of the Law ; and below, a spread eagle, and Joseph meeting Jacob.

¶ 157 × 93 mm.
With Metrical Psalms (1664).
Contemporary binding.   [F. F.]

                                                                                      541.

1664. The New Testament . . .

                      Bill and Barker : London. 1664. 8°.

Title plain, with small cut of royal arms; list of books on verso. Text, Aa 2 to Zz 8 *b*; printed in double columns. Name of book and chapter number in headlines in black-letter.

¶ 167 × 105 mm.
With Prayer Book (1664).
Contains many plates.   [F. F.]

                                                                                    542.

1665. The Holy Bible . . .

                    Bill and Barker : London. 1665, 62. 12°.

General title engraved, and dated 1665 ; N. T. dated 1662.
Text ends on Ss 2 *b*. No Apocrypha.

¶ 150 × 81 mm.   [F. F.]

                                                                                      543.

1665. The Holy Bible . . .
J. Field: Cambridge. 1663. Bill and Barker: London. 1665. 8°.

General title engraved, with Field's name, and dated 1663. N. T. title, with Bill and Barker's names, dated 1665. Text: O. T. ends on Ppp 2 b; N. T. ends on Kkkk 8 b. No Apocrypha.

¶ 170 × 109 mm.
The general title is mounted, and may have been inserted. But according to Loftie (p. 143) London and Cambridge editions of the period are often mixed. And probably the book was originally published in this state. [F. F.]
544.

1665. The Holy Bible . . .
Bill and Barker: London. 1665. 8°.

Text ends on Kkkk 8 b. No Apocrypha. General title engraved by *P. Williamson*; architectural design, with royal arms supported by lion and unicorn.

¶ 163 × 111 mm. Wants N. T. title.
Apocrypha inserted, and a second copy added at the end.
With Prayer Book (? date). [F. F.]
545.

1666. The Holy Bible . . .
Bill and Barker: London. 1666. 12°.

Both titles within woodcut border. Text ends on Qq 12 b. The Apocrypha section (A–G) interrupts the signatures.

¶ 149 × 79 mm. [F. F.]
546.

1666. Solomons Proverbs, alphabetically collected out of his Proverbs and Ecclesiastes, for help of Memory. With an additional Collection of other Scripture-Proverbs out of the Old and New Testament. By H. D. . . .
London. 1666. 8°.

The B. M. Catalogue ascribes this collection of Proverbs to Henry Danvers, the Anabaptist and politician, who died in 1687.

Printer's name not given.
The preliminary matter includes *To the Reader* (dated *1. Moneth, 1666,* and signed *H. D.*)— 11 pp.; Verses, *Of Wisdom* and *Of a Pearl* (by *S. P.*); and list of *errata*. Solomon's Proverbs (grouped under headings in alphabetical order, e.g. *Adversity, Adultery, Affliction, Anger,* etc.), B 1 a to F 7 a; followed by two indexes. Other Proverbs, with separate title: *Additional Proverbs to those of Solomons, collected out of the Old and New Testament. With an Addition of about Eighty Proverbs more, omitted in the former, and gathered since the Impression* . . . ending on K 7 b; followed by index, ending on L 3 a.
See No. 727.

¶ 139 × 84 mm. [F. F.]
547.

1666. B. 4°. See 1668.

1668. The Holy Bible . . .
J. Field: Cambridge. 1668,66. 4°.

This edition is sometimes known as the 'Preaching Bible,' being well adapted for pulpit use; it is printed in small type, with a very full page.

General title engraved by *Chantry*, and dated 1668; N. T. title dated 1666.
Text: O. T. ends on Qq 3 *b*; Apocrypha end on I 4 *b*; N. T. ends on M 4 *a*.

¶ 226 × 171 mm.
With Prayer Book (1666), and Metrical Psalms (1666). [F. F.]

—— Another copy.

With Prayer Book (1666), and Metrical Psalms (1666), and Jackson's *Index Biblicus* (1668).
548.

1668. The Holy Bible . . .
Bill and Barker : London. 1668. 12°.

General title engraved; N. T. title plain, . . . *In the Savoy, Printed by the Assigns of John Bill and Christopher Barker* . . . Text ends on Qq 12 *b*. Apocrypha mentioned in list of books, but not required by signatures.

¶ 153 × 83 mm.
Wants Apocrypha?
With Prayer Book (? date), and Metrical Psalms (1668).
Covers of inlaid leather-work. [F. F.]
549.

1669. The Holy Bible . . .
Bill and Barker : London. 1669. 8°.

General title engraved; architectural design, with angel holding book and trumpet, at the top. N. T. title printed, with cut of royal arms; the imprint reads: *In the Savoy, Printed by the Assigns of John Bill and Christopher Barker* . . . *1669*. Text ends on Aaa 3 *b*. No Apocrypha.
Xx 8 *a* headline, *Pauls ministery*.

¶ 172 × 110 mm. [F. F.]

—— Another copy.

Apocrypha inserted. [F. F.]

—— Another copy.

Imperfect. Contains many plates, some of which are signed *F. H. Van Hove fecit*. Two in the Psalms represent *The Powder Plot November the V* (illustrating Ps. ix. 16, and x. 14); and *King Charles the First Murthered* (Ps. xxxi. 13). [F. F.]
550.

—— ANOTHER EDITION.

This closely resembles the above, reading with it generally page for page. But it is quite distinct, being printed in smaller and inferior type. Possibly a foreign edition, produced in Holland.
Xx 8 *a* headline, *Pauls ministry*.

¶ 171 × 112 mm. Wants general title.
With Scotch Metrical Psalms (? date). [F. F.]
551.

1669. The Holy Bible . . .
Bill and Barker : London. 1669. 12°.

'Apparently printed abroad' (Lea-Wilson). *Cf.* No. 592.
General title has woodcut border—architectural design, with royal arms, and picture of the Ark; N. T. title-border has similar design, but the bottom block represents King David. Text ends on Mm 6 *b*. No Apocrypha.
Headlines on Ll 1 *b* and 2 *b*, *Tmothy, Thimothy*.

¶ 149 × 86 mm.
With Metrical Psalms (1669). [F. F.]
552.

1669. B. 8°. See 1671 and 1676.
B. 12°. See 1680.

1670. The Holy Bible . . .
John Hayes, Printer to the University : Cambridge. 1670. 4°.

General title engraved by *Chantry*. Text: O. T. ends on Ppp 4 *a*; Apocrypha end on p 4 *a*; N. T. ends on T 4 *a*.

¶ 230 × 171 mm.
With Prayer Book (1670), and Metrical Psalms (1670). [F. F.]
553.

1671. The Holy Bible . . .
Bill and Barker : London. 1671,69. 8°.

General title engraved; dated 1671. N. T. title (*In the Savoy, Assigns of Bill and Barker*) dated 1669. Text ends on Aaa 3 *b*. No Apocrypha.

¶ 167 × 110 mm. Very possibly a copy of the 1669 edition, with a 1671 title inserted; but probably it was issued in this state. The octavo Bibles of the period are often curiously mixed (see note, No. 333).
Apocrypha inserted.
With Metrical Psalms (1669), and Prayer Book (1671).
With painted edges. [F. F.]

—— Another copy.
Differs very slightly from the above in parts, e.g. in sheet Zz. Perhaps a mixed copy.
Apocrypha inserted.
With Metrical Psalms (1669), and Prayer Book (1671). [F. F.]
554.

1671. The Holy Bible . . .
Bill and Barker : London. 1671. 8°.

Engraved general title. N. T. title, *In the Savoy, Printed by the Assigns* . . . Text ends on Kkkk 8 *b*. No Apocrypha.

¶ 173 × 114 mm.
With Metrical Psalms (1677).
With painted edges. [F. F.]
555.

1671. B. 12°. See 1672.

1672. The Holy Bible . . .
Assigns of Bill and Barker : London. 1671,72. 12°.

General title dated 1671; N. T. title (*In the Savoy* . . .) dated 1672. Text ends on Qq 12 *b*. No Apocrypha.

¶ 146 × 80 mm. Wants two leaves.
556.

1672. The Holy Bible . . . With most profitable Annotations . . .
[*Amsterdam.*] 1672. f°.

Text of King James' version, with Geneva notes, etc.

This edition closely agrees with that printed by Broerss in 1642 (No. 438).
Loftie (p. 149) states that some copies give the printer's name: *Stephen Swart, bookseller near the Exchange, Amsterdam.* See Nos. 583 and 584.

An engraved title (representing Moses and Aaron, the royal arms, a view of London, etc.) precedes the ordinary title. The printed title has a cut of the royal arms, and the N. T. title has a cut of the crossing of the Red Sea. Text: O. T., pp. 1 to 710 (really 712); N. T., 248 pp. No Apocrypha.

¶ 384 × 231 mm.
With a Map of the World and two other maps (by *Jacob Savry*). [**F. F.**]
557.

1672. The Holy Bible . . .
Assigns of Bill and Barker: London. 1672. 24°.

General title engraved. N. T. title, *In the Savoy* . . . Text ends on Ddd 12 *a*. No Apocrypha.

¶ 115 × 54 mm.
With Metrical Psalms (1672).
Contemporary binding; with edges goffered and painted. [**F. F.**]
558.

1672. B. 12°. See 1673.
B. 24°. See 1673.

1673. The Holy Bible . . .
Assigns of Bill and Barker: London. 1672,73. 12°.

General title dated 1672; N. T. dated 1673. Text ends on Oo 12 *b*. Apocrypha mentioned in list of books, but not required by signatures.

¶ 150 × 79 mm.
Wants Apocrypha? [**F. F.**]
559.

1673. The Holy Bible . . .
Assigns of Bill and Barker: London. 1672,73. 24°.

General title dated 1672; N. T. title dated 1673. Text ends on Ddd 12 *a*. No Apocrypha.

¶ 111 × 54 mm. [**F. F.**]
560.

1673. The Holy Bible . . .
J. Hayes: Cambridge. 1673. 4°.

Closely agrees with Hayes' quarto of 1670 (No. 553).
Eph. ii. 13, *sometime*—not *sometimes* as it is often wrongly printed.

¶ 228 × 167 mm. [**F. F.**]
561.

1673. The Holy Bible . . .
R. Barker and Assigns of J. Bill: London. 1673. 12°.

Text ends on Nn 6 *b*. No Apocrypha.

¶ 152 × 88 mm.
With Prayer Book (1670), and Metrical Psalms (1673). [**F. F.**]

—— Another copy.

Wants N. T. titleleaf.
With Prayer Book (1670), and Metrical Psalms (1673).
In tortoise-shell covers, with silver corners and clasps. [**F. F.**]

―― Another copy.
A fragment, containing title and a few leaves. [F. F.]
562.

1673. The Holy Bible . . .
Assigns of J. Bill and C. Barker: London. 1673. 12°.

Text ends on Oo 12 b. Apocrypha mentioned in list of books, but not required by signatures.

¶ 151 × 84 mm.
Wants Apocrypha?
With Metrical Psalms (1673), and Prayer Book (1674).
Covers embroidered with coloured silks and silver thread. [F F.]
563.

1673. B. 4°. See 1675.
B. 24°. See 1674.

1674. The Holy Bible . . .
Assigns of Bill and Barker: London. 1674,73. 24°.

General title dated 1674; N. T. title dated 1673. Text ends on Ddd 12 a. No Apocrypha.

¶ 116 × 57 mm. Imperfect: wanting general title and following leaf; but it exactly agrees with the B. M. copy (336. a. 3) of the edition of 1674,73.
With Metrical Psalms (1674).
Binding of inlaid leather-work. [F. F.]
564.

1674. The Holy Bible . . .
Assigns of Bill and Barker: London. 1674. 12°.

Text ends on Ff 12 a. No Apocrypha.

¶ 151 × 81 mm.
With Metrical Psalms (1675). [F. F.]
565.

1675. The Holy Bible . . .
At the Theater, Oxford. 1675,73. 4°.

The first English Bible printed at Oxford.

An engraved title precedes the printed general title; it represents the Transfiguration above a mountain inscribed *Mt. Tabor Matt. 17. 1*; across the centre is a label *The Holy Bible*; in the foreground are seated two symbolical female figures:—one, veiled, representing *The Law*; the other with a nimbus, *The Gospel*; on the base of a broken column to the left are the words *At the Theater in Oxon*. The printed N. T. title is also preceded by an engraved title: three cherubs carry the label *The New Testament*; an obelisk rests on a square base, on the former an angel writes with an arrow the words *The Law of Loue from The hill of Sion*, on the latter is inscribed *The Law of fear from mount Sinai;* the step, on which the angel kneels, bears the words *At the Theater in Oxford A° 1675*.

No Dedication or Preface; list of books on verso of printed title. Text: O. T., A 1 to Ccc 4 b; Apocrypha (in smaller type), A 1 to I 3 b; N. T., A 1 to P 7 b, ending with colophon; 1 f. blank.

Two varieties occur, differing in the colophon, and very slightly elsewhere.

A.
Colophon dated 1673.

ENGLISH

¶ 228 × 167 mm.
With Prayer Book (1675), and Metrical Psalms (1675).   [F. F.]

—— Another copy.
566.

—— ANOTHER EDITION.
B.
Colophon dated 1675. The printed general title also slightly differs.
¶ 213 × 156 mm.   [F. F.]
567.

1675. The Holy Bible . . .
       J. Hayes: Cambridge. 1675. 4°.

General title engraved by *Chantry*. Text: O. T. ends Aaa 4 *b*; Apocrypha end on l 8 *a*; N. T. ends on P 4 *b*.
¶ 227 × 168 mm.   [F. F.]
568.

1675. The Holy Bible . . .
     Assigns of Bill and Barker: London. 1675. 8°.

Titles plain. Text ends on Aaa 3 *b*. Apocrypha mentioned in list of books, but not required by signatures.
Deut. xxxii. 39, *even I am* (*he* omitted).
¶ 166 × 111 mm.
Wants Apocrypha?   [F. F.]

—— Another copy.
Wants first two leaves, and Apocrypha (?).
With Scotch Metrical Psalms (1693).
Binding stamped inside cover, *Sepr. 21. 1699.*   [F. F.]

—— Another copy.
General title dated 1669. All the rest of the book seems to belong to the 1675 edition.
Wants Apocrypha?
569.

1675. (The Holy Bible.)
     Assigns of Bill and Barker: London. 1675. 12°.

Text ends on Oo 12 *b*. Apocrypha mentioned in list of books, but not required by signatures.
¶ 151 × 85 mm. Wants general title.
Wants Apocrypha?   [F. F.]
570.

1675. (The Holy Bible.)
   Andrew Anderson and his Partners: Edinburgh. 1675. 12°.

In 1671 Anderson 'obtained a gift under the Great Seal, which was soon ratified in Parliament, appointing and constituting him, his heirs and assignees, to be His Majesty's sole, absolute, and only printer,' in Scotland. (See Lee, *Memorial*, p. 118, etc.)

Text ends on Nn 12 *b*. No Apocrypha.
¶ 135 × 69 mm.
An odd volume, containing the second half of the Bible, Psalms–Revelation. The N. T. title gives the printer's name, etc.: *Edinburgh, Printed by Andrew Anderson, and his Partners, Printers to the Kings most Excellent Majesty: Anno Dom. 1675.*   [F. F.]
571.

1675. B. 8°. See 1676, 1680, and 1682.
VOL. I.   Q

1676. The Holy Bible . . .
Bill and Barker : London. 1676,69. 8°.

General title engraved; dated 1676. N. T. title (*In the Savoy, Assigns of Bill and Barker*) dated 1669. Text ends on Aaa 3 b. Apocrypha mentioned in list of books, but not required by signatures.

¶ 167 × 110 mm.
Wants Apocrypha ?
Contains many MS. notes—some in short-hand. [F. F.]
572.

1676. The Holy Bible . . .
Bill and Barker : London. 1676,75. 8°.

General title engraved; dated 1676. N. T. title (*Assigns of Bill and Barker*) dated 1675. Text ends on **Aaa** 3 b. Apocrypha mentioned in list of books, but not required by signatures.

¶ 172 × 114 mm.
Wants Apocrypha ? [F. F.]
573.

1676. The Holy Bible . . .
C. Barker : London. 1676. 4°.

Loftie (p. 155) states that this edition was ' probably printed in Holland.'

General title engraved, like that in No. 532. Text : O. T. ends on Eee 2 b ; N. T. ends on Q 4 b, with colophon. Apocrypha mentioned in list of books.

¶ 231 × 181 mm.
Wants Apocrypha ? [F. F.]
574.

1676. The Holy Bible . . .
Edinburgh. Andrew Anderson, Printer to His most Sacred Majesty, King Charles the second, in the 28 year of His reign.
Anno Dom. 1676. 8°.

Lee (*Memorial*, p. 163) praises this as one of the best editions printed in Scotland.
Both titles plain. The N. T. title has the royal arms on verso. Text: O. T. ends on Ll 1 b ; N. T. ends on Xx 4 b, with colophon. No Apocrypha.
1 Tim. iv. 16, *thy.*

¶ 171 × 111 mm.
With Scotch Metrical Psalms (1676).
Contemporary binding, with elaborate design ; painted edges. Fastened inside the covers are two ornamental leather name-labels: (1) *Mistres Anne Curry Aught This Bible 1688* ; (2) *Ianet Mitchel Aught This Bible 1705.* [F. F.]
575.

1676. The Holy Bible . . .
Assigns of Bill and Barker : London. 1676. 12°.

Text ends on Oo 12 b. Apocrypha mentioned in list of books, but not required by signatures.

¶ 151 × 85 mm. Wants one leaf.
Wants Apocrypha ?
With Prayer Book (? date), and Metrical Psalms (1678).
Binding of inlaid leather-work. [F. F.]
576.

1676. The Holy Bible . . .

Assigns of Bill and Barker : London. 1676. 24°.

Text ends on Ddd 12 *a*. No Apocrypha.

Two varieties occur.

A.
Gen. i. 2, *the face of the deep.*

¶ 114 × 54 mm. [F. F.]

—— Another copy.

Silver corners.

577.

—— Another edition.

B.
Gen. i. 2, *ye face* . . .

¶ 109 × 54 mm.
With Metrical Psalms (1672).

578.

1676. The New Testament . . .

Assigns of Bill and Barker : London. 1676. 8°.

List of books on verso of title. Text, Aa 2 to Aaa 8 *b*. Double columns. Name of book and chapter-numbers in headlines in black-letter.

¶ 171 × 109 mm.
Silver clasps. [F. F.]

579.

1676. B. 4°. See 1677.

1677. The Holy Bible . . .

C. Barker : London. 1677,76. 4°.

A reissue of No. 574, with a general title dated 1677. Perhaps printed abroad.

¶ 229 × 184 mm.
Wants Apocrypha? [F. F.]

580.

1677. The Holy Bible . . .

J. Hayes : Cambridge. 1677. 4°.

Closely agrees with Hayes' quarto of 1670 (No. 553).

¶ 225 × 166 mm.
With Prayer Book (1676), and Metrical Psalms (1676). [F. F.]

581.

1678. The Holy Bible . . .
J. Bill, C. Barker, T. Newcomb, and H. Hills : London. 1678. 4°.

An engraved title (with architectural design) precedes the printed general title. Text: O. T. ends on Mmm 4 *b*; Apocrypha end on p 2 *a*; N. T. ends on T 2 *b*.

¶ 233 × 177 mm.
With Prayer Book (1678), and Metrical Psalms (1678). [F. F.

—— Another copy.

In two volumes. Apocrypha bound up separately, with Prayer Book (1678) and Metrical Psalms (1678).

—— Another copy.

With Prayer Book (1678), and Metrical Psalms (1678).   [F. F.]
582.

1679. The Holy Bible . . . With most profitable Annotations . . . *For Stephen Swart, at the Crowned Bible, on the Westside of the Exchange: Amsterdam.* 1679. f°.

Text of King James' version, with Geneva notes, etc.

A reprint of the 1672 edition (No. 557).
Engraved title as before; each of the two printed titles bears a cut of the royal arms. Text: O. T. ends on p. 710 (really 712); N. T., 248 pp. No Apocrypha.

Two varieties occur.

A.
With place and printer's name on the printed general title.

¶ 354 × 221 mm.
A map of the Holy Land (by *Iacob Savery*, 1648) is inserted before the N. T.
[F. F.]
583.

—— Another edition.

B.
Without place and printer's name. The engraved title also slightly differs.

¶ 394 × 250 mm.
With Apocrypha (108 pp.), printed in smaller type, supplied. Contains two maps by *J. Moxon*.
A copy of the engraved title belonging to the first variety is inserted.
With Prayer Book (1679), and Metrical Psalms (1679).
In original boards. According to a MS. note on a fly-leaf this copy was bought at Rotterdam in 1704. Another copy is in the Library of Edinburgh University; and an entry in the Library accounts shows that its price was *18 lib.* (= 30s. in contemporary English currency, or about £6 to-day). Loftie, p. 161.   [F. F.]
584.

1679. The Holy Bible . . .
At the Theater in Oxford. 1679. 4°.

The second edition printed at Oxford. See No. 566.

General title engraved (with figures of Moses, Aaron, Jeremiah, and Isaiah, and a view of the Theatre, etc.). Some copies have two N. T. titles: (1) engraved, like the general title; (2) printed, with the following imprint (given also in the colophon): *Printed at the Theater in Oxford, and are to be sold by Moses Pitt at the Angel in St. Paul's Churchyard, Peter Parker at the Leg and Star over against the Exchange in Cornhill, Thomas Guy at the Corner of Little Lumbard-street, and William Leak at the Crown in Fleet-street, London. Anno 1679.*
The names Pitt, Parker, Leak, and Guy often occur, conjointly or separately, as the London publishers of Bibles printed at the Theatre, Oxford, in the last quarter of the seventeenth century. Regarding Guy's Bible-trade W. Maitland (*History of London*, 1775 edition, p. 1306) writes: 'Mr. *Guy*, being out of his Apprenticeship [Sept. 1668], set up his Trade, in the little Corner-House betwixt *Cornhill* and *Lombard-street*, with a Stock of about two hundred Pounds. At which Time, the *English* Bibles printed in this Kingdom being very bad, both in the Letter and Paper, occasioned divers of the Booksellers of this City to encourage the Printing thereof in *Holland*, with curious Types, and fine Paper; and imported vast Numbers of the same, to their no small Advantage. Mr. *Guy*, soon coming acquainted with this profitable Commerce, became a large Dealer therein. But this Trade proving very detrimental to the King's Printer, all Ways and Means were devised to quash the same;

which being vigorously put in Execution, the Booksellers, by frequent Seizures and Prosecutions, became so great Sufferers, that they judged a farther Pursuit thereof inconsistent with their Interest. Wherefore our Founder contracted with the University of *Oxford*, for their Privilege to print Bibles; and having furnished himself with Types from *Holland*, carried on a very great Trade in Bibles for divers Years, to his very great advantage.' Thomas Guy, having grown rich by this trade in Bibles, greatly increased his fortune by successful speculation in South Sea stock; and, before his death in 1724, he founded and endowed the famous Hospital known by his name.

Dedication, with list of books on verso, on A 1. Text: O. T., A 2 to Ccc 2 b; Apocrypha (in smaller type), A 1 to K 8 b; N. T., A 1 to P 8 a, with colophon; on verso of last page are printed four tables of *Kindred and Affinity, Weights and Mesures, Money,* and *Time*.

This is perhaps the earliest edition of the English Bible which has dates added in the margins. Job is dated 2400, and the Nativity 4000, years after the Creation. See note on No. 678.

Three varieties occur.

A.

The leaves of text before sheet F are printed in the smaller type used in the Apocrypha; A (2 to 8), B–E⁸—39 ff. The N. T. engraved title is a general title with a fresh centre, *The New Testament* . . . pasted on, apparently thus issued.

¶ 201 × 146 mm.
With both N. T. titles. [F. F.]

—— Another copy.

Wants N. T. titles, and other leaves. [F. F.]
585.

—— ANOTHER EDITION.

B.

The leaves before sheet F are printed in the same type as the rest of the O. T. and the N. T., but with a fuller page, containing 63 lines to the column; A⁴ B–E⁸ (E)⁴—40 ff. The printed N. T. title bears the device of three crowns and an open book inscribed *Dominus Illuminatio Mea*, within a circle of light.

¶ 191 × 140 mm.
Without leaf containing Dedication and list of books, and the engraved N. T. title; possibly thus issued. [F. F.]

—— Another copy.

Called by Fry a third variety; but apparently merely a mixture of A and B. It has the Dedication-leaf and printed N. T. title like A, but the first sheets of text like B. Wants engraved N. T. title, which was probably inserted in only a few copies.
With Prayer Book (1679), and Metrical Psalms (1679). [F. F.]
586.

—— ANOTHER EDITION.

C.

This is printed from the same setting of type as A; but, unlike either A or B, it has no marginal matter. This omission makes the page much narrower, so that the book looks like an octavo.

¶ 182 × 121 mm.
Without the engraved N. T. title.
Wants the Apocrypha.
587.

1679. The Holy Bible . . .
J. Bill, T. Newcomb, and *H. Hills : London.* 1679. 8°.

General title engraved. Text ends on Bbbb 8 b. No Apocrypha.

¶ 184 × 120 mm.
With Metrical Psalms (1689).
Silver corners, and plate inscribed M R. [F. F.]
588.

—— ANOTHER EDITION.

With titles similar to those in the foregoing edition, but otherwise totally distinct, being printed in larger type, without marginal references, etc. Text: O. T. ends on Bbb 8 a; N. T. ends on P 8 b. No Apocrypha.

¶ 183 × 116 mm.
Apocrypha inserted. [F. F.]

—— Another copy.
With Prayer Book (? date), and Metrical Psalms (? date). [F. F.]
589.

1679. The Holy Bible . . .
Bill, Newcomb, and Hills: London. 1679. 12°.

Text ends on Oo 6 a. No Apocrypha.

¶ 135 × 70 mm.
In two volumes.
590.

1679. The Holy Bible . . .
Bill, Barker, Newcomb, and Hills: London. 1679. 12°.

N. T. title omits C. Barker's name. Text ends on Ff 12 a. No Apocrypha.

¶ 145 × 77 mm. [F. F.]
591.

1680. The Holy Bible . . .
J. Bill and C. Barker: London. 1680,69. 12°.

'No doubt printed abroad' (Fry). Closely resembles the duodecimo of 1669 (No. 552). General title dated 1680; N. T. dated 1669. Title-borders as in the N. T. of No. 552. Text ends on Mm 6 b. No Apocrypha.

¶ 150 × 84 mm.
With Metrical Psalms (1669). [F. F.]
592.

1680. The Holy Bible . . .
Bill and Barker: London. 1680,75. 8°.

General title engraved; dated 1680. N. T. title (*Assigns of Bill and Barker*) dated 1675. Text ends on Aaa 3 b. Apocrypha mentioned in list of books, but not required by signatures.

¶ 173 × 111 mm.
Wants Apocrypha?
With Scotch Metrical Psalms (1676).

Contains many plates, with a separate titlepage: *The History of ye Old & New Testament in Cutts (Printed by W^m R: for Iohn Williams in Crosse-keyes Court in Little Brittaine F: H: Van Houe Sculpsit. 1672)*. These include the plates entitled *The Powder Plot November the V.*, and *King Charles the First Murthered*; also another, *King Charles the II his Returne* (illustrating 2 Sam. xxii. 44, 51). [F. F.]
593.

1680. The Holy Bible.
The Theatre, Oxford. 1680. f°.

The colophon gives the date, and the names of the London publishers *Pitt, Parker, Leak,* and *Guy*.

Both titles engraved. The general titlepage represents the veil of the Temple rent in twain, and below a small view of the Theatre. The N. T. titlepage (engraved by *Burghers*) pictures St. John in Patmos. Text ends on Rrrr 1 *b* ; followed by chronological Index. Dates in margins.

¶ 452 × 289 mm.
Contains maps by *J. Savry* (1648). [F. F.]
594.

1680. The Holy Bible . . .
The Theatre, Oxford. 1680. 8°.

General title engraved (representing a figure pointing to an open book). N. T. title has cut containing the three crowns and open book inscribed *Dominus Illuminatio Mea*, and four small shields ; below is the imprint, giving the names of the London booksellers *Pitt, Parker, Guy*, and *Leake*, as in the 1679 quarto (except that Leake is *at the Crown, between the two Temple-gates in Fleet-street*). Text : O. T. ends on Hhh 2 *b* ; N. T. ends on Bbbb 3 *a*, followed by various tables filling 3 pp. No Apocrypha. Dates in margins.

¶ 164 × 102 mm.
With Prayer Book (1682), and Metrical Psalms (? date).
595.

1680. The Holy Bible . . .
Bill, Newcomb, and Hills : London. 1680. 12°.

Text ends on Oo 6 *a*. No Apocrypha.

¶ 137 × 68 mm.
With Metrical Psalms (1680). [F. F.]
596.

1680. B. 4°. See 1682 and 1683.
B. 24°. See 1683 and 1684.

1681. The Holy Bible . . .
Assigns of Bill, Newcomb, and Hills : London. 1681. 12°.

Text ends on Oo 12 *b*. Apocrypha mentioned in list of books, but not required by signatures.

¶ 150 × 86 mm.
Wants Apocrypha ?
With Prayer Book (1680), and Metrical Psalms (1681).
Vellum covers, with leather patches. [F. F.]
597.

1681. The Holy Bible . . .
The Theatre, Oxford ; for T. Guy, London. 1681. 12°.

General title engraved (with figures of Moses, Aaron, Jeremiah, and Isaiah) ; N. T. title gives the date, and the names of the London publishers, *Pitt, Parker, Leake*, and *Guy*. N. T. ends on O 1 *b*. No Apocrypha.

¶ 143 × 75 mm. [F. F.]
598.

1681. The Holy Bible . . .
Assigns of Bill, Newcomb, and Hills : London. 1681. 24°.

Text ends on Eee 6 *a*. No Apocrypha.

¶ 117 × 55 mm. [F. F.]
599.

1681. The New Testament . . .
    Assigns of Bill, Newcomb, and Hills : London. 1681.
                              8°. 𝔅. 𝔏.

Text ends on Y 8 b. Double columns.
Acts vi. 3, *ye* ; 1 Tim. iv. 16, *thy*.

¶ 152 × 92 mm. Wants title (supplied in facsimile) and two other leaves.   [F. F.]

—— Another copy.
Wants title and some other leaves.   [F. F.]
                              600.

—— ANOTHER EDITION.
Date not known ; but probably by the same printers.

Through the bulk of the book, this agrees closely with the above edition. Text ends on Z 4 b.
Acts vi. 3, *ye*.

¶ 151 × 95 mm. Wants title and other leaves.   [F. F.]
                              601.

—— ANOTHER EDITION.
Date not known ; but probably by the same printers.

Closely resembles the preceding edition, with text ending on Z 4 b.
Acts vi. 3, *we*.

¶ 150 × 91 mm. Wants title and other leaves.   [F. F.]
                              602.

1682. The Holy Bible . . .
    Assigns of Bill, and Hills and Newcomb : London. 1682,75. 8°.

General title engraved ; dated 1682. N. T. title, dated 1675, gives the *Assigns of Bill and Barker.* Text ends on Aaa 3 b. Apocrypha mentioned in list of books, but not required by signatures.

¶ 168 × 112 mm.
Wants Apocrypha ?   [F. F.]
                              603.

1682. The Holy Bible . . .
         J. Hayes : Cambridge. 1682,80. 4°.

General title dated 1682 ; N. T. title dated 1680.
Closely resembles Hayes' quarto of 1675 (No. 568).

¶ 225 × 165 mm.   [F. F.]
                              604.

1682. The Holy Bible . . .
         The Theatre, Oxford. 1682. f°.

A cut of the royal arms occurs on both titlepages. The names of the London booksellers *Pitt, Parker, Guy,* and *W. Leake,* are given on the N. T. title and in the colophon.
Text : O. T. ends on Nnn 6 b, Apocrypha (in smaller type) on I 3 b, and N. T. on P 8 b ; followed by chronological Index and tables—14 ff. Dates in margins.

Varieties occur of this Bible, differing only in the general title.

A.
The general title bears the words ... *and are to be sold by Ann Leake over against Dean street in Fetter lane London.*

¶ 303 × 203 mm.
With Prayer Book (1682), and Metrical Psalms (1682). [F. F.]
605.

—— ANOTHER EDITION.
B.
General title : ... *and are to be sold by Moses Pitt at the Angel in St. Pauls Churchyard London.*

¶ 313 × 211 mm.
With Metrical Psalms (1682). [F. F.]
606.

—— ANOTHER EDITION.
C.
General title : ... *and are to be sold by Peter Parker at the Leg and Star over against the Royal Exchange in Cornhil, London.*

¶ 315 × 218 mm.
With Prayer Book (1681), and Metrical Psalms (1682).

—— Another copy.

Wants Apocrypha and N. T. title.
With Prayer Book (1682) and Metrical Psalms (1682). [F. F.]
607.

1682. The Holy Bible ...
        Assigns of Bill, and Hills and Newcomb : London. 1682. 8°.

General title engraved. Text ends on Eeee 4 a. No Apocrypha.

¶ 181 × 116 mm. [F. F.]
608.

1682. The Holy Bible ...
        The Theatre, Oxford ; for T. Guy : London. 1682. 8°.

General title engraved (with figures of Moses, Aaron, Jeremiah and Isaiah). N. T. title gives the date, and the names of the London publishers *Pitt, Parker, Guy,* and *Leake.* Text: O. T. ends on Hh 2 b ; N. T. ends on Mmm 4 a, with two tables on verso. No Apocrypha. The signatures are generally in sixteens ; the size of the book is small octavo.

¶ 154 × 100 mm.
With Metrical Psalms (n. d.). [F. F.]

—— Another copy.

Wants general title.
With Metrical Psalms (n. d.). [F. F.]
609.

—— ANOTHER EDITION.

With titles as in the foregoing edition ; but quite distinct, having a longer page. Text ends on Kkk 7 a, followed by 3 pp. of tables. Signatures generally in sixteens ; size—small octavo.

¶ 167 × 103 mm. [F. F.]
610.

1682. The Holy Bible . . .
   Assigns of Bill, Newcomb, and Hills : London. 1682. 12°.

Similar to the duodecimo of 1680,69 (No. 592), and like it probably printed abroad. Text ends on Mm 6 b. No Apocrypha.
N. T. title, *Assings* for *Assigns*.

¶ 146 × 81 mm.
With Prayer Book (1670), and Metrical Psalms (1680).   [F. F.]
                         611.

1682. The Holy Bible . . . With Marginal notes, shewing Scripture to be the best Interpreter of Scripture.
                [*Amsterdam?*] 1682. 12°.

Probably printed abroad. With Canne's marginal matter.

General title engraved: architectural design, above—open book, below—sword and palm-branch crossed; list of books on verso; *To the Reader* signed by *John Canne*—1 f. Text, A 1 to Ccc 4 b. No Apocrypha.
A very inaccurate edition. Deut. xxiv. 3, *if the latter husbhand ate her*; Esther vi. 2, *kings* for *keepers*; Jer. xiii. 27, *adversaries* for *adulteries*; xvi. 6, *glad* for *bald*; xviii. 21, *swine* for *famine*; Ezek. xviii. 25, *is equal* for *is not equal*; etc.

¶ 166 × 94 mm.
With Metrical Psalms (1682).
Contemporary binding.   [F. F.]

—— Another copy.

—— Another copy.
Wants Canne's Preface.   [F. F.]

—— Another copy.
Wants title, Preface, and other leaves.   [F. F.]
                         612.

1682. The Holy Bible . . .
   Assigns of Bill, Newcomb, and Hills: London. 1682. 12°.

General title engraved (having a design similar to that in the foregoing edition, but with the royal arms below); list of books on verso; Dedication—1 f. Text, A 1 to Ccc 4 b. No Apocrypha.
This Bible appears to have been printed abroad from the same type as the foregoing edition. Canne's marginal matter has been removed; but the text agrees generally line for line, except where the removal of an italic reference letter necessitates closing up the type. Some of these italic letters have been carelessly left in the text; e.g. in Gen. iii. 24, xxv. 14, xxvii. 35, etc. The gross errors are retained; *vide passim,* esp. Deut. xxiv. 3, *husbhand ate* for *husband hate*, and 19, *sha eaf* for *a sheaf.*
It is possible that this edition was produced abroad for the King's Printers in London, who sold it with a new title and the Dedication. But more probably it is a pirated edition with a fictitious title.

¶ 160 × 95 mm. In two volumes.   [F. F.]
                         613.

1683. The Holy Bible . . .
     J. Hayes: Cambridge. 1683,80. 4°.

General title dated 1683; N. T. title dated 1680.
Apparently identical with Hayes' quarto of 1682,80 (No. 604), except for the date on the engraved title, which has been obviously altered from 1682.

¶ 219 × 156 mm.
                         614.

1683. The Holy Bible . . .
     C. Bill, Hills, and Newcomb : London. 1680,83. 24°.

General title apparently dated 1680 (though the last numeral in the copy described below is indistinct); N. T. title (*Assigns of John Bill deceas'd, and Hills and Newcomb*) dated 1683. Text ends on Eee 6 *a*. No Apocrypha.

¶ 120 × 57 mm.
With Metrical Psalms (1683).   [F. F.]
                             615.

1683. The Holy Bible . . . With most profitable Annotations . . .
                    [*Amsterdam* ?] 1683. f°.
King James' version, with Geneva notes, etc.

A reprint of the 1672 folio (No. 557).
Place and printer's name not given. Probably by, or for, Swart in Amsterdam.
Titles as before. Text: O. T. ends on p. 710 (really 712); N. T., 248 pp. No Apocrypha.

¶ 385 × 237 mm.
Contains maps by *J. Moxon*.
With Metrical Psalms (1679).
In original boards, with brass corners and clasps.   [F. F.]
                             616.

1683. The Holy Bible . . .
          J. Hayes : Cambridge. 1683. 4°.

Closely resembles Hayes' quarto of 1670 (No. 553). The date on the general title has been obviously altered from 1682.

¶ 229 × 171 mm.   [F. F.]
                             617.

1683. The Holy Bible . . .
          The Theatre, Oxford. 1683. 4°.

General title resembles that in the first Oxford quarto (No. 566), but has been re-engraved by *Sturt*. The N. T. title (with cut of royal arms) gives the full imprint . . . *and are to be sold by Thomas Guy . . . London,* and the date. Text ends on Rrrr 6 *b*; followed by chronological Index and tables.

¶ 219 × 168 mm. Wants one leaf (Sss 6).   [F. F.]
                             618.

1683. The Holy Bible . . .
   Assigns of Bill, and Hills and Newcomb : London. 1683. 12°.

Text ends on Zz 11 *b*. No Apocrypha.

¶ 160 × 95 mm. Slightly imperfect.
With Metrical Psalms (1682).   [F. F.]
                             619.

1684. The Holy Bible . . .
     C. Bill, Hills, and Newcomb : London. 1680,84. 24°.

General title dated 1680; N. T. title (*Assigns of J. Bill deceas'd, and Hills and Newcomb*) dated 1684. Text ends on Eee 6 *a*. No Apocrypha.

¶ 121 × 60 mm.
With Metrical Psalms (1683).   [F. F.]
                             620.

1684. The Holy Bible . . .
The Theatre, Oxford. 1684. f°.

Engraved title like that in No. 566, but has a small view of the Theatre at the base, and an imprint . . . *Sold by Thomas Guy at yᵉ Oxford Arms* . . . No separate titlepage to the N. T. Text: O. T. ends on Zzz 1 b; Apocrypha end on Lll 1 b; N. T. ends on Oooo 2 a, followed by tables and chronological Index.

¶ 340 × 211 mm.
With Metrical Psalms (n. d.). [F. F.]
621.

1684. The Holy Bible . . .
Assigns of Bill, Newcomb, and Hills: London. 1684. 12°.

~~Probably~~ printed abroad.
Text ends on Nn 6 b. No Apocrypha.
General title, *Assings* for *Assigns*. Headline on Gg 12 b, *S. Jean* for *S. John*.

¶ 161 × 86 mm.
With Metrical Psalms (1682).
On two blank leaves at the end of the volume is written a table of the Epistles and Gospels for Sundays and Holydays.
Bound in vellum, stamped on the side M. I. A. W. 1718. [F. F.]

—— Another copy.

With Metrical Psalms (1682).
Bound in vellum. [F. F.]

—— Another copy.

With Metrical Psalms (1726). [F. F.]
622.

1684. The Holy Bible . . .
Assigns of Bill, Newcomb, and Hills: London. 1684. 24°.

N. T. title gives *the Assigns of J. Bill deceas'd, and Hills and Newcomb*. Text ends on Eee 6 a. No Apocrypha.

Three varieties occur.

A.
General title : . . . *Printed by the Assigns of J. Bill*, etc.

¶ 121 × 57 mm.
In two volumes. [F. F.]

—— - Another copy. [F. F.]
623.

—— Another edition.
B.
General title : . . . *Printed by C. Bill*, etc. . . . *168* (last figure omitted). This engraved title appeared in many of these 24° editions, the plate being altered from time to time.

¶ 121 × 58 mm.
With Metrical Psalms (1683), and Prayer Book (1689).
Silver clasps and plates engraved *S. L.* and *1699*. [F. F.
624.

—— Another edition.
C.
Very like A, but differing slightly in the setting-up of the type, e.g. Ll 9 a, first column ends: . . . *when those*, instead of . . . *the earth* in A.

¶ 122 × 59 mm. Contains the O. T. only. [F. F.]
625.

1684. The New Testament . . .
   The Widow of Steven Swart, etc.: Amsterdam. 1684. 12°.

With the Dutch and French versions, in parallel columns. Pp. 601.
(See Dutch section, 1684.)

¶ 155 × 94 mm.   [F. F.]
                                  626.

1684. B. 12°. See 1685 and 1704.

ACCESSION OF KING JAMES II: 6 FEBRUARY 1685.

1685. The Holy Bible . . .
   Assigns of Bill, and Hills and Newcomb: London. 1684,85. 12°.

General title dated 1684; N. T. title dated 1685. Text ends on Oo 6 *a*. No Apocrypha.

¶ 138 × 75 mm.
With Metrical Psalms (1684), and Prayer Book (1685).   [F. F.]
                                  627.

1685. The Holy Bible.
            The Theatre, Oxford. 1685. f°.

Both titles engraved as in the Oxford folio of 1680 (No. 594); but the words *By P. Parker and Thomas Guy* are added on the general title. Text ends on Dddddd 1 *b*, with *A Table of Kindred* . . . on the same page. No colophon.

¶ 419 × 270 mm.   [F. F.]
                                  628.

1685. The Holy Bible . . .
   Assigns of Bill, and Hills and Newcomb: London. 1685. 4°.

Each title bears a cut of the royal arms with the initials I² R.
Text: O. T. ends on Kkk 8 *b*; Apocrypha end on o 4 *a*; N. T. ends on S 2 *b*.

¶ 244 × 186 mm.
With Prayer Book (1682), and Metrical Psalms (1682).   [F. F.]
                                  629.

1685. The Holy Bible . . .
   Assigns of Bill, and Hills and Newcomb: London. 1685. 12°.

Text ends on Oo 12 *b*. Apocrypha mentioned in list of books, but not required by signatures.

¶ 152 × 86 mm. Wants both titles, and some other leaves.
Wants Apocrypha?
With Metrical Psalms (1688).   [F. F.]

—— Another copy.
Contains the O. T. only.   [F. F.]

—— Another copy.
Contains the O. T. only; wanting titleleaf.   [F. F.]
                                  630.

1685. B. 12°. See 1686.

1686. The Holy Bible . . .
   The Theatre, Oxford; for T. Guy: London. **1685,86. 12°.**

General title dated 1685; N. T. title dated 1686. Text ends on Vv 12 b. No Apocrypha.
¶ 120 × 62 mm.
With Metrical Psalms (1685).
Silver clasps.

—— Another copy.
With Prayer Book (? date), and Metrical Psalms (? date).   [F. F.]
631.

1686. The Holy Bible . . .
   The Theatre, Oxford; for P. Parker: London. **1686. 4°.**

Resembles the Oxford quarto of 1683 (No. 618). Both titles give the name of the London publisher, *P. Parker*. Text ends on Rrrr 6 b; followed by chronological Index and tables.
¶ 222 × 172 mm.   [F. F.]

—— Another copy.
Very imperfect.
With Prayer Book (? date).
632.

1686. The Holy Bible . . .
   C. Bill, Hills, and Newcomb: London. **1686. 12°.**

Text ends on Oo 12 b. Apocrypha mentioned in list of books, but not required by signatures.
¶ 149 × 82 mm.
Wants Apocrypha?   [F. F.]
633.

1686. The New Testament . . .
   Bill, Hills, and Newcomb: London. **1686. 8°.**

Resembles the octavo of 1676 (No. 579). Text ends on Aaa 8 b.
¶ 167 × 104 mm.   [F. F.]
634.

1686. B. 4°. See 1687.
* B. 12°. See 1687.*

1687. The Holy Bible . . .
   The Theatre, Oxford; for T. Guy: London. **1687,86. 4°.**

General title engraved (resembling that in No. 566), and dated 1687; N. T. title dated 1686. Text ends on Rrrr 6 b.
¶ 231 × 179 mm.   [F. F.]
635.

1687. The Holy Bible . . .
   The Theatre, Oxford; for T. Guy: London. **1686,87. 12°.**

General title dated 1686; N. T. title dated 1687. Text ends on Tt 8 b, the last page being filled up with *A Table of Kindred and Affinity* . . . No Apocrypha.

¶ 146 × 81 mm.
With Prayer Book (1687), and Metrical Psalms (1688). [F. F.]
636.

1687. The Holy Bible . . .
  The Theatre, Oxford ; for T. Guy : London. 1687. 12°.

Text ends on Hhh 12 *b*. No Apocrypha. No separate N. T. titlepage.

¶ 121 × 63 mm.
With Prayer Book (1689), and Metrical Psalms (n. d.). [F. F.]
637.

1687. (The Holy Bible in short-hand.)
  Printed for the Author, and others : London. 1687. 16°.

The Bible (with the Metrical Psalms) written in short-hand by William Addy, and engraved by John Sturt.

A MS. note affixed to the last leaf of the B. M. copy 3049. a. 4 explains the method in which this work was executed : ' This Bible in Stenography, my Brethren at sight, and all others skill'd in ye Art of Sculpture know it's Engraven ; but in a Peculiar Manner. It was written by Mr. Addy in ungum'd Ink burnished on the wax and then run thrô with the Engraver by John Sturt.'

William Addy based his system of short-hand on that of Cartwright and Rich (see above, No. 529). He published ' Stenographia ' in 1695.

For a full description of this Bible see the *Phonetic Journal*, 1885, pp. 158–160, and *cf.* pp. 184, 196–7.

Although some copies contain a dedication to King William III., these, also, bear the date 1687 on the title.

DESCRIPTION. Frontispiece ; title (' Holy Bible, containing the Old and New Testaments with Singing Psalms in Shorthand written by William Addy ' and ' The Bible engraved by John Sturt,' in short-hand), verso blank ; [in some copies :—1 p. blank, 1 p. containing a short note and imprint : *London Printed for the Author, and Peter Story. and sold by, Tho : Fabian at the Bible in Pauls Churchyard. Dorman Newman at y^e. King's Armes in the Poultry. Sam : Crouch at y^e. Flower-de-luce in Cornhill. W^m. Marshall at the Bible in Newgate street. Thomas Cockerill at y^e. 3. Leggs over against y^e. Stocks Market. I. Lawrence at y^e. Angel in y^e. Poultry* ; Dedication—1 p., 1 p. blank]. Text : Bible, 358 pp. ; the Metrical Psalms, which follow, end on p. 396 ; 1 f. blank.

Some copies (e.g. B. M. copy 1159. b. 22) exhibit differences in the third and fourth leaves, containing the prefatory matter. On the page opposite the dedication is what appears to be an address to the reader ; and across the bottom of both pages runs a different imprint from that given above : *London Printed for the Author, and sold by Dorman Newman at the Kings Armes in ye Poultry Tho Fabian in Pauls Church yard Sam : Crouch at ye Flower de luce in Cornhill Wm Marshall at ye Bible in Newgate street Tho : Cockerill at ye 3 Leggs over against ye Stocks market I. Lawrence at ye Angel in ye Poultry &c^t.* Another variety gives only one bookseller : *Sold by I. Lawrence at ye Angel in the Poultry* (see the *Phonetic Journal*, 1885, p. 184).

A portrait of *Gulielmus Addy* (engraved by Sturt) stands as frontispiece. The general title is an architectural design, with figures of Moses and Aaron. The N. T. title represents the Holy Dove, and the four Evangelists with their emblems. The title to the Metrical Psalms shows King David playing the harp.

All copies are ruled by hand with red lines.

¶ 111 × 73 mm.
Without prefatory matter after title.

—— Another copy.

Without prefatory matter after title.
Wants portrait of Addy.

—— Another copy.
With prefatory matter.
Agrees with the B. M. copy 3049. a. 4.
638.

1688. The Holy Bible . . .
The Theatre, Oxford. 1688. f°.

Large cut of royal arms on general title ; . . . *are to be sold by Peter Parker . . London.* Smaller cut with initials J. R. on N. T. title. Text ends on Tttt 6 *b.* Columns divided by double rules.

¶ 342 × 215 mm.
Apocrypha supplied from another copy. [F. F.]
639.

1688. The Holy Bible . . .
Bill, Hills, and Newcomb : London. 1688. 12°.

Text ends on Oo 12 *b.* Apocrypha mentioned in list of books, but not required by signatures.

¶ 149 × 83 mm.
Wants Apocrypha ? [F. F.]
640.

1688. The Holy Bible . . .
The Theatre, Oxford ; for T. Guy : London. 1688. 12°.

Text ends on Hhh 12 *b.* No Apocrypha.

¶ 121 × 62 mm.
With Metrical Psalms (n. d.). [F. F.]
641.

ACCESSION OF KING WILLIAM III AND QUEEN MARY : 13 FEBRUARY 1689.

1689. The Holy Bible . . .
The Theatre, Oxford ; for P. Parker : London. 1689. 8°.

Text ends on Dddd 7 *b*, followed by tables. No Apocrypha.
N. T. title has a cut of the Theatre.

¶ 181 × 112 mm.
With Metrical Psalms (1679). [F. F.]

—— Another copy.
The N. T. title in this copy substitutes the name of T. Guy for P. Parker.
Wants two leaves.
Apocrypha inserted.
With Prayer Book (1679), and Metrical Psalms (1689). [F. F.]
642.

1689. B. 12°. See 1694.

1690. The Holy Bible . . . With Annotations and Parallel Scriptures. To which is annex'd the Harmony of the Gospels : as also the Reduction of the Jewish Weights Coins and Measures, to our English Standards. And a Table of the Promises in Scripture. By Samuel Clark.
J. Rawlins for Richard Chiswell and Jonathan Robinson in St. Paul's Church-yard; and Brabazon Aylmer in Cornhill: London. 1690. f°.

S. Clark, or Clarke (1626-1701), was Fellow of Pembroke College, Cambridge, and for a time held the rectory of Grendon Underwood, Bucks, from which, however, he was ejected in 1662. He afterwards settled at High Wycombe, where he gathered an Independent congregation. His commentary has won the praise of such men as Owen, Baxter, Doddridge, Whitefield, and Bishop Cleaver.

The N. T. title bears the imprint *J. Heptinstall for Brabazon Aylmer at the Three Pigeons against the Royal Exchange in Cornhill.*

With Preface by Clark, explaining the scope of the work. The editor states that in some passages he has made use of the marginal reading, and in one case he has adopted an independent rendering.

Text: O. T. ends on Xxxxx 1 *a*; N. T. ends on Xx 4 *a*; followed by tables, *A Poetical Meditation* . . . (by J. C.), the Harmony, etc. No Apocrypha. The short notes are placed between the verses. Some dates in margins.

¶ 387 × 237 mm.

643.

1690. The Holy Bible . . .
C. Bill and T. Newcomb: London. 1690. 8°.

General title engraved. Text: O. T. ends on Bbb 8 *a*; N. T. ends on P 8 *b*. No Apocrypha.

¶ 190 × 120 mm. [F. F.]

644.

1691. (The Holy Bible.)
Bill and Newcomb: London. 1691. 12°.

Text ends on Ddd 12 *a*. No Apocrypha.
Distinct from No. 653; Ps. lxxiv. 15, *driest.*

¶ 121 × 51 mm. Wants general title, and last leaf.
With Metrical Psalms (1694). [F. F.]

645.

—— ANOTHER EDITION.
Date not known. Probably by the same printers.

Resembles the above; but the text ends on Tt 11 *b*. General title engraved by *F. H. Van Hove*; dated 169 (last numeral missing).

¶ 123 × 63 mm. Wants N. T. title, in place of which is inserted a N. T. title dated 1744.
[F. F.]

646.

1691. The Holy Bible . . .
C. Bill and Executrix of T. Newcomb: London. 1691. 12°.

Text ends on Oo 12 *b*. Apocrypha mentioned in list of books, but not required by signatures.

¶ 148 × 82 mm.
Wants Apocrypha? [F. F.]

647.

1691. The Holy Bible . . .
  The Theatre, Oxford ; for T. Guy : London. 1691. 12°.

Text ends on Hh 6 *b*. No Apocrypha. No separate N. T. titlepage.

¶ 140 × 71 mm. [F. F.]
648.

1691. (The Holy Bible.)
  The Theatre, Oxford ; for T. Guy : London. 1691. 12°.

Distinct from No. 648. Text ends on Vv 12 *b*. No Apocrypha.

¶ 119 × 56 mm. Wants title and following leaf. [F. F.]
649.

1691. The New Testament . . .
  Robert Sanders : Glasgow. 1691. 12°. B. L.

R. Sanders published his first Glasgow edition in 1670 (see Loftie, No. 289). For his disputes with A. Anderson, the King's printer in Scotland, in 1671, and with Anderson's widow in 1680, see Lee, *Memorial,* App. xxiv and xxvi.
Titlepage bears a device surrounded by the motto, *Lord let Glasgow flourish through the preaching of Thy Word*; list of books on verso. Text, A 2 to R 2 *b*. Signatures in twelves. No chapter-contents; subject-headings in headlines printed in roman type. Double columns. Acts vi. 3, *ye*; 1 Tim. iv. 16, *thy*.

¶ 145 × 80 mm. [F. F.]
650.

—— ANOTHER EDITION.
Date not known. Probably printed by R. Sanders.

Resembles the above edition. Text ends on O 12 *b*. Subject-headings in headlines printed in italics.

¶ 143 × 85 mm. Wants title, last leaf, and other leaves. [F. F.]
651.

1691. B. 12°. See 1693.

1692. The Holy Bible . . .
  Bill and Executrix of Newcomb : London. 1692. 12°.

Text ends on Oo 12 *b*. Apocrypha mentioned in list of books, but not required by signatures.

¶ 150 × 83 mm.
Wants Apocrypha?
With Prayer Book (1692), and Metrical Psalms (1692). [F. F.]

—— Another copy.

Wants Apocrypha?
With very many plates, including as frontispiece a portrait of King William III, with inscription *Sold by William Leake and Thomas Guy.*
With Metrical Psalms (1693).
Contemporary binding; with silver corners and clasps. [F. F.]

—— Another copy.

Wants Apocrypha?
With Prayer Book (1692), and Metrical Psalms (1693).
652.

1693. The Holy Bible . . .
               Bill and Newcomb: London. 1693,91. 12°.

General title (engraved by *F. H. Van Hove*) is dated 1693, and bears the name of T. Newcomb (the younger), though he had died in 1691. N. T. title dated 1691.
Text ends on Ddd 12 *a*. No Apocrypha.
Distinct from No. 645; Ps. lxxiv. 15, *driedst*.

¶ 124 × 55 mm. [F. F.]

—— Another copy.
Contains the O. T. only. The numeral 3 is missing in the date.
Silver clasps. [F. F.]
653.

1693. Holy Bible . . .
               Bill and Executrix of Newcomb: London. 1693. 12°.

Text ends on Yy 11 *b*. No Apocrypha.

¶ 162 × 95 mm.
With Metrical Psalms (1693). [F. F.]
654.

1693. FACSIMILE. The Christian Soldier's Penny Bible. Shewing from the Holy Scriptures, the Soldier's Duty and Encouragement. Being a Brief Collection of pertinent Scriptures, under XX Heads, fit for the Soldier's, or Seaman's Pocket, when he is not furnish'd with, or cannot well carry a larger Volume, in time of War. Ephes. vi. 11, 16. Put on . . . of the Wicked.
    Printed by R. Smith, for Sam. Wade, under the Piazza of the Royal Exchange in Cornhil, and Sold by him and Rich. Baldwin, near the Oxford-Arms in Warwick-Lane: London. 1693. 8°.

A reprint, with slight alterations and additions, of the *Souldiers Pocket Bible* printed in 1643. See No. 447.
Facsimile reproduction; with a preface by F. Fry. (Willis and Sotheran, London, 1862.)

This edition is believed to have been published for the use of 'our army in Flanders.' The Scripture passages are here quoted from King James' version, and some fresh texts are added. The only known copy formerly belonged to Mr. Fry, and is now in the British Museum.
Title, with *Imprimatur, March 17, 169$\frac{2}{3}$. C. Alston.* on verso. Text, pp. 3 to 16 (A 2 to A 8 *b*).
655.

1694. The Holy Bible . . .
               Bill and Executrix of Newcomb: London. 1694,89. 12°.

Perhaps printed abroad.
General title dated 1694; New Testament title (. . . *by the Assings of J. Bill, Thomas Newcomb and Henry Hills* . . .) dated 1689 (see Loftie, No. 422). Text ends on Mm 6 *b*. No Apocrypha.

¶ 155 × 87 mm.
656.

1694. (The Holy Bible.)
Bill and Executrix of Newcomb: London. 1694. 8°.

Text ends on Cccc 4 b.
2 Pet. i. 19, *a most sure word* . . . for *a more sure word*.

¶ 195 × 122 mm. Wants general title (presumably dated 1694), and following leaf.
[F. F.]
657.

1694. The New Testament . . .
University-Printers: Oxford. 1694. 8°.

Printed title with list of books on verso. Text, A 2 to Gg 8 b, printed in double columns.

¶ 185 × 115 mm. [F. F.]
658.

1694? (The Holy Bible.)
Qu. *Edinburgh.* 1694? 8°.

O. T. ends on Mm 8 b; N. T. ends on Zz 8 b. No Apocrypha? Signatures in eights.

¶ 145 × 93 mm. Wants both titles and some other leaves.
With Scotch Metrical Psalms (1695). [F. F.]
659.

1695. The Holy Bible . . .
Bill and Executrix of Newcomb: London. 1695. 8°.

Text ends on Rrr 3 b. No Apocrypha.

¶ 177 × 113 mm. [F. F.]
660.

1695. The Holy Bible . . .
Bill and Executrix of Newcomb: London. 1695. 12°.

Text ends on Oo 12 b. Apocrypha mentioned in list of books, but not required by signatures.

¶ 149 × 87 mm.
Wants Apocrypha?
With Metrical Psalms (1696).
In two volumes. [F. F.]
661.

1695. The Holy Bible . . .
University-Printers: Oxford. 1695. 12°.

Text ends on Vv 11 b, followed by one leaf of tables. No Apocrypha.
Luke chap. xi is numbered xii.

¶ 152 × 83 mm. [F. F.]
662.

1696. The Holy Bible . . .
University-Printers: Oxford. 1696. 12°.

O. T. ends on Vv 6 b. No Apocrypha.

¶ 123 × 63 mm. Contains only the O. T., of which one leaf is wanting.
With Metrical Psalms (1696).
In two volumes. [F. F.]
663.

ENGLISH 245

1697. The Holy Bible . . .
       University-Printers : Oxford. 1697. 4°.

General title, engraved by *M. Burghers*, represents the giving of the Law, the Baptism of our Lord, etc., with the device *Dominus Illuminatio Mea*. Text: O. T. ends on Kkk 8 *b*; Apocrypha (in smaller type) end on k 8 *b*; N. T. ends on S 2 *b*.

¶ 264 × 202 mm.
With Prayer Book (? date), and Metrical Psalms (1696).   [F. F.]

—— Another copy.
Wants Apocrypha.
With Metrical Psalms (1696).
Contemporary binding; with elaborate design.   [F. F.
                   664.

1698. The Holy Bible . . . With Marginal Notes, shewing the Scripture to [be] the best Interpreter of Scripture.
     Bill and Executrix of Newcomb : London. 1698. 12°.

With Canne's Preface and marginal matter.
Text ends on Ii 6 *a*. No Apocrypha.

¶ 156 × 85 mm.   [F. F.]

—— Another copy.

—— Another copy.

—— Another copy.
Wants general title.

—— Another copy.
Wants general title.

—— Another copy.
On thin paper.   [F. F.]
                   665.

1698. The Holy Bible . . .
   Heirs and Successors of Andrew Anderson : Edinburgh. 1698. 12°.

For the abuses of the monopoly held by the widow of Anderson see Lee, *Memorial*, pp. 119–122, etc.; her duodecimo Testament of 1694 abounds in errors.

Rude woodcut border to both titles: architectural design, with open book and cherub's head above, and thistle and crown below. Text ends on Nnn 10 *a*. No Apocrypha.
Incorrectly printed. Lee (*Memorial*, p. 164) mentions many mistakes, e.g. Rom. vi. 17, *ye were not the servants of sin* (*not* inserted).

¶ 116 × 51 mm.   [F. F.]
                   666.

1698. *B.* *12°.* See 1700.
   B. *18°.* See 1699.

1699. The Holy Bible . . .
   Bill and Executrix of Newcomb : London. 1698,99. 18°.

General title dated 1698; N. T. title dated 1699. Text ends on Ee 17 b. No Apocrypha.

¶ 126 × 65 mm.
In two volumes. [F. F.]

—— Another copy.
Contains the O. T. only.
                     667.

—— ANOTHER EDITION.
Somewhat like the above edition ; but with text ending on Ff 5 b.
General title (with view of London, etc.) engraved by *L. Lucas.*

¶ 124 × 64 mm. [F. F.]

—— Another copy.
                     668.

1699. The Holy Bible . . .
   Bill and Executrix of Newcomb : London. 1699. 8°.

General title engraved. Text ends on Cccc 4 b. No Apocrypha.

¶ 193 × 120 mm.

—— Another copy.
The general title differs slightly in this copy.
Apocrypha inserted.
With Metrical Psalms (1699). [F. F.]
                     669.

1699. (The Holy Bible.)
   Bill and Executrix of Newcomb : London. 1699. 12°.

Text ends on Oo 12 b. Apocrypha mentioned in list of books, but not required by signatures.

¶ 148 × 85 mm. Wants general title.
Wants Apocrypha ?
With Metrical Psalms (1698). [F. F.]
                     670.

1699. B. 12°. See 1701.

1700. The Holy Bible . . .
   Bill and Executrix of Newcomb : London. 1698,1700. 12°.

General title dated 1698; N. T. title dated 1700. Text ends on Aaa 5 b. No Apocrypha.

¶ 121 × 60 mm. [F. F.]
                     671.

1700. The Holy Bible . . . With Marginal Notes, Shewing, That Scripture is the best Interpreter of Script:
   Bill and Executrix of Newcomb : London. 1700. 4°.

With Canne's Preface and marginal matter.

Apparently printed abroad.

ENGLISH

General title engraved. N. T. title has the royal arms with initials W R. No Dedication. Text: O. T. ends on Eee 2 b; N. T. ends on Q 4 b, followed by chronological Index and tables. Apocrypha.

¶ 240 × 185 mm.
With Scotch Metrical Psalms (1661).

—— Another copy.
Without Index and tables.
With Prayer Book (1676), and Metrical Psalms (1698). [F. F.]
672.

1700. The Holy Bible . . .
    Bill and Executrix of Newcomb: London. 1700. 12°.

Text ends on Yy 11 b. No Apocrypha.
¶ 163 × 99 mm. Wants one leaf (A 12).
With Prayer Book (1700), and Metrical Psalms (1700). [F. F.]
673.

1700. The New Testament . . .
    Bill and Executrix of Newcomb: London. 1700. 12°.

Text: A 2 to S 2 b; double columns.
¶ 150 × 82 mm. [F F.]
674.

1700. The New Testament . . .
    The Widow of Steven Swart: Amsterdam. 1700. 12°.

With the Dutch version, in parallel columns. Pp. 580.
(See Dutch section, 1700.)
The same printer issued a French-English diglot in 1700.
¶ 163 × 90 mm. [F. F.]
675.

1700 ? (The New Testament in short-hand.)
 Printed for W^m. Marshall at ye Bible in newgate street & Jno.
 Marshall at ye Bible in gracechurch streete nere Cornehill:
        London. [1700 ?]. 64°.

By J. Rich. The first edition appeared in 1659. (See No. 529.)

DESCRIPTION. Frontispiece; title, verso blank; Address *To his Grace The Duke of Buckingham And my Honoured freinds* . . . (signed by Rich)—7 pp., 1 p. blank. Text, 570 pp.; followed by list of subscribers—2 ff., and 1 f. containing what appears to be an Epilogue (the last page is numbered 576).

¶ 59 × 38 mm.
The bottom of the titleleaf has been shaved, but this is apparently the same edition as the B. M. copy 3051. a. 1, dated in the catalogue [1700 ?], in which the title has the inscription *Y^e twentieth Impression* below the imprint. [F. F.]
676.

1701. The Holy Bible . . .
    University-Printers: Oxford. 1699, 1701. 12°.

General title dated 1699; N. T. title dated 1701. Text: O. T. ends on Vv 6 b; N. T. ends on N 12 b. No Apocrypha.

¶ 124 × 63 mm. [F. F.]
677.

1701. The Holy Bible . . .
University-Printers : Oxford. 1701. f°.

It is commonly admitted that William Lloyd (1627-1717), created Bishop of Worcester in 1700, undertook, apparently on the motion of Archbishop Tenison and at the request of Convocation in 1699, to prepare an improved edition of King James' version; and that his Bible appeared in 1701. But there has been considerable confusion as to which should be called ' Lloyd's edition.'

Some authorities (e.g. Loftie, the B. M. Catalogue, and the D. N. B.) ascribe this Oxford folio to Lloyd. Others (e.g. Lewis and Scrivener) assert that a London folio of 1701 is the special edition prepared by the Bishop. Now the Oxford Bible of 1701 does not materially differ from Bibles printed at that University during the previous twenty years. The dates given in its margin had appeared in Oxford Bibles as early as 1679 (see No. 585), its chronological Index had been appended to more than one Oxford edition before 1701 (see Nos. 594, 605, 618, etc.), and the years throughout are reckoned from the Creation. The London folio of 1701, however, exhibits a striking change. In its dates the Nativity is taken as the central event in history, and—apparently for the first time in any English Bible—the years are reckoned as either ' Before Christ ' or ' Anno Domini.'
The Welsh folio Bible of 1690 is sometimes called ' Bishop Lloyd's Bible,' presumably because ' its chronology is Lloyd's ' (so D. N. B., art. *William Lloyd*, and B. M. Catalogue). Now this Welsh edition merely reproduces the dates (reckoned ' Anno Mundi ') which had already appeared in certain Oxford-printed English Bibles since 1679: for those dates the Bishop is thus made responsible. As Lloyd was a keen student of the subject, and compiled ' A System of Chronology,' it is more than probable that he himself also prepared the revised Biblical chronology, giving dates B.C. and A.D., which first appeared in the London folio of 1701, and has since been reproduced in most editions of King James' version down to the present day.

It should be noted that this chronology of the London folio of 1701, which has been inserted without any authority in English Bibles for the last two centuries, was based on the famous work *Annales Veteris et Novi Testamenti* (1650-4), compiled by the learned James Ussher (1581-1656), Archbishop of Armagh.

With additional general and N. T. titles engraved, the latter by *Burghers*. Text: O. T. ends on Iii 1 *b* ; Apocrypha (in rather smaller type) end on s 2 *a* ; N. T. ends on R 6 *b*, followed by chronological Index.

¶ 468 × 292 mm.
At Romans xiii is inserted a small four-leaved tract, entitled *St. Paul and Her Majesty vindicated. In proving from the Apostle's own words, Rom. xiii that the doctrine of Non-resistance, as commonly taught, is none of his. Not done before* (London, 1710). [**F. F.**]
678.

[1701. The Holy Bible.
Bill and Executrix of Newcomb : London. 1701. f°.**]**

This is probably the edition supervised by William Lloyd, Bishop of Worcester. See note above, No. 678.

The text, printed in large type, fills 1456 pp. Besides the revised marginal dates and chronological Index (see above), the book contains a long note on Jewish Weights and Measures etc., compiled by Richard Cumberland (1631-1718), Bishop of Peterborough, whose Essay on this subject, dedicated to his friend Samuel Pepys, as President of the Royal Society, appeared in 1686. This matter is sometimes appended, with other tables, to subsequent editions of the Bible.
Lewis (p. 350) states that this Bible was included among those condemned by the Lower House of Convocation in 1703 for their gross errors.
The B. M. possesses a copy [3061. k. 1.] of this Bible ; and also a copy [3035. f. 4.] of another London folio of 1701, by the same printers, which agrees generally with the other, but is printed in smaller type (1143 pp.). From both these London folios the Oxford folio of 1701 (No. 678), as has been shown, is quite distinct.

ACCESSION OF QUEEN ANNE: 8 MARCH 1702.

1702. The Holy Bible . . .
    Bill and Executrix of Newcomb : London. 1702. 4°.

Lee (*Memorial*, pp. 203-4 *n*.) states that many copies of this edition were sent to the libraries established in the Highlands early in the eighteenth century.
 Additional general title engraved. Text ends on [Kkkk] 2 *b*, followed by Index and tables, including Bishop Cumberland's note mentioned above. The dates are B.C. and A.D. (See No. 678.)

¶ 264 × 194 mm.
With Prayer Book (1702), and Metrical Psalms (1702).
                        679.

1702. B. 8°. See 1703.

1703. The Holy Bible . . .
    Bill and Executrix of Newcomb : London. 1703,02. 8°.

General title engraved, and dated 1703; N. T. title dated 1702. Text ends on Cccc 4 *b*. No Apocrypha. The dates are B.C. and A.D. (see No. 678).

¶ 191 × 116 mm.
Apocrypha inserted.
With Metrical Psalms (1701).   [F. F.]
                        680.

1703. The Holy Bible . . .
    University-Printers : Oxford. 1703. 4°.

General title engraved by *M. Burghers*. N. T. ends on Q 4 *b*, followed by Index and tables. Apocrypha in smaller type.

¶ 238 × 185 mm.
                        681.

1703. The Holy Bible . . .
    Bill and Executrix of Newcomb : London. 1703. 8°.

General title engraved. Text ends on Cccc 4 *b*. No Apocrypha.

¶ 193 × 116 mm.
Apocrypha inserted.   [F. F.]

—— Another copy.
Apocrypha inserted.   [F. F.]
                        682.

1703. The Holy Bible . . .
    Bill and Executrix of Newcomb : London. 1703. 12°.

Text ends on Oo 12 *b*. Apocrypha mentioned in list of books, but not required by signatures.

¶ 154 × 80 mm.
Wants Apocrypha?
With Metrical Psalms (1703), and Prayer Book (1704).
Silver corners, clasps, and plates.   [F. F.]
                        683.

1703. B. f°. See 1704.

1704. The Holy Bible . . .
Bill and Executrix of Newcomb : London. 1704,1684. 12°.

Apparently a reissue, with a fresh title dated 1704, of an edition printed in 1684. The N. T. title is dated 1684, and bears the names of the *Assigns of J. Bill, and H. Hills and T. Newcomb*.
General title engraved. Text ends on Eee 6 a. No Apocrypha.

¶ 119 × 58 mm. Wants two leaves. [F. F.]
684.

1704. The Holy Bible . . .
Bill and Executrix of Newcomb : London. 1704,08. f°.

Additional general title engraved by *I. Sturt*, and dated 1704. Dated 1703 elsewhere. Text ends on Tttt 4 a, followed by tables and Index, etc.

¶ 320 × 203 mm.
Covers stamped with portraits of Luther and Melanchthon. [F. F.]
685.

1704. The Holy Bible . . .
Bill and Executrix of Newcomb : London. 1704. 12°.

Text ends on Oo 12 b. Apocrypha mentioned in list of books, but not required by signatures.

¶ 153 × 88 mm.
Wants Apocrypha?
With Prayer Book (1705), and Metrical Psalms (1705).
686.

1704. The Holy Bible . . .
University-Printers : Oxford. 1704. 12°.

O. T. ends on Vv 6 b ; N. T. ends on N 12 b. No Apocrypha.

¶ 122 × 63 mm.
Silver clasps. [F. F.]

—— Another copy.
With Prayer Book (1711), and Metrical Psalms (1711).
687.

1704. The New Testament . . .
Bill and Executrix of Newcomb : London. 1704. 8°. 𝕭. 𝕷.

A late black-letter edition. Loftie (p. 199) suggests that it was printed in Holland.

Text ends on X 6 b.

¶ 165 × 96 mm. [F. F.]
688.

—— ANOTHER EDITION.
Date not known. Probably issued by the same printers.

Agrees closely with the above edition ; with the same signatures.

¶ 164 × 101 mm. Imperfect : wanting leaves at beginning and end. [F. F]
689.

1704? (The New Testament.)
    [Qu. *Bill and Executrix of Newcomb : London.* 1704 ?] 12°. 𝔅. 𝔏.

Perhaps Loftie's No. 489; and possibly printed in Holland.

Somewhat resembles Nos. 688 and 689 ; but the signatures are in twelves, not eights. Text ends on O 10 *b*.

¶ 157 × 94 mm. Wants title. [F. F.]
690.

—— Another edition.

Date not known. Probably issued by the same printers.

Differs from No. 690 in having a shorter page and rather longer lines. Revelation begins on N 8 *a*.

¶ 150 × 94 mm. Imperfect: wanting title and many other leaves. [F. F.]
691.

1705. The Holy Bible . . .
    Heirs and Successors of A. Anderson : Edinburgh. 1705. 4°.

Very incorrectly printed, according to Lee (*Memorial*, p. 167).

N. T. title dated 1605 by error. Text ends on Lll 4 *b*, followed by tables. No Apocrypha. Many of the initials at the beginning of the books appear to be battered specimens of those originally used in English Bibles of the mid-sixteenth century.

¶ 229 × 170 mm.
Date on N. T. title altered by pen to 1705. [F. F.]

—— Another copy.
Imperfect: wanting general title and other leaves. [F. F.]
692.

1705. The Holy Bible . . .
    Bill and Executrix of Newcomb : London. 1705. 12°.

Text ends on Yy 11 *b*. No Apocrypha.

¶ 194 × 161 mm.
With Metrical Psalms (1704).
Silver corners and clasps. [F. F.]
693.

1705. The New Testament . . .
    Bill and Executrix of Newcomb : London. 1705. 12°.

Text ends on S 2 *b*.

¶ 148 × 85 mm. [F. F.]
694.

1706. The Holy Bible . . .
    Bill and Executrix of Newcomb : London. 1706. f°.

Additional general title engraved by *I. Sturt*. Text ends on Tttt 4 *a*, followed by tables and Index, etc., as in the folio of 1704,03 (No. 685).

¶ 325 × 218 mm.
With Prayer Book (1706), and Metrical Psalms (1706).
Binding stamped *Iohn Forde 1707*. The cost of the book is given, in a contemporary hand, as £1.12*s*.0*d*.

Two curious printed labels are pasted inside the cover : (1) *Mr. John Forde of the Six Clarks Office London. Printed on the Frozen Thames. January the 30th. 1683.* (2) *Mr. John Forde Printed on the Ice on the Thames, Jan. 18. 1715–6.* [F. F.]

—— Another copy.
Wants engraved title.
With Metrical Psalms (1706).

695.

1706. (The Holy Bible.)
Bill and Executrix of Newcomb : London. 1706. 12°.

Text ends on Aaa 5 *b*. No Apocrypha.

¶ 121 × 65 mm. Wants general title.
With Prayer Book (1706), and Metrical Psalms (1708). [F. F.]

696.

1706. The Holy Bible . . .
University-Printers : Oxford. 1706. 12°.

Text ends on Ll 12 *a*, with tables on verso. No Apocrypha.

¶ 156 × 93 mm.
With Metrical Psalms (1707). [F. F.]

697.

1706. Select Moral Books of the Old Testament and Apocrypha, paraphras'd. Viz. Proverbs. Ecclesiastes. Wisdom. Ecclesiasticus.
*Printed for A. and J. Churchill at the Black Swan in
Paternoster-Row :* London. 1706. 12°.

An original translation into ' modern English ' of the four books Proverbs, Ecclesiastes, Wisdom, and Ecclesiasticus. The B. M. Catalogue suggests that the author was H. Locke.

The preface (5 ff.) explains the design of the work, and contains a short notice of each of the four books which it contains. King James' version and the ' Paraphrase ' are given in parallel columns, the new translation being printed in paragraphs ; 463 pp.

¶ 157 × 93 mm.
[F. F.]

698.

1707. The Holy Bible . . .
University-Printers : Oxford. 1707. 12°.

O. T. ends on Ii 10 *b*, followed by 1 f. containing tables. No Apocrypha.

¶ 121 × 63 mm. Imperfect : containing the O. T. only. [F. F.]

699.

1707. B. f°. See 1708.
B. 8°. See 1708.
B. 12°. See 1710.

1708. The Holy Bible . . . With most profitable Annotations . . .
[*Amsterdam* ?] 1708,07. f°.

King James' version, with the Geneva notes, etc.

ENGLISH 253

Resembles Nos. 557, 583, and 616. No doubt printed abroad, probably at Amsterdam. Additional general title engraved (with figures of Moses and Aaron, and view of London) and, with the other, dated 1708 ; N. T. title dated 1707.
Text: O. T. ends on p. 710 ; N. T. ends on p. 248. No Apocrypha.
With maps by *N. Visscher, Amsterdam,* and *J. Moxon, London.*

¶ 397 × 241 mm.
Apocrypha inserted.
With Metrical Psalms (1702), and Prayer Book (1711). [F. F.]

—— Another copy.

Apocrypha inserted.
With Metrical Psalms (1702), and Prayer Book (1711).
700.

1708. The Holy Bible . . .
Bill and Executrix of Newcomb : London. 1708,07. 8°.

General title engraved, and dated 1708 ; N. T. title dated 1707. Text ends on Cccc 4 *b.* No Apocrypha.

¶ 192 × 123 mm.
With Prayer Book (1704), and Metrical Psalms (1709). [F. F.]
701.

1708. The Holy Bible . . .
Bill and Executrix of Newcomb : London. 1708. 4°.

N. T. ends on P 4 *b,* followed by Index and tables.

¶ 245 × 180 mm.
Contains a series of plates.
With Prayer Book (1709), and Metrical Psalms (1709). [F. F.]
702.

1708. The Holy Bible . . .
Bill and Executrix of Newcomb : London. 1708. 12°.

Text ends on Yy 11 *b.* No Apocrypha.

¶ 159 × 99 mm. Wants N. T. title.
With Metrical Psalms (? 1708). [F. F.]
703.

1708. The Holy Bible . . .
University-Printers : Oxford. 1708. 12°.

Text ends on Ss 2 *b.* No Apocrypha.

¶ 165 × 100 mm.
With Prayer Book (1707), and Metrical Psalms (1708).
704.

1708. The Holy Bible . . .
University-Printers : Oxford. 1708. 12°.

Quite distinct from No. 704. Text ends on Tt 10 *b.* No Apocrypha. One leaf of tables after the O. T., and another at the end of the N. T.

¶ 121 × 63 mm. Wants two leaves. [F. F.]
705.

1708. B. 12°. See 1712.

1709. The Holy Bible . . .
    Bill and Executrix of Newcomb : London. 1709. f°.

The patent to print English Bibles may be traced down from Christopher Barker, who purchased a very extensive patent in 1577, and obtained an exclusive patent from the Queen in 1589. It remained nominally in the Barker family down to 1709. 'The patent was then held by Thomas Newcomb and Henry Hills, from whose executors John Baskett and some others purchased the remainder of their term. In 1713 Benjamin Tooke and John Barber were constituted Queen's printers, to commence after the expiration of the term purchased by Baskett, i.e. thirty years from 1709, or January 1739. Baskett bought from Tooke and Barber their reversionary interest, and obtained a renewal of sixty years, the latter thirty of which were subsequently conveyed by the representatives of the Baskett family to Charles Eyre and his heirs' (D. N. B., art. *John Baskett*). For the subsequent history of the patent see note at 1772 (No. 900).

O. T. ends on Kkk 6 *b* ; Apocrypha end on N 6 *b* ; N. T. ends on S 4 *a*, followed by Index and tables.

¶ 358 × 221 mm.
With Prayer Book (1709), and Metrical Psalms (1710). [F. F.]
706.

1709. The Holy Bible . . .
    University-Printers : Oxford. 1709. 12°.

Text ends on Ll 12 *a*, with tables on verso. No Apocrypha.

¶ 158 × 93 mm.
With Metrical Psalms (1704), and Prayer-Book (1708). [F. F.]
707.

1709. The New Testament . . .
    Bill and Executrix of Newcomb : London. 1709. 8°.

Text ends on Gg 8 *b*. Name of book and chapter-number in headlines in black-letter.

¶ 193 × 116 mm. [F. F.]

—— Another copy. [F. F.]
708.

1710. The Holy Bible . . .
    Bill and Executrix of Newcomb : London. 1707,10. 12°.

General title engraved, and dated 1707 ; N. T. title (*Assigns of Newcomb and Hills*) dated 1710. Text ends on Aaa 5 *b*. No Apocrypha.

¶ 122 × 64 mm.
With Metrical Psalms (1715). [F. F.]
709.

1710. The Holy Bible . . .
    Heirs of A. Anderson : Edinburgh. 1710. 12°.

General title within woodcut border containing the royal arms, and the device *Frustra nisi Dominus*. Lee gives a facsimile of this border (see *Memorial*, pp. 161-3). No Apocrypha.

¶ 150 × 87 mm. A fragment, containing only the first sheet A.
710.

ENGLISH

1710. The New Testament . . .
Assigns of T. Newcomb and H. Hills : London. 1710. 12°.

Text ends on S 2 a.

¶ 151 × 84 mm.
With Prayer Book (1712), and Metrical Psalms (1713).

711.

1710. B. 8°. See 1711.
B. 12°. See 1711.

1711. The Holy Bible . . .
Assigns of Newcomb and Hills : London. 1711,10. 8°.

General title engraved, and dated 1711; N. T. dated 1710. Text ends on Cccc 4 b. No Apocrypha.

¶ 195 × 124 mm.

712.

1711. The Holy Bible . . .
Assigns of Newcomb and Hills : London. 1711,10. 12°.

General title engraved, and dated 1711; N. T. title dated 1710. Text ends on Aaa 5 b. No Apocrypha.

¶ 121 × 63 mm. Slightly imperfect.
In two volumes.   [F. F.]

713.

1711. The Holy Bible . . .
University-Printers : Oxford. 1711. 12°.

Text ends on Ll 12 a, with tables on verso. No Apocrypha.
Is. lvii. 12, *I will declare thy righteousness, and thy works, for they shall profit thee* (not omitted).

¶ 159 × 97 mm. Wants one leaf.   [F. F.]

714.

1711. B. 8°. See 1712 and 1740.
B. 12°. See 1713.

1712. The Holy Bible . . .
University-Printers : Oxford. 1708,12. 12°.

General title dated 1708; N. T. title dated 1712. Text ends on Tt 10 b. No Apocrypha. Two leaves of tables.

¶ 124 × 64 mm.

715.

1712. The Holy Bible . . .
Assigns of Newcomb and Hills : London. 1711,12. 8°.

General title engraved, and dated 1711; N. T. title (*John Baskett and Assigns of Newcomb and Hills*) dated 1712. Text ends on Cccc 4 b. No Apocrypha.

¶ 195 × 122 mm.
Apocrypha inserted.
With Prayer Book (1709), and Metrical Psalms (1709).   [F. F.]

716.

1712. The Holy Bible . . .
                Assigns of Newcomb and Hills : London. 1712. 4°.

N. T. ends on P 4 b, followed by Index and tables.

¶ 254 × 195 mm.
With Metrical Psalms (1712), and Prayer Book (1713).   [F. F.]

717.

1712. The Holy Bible . . .
                University-Printers : Oxford. 1712. 4°.

General title engraved by *Burghers*. N. T. ends on P 7 a, followed by Index and tables. One leaf of tables after Apocrypha.

¶ 253 × 196 mm.   [F. F.]

718.

1712. The New Testament . . .
                Assigns of Newcomb and Hills : London. 1712. 12°.

Text ends on N 12 b.

¶ 119 × 59 mm.

719.

1712. An Exposition of the Prophetical Books of the Old Testament . . . by Matthew Henry . . .
                Printed for J. Lawrence, and others : London. 1712. f°.

Matthew Henry (1662–1714), a Presbyterian minister at Chester, began his 'Exposition of the Old and New Testament' in Nov. 1704. The first volume was published in 1708; and five uniform volumes completing the Old Testament and Gospels appeared during the author's lifetime. Before his death he had reached the end of Acts, and the New Testament was afterwards finished by a number of Nonconformist divines. This most popular of English commentaries was frequently reprinted in the eighteenth and nineteenth centuries. The edition of 1811 contains additional matter from Henry's manuscripts. See No. 856.

With Preface (pp. x) dated 18 July 1712. The text is printed with the Commentary, but in larger type.

¶ 353 × 220 mm.

720.

1712. B. 8°. See 1715.
B. 12°. See 1713.

1713. The Holy Bible . . .
                University-Printers : Oxford. 1713,11. 12°.

General title dated 1713; N. T. title dated 1711. Text ends on Tt 10 b. No Apocrypha. Two leaves of tables.

¶ 123 × 65 mm.   [F. F.]

721.

1713. The Holy Bible . . .
    John Baskett, and Assigns of Newcomb and Hills :
                              London. 1712,13. 12°.

The earliest Bible in this Catalogue which bears on its titlepage the name of John Baskett, 'one of the greatest monopolists of Bibles who ever lived.'

ENGLISH

For J. Baskett (d. 1742) see note at 1709 (No. 706). He printed also at Oxford (see No. 730), and at Edinburgh (see No. 759).
General title dated 1712; N. T. title dated 1713. Text ends on Oo 12 b. Apocrypha mentioned in list of books, but not required by signatures.

¶ 150 × 88 mm.
Wants Apocrypha?
With Prayer Book (1713), and Metrical Psalms (1713).

722.

1713. The Holy Bible . . .
Baskett and Assigns of Newcomb and Hills: London. 1713. 12°.

Text ends on Oo 12 b. Apocrypha mentioned in list of books, but not required by signatures.

¶ 150 × 89 mm.
Wants Apocrypha?
With Prayer Book (1713), and Metrical Psalms (1713). [F. F.]

723.

1713. The Holy Bible . . .
University-Printers: Oxford. 1713. 12°.

Text ends on Ss 2 b. No Apocrypha.

¶ 162 × 94 mm. [F. F.]

724.

ACCESSION OF KING GEORGE I: 1 AUGUST 1714.

1714. The Holy Bible . . .
Printed by A. Rhames; for William Binauld, at the Bible in Eustace-street, and Eliphal Dobson, at the Stationers-Arms in Castle-street: Dublin. 1714. f°.

One of the earliest editions of the English Bible printed in Ireland.

An edition of the English New Testament (probably the Rheims version) was certainly printed at Dublin in 1699, or possibly in 1698, by *Bryan Wilson* and *Cornelius Carter* for *James Malone* and his Partners. It was apparently suppressed on account of its alleged naccuracy; and no copy is now known. In an advertisement of books printed 'by and for' *Patrick Neill*, of Belfast, in 1700, appears 'New Testament.'
It is asserted in two Histories of Belfast and in Hardy's 'Tour' that 'The Holy Bible' was printed by *James Blow* (or *Blaeu*) at Belfast in 1704. Dr. Robert Travers, Assistant Librarian of Marsh's Library, Dublin, recorded in writing that he had seen an octavo Bible printed several years before 1714 at Belfast by *Blaeu*. And in 1714 Blow advertised an edition of 'The Holy Bible in several volumes' as printed and sold by him. But no copy of an Irish edition of the English Bible before that printed by Rhames in 1714 is known to survive.
We are indebted for this note to Mr. E. R. McC. Dix.
Royal arms on both titles. Text: O. T. ends on Zzzz 3 b; Apocrypha end on Y 2 a; N. T. ends on Ff 4 b, followed by Index and tables.

¶ 346 × 223 mm.
With Prayer Book (1714), and Metrical Psalms (1714). [F. F.]

725.

1714. The Holy Bible . . .
Baskett and Assigns of Newcomb and Hills: London. 1714. 12°.

Text ends on Yy 4 b. No Apocrypha.

¶ 169 × 96 mm. [F F.]

726.

VOL. I. S

1714. Solomon's Proverbs English and Latin, alphabetically collected for help of Memory. In English by H. D. And since made Latin by S. Perkins, late School-master of Christs-Church Hospital. Fitted for the use of Schools. Very much corrected and amended . . .
Printed for George Mortlock, at the Phœnix in
St. Paul's Church-yard : London. 1714. 12°.

H. Danvers' collection of Proverbs (see above, No. 547), with a Latin version by S. Perkins.

Previous editions of this diglot appeared in 1689, 1699, and 1704. It was republished in an improved form, edited by P. Selby, in 1728.
With *imprimatur*, dated *May 15th, 1688*, and signed by *Rob. Midgley*. The Proverbs—English and Latin on opposite pages—end on p. 121. The volume contains two catalogues of schoolbooks sold by G. Mortlock.

¶ 138 × 78 mm. [F. F.
727.

1714. B. 8°. See 1715.

1715. The Holy Bible . . .
Baskett and Assigns of Newcomb and Hills : London. 1715,12. 8°.

General title engraved, and dated 1715; N. T. title dated 1712. Text ends on Cccc 4 b. No Apocrypha.

¶ 195 × 120 mm.
Apocrypha inserted.
With Metrical Psalms (1717), and Prayer Book (1719).
Pasted on the inside of the cover is a tract: *On the Reverence required in Praying to God.* [F. F.]
728.

1715. The Holy Bible . . .
James Watson, One of His Majesty's Printers : Edinburgh.
1715,14. 8°.

Lee (*Memorial*, pp. 187-8) commends the execution and accuracy of Watson's editions.
Titles dated 1715; colophon dated 1714.
General title engraved by *Rot: Wood*. Text ends on Xx 4 b. No Apocrypha.

¶ 170 × 112 mm. [F. F.]
729.

1715. The Holy Bible . . .
J. Baskett, Printer to the King's most Excellent Majesty,
and the University : Oxford. 1715. f°.

Lee (*Memorial*, p. 179 n.) states that Baskett received a licence from the University of Oxford to print Bibles for twenty-one years, on payment of £200 a year.

The N. T. title gives the names of *J. Baskett and the Assigns of Newcomb and Hills, London.* ' Text ends on Tttt 4 a, followed by Index and tables.

¶ 321 × 199 mm.
With Prayer Book (? date), and Metrical Psalms (1715).

730.

ENGLISH 259

1715. The Holy Bible . . .
[*Amsterdam ?*] 1715. f°.

King James' version, with the Geneva notes.

Like No. 700, probably printed at Amsterdam.
Text : O. T. ends on p. 712 ; N. T. ends on p. 248. No Apocrypha.
With Moxon's maps.

¶ 390 × 244 mm.
Apocrypha (160 pp.), with separate titleleaf, inserted.
With Prayer Book (1715), and Metrical Psalms (1715).
Binding stamped *Christopher Ward. 1725.*
[F. F.]
731.

1715. The Holy Bible . . .
J. Baskett : Oxford. 1715. 4°.

N. T. title gives the names of *J. Baskett, and Assigns of Newcomb and Hills, London.*
Text ends on Llll 2 *b*, followed by Index and tables.

¶ 265 × 197 mm.
[F. F.]
732.

1716. The Holy Bible . . .
Baskett and Assigns of Newcomb and Hills : London. 1716. 4°.

N. T. ends on P 4 *b*, followed by Index and tables.

¶ 238 × 188 mm.
[F. F.]
733.

1716. The Holy Bible . . .
Printed by James Watson, One of His Majesty's Printers ; sold at his Shop, opposite to the Lucken-Booths : Edinburgh. 1716. 12°.

Closely resembles certain contemporary editions printed at Oxford.
Text ends on Tt 10 *b*. No Apocrypha. Two leaves of tables.

¶ 119 × 62 mm.
[F. F.]
734.

1716. B. f°. See 1717.

1717. The Holy Bible . . .
J. Baskett : Oxford. 1717,16. f°.

General title dated 1717 ; N. T. title dated 1716.
The preliminary matter includes table of Lessons and Kalendar. Text: O. T. ends on Zzz 2 *a* ; Apocrypha end on Qqqq 3 *b* ; N. T. ends on Y 4 *b*.
A magnificent edition, printed in large type. With many plates at the beginning and end of books, engraved on steel from the designs of various artists. Some of the initial letters are similarly engraved. Unfortunately the book contained many misprints, and earned the nickname *A Baskett-ful of Errors.* See Acts iii. 24 . . . *and the prophets* . . . *and all those* . . . for *and all the prophets* . . . *and those* . . . , and iv. 24 *had* for *heard*, etc. From the misprint *The parable of the vinegar* (for *vineyard*) in the headline above Luke xx, this edition is commonly known as the 'Vinegar Bible.'

Two distinct varieties occur.

A.
The additional general title, engraved by *Du-Bose,* represents Moses writing the first words of Genesis ; below is the imprint *Printed by Jn°. Baskett at the Clarendon Printing-*

house in Oxford. The other general title has a view of Oxford. The N. T. title bears an engraving of the Annunciation.

¶ 490 × 307 mm.
Enclosed is a MS. list of errors. [F. F.]

—— Another copy.
Wants the engraved general title, and one leaf of text.
735.

—— ANOTHER EDITION.
B.
The additional general title, engraved by *Sturt*, represents a church-interior, with figures of Moses and Aaron, etc.; and is dated 1716. The other general title and the N. T. title have small engravings. In the text the columns are separated by a double rule. The engravings differ considerably from those in A; many represent allegorical subjects, and others are merely ornamental pieces, and do not, as in A, generally illustrate Bible incidents.

¶ 503 × 305 mm.
736.

The Bodleian Library possesses a copy of this folio Bible printed on vellum, which was presented by Baskett to the University. Another vellum copy is in the B. M., and a third at Blenheim.

1717. The Holy Bible . . .
Baskett and Assigns of Newcomb and Hills : London. 1717. 12°.

Text ends on Oo 12 *b.* Apocrypha mentioned in list of books, but not required by signatures.

¶ 149 × 82 mm.
Wants Apocrypha ?
With Prayer Book (? date), and Metrical Psalms (1717). [F. F.]
737.

1717. The New Testament . . .
Baskett and Assigns of Newcomb and Hills : London. 1717. 12°.

Text ends on R 7 *b.*

¶ 152 × 87 mm. [F. F.]

—— Another copy.
Wants one leaf. [F. F.]
738.

1718. The Holy Bible . . .
Baskett·and Assigns of Newcomb and Hills : London. 1718. 12°.

Text ends on Xx 2 *b.* No Apocrypha.

¶ 127 × 64 mm.
With Prayer Book (1712), and Metrical Psalms (1721). [F. F.]
739.

1718. B. 8°. See 1719.

1719. The Holy Bible . . .
Baskett and Assigns of Newcomb and Hills : London. 1718,19. 8°.

General title dated 1718; N. T. title (*J. Baskett, Oxford*) dated 1719. Text ends on Nnn 8 *b.* No Apocrypha. One page of tables after the O. T.

ENGLISH 261

¶ 192 × 117 mm.
Apocrypha inserted. [F. F.]
740.

1719. The Holy Bible . . .
J. Baskett : Oxford. 1719. 4°.

N. T. ends on O 4 *a*, followed by Index and tables.

¶ 239 × 176 mm.
741.

1719. The Holy Bible . . .
Baskett and Assigns of Newcomb and Hills : London. 1719. 12°.

Text ends on Oo 12 *b*. Apocrypha mentioned in list of books, but not required by signatures.

¶ 156 × 90 mm.
Wants Apocrypha ?
With Metrical Psalms (1718), and Prayer Book (1719). [F. F.]
742.

1719. The Holy Bible . . .
J. Watson : Edinburgh. 1719. 12°.

Text ends on Tt 10 *b*. No Apocrypha. Two leaves of tables.

¶ 123 × 61 mm. In two volumes. [F. F.]
743.

1719. The New Testament . . . Newly translated out of the Latin Vulgat; and with the original Greek, and divers translations in vulgar languages diligently compared and revised. Together with Annotations . . . and Marginal Notes . . . By C. N., C. F. P. D.
[*Dublin* ?] 1719. 8°.

An original version by Cornelius Nary, a Roman Catholic priest.

C. Nary (1660–1738), *Consultissimæ Facultatis Parisiensis Doctor*, was parish priest of St. Michan's, Dublin. In his remarkable preface (printed in full by Cotton, *R. and D.*, pp. 298–304) he complains that the Rheims-Douai version is unintelligible, and that its editions are bulky and expensive. Yet his praiseworthy attempt to provide a simpler version, in a convenient octavo, seems to have proved a failure. Witham (see below, No. 776) speaks slightingly of Nary as a translator.
Some copies are dated 1718, and a few of these have a second title *A Paraphrase and Annotations upon the New Testament. London, printed for J. Moore in Cornhill. 1718.* But perhaps the real place of printing was Dublin, as stated by Geddes. Cotton asserts that the issue of 1719 is identical with that of the previous year, with the exception of two or three slight alterations. The book was never reprinted.
Title, verso blank, preface—5 ff., Approbations (dated 1714 and 1715, and signed by *Joannes Farely, M. Fogarty, Mich. Morus*, and *Francis Walsh*)—3 pp., list of books—1 p.; text, A 2 to Ll 8 *b*; table of Epistles and Gospels, 4 ff. An extra leaf contains a list of *Errata*.

¶ 194 × 113 mm. [F. F.
744

1719. B. 4°. See 1723.

1720. The Holy Bible . . .
                            J. Baskett : Oxford. 1720. 12°.

O. T. ends on Kk 10 *a* ; followed by two leaves, with tables printed on the recto of each. N. T. ends on L 5 *b*. No Apocrypha.

Two varieties occur.

A.
General title : *The Holy Bible containing* . . .

¶ 172 × 99 mm. [F. F.]
                                                                 745.

—— Another edition.

B.
General title : *The Holy Bible, containing* . . .

¶ 180 × 104 mm.   A fragment, containing only the first two sheets. [F. F.]
                                                                 746.

1720. The Holy Bible . . .
                            J. Baskett : Oxford. 1720. 18°.

Text ends on Aa 2 *b*.   No Apocrypha.   Signatures in eighteens.

¶ 134 × 74 mm. [F. F.]
                                                                 747.

1721. (The Holy Bible.)
     Baskett and Assigns of Newcomb and Hills : London. 1721. 12°.

Text ends on Oo 12 *b*.

¶ 150 × 87 mm.   Imperfect : containing the N. T. only. [F. F.]
                                                                 748.

1721. The New Testament . . .
     Baskett and Assigns of Newcomb and Hills : London. 1721. 8°.

Text ends on Gg 8 *b*.   Name of book and chapter-number in headlines in black-letter.

¶ 190 × 112 mm. [F. F.]
                                                                 749.

1722. The Holy Bible . . .
                            J. Watson : Edinburgh. 1722. f°.

This edition is specially commended for its accuracy by Lee (*Memorial*, pp. 188–193) ; it contains, however, a misprint in Ps. liii. 1, *on God* for *no God*.
Text ends on Xxxxx 2 *b*.   The insertion of the Apocrypha interrupts the signatures.

¶ 385 × 247 mm. [F. F.]
                                                                 750.

1722. The Holy Bible . . .
                            J. Watson : Edinburgh. 1722. 8°.

General title engraved by *Ro*^{t}. *Wood*.   Text ends on Xx 4 *b*.   No Apocrypha.

¶ 170 × 110 mm. [F. F.]
                                                                 751.

1722. The Holy Bible . . .
A. Rhames, for J. Hyde, R. Gunne, R. Owen, and E. Dobson:
Dublin. 1722. 12°.
No Apocrypha.

¶ 185 × 102 mm. A fragment, containing only sheet A. [F. F.]
752.

1722. B. f°. See 1723.
B. 12°. See 1723.

1723. The Holy Bible . . .
J. Baskett: Oxford. 1719,28. 4°.

General title dated 1719; N. T. title dated 1723. N. T. ends on O 4 a, followed by Index and tables.

¶ 242 × 175 mm. Slightly imperfect.
Contains a series of plates, arranged four on a page.
With Prayer Book (1720), and Metrical Psalms (1720). [F. F.]
753.

1723. The Holy Bible . . .
Baskett and Assigns of Newcomb and Hills: London. 1723,22. f°.

General title dated 1723; N. T. title dated 1722. Text ends on Tttt 4 a. With Index and tables.

¶ 359 × 233 mm.
Contains a series of plates, arranged four on a page, with a special engraved title: *The Historical Part of the Holy Bible . . . describ'd in near Three Hundred Historys Engraven by John Sturt . . . Sold by Richd Ware at the Bible and Sun in Amen Corner . . .*; opposite this is placed a general title to the whole Bible engraved by Sturt. There are also six maps with separate title: *Sacred Geography Contained in Six Maps . . . Printed for Richard Ware . . . 1727.*
With Downame's Concordance (1726).
With Prayer Book (1721), and Metrical Psalms (1723). [F. F.]

—— Another copy.
With Maps (1727), and Downame's Concordance (1726).
With Prayer Book (1721). [F. F.]

—— Another copy.
Additional engraved title.
With Downame's Concordance (1726).
With Prayer Book (1726).

—— Another copy.
379 × 240 mm. Marked by Fry as a 'large-paper' copy, but apparently only an uncut specimen.
With Prayer Book (1721). [F. F.]
754.

1723. The Holy Bible . . .
J. Baskett: Oxford. 1722,23. 12°.

General title dated 1722; N. T. title dated 1723. Text ends on Qq 9 b, followed by two leaves of tables. No Apocrypha.

¶ 129 × 65 mm. [F. F.]
755.

1725. The Holy Bible . . .
> For J. Baskett: London. 1725. 8°.

Before this date complaints had arisen as to the quality of paper used in printing Bibles, the incorrectness of many editions, and the unreasonable prices at which they were sold. To amend such abuses a royal order, dated Whitehall, 24 April 1724, gave strict injunctions to the holders of the patent with regard to the printing of Bibles, and among other provisions commanded them to set forth clearly ' on the titlepage of each book the exact price at which such book is by them to be sold to the booksellers' (Lewis, *History*, p. 851). Accordingly most of the subsequent eighteenth-century Bibles have this price printed at the foot of the general titlepage.

General title engraved, bearing below the words: *Price Six Shillings Unbound.* N. T. title gives the names of *Baskett and Assigns of Hills.* Text ends on Cccc 4 b. No Apocrypha.

¶ 196 × 123 mm.
Apocrypha inserted.
With Prayer Book (1719), and Metrical Psalms (1724). [F. F.]
756.

1725. The Holy Bible . . .
> J. Baskett: Oxford. 1725. 12°.

Text ends on Qq 9 b, followed by two leaves of tables. No Apocrypha.

¶ 131 × 67 mm.
Contains many plates, arranged two on a page, inserted in the text.
In two volumes. [F. F.]
757.

1725. B. 4°. See 1726.
B. 8°. See 1734.

1726. The Holy Bible . . .
> J. Baskett: Oxford. 1726,25. 4°.

Price 9s. Unbound.
Additional general title, engraved by Sturt, bears the words *Printed and Sold by Richard Ware at ye Bible & Sun in Amen Corner.* General title dated 1726; N. T. title dated 1725. N. T. ends on O 4 a, followed by Index and tables.

¶ 241 × 175 mm.
With Metrical Psalms (1725). [F. F.]
758.

1726. The Holy Bible . . .
> J. Baskett: Edinburgh. 1726. 4°.

Apparently the earliest Edinburgh Bible which bears J. Baskett's name on the titlepage.

Baskett purchased a third part of the gift to Robert Freebairn, the Edinburgh printer, in 1711, and tried with him later to annul the right of James Watson, the other partner, but failed in this attempt. In 1716, however, he obtained a commission as royal printer for Scotland, in conjunction with Agnes Campbell, the widow of A. Anderson. (See Lee, *Memorial*, p. 179 n., and App. xxxi; and *cf.* note at 1713, No. 722.)
Text ends on Lll 4 a, with tables on verso, followed by Index and other tables. The insertion of the Apocrypha interrupts the signatures.

¶ 254 × 195 mm.
With Scotch Metrical Psalms (n. d.). [F. F.]
759.

ENGLISH

1726. The Holy Bible . . .
          J. Baskett : Oxford. 1726. 8°.

Price Three Shillings Unbound.
N. T. ends on O 8 *b*. No Apocrypha. One leaf of tables after N. T. title.

¶ 169 × 100 mm.
Apocrypha inserted.
With Prayer Book (1726), and Metrical Psalms (1726).   [F. F.]
                          760.

1726. The Holy Bible . . .
        J. Baskett and Company : Edinburgh. 1726. 8°.

Text ends on Ppp 9 *a*, followed by three pages of tables. No Apocrypha.

¶ 168 × 109 mm.   [F. F.]
                          761.

ACCESSION OF KING GEORGE II: 11 JUNE 1727.

1727. The Holy Bible . . .
            J. Baskett : Oxford. 1727. 8°.

Price Three Shillings Unbound.
N. T. ends on P 8 *b*. No Apocrypha.

¶ 164 × 95 mm.
Apocrypha inserted.   [F. F.]
                          762.

1727. The Holy Bible . . .
*John Mosman and William Brown, Printers to the Kings
    most excellent Majesty : Edinburgh.* 1727. 8°.

With Canne's preface and marginal matter—revised.

 The following note is appended to the Preface in this edition: 'There are, in this Edition of the Holy Bible, several Thousands of Errors amended and corrected in the Notes on the Old Testament, which were in all, or most of the former Editions, whether printed at Edinburgh or elsewhere. It was the Labour of a judicious Gentleman for several Years at his Leisure-hours, who was so kind as to make us an Offer of them, which we accepted. As for the Notes on the New Testament, we were recommended by a learned and worthy Gentleman, our very good Friend, to make choice of those subjoyned to Wetsten's Edition of his Greek New Testament, printed Anno 1711, as the most copious and best extant.'
Text ends on Ooo 8 *b*. No Apocrypha.

¶ 186 × 120 mm.
With Scotch Metrical Psalms (n. d.).   [F. F.]
                          763.

1727. The Holy Bible . . .
      Baskett and Assigns of Hills : London. 1727. 12°.

Price Two Shillings Unbound.
 Text ends on Mm 12 *b*. Apocrypha mentioned in list of books, but not required by signatures.

¶ 151 × 88 mm.
Wants Apocrypha?
                          764.

1727. A Commentary upon the Historical Books of the Old Testament . . . by . . . Symon Lord Bishop of Ely. The third edition corrected.
For John Darby, and others: London. 1727. f°. 2 vols.

Simon Patrick (1626-1707) was Bishop first of Chichester and then of Ely. He issued a long series of paraphrases on books of the Bible.
This edition contains the section Genesis-Esther. The preface is dated 1694. The text and notes are mixed together, the former being printed in italics. Pp. 888, 731. With list of subscribers and index. A portrait of the author occurs as frontispiece; and a small engraving precedes each book.

¶ 345 × 220 mm. Imperfect: wanting vol. i, containing the Pentateuch.

765.

1727. The Books of Job, Psalms, Proverbs, Ecclesiastes, and the Song of Solomon, paraphras'd, with Arguments . . . and Annotations . . . By . . . Symon, late Lord Bishop of Ely.
For J. Walthoe, and others: London. 1727. f°.

Uniform with No. 765.
On the page facing the title is the *Imprimatur*, dated 1678. The Epistle Dedicatory is signed *Sy. Patrick*, and is dated 1679. With Prefaces, etc.; 540 pp. A small engraving precedes each book.

¶ 347 × 213 mm.

766.

1727. A Commentary upon the Larger and Lesser Prophets: being a continuation of Bishop Patrick. By William Lowth . . .
For R. Knaplock, and others: London. 1727. f°.

W. Lowth (1660-1732) was Prebendary of Winchester, and held the livings of Buriton and Petersfield in Hampshire.
This commentary, originally published in parts between 1714 and 1725, is printed uniformly with Nos. 765 and 766, which it supplements.
Pp. 526; with index. A few engravings.

¶ 345 × 220 mm.

767.

1728. The Holy Bible . . .
J. Baskett: Oxford. 1728. 4°.

General title, engraved by *Sturt*, bears the words *Printed and Sold by Richard Ware at ye Bible & Sun in Amen Corner. Just Published fitted to Bind up with all Sorts of House Bibles a Brief Concordance for the more easy finding out of the useful Places therein Contained, by I. Downame B.D.* The N. T. title gives the name of the actual printer, with place and date. N. T. ends on O 4 a, followed by Index and tables.

¶ 238 × 176 mm. Perhaps wants Baskett's general title.
With Downame's Concordance (1726).
With Prayer Book (1726). [F. F.]

768.

1728. B. *4°. See 1730.*
B. *12°. See 1729.*

1729. The Holy Bible . . .
Baskett and Assigns of Hills: London. 1728,29. 12°.

Price Three Shillings Unbound.
General title dated 1728; N. T. title dated 1729. Text ends on Mm 12 b. Apocrypha mentioned in list of books, but not required by signatures.

¶ 157 × 89 mm.
Wants Apocrypha?
With Metrical Psalms (1732). [F. F.]
769.

1729. (The Holy Bible.)
J. Mosman and W. Brown, the Assigns of
J. Watson deceast: Edinburgh. 1729. 4°.

Text ends on Iii 5 a, followed by one leaf containing *A Description of Canaan, and the bordering Countries*. No Apocrypha?

¶ 240 × 180 mm. Wants general title and following leaf. [F. F.]
770.

1729. The Holy Bible . . .
University-Printer: Oxford. 1729. 8°.

Price Six Shillings.
General title engraved. N. T. title gives the name *John Baskett*. N. T. ends on Q 4 b. No Apocrypha.

¶ 209 × 126 mm.
Apocrypha inserted.
With Prayer Book (1729), and Metrical Psalms (1729).

771.

1729. The Holy Bible . . .
Mr. Baskett and Company, His Majesty's Printers: Edinburgh.
1729. 12°.

Text ends on Oo 10 b, followed by three pages of tables. Colophon after the O. T., and at the end of the book. No Apocrypha.
The woodcut border to the general title contains figures of Moses and Aaron, and the royal arms.

¶ 148 × 84 mm. Wants one leaf. [F. F.]
772.

1729. The New Testament in Greek and English. Containing the Original Text corrected from the Authority of the most Authentic Manuscripts: and a New Version form'd agreeably to the Illustrations of the most Learned Commentators and Critics: with Notes and Various Readings, and a Copious Alphabetical Index . . .
For J. Roberts, near the Oxford-Arms in Warwick-Lane:
London. 1729. 8°. 2 vols.

A diglot New Testament containing the Greek text with an original English version by William Mace.

For some account of this curious version, which Cotton styles 'Arian,' see Leonard Twells' *Critical Examination*, published in three parts, 1731-2. *Cf.* also Lewis, pp. 365-72.
Dedication *To the Right Honourable Peter Lord King, Baron of Ockham, Lord High-Chancellor of Great-Britain* and *Premonition to the Reader*—3 ff. Text, 1022 pp.; followed by index ending on p. 1058, and one extra leaf. The two texts are printed in parallel columns with verse-numbers in the margins. Many notes, including a long discussion as to the authenticity of 1 John v. 7.

¶ 199 × 120 mm.
With MS. notes by W. Blair.

773.

1729. B. 12º. See 1735.

1730. The Holy Bible . . .
[*Amsterdam.*]   1730,28.   4°.

No place or printer. From a note in the B. M. Catalogue it appears that this edition is identical with one printed at Amsterdam in 1730, with the exception of the general title (dated 1730) and following leaf, and the N. T. title (dated 1728), which supplant the original leaves, while the original leaf containing the list of books has been cancelled.
The preliminary matter includes Index and tables.   N. T. ends on Q 4 b.
In Gen. xxix, v. 23 is omitted.

¶ 266 × 203 mm.
With Prayer Book (1728), and Metrical Psalms (1728).   [F F.]
774.

1730. The New Testament . . . According to the Antient Latin Edition. With Critical Remarks . . . From the French of Father Simon. By William Webster . . .
For John Pemberton, in Fleet-street; and Charles Rivington, in St. Paul's Church-yard: London.   1730.   4°.   2 vols.

A translation of Richard Simon's French version of the New Testament, and his Annotations thereon.

Webster (1689-1758) was Curate of St. Dunstan's in the West. Simon's version appeared in 1702. See Lewis, pp. 372-5, and Cotton, *R. and D.*, pp. 45-6, and p. 227.
Vol. 1: title; the translator's preface, addressed *to the Honourable and Reverend Mr. Edward Finch, Prebendary of Canterbury and York*—2 ff.; *The Author's Preface, with a Letter to M. L. J. D. R.* (dated *Paris, June 15, 1697*)—pp. 1 to 42; Matthew-Acts, pp. 43-562.
ol. 2: title; Acts-Revelation, pp. 563-1044. The notes are printed below the text.

¶ 220 × 175 mm.   [F. F.]

—— Another copy.
In one volume.   The titleleaf to vol. 2 is placed before Acts.
775.

1730. Annotations on the New Testament . . . By R. W. D. D. . . .
[*Douai.*]   1730.   8°.   2 vols.

The New Testament newly translated from the Vulgate text with Annotations by Robert Witham (d. 1738), appointed President of the English College at Douai in 1714.

In this original and annotated version, the author professes to explain the literal sense, according to the ancient Fathers; to examine and disprove false interpretations; and to show the differences between the Vulgate and the Greek text. Cotton (*R. and D.* pp. 305-14) prints his preface in full. His work seems to have attracted more notice than Nary's version (see No. 744). It was severely criticised in a pamphlet entitled *Popery an enemy to Scripture* . . . (1736) by James Serces. The annotations were reprinted in Oswald Syers' Bible, Manchester, 1813 (No. 1034).
Apparently printed at Douai.
Vol. 1: title, verso blank, preface—4 ff., *Errata*—1 p., Approbations on vol. 1 (dated 1730 and 1729, and signed by *Ambrosius Burgis* and *F. Antonius Codrington*)—1 p., index—5 ff.; text (Matthew–Acts), 506 pp.; followed by 3 ff. containing chronological table, 'Chronotaxis,' and short list of *errata*. [Vol. 2: title, verso blank, table of Epistles and Gospels—9 pp., 1 p. blank; preface, and Argument to Romans—2 pp.; text (Romans–Revelation), pp. 5 to 536; followed by list of *errata*—1 p., Approbations on both volumes (dated 1730, and signed by

Joannes Ingleton, Ricardus Challoner, F. Philippus Loraine, Georgius Kendal, and Gulielmus Thornburgh)—2 pp., 1 p. blank.]

¶ 187 × 115 mm. Imperfect: vol. 1 only. The description of vol. 2 is from Cotton.

—— Another copy.
Vol. 1 only, wanting six leaves at the beginning.

776.

1731. The New Testament . . . Translated out of the Latin Vulgat by John Wiclif . . . about 1378. To which is Praefixt a History of the several Translations of the H. Bible and N. Testament, &c. into English, both in MS. and Print, and of the most remarkable Editions of them since the Invention of Printing. By John Lewis . . .
Printed by John March. Sold by Thomas Page and William Mount on Tower-Hill; and William Parker at the King's Head in St. Paul's Church-Yard: London. 1731. f°.

The earliest printed edition of Wycliffe's version of the New Testament.

Though it was proposed as early as 1719 to print Wycliffe's translation of the complete Bible, this was not accomplished until 1850. For a notice of the version, see No. 1178, 1850.
Lewis (1675–1747) was for upwards of 37 years vicar of Minster, in Kent.
Title, Dedication *To the Right Honourable Thomas Lord Malton* . . ., Advertisement, List of Subscribers and *Errata*, etc.—5 ff.; *The History* . . . with *A Particular Account of the several MSS.* . . . *made use of in this Edition of the New Testament*, 108 pp.; *The New Testament . . . Translated . . . by John Wiclif* . . ., 156 pp.; Glossary, viii pp. With engraved portraits of Lewis and of Wycliffe, and a reproduction of the titlepage to the Great Bible.
The printer's name is given in the colophon on p. 153 of the N. T.: *Printed by John March in George-yard near the Postern on Tower-hill, and finished the Sixth day of June, MDCCXXXI.*
The text was obtained by Lewis from two MSS., both representing the later Wycliffite version:—(1) an early fifteenth-century MS., belonging to himself, now in the Bodleian (Gough Eccl. top. 5); (2) a MS. written about 1420, belonging to Sir Edw. Dering, and in 1850 the property of W. Conybeare, Dean of Llandaff. (See Forshall and Madden's edition of the complete Bible, 1850, Preface, p. i n., p. 1, and p. lxiv.)
Only 160 copies of this book were issued, sold at one guinea in sheets. For a reprint, see No. 1014, 1810. Lewis' *History* was published separately in 1739, and again in 1818.

¶ 368 × 233 mm.

777

1731. The New Testament . . .
Assigns of His Majesty's Printer, and of Henry Hills, deceas'd :
London. 1731. 12°.
Text ends on R 7 b.

¶ 154 × 91 mm.
With Prayer Book (1732), and Metrical Psalms (1733). [F. F.]

778.

1731. B. 4°. See 1732.

1732. The Holy Bible . . .
J. Baskett : Oxford. 1732,31. 4°.

General title dated 1732; N. T. title (*the Assigns of His Majesty's Printer, and Henry Hills deceased*) dated 1731. Text ends on Iiii 2 b, followed by Index and tables.

¶ 282 × 219 mm.
In two volumes.

—— Another copy.

The general title in this copy adds *Price Fourteen Shillings, Unbound.*
With Prayer Book (? date), and Metrical Psalms (1732)

779.

1732. The Holy Bible . . .
J. Baskett : London. 1732. 12°.

Price Two Shillings Unbound.
Text ends on Mm 12 b. Apocrypha mentioned in list of books, but not required by signatures.

¶ 156 × 90 mm.
Wants Apocrypha?
With Metrical Psalms (1731), and Prayer Book (1732). [F. F.]

780.

1732. The Holy Bible . . .
[*Amsterdam* ?] 1732. 12°.

Probably printed abroad; perhaps in Amsterdam.
Text ends on Kkk 5 b. No Apocrypha. The woodcut border to the general title is copied from the engraved titles of R. Daniel's Cambridge editions of 1648.

¶ 126 × 70 mm.
With Metrical Psalms (n. d.). [F. F.]

781.

1732. The New Testament . . .
J. Baskett: London. 1732. 8°.

Price One Shilling, and Eight Pence, Unbound.
Text ends on Gg 4 b. Name of book and chapter-number in headlines in black-letter.

¶ 189 × 114 mm. [F. F.]

782.

1733. The Holy Bible . . .
J. Baskett : London. 1733. 12°.

Text ends on Mm 12 b. Apocrypha mentioned in list of books, but not required by signatures.

¶ 160 × 93 mm.
Wants Apocrypha? [F. F.]

783.

1733. (Annotations on the New Testament.)
[*Douai.*] 1733. 8°. 2 vols.

A reprint of R. Witham's annotated translation, first published in 1730. See No. 776.

This is quite a distinct edition, and not merely a reissue of the first edition with new titles, as stated by Cotton (*R. and D.*, p. viii).
[Vol. 1 : —.] Vol. 2 : engraved frontispiece, representing St. Paul ; title, verso blank, preface—1 p. ; Argument to Romans—1 p. ; text, pp. 5 to 541 ; Approbations—1 p. ; index, pp. 1 to 6.

¶ 198 × 117 mm. Imperfect: vol. 2 only.

784.

1733. B. 8°. See 1734.

ENGLISH 271

1734. The Holy Bible . . .
For J. Baskett : London. 1725,34. 8°.

Price Six Shillings Unbound.
General title engraved, and dated 1725; N. T. title (*printed by Baskett*) dated 1734. Text ends on Cccc 4 *b.* No Apocrypha.

¶ 197 × 125 mm. [F. F.]
785.

1734. The Holy Bible . . .
J. Baskett : London. 1733,34. 8°.

Price Three Shillings Unbound.
General title dated 1733; N. T. title (*J. Baskett : Oxford*) dated 1734. Text ends on Sss 8 *a.* No Apocrypha.

¶ 170 × 100 mm.
Apocrypha inserted.
With Metrical Psalms (1732), and Prayer Book (1733).
Leather name-label *Charles Bigg. 17. Feb^{ry} 1757* inside cover. [F. F.]
786.

1734. The Holy Bible . . .
J. Baskett : London. 1734. 12°.

Price Two Shillings Unbound.
Text ends on Mm 12 *b.* Apocrypha mentioned in list of books, but not required by signatures.

¶ 159 × 92 mm.
Wants Apocrypha? [F. F.]
787.

1734. B. 8°. See 1735.

1735. The Holy Bible . . .
J. Baskett : London. 1735,29. 12°.

Price Two Shillings Unbound.
General title dated 1735; N. T. title (*Baskett and Assigns of Hills*) dated 1729. Text ends on Mm 12 *b.* Apocrypha mentioned in list of books, but not required by signatures.

¶ 157 × 90 mm.
Wants Apocrypha? [F. F
788.

1735. The Holy Bible . . .
For J. Baskett : London. 1735,34. 8°.

Price Six Shillings Unbound.
General title engraved, and dated 1735; N. T. title (*by J. Baskett*) dated 1734. Text ends on Cccc 4 *b.* No Apocrypha.

¶ 198 × 125 mm.
Apocrypha inserted. [F. F.]

—— Another copy.
With Scotch Metrical Psalms (1738).
789.

1735. The Holy Bible . . .
J. Baskett: London. 1735. 12°.

Price Two Shillings Unbound.

Text ends on Mm 12 b. Apocrypha mentioned in list of books, but not required by signatures.

¶ 156 × 91 mm. Wants one leaf, and perhaps the Apocrypha. [F. F.]
790.

1736. The Holy Bible . . .
Robert Freebairn, His Majesty's Printer: Edinburgh. 1786. 8°.

For R. Freebairn's commission of 1711 see Lee, *Memorial,* App. xxx; and *cf.* note on No. 759.
Text ends on Bbb 4 a, with table on verso. No Apocrypha.

¶ 176 × 108 mm.
With Scotch Metrical Psalms (n. d.). [F. F.]
791.

1737. The Holy Bible . . .
J. Baskett: London. 1787. 12°.

Price Two Shillings Unbound.
Text ends on Mm 12 b. Apocrypha mentioned in list of books, but not required by gnatures.

¶ 161 × 87 mm.
Wants Apocrypha? [F. F.]
792.

1737. (The Holy Bible.)
R. Freebairn: Edinburgh. 1787. 12°.

Text ends on Oo 10 b, followed by three pages of tables, with colophon. No Apocrypha.

¶ 143 × 90 mm. Imperfect: wanting general title and following leaf. [F. F.]
793.

1737. The New Testament . . .
Printed by Alex. Carmichael, and Alex. Millar in Company :
Glasgow. 1737. 12°.

A school-edition of the New Testament.

In Scotland during the eighteenth century 'children were generally taught to read in country schools, by using first the *Shorter Catechism,* then the *Proverbs,* afterwards the *New Testament,* and lastly the *Bible.* The New Testaments (as well as the Catechism and Proverbs) used in schools were very commonly printed at Glasgow' (Lee, *Memorial,* p. 195 n., where this edition is mentioned, and also another printed in 1748 'by John Robertson and Mrs. M'Lean in Company'). For a school-edition of *Proverbs* see No. 928. The 'Society in Scotland for Propagating Christian Knowledge,' which circulated large numbers of these and similar books, purchased many of its editions of the Bible and of the Proverbs from the royal printers in Edinburgh, paying twenty-two pence for each Bible, and one shilling per dozen for the Proverbs.
Text ends on p. 376 (Q 8 b). The last three verses of Rev. xxii are printed in smaller type, so as not to run on to another page.

¶ 146 × 86 mm. Title mended.
With Scotch Metrical Psalms (1735). [F. F.]
794.

1738. The Holy Bible . . .
J. Baskett: London. 1788. f°.

Price One Pound Five Shillings Unbound.
N. T. title gives the names *Baskett and Assigns of Newcomb and Hills.* N. T. ends on R 4 b, followed by Index and tables.

¶ 375 × 237 mm.
With Downame's Concordance (1726).
With Prayer Book (1738).

ENGLISH

—— Another copy.
With Prayer Book (? date), and Metrical Psalms (1745). [F. F.]
795.

1738. The New Testament . . . with arguments of books and chapters; with annotations, and other helps, for the better understanding the text, and especially for the discovery of corruptions in divers late translations, and for clearing up religious controversies of the present times; to which are added tables of the Epistles and Gospels, controversies, and heretical corruptions. The text is faithfully translated into English, out of the authentical Latin, diligently conferred with the Greek, and other editions in divers languages, and the annotations etc. are affix'd to it by the English College then resident in Rhemes. The fifth edition (the first in folio) adorn'd with cuts . . .
[*Douai?*] 1738. f°.

No edition of the Rheims New Testament of 1582 had appeared since 1633.

Cotton (*R. and D.*, p. 47) suggests that this reprint was edited by Richard Challoner and Francis Blyth. For Challoner, see No. 824, 1750. Blyth was a 'Discalced Carmelite.'

Printed *permissu superiorum*, perhaps at Douai, but Cotton says 'most probably in London.'

Pp. xx, 646; followed by tables.

The editors prefix the following note to their reprint of the table of 'Heretical Corruptions': 'The following table has had so good an effect, that since the first edition of it the Protestants have had the grace to correct, by it, their edition of the N. Testament of 1660 in many places. But as falsehood is inseparable from heresy, and none can be fit to translate faithfully the Word of God, who have not first the Spirit of God in them, they have left many other passages here taken notice of, either totally unalter'd, or not alter'd for the better, sometimes even for the worse. We thought therefore it could not but be beneficial to the Publick to point those places out to them; which we have done by prefixing an asterism * at the beginning of every paragraph, which they have vouchsafed to amend. And where they have made any alterations, we have inserted them in the margin. Those texts which are here found with this mark † annex'd to them, are such as still remain corrupt in the latest edition of the P. Testament.'

The 'cuts' are an additional title and figures of the Evangelists, engraved by *G. van der Gucht.*

¶ 371 × 233 mm. [F. F.]

—— Another copy.
Wants the 'cuts.'
796.

1739. The Holy Bible . . .
J. Baskett: Oxford. 1739. 4°.

N. T. title gives *J. Baskett, London.* Text ends on Iiii 2 *b*, followed by Index and tables.

¶ 266 × 201 mm.
797.

1739. The Holy Bible . . .
George Grierson, Printer to the King's Most Excellent Majesty, at the King's-Arms and Two-Bibles in Essex-Street:
Dublin. 1739. 4°.

For G. Grierson see Lee, *Memorial*, App. xxxix.
Text ends on [6] R 2 *b*. The insertion of the Apocrypha interrupts the signatures.

¶ 252 × 198 mm. Wants two leaves. [F. F.]
798.

VOL. I. T

1739. The Holy Bible . . .
J. Baskett : Oxford. 1739. 12°.

Text ends on Qq 6 b. No Apocrypha.

¶ 131 × 68 mm.
With Prayer-Book (1736), and Metrical Psalms (1739). [F. F.]
799.

1740. The Holy Bible . . .
G. Grierson : Dublin. 1740. [1711.] 8°.

Possibly a reissue by the Dublin printer of an earlier London edition; since it contains a second general title (not engraved) bearing the names of *the Assigns of Thomas Newcomb and Henry Hills, London,* and dated 1711. But it does not exactly agree with either No. 712 or No. 716. The N. T. title has the Dublin imprint, and the date 1740. General title engraved. Text ends on Cccc 4 b. No Apocrypha.

¶ 201 × 124 mm.
With Scotch Metrical Psalms (1741). [F. F.]
800.

1741. The Holy Bible . . .
G. Grierson : Dublin. 1741. f°.

Text ends on Pppppp 4 a, followed by Index and tables.

¶ 350 × 227 mm.
With Prayer Book (1740), and Tate and Brady's Metrical Psalms (1741). [F. F.]
801.

1741. The Holy Bible . . .
J. Baskett : Oxford. 1741. 8°.

O. T. ends on Ccc 8 b. The list of books includes the Apocrypha.
Resembles the octavo of 1745,44 (No. 812).

¶ 172 × 102 mm. Imperfect: containing the O. T. only.
In two volumes. [F. F.]
802.

1741. A new version of St. Matthew's Gospel: with select notes . . . To which is added, A review of Dr. Mill's notes on this Gospel. By Daniel Scott, I.U.D.
J. Noon, at the White Hart in Cheapside near Mercers Chapel :
London. 1741. 4°.

Daniel Scott (1694–1759), theological writer and lexicographer, graduated LL.D. at Leyden in 1719. While at Utrecht he became a Baptist, and joined the Mennonite communion. In this work he makes a point of showing that the Hebraisms of the N. T. have their parallels in classic Greek, and improves Mill's collection of various readings, especially by a more accurate citation of oriental versions.
Pp. vi, 61, 207, 88.

¶ 271 × 198 mm.

803.

1741. B. *8°. See 1742.*

1742. The Holy Bible . . .
For J. Baskett : London. 1741,42. 8°.

Very incorrect. See Lee, *Memorial,* p. 184 n. Matt. ix. 22, *me whole* for *thee whole,* etc. Price *Six Shillings Unbound.*

General title engraved, and dated 1741; N. T. title (*by J. Baskett*) dated 1742. Text ends on Cccc 4 *b*. No Apocrypha.

¶ 203 × 124 mm.
Apocrypha inserted. [F. F.]
804.

1742. B. 12°. See 1743.

1743. The Holy Bible . . .
Thomas Baskett, and Robert Baskett: Oxford. 1743,42. 12°.

General title dated 1743; N. T. title (*John Baskett*) dated 1742. Text ends on Qq 6 *b*. No Apocrypha.

¶ 130 × 67 mm. [F. F.]
805.

1743. The Holy Bible . . .
G. Grierson: Dublin. 1742,43. 12°.

General title dated 1742; N. T. title dated 1743. Text ends on Llll 8 *a*. Apocrypha mentioned in list of books, but not required by signatures.

¶ 170 × 101 mm.
Wants Apocrypha? [F. F.]
806.

1743. The Holy Bible . . .
Joseph Bentham, Printer to the University: Cambridge. 1743. 12°.

Price Two Shillings unbound.
Text ends on Mm 12 *b*. No Apocrypha. One page of tables at end of O. T.

¶ 158 × 92 mm. [F. F.]

—— Another copy.
On the general title are printed the words *Price 2s. 6d. unbound.*

¶ 171 × 99 mm.
807.

1743. B. 12°. See 1744.

1744. (The Holy Bible . . .)
Richard Watkins, One of His Majesty's Printers:
Edinburgh. 1743,44. 12°.

The date 1744 appears only in the colophon. Text ends on Rr 5 *a*, followed by three pages of tables, with colophon. No Apocrypha.

¶ 130 × 67 mm. Imperfect: the second of two volumes, containing Ecclesiastes to Revelation.
With Scotch Metrical Psalms (1744). [F. F.]
808.

1744. (The Holy Bible.)

1744. 12°.

Printer and place not known.

¶ 123 × 63 mm.
N. T. titleleaf only. Inserted in a Bible with general title dated 169 (last numeral omitted). See No. 646. [F. F.]

809.

1744. The New Testament . . .

T. and R. Baskett: London. 1744. 12°.

Price One Shilling, Unbound.
Text ends on R 7 b.

¶ 146 × 88 mm.
Apocrypha added.

810.

1744. B. 4°. See 1745.
B. 8°. See 1745.

1745. The Holy Bible . . .

T. and R. Baskett: Oxford. 1744,45. 4°.

General title dated 1744; N. T. title (*T. Baskett* only) dated 1745. N. T. ends on O 4 a followed by Index and tables.

¶ 264 × 204 mm.
In three volumes, interleaved with writing paper containing many MS. notes.

811.

1745. The Holy Bible . . .

T. and R. Baskett: Oxford. 1745,44. 8°.

General title dated 1745; N. T. title (*T. and R. Baskett: London*) dated 1744. Text ends on Sss 8 a. Apocrypha mentioned in list of books, but not required by signatures.

¶ 174 × 106 mm.
Wants Apocrypha?

812.

1745. Mr. Whiston's Primitive New Testament. Part I. containing the Four Gospels, with the Acts of the Apostles. Part II. containing XIV. Epistles of Paul. Part III. containing VII. Catholick Epistles. Part IV. containing the Revelation of John.

Stamford and London: Printed for the Author, and sold by the Booksellers of London and Westminster. 1745. 8°.

An original version of the New Testament by William Whiston (1667-1752), the translator of Josephus, known also for his book entitled *Primitive Christianity Revived.*

In this edition the Gospels and Acts are translated from 'the MS. of Beza' in Cambridge University Library, the 'imperfections' being 'supplied from the vulgar Latin'; St. Paul's Epistles from 'the Clermont Manuscript . . . in the King of France's Library at Paris'; and the rest of the New Testament from 'the Greek Alexandrian MS. . . . in the King's Library at St. James's.'

General title (as above). Title to Pt. I; text, Matthew-Acts, A 1 to Z 3 a, with a note on verso. Title to Pt. II; text, Romans-Hebrews, A 2 to M 2 a. Title to Pts. III and IV;

text, James–Jude and Revelation, M 4 to R 2 *b*; followed by a note *Of the Resurrection of Jesus Christ* . . ., pp. 1 to 16, signed *William Whiston, July 23, 1744.*

On a leaf at the end is printed a notice of the remainder of the work: *Mr. Whiston's Primitive New Testament. Part V. containing the Epistle of the Corinthians to Paul, and his Answer, preserved by the Armenians. The Epistle of Timothy to Diognetus, and the Homily. With the two Epistles of Clement to the Corinthians. Part VI. containing the Constitutions of the Apostles, in VIII Books. Part VII. containing the Catholick Epistle of Barnabas. With the Shepherd of Hermas, in III. Books. Part VIII. containing the X. Epistles of Ignatius. The Epistle of Polycarp to the Philippians. Josephus's Homily concerning Hades. With the Martyrdom of Polycarp.* It is more than doubtful whether these additional parts of the work were ever published.

¶ 202 × 117 mm. [F. F.]

—— Another copy.

813.

1746. The Holy Bible . . .
Printed for John Grosse's Heir: Leipzig. 1746. 8°.

General title engraved, verso blank, 1 p. blank, list of books—1 p. Text: O. T., pp. 5 to 784; N. T., 239 pp. No Apocrypha.

¶ 207 × 127 mm. [F. F.]

814.

1746. B. 8°. See 1747.

1747. The Holy Bible . . .
T. Baskett and Assigns of R. Baskett: London. 1747,46. 8°.

General title dated 1747; N. T. title dated 1746. Text ends on Sss 8 *a*. Apocrypha mentioned in list of books, but not required by signatures.

¶ 176 × 105 mm.
Wants Apocrypha?
In two volumes. [F. F.]

815.

1747. The Holy Bible . . .
T. Baskett: Oxford. 1747. 4°.

Text ends on Llll 8 *b*, followed by Index and tables.

¶ 259 × 193 mm. [F. F.]

816.

1747. The Holy Bible . . .
J. Bentham: Cambridge. 1747. 12°.

Price *2s. 6d. unbound.*
Text ends on Mm 12 *b*. No Apocrypha. Tables after O. T.

¶ 161 × 96 mm.
In two volumes. [F. F.]

—— Another copy.

The general title bears the words *Price 2s. unbound.* N. T. title: . . . *and sold by Charles Bathurst in Fleet-street, London.*

817.

1747. The Holy Bible . . .
R. *Watkins, His Majesty's Printer: Edinburgh.* 1747. 12°.

With Canne's Preface and marginal matter.
Text ends on Ppp 7 a. No Apocrypha.

¶ 166 × 100 mm. [F. F.]
818.

1748. The Holy Bible . . .
T. Baskett and Assigns of R. Baskett : London. 1748. 8°.

Text ends on Sss 8 a. Apocrypha mentioned in list of books, but not required by signatures.

¶ 171 × 106 mm.
Wants Apocrypha ?
With Prayer Book (1746), and Metrical Psalms (1747).
819.

1749. The Holy Bible . . .
T. Baskett: Oxford. 1749. 4°.

N. T. ends on O 4 a, followed by Index and tables.

¶ 243 × 187 mm.
With Downame's Concordance (1745).
With Prayer Book (1749). [F. F.]
820.

1749. The New Testament . . .
T. Baskett and Assigns of R. Baskett : London. 1749. 12°.

Price One Shilling, Unbound.
Text ends on R 7 b.

¶ 150 × 87 mm. [F. F.]

——— Another copy.
With Prayer Book (1749), and Metrical Psalms (1750). [F. F.]
821.

[1749. The New Testament . . .
[Dublin ?] 1749. 12°.**]**

The first edition of Challoner's revision of the Rheims New Testament. See below, No. 825.

Pp. 500. See Cotton, *R. and D.*, pp. 228-9.

1750. The Holy Bible . . .
T. Baskett and Assigns of R. Baskett : London. 1750. 8°.

Text ends on Sss 8 a. The insertion of the Apocrypha interrupts the signatures.

¶ 169 × 107 mm. Wants one leaf.
With Prayer Book (? date), and Metrical Psalms (1749). [F. F.]
822.

ENGLISH 279

1750. The Holy Bible . . .
T. Baskett : Oxford. 1750. 12°.
Text ends on Qq 6 b. No Apocrypha.
¶ 126 × 65 mm.
With Prayer Book (1736), and Metrical Psalms (1750). [F. F.]

823.

1750. The Holy Bible, translated from the Latin Vulgat . . . first published by the English College at Doway, Anno 1609. Newly revised, and corrected, according to the Clementin Edition of the Scriptures. With annotations for clearing up the principal difficulties of Holy Writ . . .
[*Dublin?*] 1750. 12°. 4 vols.

This revision of the Douai Old Testament was the work of Richard Challoner. The last previous edition appeared in 1635.

R. Challoner, D.D. (1691–1781) was educated at Douai, where he held important offices. In 1730 he joined the 'London Mission,' subsequently becoming Bishop of Debra, and later Vicar Apostolic of the London District. He 'inaugurated a new era in English Catholic literature, and many of his publications are to this day regarded by his co-religionists as standard works of doctrine or devotion.'
The 'Clementin Edition of the Scriptures,' referred to in the title, is the authorised recension of the Vulgate published under the authority of Clement VIII in 1592. Challoner's alterations tended to simplify and to modernise the version, and in the process made it approximate more closely to King James' Bible. This revision was issued without any special 'Approbations.'
Challoner's corresponding revision of the Rheims New Testament had appeared in 1749. The two volumes of the third (1752) edition of that N. T. (see No. 829) are often added to the four volumes of this first (1750) edition of the O. T. in order to complete a uniform Bible.
Vol 1: title, with list on verso *The Order of the Books of the Old Testament, received by the Catholick Church* . . ., *Approbations of the old Edition*—1 f.; text (Genesis–Ruth), pp. 1 to 407 (really 507). Vol. 2: text (1 Sam.–Esther) with chronological table, 492 pp. Vol. 3: text (Job–Isaiah), with table of Psalms, 484 pp. Vol. 4: text (Jeremiah–2 Maccabees), with note at end explaining the omission of certain books—3 and 4 Maccabees, 3 and 4 Esdras, and the Prayer of Manasses—pp. 3 to 411 (really 511); list of *errata*, 1 p.
Text printed in double columns, with occasional foot-notes.

¶ 174 × 100 mm.
The 'Approbations' are placed before the title in vol. 1 in this copy.

——— Another copy.

Vols. 2 and 4 are misbound.

824.

1750. The New Testament . . . translated out of the Latin Vulgat . . . first published by the English College of Rhemes, Anno 1582. Newly revised, and corrected according to the Clementin Edition of the Scriptures. With Annotations . . .
[*Dublin?*] 1750. 12°.

The second edition of Challoner's revision of the Rheims New Testament, which appeared first in 1749.

For R. Challoner see note above, No. 824.
According to Cotton's careful collation (*R. and D.*, pp. 315–370), this differs but slightly from the first edition. It is not, however, as Cotton (p. 200) implies, the fifth volume of a Bible, of which Challoner's edition of the O. T. described above (see No. 824) forms four volumes, but a distinct publication.

Title, the Approbations of the editions of 1582 and 1600 on verso, *Approbations of this present edition* (dated 1748, and signed by *Gulielmus Green* and *Gulielmus Walton*)—1 p.; list of books—1 p.; text, 488 pp.; followed by table of Controversies, table of Epistles and Gospels, chronological table, and list of *errata*, ending on p. 500.

¶ 179 × 105 mm.

825.

1751. The Holy Bible . . .
  T. Baskett and Assigns of R. Baskett: London. 1751. 8°.

Text ends on Sss 8 *a*. Apocrypha mentioned in list of books, but not required by signatures.

¶ 172 × 107 mm.
Wants Apocrypha?
In one volumes.   [F. F.]

826.

1752. The Holy Bible . . .
            T. Baskett: Oxford. 1752. 4°.

Text ends on Llll 8 *b*, followed by Index and tables.

¶ 263 × 202 mm.
With Metrical Psalms (1746), and Prayer Book (1752).
Cover stamped *Portsmouth Lodge 1754*.

827.

1752. The Holy Bible . . .
  Adrian Watkins, His Majesty's Printer: Edinburgh. 1752. 4°.

Adrian Watkins succeeded R. Watkins in 1747; he died in 1766 (Lee, *Memorial*, p. 185 *n*). Text ends on Ggg 3 *b*, followed by 1 p. of tables, and 12 ff. containing Index and tables. The insertion of the Apocrypha interrupts the signatures.

¶ 245 × 191 mm.   [F. F.]

828.

1752. The New Testament . . . translated out of the Latin Vulgat . . . first published by the English College of Rhemes, anno 1582. Newly revised . . . With Annotations . . .
           [*Dublin?*] 1752. 12°. 2 vols.

The third edition of Challoner's revision of the Rheims New Testament, first published in 1749.

See above, Nos. 824 and 825. Cotton by careful collation (*R. and D.*, pp. 315-370) has shown that this edition differs in at least 2000 places from the first and second; yet no notice is given of this extensive further revision, and the Approbation of the 1749 edition is reprinted before the text.
 Vol. 1: title; Approbations (as in the 1750 edition)—2 pp.; list of books—1 p.; text (Matthew-Acts), 296 pp. Vol. 2: title, verso blank, text (Romans-Revelation), pp. 3 to 229; followed by tables ending on p. 239; list of *errata* —1 p.
 Neither of the two copies below contains the error in 1 John i. 5 which Cotton (p. 230) mentions.

¶ 174 × 100 mm.
In one volume.

—— Another copy.
In one volume.

829.

1752. B. 4°. See 1754.

1753. The Holy Bible . . .
    T. *Baskett and Assigns of R. Baskett : London.* 1753. 12°.

Price Two Shillings unbound.
Text ends on Mm 12 *b*. Apocrypha mentioned in list of books, but not required by signatures.
Matt. xxiii. 24, *strain out* (for *at*).

¶ 161 × 92 mm.
Wants Apocrypha? [F. F.]
830.

1754. The Holy Bible . . .
    G. Grierson : Dublin. 1752,54. 4°.

General title dated 1752; N. T. title dated 1754; N. T. ends on Cc 4 *b*.

¶ 249 × 199 mm. [F. F.]
831.

1754. The Holy Bible . . .
    T. Baskett : Oxford. 1754. 4°.

Text ends on Llll 8 *b*, followed by Index and tables.

¶ 271 × 213 mm.
With Downame's Concordance (1752).
With Prayer Book (1754), and Metrical Psalms (1754).
832.

1754. The Holy Bible . . .
    A. Watkins : Edinburgh. 1754. 8°.

With Canne's Preface and marginal matter.

Text ends on Nnn 6 *b*. No Apocrypha.

¶ 191 × 117 mm. [F. F.]
833.

1754. The Holy Bible . . .
    T. Baskett and Assigns of R. Baskett : London. 1754. 12°.

Price Two Shillings unbound.
Text ends on Mm 12 *b*. The insertion of the Apocrypha interrupts the signatures.
Matt. xxiii. 24, *strain out*.

¶ 158 × 93 mm.
With Metrical Psalms (1753).
In three volumes. [F. F.]
834.

1755. The Holy Bible . . .
    T. Baskett and Assigns of R. Baskett : London. 1755. 8°.

Price Three Shillings Unbound.
Text ends on Sss 8 *a*. The insertion of the Apocrypha interrupts the signatures.
Matt. xxiii. 24, *strain out*.

¶ 160 × 102 mm.
With Prayer-Book (? date), and Metrical Psalms (1754). [F. F.]
835.

1755. The Holy Bible . . .
  James Blow : Belfast ; for George Abraham Grierson :
                  Dublin. 1755. 12°.

Text ends on Kk 12 b. No Apocrypha.

¶ 156 × 90 mm. Apparently wants either a leaf before text (which begins on A 3), or a blank leaf before title.
With Scotch Metrical Psalms (n. d.).   [F. F.]
                            836.

1755. The New Testament . . . Adapted to the Capacities of Children. To which is added, an historical Account of the Lives . . . of the Apostles and Evangelists . . . With a Preface . . . Adorned with Cuts . . . *Printed for J. Newbery, at the Bible and Sun in St. Paul's Church-yard : London.* 1755. 12°.

A harmony of the Evangelists, with lives of the Apostles ' as much as possible set forth in the Words of the sacred Text.'

Printed for John Newbery (1713–1767), publisher and medicine-vendor in St. Paul's Churchyard, who was the first to make the issue of books specially intended for children an important branch of the publishing business. His 'Juvenile Library' included such classics of the nursery as 'Mrs. Margery Two Shoes' and 'Tommy Trip and his Dog Jowler.'
Title; Preface, pp. iii to xi; Advertisement. *The History and Harmony of the Evangelists*, pp. 1 to 174; *A Summary Account of the Life of St. Peter. Agreeable with the Sacred Text*, followed by the other Lives, pp. 175 to 288. The eight Cuts are described as 'designed by the celebrated Raphael, and engraved by Mr. Walker.'

¶ 151 × 85 mm.   [F. F.]
                            837.

1755. B. 12°. See 1756.

1756. The Holy Bible . . .
  T. Baskett and Assigns of R. Baskett : London. 1756,55. 12°.

Price Two Shillings unbound.
General title dated 1756 ; N. T. title dated 1755. Text ends on Mm 12 b. Apocrypha mentioned in list of books, but not required by signatures.

¶ 157 × 91 mm.
Wants Apocrypha ?
In two volumes.   [F. F.]
                            838.

1756. The Holy Bible . . .
         T. Baskett : Oxford. 1756. 4°.

N. T. ends on O 4 a, followed by Index and tables.

¶ 251 × 198 mm.
With Downame's Concordance (1752).
With Prayer Book (1755).
Inserted are a series of engravings, arranged four on a page, by *J. Cole*, and a few maps. An engraved title is inserted before the Prayer Book, and another before the Bible, bearing the name of *Richard Ware*, the bookseller of Ludgate Hill.
Binding stamped *John Jenkins 1766.*   [F. F.]
                            839.

1756. The Holy Bible . . .
           T. Baskett and Assigns of R. Baskett : London. 1756. 8°.

Price Three Shillings Unbound.
Text ends on Sss 8 a. Apocrypha mentioned in list of books, but not required by signatures.
Matt. xxiii. 24, *strain out*.

¶ 174 × 111 mm.
Wants Apocrypha?
With Metrical Psalms (1755), and Prayer Book (1756).
                                                                             840.

1756. The Holy Bible . . .
                      T. Baskett : Oxford. 1756. 12°.

Text ends on Qq 6 b. No Apocrypha.

¶ 128 × 69 mm.   [F. F.]
                                                                              841.

1757. The Holy Bible . . .
           T. Baskett and Assigns of R. Baskett : London. 1757. 8°.

Price Three Shillings Unbound.
Text ends on Sss 8 a. The insertion of the Apocrypha interrupts the signatures.
Matt. xxiii. 24, *strain out*.

¶ 171 × 108 mm.
With Metrical Psalms (1754), and Prayer Book (1756).
                                                                            842.

1758. The Holy Bible . . .
    Boulter Grierson, Printer to the King's most Excellent Majesty :
                                                             Dublin. 1758. 8°.

B. Grierson, who succeeded his father G. Grierson, obtained the office of Printer-General for Ireland in 1766 (Lee, *Memorial*, App. xxxix).
General title engraved. Text ends on Cccc 4 b. No Apocrypha.

¶ 213 × 131 mm.   [F. F.]

—— Another copy.

Differs slightly from the preceding. The Apocrypha are included in the list of books, though not required by the signatures and omitted from the volume.
                                                                             843.

1758. The Holy Bible . . .
      Alexander Kincaid, His Majesty's Printer : Edinburgh. 1758. 12°.

For Kincaid's commission, dated 1749, see Lee, *Memorial*, App. xxxii.
Text ends on Ggg 5 a, followed by 3 pp. of tables. No Apocrypha.

¶ 133 × 72 mm.
With Scotch Metrical Psalms (1758).   [F. F.]

—— Another copy.

With Scotch Metrical Psalms (1758).   [F. F.]
                                                                             844.

1759. The Holy Bible . . .
   T. Baskett, and Assigns of R. Baskett : London. 1759. f°.

Price One Pound Five Shillings Unbound.
N. T. ends on R 4 *b*, followed by 12 ff. containing Index and tables.
Matt. xxiii. 24, *strain out*.

¶ 388 × 256 mm.
With Prayer Book (1760), and Metrical Psalms (1763).

                    845.

1759. The Holy Bible . . .
   T. Baskett and Assigns of R. Baskett : London. 1759. 8°.

Price Three Shillings Unbound.
Text ends on Sss 8 *a*. Apocrypha mentioned in list of books, but not required by signatures.
Matt. xxiii. 24, *strain out*.

¶ 170 × 112 mm. Wants one leaf.
Wants Apocrypha?
With Prayer Book (1758), and Metrical Psalms (1758).   [F. F.]
                    846.

1759. The Holy Bible . . .
        J. Bentham : Cambridge. 1759. 12°.

Price 2s. unbound.
Sold also by *Benj. Dod, Bookseller in Ave-Mary Lane, London.*
Text ends on Mm 12 *b*. No Apocrypha. One page of tables after O. T.

¶ 162 × 95 mm.   [F. F.]
                    847.

    ACCESSION OF KING GEORGE III: 25 OCTOBER 1760.

1760. The Holy Bible . . .
        J. Bentham : Cambridge. 1760. 8°.

Price 4s. unbound. Sold by *B. Dod*, London.
Text ends on Vvv 2 *a*. Apocrypha mentioned in list of books, but not required by signatures. One page of tables after O. T., and another after N. T.

¶ 206 × 124 mm.
Wants Apocrypha?   [F. F.]
                    848.

1760. The Holy Bible . . .
        T. Baskett : Oxford. 1760. 12°.

Text ends on Qq 6 *b*. No Apocrypha.

¶ 129 × 68 mm.
In two volumes.   [F. F.]
                    849.

1761. The Holy Bible . . .
 T. Baskett: Oxford. 1761. 4°.

Additional general title engraved by *Mynde*. N. T. ends on S 4 b, followed by Index and tables.

¶ 273 × 222 mm. [F. F.]
850.

1761. The Holy Bible . . .
 T. Baskett and Assigns of R. Baskett: London. 1761. 8°.

Price Three Shillings Unbound.
Text ends on Sss 8 a. Apocrypha mentioned in list of books, but not required by signatures.
Matt. xxiii. 24, *strain out*.

¶ 171 × 112 mm.
Wants Apocrypha? [F. F.]
851.

1761. The Holy Bible . . .
 Mark Baskett, Printer to the King's most Excellent Majesty,
  and the Assigns of R. Baskett: London. 1761. 12°.

Text ends on Mm 12 b (?).
Matt. xxiii. 24, *strain out*.

¶ 159 × 100 mm. Imperfect, wanting general title and other leaves.
Wants Apocrypha? [F. F.]
852.

1761. The Holy Bible . . .
 J. Bentham: Cambridge. 1761. 12°

Price 2s. unbound.
Text ends on Mm 12 b. No Apocrypha. One leaf of tables after O. T.

¶ 160 × 96 mm. [F. F.
853.

1761. B. f°. See 1763.

Note on the earliest English Bible printed in America.

Under this date 1761, when we first meet with Mark Baskett's name, it is fitting to cite the following passages from Isaiah Thomas' *History of Printing in America* (published at Worcester, Massachusetts, in 1810), which bear upon the printing of the first English Bible in America:

'Kneeland and Green [of Boston] printed, principally for Daniel Henchman, an edition of the Bible in small 4to. This was the first Bible printed, in the English language, in America. It was carried through the press as privately as possible, and had the London imprint of the copy from which it was reprinted, viz. "London: Printed by Mark Baskett, Printer to the King's Most Excellent Majesty," in order to prevent a prosecution from those in England and Scotland, who published the Bible by a patent from the crown; or, *Cum privilegio*, as did the English universities of Oxford and Cambridge. When I was an apprentice, I often heard those who had assisted at the case and press in printing this Bible, make mention of the fact. The late governor Hancock was related to Henchman, and knew the particulars of the transaction. He possessed a copy of this impression. As it has a London imprint, at this day it can be distinguished from an English edition, of the same date, only by those who are acquainted with the niceties of typography. This Bible issued from the press about the time that the partnership of Kneeland and Green expired [i.e. in 1752]. The edition was not large; I have been informed that it did not exceed seven or eight hundred copies. Not long after the time that this impression of the Bible came from the press, an edition of the New Testament, in duodecimo, was printed by Rogers and Fowle, for those, at whose expense the Bible issued. Both the Bible and the Testament were well executed. These were heavy undertakings for that day, but Henchman was a man of property; and, it is said, that several other principal booksellers, in Boston, were concerned with him in this business. The credit of this edition of the Testament was, for the reason I have mentioned, transferred to the king's printer, in London, by the insertion of his imprint.' (Vol. i, pp. 305-6.)

'During the partnership of Rogers and Fowle, they printed an edition of about two thousand copies of the New Testament, 12mo. for D. Henchman and two or three other principal booksellers, as has been already observed. This impression of the Testament, the first in the English language printed in this country, was, as I have been informed, completed at the press, before Kneeland and Green began the edition of the Bible which has been mentioned. Zechariah Fowle, with whom I served my apprenticeship, as well as several others, repeatedly mentioned to me this edition of the Testament. He was, at the time, a journeyman with Rogers and Fowle, and worked at the press. He informed me, that on account of the weakness of his constitution, he greatly injured his health by the performance. Privacy in the business was necessary; and as few hands were intrusted with the secret, the press work was, as he thought, very laborious. I mention these minute circumstances in proof that an edition of the Testament did issue from the office of Rogers and Fowle, because I have heard that the fact has been disputed.' (Pp. 324-5.)

In spite of the explicit character of these statements, their accuracy has been questioned by more than one writer. They are based on second-hand information, they are not wholly consistent, and they are directly contradicted by other evidence. Bancroft in his *History of the United States* (11th ed., vol. v, p. 266) refuses them credit till a copy of the actual book has been found. For similar reasons E. B. O'Callaghan declines to admit the editions mentioned by Thomas into his *List of editions of the Holy Scriptures and parts thereof, printed in America previous to 1860* . . . (Albany, 1861). Cf. J. Wright's *Early Bibles of America* (New York, 1892). It may be noted further that Mark Baskett's name does not occur on the titlepage of any Bible or Testament before 1761; and, when it does occur, in the case of *London* editions it is joined with the 'Assigns of Robert Baskett.' The truth seems to be that, in spite of more than one attempt made by Cotton Mather, and again by John Fleming, a printer of Boston, and possibly by others, to get an English Bible printed in their own country, America before the War of Independence was supplied with English Scriptures solely from abroad. Great numbers must have been imported from Great Britain during the seventeenth and eighteenth centuries.

To this day, no English Bibles are printed in the Colonies; and the only copies of King James' version which can be legally sold there are those which have been printed in Great Britain.

The earliest English New Testament, avowedly printed in America, was issued by R. Aitken of Philadelphia, in 1777. The complete Bible was first published by the same printer in 1782,81. The B. M. copy (C. 51. b. 7) contains a note in Aitken's writing which certifies it to be the 'first copy of the first edition of the Bible ever printed in America in the English language.' Both editions were of King James' version.

1762. The Holy Bible . . .

J. Bentham : Cambridge. 1762. 4°.

The 'standard' edition prepared by Dr. Thomas Paris, of Trinity College, Cambridge. In this Bible a serious attempt was made to correct the text of King James' version by amending the spelling and punctuation, unifying and extending the use of italics, and removing printers' errors. Marginal annotations, which had been growing in some Bibles since 1660, although excluded from others, were finally received into the place they have occupied ever since, sundry new ones being added. Lloyd's dates and chronological notes (see No. 678) were also adopted and increased, and the marginal references were much enlarged. Cf. Scrivener, *The Authorized Edition* . . ., 1884.

' Sold by *Benjamin Dod*, Bookseller, at the Bible and Key, in Ave-Mary Lane, near St. Paul's, London.'
Engraved frontispiece. Text ends on Xxx 6 *b*, followed by Index and tables, ending on Zzz 4 *b*. The insertion of the Apocrypha (A to M) interrupts the signatures.
In 1 Tim. iv. 16 the incorrect rendering *thy doctrine* is retained.

¶ 272 × 222 mm.
With Prayer Book (1762), and Metrical Psalms (1762).　　　　　　　　　　　[F. F.]

—— Another copy.

—— Another copy.　L. P.
In two volumes; with a separate title to vol. 2.　　　　　　　　　　　　　[F. F.]
854.

[A folio edition of this Bible was also printed in the same year, but copies are very scarce; it is said that only six survived a fire at Dod's warehouse. The B. M. possesses a copy.]

1762. The Holy Bible . . .
　　　　　　　　　　　T. Baskett: Oxford. 1762. 12°.

N. T. title bears the name of *M. Baskett*, as *Printer to the University.* Text ends on Qq 6 *b*. No Apocrypha.

¶ 130 × 68 mm.　　　　　　　　　　　　　　　　　　　　　　　　　　[F. F.]
855.

1762.　B.　f°.　See 1763.
*　　　B.　4°.　See 1769.*

1763. An Exposition on the Old and New Testament . . . by Matthew Henry . .
　　　　For J. Knapton, and others: London. 1761,62,63. f°. 5 vols.

The fifth edition. With portrait by *Geo: Vertue.* See above, No. 720, 1712.

¶ 403 × 250 mm.
856.

1763. The Holy Bible . . .
　　　John Baskerville, Printer to the University: Cambridge. 1763. f°.

This edition ' has always been regarded as Baskerville's *magnum opus*, and is his most magnificent as well as his most characteristic specimen' (T. B. Reed, *A History of the Old English Letter Foundries* . . ., p. 279). Baskerville's name also appears on editions published in 1760, 1769, and 1772.

Text ends on 13 E 1 *a*, followed by Index and tables. The matter usually printed in the margin is placed at the foot of the page.

¶ 483 × 308 mm.
A List of Subscribers is inserted before the text, together with a specimen leaf of another edition.

857.

1763. The Holy Bible . . .
M. Baskett and Assigns of R. Baskett : London. 1763. 12°.

Price Two Shillings unbound.
Text ends on Mm 12 b. Apocrypha mentioned in list of books, but not required by signatures.
Matt. xxiii. 24, *strain out.*

¶ 159 × 92 mm. Wants leaf after general title.
Wants Apocrypha?

858.

1763. B. 12°. See 1764.

1764. The Holy Bible . . .
M. Baskett and Assigns of R. Baskett : London. 1763,64. 12°.

Price Two Shillings unbound.
General title dated 1763; N. T. title dated 1764. Text ends on Mm 12 b. Apocrypha mentioned in list of books, but not required by signatures.
Matt. xxiii. 24, *strain out.*

¶ 167 × 94 mm.
Wants Apocrypha? [F. F.]

—— Another copy.

Differs slightly in one or two sheets. Perhaps a mixed copy.
Imperfect: wanting general title, and last leaf.
Wants Apocrypha? [F. F.]

859.

1764. The Holy Bible . . .
M. Baskett : Oxford. 1764. 8°.

General title engraved by *Mynde.* Text ends on Cccc 4 b. No Apocrypha.

¶ 210 × 133 mm.
With Prayer Book (1766), and Metrical Psalms (1767). [F. F.]

—— Another copy.
Wants leaf after general title. [F. F.]

860.

1764. The Holy Bible . . .
A. Kincaid : Edinburgh. 1764. 12°.

Text ends on Fff 4 a, followed by 3 pp. of tables. Apocrypha mentioned in list of books, but not required by signatures.

¶ 129 × 73 mm.
With Scotch Metrical Psalms (1758). [F. F.]

—— Another copy.
With Scotch Metrical Psalms (1764). [F. F.]

861.

1764. A new and literal translation of all the books of the Old and New Testament; with notes, critical and explanatory. By Anthony Purver . . .
Printed by W. Richardson and S. Clark ; and sold by William Johnston in Ludgate-Street : London. 1764. f°. 2 vols.

An original version, by a member of the Society of Friends, who is said to have spent 30 years in its preparation.

ENGLISH

For a notice of his life see the Editor's Preface to Bishop Wilson's Bible, 1785 (No. 937). Purver (1702–1777) began his translation about 1733. A portion of it was published in parts about 1742 by Felix Farley, the Bristol printer; but it received little support. Subsequently, in 1763, Dr. John Fothergill gave Purver £1000 for the copyright, and published the complete version at his own expense.

Vol. 1: title; *Introductory remarks on Translations of the Scripture* . . ., pp i to xvi; Appendix, pp. xvii to xxx; *Errata*, pp. xxxi to xxxviii. Text, Genesis–Psalms, pp. 1 to 745. Vol. 2: title; text, Proverbs–Malachi, pp. 1 to 334; *Additional remarks* . . . and Appendix, pp. i to viii; text, N. T., pp. 1 to 339. No Apocrypha. Notes printed at the foot of the page.

¶ 357 × 230 mm. [F. F.]

—— Another copy.

With the *Additional Remarks* . . . and Appendix misplaced after the title in vol. 2.

862.

1764. The New Testament . . .
　　　　　　　　　　　　　　　M. Baskett : Oxford. 1764. 8°.

Text ends on Gg 4 b. Names of books and chapter-numbers in headlines in black-letter.

¶ 196 × 120 mm. [F. F.]

863.

1764. The New Testament: carefully collated with the Greek, and corrected; divided and pointed according to the various subjects treated of by the inspired writers, with the common division into chapters and verses in the margin; and illustrated with notes . . . By Richard Wynne, A.M. . . . *Printed for R. and J. Dodsley in Pall-Mall :*
　　　　　　　　　　　　　　　　London. 1764. 8°. 2 vols.

An original version of the New Testament by R. Wynne, 'Rector of St. Alphage, London,' in which he endeavoured 'to steer in a just medium between a servile literal translation, and a paraphrastic loose version; between low, obsolete, and obscure language, and a modern enervated stile.'

Vol. 1: title; Preface, table, etc., pp. iii to xviii; text, Matthew–John, pp. 1 to 489. Vol. 2: title; table, pp. iii to vi; text, Acts–Revelation, pp. 1 to 530. Short notes at the foot of the page, many of which are taken from Doddridge's *Family Expositor*.

¶ 201 × 121 mm.

864.

1765. The Holy Bible . . .
　　　　M. Baskett and Assigns of R. Baskett : London. 1765. 8°.

Price *Three Shillings Unbound.*
Text ends on Sss 8 a. Apocrypha mentioned in list of books, but not required by signatures.
Matt. xxiii. 24, *strain out.*

¶ 179 × 113 mm.
Wants Apocrypha? [F. F.]

865.

1765. The Holy Bible . . .
　　　　　　　　　　　J. Bentham : Cambridge. 1765. 8°.

Price *4s. unbound.* Sold by *B. Dod*, London.
Text ends on Vvv 2 a. The insertion of the Apocrypha interrupts the signatures. One page of tables at end of O. T., and another at end of N. T.

¶ 195 × 120 mm.
With Prayer Book (1760), and Metrical Psalms (1760).

—— Another copy.
Wants general title. Apocrypha omitted.

866.

1765. The Holy Bible . . .
J. Bentham: Cambridge. 1765. 12°.

Sold by *John Beecroft, John Rivington, James Waugh, Benjamin White,* and *Edward Dilly,* in London; and by *T. and J. Merrill,* in Cambridge.
Text ends on Mm 12 b. No Apocrypha. One page of tables after O. T.

¶ 164 × 98 mm. Slightly imperfect. [F. F.]

867.

1765. (The Holy Bible.)
Printed by and for Daniel Blow: Belfast; and for
Boulter Grierson: Dublin. 1765. 12°.

Text ends on Ggg 5 a, followed by 3 pp. of tables.

¶ 132 × 72 mm. Imperfect: containing the N. T. only. [F. F.]

868.

1765. The New Testament . . .
M. Baskett: Oxford. 1765. 12°.

Text ends on O 4 a. No list of books, so this may possibly be part of a complete Bible; the signatures, however, begin with A.

¶ 132 × 68 mm.

869.

1765. A new translation of the New Testament . . . extracted from the paraphrase of the late Philip Doddridge, D.D. and carefully revised. With an introduction and notes.
For J. Rivington, W. Johnston, R. Baldwin, and C. Rivington:
London. 1765. 12°. 2 vols.

Doddridge (1702-1751), the celebrated Independent divine and hymn-writer, of Northampton, compiled a New Testament commentary with a paraphrase, published in six volumes between 1739 and 1756, under the title of 'The Family Expositor,' from which this translation was extracted.

Vol. 1 contains *The confession of a freethinker* (i.e. J. J. Rousseau), Preface, Introduction, and the text of the Four Gospels, ending on N 5 a. Vol. 2 contains the rest of the text, Acts–Revelation, ending on Q 2 b.

¶ 166 × 95 mm.

870.

1766. The Holy Bible . . .
M. Baskett and Assigns of R. Baskett: London. 1766. 4°.

N. T. ends on O 4 a, followed by Index and tables.
Matt. xxiii. 24, *strain out.*

¶ 246 × 202.

871.

1766. The Holy Bible . . .
  M. Baskett and Assigns of R. Baskett : London. 1766. 8°.

Price Three Shillings Unbound.
Text ends on Sss 8 a. Apocrypha mentioned in list of books, but not required by signatures.
Matt. xxiii. 24, *strain out.*

¶ 173 × 110 mm.
Wants Apocrypha? [F. F.]

872.

1766. (The Holy Bible.)
  A. Kincaid : Edinburgh. 1766. 12°.

Text ends on Mm 12 b (?). Apocrypha mentioned in list of books, but not required by signatures.

¶ 156 × 95 mm. Imperfect: wanting general title, and some other leaves.
Wants Apocrypha?
With Scotch Metrical Psalms (? date).
This copy formerly belonged to Jesse Sidwell, a private in the 3rd regiment of Foot Guards, who was wounded and taken prisoner at the battle of Talavera (1809). He seems to have bought this tattered copy at Verdun for 7s. 3½d. from a fellow-prisoner, who had supplied the missing portion of the text in manuscript. Sidwell's autograph appears on the fly-leaf, dated *January the 1st 1813. Briançon Prison, France.* On his release in 1814 he exchanged the book for a fresh copy obtained from the Bible Society, and carried the latter with him to Brussels in 1815, when the Waterloo campaign began.

873.

1766. B. 12°. See *1767 and 1796.*

1767. The Holy Bible . . .
  A. Kincaid : Edinburgh. 1766,67. 12°.

With Canne's Preface and marginal matter.

Titles dated 1766; colophon dated 1767. Text ends on Hh 3 a; followed by 7 pp. of tables, and the Scotch Metrical Psalms, ending on Ii 12 b, with colophon. The Metrical Psalms have no separate titleleaf and the signatures run on. Apocrypha mentioned in list of books, but not required by signatures.
See No. 968.

¶ 175 × 102 mm.
Wants Apocrypha? [F. F.]

—— Another copy.

Wants one leaf in text (Z 10), and the Metrical Psalms.
Wants Apocrypha? [F. F.]

—— Another copy.

Wants general title, and the Metrical Psalms.
Wants Apocrypha?

874.

1767. The Holy Bible . . .
  M. Baskett and Assigns of R. Baskett : London. 1767. 4°.

Additional general title engraved by *Mynde.* N. T. ends on S 4 b, followed by Index and tables.

¶ 274 × 222 mm.

—— Another copy. L. P.
In two volumes. [F. F.]
875.

1767. The Holy Bible . . .
   M. Baskett and Assigns of R. Baskett: London. 1767. 8°.

Price Three Shillings Unbound.
Text ends on Sss 8 a. The insertion of the Apocrypha interrupts the signatures.
Matt. xxiii. 24, *strain out*.

¶ 171 × 108 mm. [F. F.]
876.

1767. The Holy Bible . . .
   John Archdeacon, Printer to the University: Cambridge. 1767. 8°.

Price 3s. unbound. Sold by *J. Beecroft, J. Rivington, B. White*, and *E. Dilly*, in London; and *T. and J. Merrill*, in Cambridge.
Text ends on Sss 6 a. Apocrypha mentioned in list of books, but not required by signatures. One page of tables at end of O. T., and another at end of N. T.

¶ 173 × 110 mm.
Wants Apocrypha? [F. F.]
877.

1767. (The Holy Bible.)
   A. Kincaid: Edinburgh. 1767. 12°.

Text ends on Fff 4 a; followed by 3 pp. of tables, and the Scotch Metrical Psalms. The Psalms form part of the book, since the signatures run on, the titleleaf (dated 1767) being Ggg 1. Apocrypha mentioned in list of books, but not required by signatures.

¶ 133 × 73 mm. Imperfect: wanting general title and other leaves.
Wants Apocrypha? [F. F.]
878.

1767. The Family Testament, and Scholar's Assistant: calculated not only to promote the reading of the Holy Scriptures in families and schools, but also to remove that great uneasiness observable in children upon the appearance of hard words in their lessons, by a method entirely new . . . With an Introductory Preface, by the Reverend Mr. Joseph Brown. The second edition, carefully corrected.
   London: Printed for T. Luckman, near the Cross, Coventry; and sold by Messrs. Johnson and Co. in Pater-noster-Row, London; C. Etherington, in York; T. Lesson, in Doncaster; etc. 1767. 12°.

First published in 1766.
This Child's book contains (1) *An introduction to spelling and reading in general . . . and directions for reading with elegance and propriety*; (2) . . . *an alphabetical table of all the proper names of persons and places . . . with the meaning . . . of each* . . . ; (3) *Proper names, and other hard words . . . ranged in columns of spelling at the head of every chapter . . . properly divided and accented* . . . ; (4) . . . *a collection of short and useful notes* . . .
Preliminary matter, xxiv pp. The complete text of the New Testament (printed in double columns with short notes at the foot of some pages), C 1 to Qq 5 b; followed by a leaf containing a list of *New books lately published by T. Luckman, in Coventry*.
See also Nos. 990 and 1009.

¶ 172 × 101 mm. [F. F.]
879.

1767. B. 4°. See 1768.

1768. The Holy Bible . . .
M. Baskett and Assigns of R. Baskett: London. 1768,67. 4°.

General title dated 1768 ; N. T. title dated 1767. N. T. ends on O 4 a, followed by Index and tables.
Matt. xxiii. 24, *strain out*.

¶ 261 × 200 mm. [F. F
880.

1768. The Holy Bible . . .
J. Archdeacon: Cambridge. 1768. 4°.

Sold by *J. Beecroft*, etc.
Engraved frontispiece. Text ends on Xxx 6 b, followed by Index and tables. The insertion of the Apocrypha interrupts the signatures.

¶ 278 × 221 mm.
With Prayer Book (1762), and Metrical Psalms (1762). [F. F.]
881.

1768. The Holy Bible . . .
T. Wright and W. Gill, Printers to the University:
Oxford. 1768. 4°.

Sold by *J. Newbery, R. Baldwin, S. Crowder*, and *J. Coote*, London; and by *W. Jackson*, Oxford.
Text ends on O 4 a, followed by Index and tables.

¶ 249 × 203 mm. [F. F.]
882.

1768. The Holy Bible . . .
B. Grierson: Dublin. 1768. 8°.

Text ends on Ooo 3 b. Apocrypha mentioned in list of books, but not required by signatures.

¶ 191 × 119 mm.
Wants Apocrypha ? [F. F.]
883.

1768. B. 4°. See 1769.

1769. The Complete Family Bible . . . With notes . . . By the Rev. Francis Fawkes . . .
For J. Cooke, at Shakespear's Head, No. 10, Pater-noster-Row:
London. 1768,62,69. 4°. 2 vols.

Fawkes (1720–1777), poet and divine, was at this time vicar of Orpington and St. Mary Cray in Kent. The 'Complete Family Bible' bearing his name was first published in 1761,62. 'To this production, which came out in sixty weekly numbers, he sold his name for money, and his name possessed sufficient value in the book-world to justify an edition in 1765 " with notes taken from Fawkes." '

The general title in vol. 1 is dated 1768. The title to vol. 2, and that to the Apocrypha, are dated 1762, and state that the book was printed for the author, and sold by *J. Fletcher* and others. The N. T. title is dated 1769.

Text: O. T., B 1 to 14 P 2 a; Apocrypha, 19 E 1 to 21 Y 2 b; N. T., 14 Q 2 to 19 D 2 a. Notes at the foot of the page. With indexes, map, and many full-page engravings. Some commendatory verses precede the text in vol. 1; and other verses are printed after the Apocrypha, and after the N. T.

¶ 270 × 207 mm.
Apparently the portions of this copy which are dated 1762 belong to the first issue; and the Apocrypha should be placed after the N. T.

884.

1769. The Holy Bible . . .
T. Wright and W. Gill: Oxford. 1769. f°.

The Oxford 'standard' edition, carefully revised by Dr. Benjamin Blayney of Hertford College, following the lines of Dr. Paris' Cambridge edition of 1762 (No. 854). Blayney quietly incorporated most of Paris' improvements, increased his marginalia, and repeated not a few of his errors.

For a critical examination of the work of these two editors, Paris and Blayney, 'the great modernizers of the diction of the version, from what it was left in the seventeenth century, to the state wherein it appears in modern Bibles,' see Scrivener, *The Authorized Edition* . . . (1884), pp. 28–35. In an appendix Scrivener reprints from the *Gentleman's Magazine*, vol. xxxix, p. 517, Blayney's Report submitted to the Vice-Chancellor and the other Delegates of the Clarendon Press 25 Oct. 1769.

Sold by *R. Baldwin* and *S. Crowder*, in Paternoster Row, London; and by *W. Jackson*, Oxford.

With Translators' Preface. Text ends on 9 Z 2 b, followed by Index and tables ending on 10 E 2 b. The insertion of the Apocrypha interrupts the signatures.

Contains many misprints, probably more than 'the commonly estimated number of 116' (Scrivener, p. 31). In Rev. xviii. 22 a whole clause *and no craftsman* . . . is omitted. Cotton (p. 98, n.) errs in stating that this omission occurs only in the quarto (No. 887). In 1 Tim. iv. 16 *thy* is corrected to *the*.

Copies of this folio are scarce, owing to the destruction of a large part of the impression by a fire in the warehouse in London (cf. the *Gentleman's Magazine, l.c.*).

¶ 413 × 252 mm.   [F. F.]

885.

1769. The Holy Bible . . .
J. Archdeacon: Cambridge. 1769. 4°.

Sold by *J. Beecroft*, etc.
N. T. ends on M 7 b, followed by Index and tables, ending on R 2 b.

¶ 257 × 203 mm.   [F. F.]

—— Another copy.

886.

1769. The Holy Bible . . .
T. Wright and W. Gill: Oxford. 1769. 4°.

A quarto edition of Dr. Blayney's 'standard' Bible, issued in folio in the same year (see No. 885). According to the editor's Report the quarto was finished first, the folio being afterwards printed from the same type, differently disposed.

Sold by *R. Baldwin*, etc.
With Translators' Preface. Text ends on 6 V 2 b, followed by Index and tables ending on 6 Z 3 b. The insertion of the Apocrypha interrupts the signatures.
In Rev. xviii. 22 the clause *and no craftsman* . . . is omitted.

¶ 275 × 219 mm.   [F. F.]

—— Another copy.

A MS. note by Josiah Pratt states that 'a great part of the folio edition of 1769 having been destroyed at Woodmason's fire, a copy of that edition is scarcely to be purchased at any

price. A copy of this edition is also very rarely to be met with; sometimes it may be found with a New Testament of later date substituted for that of 1769' (see below, No. 899, 1772).
Contains a MS. copy of Dr. Blayney's Report.

887.

1769. The Holy Bible . . .
      T. Wright and W. Gill: Oxford. 1769. 8°.

Price Three Shillings unbound. Sold by *R. Baldwin*, etc.
Text ends on Sss 6 *a*. Apocrypha mentioned in list of books, but not required by signatures. One page of tables after O. T., and another after N. T.

¶ 175 × 113 mm. Wants general title, and last leaf.
Wants Apocrypha?   [F. F.]

888.

1769. The Holy Bible . . .
      J. Archdeacon: Cambridge. 1769. 12°.

Sold by *J. Beecroft*, etc.
Text ends on Fff 3 *b*, followed by 3 ff. containing the *History of the Bible Epitomized*, and a table. No Apocrypha.

¶ 134 × 71 mm.
In two volumes.   [F. F.]

889.

1769. The New Testament . . .
    M. Baskett and Assigns of R. Baskett: London. 1769. 8°

Price One Shilling and Eight Pence Unbound.
Text ends on Gg 4 *b*. Names of books and chapter-numbers in headlines in black-letter.
Matt. xxiii. 24, *strain out*.

¶ 200 × 123 mm.

890.

1769. The New Testament . . .
      J. Archdeacon: Cambridge. 1769. 12°.

Sold by *J. Beecroft*, etc.
Text ends on N 3 *b*, followed by one leaf, containing the *History of the New Testament Epitomized*.

¶ 129 × 68 mm.   [F. F.]

891.

1769. B. *f°*. *See 1770.*
    B. *4°*. *See 1772.*

1770. An Illustration of the Holy Bible, containing the Sacred Texts of the Old Testament, and the New; together with the Apocrypha. The Notes are carefully selected from the most eminent Commentators.
      N. Boden and O. Adams: Birmingham. 1769,70. f°.

General title dated 1769; titles to Apocrypha and N. T. (*Printed at the Verulam Press, by N. Boden and T. Appleby*) dated 1770. N. T. ends on 3 S 3 *b*, followed by chronological Index.

¶ 408 × 262 mm.

892.

1770. The Holy Bible . . .
       T. Wright and W. Gill : Oxford. 1770. 8°.

Sold by *R. Baldwin*, etc.
Text ends on Sss 6 *a*. The insertion of the Apocrypha interrupts the signatures. One page of tables after O. T., and another after N. T.

¶ 211 × 131 mm.   [F. F.]
                               893.

1770. The Holy Bible . . .
       J. Archdeacon : Cambridge. 1770. 12°.

Price 2s. unbound. Sold by *J. Beecroft*, etc.
Text ends on Mm 12 *b*. No Apocrypha. One page of tables after O. T.

¶ 162 × 100 mm. Wants one leaf.   [F. F.]
                               894.

1770. The New Testament or New Covenant . . . Translated from the Greek according to the present idiom of the English tongue. With notes and references . . . By the late Mr. John Worsley . . .
   Printed by R. Hett ; sold by T. Cadell, etc. : London. 1770. 8°.

An original version by J. Worsley (d. 1767), who was for fifty years a successful schoolmaster at Hereford. Published after his death by subscription, and edited by his son, Samuel Worsley, and Matthew Bradshaw.

Preliminary matter includes Editors' Preface, Author's Advertisement, list of Subscribers, etc. Text, B 1 to Ii 3 *b*. The foot-notes on each page refer almost entirely to the rendering of the Greek. Obsolete words and phrases are altered. Among peculiarities of spelling may be noticed *-or* for *-our* as a termination, except in verbs ; *lest* for *least*, and *least* for *lest*, etc.

¶ 208 × 127 mm.
                               895.

1770. B. 8°. See 1771.

1771. The Holy Bible.
       T. Wright and W. Gill : Oxford. 1771,70. 8°.

Price Three Shillings unbound. Sold by *S. Crowder*, London, and *W. Jackson*, Oxford. General title dated 1771 ; N. T. title dated 1770. Text ends on Sss 6 *a*. The insertion of the Apocrypha interrupts the signatures. One page of tables after O. T., and another after N. T.

¶ 180 × 115 mm.   [F. F.
                               896.

1771. The New Testament.
       B. Grierson : Dublin. 1771. 12°.

Text ends on T 12 *b*. Double columns.

¶ 171 × 103 mm.   [F. F.]
                               897.

1771 ? The Complete Family Bible . . . With . . . notes . . . By . . . Samuel Newton . . .
Printed for the author by Brewman and Co. ; sold by T. Evans, etc. : London. [1771 ?] f°.

The editor is described as rector of Clifton.

O. T. and Apocrypha, 557 pp. ; N. T., not paged, ends on Ii 2 a. With many full-page engravings, including a portrait of the King as frontispiece.

¶ 363 × 228 mm.
The B. M. Catalogue mentions two copies, one dated 1771, the other with the undated title-page found in this copy,—possibly a slightly later issue.

898.

1772. The Holy Bible . . .
T. Wright and W. Gill : Oxford. 1769,72. 4°.

Sold by *R. Baldwin*, etc.
General title dated 1769 ; N. T. title dated 1772. With Translators' Preface. N. T. ends on 6 V 2 b, followed by Index and tables. The insertion of the Apocrypha interrupts the signatures.
A clause is omitted in Rev. xviii. 22. See No. 885.

¶ 280 × 226 mm.
Apparently some copies were issued in this mixed state. See note above, No. 887, 1769.

899.

1772. The Holy Bible . . .
Charles Eyre and William Strahan, Printers to the King's most Excellent Majesty : London. 1772. 4°.

The last thirty years of Baskett's patent (see No. 706) ' were conveyed to Charles Eyre and his heirs for 10,000*l*. Eyre took possession of his reversion in 1769, and assumed William Strahan as his partner.' A new patent was granted in 1799 to George Eyre, Andrew Strahan, and John Reeves. This was subsequently renewed, and has come in course of time into the hands of its present holders, Messrs. Eyre and Spottiswoode. (See Lee, *Memorial*, p. 179 *n.*, and App. xxxiv.)

N. T. ends on Aa 3 b, followed by Index and tables.

¶ 263 × 209 mm.

900.

1772. The Holy Bible . . .
T. Wright and W. Gill : Oxford. 1772. 4°.

Sold by *S. Crowder*, London, and *W. Jackson*, Oxford.
With Translators' Preface. N. T. ends on 6 V 2 b, followed by Index and tables. The insertion of the Apocrypha interrupts the signatures.
A clause is omitted in Rev. xviii. 22. See No. 885.

¶ 287 × 220 mm.
In two volumes, with separate title to vol. 2. [F. F.]

—— Another copy. L. P.

In two volumes, with separate title to vol. 2.
Contains a series of engravings, dedicated to King George III, the Bishops, and the Clergy and Congregations of various counties, by *F. Willoughby*. [F. F.]

901.

1772. The Holy Bible . . .
       T. Wright and W. Gill: Oxford. 1772. 8°.

Sold by *S. Crowder*, London, and *W. Jackson*, Oxford.
Text ends on Cccc 4 *b*. Apocrypha with separate register.

¶ 214 × 134 mm.
Apocrypha placed after N. T.
With Tate and Brady's Metrical Psalms (1773).
In two volumes.   [F. F.]
                           902.

1772. The New Testament . . . translated out of the Latin Vulgat . . . first published by the English College of Rhemes, anno 1582. Newly revised . . . With Annotations . . .
       [*For J. P. Coghlan* :] *London.* 1772. 12°.

The fifth edition of Challoner's revision of the Rheims New Testament, first published in 1749. See Nos. 824 and 825.

According to Cotton (*R. and D.*, pp. 231-2), this is a reprint of the fourth edition issued in 1764. Some copies have a title bearing the words 'Printed for J. P. Coghlan, 1772,' and a second title with a list of books on verso.
Title (with small engraving of the Crucifixion), verso blank, Approbations—1 f.; text, 523 pp.; followed by tables, which end on p. 533; list of *errata*—1 p.

¶ 171 × 101 mm.   [F. F.]
                           903.

1773. The Holy Bible . . .
       J. Archdeacon: Cambridge. 1773. 8°.

Sold by *J. Beecroft*, etc.
Text ends on Vvv 2 *a*. The insertion of the Apocrypha interrupts the signatures. One page of tables after O. T., and another after N. T.

¶ 214 × 143 mm.   [F. F.]
                           904.

1773. The Holy Bible . . .
       T. Wright and W. Gill: Oxford. 1773. 8°.

Price Three Shillings unbound. Sold by *S. Crowder*, etc.
Text ends on Sss 6 *a*. Apocrypha mentioned in list of books, but not required by signatures. One page of tables after O. T., and another after N. T.

¶ 182 × 117 mm.
Wants Apocrypha?   [F. F.]
                           905.

1773. The Holy Bible . . .
       J. Archdeacon: Cambridge. 1773. 12°.

Price 2s. unbound. Sold by *J. Beecroft*, etc.
Text ends on Mm 12 *b*. No Apocrypha. One page of tables after O. T.

¶ 162 × 97 mm.   [F. F.]
                           906.

1773. The Book of Job, in English verse, translated from the original Hebrew; with remarks . . . By Thomas Scott. The second edition . . . *Printed for James Buckland, at the Buck in Pater-noster-Row : London.* 1773. 8°.

Scott (1705–1775) was a hymn-writer and Nonconformist minister. His metrical version of Job first appeared in 1771.

Engraved frontispiece. Pp. vii, 442. With footnotes.

¶ 219 × 129 mm.

907.

1773? The Universal Family Bible: or Christian's Divine Library . . . Illustrated with notes . . . by . . . Henry Southwell . . . *For J. Cooke : London.* [1773?] f°.

H. Southwell, LL.D., rector of Asterby, Lincolnshire, lent his name to this work for a fee of a hundred guineas. The real compiler was Robert Sanders (1727–1783), a hack-writer with a fair knowledge of Hebrew and Greek, who received twenty-five shillings a sheet for his work.

The B.M. Catalogue places this Bible under the date 1773; the D. N. B. states that it was first published in numbers, and then reissued in two folio volumes in 1774.
N. T. title gives the publisher's name as *J. Cooke.* Text ends on 11 Y 1 *b*; the Apocrypha have a separate register. The book is 'embellished with one hundred elegant copperplates executed from original designs, and capital foreign paintings.' With tables, indexes, etc.

¶ 375 × 236 mm.

908.

1774. The Holy Bible . . . *T. Wright and W. Gill : Oxford.* 1774. 8°.

Sold by *S. Crowder*, London, and *W. Jackson*, Oxford.
Text ends on 8ss 6 *a*. Apocrypha mentioned in list of books, but not required by signatures. One page of tables after O. T., and another after N. T.

¶ 201 × 123 mm.
Wants Apocrypha ?

[F. F.]
909.

1774. The Holy Family Bible . . . With concise explanatory notes . . . wherein the objections of Infidels are obviated, and the obscure passages explained to the meanest capacity . . . By the Reverend Alexander Fortescu, D.D., Rector of Stretton.
Winchester : Printed for the proprietor by John Wilkes, and sold by him, and William Harris, in Saint Paul's Church Yard, London. 1774. 8°.

Text, A 3 to 4 R 6 *a*; followed by tables, *A new Explanation of the Holy Bible, by question and answer* and *A new accented Dictionary of the names and places mentioned in the Holy Bible*, ending on 4 X 1 *b*.
According to the Preface, the text was printed with the greatest care from *the Folio Edition of Field*, i.e., apparently, the Cambridge edition of 1659 (see No. 525). Short notes with some references are given at the foot of many pages. Engraved frontispiece, and other plates in the text.

¶ 214 × 148 mm.

[F. F.]
910.

1774. The Holy Bible . . .
T. Wright and W. Gill: Oxford. 1774. 12°.

Sold by *S. Crowder*, London, and *W. Jackson*, Oxford.
Text ends on Qq 12 b. No Apocrypha.

¶ 136 × 74 mm. [F. F.]
911.

1774. A Commentary on the Holy Bible: Containing the whole sacred text . . . with notes . . .
William Pine: Bristol. 1774. 12°.

The Preface states that 'though there are several thousand notes, (and indeed more than in some folio commentaries,) besides the whole of the sacred text, yet through the smallness of the type, (it being the smallest a bible was ever printed with, and made on purpose for this work,) and the remarkable fineness of the paper, it is brought into a portable compass for the pocket; and must therefore be of peculiar use to those who wish daily to read the scriptures, abroad as well as at home, to edification.'
William Pine was connected with the firm of I. Moore and Co. (afterwards J. Fry and Co.), which printed two folio and two octavo Bibles. (See below, No. 915, 1776.)
Text ends on 4 F 6 b, followed by 6 ff. containing *A Collection of the Names and Titles given to Jesus Christ*, and a table of Proper Names. No Apocrypha. Brief notes are printed at the end of the chapters.

¶ 132 × 73 mm. [F. F.]
912.

1774. The New Testament . . .
T. Wright and W. Gill: Oxford. 1774. 12°.

Sold by *S. Crowder*, London, and *W. Jackson*, Oxford.
Text ends on I 12 b.

¶ 135 × 73 mm.
With Tate and Brady's Metrical Psalms (1780), and Prayer Book (1781). [F. F.]
913.

1774. B. f°. See 1776.
B. 8°. See 1776.

1775. The Holy Bible . . .
J. Archdeacon: Cambridge. 1775. 12°.

Price *2s. unbound.* Sold by *J. Beecroft*, etc.
Text ends on Fff 3 b, followed by 3 ff. containing the *History of the Bible Epitomized* and a table. No Apocrypha.

¶ 136 × 71 mm.
In two volumes. [F. F.]
914.

1775. B. f°. See 1776.
B. 8°. See 1776.
B. 12°. See 1777.

1776. The Holy Bible . . . With notes . . . selected from the works of several eminent divines . . .
Printed and sold by I. Moore and Company, Letter-Founders and Printers, in Queen-Street, near Upper-Moorfields: London. 1774,76. f°.

According to the Preface the editors selected the notes 'from the most eminent commentators, viz. Bishop Patrick; Pool, Clarke, Henry, Doddridge, Dodd, etc.,' and took great care

ENGLISH

that they should 'be free from party reflections, and tenets hurtful to peace and benevolence, and have a real tendency to promote useful knowledge and genuine piety.'

General title dated 1774; N. T. title dated 1776. Text ends on 11 F 1 *a*, followed by tables and Index ending on 11 L 2. Apocrypha not included in list of books. The notes are printed at the foot of each column.

The type much resembles that used in Baskerville's Bible of 1763. For a notice of the firm of letter-founders and printers known at first as Isaac Moore and Co., and later styled Joseph Fry and Co., see T. B. Reed, *A History of the Old English Letter Foundries* . . . (1887), pp. 298–302. Joseph Fry was grandfather of the Francis Fry whose name recurs on so many pages of this Catalogue. The firm printed two folio and two octavo Bibles between 1774 and 1777; and William Pine of Bristol, who was connected with the same firm, printed a small duodecimo Bible in 1774. (See Nos. 912, 915, 916, 921, and 922.)

¶ 471 × 292 mm.
Apocrypha (A to Rr) inserted. [F. F.]

915.

1776. The Holy Bible . . . With notes . . . selected from the works of several eminent divines . . .
   I. Moore and Co. : London. 1774,76,75. 8°. 5 vols.

An octavo edition of the Bible printed in large folio with the same type by *I. Moore and Co.*, 1774,76 (No. 915).

Vols. 1–3 (containing the O. T.) are dated 1774; vol. 4 (the N. T.), 1776; and vol. 5 (the Apocrypha—not included in the list of books), 1775. An index is given at the end of each volume.

¶ 229 × 140 mm.
Contains a series of small engravings, mounted and inserted in the text. These represent the principal characters in the O. T. Some are signed; e.g. that of *Seth* is inscribed *Crispin J. Vent* and *J. Saedeler fecit*, and is dated *1579*. The N. T. has only a large engraving of our Lord, by *C. J. Visscher* and *J. Wirix*.
Bound in nine volumes. The volume containing the Apocrypha was added by Fry.
[F. F.]

—— Another copy.
Vol. 5 (the Apocrypha) only. See below, No. 922, 1777.

916.

1776. The Holy Bible . . . With most profitable annotations . . . By the Archbishops, Bishops, etc. etc. . . .
  Printed by M. Lewis, Paternoster-Row, for Mess. Buckland, Keith, Vallance and Simmons : London. 1775,76. f°.

A reprint of the Geneva Bible, with Tomson's revised New Testament and Junius' Revelation.

General title dated 1775; N. T. title dated 1776.
The preliminary matter includes *Archbishop Parker's Preface, How to take Profit* . . . (by *T. Grashop*), and list of books. The N. T. ends on 4 N 2 *b*, followed by 13 pp. of tables. No Apocrypha. Printed in double columns, with notes at the foot of the page.
Gen. iii. 7, *aprons*. This and a similar reprint of 1778 are the only editions of the Geneva version in which the rendering *breeches* does not occur.
With many engravings.

¶ 365 × 229 mm. [F. F.]

917.

1776. The Holy Bible . . .
   T. Wright and Gill : Oxford. 1776. 4°.

Sold by *S. Crowder*, etc.
N. T. ends on O 3 *b*, followed by Index and tables ending on S 2 *b*.

¶ 263 × 204 mm.
With Metrical Psalms (1770), and Prayer Book (1773). [F. F.]
918.

1776. The Holy Bible . . . with Notes.
J. W. Pasham: London. 1776. 12°.

General title engraved by *Is. Taylor*. Text ends on Ddd 8 *a*. No Apocrypha. One leaf of tables after O. T.
The Notes are evidently added merely to evade the provisions of the Bible-patent, whose prohibitions apparently did not apply to texts with a commentary. They generally occupy only five lines, and are printed at the bottom of the page, leaving a broad space below the text, so that they may be cut off, if desired, by the binder. See No. 985.

¶ 131 × 63 mm.
With the notes intact. [F. F.]

—— Another copy.
112 × 62 mm. With the notes cut off. [F. F.]
919.

1777. The Holy Bible . . .
J. Archdeacon: Cambridge. 1775, 77. 12°.

Price 2s. unbound. Sold by *J. Beecroft*, etc. The N. T. gives the names of the London publishers as follows: *John, Francis and Charles Rivington, Benjamin White, Edward Dilly, and Thomas Beecroft.*
General title dated 1775; N. T. title dated 1777. Text ends on Mm 12 *b*. No Apocrypha. One page of tables at end of O. T.

¶ 167 × 98 mm. Wants two leaves.
With Prayer Book (? date), and Metrical Psalms (1773). [F. F.]
920.

1777. The Holy Bible . . . With notes . . . selected from the works of several eminent authors . . .
J. Fry and Company: London. 1777. f°.

A reissue of the folio edition of 1774, 76 which bore the imprint of *I. Moore and Co.* (No. 915).

¶ 473 × 284 mm.
With the Apocrypha (not included in the list of books). [F. F.]

—— Another copy. [F. F.]
921.

1777. The Holy Bible . . . With notes . . . selected from the works of several eminent authors . . .
J. Fry and Co.: London. 1777. 8°. 4 vols.

A reissue of the octavo edition of 1774, 76 which bore the imprint of *I. Moore and Co.* (No. 916).
Apparently the Apocrypha (vol. 5) were not included in this edition.

¶ 228 × 138 mm.
The Apocrypha (vol. 5) of the edition of 1774, 76 are added as a fifth volume.
This copy originally belonged to Joseph Fry, its printer and publisher. [F. F.]
922.

1777. B. 12°. See 1778.

ENGLISH

[1777. The New Testament . . .
R. Aitken : Philadelphia. 1777. 12°.]

The earliest edition of the English New Testament avowedly printed in America. See note after 1761, and O'Callaghan, *List*, p. 80.

Pp. 353.

1778. The Holy Bible . . .
J. Archdeacon : Cambridge. 1778,77. 12°.

Price 2s. unbound. Sold by J., F., and C. Rivington, etc.
General title dated 1778; N. T. title dated 1777. Text ends on Fff 3 *b*, followed by 3 ff. containing the Epitome and table. No Apocrypha.

¶ 137 × 72 mm.
In two volumes. [F. F.]
923.

1778. The Holy Bible . . .
T. Wright and W. Gill: Oxford. 1778. 8°.

Sold by *S. Crowder*, London, and *W. Jackson*, Oxford.
Text ends on Sss 6 *a*. Apocrypha mentioned in list of books, but not required by signatures. One page of tables after O. T., and another after N. T.

¶ 178 × 118 mm.
Wants Apocrypha ?
With Prayer Book (1766), and Metrical Psalms (1766). [F. F.]
924.

1779. The Holy Bible . . .
J. Archdeacon : Cambridge. 1779. 8°.

Price 4s. unbound. Sold by J., F., and C. Rivington, etc.
Text ends on Vvv 2 *a*. The insertion of the Apocrypha interrupts the signatures. One page of tables after O. T., and another after N. T.

¶ 203 × 122 mm. [F. F.]
925.

1779. Isaiah. A new translation, with a preliminary dissertation and notes . . . By Robert Lowth . . . The second edition.
J. Nichols, for J. Dodsley and T. Cadell : London. 1779. 4°.

Dr. R. Lowth (1710-1787), Bishop of London, was an accomplished Hebrew scholar, whose work on Isaiah first appeared in 1778, and was many times reprinted.

Pp. lxxiv, 174, 283. With indexes.

¶ 273 × 208 mm.
926.

1779. Essay towards a literal English version of the New Testament, in the Epistle of the Apostle Paul directed to the Ephesians.
Andrew Foulis, Printer to the University : Glasgow. 1779. 4°.

By John Callander (d. 1789), a Scottish antiquary, of Craigforth, Stirlingshire.

Cf. Orme's *Bibliotheca Biblica*, 1824, pp. 73-4.
The Greek text is given with an interlinear literal English version; the foot-notes are in Greek. Pp. 32.

¶ 250 × 194 mm.
927.

1780. The Proverbs of Solomon . . . Very necessary for the use of young children.
J. Chalmers and Co. : Aberdeen. 1780. 8°.

A school-edition of Proverbs. See note on No. 794.
At the end of Proverbs are added four Psalms (xxiii, and cx–cxii), printed in smaller type. Pp. 40. Royal arms on title.

¶ 223 × 135 mm.
In paper covers inscribed *From Northesk, 1785.*

928.

[1782. The Holy Bible . . .
R. Aitken : Philadelphia. 1782,81. 12°.**]**

The earliest edition of the English Bible avowedly printed in America. See note after 1761, and O'Callaghan, *List*, p. 81.

The second leaf bears the Recommendation of Congress. N. T. ends on Dd 6 a. No Apocrypha. See B. M. copy, C. 51. b. 7.

1782. The Holy Bible . . .
Executors of David Hay, Assignee of the late Boulter Grierson, Printer to the King's Most Excellent Majesty : Dublin. 1782. 4°.

With the Translators' Preface. Text ends on 6 V 2 b, followed by Index and tables, ending on 6 Z 3 b. The insertion of the Apocrypha interrupts the signatures.

¶ 295 × 231 mm. Wants one leaf.
With Tate and Brady's Metrical Psalms (1797). [F. F.]

929.

1782. The Holy Bible . . .
J. Archdeacon : Cambridge. 1782. 12°.

Price 2s. unbound. Sold by J., F., and C. Rivington, B. White, C. Dilly, and John Fielding, London, and J. and J. Merrill, Cambridge.
Text ends on Fff 3 b, followed by 3 ff. containing Epitome and table. No Apocrypha.

¶ 132 × 71 mm.
In two volumes. [F. F.]

930.

1782. The Holy Bible . . .
W. Jackson and A. Hamilton, Printers to the University, Clarendon Press : Oxford. 1782. 12°.

Sold by W. Dawson at the Oxford Bible Warehouse, Paternoster Row, London.
Text ends on Qq 12 b. No Apocrypha.

¶ 135 × 71 mm. [F. F.]

931.

1782. The New Testament . . .
W. Jackson and A. Hamilton, Clarendon Press : Oxford. 1782. 8°.

Sold by W. Dawson, London.
Text ends on Ff 8 a. Some black-letter in headlines.

¶ 205 × 129 mm. [F. F.]

932.

1782. A new translation of the Gospel of St. Matthew; with notes . . .
By Gilbert Wakefield . . .
Warrington: Printed by William Eyres for the author; and sold by Joseph Johnson: London. 1782. 4°.

An original version by G. Wakefield (1756–1801), better known for his edition of Lucretius, 1796-9. He published a translation of Thessalonians in 1781, and this edition of St. Matthew in the following year. His complete translation of the New Testament appeared in 1792 and was reprinted in 1795 and in 1820.

Pp. xii, 417. With index.

¶ 275 × 218 mm.

933.

1783. The Holy Bible . . .
W. Jackson and A. Hamilton, Clarendon Press: Oxford. 1783. 8°.

Sold by *W. Dawson*, London.
Text ends on Sss 6 a. Apocrypha mentioned in list of books, but not required by signatures. One page of tables after O. T., and another after N. T.

¶ 206 × 129 mm. N. T. title mutilated.
Wants Apocrypha?

934.

1783. B. 12°. See 1784.

1784. The Holy Bible . . .
J. Archdeacon: Cambridge. 1783,84. 12°.

Price 2s. unbound. Sold by *J., F., and C. Rivington*, etc. The N. T. title omits the name of *J. Fielding* from the list of London publishers.
General title dated 1783; N. T. title dated 1784. Text ends on Fff 3 *b*, followed by 3 ff., containing Epitome and table. No Apocrypha.

¶ 138 × 73 mm.
In two volumes.
[F. F.]

935.

1784. Jeremiah and Lamentations. A new translation, with notes . . . By Benjamin Blayney . . .
Clarendon Press: Oxford. 1784. 4°.

For Dr. Blayney (1728–1801) and his 'standard' Oxford Bible see above, No. 885, 1769. He was at this time rector of Poulshot in Wilts. He also translated Zechariah (published in 1797), and the Psalms (unpublished).

Sold by *T. Cadell*, London; and by *D. Prince and J. Cooke*, Oxford.
Pp. xiv, 165, 361. With indexes.

¶ 269 × 197 mm.

936.

1785. The Holy Bible . . . Carefully printed from the first edition (compared with others) of the present translation. With notes by . . . Thomas Wilson, D.D., Lord Bishop of Sodor and Man. And various renderings, collected from other translations by . . . Clement Cruttwell, the editor . . .
R. Cruttwell: Bath. 1785. 4°. 8 vols.

Dr. Thomas Wilson (1663–1755), Bishop of Sodor and Man, was responsible for the publication of some of the earliest books in Manx, including the Gospel of

St. Matthew printed in 1748. The notes in this edition of the Bible are apparently taken from Wilson's 'Abstract of the Historical Part of the Old Testament' (1785) and other writings.

C. Cruttwell (1743–1808) edited Wilson's complete works under the direction of the Bishop's son, Thomas.

Sold by *Rivingtons*, etc., London.
The preliminary matter includes the Dedication, the editor's Preface (giving a sketch of the history of the English Bible), a list of the various editions since 1526 (based on a MS. in Lambeth Library), Bp. Wilson's *Preamble*, Dedication and Translators' Preface. Vol. 1 contains Genesis–2 Chronicles; Vol. 2, Ezra–Malachi; vol. 3, N. T. and Apocrypha, with chronological Index and tables, followed by List of Subscribers. The text has a running analysis in the margin; below are given the parallel texts, the various renderings, and Bp. Wilson's notes.

The Apocrypha include 3 Maccabees, which had not appeared in an English Bible since 1551 (see No. 66).

¶ 310 × 230 mm.

937.

1786. The Holy Bible . . .
J. Archdeacon : Cambridge. 1786. 12°.

Price 2s. 2d. unbound. Sold by J., F., and C. Rivington, etc.
Text ends on Fff 3 b, followed by 3 ff., containing Epitome and table. No Apocrypha.

¶ 138 × 73 mm. [F. F.]

938.

1786. The Holy Bible . . .
Assigns of A. Kincaid : Edinburgh. 1786. 12°.

Text ends on Ss 10 a, followed by 3 pp. of tables. Apocrypha mentioned in list of books, but not required by signatures. The Scotch Metrical Psalms follow the text, with continuous register, ending on Xx 12 b, with colophon.

¶ 127 × 66 mm.
Wants Apocrypha ? [F. F.]

939.

1787. The Holy Bible . . .
W. Jackson and A. Hamilton, Clarendon Press : Oxford. 1787. 8°.

Sold by W. Dawson, London.
Text ends on Sss 6 a. Apocrypha mentioned in list of books, but not required by signatures. One page of tables after O. T., and another after N. T.

¶ 209 × 129 mm.
Wants Apocrypha ? [F. F.]

940.

1788. The Holy Bible . . .
J. Archdeacon : Cambridge. 1788. 8°.

Price 3s. 3d. unbound. Sold by J., F., and C. Rivington, etc.
Text ends on Sss 6 a. Apocrypha mentioned in list of books, but not required by signatures. One page of tables after O. T., and another after N. T.

¶ 180 × 107 mm.
Wants Apocrypha ? [F. F.]

941.

1788. The Holy Bible . . .
   W. Jackson and A. Hamilton, Clarendon Press: Oxford. 1788. 12°.

Sold by *W. Dawson*, London.
Text ends on Qq 12 *b*. No Apocrypha.

¶ 136 × 70 mm.
In two volumes. [F. F.]
942.

1788. B. 4°. *See 1792.*

1789. The Holy Bible . . .
   W. Jackson and A. Hamilton, Clarendon Press: Oxford. 1789. 4°.

Sold by *W. Dawson*, London.
N. T. ends on O 3 *b*, followed by Index and tables, ending on S 2 *b*.

¶ 253 × 206 mm. [F. F.]
943.

1789. The Holy Bible . . .
   Assigns of A. Kincaid: Edinburgh. 1789. 12°.

Apocrypha included in list of books.

¶ 165 × 105 mm. A fragment, containing only the first eight leaves.
Bound with a copy of No. 488.

944.

1789. A curious Hieroglyphick Bible; or, select passages in the Old and New Testaments, represented with emblematical figures, for the amusement of youth: designed chiefly to familiarize tender age, in a pleasing and diverting manner, with early ideas of the Holy Scriptures. To which are subjoined, a short account of the Lives of the Evangelists, and other pieces, illustrated with cuts. The fourth edition; with additions, and other great improvements.
   B. Dugdale: Dublin. 1789. 12°.

A child's book; containing short passages of Scripture in which some of the words are represented by small cuts.

This little book, dedicated 'to the parents, guardians, and governesses, of Great Britain and Ireland,' must have proved very popular, since a 'thirteenth edition' was printed in 1796. The B. M. has a 'second edition' of 1784, a 'third' of 1785, a 'fourth' of 1786, a 'sixth' of 1788, and a 'ninth' of 1791—all of which were printed for *T. Hodgson*, London, and sold for 'One Shilling bound'; and also *A New Hieroglyphic Bible* . . . (1794), with a recommendation from the Rev. Rowland Hill, 'Price One Shilling Plain, & Two Shillings Colloured.' E. B. O'Callaghan, in his *List of Editions . . . printed in America . . .*, pp. 47–8, mentions a Boston edition of this last-named work, and ascribes its authorship to 'a Mr. Thompson.'
The edition here described was apparently the fourth printed in Ireland.
Frontispiece, title, [dedication?], preface; text, pp. 7 to 132; followed by a hymn, Lives of the Evangelists, another hymn, a prayer, and Questions and Answers, ending on p. 142.

¶ 140 × 90 mm. Apparently lacks a dedication-leaf after the title. Sheet K is duplicate
[F. F.]
945.

1790. The Holy Bible . . . with notes.
   T. Rickaby, for Scatcherd and Whitaker: London. 1790. 12°.

General title and frontispiece engraved. N. T. ends on M 5 *a*. No Apocrypha. One leaf of tables after O. T.

The notes were printed low down at the foot of the page, so that they might be cut off by the binder. See No. 985.

¶ 111 × 64 mm.
With notes cut off. [F. F.]

946.

1790. The Holy Bible . . .
    J. Archdeacon : Cambridge. 1790. 12°.

Price 2s. 2d. unbound. Sold by J., F., and C. Rivington, etc.
Text ends on Fff 3 b, followed by 3 ff. containing Epitome and table. No Apocrypha.

¶ 136 × 74 mm. [F. F.]

947.

1790. The Holy Bible . . .
  Mark and Charles Kerr, His Majesty's Printers :
        Edinburgh. 1790. 12°.

Text ends on Ss 10 a, followed by 3 pp. of tables. The Scotch Metrical Psalms follow, with continuous register, ending on Xx 12 b. No Apocrypha.

¶ 129 × 68 mm.
In two volumes. [F. F.]

948.

1790. A new literal version of the Book of Psalms, with a preface and notes. By the Rev. Stephen Street . . .
    J. Davis, for B. White and Son : London. 1790. 8°. 2 vols.

The title describes the author as ' of Queen's College, Oxford, Rector of Treyford in Sussex.'

Vol. 1: Preface, List of Subscribers, and text; pp. xxviii, 326. Vol. 2: Notes, etc.; 374 pp.

¶ 210 × 125 mm.

949.

1790. B. 12°. See 1791 and 1792.

[1790. The Holy Bible, translated from the Latin Vulgate . . .
   Carey, Stewart, and Co. : Philadelphia. 1790. 4°. 2 vols.]

The earliest edition of the Douai-Rheims version printed in America. Challoner's revision. See note after 1761, and O'Callaghan, *List*, pp. 34-5.

Pp. 487, 490.

1791. The Holy Bible . . .
    J. Archdeacon : Cambridge. 1790,91. 12°.

Sold by J., F., and C. Rivington, etc.
General title dated 1790; N. T. title dated 1791. Text ends on Mm 12 b. No Apocrypha. One page of tables after O. T.

¶ 167 × 99 mm. [F. F.]

950

1791. The Holy Bible . . .
   W. Jackson and A. Hamilton, Clarendon Press: Oxford. 1791. 12°.

   Sold by *W. Dawson*, London.
   Text ends on Kk 12 *b*. No Apocrypha. One page of tables after O. T.

   ¶ 169 × 101 mm. [F. F.]
   951.

1791. B. 4°. See 1792.

1792. The Holy Bible . . . With original Notes . . . by the Rev. Thomas Scott . . . to which are added a Concordance, General Index, and Tables.
   For Bellamy and Robarts: London. 1788,92,91. 4°. 4 vols.

   Thomas Scott (1747-1821), who was appointed in 1785 joint-chaplain at the Lock Hospital, agreed to prepare for Bellamy the publisher a Commentary on the Bible in a hundred weekly numbers, for which he was to receive a guinea a number. The first part appeared in March 1788. But financial difficulties soon arose; and by the time the Commentary was finished (June 1792) in 174 numbers, Bellamy was bankrupt, and Scott had not only lost his money, but was saddled with a debt, from which he was finally released by the aid of Charles Simeon and other friends in 1813. Sir James Stephen characterised his Commentary as 'the greatest theological performance of our age and country.'

   Other editions appeared in 1809, 1810, 1812, etc.
   Vol. 1, dated 1788, contains Preface, and Genesis-2 Samuel; vol. 2 (1792), 2 Kings-Song of Solomon; vol. 3 (1792), Isaiah-Malachi, and Apocrypha; vol. 4 (1792), N. T. (with separate title dated 1791). With Concordance, chronological Index, tables, etc.

   ¶ 270 × 210 mm.

   The Concordance (by the Rev. V. Powell; 3rd edition, 1792) in this copy is inserted immediately before the text. At the end is a List of Subscribers.
   952.

1792. The Holy Bible . . .
   W. Jackson and A. Hamilton, Clarendon Press: Oxford. 1790,92. 12°.

   Sold by *W. Dawson*, London.
   General title dated 1790; N. T. title dated 1792. Text ends on Fff 3 *b*, followed by 3 ff. containing Epitome and table. No Apocrypha.

   ¶ 135 × 74 mm. [F. F.]
   953.

1792. The Holy Bible . . .
   J. Archdeacon: Cambridge. 1792. 12°.

   Sold by *J., F., and C. Rivington*, etc. The N. T. title omits the name of *John Rivington*. Text ends on Fff 3 *b*, followed by 3 ff. containing Epitome and table. No Apocrypha.

   ¶ 139 × 75 mm. [F. F.]
   954.

1792. The New Testament . . . with short Notes.
   Printed and sold by Darton and Harvey: London. 1792. 8°.

   'Sold also by *W. Bleckly*, Stretton, Norfolk; *M. Stevenson*, Norwich; *D. Boulter* Yarmouth, and the booksellers in general.'

Text ends on Mmm 1 b. Some black-letter in headlines. Brief notes occur at the bottom of a very few pages. See No. 985.

¶ 232 × 140 mm.

955.

1792. The New Testament . . .
W. Jackson and A. Hamilton, Clarendon Press: Oxford. 1792. 12°.

Sold by W. Dawson, London.
Text ends on M 12 b. The type from M 4 b to end is smaller than that used for the rest of the book.

¶ 130 × 72 mm.
With Prayer Book (? date), and Tate and Brady's Metrical Psalms (1796).

956.

1793. The Holy Bible . . .
M. and C. Kerr: Edinburgh. 1793. f°.

Text ends on 9 R 2 b, followed by 9 ff. containing Index and tables. The insertion of the Apocrypha interrupts the signatures.

¶ 379 × 236 mm.
With Scotch Metrical Psalms (1795). [F. F.]

957.

1793. The Holy Bible, containing the Old and New Testaments, together with the Apocrypha: translated out of the Original Tongues, and with the former translations diligently compared and revised, by the Special Command of King James I., of England.
Isaiah Thomas: Worcester, Massachusetts, United States of America.
1793. 8°.

One of the early Bibles printed in the United States. Produced by Isaiah Thomas of Worcester, Massachusetts, whom Benjamin Franklin called 'the Baskerville of America.'
See note after 1761; and *cf.* O'Callaghan's *List*, pp. 46–7, and Wright's *Early Bibles of America*, p. 82 f.

Sold by Thomas in Worcester. 'Sold also by said *Thomas*, and *Andrews*, at Faust's Statue, No. 45, Newbury Street, *Boston*, and by said *Thomas, and Co.* in *Walpole*, Newhampshire.'
Text ends on p. 959. The insertion of the Apocrypha (A–Y, pages not numbered) interrupts the signatures and the pagination. One page of tables after O. T., and another after N. T.

¶ 214 × 128 mm. Wants six leaves after general title.

958.

1794. The New Testament . . .
W. Jackson and W. Dawson, Printers to the University,
Clarendon Press: Oxford. 1794. 8°.

Text ends on Dd 7 b, followed by 1 f. containing table. Some black-letter in headlines.

¶ 212 × 133 mm. [F. F.]

959.

1794. B. 12°. See 1795.

1795. The Holy Bible . . .
J. Archdeacon and John Burges, Printers to the University: Cambridge. 1794,95. 12°.

The N. T. title gives the publishers as follows: *C. Dilly, F. and C. Rivington, and B. and J. White*, London; and *J. and J. Merrill*, Cambridge.
General title dated 1794; N. T. title dated 1795. Text ends on Mm 12 *b*. No Apocrypha One page of tables after O. T.

¶ 162 × 98 mm.

960.

1795. The Holy Bible, ornamented with engravings by James Fittler from celebrated pictures by old masters. The letterpress by Thomas Bensley.
T. Bensley, for R. Bowyer and J. Fittler: London. 1795. 4°.

Text ends on 9 I 2 *b*. No Apocrypha.
The engravings are after pictures by *Dürer, Rembrandt, Rubens*, etc.

¶ 315 × 245 mm. L. P.
In two volumes, with separate title to vol. 2.

961.

1795. The Holy Bible . . .
J. Archdeacon and J. Burges: Cambridge. 1795. 8°.

Sold by *C. Dilly*, etc.
Text ends on Vvv 2 *a*. Apocrypha mentioned in list of books, but not required by signatures. One page of tables after O. T., and another after N. T.

¶ 209 × 123 mm.
Wants Apocrypha?
In two volumes. [F. F.]

962.

1795. The Holy Bible . . .
J. Archdeacon and J. Burges: Cambridge. 1795. 12°.

Sold by *C. Dilly*, etc. The N. T. title omits the name of *J. White*.
Text ends on Fff 3 *b*, followed by 3 ff. containing Epitome and table. No Apocrypha.

¶ 133 × 74 mm.

963.

1795. The Holy Bible . . .
M. and C. Kerr: Edinburgh. 1795. 12°.

Text ends on Ll 12 *a*. No Apocrypha. One page of tables after O. T., and another after N. T.

¶ 161 × 102 mm. Wants two leaves. [F. F.]

964.

1795. A Translation of the New Testament from the original Greek. Humbly attempted with a view to assist the unlearned with clearer and more explicit views of the mind of the Spirit in the Scriptures of Truth. By T. Haweis, LL.B. . . .
Printed for T. Chapman: London. 1795. 8°.

An original version by Thomas Haweis (1734–1820), who was rector of Aldwinkle,

Northamptonshire, chaplain to Selina Countess of Huntingdon, the intimate friend of John Newton of Olney, and one of the founders of the London Missionary Society in 1794.

With Preface. Text, printed in double columns, ends on Ff 8 a.

¶ 214 × 130 mm.

965.

1796. The Holy Bible . . .
  W. Dawson, T. Bensley, and J. Cooke, Printers to the University,
          Clarendon Press: Oxford. 1796. 8°.

Price unbound, 4s. 8d. Sold by *W. Dawson*, London.
Text ends on 8ss 6 a. The insertion of the Apocrypha interrupts the signatures. One page of tables after O. T., and another after N. T.

¶ 204 × 126 mm.   [F. F.]

966.

1796. The Holy Bible . . .
  R. Bowyer, Historic Gallery, Pall Mall: London. 1796. 12°.

The general title, the page containing list of books and the N. T. title are engraved. Text ends on 3 K 6 b. No Apocrypha.
A few short notes are printed low down at the foot of the page, doubtless intended to be cut off by the binder. See No. 985.

¶ 172 × 106 mm.

—— Another copy.
On very thin paper. Without list of books.

—— Another copy.
On very thin paper. Without list of books.
Some of the notes have been cut off.   [F. F.]

967.

1796. The Holy Bible . . .
    M. and C. Kerr: Edinburgh. 1796. [1766.] 12°.

With Canne's Preface and marginal matter.

Apparently a reissue of A. Kincaid's edition of 1766,67 (No. 874), with a new general title; the N. T. title still bears Kincaid's name and the date 1766.

·¶ 175 × 100 mm. Wants last leaf.
Wants Apocrypha?   [F. F.]

968.

1796. The Holy Bible . . .
    M. and C. Kerr: Edinburgh. 1796. 12°.

With Canne's Preface and marginal matter.
A specimen of the marked Bibles, known as 'Porteusian Bibles.' Beilby Porteus (1731–1808), Bishop of London, who apparently suggested this plan of denoting the relative importance of chapters of the Bible by special marks, was one of the original Vice-Presidents of the Bible Society.

 A printed slip inserted after the titleleaf explains that *those chapters which are of a more spiritual and practical nature are distinguished . . . by the figure (†) being printed at the head of each chapter . . . leading historical chapters . . . by the figure (2) . . . Our Lord's Discourses . . . and other chapters of more peculiar interest . . . by a Star being added . . .*

Distinct from No. 968. Text ends on Pp 3 b, followed by 3 ff. of tables. Apocrypha mentioned in list of books, but not required by signatures.

¶ 175 × 99 mm.
Wants Apocrypha ? [F. F.]
969.

1796. The Holy Bible translated from the Latin Vulgate . . . first published by the English College at Douay, Anno 1609. Newly revised and corrected . . . With Annotations . . .
  John Moir, Paterson's Court, Edinburgh. 1796. 12°. 4 vols.

An Edinburgh edition of Challoner's revision of the Douai Old Testament, first published in 1750 (see No. 824), and reprinted in 1763,64.

'Published under the inspection of Dr. Hey, one of the Vicars Apostolic in Scotland' (Cotton, *R. and D.*, p. 77). The edition consisted of about 3000 copies, which were sold chiefly in England and Ireland.
An edition of the N. T. of Challoner's revision was issued by the same printer in 1797.
Vol. 1 : title, with list of books on verso, Approbations —1 f. ; text, 507 pp. Vol. 2 : 492 pp. Vol. 3 : 484 pp. Vol. 4 : 511 pp. ; list of *errata* —1 p.

¶ 176 × 102 mm. [F. F.]
970.

1796. Jonah, a faithful translation from the original, with philological and explanatory notes ; to which is prefixed a preliminary discourse, proving the genuineness, the authenticity and the integrity of the present text. By George Benjoin . . .
  J. Burges, Printer to the University : Cambridge. 1796. 4°.

In this diglot, the Hebrew text is given, together with the A. V., an original translation, and a very literal version.
Sold by *W. H. Lunn and J. Deighton*, Cambridge, etc.
With copious notes, etc. Pp. 198.

¶ 276 × 213 mm.
971.

1796. B. 8°. See 1798.

1797. The New Testament . . .
  M. and C. Kerr : Edinburgh. 1797. 12°.

Text ends on O 12 a, with table on verso.

¶ 162 × 101 mm.
972.

1798. The Holy Bible . . .
  J. Archdeacon and J. Burges : Cambridge. 1796,98. 8°.

General title dated 1796 ; the N. T. title, dated 1798, bears the name of *J. Burges* alone (*cf.* imprint of No. 971). Text ends on 5 T 1 b. The insertion of the Apocrypha interrupts the signatures.

¶ 239 × 149 mm.
In two volumes. At the beginning of vol. 2 is inserted a general title, dated 1798, and bearing the name of *J. Burges* alone. [F. F.]
973.

1798. The Holy Bible . . .
University Press: Cambridge. 1798. 8°. 2 vols.

'Sold by *John Deighton*, Cambridge, and all other booksellers.'
The body of the book appears to be identical with the octavo of 1796,98 (No. 973).
Vol. 1 contains Genesis-Song of Solomon ; vol. 2, Isaiah-Malachi, [Apocrypha,] and N. T. Text ends on 5 T 1 *b*. Apocrypha mentioned in list of books, but not required by signatures.

¶ 223 × 146 mm.
Wants Apocrypha?
[F. F.]
974.

1798. The Holy Bible . . .
J. Burges: Cambridge. 1798. 12°.

Sold by *C. Dilly*, etc.
N. T. ends on I 8 *b*. No Apocrypha.

¶ 142 × 79 mm.
[F. F.]
975.

1798. The New Testament . . .
Dawson, Bensley, and Cooke, Clarendon Press: Oxford. 1798. 12°.

Price 9d. Sold by *W. Dawson*, London.
Text ends on O 12 *b*.

¶ 170 × 103 mm.
[F. F.]
976.

1798. The New Testament . . .
Dawson, Bensley, and Cooke, Clarendon Press: Oxford. 1798. 12°.

Price 9d.; though a much smaller book than No. 976. Sold by *W. Dawson*, London.
Text ends on N 12 *b*.

¶ 131 × 70 mm.
[F. F.]
977.

1798. A Translation of the New Testament from the Original Greek, humbly attempted by Nathaniel Scarlett, assisted by men of piety & literature: with notes.
T. Gillet: London. 1798. 8°.

This original version is of composite authorship. Scarlett (1753–1802) was a bookseller in the Strand. His work is based on a manuscript translation of the New Testament by James Creighton, an Anglican clergyman. Once a week Creighton, William Vidler (a Universalist), and John Cue (a Sandemanian), met Scarlett at his house, 349 Strand, to revise this translation. The final arrangement of the text, and the headings and notes are Scarlett's own work.

'Sold by *Nathaniel Scarlett* No. 349 (near Exeter 'Change) Strand ; also *F. & C. Rivington*, St. Paul's Church Yard.'
The preface tells us that ' whilst an attempt is made to bring this sacred Book somewhat nearer to the English idiom at this day, still care is taken to steer between the two extremes, of being too servile and literal on the one hand, or too periphrastic on the other.'
Text printed in paragraphs, and divided into sections; the names of the speakers are given at the side—*Jesus, Pharisees, Disciples*, etc. or *Historian*; O. T. references occur in brackets in the text; and a few short notes are printed at the foot of some pages. The text is followed by *Observations on some terms used in this translation*, viz. *immersion*,

restore etc., *ages*, and *æonian.* Pp. xi, 483, vi. The table of Contents states that the whole N. T. may be read distinctly in 14 hours, and the O. T. in about 48 hours.

This edition has the title and table of Contents engraved; and also a frontispiece and three other plates, and an engraved folding table 'shewing the harmony of Matthew and Luke in their account of Christ's Genealogy.'

¶ 219 × 137 mm.

978.

1798. A Translation of the New Testament . . . by Nathaniel Scarlett . . .
T. Gillet: London. 1798. 12°.

A smaller edition of Scarlett's version. See No. 978.
Pp. xi, 483, vi. No engravings.

¶ 175 × 100 mm.

—— Another copy.

Inserted in this copy is an advertisement of the book, giving an extract from a contemporary review; the price of this edition was 6*s.*, and of the other (No. 978), 10*s.* 6*d.*, in boards.

979.

1799. The Holy Bible . . .
Dawson, Bensley, and Cooke, Clarendon Press: Oxford. 1799. 12°.

Price 2s. 4d.
Text ends on Qq 12 *b*. No Apocrypha.

¶ 132 × 73 mm.
In two volumes.

[F. F.]
980.

1799. The Holy Bible . . .
Sir J. H. Blair and J. Bruce, Printers to the King's Most Excellent Majesty: Edinburgh. 1799. 12°.

Sir J. H. Blair and J. Bruce were apparently appointed His Majesty's Printers for Scotland in 1785, though Kincaid's original patent did not terminate before 1798, and until that date his representatives enjoyed the privileges of the office. (Lee, *Memorial*, pp. vi–ix, and App. xxxiii and xxxviii.)

Text ends on 4 P 3 *a*. No Apocrypha. One page of tables after O. T.; and 7 pp. containing Epitome and tables after N. T.

¶ 146 × 83 mm.
With Scotch Metrical Psalms (1799).
In two volumes.

[F. F.]
981.

1800. The Holy Bible.
Thomas Bensley, for Thomas Macklin: London. 1800. f°. 6 vols.

Macklin's sumptuous edition, 'embellished with engravings, from pictures and designs by the most eminent English artists.'

Vols. 1–4 contain the O. T., and vols. 5 and 6 the N. T. The Apocrypha were issued in a similar form in 1816 (see No. 1066).

Preliminary matter includes Dedication to the King (dated 1791), and List of Subscribers. Text printed in very large type; double columns, with 29 lines to the full column; the words generally printed in italics are distinguished in this edition only by a dot placed under the first vowel.

982.

1800. An Analysis of the Holy Bible, containing the whole of the Old and New Testaments : collected and arranged systematically, in thirty books, each book being divided into chapters, and every chapter sub-divided into sections, whereby the dispersed rays of truth are concentrated, and every Scriptural subject defined and fully exhibited. By Matthew Talbot . . .
Printed by and for Edward Baines : Leeds ; and for
Thomas Conder : London. [1800.] 4°.

This work contains all the verses of the Bible arranged, according to the subject-matter, in thirty books bearing such titles as *Deity, Christ, Scripture, Providence, Holy Days*, etc., and subdivided into 285 chapters and 4144 sections.

The Preface by Talbot is dated *Leeds, May, 1800.* Analysis, B 1 to 10 Q 2 a, followed by ndexes.

983.

NOTE.

AFTER THE YEAR 1800, THE SIZE OF EACH EDITION IS GIVEN IN CENTIMETRES, MEASURED ON THE OUTSIDE OF THE BINDING OF THE COPY DESCRIBED—IN PLACE OF THE DESIGNATIONS *folio, quarto, octavo,* ETC.

IT IS ALSO TO BE UNDERSTOOD, UNLESS THE CONTRARY IS STATED, THAT EACH EDITION, OTHER THAN THE DOUAI VERSION, FROM THIS DATE ONWARDS OMITS THE APOCRYPHA.

1801. B. See 1802.

1802. The Holy Bible . . .
J. Burges : Cambridge. 1801,02. 21·5 × 14·5 cm.

'Sold by *F. & C. Rivington, J. White,* and *J. Mawman,* in London ; and *J. Deighton,* in Cambridge.'
General title dated 1801 ; N. T. title dated 1802.
Text ends on Vvv 2 a. Apocrypha mentioned in list of books. One page of tables after O. T., and another after N. T.

984.

1802. The Holy Bible . . .
J. Crowder and others, for J. Reeves : London. 1802.
19 × 12·5 cm. 10 vols.
This edition is known as Reeves' Bible.

In the Preface Reeves explains his design 'to put to the press an edition of the Bible in separate volumes, that would make a manual, commodious for perusal, like the editions of our best English books.' The text is a careful reprint of Blayney's Bible of 1769 (No. 885), with certain changes. It is here printed in paragraphs, and divided into sections, though the chapter- and verse-numbers are retained, and 'metre' is distinguished from 'prose.' The sectional headings and marginal summary take the place of the usual chapter-contents. With regard to the marginal matter in Blayney's Bible, the references to parallel passages are here omitted, but the alternative renderings etc. are printed at the foot of the page. Explanatory notes are appended ; these are based on Wells' Paraphrase, and the commentaries of Patrick, Lowth, Whitby, and others. In alluding to this last feature Reeves says : 'all our authorized Bibles, published by the King's printer, and the universities, are wholly without explanatory notes. These privileged persons have confined themselves to reprinting the bare text, in which they have an exclusive right ; forbearing to publish it with notes, which, it is deemed, may be done by any of the King's subjects as well as themselves.' And he adds the significant comment : 'I mean such notes, as are *bonâ fide* intended for annotation, not the pretence of notes, which I have seen in some editions of the Bible and Common Prayer, placed there merely as a cover to the piracy of printing upon the patentees,

ENGLISH

as if fraud could make legal anything that was in itself illegal. In some of these editions the notes are placed purposely so as to be cut off by the binder.' (See Nos. 919, 946, 955, 967, and 988.)

'For the sake of correctness, as well as dispatch,' Reeves divided the work among several printers, whose names are given on p. xiii of his Preface: *J. Crowder, H. Baldwin and Son, S. Gosnel, Wilks and Taylor, Cox, Son, and Baylis,* and *T. Bensley.* The completed book was 'published for *John Reeves Esq.*, one of the patentees of the office of King's printer; sold by *George and William Nicol*, booksellers to His Majesty, Pall Mall.' (See note on No. 900.)

Besides Reeves' Dedication to the King and Preface, the preliminary matter includes the Translators' Preface, chronological Index, tables, etc. With Apocrypha. The Prayer Book version of the Psalms is printed side by side with King James' version. A full page contains 39 lines. Issued apparently in ten volumes: O. T., 6 vols.; Apocrypha, 1 vol.; N. T., 2 vols.; Notes, 1 vol.

Two other editions appeared in 1802: (1) with 42 lines to the full column, in nine volumes; (2) without Apocrypha and explanatory notes, in four volumes.

¶ Bound in five volumes; with the notes placed at the end of each volume, and some of the separate titles omitted.

—— Another copy.

Imperfect: wanting the N. T.
Bound in four volumes. The matter is arranged somewhat differently, and the Index and tables are omitted. [F. F.]

985.

1802. The Holy Bible . . .
Richard Edwards: Bristol. 1802. 12 × 7·5 cm.

N. T. ends on T 6 a.

¶ [F. F.]

986.

1803. The Holy Bible . . .
Dawson, Bensley, and Cooke, Clarendon Press:
Oxford. 1803. 14 × 7·5 cm.

Price *3 s.*
Text ends on Qq 12 b.

¶ [F. F.]

987.

1803. The Holy Bible . . . with notes by the editor.
Printed by John Fenley, Jun.; and sold by the proprietor,
John Parsons: Bristol. 1803. 14 × 8 cm.

Described as 'Parsons's Bible' on the half-title.

Text ends on Gggg 2 a. The list of books and 'A collection of names given to Jesus Christ' are placed after the O. T. Brief notes, printed at the foot of each page below the signatures. See No. 985.

¶ An uncut copy. [F. F.]

—— Another copy.

With the notes cut off, and the half-title removed.

988.

1803. The New Testament . . .
R. Watts, Printer to the University: Cambridge. 1803. 17·5 × 10·5 cm.

Price *One Shilling.* Sold by *F. and C. Rivington*, and *J. Mawman*, London, and *J. Deighton*, Cambridge.
Text ends on O 12 b.

989.

1803. The Family Testament and Learner's Assistant . . . by the Rev. Joseph Brown.
Printed by M. Vint, Ave-Maria-Lane, for W. Lowndes, etc.:
London. 1803. 18 × 10·5 cm.

See above, No. 879, 1767. *Price Three Shillings, bound.*
Preliminary matter, xxiv pp., ending with a list of *Books printed for W. Lowndes.*
Text, B 1 to T 12 b.

¶ Two leaves (A 6 and 7) are mutilated. [F. F
990.

1804. (The Holy Bible.)
R. Watts : Cambridge. 1804. 18·5 × 11·5 cm.

Sold by *F. and C. Rivington*, etc.
Text ends on Sss 6 a, with table on verso.

¶ Imperfect: containing only the N. T.
991.

1804. The Holy Bible . . .
Dawson, Bensley, and Cooke, Clarendon Press :
Oxford. 1804. 17 × 10·5 cm.
Price 3s. Sold by *W. Dawson*, London.
Text ends on Kk 12 b. One page of tables after O. T.

¶ With Prayer Book (1801), and Metrical Psalms (? date).
'Bound at the Expence of The Society for Promoting Christian Knowledge, No. 5, in Bartlett's Buildings, Holborn, London.' [F. F.]
992.

FOUNDATION OF THE BRITISH AND FOREIGN BIBLE SOCIETY: 7 MARCH 1804.

NOTE ON THE EARLY ENGLISH EDITIONS PUBLISHED BY THE BIBLE SOCIETY.

The primary object of the British and Foreign Bible Society, founded 7 March 1804, was to multiply and cheapen copies of the Scriptures in the United Kingdom. As regards English Bibles, it was proposed at first to purchase a supply for immediate circulation. The Committee, however, determined that editions should be printed expressly for the Society. Early in 1804 Andrew Wilson, who, aided by Earl Stanhope, had improved Ged's method of stereotype-printing, began negotiations with the Cambridge University Press for adapting his process to Bible-printing (see note on No. 995). On learning that the Cambridge Press had decided to employ Wilson's process, the Committee in September 1804 ordered large editions of the New Testament and the Bible to be printed from stereotype plates. The delay thus entailed was fully recompensed by the gain in cheapness and accuracy. In September 1805 ' an impression of an octavo English Testament was announced as ready for delivery.' As this was asserted to be ' the first specimen of the application of stereotype to any part of the Holy Scriptures ' (in English), it must have been printed from the same plates as the Cambridge Long Primer Testament bearing the date July 1805 (see No. 995). The Society's Second Report (1806) announces a duodecimo Testament, in Brevier type, and states that a large edition of the Bible was nearly ready. Up to the end of March 1806, the Society had paid the Cambridge Press £219 6s. 5d. for printing English Testaments. During the next twelvemonth this amount was trebled, and in the following year the Society's payments for English and Welsh Scriptures amounted to £5880. The Third Report (1807), which contains the earliest list of 'Editions of the Scriptures on sale to Subscribers at the Depository,' enumerates five English books:— (1) Brevier Testament 12° . . . 1s. 0d., (2) Bourgeois Testament 8° . . . 1s. 6d., (3) Long Primer Testament 8° . . . 1s. 9d., (4) Pica Testament 8° . . . 2s. 6d. (these prices are for copies '*strongly* bound in sheep': copies in calf cost 6d. extra), (5) Nonpareil Bible 12° in calf . . . 3s. 0d. During 1807 an octavo Brevier Bible (price in calf 5s. 3d.) was added to the list. The Fifth Report (1809) omits the Bourgeois Testament, but mentions a *cloth* edition (price 10d.) of the Brevier 12° Testament, and a new Minion Bible Crown 8° in calf . . . 4s. 4d.; while it states that the sale prices 'are fixed upon an average of 20l. per cent. below the cost prices.' The Sixth Report (1810) announces the first Bible with marginal references published by the Society (Brevier 8° . . . 8s. 6d.), and alludes to a Small Pica 8° Bible, which appeared during 1810 and cost 8s. 6d. This Report also gives specimens of the types used. Owing to a rise in the price of paper, and in the expense of printing, the loss on each copy sold now represented two-fifths of the cost price. The year's bill for printing and binding English and Welsh Scriptures now exceeded £10,000.

By 1810 the Oxford University Press also was engaged in printing for the Society; and the Eighth Report (1812) announces that the Committee 'have now obtained the assistance of his Majesty's Printers, Messrs. Eyre and Strahan, for a large assortment of Bibles and Testaments.' Nevertheless the supply hardly met the demand. The Price List for 1812 includes some new editions:—a Pocket Bible Nonpareil 24° 'with hollow back, rebacked' (3s. 6d.), and a corresponding Testament (1s. 0d.), with another Pocket Bible Pearl type (3s. 6d.); the octavo Bibles in Small Pica and in Brevier (with references), printed on 'medium paper,' now cost 8s. 6d. and 8s. 0d. An appended note states that 'the Committee having adopted a more expensive method of Sewing and Binding, in order to render their Books more serviceable, this, together with the additional Duty on Leather, has augmented the Cost of their Bibles and Testaments.' During the next year it was found necessary to raise the sale prices of all the Society's editions, and from July 1813 they were 'calculated at an average of 20l. per cent. below the cost prices.' Thus the Brevier 12° Testament in sheep now sold at 1s. 4d., and the Nonpareil 12° Bible in calf at 3s. 7d. Three octavo Bibles—the Brevier demy paper, the Small Pica medium paper, and the Small Pica royal paper (a new edition, sold at 21s.)—were supplied between 1813 and 1815 'with references at the end' (i.e. after each verse), and offered at 7s. 8d., 11s. 1d., and 24s. 6d.

The foregoing are all the editions of the English Scriptures printed for, and published by, the Bible Society during the first eleven years of its existence. Down to 31 March 1815 it issued 429,768 copies of the Bible, and 481,840 of the New Testament, in English. These were sold at reduced prices to Subscribers 'according to their privileges.' The rule states that 'each Annual Subscriber of One Guinea has the privilege of purchasing Bibles and Testaments, within the year, to the amount of Five Guineas; and in like proportion for every Guinea subscribed. A further quantity may also be had (upon application to the Committee) at the Cost Prices.' The poor were supplied with copies on favourable terms by the local Associations; and large grants of free Bibles and Testaments were made by the Committee to meet special cases at home and abroad. All these editions bear on their titlepages the name of the Bible Society, and the words 'sold to Subscribers only, by *L. B. Seeley*, at the Society's Depository, No. 169, Fleet Street, London.' Seeley was appointed full agent in June 1808, and held this office till 1816, when the Depository was moved. The address thereafter became 'Earl Street, Blackfriars.' The bindings bear a small circular stamp, giving the Society's name.

Certain of these editions unfortunately are not represented in the Bible House

Library; and many of the earlier issues are undated. For these reasons it has seemed advisable to summarize the above information as a Note at this point in the Catalogue. All the editions published by the Bible Society during the first twenty years of its existence (1804–1824), which are represented in the Library, appear in the following pages. The prices, which vary from year to year, are quoted in each case from the list in the Society's contemporary Report.

1805. The Holy Bible . . .
    Dawson, Bensley, and Cooke, Clarendon Press:
                                 Oxford. 1805. 17 × 10·5 cm.
Price 3s. Sold by *W. Dawson*, London.
Text ends on Kk 12 b. One page of tables after O. T.

¶   [F. F.]
                                                                                     993.

1805. The Holy Bible, translated from the Latin Vulgate . . . first published by the English College at Douay, Anno 1609: newly revised . . . With Annotations . . .
    Printed by and for John Moir: Royal Bank Close, Edinburgh;
        for Keating, Brown, and Keating: London; and for
            W. Green: Dublin. 1805. 18·5 × 11 cm. 4 vols.

A reprint of Challoner's revision, first published in 1750, of the Douai Old Testament. See No. 824.

    Closely resembles the edition of 1796 (No. 970), by the same printer. Challoner's revision of the Rheims N. T. was also reprinted in 1804.
    This edition, of about 2000 copies, circulated chiefly in England and Ireland. The London publishers subsequently sold a number of copies to *R. Coyne* of Dublin, who republished them with a Dublin imprint in 1811. (Cotton, *R. and D.*, pp. 77–8, and p. 205.)

¶   [F. F.]
                                                                                     994.

1805. The New Testament . . .
                R. Watts: Cambridge. July, 1805. 22 × 13·5 cm.

Apparently the earliest edition of the New Testament, in English, printed from stereotype plates.
    William Ged (1690–1749), the inventor of stereotyping, obtained in 1731 a contract for printing Prayer Books and Bibles for Cambridge University. But he completed only two Prayer Books, and surrendered his lease in 1738. Thwarted at every turn by trade jealousy, he failed in all his attempts to establish a business. 'Subsequently Andrew Wilson, the Earl of Stanhope's practical man, starting where Ged left off, worked out the plaster-of-Paris plan that preceded the papier-mâché system, which has established stereotyping in its present position.' (See note after 1804.)

'Cambridge stereotype edition.' Sold by *Messrs. Rivington*, etc.
Pp. 300; with table on last page.

¶   [F. F.]
                                                                                     995.

1805. B. See 1806.

1806. The Self-Interpreting Bible, containing the Old and New Testaments; to which are annexed an . . . introduction, marginal references and illustrations . . . explanatory notes . . . etc. etc. By the late Rev. John Brown, Minister of the Gospel at Haddington. The third edition, with many additional references . . .
W. Flint, for D. Ogilvy and Son, etc.: London.
1806,05. 31 × 24 cm. 2 vols.

Previous editions had appeared in 1778 and 1791.
J. Brown (1722-1787), the son of a Perthshire weaver, became minister to the Burgher Secession Congregation, at Haddington, and Professor of Divinity to the Associate Burgher Synod. He also compiled a Dictionary of the Bible, a Concordance, and a metrical version of the Psalms.

This Bible was many times reprinted, and proved almost as popular south as north of the Tweed. Its vogue in Scotland is attested by some characteristic lines of Burns:—

> For now I'm grown sae cursed douse,
> I pray an' ponder butt the house,
> My shins, my lane, I there sit roastin',
> Perusing Bunyan, Brown, an' Boston.
> *Letter to James Tennant of Glenconner*, ll. 19-22.

General title dated 1806; N. T. title dated 1805. Text ends on 6 B 2 a.

996.

1806. The Holy Bible . . .
G. Woodfall, for George Eyre and Andrew Strahan, printers to the King's most excellent Majesty: London. 1806. 29 × 22·5 cm.

Text ends on 6 T 2 b, followed by chronological Index and tables. With Translators' Preface, and Apocrypha (having separate register).
Elaborate precautions were taken to secure the accuracy of this edition, and of the similar Bible of 1813 (No. 1035), also printed by G. Woodfall for the King's printers. Horne, pp. 84–5. It contains, however, a few errors, e.g. Ezek. xlvii. 10, *the fishes shall stand* for *the fishers* . . .
Of this edition 500 copies were in imperial quarto, 2000 in royal quarto, and 3000 in medium quarto size.

¶ [F. F.]

—— Another copy.
L. P. In two volumes. [F. F.]

—— Another copy.
L. P. Without Woodfall's name on verso of title.
Bound in red morocco; the sides and back decorated with symbolic devices and monograms in gold; watered silk linings, with leather border, similarly ornamented; the edges stamped *Shiloh* and *I H S*. A leather label inserted gives an explanation of the various symbols. The back is inscribed *This Holy Bible is the gift of a family by faith to the Promised Seed.*
This volume was prepared by followers of Joanna Southcott (born 1750, died 27 Dec. 1814), in view of the expected birth of 'the Prince of Peace,' which she announced would occur on 19 Oct. 1814.

997.

1806. The Holy Bible . . .
Printed for the B. F. B. S. by R. Watts:
Cambridge. 1806. 17·5 × 10·5 cm.

'Stereotyped and printed . . . for the British and Foreign Bible Society, instituted in London in the Year 1804; and sold, to Subscribers only, by L. B. Seeley, at the Society's Depository, No. 169, Fleet Street, London.' Apparently the earliest English Bible to bear the Bible Society's name on its title. See note after 1804.

'Cambridge Stereotype Edition.' 'Nonpareil 12° in calf . . . 3s. 0d.'
Pp. 633, 192.

998.

—— ANOTHER EDITION.

Printed from the same plates as No. 998, but *J. Smith* is given on both titles as the University printer, and the date is omitted. A somewhat later issue.

999.

1806. The New Testament . . .
Printed for the B. F. B. S. by J. Smith : Cambridge. [1806.] 22 × 14 cm.

'Cambridge Stereotype Edition.' Pica 8°. In sheep, 2s. 6d.; in calf, 3s. 0d. Issued in 1806, or early in 1807.
Pp. 429. With one-page 'Table of Offices and Conditions of Men,' on extra leaf.

1000.

1807. The Holy Bible . . .
Dawson, Bensley, and Cooke, Clarendon Press :
Oxford. 1807. 32 × 26 cm.

Text ends on 8 R 2 b, followed by chronological Index and tables. With Translators' Preface, and tables of Marginal Readings and Parallel Passages from the edition of 1611; also the Apocrypha.

1001.

1807. The Gothic Gospel of Saint Matthew, from the Codex Argenteus of the fourth century; with the corresponding English, or Saxon, from the Durham Book of the eighth century, in roman characters; a literal English lesson of each; and notes, illustrations, and etymological disquisitions on organic principles. By Samuel Henshall, M.A. . . .
Printed for the author, and sold by J. White :
London. 1807. 21·5 × 13 cm.

Contains a literal English translation of the Gothic and Anglo-Saxon versions of St. Matthew's Gospel mentioned in the title.

See the Gothic and Anglo-Saxon sections of this Catalogue.

¶ [F. F.]

—— Another copy.
Very imperfect.

1002.

1808. The Holy Bible . . .
Dawson, Bensley, and Cooke, Clarendon Press :
Oxford. 1808. 21 × 12·5 cm.

Price 6s. 6d. in Sheets. Sold by *W. Dawson*, London.
Text ends on Sss 6 a. The insertion of the Apocrypha interrupts the signatures. One page of tables after O. T., and another after N. T.

¶ [F. F.]

1003.

1808. The Holy Bible . . .
　　　　Dawson, Bensley, and Cooke, Clarendon Press :
　　　　　　　　　　　　Oxford.　1808.　18·5 × 10·5 cm.

Stereotype edition. Sold by *W. Dawson*, London.
Pp. 772. One page of tables after O. T.

¶　　　　　　　　　　　　　　　　　　　　　　　　　　[F. F.]
　　　　　　　　　　　　　　　　　　　　　　　　　　　1004.

1808. The Holy Bible . . .
　　　　Dawson, Bensley, and Cooke, Clarendon Press :
　　　　　　　　　　　　Oxford.　1808.　14 × 8 cm.

Price *4s.*
Text ends on Qq 12 *b.*

¶　　　　　　　　　　　　　　　　　　　　　　　　　　[F. F.]
　　　　　　　　　　　　　　　　　　　　　　　　　　　1005.

1808. The Holy Bible, containing the Old and New Covenant, commonly called the Old and New Testament : translated from the Greek. By Charles Thomson, late Secretary to the Congress of the United States. *Printed by Jane Aitken, No. 71, North Third Street,*
　　　　　　　　Philadelphia.　1808.　22·5 × 13·5 cm.　4 vols.

　　This edition, generally known as 'Thomson's Bible,' contains the earliest translation of the Septuagint into English.
　　Charles Thomson (1729–1824) was Secretary to Congress from 1774 to 1789, when he retired to devote himself to Biblical study.
　　　J. F. Watson in his *Annals of Philadelphia* . . . (1844, vol. i. pp. 568–9) says of Thomson : ' He told me that he was first induced to study Greek from having bought a part of the Septuagint at an auction in this city. He had bought it for a mere trifle, and without knowing what it was, save that the crier said it was outlandish letters. When he had mastered it enough to understand it, his anxiety became great to see the whole ; but he could find no copy. Strange to tell, in the interval of two years, passing the same store, and chancing to look in, he then saw the remainder actually crying off for a few pence, and he bought it. I used to tell him that the translation which he afterwards made should have had these facts set at the front of that work as a preface ; for that great work, the first of the kind in the English language, strangely enough, was ushered into the world without any preface.'
　　The original MS. of his translation is preserved at Allegheny College ; three of his notebooks containing suggestions and alterations are in the Library of the Pennsylvania Historical Society ; while his own copy of the Bible, with manuscript notes in the margins, is the property of the Library Company of Philadelphia. See O'Callaghan's *List*, pp. 91–2, and Wright's *Early Bibles of America*, pp. 91–6.
　　Text printed in paragraphs, with a few foot-notes. No preface. Each volume contains a general title, as well as its own part title.

　　—— Another copy.
　　　　　　　　　　　　　　　　　　　　　　　　　　　1006.

1808. The New Testament, in an improved version, upon the basis of Archbishop Newcome's new translation : with a corrected text, and notes critical and explanatory. Published by a Society for promoting Christian knowledge and the practice of virtue, by the distribution of books.
　　　　Richard Taylor and Co. : London.　1808.　21·5 × 13 cm.

　　This original version is supposed to show a Unitarian bias

For an account of its production, and Mr. Thos. Belsham's share therein, 'consult the advertisement prefixed to Mr. Belsham's translation of St. Paul's Epistles, 4° 1822' (Cotton, p. 113 *n*.). See also Orme, pp. 328-9; and Horne, p. 304, who cites certain pamphlets and articles criticising this version, for which Archbishop Newcome seems to have been in no way responsible.

William Newcome (1729-1800), Archbishop of Armagh, devoted most of his leisure to Biblical studies with a view to an amended edition of the English Scriptures, and he set forth a plan for revision in his 'Historical View of the English Biblical Translations' (1792). His 'Attempt towards an improved version . . . of the Twelve Minor Prophets . . .' appeared in 1785; and his version of Ezekiel in 1788. His New Testament was printed at Dublin in 1796, under the title 'An attempt towards revising our English translation of the Greek Scriptures,' the Greek text adopted being Griesbach's first edition of 1775-7. The work was not published till after his death in 1800. His interleaved Bible, in four folio volumes, containing his collections for a revised version of the Old Testament, is preserved in Lambeth Palace Library.

Pp. xxxiv, 612. Printed in paragraphs, with foot-notes. The Introduction deals with the 'Origin, Progress and Design of the Work - Canon of the N. T. . . .—Brief Account of the Received Text . . .—Means of improving the Received Text . . .—Critical Editions of the Greek Testament . . . — . . . Propriety of editing a Correct Text . . .,' etc. A table is given of *Undisputed* and *Disputed Books* according to Eusebius. With maps.

1007.

1808. The New Testament, in an improved version, upon the basis of Archbishop Newcome's new translation . . . .
    R. Taylor and Co.: London. 1808. 15·5 × 9·5.

A small edition of the preceding book (No. 1007), without the Introduction, and other matter. Text ends on 2 M 5 *a*.

¶   [F. F.]
1008.

1808. The Family Testament and Learner's Assistant . . . by the Rev. Joseph Brown.
    Printed for J. Johnson, etc.: London. 1808. 18·5 × 11 cm.

See above, No. 879 (1767), and No. 990 (1803).
Printed by *S. Hamilton, Weybridge, Surrey.*
Preliminary matter, xxiv pp. Text, B 1 to T 12 *b*.

¶   [F. F.]
1009.

1809. The Holy Bible. . .
    Sir D. Hunter Blair and J. Bruce, printers to the King's most excellent Majesty: Edinburgh. 1809. 16·5 × 10 cm.

On inferior paper. Condemned for its illegibility by Lee (*Memorial*, p. 206 *n*.).
O. T. ends on Aa 9 *a*, followed by 2 pp. of tables.

¶ Imperfect: wanting the N. T.

1010.

1809. The Holy Bible . . .
    Sir D. Hunter Blair and J. Bruce: Edinburgh. 1809. 13·5 × 7·5 cm.

Text ends on Ss 11 *a*; with table on verso.

1011.

ENGLISH

1810. The Holy Bible . . .
Printed for the B. F. B. S. by J. Smith .
Cambridge. [1810.] 28 × 14·5 cm.

Stereotype edition. Small Pica demy paper 8°, in calf, 8s. 6d.
Pp. 1290.
Lee noticed some errors in this Bible, e.g. in 2 Cor. xi. 32 the words *of the Damascenes* are omitted.

1012.

1810. The Holy Bible. . . .
Dawson, Bensley, and Cooke, Clarendon Press:
Oxford. 1810. 18·5 × 11 cm.

Stereotype edition. Sold by *W. Dawson*, London.
Pp. 772. One page of tables after O. T.

¶   [F. F.]

—— Another copy.

1013.

1810. The New Testament, translated from the Latin, in the year 1380, by John Wiclif, D.D. To which are prefixed Memoirs of the life, opinions, and writings of Dr. Wiclif; and an historical account of the Saxon and English Versions of the Scriptures, previous to the opening of the fifteenth century. By the Rev. Henry Hervey Baber, M.A. . . .
Richard Edwards: London. 1810. 27·5 × 21·5 cm.

A reprint of the later Wycliffite version, as edited by Lewis, and published in 1731 (see No. 777). Edited, with new preliminary matter, by H. H. Baber, 'Assistant Librarian of the British Museum.'

A portrait of Wycliffe stands as frontispiece. Preliminary matter, lxxii pp. Text, with Glossary, 275 pp.

1014.

1810. The New Testament . . . translated from the Latin Vulgat . . . first published by the English College at Rhemes, Anno 1582. With Annotations. The eighth edition, newly revised . . .
H. Fitzpatrick, printer and bookseller to the R. C. College, Maynooth:
Dublin. 1810. 18·5 × 10·5 cm.

The third issue of MacMahon's amended edition of Challoner's revision.

This revision of Challoner's New Testament (see Nos. 824 and 825) was undertaken by Bernard MacMahon, a Dublin priest, with the approval of James Carpenter, R. C. Archbishop of Dublin. It was first published in 1783; and in 1803 a corrected edition appeared, from which the present issue was printed. For some obscure reason this is styled 'the eighth edition.' See Cotton, *R. and D.*, pp. 54-6, 78, and 82.

MacMahon was also employed in superintending the revision of the complete Douai-Rheims Bible published in 1791 with the sanction of John Thomas Troy (1789-1823), who became R. C. Archbishop of Dublin in 1784. The New Testament of 1803 conforms generally to that Bible.

According to Cotton some copies give the name *Wogan*, instead of *Fitzpatrick*, as the printer. The Approbations are:—(1) that signed by *Green* and *Watson* [Walton], which appeared in the first edition of Challoner's revision (1749); and (2) an 'Approbation of the eighth edition,' dated 1810 and signed by Archbishop Troy. These are followed by an 'Admonition,' and 'A Prayer before the reading of any part of the Holy Scripture.' Text, 523 pp.; followed by tables, and list of *errata*.

1015.

1811. The Holy Bible . . .
 Bensley, Cooke, and Collingwood, Printers to the University,
     Clarendon Press: Oxford. 1811. 22 × 13·5 cm.

 Stereotype edition. *Price 6s. 6d. Sheets.* Sold by *E. Gardner*, London.
 Pp. 976. Apocrypha mentioned in list of books.

¶ Bound in seven volumes.

1016.

1811. The Holy Bible . . .
 Printed for J. Reeves by C. Whittingham, at the
     Chiswick Press: London. 1811. 15 × 9 cm.

 A small edition of Reeves' Bible (see No. 985), without the Apocrypha, explanatory notes, and other matter.

 Sold by *G. and W. Nicol*, and *Scatcherd and Letterman*.
 Text ends on 3 Y 4 *a*. One page of tables after O. T.

¶ With 'Index to the Bible' (1825).   [F. F.]

1017.

1811. The Holy Bible . . .
 Printed for J. Reeves by C. Whittingham, at the
     Chiswick Press: London. 1811. 14·5 × 9·5 cm.

 Sold by *G. and W. Nicol*, etc.
 Quite distinct from No. 1017. The text is not divided into paragraphs.
 Text ends on 4 B 2 *b*.

1018.

1811. The Holy Bible . . .
 Sir D. Hunter Blair and J. Bruce: Edinburgh. 1811. 16·5 × 10 cm.

 Text ends on 4 F 8 *b*.
 Headline over Neh. x, on 2 K 6 *b*, *Hemiah* for *Nehemiah*.

¶ L. P. In two volumes.   [F. F.]

1019.

1811. The Holy Bible . . .
 Sir D. Hunter Blair and J. Bruce: Edinburgh. 1811. 12 × 7 cm.

 Though this edition reads line for line with No. 1019, the signatures run in twelves, not in eights. According to Brunet the other was a special issue consisting of 25 copies only. Text ends on 3 D 12 *b*. The headline over Neh. x. is correct.

¶ In two volumes. With silver clasps.   [F. F.]

1020.

1811. The New Testament . . .
 Sir D. Hunter Blair and J. Bruce: Edinburgh. 1811. 18 × 11 cm.

 Text ends on M 12 *a*; with table on verso.

1021.

1812. The Holy Bible . . .
*Printed for the B. F. B. S., by Bensley, Cooke, and Collingwood,
Clarendon Press : Oxford.* 1812. 17·5 × 10·5 cm.

Stereotype edition. Nonpareil 12°. Cost price 4s. 5d.; sale price 3s. 0d.
The N. T. title omits all mention of the B. F. B. S., and gives the name of *E. Gardner,* London.
Pp. 772. One page of tables after O. T.

¶ [F. F.]

1022.

1812. The Holy Bible . . .
J. Smith : Cambridge. 1812. 14·5 × 8·5 cm.

Stereotype edition. *Price 5s. 6d. in Sheets.* Apparently the N. T. was also issued separately, *price 1s. 3d. in Sheets.* Sold by *F. and C. Rivington,* etc.
Pp. 684, 208.

1023.

1812. The Holy Bible . . .
*Printed for the B. F. B. S. by Bensley, Cooke, and Collingwood,
Clarendon Press : Oxford.* 1812. 14 × 8 cm.

Stereotype edition. Nonpareil 24° Pocket Bible. Cost price 5s. 1d.; sale price 3s. 6d.
The N. T. title omits all mention of the Bible Society, and gives the name of *E. Gardner,* London.
Pp. 839, 252. Two pages of tables after O. T.

¶ Wants general title, which undoubtedly bore the name of the Bible Society. This copy bears the Society's stamp. See the similar edition of 1817 (No. 1079).

1024.

1812. The New Testament . . . translated out of the Latin Vulgat . . . first published by the English College of Rhemes, Anno 1582. Newly revised . . . With Annotations . . .
Preston and Heaton : Newcastle upon Tyne. 1812. 16·5 × 9·5 cm.

Edited by John Worswick, a Roman Catholic priest of Newcastle.

For a full account of this remarkable edition see Cotton, *R. and D.,* pp. 91–3, 397–8. In appearance this cheap and handy book resembles the editions of Challoner and of MacMahon. It contains an ' Admonition ' (first printed in the New Testament of 1783); a translation of the Letter (dated 1778) from Pope Pius VI. to Antonio Martini, author of an Italian version of the Bible (this appeared first in Troy's Bible of 1791, and was reprinted in many later editions); and the Approbations, as given in Challoner's Testament of 1749. But in reality the text throughout a considerable portion of this book differs entirely from any of the ordinary R.C. editions. In some passages words are added in brackets, e.g. Matt. xvi. 7 : . . . [*This he says*] *because we have taken no bread* . . .; and the words *repentance, passover, cup,* and *elders* are generally substituted for *penance, pasch, chalice,* and *ancients.* For some reason these peculiarities occur only in the first part of the New Testament; from Romans iii to the end the book is a mere reprint of Challoner's edition of 1752. But in the Gospels and Acts Cotton noted no fewer than 395 variations from the text of 1752; many of the notes are changed, or even omitted, while in some places fresh notes are added. Cotton afterwards discovered a Rheims New Testament dated 1792, which also contained these peculiar ren-

derings etc., with similar changes carried through from Romans to Revelation. Evidently it was from that New Testament that this Newcastle edition was printed.
Pp. 412.

¶ The fly-leaf is inscribed ' Francis Fry, from Henry Cotton, October 17th. 1856.'
[F. F.]
1025.

1812. The New Testament . . .
    Sir D. Hunter Blair and J. Bruce : Edinburgh. 1812. 22 × 14 cm.

Text ends on Ee 3 a. With 'A Summary of the Christian Religion,' and table, on extra leaf.

—— Another copy.
On inferior paper.
1026.

1812. The New Testament . . .
    Sir D. Hunter Blair and J. Bruce : Edinburgh. 1812. 12·5 × 6·5 cm.

Text ends on M 9 b.

¶
[F. F.]
1027.

1812. A modern, correct, and close translation of the New Testament; with occasional observations, and arranged in order of time; with a special explanation of the Apocalypse. By the author of the 'Christian Code,' and ' Primitive History.'
    T. Bensley, for John Stockdale : London. 1812. 28 × 21·5 cm.

Ascribed by Cotton (p. 114) to W. Williams.

Pp. xix, 491. On a last page is printed *A Morning Prayer ;— made Extempore, on the Fast-day, Feb. 27, 1799,* etc., *by W. W.*
1028.

1812. The Book of Job, literally translated from the original Hebrew, and restored to its natural arrangement; with notes . . . and an introductory dissertation . . . By John Mason Good . . .
    R. Watts, Broxbourn Press, for Black, Parry, and Co. :
    London. 1812. 28 × 14·5 cm.

J. M. Good (1764 1827), physician and miscellaneous writer, was elected F.R.S. in 1805. He also translated and published the Song of Solomon (1803), and the Psalms (see below, No. 1191, 1854), and left a MS. version of Proverbs.

Introductory dissertation, xcii pp.; text, divided into six parts; notes, 491 pp.
1029.

1812 ? (The Holy Bible.)
    Eyre and Strahan : London. [1812 ?] 20·5 × 13 cm.

Stereotype edition. Sold by *Longman,* etc.
Text ends on p. 936.

¶ Imperfect: containing the N. T only.
[F. F.]
1030.

ENGLISH

1812? The New Testament . . .
Printed for the B. F. B. S. by Bensley, Cooke, and Collingwood,
Clarendon Press: Oxford. [1812?] 22 × 14 cm.

Stereotype edition. Long Primer 8°. Cost price, in sheep 2s. 4d., in calf 3s. 2d.; sale price, in sheep 1s. 9d., in calf 2s. 3d.
Pp. 319. Four pages of tables follow the text, which ends on p. 315.
This and the two following editions (Nos. 1032 and 1033) are placed under the date 1812. They may have been issued a little later, but certainly not after 1816, otherwise the address of the Society's Depository on the titlepage would be Earl Street. (See Note after 1804.)

1031.

1812? The New Testament . . .
Printed for the B. F. B. S. by Bensley, Cooke, and Collingwood,
Clarendon Press: Oxford. [1812?] 18·5 × 11 cm.

Stereotype edition. Brevier 12°. Cost price, in cloth 1s. 5d., in sheep 1s. 9d., in calf 2s. 4d.; sale price, in cloth 10d., in sheep 1s. 0d., in calf 1s. 6d.
Text ends on p. 333, followed by two pages of tables.

1032.

1812? The New Testament . . .
Printed for the B. F. B. S. by Bensley, Cooke, and Collingwood,
Clarendon Press: Oxford. [1812?] 13·5 × 8 cm.

Stereotype edition; apparently from the same plates as the N. T. of No. 1024. Nonpareil 24° Pocket N. T. Cost price, in sheep 1s. 7d., in calf 2s. 0d.; sale price, in sheep 1s. 0d., in calf 1s. 6d.
Pp. 252.

1033.

1812. B. See *1815*.

1813. The Holy Bible, translated from the Latin Vulgat . . . The Old Testament, first published by the English College at Doway, A.D. 1609. And the New Testament, first published by the English College at Rhemes, A.D. 1582. With annotations, references, and an historical and chronological index.
Oswald Syers: Manchester. 1813. 40 × 25·5 cm.

Douai-Rheims version.

The text generally follows that of Challoner. The O. T. notes are Challoner's, with some taken from Troy's Dublin Bible of 1791; the N. T. notes are borrowed from Witham's edition (see No. 776).
Published in numbers, 1811-3. The first number appeared in March, 1811. General title dated 1813.
In the year 1806 Thomas Haydock, a Manchester printer, conceived the design of publishing a new edition of the Douai-Rheims Bible with notes from various commentators. On Haydock's removal to Dublin, the R. C. priests of Manchester, supposing that he had abandoned his project, persuaded Syers to undertake it. Syers secured the patronage of Dr. Gibson, Vicar Apostolic of the District, and in 1811 began printing. Haydock meantime returned to Manchester, and in July 1811 began to issue his Bible, edited by the printer's brother, George Leo Haydock, a R. C. priest of Ugthorpe, near Whitby. The book was printed at Manchester and at Dublin, and completed in 1814. Dr. Gibson withdrew his patronage from Syers' publication, when Haydock returned to Manchester; and, whether from this fact, or the competition of Haydock's Bible, Syers' unlucky work appears to have had but a limited circulation, and copies are scarce. See Cotton, *R. and D.*, pp. 83-91.
The preliminary matter includes a translation of the Decree of the Council of Trent, Admonition, Pius VI.'s letter to Martini, a Prayer, and list of books. Text: O. T., B 1 to

11 S 1 *b*. N. T. ends on 5 H 1 *a*, followed by index and tables, ending on 5 L 2 *b*. With frontispiece, and other full-page engravings.

¶ Imperfect: wanting the N. T. In two volumes. [F. F.]

1034.

1813. The Holy Bible . . .
G. Woodfall, for Eyre and Strahan: London. 1813. 30 × 23 cm.

A reprint of Eyre and Strahan's quarto edition of 1806 (see No. 997). Horne (p. 85) states that the General Convention of the Protestant Episcopal Church in the United States of America recommended that this should be adopted as its standard edition. The error in Ezek. xlvii. 10, *fishes* for *fishers*, still remains. Lee (in the lists appended to his *Additional Memorial* in 1839, p. 7) asserts that this Bible is very far from faultless; he noticed '51 deviations from the best of the old editions,' and cites among others an error in Eph. iv. 16, *holy body* for *whole body*.

Text ends on 6 T 2 *b*, followed by chronological Index and tables. With Translators' Preface, and Apocrypha (having separate register).

1035.

1813. The Holy Bible . . .
Sir D. Hunter Blair and J. Bruce : Edinburgh. 1813. 22 × 14 cm.

Text ends on 4 A 5 *a*. One page of tables after O. T., and 7 pp. of tables after N. T. Apocrypha mentioned in list of books.

1036.

1813. The Holy Bible . . .
Printed for the B. F. B. S. by Eyre and Strahan :
London. 1813. 18 × 10.5 cm.

Stereotype edition. Nonpareil 12°. Cost price 4*s*. 6*d*.; sale price 3*s*. 7*d*. (after 1 July 1813).
Pp. 633, 192. One page of tables after O. T.

1037.

1813. The New Testament . . .
Printed for the B. F. B. S. by Eyre and Strahan :
London. 1813. 18 × 10.5 cm.

Stereotype edition. Brevier 12°. Cost price, in cloth 1*s*. 5*d*., in sheep 1*s*. 8*d*., in calf 2*s*. 5*d*.; sale price, in cloth 1*s*. 2*d*., in sheep 1*s*. 4*d*., in calf 2*s*. 0*d*.
Pp. 321.

1038.

1813 ? The Holy Bible . . .
Printed for the B. F. B. S. by Eyre and Strahan :
London. [1813 ?] 22 × 13.5 cm.

Stereotype edition. Brevier 8°. Cost price 7*s*. 9*d*.; sale price 6*s*. 3*d*.
Pp. 968.

1039.

1813 ? The New Testament . . .
Printed for the B. F. B. S. by Eyre and Strahan :
London. [1813 ?] 22.5 × 14 cm.

Stereotype edition. Long Primer 8°. Cost price, in sheep 2*s*. 4*d*., in calf 3*s*. 4*d*.; sale price, in sheep 1*s*. 11*d*., in calf 2*s*. 8*d*.
Pp. 286.

1040.

1813. B. See 1816.

1814. The Self-Interpreting Bible . . . by . . . John Brown . . .
Brightly and Childs: Bungay. 1814. 44 × 27 cm.

See above, No. 996, 1806.
With forty engravings, published by *Brightly and Co.*, and by *T. Kinnersley*, Bungay, and dated 1810 etc. Introduction, notes, etc.

1041.

1814. The Holy Bible . . .
Printed for the B. F. B. S. by Eyre and Strahan:
London. 1814. 20 × 12·5 cm.

Stereotype edition. Minion 8°. Cost price 6s. 5d.; sale price 5s. 2d.
Pp. 936.

1042.

1814. The New Testament . . .
Sir D. Hunter Blair and J. Bruce: Edinburgh. 1814. 18·5 × 7·5 cm.

Text ends on M 12 b.

¶ Perhaps the N. T. of a complete Bible.
With Scotch Metrical Psalms (1814), and *Translations and Paraphrases in verse* . . .
(1814). [F. F.]

—— Another copy.

1043.

1814. Extracts from the Old and New Testaments, for the use of schools in Ireland, according to the respective translations of the Church of England, and the Church of Rome.
Graisberry and Campbell: Dublin. 1814. 21·5 × 13 cm.

According to the Preface, the Fourteenth Report of the Commissioners of Education in Ireland condemned the school-books generally adopted, which, 'instead of improving, corrupt the mind; being calculated to incite to lawless and profligate adventure, to cherish superstition, and to lead to dissention and disloyalty'; and recommended for the use of schools a selection of 'Extracts from the Sacred Scriptures, an early acquaintance with which we deem of the utmost importance, and indeed indispensable in forming the mind to just notions of duty and sound principles of conduct.' To supply a suitable school-book, this volume was compiled.

The two texts—King James' and the Douai-Rheims—are printed on opposite pages.
Pp. 319.

1044.

1814. B. See 1816.

1815. The Self Interpreting Bible, with an Evangelical Commentary, by the late Rev[d]. John Brown . . .
Printed for, and published by, Richard Evans:
London. 1812,15. 44·5 × 27 cm.

See above, No. 996, 1806.
General title dated 1812; N. T. title dated 1815.
Reprinted from the second edition, issued in 1791 by *Bensley*. Introduction, notes, etc., and plates. With Apocrypha.
Sold 'in 77 double Nos. in boards, 5l. 8s.' or in 154 Nos. at 8d. each; Apocrypha in 18 Nos. at 8d. each.

1045.

1815. The Holy Bible . . .
Printed for the B. F. B. S. by Eyre and Strahan :
London. 1815. 25 × 16 cm.

Stereotype edition. Small Pica 8°, royal paper. Cost price 21s. 0d. ; sale price 21s. 0d. Pp. 1271 ; with one page of tables.

1046.

1815. The Holy Bible . . .
Printed for the B. F. B. S. by J. Smith :
Cambridge. 1815. 23 × 14·5 cm.

Stereotype edition. Small Pica 8°, medium paper. Cost price 12s. 0d. ; sale price 9s. 8d. Pp. 1290.

1047.

1815. The Holy Bible . . .
Printed for the B. F. B. S. by J. Smith :
Cambridge. 1815. 22·5 × 13·5 cm.

Stereotype edition. Brevier 8°. Cost price 7s. 9d. ; sale price 6s. 3d.
Pp. 556, 196, 224. The pagination in the O. T. begins afresh at Isaiah. Apocrypha mentioned in list of books.

1048.

1815. A revised translation and interpretation of the Sacred Scriptures, after the Eastern manner, from concurrent authorities of the critics, interpreters and commentators, copies and versions ; shewing that the inspired writings contain the seeds of the valuable sciences . . . With an Appendix . . .
Printed for R. Hutchinson and Co., and others :
Glasgow. 1815. 22 × 14 cm. 3 vols.

This original version was first published in 1799,98. Orme (p. 303) and Horne (p. 260) ascribe it to *David Macrae*. D. McRae was a licentiate preacher in the Church of Scotland.

Preface signed *J. M. Ray*, and dated London, 1802. Vol. 3 has a slightly different title, bearing the words ' A new edition, corrected and improved,' and giving the printer's name *W. Lang, Glasgow.* Pp. xx, 837, 814, 596.

1049.

1815. The Holy Bible . . .
Sir D. Hunter Blair and J. Bruce : Edinburgh. 1815. 18 × 11 cm.

Text ends on Ii 5 a, followed by Epitome (3 pp.). Two pages of tables after O. T.

— Another copy.
On inferior paper.

1050.

1815. The New Testament of our Lord and Saviour Jesus Christ : translated out of the Latin Vulgate ; and diligently compared with the original Greek. Stereotyped from the edition published by authority in 1749.
Stereotyped and printed by A. Wilson, Camden Town ; and sold by J. Booker, New Bond Street : London. 1815. 18 × 10·5 cm.

For a full account of the steps which led to this edition of the Rheims New Testament, see Cotton, *R. and D.*, pp. 94–110.

It was published by the 'Roman Catholic Bible Society,' formed in 1813 by Bishop Poynter, Lord Clifford, Peter Gandolphy, and other Roman Catholics in London. With this association the Protestant founders of the 'Catholic Fund,' for the circulation of the Rheims version without note or comment, endeavoured at first to co-operate; but the scheme, promoted mainly by William Blair, fell through. The Roman Catholic Bible Society encountered bitter opposition from Dr. Milner and other Roman Catholics, and soon came to an end.

This edition contains the Approbation prefixed to Challoner's first edition, list of *errata*, Address (by Bp. Poynter), Historical Index, list of books, and Advertisement; text, pp. 3 to 641; table, 13 pp.

The text follows the edition of 1749; the notes, too, are Challoner's, but their controversial parts are generally omitted.

According to Cotton, the book was reprinted at least three times.

¶ Henry Cotton's copy. In the original boards; with the Laws and Regulations of the R. C. Bible Society printed on the back.

1051.

1815. The New Testament . . .
   Sir D. Hunter Blair and J. Bruce :
          Edinburgh. 1815. 17·5 × 10·5 cm.

Text ends on N 12 *b*.

1052.

1815. B. See 1816.

1816. The Devotional Diamond Pocket Bible: with notes and reflections, by the Rev. W. Gurney . . . Embellished with engravings.
   Printed by and for J. Jones, Lambeth : London. 1813,16. 13 × 7 cm.

With additional general title engraved. General title dated 1813. N.T. title, dated 1816, bears the name *J. White* in place of *J. Jones*. W. Gurney was 'Rector of Saint Clement Danes, Strand.'

Pp. 874, 263. With short notes at the end of some chapters, and a few engravings.

1053.

1816. The Self-Interpreting Bible . . . by . . . John Brown . . .
   Brightly and Childs, for T. Kinnersley :
         Bungay. 1814,16. 43·5 × 26·5 cm.

See above, No. 996, 1806.

With additional engraved titlepage, bearing the name *R. Evans* (see No. 1045), and dated 1814. Introduction, notes, etc.; and many engravings. With Apocrypha.

¶ Slightly imperfect: wanting some preliminary matter.

1054.

1816. The Holy Bible . . .
   Sir D. Hunter Blair and J. Bruce :
         Edinburgh. 1816,15. 13·5 × 7·5 cm.

General title dated 1816; N. T. title dated 1815.
Text ends on Ss 11 *a*, with table on verso.

1055.

1816. The Holy Bible, translated from the Latin Vulgat . . . The Old Testament first published by the English College at Doway, A.D. 1609. And the New Testament, first published by the English College at Rhemes,

A.D. 1582. With Annotations . . . Revised . . . and approved of by the Most Reverend Doctor Troy, R. C. A. D.
Printed and published by Richard Coyne : Dublin ; and sold by Keating, Brown, and Keating : London. 1816. 38 × 26 cm.

Douai-Rheims version.

For a full account of this edition see Cotton, *R. and D.*, pp. 110–6.

J. A. McNamara, a Cork bookseller, supported by influential patronage, began in 1813 to issue the R. C. Bible in parts, at 1s. 8d. each, to subscribers only, the Rev. P. Walsh of Dublin having been appointed to revise the work. In 1814 McNamara, who had removed to Dublin, became bankrupt, and R. Coyne was persuaded to complete the publication. The finished Bible appeared in 1816, with the approval of Archbishop Troy, as stated on the title.

In the O. T. the text and notes generally follow Challoner's edition; the text of the N. T. appears to be copied from a folio edition printed at Liverpool in 1788, with the original notes Text, 927, 424 pp. With the preface of 1582, tables, etc.

The re-issue of the controversial notes of the original Rheims New Testament aroused much indignation, and Dr. Troy eventually withdrew his approbation.

In 1818 McNamara, who had returned to Cork, published another edition of this Bible in that city, reprinting many sheets, and adding fresh matter, including an acrimonious work entitled *The Errata to the Protestant Bible* . . ., by Thomas Ward, first published in 1688.

The following error occurs in 1 Cor. i. 25 : *the wickedness of God* . . ., for *the weakness of God* . . .

¶ [F. F.]

—— Another copy.

1056.

1816. The Holy Bible . . .
Printed for the B. F. B. S. by Eyre and Strahan :
London. 1816. 31 × 24 cm.

Stereotype edition. 'Small Pica 4°.' This is the Small Pica 8° edition, printed on large paper, 'with broad margins for writing upon.' It is marked in the price list for 1817 at 52s. 6d. in boards.
Pp. 1271.

1057.

1816. The Holy Bible . . .
Printed for the B. F. B. S. by J. Smith :
Cambridge. 1816. 19·5 × 12·5 cm.

Cambridge Stereotype edition. Minion 8°.
Pp. 988.

—— Another copy.

The fly-leaf bears two inscriptions : (1) 'Francis Fry, Frenchay,' and (2) 'This Bible was given to me when I went to Joel Lean's School, Fishponds, 1817. The writing above is by Joel Lean. Francis Fry, Cotham, 1856.' [F. F.]

1058.

1816. The Holy Bible . . .
Corrall, Charing Cross, for Eyre and Strahan :
London. 1816. 12 × 7 cm.

Sold by *Longman*, etc.
Text ends on Qq 3 a.

¶ [F. F.]

1059.

1816. The New Testament . . .
  Printed for the B. F. B. S. by Eyre and Strahan :
    London. 1816. 22 × 14 cm.

Stereotype edition. Pica 8°. Cost price, in sheep 3s. 6d., in calf 4s. 6d.; sale price, in sheep 2s. 10d., in calf 3s. 8d.
Pp. 448.
                                                                               1060.

1816. The New Testament . . .
  Printed for the B. F. B. S. by J. Smith :
    Cambridge. 1816. 21·5 × 13·5 cm.

Cambridge Stereotype edition. Long Primer 8°. Cost price, in sheep 2s. 4d., in calf 3s. 4d.; sale price, in sheep 1s. 11d., in calf 2s. 8d.
Pp. 296; with table on last page.

¶ Bound in sheep. In this copy quotation-marks are added by hand to all the words of our Lord. [**F. F.**]

—— Another copy.
Bound in calf.
                                                                               1061.

1816. The New Testament . . .
  Printed for the B. F. B. S. by J. Smith :
    Cambridge. 1816. 14·5 × 8 cm.

Stereotype edition. Nonpareil 24° Pocket N. T. Cost price, in sheep 1s. 7d., in calf 2s. 2d.; sale price, in sheep 1s. 3d., in calf 1s. 9d.
Pp. 251; with table, 1 p.
                                                                               1062.

1816. The Holy Bible . . .
  Printed for the B. F. B. S. by Bensley, Cooke, and Collingwood,
    Clarendon Press : Oxford. 1816. 25·5 × 16 cm.

Small Pica, royal paper, with marginal references. Cost price 16s. 0d.; sale price 12s. 9d. (B. F. B. S. list for 1817.)
The N. T. title omits all mention of the B. F. B. S., and gives the name of *E. Gardner*, London.
Text ends on 4 H 1 b. Apocrypha mentioned in list of books.
This Bible and No. 1064 are placed after the other B. F. B. S. editions of 1816, because their general titles give a new address for the Society's Depository, 'Earl Street, Blackfriars,' showing that they were published later in the same year. After 1816 L. B. Seeley's name disappears from the titlepages of the Bible Society's editions. See Note after 1804.
                                                                               1063.

1816. The Holy Bible . . .
  Printed for the B. F. B. S. by J. Cooke and S. Collingwood,
    Clarendon Press : Oxford. 1816. 22 × 13·5 cm.

Stereotype edition. Long Primer 8°. Cost price 10s. 10d.; sale price 8s. 8d. (B. F. B. S. list for 1817.)
The N. T. title omits all mention of the B. F. B. S., and gives the name of *E. Gardner*, London; it also gives *Bensley, Cooke, and Collingwood* as the printers.
Pp. 976. Apocrypha mentioned in list of books.
                                                                               1064.

1816. The New Testament . . .
   C. Corrall, Charing Cross, for Eyre and Strahan :
   London. 1816.   9·5 × 5·5 cm.
Sold by *Longman*, etc.
In minute type on thin paper.   Text ends on Dd 3 *b*.

¶ Bound in silk. [F. F.]

1065.

1816. The Apocrypha, embellished with engravings, from pictures and designs by the most eminent English artists.
   T. Bensley, for T. Cadell and W. Davies : London. 1816.   49 × 39 cm.

A supplementary volume, completing Macklin's Bible published in 1800. (See No. 982.)

Preliminary matter includes a List of Subscribers, and 'Explanations of the head and ail-pieces to the Apocrypha.'   Type etc. exactly as in Macklin's Bible.

¶ Uncut, in publishers' boards.

1066.

1816. A new literal translation from the original Greek of all the Apostolical Epistles ; with a commentary, and notes . . . to which is added a history of the life of the Apostle Paul. By James Macknight, D.D. A new edition ; to which is prefixed an account of the life of the author.
   Walker and Greig : Edinburgh, for Longman, etc. and others :
   London, etc.   1816.   23 × 14 cm.   6 vols.

First published in 4 vols. at Edinburgh, 1795, and reprinted in 6 vols. at London, 1806, etc.   A specimen containing 1 and 2 Thessalonians, appeared as early as 1787.
J. Macknight (1721-1800) was a minister of the Church of Scotland.

The preface states that this work was the result of unremitting labour of seldom less than eleven hours a day for almost thirty years ; during which the whole manuscript was written no less than five times with the translator's own hand.
Four columns give (1) 'Old Translation' (King James' version), (2) 'Greek Text,' (3) 'New Translation,' and (4) 'Commentary' (or paraphrase). With foot-notes, and much supplementary matter ; and a map.

1067.

1816 ?   The Holy Bible . . .
   Printed for the B. F. B. S. by Eyre and Strahan :
   London.   [1816 ?]   22 × 13·5 cm.

Stereotype edition.   Brevier 8°.   Cost price 7*s.* 9*d.* ; sale price 6*s.* 3*d.*
Pp. 968.
This and the two following editions were issued perhaps at the end of 1816, or early in 1817.   The titles give the Earl Street address.   See note on No. 1063.

1068.

1816 ?   The Holy Bible . . .
   Printed for the B. F. B. S. by Eyre and Strahan :
   London.   [1816 ?]   17·5 × 11 cm.

Stereotype edition.   Nonpareil 12°.   Cost price 4*s.* 6*d.* ; sale price 3*s.* 7*d.*
Pp. 633, 192.   One page of tables after O. T.

1069.

1816? The New Testament . . .
  Printed for the B. F. B. S. by Bensley, Cooke, and Collingwood,
  the Clarendon Press: Oxford. [1816?] 21·5 × 18·5 cm.

Stereotype edition. Pica 8°. Cost price, in sheep 3s. 6d., in calf 4s. 6d.; sale price, in sheep 2s. 10d., in calf 3s. 8d.
Pp. 464. Four pages of tables follow the text, which ends on p. 460.

1070.

1817. The Self-interpreting Bible . . . by the late Rev. J. Brown . . . revised . . . by the Rev. Thomas Raffles.
  Barnard and Farley, for Walker and Edwards, etc.:
  London. [1817.] 28 × 22 cm. 2 vols.

See above, No. 996, 1806.
No date on the titlepage, but the 'Advertisement to the present edition' is dated April 1817. A new edition of Brown's Bible, with additional matter. With plates.

1071.

1817. The Holy Bible . . . with Notes . . . together with . . . introductions, tables, indexes, maps, and plans: prepared and arranged by the Rev. George D'Oyly, B.D., and the Rev. Richard Mant, D.D. . . . under the direction of the Society for Promoting Christian Knowledge. For the use of families.
  Printed for the Society by Bensley, Cooke, and Collingwood,
  Clarendon Press: Oxford. 1817. 29 × 22 cm. 3 vols.

The first edition of this Bible, prepared at the instance of Archbishop Manners-Sutton, appeared in 1814; the editors were his Domestic Chaplains.
  D'Oyly (1778–1846) was rector of Buxted in Sussex, and later became rector of Lambeth; Mant (1776–1848) subsequently became Bishop of Down, Connor, and Dromore.

Text ends on 15 G 1 b. With Apocrypha. Many plates, chiefly after old masters.

¶ Bound up at the end is 'A Concordance . . . published under the direction of the Society for Promoting Christian Knowledge. Edited by James W. Bellamy . . . Second Edition' (1818).

1072.

1817. The Holy Bible . . .
  Printed for the B. F. B. S. by Eyre and Strahan:
  London. 1817. 28 × 18 cm.

Stereotype edition.
  The N. T. title omits all mention of the B. F. B. S., and gives the names *Longman*, etc. as publishers.
  O. T. and Apocrypha, pp. 5 to 1120; N. T., 279 pp.; followed by chronological Index and tables, ending on p. 308. With Translators' Preface.
  The only edition of the English Bible with the Apocrypha ever printed with the name of the Bible Society on the titlepage. The inclusion of the Apocrypha was due to an error, and the volume apparently never passed into circulation in this form. (See below.)

¶ In two volumes. Uncut, in paper-covered boards.

1073.

—— ANOTHER EDITION.

The same as No. 1073, with the omission of the Apocrypha and the Translators' Preface. This is the edition advertised in the Price List of 1817 as 'Long Primer, imperial paper, 8vo. with the full references of the authorised 4to. Bible, in the margin, fine edition, 2 vols. boards . . . 36s. 0d.'
Pp. 907, 308.

1074.

1817. The Holy Bible . . .
Printed for the B. F. B. S., by Eyre and Strahan:
London. 1817. 23 × 15·5 cm.

Stereotype edition. Brevier 8°, 'medium paper, with full references in the margins, as in the authorised 4to. Bibles.' Cost price 11s. 10d.; sale price 9s. 6d.
Pp. 1008. One page of tables after O. T., and another after N. T.

1075.

1817. The Holy Bible . . .
Printed for the B. F. B. S. by Eyre and Strahan :
London. 1817. 22 × 14 cm.

Stereotype edition. Long Primer 8°. Cost price 10s. 10d.; sale price 8s. 8d.
Pp. 927, 286. One page of tables after O. T.

1076.

1817. The Holy Bible . . .
J. Smith: Cambridge. 1817. 18 × 10·5 cm.

Cambridge Stereotype edition. *Price 3s. in Sheets.* Sold by *Messrs. Rivington,* etc.
Pp. 633, 192.

¶
[**F. F.**]
1077.

1817. The Holy Bible . . .
Printed for the B. F. B. S. by Bensley, Cooke, and Collingwood,
Clarendon Press: Oxford. 1817. 17·5 × 10·5 cm.

Stereotype edition. Nonpareil 12°. Cost price 4s. 6d.; sale price 3s. 7d.
The N. T. title omits all mention of the B. F. B. S., and gives the name of *E. Gardner*, London.
Pp. 772. One page of tables after O. T.

1078.

1817. The Holy Bible . . .
Printed for the B. F. B. S. by J. Cooke and S. Collingwood,
Clarendon Press: Oxford. 1817. 14 × 7·5 cm.

Stereotype edition. Nonpareil 24°. Cost price 5s. 2d.; sale price 4s. 2d.
The N. T. title omits all mention of the Bible Society, and gives the name of *E. Gardner*, London; it also gives *Bensley, Cooke, and Collingwood* as the printers.
Pp. 839, 252. Two pages of tables after O. T.

—— Another copy.

In this the list of N. T. books is printed by mistake on verso of the general title.

[**F. F.**]
1079.

ENGLISH

1817. The New Testament . . .
Printed for the B. F. B. S. by J. Smith:
Cambridge. 1817. 18 × 10·5 cm

Stereotype edition. Brevier 12°. Cost price, in cloth 1s. 5d., in sheep 1s. 8d., in calf 2s. 5d.; sale price, in cloth 1s. 2d., in sheep 1s. 4d., in calf 2s. 0d.
Pp. 324.

1080.

1817. The New Testament of the English version of the Polyglott Bible; having a centre column of . . . references; interpaged with the Biblical Concordance entitled 'Scripture Harmony' . . .
R. Watts, for Samuel Bagster, No. 15 Paternoster Row,
London. 1817. 17 × 10·5 cm.

With Prefaces to text and Concordance. Pp. 188. The Concordance is interleaved with the text.

¶ [F. F.]

1081.

1817. The New Testament . . .
Printed for the B. F. B. S. by Eyre and Strahan:
London. 1817. 14·5 × 8·5 cm.

Stereotype edition. Minion 24° Pocket N. T. Cost price, in sheep 1s. 7d., in calf 2s. 2d.; sale price, in sheep 1s. 3d., in calf 1s. 9d.
Pp. 343.

1082.

1817. B. See 1818.

1818. The Holy Bible . . .
J. Cooke and S. Collingwood, Clarendon Press:
Oxford. 1818, 17. 14 × 7·5 cm.

Stereotype edition. *Price 4s. in Sheets.* Nonpareil 24°. Sold by *E. Gardner*, London. General title dated 1818; N. T. title, dated 1817, gives the names *Bensley, Cooke, and Collingwood*.
Pp. 839, 252. Two pages of tables after O. T.

1083.

1818. The New Testament . . . translated out of the Latin Vulgat . . . first published by the English College of Rhemes, Anno 1582. Newly revised . . . With Annotations . . .
Keating and Brown: London. 1818. 18 × 10·5 cm.

According to Cotton (*R. and D.*, p. 237), a close reprint of Challoner's first edition of 1749.
Pp. 500.

1084.

1818. The New Testament . . .
Printed for the B. F. B. S. by Eyre and Strahan:
London. 1818. 17·5 × 11 cm.

Stereotype edition. Brevier 12°. Cost price, in cloth 1s. 4d., in sheep 1s. 7d., in calf 2s. 4d.; sale price, in cloth 1s. 0d., in sheep 1s. 2d., in calf 1s. 9d.

1085.

1818. Arrangements of passages in the Scriptures; in prose, and in poetry. By Smith Travers.
Printed for the author by William Fry :
Philadelphia. 1818. 31 × 24·5 cm.

Selections from the Old and New Testaments, the poetry printed in 'parallelisms.' Pp. 84.
1086.

1819. The Holy Bible . . .
J. Cooke and S. Collingwood, Clarendon Press :
Oxford. 1819. 23 × 15 cm.

Small Pica 8°. Sold by *E. Gardner*, London.
Text ends on 4 L 4 a, with table on verso. Apocrypha included in list of books.

¶ In two volumes, to each of which are appended the Scotch Metrical Psalms (1809) with the 'Translations and Paraphrases.' The price on the titlepage is erased.
[F. F.]
1087.

1819. The Holy Bible . . .
J. Cooke and S. Collingwood, Clarendon Press :
Oxford. 1819. 14 × 8 cm.

Stereotype edition. *Price 5s. 6d. in Sheets.* Sold by *E. Gardner*, London.
Pp. 839, 252. Two pages of tables after O. T.
1088.

1819. The Epistles of St. Paul to the Colossians, to the Thessalonians, to Timothy, and to Titus, and the general Epistle of St. James : a new version from the Greek, and chiefly from the text of Griesbach; by Philalethes.
Richards and Co., for Rowland Hunter :
London. 1819. 16·5 × 10 cm.

Horne (p. 325) identifies Philalethes with *John Jones, LL.D.* (1766?-1827), who also translated Isaiah (pub. 1830).

Pp. viii, 70.
1089.

ACCESSION OF KING GEORGE IV: 29 JANUARY 1820.

1820. The New Testament . . . translated out of the Latin Vulgate . . . first published by the English College of Rhemes, Anno 1582; newly revised . . . Stereotype edition.
R. Coyne, 16 Parliament St. : Dublin. 1820. 18 × 11 cm.

Rheims version.

This remarkable Testament appeared without a single note, comment, various reading, or marginal reference. An edition of 20,000 copies was printed for a body of Dublin gentlemen, both Roman Catholics and Protestants (though the latter predominated), for general distribution in Ireland at low prices, especially in schools, hospitals, etc. (Cotton, *R. and D.* pp. 119-122.)

The title, with list of books on verso, is immediately followed by the text, pp. 3 to 311. On verso of the last leaf, according to Cotton, appear the names of the printer and stereotyper; but in the copy mentioned below, this page contains a certificate by Dr. Troy and 'An Extract of a Rescript' (dated 18 April 1820), commending the reading of the Holy Scriptures, addressed by Pius VII. to the Vicars Apostolic of Great Britain. A replica of this page was also pasted inside the cover of each copy.

Dr. Troy's certificate, dated Dublin, 9 Feb. 1820, runs :—'I Certify, that the Sacred Text of the New Testament, in *this Edition* of it, is conformable to that of former approved Editions; and particularly to that of the Douay English Version sanctioned by me, and published by R. Cross, in the year 1791.' Cotton, however, states that the text is taken from Challoner's second edition of 1750.

Not long after the publication of this New Testament, Coyne printed a small tract (36 pp.), headed 'Supplement to the Douay Testament without Note or Comment.'

¶ A printed slip is pasted on the title in this copy, hiding the date, and bearing the words and sold by R. M. Tims, 85, Grafton-street; and in London, sold by Robert Henry C. Tims, 21, Wigmore-street, Cavendish-square; and Messrs. J. Nisbet and Co., Berners-street.' A number of Coyne's unsold copies apparently passed later into the hands of certain London booksellers, one of whom in 1825 issued the book with a false title bearing the words . . . *with Annotations.*

1090.

—— ANOTHER EDITION.

Apparently the same book as the above, with the title and last leaf reprinted—issued perhaps some years later. The titlepage bears the name of *Richard Coyne, 4 Capel-street* . . ., and is not dated; on verso are the 'Recommendation' of Dr. Troy, and the Extract from Pius VII.'s Rescript. On verso of the last leaf of text is printed the list of books.

1091.

1820. The New Testament . . .
Stereotyped for, and printed by, George Grierson and Martin Keene, printers to the King's most excellent Majesty:
Dublin. 1820. 18 × 10·5 cm.

Stereotyped by *Andrew Wilson*, London.
Pp. 324; with table on last page.

¶ [F. F.]

1092.

1820. Scripture Lessons for schools on the British system of mutual instruction. Adopted in Russia, by order of the Emperor, Alexander I.
J. B. G. Vogel : London. 1820. 21 × 13·5 cm.

According to the preface, these selections were originally made in Russian at St. Petersburg in 1818–9, and adopted in Russian schools at the instance of Prince Alexander Galitzin, Minister of Instruction. The Committee of the British and Foreign School Society then determined to issue them in the chief languages of Europe. This volume is the English edition.

The extracts are divided into :—(1) Historical Lessons from the O. T.; (2) Lessons on Duty towards God and Man; (3) Lessons from the Evangelists and the Acts.
Pp. 160.

1093.

1821. The Holy Bible . . .
Printed for the B. F. B. S. by Samuel Collingwood and Co., Clarendon Press: Oxford. 1821. 19·5 × 12·5 cm.

Stereotype edition. Minion 8°, with marginal references. Cost price 9s. 0d.; sale price 6s. 9d. (B. F. B. S. list for 1822.)
Text ends on p. 1038, followed by 2 pp. of tables.

1094.

1821. The New Testament . . .
Eyre and Strahan: London. 1821. 14 × 8·5 cm.

Stereotype edition. Sold by *Longman*, etc.
Pp. 343.

¶ [F. F.]
1095.

1822. The Holy Bible . . .
Printed for the B. F. B. S., by J. Smith:
Cambridge. 1822. 22 × 13·5 cm.

Stereotype edition. Long Primer 8°. Cost price 8s. 7d.; sale price 6s. 6d.
Pp. 1032. One page of tables after O. T., and another after N. T. Apocrypha mentioned in list of books.

1096.

1822. The New Testament . . .
Printed for the Porteusian Bible Society (and sold at their
Depository, 40 Frith-Street, Soho), by Eyre and Strahan:
London. 1822. 18·5 × 10·5 cm.

Stereotype edition.
With the special marks at the beginning of each chapter. See above, No. 969. Pp. 336.

¶ With 'The Porteusian Index; or Family Guide to the Holy Scriptures' (1823).
1097.

1822. B. See 1823.

1823. The Holy Bible . . .
Printed for the B. F. B. S. by S. Collingwood and Co.,
Clarendon Press: Oxford. 1823,22. 31·5 × 24·5 cm.

'Pica, royal paper, 4to. with marginal references, calf lettered . . . 21s. 0d.'
The N. T. title omits all mention of the B. F. B. S.
General title dated 1823; N. T. title dated 1822. Text ends on 7 G 1 b, followed by chronological Index and tables. With Translators' Preface.

1098.

1823. The Holy Bible . . .
S. Collingwood and Co., Clarendon Press: Oxford. 1823. 22 × 14 cm.

Stereotype edition. Brevier 8°. Sold by *E. Gardner*, etc.
Pp. 975. Table at end. Apocrypha mentioned in list of books.

¶ [F. F.]
1099.

1823. The Holy Bible . . .
Eyre and Strahan: London. 1823. 17·5 × 11 cm.

Stereotype edition. Nonpareil 12°. Sold by *Longman*, etc.
Pp. 736, 188. Tables at the end of O. T. and N. T. With Apocrypha.

¶ [F. F.]
1100.

1823. B. See 1824 and 1825.

ENGLISH 343

1824. The Holy Bible . . .
Sir D. Hunter Blair and J. Bruce : Edinburgh. 1824,23. 13·5 × 7·5 cm.

General title dated 1824; N. T. title dated 1823. Text ends on Ss 11 a, with table on verso.

¶ The cover is stamped *Hibernian Bible Society*. [F. F.]
1101.

1824. A new family Bible, and improved version, from corrected texts of the originals; with notes critical and explanatory, and short practical reflections . . . with a general introduction . . . By the Rev. B. Boothroyd . . .
Printed for the author, and others, by William Moore :
Huddersfield. 1824. 29·5 × 24 cm. 3 vols.

First published in 1818.
Benjamin Boothroyd (1768–1836) was a Nonconformist minister at Halifax, and afterwards at Huddersfield. The idea of this Family Bible was suggested to him by Henry Tuke, of York, a member of the Society of Friends.

Introduction, 63 pp. Text, 739, 722, 505 pp. With prefaces, foot-notes, tables, indexes, etc.
1102.

1824. The New Testament . . .
Sir D. Hunter Blair and J. Bruce : Edinburgh. 1824. 21 × 13 cm.

Text ends on Ee 3 a, followed by one leaf containing 'A Summary of the Christian Religion,' and table.
An incorrect edition: e.g. Mark xi. 8, *strayed* for *strawed*; Luke vi. 29, *forbid* for *forbid not*; 1 Pet. iii. 18, *offered* for *suffered*.

¶ This copy formerly belonged to Dr. John Lee. It has the following MS. note on the fly-leaf: 'This is one of the Editions of the New Testament printed by His Majesty's Printer for Scotland, produced by me when required to give evidence before a Committee of the House of Commons in 1831. John Lee.'
With Scotch Metrical Psalms (1823) and ' Translations and Paraphrases.' [F. F.]
1103.

1824. The Gospel . . . according to Saint Luke : the Authorised version . . . and the Douay version . . . in parallel columns.
Goodwin, for William Curry, Junior, and Co. :
Dublin. 1824. 14·5 × 8·5 cm.

Evidently a Protestant publication.

Pp. 129. In the case of certain words (e.g. *repentance, penance*, etc.) the Greek and the Latin are given at the foot of the page.

¶ Bound with a copy of the uniform edition of Acts (No. 1107).
1104.

See Appendix for certain American editions printed between 1809 and 1824.

NOTE.
AFTER THE DATE 1824 THIS CATALOGUE REGISTERS ONLY SUCH EDITIONS OF THE ENGLISH BIBLE AS PRESENT SOME FEATURE OF IMPORTANCE OR INTEREST.

1825. The Holy Bible . . .
Printed for the Naval and Military Bible Society (instituted in 1780) by Eyre and Strahan : London. 1825,23. 13·5 × 8 cm.

Stereotype edition. Pearl 24°. Sold at the Society's Depository, No. 32, Sackville Street. General title dated 1825. N. T. title, dated 1823, omits all mention of the N. M. B. S., and gives *Longman*, etc. as the publishers.
Pp. 936 ; with 5 pp. of tables at end.

¶ Covers stamped with the name of the publishing Society.

1105.

1825. The New Testament . . .
Printed for the Hibernian Bible Society by Sir D. Hunter Blair and J. Bruce : Edinburgh. 1825. 14 × 8 cm.

Text ends on T 4 b.

1106.

1825. The Acts of the Apostles : the Authorised version . . . and the Douay version . . . in parallel columns.
Goodwin, for W. Curry, Jun. and Co. : Dublin. 1825. 14·5 × 8·5 cm.

Uniform with the edition of St. Luke's Gospel printed in 1824 (No. 1104).
Pp. 124.

¶ Bound with a copy of No. 1104.

1107.

1826. The Holy Bible . . .
Eyre and Strahan : London. 1826. 14·5 × 8·5 cm.

Stereotype edition. Sold by *Longman*, etc.
Pp. 1119, 343.

¶   [F. F.]

1108.

1826. The Holy Bible . . .
Sir D. Hunter Blair and J. Bruce : Edinburgh. 1826. 14 × 8 cm.

Text ends on Ss 11 a, with table on verso.

¶ With Scotch Metrical Psalms (1826), and 'Translations and Paraphrases.'   [F. F.]

1109.

1826. The Book of Psalms.
Printed for the Hibernian Bible Society by Sir D. Hunter Blair and J. Bruce : Edinburgh. 1826. 14 × 8 cm.

Text ends on E 6 b.

1110.

1826. The New Testament ...
Printed for the Hibernian Bible Society by Sir D. Hunter Blair and M. S. Bruce: Edinburgh. 1826. 17·5 × 10·5 cm.

The name *M. S. Bruce* now takes the place of *J. Bruce* in the imprint.
Text ends on S 11 *a.* Double columns, with marginal references.

1111.

1826. The Gospel according to St. Luke, and the Acts of the Apostles.
Printed for the Hibernian Bible Society by Sir D. Hunter Blair and M. S. Bruce: Edinburgh. 1826. 12 × 7 cm.

Text ends on M 4 *a.*

1112.

1826. B. See 1827.

1827. The Comprehensive Bible ... with the various readings ... a general introduction ... introductions and concluding remarks to each book: the parallel passages ... systematically arranged: philological and explanatory notes ...
Bagster and Thoms, for S. Bagster: London. 1827,26. 32 × 25 cm.

Edited by William Greenfield (1799–1831), who became Editorial Superintendent of the Bible Society in 1830.

General title dated 1827; N. T. title dated 1826. With Dedication to King George IV., Translators' Preface, Introduction, indexes, tables, etc. Text ends on p. 1338.

—— Another copy.

With *Boydell's Illustrations of Holy Writ: being a series of one hundred copper-plate engravings, from original drawings by Isaac Taylor, Junior, of Ongar* ... (*London*, 1820 and *Scripture Genealogy* ... (*S. Leigh, London*, 1817).
In two volumes.

1113.

1827. The Holy Bible ...
S. Collingwood and Co., Clarendon Press: Oxford. 1827. 41 × 33 cm.

Sold by *E. Gardner,* London.
Text ends on 14 C 2 *b.* With Apocrypha.

¶ A label on the cover is inscribed: 'St. Laurence Thanet, 1835.'

1114.

1827. An English Harmony of the four Evangelists, disposed after the manner of the Greek of William Newcome ... with explanatory notes and indexes, and a new map of Palestine ...
Bagster and Thoms, for S. Bagster: London. 1827. 23·5 × 14·5 cm.

Compiled by William Phillips (1775–1828) a member of the Society of Friends.

First published in 1802.
Text and notes, 467 pp.

1115.

1827. The Book of Psalms.
Printed for the B. F. B. S. by S. Collingwood and Co.,
Clarendon Press: Oxford. 1827. 22 × 14 cm.

Stereotype edition. Pica 8°. Cost price 1s. 8d., sale price 1s. 3d.
Pp. 112.

1116.

1827. Liber Ecclesiasticus, the Book of the Church; or Ecclesiasticus: translated from the Latin Vulgate, by Luke Howard, F.R.S.
Printed for the translator, by A. and R. Spottiswoode:
London. 1827. 26 × 16 cm.

The author (1772-1864) was a member of the Society of Friends, and a meteorologist of repute. As a member of the Committee of the Bible Society, he took an active part in the 'Apocrypha' controversy.

See Nos. 1118, 1121, and 1123.
Pp. xi, 127.

—— Another copy.
Bound with other books. (See No. 1123, 1829.)

1117.

1827. Liber Sapientiæ, the Book of Wisdom; commonly called the Wisdom of Solomon: translated from the Latin Vulgate, by Luke Howard . . .
Printed for the translator, by A. and R. Spottiswoode:
London. 1827. 25 × 15·5 cm.

See No. 1117.
Pp. viii, 48.

¶ Bound with other books. (See No. 1123, 1829.)

1118.

1828. The Holy Bible . . . principally designed to facilitate the audible or social reading of the Sacred Scriptures; illustrated with notes, historical, geographical, and otherwise explanatory, and also pointing out the fulfilment of various prophecies. By William Alexander. In three volumes—Vol. 1.
W. Alexander and Son: York. 1828. 27 × 18 cm.

This revised Bible owed its origin to efforts of members of the Society of Friends.

Passages 'unsuitable for a mixed audience' are printed in italics below the text. In some parts a 'lineal arrangement' of the text is also given, in order to exhibit the characteristic features of Hebrew poetry. Besides the notes on each page, many dissertations and longer notes are scattered throughout the volume.
The Pentateuch (with separate title), vol. 1. 792 pp. Vols. 2 and 3 were advertised, but, owing to the lack of adequate support, were never published.

¶ Bound up at the end of this copy are Prospectuses of the work, a specimen leaf, and the covers of the six parts in which the first volume was originally published. Each part cost 4s., 5s., or 6s., according to the quality of the paper. The present copy represents the best quality. Part 1 is dated 1823; part 2, 1824; and parts 3-6, 1827.

[F. F.]

Cotton (p. 124) describes this edition under the date 1835. His copy, apparently had an undated title.

1119.

1828. The Gospel of God's Anointed, the Glory of Israel, and the Light of Revelation for the Gentiles: or, the Glad Tidings of the Service, Sacrifice, and Triumph of our Lord and Saviour Jesus Christ, the only begotten Son of God; and of the gracious and mightily operative powers of the Holy Spirit, which were the first-fruits of that labour of divine love: being a recent version, in two parts, of the Greek Scriptures, (commonly called the New Testament,) in which is plainly set forth the New Covenant promised by God through Moses and the Prophets.
A. Macintosh, for Alexander Greaves: London. 1828. 16 × 10 cm.

An original version by Alexander Greaves.

With preface, indexes, etc. Text ends on 3 A 6 a.
A variety occurs with a first titlepage dated 1827, and differences in the preliminary matter.

—— Another copy.
With the autograph of *H. Cotton*.

1120.

1828. The Book of Tobias; commonly called the Book of Tobit: translated from the Latin Vulgate, by Luke Howard . . .
Printed for the translator, by A. and R. Spottiswoode:
London. 1828. 25 × 15·5 cm.

See No. 1117.
Pp. viii, 38.

¶ Bound with other books. (See No. 1123, 1829.)

1121.

1829. The Holy Bible . . .
Eyre and Strahan: London. 1829. 49 × 31 cm.

Sold by *Longman*, etc.
Pp. 752. With tables of Lessons, etc., before the text, and one leaf of tables at the end.

1122.

1829. The Apocrypha of the Book of Daniel; containing the Story of Susannah; the Prayer of Azariah, with the Hymn of the Three Children; and the History of Bel and the Dragon: translated from the Vulgate Latin; with notes; and a short treatise on the matter contained in these pieces, by Luke Howard . . .
Printed for the translator, by Harvey and Darton:
London. 1829. 25 × 15·5 cm.

See No. 1117.
Pp. viii, 32.

¶ Bound with Ecclesiasticus, Wisdom, and Tobit, also translated by L. Howard (see Nos. 1117, 1118, and 1121). The volume has a general titlepage, dated 1827-29.

1123.

ACCESSION OF KING WILLIAM IV.: 26 JUNE 1830.

1830. The Holy Bible . . .
  Sir D. Hunter Blair and M. T. Bruce:
    Edinburgh. 1830. 14 × 8 cm.

Text ends on 2 S 11 a, with table on verso.

¶ With Scotch Metrical Psalms (1831), and Translations and Paraphrases (1831).
This copy was transmitted in 1880 by the India Office to the Bible Society. It had belonged to an officer of the Indian army—apparently *James Anderson,* whose name, with the date 1832, is inscribed on the fly-leaf.

1124.

1830. The New Testament in the Common Version, conformed to Griesbach's Standard Greek Text.
  Gray and Bowen: Boston, U. S. A. 1830. 20 × 12 cm.

An attempt to exhibit to the ordinary reader the results of Griesbach's critical labours. King James' version is only modified so as to conform with Griesbach's amended Greek text (Leipzig, 1805).

Cotton (p. 122) ascribes this work to *Nathan Hale,* who, however, was apparently merely the 'proprietor.' According to Horne (p. 23), *J. G. Palfrey* was the editor.
Pp. 491.

1125.

1830 ? The Holy Bible . . . With Chronological Notes.
  G. F. Isaac and Co.: London. [1830 ?] 28 × 14·5 cm.

Stereotype edition. Pp. 758; followed by one leaf of tables. Short notes at the foot of some pages. Contains four engravings.

1126.

1831. The Holy Bible . . .
  Wm. Brown, for the Bible Association of Friends in
    America: Philadelphia. 1831. 26 × 17·5 cm.

'Stereotyped by J. Howe, Philad.'
Text, 1061 pp., with table—1 p.; references placed in a central column. The text is followed by 'Index to the subjects contained in the Old and New Testaments' ('copied, with a few alterations, from Bagster's Comprehensive Bible'), xxxiii pp., with tables—1 p.; and 'A Brief Concordance . . . by John Brown . . . revised and corrected,' 92 pp.

—— Another copy.

Printed on superior paper; and bound in two volumes.

1127.

1831. The Holy Bible . . .
  Wm. Brown, for the Bible Association of Friends in
    America: Philadelphia. 1831. 25 × 15·5 cm.

'Stereotyped by J. Howe, Philad.'
Pp. 1080; with table—1 p.

1128.

1831. The New Testament . . .
  Wm. Brown, for the Bible Association of Friends in
            America : Philadelphia. 1881. 20·5 × 12·5 cm.

'Stereotyped by J. Howe, Philad.'
Pp. 386.

1129.

1831. The New Testament . . .
  Printed for the B. F. B. S. by J. Smith :
            Cambridge. 1831. 18 × 11 cm.

Brevier 12°. Cost price (in sheep) 1s. 5d.; sale price 1s. 1d.
Pp. 336.

¶ [F. F.]

1130.

1832. The Biblical Annual; containing a fourfold translation of the book of Ecclesiastes, or the Preacher; viz. (1) the common English version, (2) a new translation from the original Hebrew, (3) . . . from the Greek of the Septuagint, (4) . . . from the Latin Vulgate. With illustrative notes.
  Hamilton, Adams, and Co., etc. : London ;
        W. Robinson : Stockton-on-Tees. 1832. 18 × 11 cm.

Preface signed 'T. W.,' 'Norton, near Stockton, December 1831.'
Pp. 93.

1131.

1833. The Holy Bible, an exact reprint page for page of the Authorized Version published in the year 1611.
        S. Collingwood and Co., University Press :
            Oxford. 1833. 30 × 23·5 cm.

A reprint in roman type of the first edition of 1611 (No. 240).
Before the text is given a collation of this text with the folio of 1613 (No. 249).

Sold by *E. Gardner*, London.

¶ Inserted is a four-page pamphlet, dated 14 Jan. 1834, which begins : 'Complaints having been made that the English Bibles printed at the Universities, besides necessary alterations in the spelling, differed greatly from the Authorized Version of the Scriptures, and a Committee of Dissenting Ministers having addressed a letter on the subject to the Vice-Chancellor, bearing date London, April 2, 1832, the Delegates of the Press took the most effectual method for enabling themselves and others to judge how far these complaints were well-founded. They commenced an exact Reprint in Roman letter of the original Edition of King James printed in the year 1611, and were able to complete and publish it in the month of November, 1833, having previously issued the Book of Genesis as a Specimen. They also caused a most minute Collation to be made of the Oxford 4to. Bible of the year 1824, with the copy of the above-mentioned Edition of 1611, which is in use at the University Press. Some doubts moreover having arisen as to the perfectness of the Copies now remaining of the early Editions, the following Bibles were examined, sheet by sheet, and the papers recording the result of this examination, together with the Collations and the Pamphlets and other Documents which appeared during the progress of the Controversy, are preserved in the Archives of the Delegates.' Then follows a list of over 50 Bibles examined.
  The controversy referred to was begun by Thomas Curtis of Islington. Copies of Curtis'

pamphlet *The Existing Monopoly* . . . and of the rejoinders by Edward Cardwell of Oxford and Thomas Turton of Cambridge, with other articles dealing with the subject, are preserved in this Library.

—— Another copy.

1132.

1833. The Holy Bible . . . in the common version; with amendments of the language; by Noah Webster, LL.D.
*Hezekiah Howe and Co., for Durrie and Peck, etc.,
New Haven, U. S. A.* 1833. 23·5 × 14·5 cm.

The American lexicographer, Noah Webster (1758–1843), professes to give a careful revision of King James' version.

The alterations affect (1) errors in grammar, (2) obsolete or unseemly words and phrases, and (3) certain mistranslations. 'To avoid giving offense to any denomination of christians, I have not knowingly made any alteration in the passages of the present version, on which the different denominations rely for the support of their peculiar tenets' (Preface, p. iv). An Introduction gives the 'principal alterations in the language of the common version of the Scriptures, made in this edition, stated and explained.'

Pp. xvi, 907. The references, alternative renderings, etc., are printed in a central column.

1133.

1833. The New Testament . . .
*Printed for the B. F. B. S. by J. Smith, Pitt Press:
Cambridge.* 1833. 22·5 × 14 cm.

Pica 8°. Cost price, in sheep 3s. 0d., in calf 4s. 0d.; sale price, in sheep 2s. 3d., in calf 3s. 0d. With Psalms, cost price, in sheep, 3s. 9d.; sale price 2s. 10d.
Text ends on Ff 4 b.

¶ Bound with a Psalter of 1834 (No. 1142).

The cover is stamped: 'Presented by the British & Foreign Bible Society in commemoration of the 1st of August 1834'—the date on which slavery was abolished throughout the British dominions. Nearly 100,000 copies of the N. T. and Psalms in English were sent by the Bible Society to the West Indies, for free distribution to such liberated negroes as were able to read. See B. F. B. S. Annual Report, 1835, pp. lxxxv–xciv. *Cf.* Nos. 1135 and 1141.

—— Another copy.

This copy belonged to Christian Allen, a native member of the Moravian Mission in Antigua, who received the book from Bennett Harvey, the Superintendent of that Mission in 1834, and presented it to the Bible Society in 1884.

1134.

1833. The New Testament . . .
*Printed for the B. F. B. S., by J. Smith, Pitt Press:
Cambridge.* 1833. 18·5 × 11 cm.

Brevier 12°. Cost price, in sheep 1s. 5d., in calf 2s. 2d.; sale price, in sheep 1s. 1d., in calf 1s. 9d. With Psalms, cost price, in sheep, 1s. 9d., sale price 1s. 4d.
Text ends on O 11 a.

¶ Bound with a Psalter of 1834 (No. 1143).
The cover is stamped: 'Presented by the British & Foreign Bible Society in commemoration of the 1st August, 1834.' See No. 1134

1135.

1833. A literal translation from the Hebrew of the twelve Minor Prophets; with some notes from Jonathan's Paraphrase in the Chaldee, and critical remarks from R. S. Yarchi, Abenezra, D. Kimchi, and Abarbenel. By A. Pick . . .
Joseph Shackell, for W. Straker, etc. : London. 1833. 22·5 × 14·5 cm.

This version by a Jewish Christian professes to give the plain grammatical sense of the original.

Pp. xii, 177.

1136.

1834. The Holy Bible . . . arranged in historical and chronological order, in such a manner that the whole may be read as one connected history, in the words of the authorized translation. By . . . George Townsend . . . New edition with select notes . . . indexes, and a table dividing the sacred volume into 365 portions, for daily reading throughout the year.
Gilbert and Rivington, for J. G. and F. Rivington : London. 1834. 23 × 14·5 cm. 2 vols.

A new edition of Townsend's Old Testament in two volumes, 1821 etc., and of his New Testament in two volumes, 1825 etc.; with most of the notes omitted.

G. Townsend (1788–1857) was at this time vicar of Northallerton.

Townsend's arrangement is based mainly on J. Lightfoot's 'Chronicle' (first printed in 1647) and similar works.
The table of contents divides the O. T. into eight 'periods,' each subdivided into 'parts'; and the N. T. into fifteen 'parts.' Vol. 1 contains O. T. periods 1–6; vol. 2 contains O. T. periods 7 and 8, and N. T. Pp. xxxiv, 1464.

1137.

1834. The New Testament . . . translated out of the Latin Vulgate . . . first published by the English College of Rheims, anno 1582. With the original preface . . . and annotations. To which are now added, an Introductory Essay; and a complete topical and textual index.
Jonathan Leavitt : New York, etc.
(*John H. Turney's stereotype*). 1834. 24 × 14 cm.

A reprint of the Rheims New Testament of 1582.

It appears from the 'Introductory Address' that this edition was published in order to provide Protestants in the United States with a full reprint of the original Rheims Testament, for purposes of controversy. Cotton, in his notice of this book (*R. and D.*, pp. 127–134), prints the Address in full.
Contains, besides the 'Introductory Address to Protestants' (dated Nov. 1833), Recommendations 'by Ministers of the Gospel, and others, of various denominations,' and a Certificate of the genuineness of the reprint; also a full index at the end of the volume. O'Callaghan (*List*, pp. 233–6) states that this reprint contains many errors.

Pp. 458.

1138.

1834. The New Testament . . . translated out of the Latin Vulgate . . . Stereotype edition.
R. Coyne : Dublin. 1834. 18·5 × 11 cm.

Rheims version.

Except for its fresh title, this is the same book as the New Testament published in 1826, which was a reprint of that issued by the R. C. Bible Society in 1815 (No. 1051), with the Address alone omitted. Similar issues appeared in 1835, 1837, and 1840. (Cotton, *R. and D.*, pp. 241-2.) The Approbation is dated 16 Dec. 1825.

Text, 367 pp. With index, tables, etc.

1139.

1834. The New Testament . . . according to the present Authorized English Version. The critical, explanatory, and practical notes, from the exposition of Matthew Henry.
Printed and enamelled by De La Rue, James, and Rudd, for
Adolphus Richter and Co. : London. 1834. 29·5 × 21·5 cm.

An *édition de luxe*, printed by *Balne, Gracechurch Street*, in gold on loaded and glazed paper. The volume weighs no less than 11 lbs. 6 ozs.

Pp. 346 ; with table after text.

1140.

1834. The New Testament . . .
Printed for the B. F. B. S. by S. Collingwood and Co.,
University Press : Oxford. 1834. 18·5 × 11 cm.

Brevier 12°. Cost price, in 'coloured calf' 2s. 2d., in basil 1s. 7d. ; sale price, in calf 1s. 8d., in basil 1s. 2d. With Psalms, cost price, in basil, 1s. 11d., sale price 1s. 6d. Text ends at O 12 b.

¶ Bound with a Psalter of 1834 (No. 1144).
The cover is stamped 'Presented by the British & Foreign Bible Society in commemoration of the 1ˢᵗ August, 1834.' See No. 1134.

1141.

1834. The Book of Psalms . . .
Printed for the B. F. B. S. by J. Smith, Pitt Press :
Cambridge. 1834. 22·5 × 14 cm.

Pica 8°. Cost price, in sheep, 1s. 8d. ; sale price 1s. 3d.
Text ends on G 8 a.

¶ Bound with a N. T. of 1833 (No. 1134).

1142.

1834. The Book of Psalms . . .
Printed for the B. F. B. S. by George Eyre and
Andrew Spottiswoode : London. 1834. 18·5 × 11 cm.

Brevier 12°. Cost price, in roan, 1s. 0d. ; sale price 9d.
Text ends on D 11 a.

¶ Bound with a N. T. of 1833 (No. 1135). [F. F.]

1143.

1834. The Book of Psalms . . .
Printed for the B. F. B. S. by J. Smith,
Pitt Press : Cambridge. 1834. 18·5 × 11 cm.

Text ends on E 2 a.

¶ Bound with a N. T. of 1834 (No. 1141).

ENGLISH

—— Another copy.
Bound with a N. T. of 1835 (No. 1146). [F. F.]
1144.

1834. Commentary on the Epistle to the Romans, by John Calvin; to which is prefixed his Life, by Theodore Beza; translated by Francis Sibson . . .
L. B. Seeley: London. 1834. 18 × 10·5 cm.

An English translation of Calvin's Commentary.
Contains portrait of Calvin, his Life, Text, Notes, etc. Pp. viii, 640.
1145.

1835. The New Testament . . .
Printed for the B. F. B. S. by J. Smith,
Pitt Press: Cambridge. 1835. 18·5 × 11 cm.

Brevier 12°. Prices as in 1834 (see No. 1143).
Text ends on O 11 a.

¶ Bound with a Psalter of 1834 (No. 1144). [F. F.]
1146.

1835. B. See 1836.

1836. The Holy Bible, with the text according to the Authorized Version and a Commentary, from Henry and Scott: with numerous observations and notes from other authors; also the marginal references, maps . . . and . . . tables.
J. R. and C. Childs: Bungay, for the Religious Tract Society:
London. 1836,35. 26 × 16·5 cm. 6 vols.

Edited by George Stokes, of Cheltenham.
Vol. 2 is dated 1835; the other volumes are dated 1836.

¶ This copy was presented by the Committee of the R. T. S. to the daughter of the editor, and given after her death to the Bible Society.
1147.

1836. The Holy Bible . . .
Brown and Sinquet, for the Bible Association of Friends
in America: Philadelphia. 1836. 15 × 9 cm.

'Stereotyped by L. Johnson.'
Pp. 1098, 342.
The N. T. was also published separately in the same year.
1148.

1836. The New Testament . . . published in 1526. Being the first translation from the Greek into English, by that eminent scholar and martyr, William Tyndale. Reprinted verbatim: with a memoir of his life and writings, by George Offor. Together with the proceedings and correspondence of Henry VIII, Sir T. More, and Lord Cromwell.
Stevens and Pardon, for S. Bagster: London. 1836. 21 × 13·5 cm.

See No. 2, 1525.
Pp. iv, 98: ff. ccxv (+ 2). With engraved portrait of Tindale as frontispiece.

VOL. I.   A A

—— Another copy.
L. P. The cuts in this copy are coloured.
1149.

1836. The Book of the New Covenant of our Lord and Saviour Jesus Christ: being a critical revision of the text and translation of the English version of the New Testament, with the aid of most ancient manuscripts unknown to the age in which that version was last put forth by authority.
James Moyes, for James Duncan: London. 1836. 23 × 14 cm.

By Granville Penn.

Pp. 470.

—— Another copy.
Bound up with this copy are Penn's 'Annotations' (1837), and 'Supplemental Annotations' (1841).
1150.

1836. B. See 1840.

ACCESSION OF QUEEN VICTORIA: 20 JUNE 1837.

1837. A free and explanatory version of the Epistles; by the Rev. Edward Barlee . . .
R. Clay, for William Pickering: London. 1837. 18 × 11 cm.

Barlee was rector of Worlingworth-cum-Southolt, Suffolk. See No. 1160, 1839.
Pp. iv, 358.
1151.

1838. The Holy Scriptures, faithfully and truly translated by Myles Coverdale . . . 1535. Reprinted from the copy in the library of . . . the Duke of Sussex.
J. Rider, for S. Bagster: London. 1838. 33 × 26 cm.

See No. 7, 1535.
With portrait of Coverdale, Bibliographical Description, etc. Text in roman type, with references etc. at foot of page.
The copy from which this edition was printed is now in the possession of Mr. W. Aldis Wright.
Another edition, containing a Memoir of Coverdale, was published by Bagster in 1847. See Appendix.
1152.

1838. The Paragraph Bible. The Holy Bible . . . arranged in paragraphs and parallelisms.
Printed for the Religious Tract Society by Eyre and Spottiswoode: London. 1838. 20 × 13 cm.

A reprint, corrected and revised, of the Paragraph Bible prepared by T. W. Coit of Cambridge (Mass.) on the lines of Reeves' Bible (see above, No. 985), and published in 1834.

The editors, who were advised by T. H. Horne and E. Henderson, endeavoured, by

collation of the best modern editions and frequent reference to the first issue of King James' version in 1611, to secure a correct text.
Pp. viii, 948, 223.

1153.

1838. The Holy Bible . . .
S. *Collingwood and Co., University Press :*
Oxford. 1838. 18 × 11 cm.

Stereotype edition. Ruby 8°. Sold by E. *Gardner*, London, etc.
Pp. 762.

¶ With Prayer Book (1839), and Tate and Brady's Metrical Psalms (1839). [F F.]
1154.

1839. The Condensed Commentary and Family Exposition of the Holy Bible : containing the Authorized Version of the Old and New Testaments, with the most valuable criticisms of the best Biblical writers, practical reflections, and marginal references, chronology, indexes, etc. By the Rev. Ingram Cobbin . . .
T. C. Savill, for T. Ward and Co. : London. [1839.] 29·5 × 20 cm.

No date on the titlepage; but the Preface (which shows this to be a second edition, containing additional matter) is dated June 1839. First published in 1837.
Pp. xx, 1396.

1155.

1839. The Holy Bible . . .
Printed for the Trinitarian Bible Society, instituted in the year 1831, by S. Collingwood and Co., University Press :
Oxford. 1839. 18 × 11 cm.

Nonpareil 12°.
Text ends on Ii 12 b.

1156.

1839. The New Testament . . . with explanatory notes by John Wesley . .
A new edition.
Joseph Smith : London. 1839. 22 × 14 cm.

First published in a quarto edition in 1755. The preface is dated 1754.

The complete Commentary on both Testaments, compiled by John Wesley (1703–1791), first appeared in four quarto volumes at Bristol in 1764 (Horne, pp. 256–7).
Pp. 800. The notes are printed below the text. With portrait of Wesley preaching, as frontispiece.

1157.

1839. The Sacred Writings of the Apostles and Evangelists of Jesus Christ, commonly styled the New Testament, translated from the original Greek, by Doctors George Campbell, James Macknight, and Philip Doddridge. With prefaces, various emendations, and an appendix, by Alexander Campbell, of Bethany, U.S.
J. H. Starie, for G. Wightman : London. 1839. 17·5 × 11 cm.

'From the fourth American edition ; third English edition.'
Pp. lx, 436, 73. The long Preface is dated *Bethany, Va., October 10th. 1832.*

—— Another copy.

1158.

1839. Explanatory notes on the Prayer Book version of the Psalms. By William Keatinge Clay . . .
    J. W. Parker : London. 1839. 19·5 × 11·5 cm.

Pp. viii, 375. Text, with notes.

1159.

1839. An explanatory version of the Minor Prophets with the text. By the Rev. Edward Barlee.
    R. Clay, for W. Pickering : London. 1839. 17 × 10 cm.

See No. 1151, 1837.
Pp. v, 195.

1160.

1840. The Holy Bible . . . with notes . . . by the Rev. Henry Stebbing . . .
    Andrew Shortrede : Edinburgh. 1836,40. 10·5 × 6·5 cm.

The printed general title is dated 1836, and gives the names of the publishers as *Allan Bell & Co. and Shepherd & Sutton : London, and Fraser & Co. : Edinburgh*; the name of the printer appears on verso. But the engraved general and N. T. titles are dated 1840, and bear only the name of *Andrew Moffat : London*. Pp. 1084, 336 (?). With Preface, introductions to each book, and foot-notes. The two frontispieces, together with the engraved titles, were evidently added by Moffat in republishing this Bible in 1840.

¶ Slightly imperfect : wanting one or two leaves at the end.

1161.

1840. The New Testament . . . revised from the authorized version with the aid of other translations and made conformable to the Greek text of J. J. Griesbach by a Layman.
    C. Whittingham, for William Pickering :
    London. 1840. 20 × 12·5 cm.

The edition of Griesbach's text adopted is that published at Leipzig in 1805. Reference is made to the original versions of Wynne, Newcome, Wakefield, Boothroyd, Penn, Campbell, Stuart, and Macknight. The author, who had edited the London edition of Griesbach's text published in 1818, died before the present work appeared. Cotton (p. 127) gives his name as Edgar Taylor.

Pp. xxxv, 522. With Index, Harmony, etc. ; and list of various readings.

1162.

1841. The Holy Bible, containing the authorized version . . . with twenty thousand emendations.
    John Childs and Son : Bungay, for Longman, etc. :
    London. 1841. 24 × 15 cm.

In his Preface the editor, J. T. Conquest, mentions about 800 authorities, from whose works his emendations have been derived.

Stereotyped and printed by *John Childs and Son*, Bungay.
With tables, index, maps, etc.
See No. 1168, 1843 (?).

1163.

1841. The English Hexapla, exhibiting the six important English translations of the New Testament Scriptures: Wiclif, 1380; Tyndale, 1534; Cranmer, 1539; Genevan, 1557; Anglo-Rhemish, 1582; Authorised 1611 . . . preceded by an Historical Account of the English translations . . .
Wertheimer and Co., for S. Bagster and Sons:
London. 1841. 29·5 × 21·5 cm.

This volume gives the New Testament in English according to 'the six important' translations down to 1611, together with 'the original Greek text after Scholz' (for which see the Greek section of this Catalogue).

The 'Wiclif' follows a MS. representing the later Wycliffite version, which belonged to the Duke of Sussex, and subsequently to the Earl of Ashburnham. The 'Tyndale' is a reprint of the edition of 1534 (No. 5). The 'Cranmer' is the first edition of the Great Bible, 1539 (No. 25). The 'Genevan' is Whittingham's Testament of 1557 (No. 76). The 'Anglo-Rhemish' is taken from the first edition of 1582 (No. 134). The 'Authorised' is apparently printed from a copy of the edition of 1613,11 (No. 246).
The long 'Historical Account' (160 pp.) was written by S. P. Tregelles (see No. 1171, 1844).
Preliminary matter, 167 pp. The English Hexapla ends on 7 H 4 a. The Greek text is printed at the top of each page, with the English versions beneath in six columns, spread over two pages.

1164.

1841. The New Testament . . .
John W. Parker, Pitt Press: Cambridge. 1841. 22 × 14 cm.

Text ends on 8 2 b.

¶ Interleaved with writing paper. [F. F.]

1165.

1842. The New Testament . . . A facsimile reprint of the celebrated Genevan Testament, 1557; with the marginal annotations and references, the initial and other wood cuts, prefaces and index.
For S. Bagster and Sons: London. [1842.] 18 × 11 cm.

See No. 76.
The date 1842 is stamped on the back of the cover.
Text etc., 455 ff.

¶ [F. F.]

—— Another copy.

1166.

1843. The Gospel according to Saint Matthew, and part of the first chapter of the Gospel according to Saint Mark, translated into English from the Greek, with original notes, by Sir John Cheke . . . Also VII. original letters of Sir J. Cheke. Prefixed is an introductory account of the nature and object of the translation; by James Goodwin . . .
C. Whittingham, for J. and J. J. Deighton: Cambridge;
W. Pickering: London. 1843. 23 × 14·5 cm.

Sir J. Cheke (1514-1557) was Regius Professor of Greek at Cambridge, tutor to King Edward VI., Privy Councillor and Secretary of State.

'Thy age, like ours, O soul of Sir John Cheek,
Hated not learning worse than toad or asp,
When thou taught'st Cambridge, and king Edward, Greek.'
Milton, Sonnet *On the detraction which followed upon my writing certain treatises*.

This version is printed from the MS. in the Library of Corpus Christi College, Cambridge. It is remarkable for the author's endeavours (1) to avoid words derived from Greek and Latin which might be unintelligible to ordinary readers (for this reason he sometimes uses strange or newly coined words, e.g. *moond* for *lunatic*, *frosent* for *apostle*, etc.), and (2) to improve the orthography by adopting certain rules of spelling to represent more nearly the accurate pronunciation of words.
Pp. 124. With three facsimiles, Glossary, etc.

1167.

1843 ? The Holy Bible . . . with many thousand emendations . . .
G. Woodfall and Son, for C. A. Bartlett :
London. [1843 ?] 14 × 9 cm.

See No. 1163, 1841. 'People's Edition, price five shillings, bound in morocco.'
With maps and tables, etc.

1168.

1844. The Septuagint version of the Old Testament, according to the Vatican text, translated into English ; with the principal various readings of the Alexandrine copy, and a table of comparative chronology ; by Sir Lancelot Charles Lee Brenton, Bart. . . .
S. Bagster and Sons : London. 1844. 24·5 × 16 cm. 2 vols.

Pp. xiv, 930. With Chronological Table, Appendix, etc.

1169.

1844. The Book of Psalms . . . Arranged in Parallelisms.
Printed for the Religious Tract Society by Eyre and Spottiswoode :
London. 1844. 18 × 12 cm.

Text ends on E 12 b.

¶ This copy, containing a few MS. notes, appears to have belonged to the seventh Earl of Shaftesbury, who became President of the Bible Society in 1851. On the flyleaf is written a large initial S, and an autograph letter of the Earl's is inserted, dated 3 July 1861. An early portrait of the Earl is pasted inside the cover.

1170.

1844. . . . The Book of Revelation in Greek, edited from ancient authorities ; with a new English version, and various readings ; by Samuel Prideaux Tregelles.
S. Bagster and Sons : London. 1844. 23 × 15 cm.

S. P. Tregelles (1813–1875), transcribed and edited in 1861 the Greek MS. of the eighth (?) century, known as Codex Zacynthius, containing part of St. Luke's Gospel, which is preserved in this Library. He was a member of the New Testament Revision Company.
With Introduction. Pp. xxxviii, 151.

1171.

1845. The Book of Psalms . . .
Printed for the B. F. B. S. by Eyre and Spottiswoode:
London. 1845. 17 × 10·5 cm.

Brevier 12°. Cost price (roan, gilt edges) 9*d.*; sale price 7*d.*
Text ends on C 16 *a.*

¶ Each page is covered with MS. notes by the former owners, V. B. and W. M. B[unting].

1172.

1845. A version of the prophecies of Ezekiel; retaining, for the most part, in English the same order of expression which occurs in the Hebrew original; by the Rev. James M'Farlan . . .
Printed for the Author by Oliver and Boyd:
Edinburgh, etc. 1845. 23 × 14·5 cm.

The author was 'Minister at Muiravonside.'
Pp. 163. With foot-notes.

1173.

1848. . . . The Way of Faith, or the Abridged Bible; containing selections from all the books of Holy Writ. By Dr. M. Büdinger; translated from the fifth German edition by David Asher . . .
S. Bagster and Sons: London. [1848.] 21 × 13·5 cm.

Contains selections from the Old Testament in an original version. 'Intended for the use of Jewish Schools and Families,' and 'specially sanctioned by the . . . chief Rabbi.'

The translator's preface is dated 5608 (=1848 A.D.). Pp. xvi. 374.

1174.

1849. The Holy Bible . . .
Printed for the Society for Promoting Christian Knowledge, at the
University Press: Oxford. 1849. 16 × 10 cm.

Nonp. 16° Refs.
Text ends on Qq 12 *b.*

¶ [F. F.]

1175.

1849. (The New Testament . . . according to the authorised version. Printed phonetically by Alexander John Ellis, B.A.)
A. J. Ellis: Bath, for Fred Pitman, Phonetic Depot:
London. 1849. 22 × 14 cm.

The title, like the rest of the book, is printed in 'phonetic spelling.' Pp. xxiv. 313. With a note on the Phonetic Alphabet, preface, and table of contents. At the end is given a list of 'Spelling Reform' publications.
See No. 1180, 1850.

¶ [F. F.]

—— Another copy.

1176.

1849. The New Testament in Lewisian Short Hand, lithographed from the manuscript of Thomas Coggin . . .
Nisbet and Co. : London. 1849. 17 × 10·5 cm.

Pp. 207 ; on the last page are the words ' Thomas Coggin Scripsit 21/12/1844.'

1177.

1850. The Holy Bible . . . in the earliest English versions made from the Latin Vulgate by John Wycliffe and his followers ; edited by the Rev. Josiah Forshall . . . and Sir Frederic Madden . . .
University Press : Oxford. 1850. 33 × 26 cm. 4 vols.

The first printed edition of the complete Wycliffite version.

Oxford in the fourteenth century had no more distinguished schoolman and reformer than John Wycliffe. After founding an order of 'poor priests,' who were ' faithfully to scatter the seed of God's word,' he and his associates conceived and carried out the great task of translating the whole Bible into the vulgar tongue. Portions of Scripture, and notably the Psalter, at that time existed in English, and the complete Bible had been rendered into the already discarded court dialect of French. Wycliffe, however, originated the first complete English Bible. He himself appears to have translated the Gospels and probably the whole New Testament. To his disciple, Nicholas of Hereford (fl. 1390), is ascribed most of the Old Testament and of the Apocrypha. By 1382 the work was certainly advanced, if not finished. The whole translation was revised, and a long general prologue prefixed, by John Purvey (1353 ?-1428 ?), Wycliffe's intimate associate at Lutterworth, where Wycliffe died 31 Dec. 1384. The result was a smoother version completed about 1388—certainly before 1400. Purvey's recension is given by five-sixths of the 170 extant MSS. of Wycliffite Scriptures enumerated by Forshall and Madden, nearly all of which were produced between 1400 and 1450. Naturally both versions were made from the current Vulgate. Wycliffe has been called the 'father of English prose.' His homely colloquial style, and Hereford's somewhat awkward literalism, were both softened by Purvey's revision.

The testimony of contemporary witnesses, such as Huss, Knighton, and Archbishop Arundel, and all available evidence support the traditional view that Wycliffe initiated, if he did not complete, this earliest English version. The contrary theory of Dom Gasquet (*Dublin Review*, July, 1894, and *The Old English Bible* . . . , 1898), has been sufficiently refuted by F. D. Matthew in the *English Historical Review*, January, 1895. See also F. G. Kenyon's *Our Bible and the Ancient Manuscripts*, 1895, pp. 204–8 ; W. W. Capes' *The English Church in the fourteenth and fifteenth centuries*, 1901, pp. 126–131 ; and T. G. Law's introduction to *The New Testament in Scots* . . . mentioned below.

Both Wycliffite versions, the earlier and the later, are here given side by side. Of the earlier version, the Song of Solomon had been published by Adam Clarke in his Bible Commentary (1810–25), and the New Testament by Lea Wilson in 1848. The New Testament of the later version had been printed by Lewis in 1731, by Baber in 1810, and by Bagster in the *English Hexapla* in 1841. (See Nos. 777, 1014, and 1164.) The New Testament of the later version was reprinted in 1879 from Forshall and Madden's edition, and the section Job–Song of Solomon in 1881. Both were edited by W. W. Skeat, and published by the Clarendon Press, Oxford.

J. Forshall (1795–1863) was Keeper of Manuscripts in, and then Secretary to, the British Museum, and subsequently became Chaplain of the Foundling Hospital. He also published editions of the Gospels of St. John (1859), St. Luke (1860), and St. Mark (1862, see No. 1213).

Sir F. Madden (1801–1873), Keeper of Manuscripts at the British Museum from 1837, edited many early English texts.

The elaborate preface is followed by a descriptive list of 170 MSS. The two texts are printed ɪn parallel columns, with various readings at the foot of the page. A Glossary is appended.

Pp. lxiv, 687, 888, 897, 749. With Apocrypha. The Epistle to the Laodiceans is inserted after the Epistle to the Colossians.

The Wycliffite Bible crossed the Tweed. Dr. T. G. Law has edited from the unique MS. in the possession of Lord Amberst of Hackney *The New Testament in Scots, being Purvey's Revision of Wycliffe's Version, turned into Scots by Murdoch Nisbet c. 1520* (printed for the Scottish Text Society, vol. 1, 1901).

1178.

1850. The Holy Bible . . .
Printed for the B. F. B. S. by Eyre and Spottiswoode : London. 1850.
17 × 10·5 cm.

Pearl Ref. 16°. Text ends on Dd 4 a.
Error in Rev. xx. 15, *lake of life* for *lake of fire*.

¶ Nearly all the copies of this edition were corrected by hand. [F. F.]

1179.

1850. (The Holy Bible . . . according to the authorised version. Arranged in paragraphs and parallelisms, and printed phonetically.)
Isaac Pitman : Bath, for F. Pitman : London. 1850. 23·5 × 14·5 cm.

Title printed in ' phonetic spelling.' See No. 1176, 1849.
Pp. 8, 580, 164. With preface and Phonetic Alphabet.

1180.

1850? The Blank-paged Bible. The Holy Scriptures . . . with copious references . . . and the alternate pages ruled for MS. notes . . .
S. Bagster and Sons : London. [1850 ?] 21 × 13·5 cm.

Pp. viii, 587, 193, 36. With maps, tables, index, etc.

1181.

1851. The Chronological New Testament, in which the text of the authorised version is newly divided into paragraphs and sections, with the dates and places of transactions marked, the marginal renderings of the translators, many parallel illustrative passages printed at length, brief introductions to each book, and a running analysis of the Epistles.
Walton and Mitchell, for Robert B. Blackader ; sold by
S. Bagster and Sons : London. 1851. 22 × 17·5 cm.

In the preface the editor acknowledges his indebtedness to the works of Townsend, Trollope, Humphrey, Kitto, and Burton.

See No. 1226, 1866.
Pp. viii, 310. With introductions, marginal notes, etc. The sections are numbered in the Gospels and Acts. Certain letters A, B, C, etc. (suggesting *Acknowledgment, Behaviour, Consolation,* etc.), ' chiefly taken from the writings of Archbishop Secker,' are placed over some of the sections, ' to assist the devotional reading of the Scriptures.'

1182.

1851. Family Bible. The New Testament . . . with brief notes and instructions, by Rev. Justin Edwards, D.D., containing the references and marginal readings of the Polyglot Bible.
American Tract Society : New York and
Boston. [1851.] 23·5 × 15 cm.

' Entered according to Act of Congress, in the year 1851, by O. R. Kingsbury . . .'
The references, notes, etc. are placed below the text on each page. Pp. 425.
With two maps.

1183.

1851. The Book of the prophet Jeremiah and that of the Lamentations, translated from the original Hebrew, with a Commentary . . . by E. Henderson, D.D.
R. Clay, for Hamilton, Adams, and Co.: London. 1851. 23 × 14·5 cm.
Pp. xvi, 303. With introduction and foot-notes.

1184.

NOTE ON THE AMERICAN BIBLE SOCIETY'S REVISION OF THE CURRENT
TEXT OF KING JAMES' VERSION, 1848-51.

It is not generally known that in the middle of the nineteenth century the American Bible Society carried out a careful revision of the current text of the 'Authorised' version. A detailed account of this recension is given in a tract entitled *Report on the History and Recent Collation of the English Version of the Bible: presented by the Committee of Versions to the Board of Managers of the American Bible Society, and adopted, May 1, 1851*. It will be convenient to insert here a short note explaining the scheme of the revision and the alterations which it involved, as described in the above-mentioned tract (printed at New York in 1851 and again in 1857, 32 pp.), and the contemporary Reports of the A. B. S.

The idea was first brought forward in October 1847, and in the following year a committee of seven was appointed, who engaged James W. M‘Lane, a Presbyterian minister of Williamsburgh, New York, to work as their collator. He was directed to compare a standard A. B. S. edition with recent Bibles printed at London, Oxford, Cambridge, and Edinburgh, and also with the original issue of 1611. The results of his collation disclosed some 24,000 variations. Where the four modern British Bibles agreed, the American edition was to be conformed to them, or in the matter of punctuation to any three combined. The 'great and leading object' was everywhere 'uniformity.' Beyond this, the Committee laid down certain rules, which resulted in the introduction of many innovations, which may be summarised as follows:—

1. In a few instances the text was altered to agree with the Hebrew or Greek. Thus in Ruth iii. 15 *she went* is altered to *he went* (thus restoring the original rendering: see No. 240); so, *she please* for *he please* in Song of Solomon ii. 7, iii. 5, and viii. 4. Again in Josh. xix. 2 *or Sheba* for *and Sheba*, in Isa. i. 16 *wash ye* for *wash you*, and in Matt. xii. 41 *in the judgment* for *in judgment*.

2. Orthography. Alterations were made where forms of words 'have become obsolete and unintelligible; or have already been changed in some places and not in others; or where in themselves they are of no importance.' Thus *assuaged* is put for *asswaged*, *axe* for *ax*, *soap* for *sope*, *didst* for *diddest*, *braided* for *broidered*, *fetched* for *fetcht*, *lain* for *lien*, etc. The *s* has been dropped in the case of Hebrew plurals; thus *cherubim* for *cherubims*, *Anakim* for *Anakims*. The form *Oh* is retained with the optative, leaving *O* as the sign of the vocative. The use of the indefinite article *a* or *an* is made consistent. The spelling of proper names has been made uniform in the O. T., except where they differ in the original Hebrew. In the N. T. unfamiliar forms are altered; thus *Korah* is substituted for *Core*, *Sinai* for *Sina*, etc. (*Jesus* for *Joshua* is explained in the margin at Acts vii. 45, and Heb. iv. 8, and is therefore retained in the text). In the use of hyphens the modern English Bibles were followed, where they agreed. When the term *Scripture* or *Scriptures* 'refers to the whole volume of inspired truth,' it begins with a capital letter. In Gen. vi. 3 *spirit* is altered to *Spirit*, in Rev. iv. 5 *Spirits* to *spirits*, and so on. Special pains were taken to secure the right use of italics. Examples may be given: Ps. lxxxix. 34 'the thing *that is* gone out of my lips,' Luke i. 35 'which shall be born *of thee*.' In Judg. ix. 53 the last clause is printed 'and *all-to* brake his skull,' with a marginal note ' That is, *altogether*.'

In punctuation 'the uniform usage of any three' of the modern British copies was followed; in cases where the rule was not applicable, the Committee 'endeavoured to decide each according to its own merits.' In five passages the changes made affected the sense: Rom. iv. 1, 1 Cor. xvi. 22 ('let him be Anathema. Maran atha '), 2 Cor. x. 8-11, Heb. xiii. 7, and Rev. xiii. 8. Finally, many parentheses, which had been inserted in modern editions were omitted, e.g. in Rom. v. 13-17; and the brackets and italics in the latter clause of 1 John ii. 23 were also dropped.

3. 'Accessories of the text.' (i) The summaries before the chapters were carefully

revised. The attention of the Committee was 'mainly directed to the change of quaint, obsolete, ambiguous, or inappropriate words and expressions; to a greater condensation and conformity with the language of the text; and to the removal of comment.' Thus, in Gen. l. *embalmed* displaces *chested*; in the O. T., *Messiah* and *Zion*, or similar words, are substituted for *Christ* and *the church*; the summaries in the Song of Solomon were entirely recast. (ii) The 'running heads of the columns' were revised in a similar manner. (iii) Marginal matter: a few fresh notes were added, e.g. one explanatory of *Selah* at Ps. iii. 2, and another, 'Gr. *the Passover*,' opposite *Easter* in Acts xii. 4; while others, inserted in some modern editions, and 'containing merely conjectural and unwarranted commentary' (e.g. at Judges iii. 31, and opposite the title of Job) were omitted. (iv) References. The Committee did not attempt any revision of these, but merely omitted some of the less important where the page was over-full. (v) Chronology. Ussher's dates were retained; but care was taken 'to have the several dates adjusted over against the paragraphs or verses to which they respectively belong.'
The Apocryphal books were not revised.

The Report of the Committee closes with a recommendation that 'the Octavo Reference Bible, now in the course of preparation . . . be adopted as the Standard Copy of this Society; to which all future editions published by the Society shall be conformed.' Several such editions were issued by the A. B. S. during the next few years. But in 1857 strong opposition to the new text among the Society's supporters induced its Committee to review the whole question; and in the following year they decided to cease printing their recension, on the ground of alleged want of constitutional authority, and popular dissatisfaction with a number of the changes made. (See a long statement in the A. B. S. Report for 1858, pp. 31–41.) Some fruit, however, of the collator's careful work remains in the later editions published by the A. B. S., which are generally commended for their accuracy.

Scrivener considers that 'the plan of operation was not sufficiently thorough to produce any considerable results.' 'No attempt seems to have been made to bridge over the wide gulf between the first issues of the Authorized version and those of modern times,' by the use of any of the important intermediate editions examined by Scrivener for his Cambridge Paragraph Bible of 1873.

1853. The Holy Bible . . .
  Printed for the B. F. B. S. by Eyre and Spottiswoode :
              London. 1858. 28 × 22 cm.

Crown 4°. Text ends on 4 B 4 *b*.

¶ A special copy, stamped on the cover 'British & Foreign Bible Society. The Year of Jubilee. 1853.' Seven leaves are inserted, containing the autograph signatures of the President (Lord Shaftesbury), Vice-Presidents, Members of Committee, Secretaries, Foreign Agents, and others connected with the Society.

1185.

1853. The Holy Bible . . .
  Printed for the B. F. B. S., University Press :
              Oxford. 1853. 27 × 18 cm.

Small Pica 8° with Ref. Pp. 1216.
A special edition, with the cover stamped 'British & Foreign Bible Society. The Year of Jubilee. 1853.'

1186.

1853. The Holy Bible . . . translated from corrected texts . . . with . . .
  introduction and . . . notes . . . By B. Boothroyd, D.D.
    Partridge and Oakey : London. 1853. 28 × 18 cm.

See No. 1102, 1824.
Pp. xxxv, 917, 308.

1187.

1853. The Holy Bible . . .
   American Bible Society : New York. 1853. 23 × 16 cm.

The revised text prepared under the auspices of the American Bible Society. See Note at 1851.

Bourgeois 8°. Pp. 1100. With marginal references, etc.

1188.

The Bible House Library also contains copies of the following editions of this same text published by the A. B. S. in 1853 : (1) Pica Royal 8° Bible (pp. 1026, 320) ; (2) Agate 32° Pocket Testament (pp. 356).

1853. The Seven Seals broke open ; or, The Bible of the Reformation reformed. Three volumes, in seven books. Containing the whole of the Old and New Testaments according to the generally received English Protestant version, but under an entirely new arrangement in every part. With preface, introduction, commentary, indexes, etc. By John Finch . . .
   Petter and Galpin, for James Rigby : London. 1853. 17·5 × 10·5 cm.

The three volumes are entitled : (1) The Old Testament reformed ; (2) The New Testament reformed ; (3) The new Apocrypha ; and the seven books : (i) Jewish History ; (ii) The Laws of Moses ; (iii) The Prophets and the Psalms ; (iv) Jewish Wisdom ; (v) The Gospels ; (vi) Mythology ; (vii) Mysteries. Books i and ii are said to form the Jews' Bible ; iii, iv, and v, the Christians' Bible ; vi and vii, the Sectarians' Bible.

¶ Bound in one thick volume.

1189.

1854. The Holy Bible . . .
   American Bible Society : New York. 1854. 25·5 × 16·5 cm.

The revised text prepared under the auspices of the A. B. S. See Note at 1851.

Pica Royal 8°. Pp. 1026, 320. Like an edition printed in 1853.

1190.

The Bible House Library also contains copies of the following editions of this same text, published by the A. B. S. in 1854 : (1) Bourgeois 8° Bible (with references, etc. : like No. 1188) ; (2) Brevier 12° Bible (pp. 835, 260) ; (3) Nonpareil 12° Bible (pp. 767) ; (4) Agate 24° Bible (pp. 965) ; (5) Great Primer Royal 8° Testament (4 vols., pp. 844) ; (6) a similar Psalter (pp. 212) ; (7) Pica 8° Testament and Psalter (pp. 447, 112) ; (8) Agate 32° Testament (pp. 356 : like an edition of 1853) ; (9) Diamond 64° Testament and Psalter (pp. 384, 100).

1854. The Book of Psalms : a new translation with notes critical and explanatory ; by . . . John Mason Good . . . edited by . . . E. Henderson.
   Seeleys : London. 1854. 23 × 14·5 cm.

For J. M. Good, M.D., F.R.S., see No. 1029, 1812.
Pp. viii, 539.

1191.

1854. The Second Epistle of Peter, the Epistles of John and Judas, and the Revelation ; translated from the Greek, on the basis of the common English version, with notes.
   Holman, Gray, and Co., for the American Bible Union :
      New York ; Trübner and Co. : London. 1854. 29·5 × 23·5 cm.

The American Bible Union was organized in June 1850 ' to procure and circulate the most faithful versions of the Sacred Scriptures in all languages throughout the world. One of the chief objects of the Union was to provide a revision of the English Bible which should ' give to the ordinary reader, as nearly as possible, the exact meaning of the inspired original; while, so far as compatible with this design, the general style and phraseology of the commonly-received version are retained.'

For full details in regard to this predominantly Baptist organization see *Documentary History of the American Bible Union* . . . (4 vols., 1857–67). Between 1850 and 1866 it circulated over 600,000 copies of Scripture. See Nos. 1195, 1200, 1227–30, and 1292.

The Introduction gives 'General rules for the direction of translators and revisers employed by the American Bible Union,' and ' Special instructions to the revisers of the English New Testament.'

A tentative edition, circulated for criticism.

The Greek text (following Bagster's octavo edition of 1851) is printed in a central column, having ' King James' version ' on one side, and the 'revised version ' on the other; with full notes. At the end is given ' the revised version in paragraphs, and according to the recommendations in the notes.' Pp. x, 253.

—— Another copy.

1192.

1855. The Annotated Paragraph Bible . . . arranged in paragraphs and parallelisms; with . . . notes, prefaces . . . and . . . references.
Religious Tract Society: London. 1855. 25 × 16·5 cm. 2 vols.

Vol. 1 contains the O. T.; viii, 1050 pp. With map.

¶ Imperfect: containing the O. T. only.

1193.

1855. The Book of the Prophet Ezekiel, translated from the original Hebrew, with a commentary . . . by E. Henderson.
R. Clay, for Hamilton, Adams, and Co.: London. 1855. 23 × 14·5 cm.

Pp. xii, 219. With introduction and foot-notes.

1194.

1855. Specimen of a revision of the English Scriptures of the Old Testament from the original Hebrew, on the basis of the common English version compared with the earlier ones on which it was founded . . . by Thomas J. Conant . . .
*Holman and Gray, for the American Bible Union:
New York; etc.* 1855. 28 × 23 cm.

See No. 1192, 1854.

A pamphlet in three parts, giving specimen pages of :—(1) · the common English version, the Hebrew text, and the revised version, with critical and philological notes '; (2) ' the revised version, with explanatory notes, for the English reader '; (3) the 'revised version.' The ' Advertisement ' explains the rules adopted, and names the works cited in the notes. Pp. iv, 12, 12, 6.

The specimens are taken from the early chapters of the Book of Job.

1195.

1856. The Holy Bible . . .
American Bible Society: New York. 1856. 39 × 27·5 cm.

The revised text prepared under the auspices of the A. B. S. See Note at 1851.

English imperial quarto. With references. Pp. 1163.

This was intended to be the standard English Bible of the A. B. S. (see the Fortieth Report, 1856, pp. 37–8).

1196.

1857. The Holy Bible . . .
    Printed for the Christian Knowledge Society by C. J. Clay,
                    University Press : Cambridge. 1857. 16 × 10 cm.
Nonpareil 16° Refs. Text ends on 78–4 a.
¶   [F. F.]
1197.

1857. The Holy Bible . . .
        American Bible Society : New York. 1857. 12·5 × 8 cm.
The revised text prepared under the auspices of the A. B. S. See Note at 1851.
Diamond 32°. Pp. 673, 211.
1198.

1857. The Four Gospels and the Acts of the Apostles, with short notes for the use of schools and young persons. By Henry Cotton, D.C.L. . . .
    John Henry and James Parker : Oxford. 1857. 16·5 × 10·5 cm.

Henry Cotton (1789–1879) was at one time sub-librarian of the Bodleian, and later became treasurer of Christ Church, Dublin, and titular Dean of Lismore. His bibliographical works on the English Bible and the Roman Catholic English versions are referred to on many pages of this Catalogue.

Text printed in paragraphs; O. T. quotations, in italics; the words of speakers, in inverted commas. The marginal readings and a few short notes are placed at the bottom of the page. Pp. xx, 364. With preface, and summary of contents.
¶   [F. F.]
—— Another copy.
1199.

1857. The Book of Job; the common English version, the Hebrew text, and the revised version of the American Bible Union, with an introduction and philological notes . . . by Thomas J. Conant . . .
    T. Holman, for the American Bible Union :
                       New York ; etc. 1857. 29 × 22·5 cm.
See No. 1192, 1854.
Pp. xxx, 165.
1200.

1857. The Book of the Prophet Isaiah, translated from the original Hebrew; with a commentary . . . to which is prefixed an introductory dissertation . . . by . . . E. Henderson . . . Second edition.
    R. Clay, for Hamilton, Adams, and Co.:
                        London. 1857. 23 × 14·5 cm.
Pp. xxxvi, 473. With preface, introduction, and foot-notes.
1201.

1857. The Gospel according to St. John, after the authorized version; newly compared with the original Greek and revised, by Five Clergymen. The second edition.
    R. Clay, for J. W. Parker and Son : London. 1857. 26 × 17·5.

Revised by J. Barrow, G. Moberly, H. Alford, W. G. Humphry, and C. J. Ellicott; and edited by E. Hawkins.

These pioneers did much to prepare English public opinion for an authoritative revision. H. Alford (1810–1871) Dean of Canterbury in 1857, G. Moberly (1803–1885) Bishop of Salisbury in 1869, C. J. Ellicott (b. 1819) the present Bishop of Gloucester, and W. G. Humphry (1815–1886) Prebendary of St. Paul's, all became members of the New Testament Revision Company (see No. 1276, 1881). J. Barrow was Principal of St. Edmund Hall. The editor, E. Hawkins, was Secretary of the Society for the Propagation of the Gospel.

The version attempts to secure a more correct rendering of the Greek, departing as little as possible from the current version, and retaining its style and rhythm. The revisers took Mill's reprint (1707) of the text of 'Stephens' (R. Estienne) as a basis, though they adopted different readings in a few important passages, where the weight of evidence appeared to be overwhelming.

Pp. xvi, 65. Preface dated 2 March 1857. The two versions are printed in parallel columns.

See Nos. 1204, 1205, and 1211; also Nos. 1214 and 1237.

1202.

1858. The Book of the Twelve Minor Prophets, translated from the original Hebrew, with a commentary . . . by E. Henderson . . . Second edition.
R. Clay, for Hamilton, Adams, and Co. :
London. 1858. 23 × 14·5 cm.

Pp. xii, 463. With prefaces and foot-notes.

1203.

1858. The Epistle of St. Paul to the Romans, after the authorized version; newly compared with the original Greek and revised, by Five Clergymen.
Savill and Edwards, for J. W. Parker and Son :
London. 1858. 26 × 17·5 cm.

Uniform with the version of St. John's Gospel by the same revisers. See No. 1202.
The Preface, dated 1 Dec. 1857, includes a list of the alterations made in the Greek text of R. Estienne. Pp. xx, 34.

1204.

1858. The Epistles of St. Paul to the Corinthians, after the authorized version; newly compared with the original Greek and revised, by Five Clergymen.
Savill and Edwards, for J. W. Parker and Son :
London. 1858. 26 × 17·5 cm.

Uniform with the versions of St. John's Gospel, and the Epistle to the Romans, by the same revisers. See No. 1202.
The Preface, dated 1 Dec. 1858, includes a list of the alterations made in the Greek text of R. Estienne. Pp. xlv, 54.

1205.

1858 ? The New Testament . . . translated from the Latin Vulgate . . . first published by the English College at Rheims, A.D. 1582. With Annotations . . . With lawful authority.
Burns and Oates : London. [1858 ?] 12·5 × 8·5 cm.

Rheims version.

This edition bears the *imprimatur* of Cardinal Wiseman, dated 'West., 29 Sept. 1858.' Pp. 446.

1206.

1859. The Commentary wholly Biblical : an Exposition in the very words of Scripture.
S. Bagster and Sons : London. [1859.] 25·5 × 19 cm. 8 vols.

Titlepages not dated : the B. M. catalogue gives 1856–59. The reference passages, which form the commentary, are printed in smaller type among the text. With maps, indexes, etc. Pp. 24, 858, 762, 644, 86.

1207.

1859. The Paragraph Bible . . .
Printed for the Religious Tract Society, by Eyre and Spottiswoode :
London. 1859. 20 × 13 cm.

A reprint of the edition of 1838 (No. 1153).

1208.

1859. The Holy Bible . . . printed in paragraphs.
University Press : Oxford. 1859. 17·5 × 11·5 cm.

Minion 16°. Sold by *E. Gardner and Son*, London.
N. T. ends on N 2 b.

1209.

1860. The Holy Bible . . .
Hector Baxter : London. 1860. 14 × 8·5 cm.

A licence to the printer, *J. A. Ballantyne : Edinburgh*, dated 11 Nov. 1859, is printed on verso of the title.
Pp. 789.

¶ Without the Scotch Metrical Psalms, mentioned in the licence.

1210.

1861. The Epistles of St. Paul to the Galatians, Ephesians, Philippians, and Colossians, after the authorized version; newly compared with the original Greek and revised, by Four Clergymen.
Robson, Levey, and Franklyn, for Parker, Son, and Bourne :
London. 1861. 26 × 17·5 cm.

Uniform with the versions of St. John's Gospel, and the Epistles to the Romans and the Corinthians, by 'Five Clergymen.' See No. 1202. One of the former revisers, J. Barrow, having left England, took no part in the present work.
The alterations made in the Greek text of R. Estienne are now indicated in the margin of the new version. Pp. iv, 37.

1211.

1862. The first New Testament printed in the English language (1525 or 1526), translated from the Greek by William Tyndale ; reproduced in facsimile with an introduction by Francis Fry, F.S.A.
Printed for the editor : Bristol. 1862. 19·5 × 13 cm.

See above, No. 2.
Contains Introduction, facsimiles, and a list of books printed by Peter Schoeffer of Worms—28 pp. ; followed by the text.
Only 177 copies were issued, of which 26 were printed upon large paper or vellum.

1212.

1862. The Gospel of S. Mark in the authorised version arranged in parts and sections, with titles and summaries of contents, marginal notes of time and place, and a preface; to which are appended cautions against the Greek Testament of Dean Alford and the Hulsean lectures of Dean Ellicott. For the use of schools and young students. By the Rev. J. Forshall . . .
    Spottiswoode and Co., for Longman, etc.: London. 1862. 19 × 12 cm.
For the editor see No. 1178, 1850.
Pp. xlviii, 70.

1213.

1862. The Gospel according to S. John, translated from the eleven oldest versions except the Latin, and compared with the English Bible; with notes on every one of the alterations proposed by the Five Clergymen in their revised version of this Gospel published in 1857. By the Rev. S. C. Malan . . .
    Joseph Masters: London. 1862. 29·5 × 23 cm.

The 'eleven oldest versions' are the Syriac, Ethiopic, Sahidic, Memphitic, Gothic, Armenian, Georgian, Slavonic, Anglo-Saxon, Arabic, and Persian. For the 'Five Clergymen,' see No. 1202, 1857.

S. C. Malan (1812-1894), vicar of Broadwindsor, Dorset, afterwards joined Dean Burgon in attacking the Revised New Testament of 1881.
Pp. xvii, 293, 134.

—— Another copy.

1214.

1862. The Souldiers Pocket Bible, printed at London by G. B. and R. W. for G. C., 1643, reproduced in facsimile with an introduction by Francis Fry, F.S.A.
    Willis and Sotheran: London. 1862. 18·5 × 12 cm.
See No. 447, 1643.
Pp. vii, 16.

1215.

1862. The Christian Soldiers Penny Bible, London, printed by R. Smith for Sam. Wade, 1693, reproduced in facsimile with an introductory note by Francis Fry, F.S.A.
    Willis and Sotheran: London. 1862. 18·5 × 12 cm.
See No. 655, 1693.
Pp. iv, 16.

1216.

1862. B. See 1863.

1863. The Holy Bible . . . With introductory remarks to each book, parallel passages, critical, explanatory, and practical notes. Illustrated with photographs by Frith.
    William Mackenzie: Glasgow, etc. 1862,63. 48 × 35 cm. 2 vols.

This Bible, edited by Gilbert McCallum, and known as 'The Queen's Bible,' was prepared for the International Exhibition of 1862. It was one of the earliest books in which machinery was used for composing, though the printing was done by hand.

Only 170 copies were published, and sold at 50 guineas apiece. The work was also issued in twenty parts at two guineas each.
The title to vol. 1 and the N. T. title are dated 1862; vol. 2 title is dated 1863. Pp. 1344. With Translators' Preface.

¶ Bound in red morocco, with embossed design (containing the royal cipher, etc.) by Leighton; with brass mountings and clasps.

1217.

1863. The Holy Bible . . . arranged in paragraphs.
Cave and Sever: Manchester. 1863,62. 28·5 × 21·5 cm.

General title dated 1863; N. T. title dated 1862.
Text, 1272 pp.; Index, 51 pp. The verse-divisions and numbers are retained, but bold numerals in the left-hand margin indicate the 5810 paragraphs into which the text is divided. The Index gives the subject of each paragraph.

1218.

1863. The Holy Bible, containing the Old and New Covenants, literally and idiomatically translated out of the original languages. By Robert Young . . .
A. Fullarton and Co.: Edinburgh, etc. 1863. 18·5 × 12·5 cm.

An attempt to reproduce the Hebrew and Greek idioms in English.

Text, 606, 178 pp. With preliminary remarks dealing with the Hebrew tenses etc.; and notices of the version.

1219.

1863. The New Testament for English readers: containing the authorized version, with marginal corrections of readings and renderings, marginal references, and a . . . commentary; by Henry Alford . . .
Gilbert and Rivington, for Rivingtons:
London, etc. 1863. 23 × 14·5 cm. 2 vols.

Vol. 1; in two parts, containing the Gospels and Acts. Pp. 839. With map.
Vol. 2 appeared in 1866.

1220.

1863. The Psalms, translated from the Hebrew, with notes chiefly critical and exegetical. By W. Kay, D.D. . . .
R. C. Lepage and Co.: Calcutta. 1863. 21·5 × 12·5 cm.

The author was 'Principal of Bishop's College, Calcutta, and Fellow of Lincoln College, Oxford.'

The idea of this translation was suggested to him in the course of his work in connection with the Bengali Bible.
Printed at the 'Bishop's College Press.'
Pp. vii, 339. With foot-notes, etc.
See No. 1254.

1221.

1863. A revision of the authorized English versions of the Book of Psalms . . . with notes by the Rev. John Noble Coleman . . .
T. Constable: Edinburgh, for J. Nisbet and Co.:
London. 1863. 29 × 20 cm.

Pp. xxxvi, 336.

1222.

1863. The Prophete Jonas with an introduction before . . . by William Tyndale. Reproduced in facsimile. To which is added Coverdale's version of Jonah, with an Introduction by Francis Fry . . .
Willis and Sotheran : London. Lasbury : Bristol.
1863. 19·5 × 13 cm.

See No. 4.
Contains Introduction (16 pp.). *The prophete Jonas* . . . (prologue and text), and 'Coverdale's Translation of Jonas . . . copied from Coverdale's Bible, folio, 1535.'

1223.

1864. The Book of Job; translated from the Hebrew, by Rev. J. M. Rodwell.
Stephen Austin : Hertford, for Williams and Norgate :
London. 1864. 21 × 13·5 cm.

Pp. viii, 104. With foot-notes.

1224.

1864. B. See 1866.

1865. The twenty four books of the Holy Scriptures : carefully translated according to the Massoretic text, after the best Jewish authorities. By Isaac Leeser.
John Childs and Co., for Trübner and Co. :
London. 5625 [=1865 A.D.]. 15·5 × 10 cm.

According to the preface (dated Philadelphia, 7 Jan. 1856), this is a revised edition of a version of the Old Testament which had appeared in quarto with fuller notes in 1854.

Pp. xii, 1243. Text arranged according to the usual Jewish division. A few notes are appended.

¶ The cover is stamped : 'Presented by the Jewish Association for the diffusion of religious knowledge.'

1225.

1866. The Chronological Bible : containing the Old and New Testaments, according to the authorised version : newly divided into paragraphs and sections ; with . . . dates and places . . . introductions . . . and notes . . . By Robert B. Blackader.
Printed for the editor, and sold by Simpkin, Marshall, and Co. :
London. 1864,66. 23 × 17·5 cm.

The preface describes the main features of this edition, which follows the same lines as Blackader's 'Chronological New Testament' of 1851 (see No. 1182).

Alexander Bell was chiefly responsible for the arrangement in paragraphs ; while F. Bosworth, S. Trail, and others contributed many of the introductions and notes. The N. T., in its improved form, was completed and published in 1858.
General title dated 1864 ; N. T. title ('Third edition, revised and enlarged') dated 1866.
Pp. xx, 628, 600, 409 ; the O. T. is in two parts. With introductions, chronological tables, marginal notes, and other matter.

1226.

1866. The New Testament . . . The common English version, corrected by the final committee of the American Bible Union. Second revision.

T. Holman, New York, for American Bible Union: New York; Trübner and Co.: London. 1866. 23 × 15 cm.

For this revision, see above, No. 1192, 1854.

The Note on verso of title states that

'This Revised Testament has been prepared under the auspices of the American Bible Union, by the most competent scholars of the day. No expense has been spared to obtain the oldest translations of the Bible, copies of the ancient manuscripts, and other facilities to make the revision as perfect as possible.

'The paragraph form has been adopted . . . But, for convenience of reference, the numbers of the verses are retained.

'All quotations from the Old Testament are distinctly indicated, and the poetic form is restored to those which appear as poetry in the original.

'The revisers have been guided in their labors by the following rules prescribed by the Union : . . .

'The received Greek text, critically edited, with known errors corrected, must be followed.

'The common English version must be the basis of revision, and only such alterations must be made as the exact meaning of the text and the existing state of the language may require.

'The exact meaning of the inspired text, as that text expressed it to those who understood the original Scriptures at the time they were first written, must be given in corresponding words and phrases, so far as they can be found in the English language, with the least possible obscurity or indefiniteness.

'The *numbering* of the *chapter* is omitted, where it would break the connection; as in John viii, 1 Cor. xi, xiii, xiv, Philipp. iv, Col. iv, 1 Pet. iii.'

'Entered according to Act of Congress, in the year 1865, by the American Bible Union. . . .'

Pica 8° Edition, 6th Thousand. 1 p. 488.

1227.

Two smaller editions were published in the same year; see below.

1866. The New Testament . . . corrected by the final committee of the American Bible Union. Second revision. [Willingham Memorial.]
American Bible Union : New York, etc. 1866. 15·5 × 10 cm.

See No. 1227.
Electrotyped by *Smith and M·Dougal*. Brevier 18°, 7th Thousand. Pp. 488.

1228.

1866. The New Testament . . . corrected by the final committee of the American Bible Union. Second Revision. [Amory Memorial.]
American Bible Union : New York, etc. 1866. 10 × 7·5 cm.

See No. 1227.
'Composed and Electrotyped by *Lange and Bro.*' Agate 32°, 20th Thousand. Pp. 488.

1229.

1866. The Book of Genesis. The common version revised for the American Bible Union, with explanatory and philological notes. By Thomas J. Conant.
American Bible Union : New York. 1866. 23 × 15 cm.

See No. 1192, 1854.
A pamphlet, giving twelve specimen pages of text (Gen. i to iv. 17), with foot-notes.

ENGLISH 373

'The following sheets are printed as a specimen of the revised translation of Genesis, with such notes as seemed to be indispensable for understanding the design of the corrections, and the meaning of the sacred narrative. The full statement of the grounds for the revised renderings, and for the readings of the text followed in the translation, is reserved for the critical and philological notes, to be printed at the end of the volume. T. J. Conant. October 1, 1866.'

—- Another copy.

1230.

1866. Ecclesiastes; a new translation, with notes . . . by the Rev. J. N. Coleman . . .
    Printed for private circulation. T. Constable :
              Edinburgh. 1866. 29 × 20 cm.
Pp. xix, 70.

1231.

1866. B. See *1867*.

1867. The Holy Bible . . .
  Printed for the B. F. B. S., at the
       University Press : Oxford. 1866,67. 16·5 × 11 cm.

Nonpareil 16°. *Sold under cost. Tenpence.*
General title dated 1866; N. T. title dated 1867. Text ends on Cc 8 b.
Error in Luke xviii. 9, *went* for *were*.

¶   [F. F.]
1232.

1867. The Holy Bible . . .
  Printed for the B. F. B. S., at the
       University Press : Oxford. 1867. 16·5 × 11 cm.

Like No. 1232. Text ends on Cc 8 b.
Error in Luke xviii. 9, *went* for *were*.

¶   [F. F.]
1233.

1867. The New Testament; translated from the original Greek, by H. T. Anderson.
  C. W. Purser : Great Bridge, Staffs., for David King :
          Birmingham. [1867.] 19 × 12·5 cm.

An English reprint of an original American version.

No date on title, but the publisher's Preface is dated January, 1867. The author's Preface is signed *H. T. Anderson*, and dated *Harrodsburg, Ky.*, March, 1864. Pp. 370.

¶   [F. F.]
1234.

1868. The Holy Bible . . .
  Printed for the B. F. B. S., at the
       University Press : Oxford. 1868. 16·5 × 11 cm.

Like No. 1232. Text ends on Cc 8 b.
Error in Luke xviii. 9, *went* for *were*.

¶   [F. F.]
1235.

1869. The Holy Bible . . .
  Printed for the B. F. B. S., at the
    University Press: Oxford. 1869. 14 × 10 cm.

Diamond 16° Refs. Text ends on Aa 16 b.
Error in John i. 48, *Pilate* for *Philip*.

1236.

1869. The New Testament . . . after the authorized version, newly compared with the original Greek, and revised, by Henry Alford . . .
  R. Clay, Sons, and Taylor, for Strahan and Co.:
    London. 1869. 17·5 × 11·5 cm.

This was practically a completion of the work begun by the 'Five Clergymen' in their versions of St. John's Gospel, and the Epistles to the Romans, Corinthians, Galatians, Ephesians, Philippians, and Colossians (see No. 1202, etc.), which are here reprinted with a very few changes. Dean Alford's wish was mainly 'to keep open the great question of an authoritative Revision, to show the absolute necessity of such a measure sooner or later, and to disabuse men's minds of the fallacies by which the Authorized Version is commonly defended.'

Pp. x, 523.

1237.

1869. The New Testament; the authorised English version; with introduction, and various readings from the three most celebrated manuscripts of the original Greek text. By Constantine Tischendorf. Tauchnitz edition, volume 1000.
  Bernhard Tauchnitz: Leipzig. 1869. 16 × 11 cm.

Issued as the thousandth volume of the 'Tauchnitz Collection.' The English equivalents of the variations of the Sinaitic, the Vatican, and the Alexandrian MSS. are printed at the foot of each page.

Pp. xvi, 414. With frontispiece.

1238.

1869. The Book of Job; translated from the Hebrew, with notes . . . by the Rev. J. N. Coleman . . .
  T. Constable: Edinburgh, for J. Nisbet and Co.:
    London. 1869. 29·5 × 22·5 cm.

Pp. xx, 118. See No. 1251.

1239.

1869. The Book of Psalms; translated from the Hebrew, by Charles Carter . . .
  Yates and Alexander, etc.: London. [1869.] 16·5 × 10·5 cm.

The translator was a Baptist missionary in Ceylon, who prepared a Sinhali version of the Scriptures for the Bible Translation Society.

The preface is dated 1869. Pp. iv, 156.

1240.

1870. The New Testament, according to the authorised version, with analysis, notes, etc.
Sold for the author by S. Bagster and Sons :
London. 1870. 23·5 × 17 cm.

By Thomas Newberry, of Crewkerne, Somerset.

The Introduction explains the design of the book. Text divided into short paragraphs, with marginal analysis, and brief foot-notes, giving more correct renderings of certain phrases, of which the Greek is added.
Text ends on 39–6 b.

¶ A copy of the original prospectus of this work is inserted.

1241.

1870. A rhymed Harmony of the Gospels; by Francis Barham and Isaac Pitman. Printed both in Phonetic and in the customary spelling, as a Transition Book from Phonetic Reading to the reading of books as now commonly printed.
F. Pitman : London. I. Pitman ; J. Davies :
Bath. 1870. 19 × 12·5 cm.

This 'rhymed paraphrase' claims to be 'very complete,' and to include almost every text in Townsend's 'Harmony of the Gospels.' It was originally prepared by F. Barham, and afterwards corrected by I. Pitman.

Pp. 262. With Phonetic Alphabet, preface, and appendix.

1242.

1870. The Writings of Solomon; comprising the Book of Proverbs, Ecclesiastes, Song of Songs, and Psalms lxxii, cxxvii. Translated by Francis Barham. Printed both in Phonetic and in the customary spelling . . .
F. Pitman : London. I. Pitman ; J. Davies :
Bath. 1870. 12·5 × 9·5 cm.

Apparently the first of F. Barham's prose versions of books of the Bible, printed by his friend Isaac Pitman at Bath. See Nos. 1244, 1252, 1253, and 1256. Sometimes, as in this case, the version was also given in phonetic spelling.

'About twenty years ago I published revised English versions of Solomon's Ecclesiastes and Canticles' (translator's preface). In this volume are added Proverbs and two Psalms attributed to Solomon.
Pp. 287.

1243.

1870. A revised version of the prophecies of Hosea and Micah. By Francis Barham.
F. Pitman : London. I. Pitman ; J. Davies :
Bath. 1870. 12·5 × 9·5 cm.

See No. 1243.
Apparently the version of Micah had been previously published by Barham (see publisher's note in his translation of the Psalms, 1871, No. 1253).
Pp. 62.

1244.

1870. The Gospel according to St. Mark: revised from the ancient Greek MSS. unknown to the translators of the authorised version; by a member of the University of Oxford.
Spottiswoode and Co., for Longmans, Green and Co. :
London. 1870. 19 × 14·5 cm.

According to a MS. note on the titlepage of the Library copy this version was made by 'Mr. Briscoe, M.P.'

Pp. 34.

1245.

1871. The Holy Bible, according to the Authorized Version, arranged in paragraphs and sections, with emendations of the text . . .
Printed for the Religious Tract Society by Eyre and Spottiswoode : London. [1871.] 32·5 × 26 cm.

Contains the text of King James' version, with emendations inserted within brackets. The Old Testament was edited by F. W. Gotch, and the New Testament by G. A. Jacob.

For the editors see No. 1269, 1877.
Published originally in parts, 1868–71. With maps, tables, etc.

—— Another copy.

—— Another copy.

In parts, with original wrappers bearing various dates between 1868 and 1871. The sections Joshua–Esther and Acts–Revelation are missing.

—— Another copy.

Containing parts 1 and 2, with a general title bearing the words 'Vol. 1. Genesis to Esther,' and dated 1869.

1246.

1871. The Hebrew Scriptures, translated by Samuel Sharpe, being a revision of the Authorized English Old Testament . . . Second Edition.
Billing : Guildford, for J. Russell Smith :
London. 1871. 17 × 10·5 cm. 3 vols.

The first edition was issued in 1865.
S. Sharpe (1799–1881), a Unitarian scholar, was also known as an Egyptologist.

Pp. iv, 524, 526, 458.
See No. 1250.

1247.

1871. The first printed English New Testament, translated by William Tyndale ; photo-lithographed from the unique fragment now in the Grenville Collection, British Museum. Edited by Edward Arber . . .
London. 1871. 22 × 17 cm.

See No. 1.
Contains Preface (70 pp), text (62 pp.), and a reproduction of part of the titlepage of Rupertus' *In Matthæum* . . . (printed by Peter Quentel at Cologne, between March and July 1526), which bears the same woodcut as that occurring at the beginning of St. Matthew's Gospel in this quarto New Testament.

—— Another copy.

1248.

1871. The New Testament . . . Printed in paragraphs.
  Printed for the B. F. B. S., at the University Press:
           Oxford. 1871. 15·5 × 11 cm.

Edited by the Rev. R. B. Girdlestone, Editorial Superintendent of the Bible Society, 1866–76.

Brevier 16°. Pp. 380. See Nos. 1261 and 1268.

1249.

1871. The New Testament, translated from Griesbach's text, by Samuel Sharpe . . .
  S. and J. Brawn, for J. R. Smith: London. 1871. 17 × 10·5 cm.

Uniform with Sharpe's translation of the Old Testament (see No. 1247).

A reissue of the Sixth edition, published in 1870.
Pp. 412.

1250.

1871. The Poem of Job . . . translated from the Hebrew with notes . . . by the Rev. J. N. Coleman . . . Second edition.
  Printed for private circulation. T. and A. Constable:
          Edinburgh. 1871. 31 × 21 cm.

First edition published in 1869. See No. 1239.
Pp. xxvi, 128.

1251.

1871. The Book of Job; newly translated from the original, by Francis Barham. Printed both in Phonetic and in the customary spelling . . .
  F. Pitman: London. I. Pitman; J. Davies:
          Bath. 1871. 12·5 × 9·5 cm.

See No. 1243.
Preface dated 10 Jan. 1871. A foot-note on p. 148 records F. Barham's death, while the eighth sheet was in the hands of the compositor, on 9 Feb. 1871.
Pp. 173.

1252.

1871. The Book of Psalms, translated from the Hebrew and the Syriac; by Francis Barham and Edward Hare.
  F. Pitman: London. I. Pitman; J. Davies:
          Bath. 1871. 12·5 × 9·5 cm.

See No. 1243.
Preface dated 4 Feb. 1871. A 'Note by the Publisher,' dated 9 Feb. 1871, records F. Barham's death, and explains that his translation from the Syriac had extended only to Ps. lviii; the book was completed by E. Hare of Bath, 'by collating the Latin translation of the Syriac given in the edition of Erpenius with the Latin version of the Syriac in Walton's Polyglot.'
Pp. 446.

1253.

1871. The Psalms, translated from the Hebrew, with notes chiefly exegetical; by William Kay . . .
   T. and A. Constable : Edinburgh, for Rivingtons :
         London, etc. 1871. 20·5 × 13·5 cm.

A revised edition of the work first published at Calcutta in 1863. See No. 1221.
Pp. 469.
                       1254.

1871. Commentary on the Book of Isaiah . . . including a revised English translation; with introduction and appendices . . . by the Rev. T. R. Birks . . .
   C. J. Clay : Cambridge, for Rivingtons :
         London, etc. 1871. 23 × 14·5 cm.

This work, in its earlier form, was intended for incorporation in the Speaker's Commentary (No. 1275).

T. R. Birks (1810–1883) was vicar of Holy Trinity, Cambridge, and afterwards Professor of Moral Philosophy.
Pp. xiv, 419.
                       1255.

1871. An elucidated translation of St. John's Epistles, from the Greek and Syriac, with a devotional commentary, by Francis Barham.
   F. Pitman : London. I. Pitman ; J. Davies :
         Bath. 1871. 12·5 × 9·5 cm.

See No. 1243.
Preface dated 2 Jan. 1871.
Pp. 62.
                       1256.

1871. B. See 1873.

1872 ? The Four Gospels and the Acts of the Apostles in paragraphs, punctuated rhetorically for reading in schools, colleges, and families; by Alexander Bell . . .
   Charles Griffin and Co. : London. [1872 ?] 19 × 12·5 cm.

The editor is described on the title as 'Professor of Elocution.' The Preface alludes to 'this edition of the New Testament,' but apparently no more was published than is given in this volume.

'Tables of Quotations' occur after the books; but there is no **Appendix** (mentioned in the Preface). Pp. iv. 315.
                       1257.

1872. B. See 1873.

1873. The Holy Bible in the Authorized Version; with notes and introductions by Chr. Wordsworth, D.D., Bishop of Lincoln.
   Rivingtons : London, etc. 1872,73,71. 28·5 × 19 cm. 6 vols.

A cheaper issue of Bishop Wordsworth's Commentary, the first part of which was published in 1864.

Contains the Old Testament only. Bishop Wordsworth (1807–1885) never completed this annotated English Bible by adding the New Testament, but he published the Greek Testament with a commentary.

Included in vol. 6 is 'An Index to the Bishop of Lincoln's Commentary on the Old Testament,' by F. H. Scrivener.

¶ Vols. 1 (1872) and 3 (1873) are styled on the titlepage 'New edition'; vols. 2 (1873), 5 (1871), and 6 (1872) omit these words; vol. 4 (1872) is the 'Third edition.'

1258.

1873. The Cambridge Paragraph Bible of the authorized English version, with the text revised by a collation of its early and other principal editions, the use of the italic type made uniform, the marginal references remodelled, and a critical introduction prefixed; by the Rev. F. H. Scrivener . . . Edited for the Syndics of the University Press.
University Press: Cambridge. 1873. 26·5 × 20 cm.

The title sufficiently indicates the method adopted in this important and elaborate attempt to publish a trustworthy text of King James' version.

The Introduction, with its valuable Appendixes, etc., was reprinted separately in 1884.
Introduction, Appendixes, Translators' Preface, and Epistle Dedicatory, cxx pp. Text in three parts: O. T., 856 pp.; Apocrypha, 198 pp.; N. T., 253 pp. Printed in paragraphs.

1259.

1873. The School and Children's Bible; prepared under the superintendence of the Rev. William Rogers . . .
Longman, Green, and Co.: London. 1873. 17 × 11·5 cm.

This edition presents the Bible in a shortened form 'adapted for the use of children.' The matter is re-arranged, sometimes in order to preserve the chronological order. The authorized version is retained, except in the Psalms, where the P. B. version is given. Four passages are taken from the Apocrypha.
Pp. xiii, 718.

1260.

1873. The New Testament . . . Printed in paragraphs.
Printed for the B. F. B. S. by C. J. Clay, University Press:
Cambridge. 1873. 14 × 9 cm.

Brevier 32°. Pp. 548. See No. 1249, 1871.

1261.

1873. The Universal Syllabic Gospel: the English of the Gospel according to St. John; with English key, and specimens in other tongues.
Gilbert and Rivington, for William Hunt and Co.:
London. 1873. 22 × 14 cm.

St. John's Gospel printed according to the system of 'Universal Syllabics,' invented by the Rev. Robert Hunt, formerly missionary in Patagonia, and then under the C.M.S. in North West America.

With Preface, Key, and 'Specimens of the Universal Syllabics in various dialects.'
Pp. xliii, 116.

1262.

1874. Ecclesiastes for English readers. The Book called by the Jews Koheleth, newly translated with introduction, analysis, and notes; by the Rev. W. H. B. Proby . . .
 Pardon and Son, for Rivingtons : London, etc. 1874. 23 × 14·5 cm.

Pp. vi, 47.
1263.

1874. The Ten Canticles of the Old Testament Canon . . . newly translated with notes . . . by the Rev. W. H. B. Proby . . .
 T. and A. Constable : Edinburgh, for Rivingtons :
London, etc. 1874. 19 × 13 cm.

Containing the Songs of Moses (2), Deborah, Hannah, Isaiah (3), Hezekiah, Jonah, and Habakkuk. Pp. 89.
1264.

1875. The Accented Bible . . . All Proper Names accented. Edited by the Rev. Alexander Taylor . . .
 Printed for the Wesleyan Methodist Sunday School Union by
Eyre and Spottiswoode : London. [1875.] 17 × 10·5 cm.

Nonpareil 12°. Preface, dated 'Easter, 1875,' vii pp. Text ends on Bb 16 a.
1265.

1875. The New Testament . . . A new translation, on the basis of the authorized version, from a critically revised Greek text, newly arranged in paragraphs, with analyses . . . by John Brown McClellan . . . Vol. I. The Four Gospels, with the chronological and analytical Harmony.
 C. J. Clay : Cambridge, for Macmillan and Co. :
London. 1875. 23 × 14·5 cm.

Pp. xciii, 763. With elaborate preface, Prolegomena, Harmony, Notes, Indexes, etc.
J. B. McClellan was vicar of Bottisham, Cambs., 1861–80.
1266.

1876. The Holy Bible . . . edited with various renderings and readings from the best authorities . . . .
Eyre and Spottiswoode : London. 1876. 20·5 × 14·5 cm.

King James' version, with various renderings and readings printed below the text on each page. The Old Testament is edited by T. K. Cheyne and S. R. Driver; and the New Testament by R. L. Clarke and A. Goodwin.

Bourgeois small 8°. Pp. 1318.
1267.

1877. The Holy Bible . . . Printed in paragraphs.
 Printed for the B. F. B. S. at the University Press :
Cambridge. 1877. 18 × 12 cm.

This edition, prepared by R. B. Girdlestone, is based on Scrivener's Cambridge edition of 1873, and other Paragraph Bibles. Two editions of the New Testament in paragraphs, prepared by the same editor, had already been published by the B. F. B. S., in 1871 and in 1873. See Nos. 1249 and 1261.

Pp. 791. No chapter headings, but short page headings. Alternative renderings and a few references at the foot of each page. With maps.

1268.

1877. Revised English Bible. The Holy Bible according to the Authorised Version, compared with the Hebrew and Greek texts, and carefully revised ; arranged in paragraphs and sections, with supplementary notes, references . . . chronological tables, and maps.
Printed for the editor by Eyre and Spottiswoode :
London. [1877.] 21 × 15 cm.

According to the Preface (dated Westminster, May, 1877, and signed *J. G.* (i.e. J. Gurney), 'this publication is the completion of a work which was commenced sixteen years ago, and was partly carried into effect by the publication in parts (in 1868–71) of a quarto Bible, containing within brackets in the text what were regarded as the more important emendations required in the Authorised Version.' In 'the present more complete revision,' the first five books of the O. T. are edited by F. W. Gotch, the rest of the O. T. by B. Davies, and the N. T. by G. A. Jacob and S. G. Green. The design 'is to correct what may be considered *indisputable* errors and inadequate renderings in our present English Bible; and in the New Testament to give also the more important emendations of the text which have been adopted by the best Editors of the Greek Testament.'

Joseph Gurney was Short-hand Writer to the House of Lords, and Treasurer of the R.T.S. (1875–80). Dr. Gotch (d. 1890) Principal of the Bapt.st College, Bristol, and Dr. Davies (d. 1875) Professor of Hebrew at Regent's Park College, were members of the Old Testament Revision Company. Dr. Green was President of Rawdon Baptist College (1863–76), and afterwards Editorial Secretary of the R.T.S. (to 1900). Dr. Jacob was Headmaster of Christ's Hospital (1853–68).

See No. 1246, 1871, edited by Drs. Gotch and Jacob.

Minion 8°. Text, divided into sections and paragraphs, ends on Kk 7 a. Marginal references, alternative renderings, etc. The dates are given according to Ussher's and Hale's chronologies. With summaries, tables, and maps.

1269.

1877. The Cambridge Bible for Schools . . . The Gospel according to St. Mark, with notes and introduction by . . . G. F. Maclear . . .
University Press: Cambridge. 1877. 17·5 × 12 cm.

The first volume of the first edition of this series, begun under the editorial supervision of the Rev. J. J. S. Perowne, D.D., Hulsean Professor of Divinity.

The text is that of King James' version. Pp. 200. With map.

1270.

1878. The Monograph Gospel; being the four Gospels arranged in one continuous narrative in the words of Scripture, without omission of fact or repetition of statement. By G. Washington Moon . . .
Hatchards: London. 1878. 13·5 × 9 cm.

Pp. vii, 273. With map and index.

1271.

1879. The Psalms from the Hebrew: translated and arranged as an English comment on the Prayerbook Psalter. By John Philip Gell . . .
  Printed for private circulation. R. Clay, Sons, and Taylor :
        London. 1879. 22 × 14 cm.

A literal rendering of the Hebrew.

Preface, xix pp.

1272.

1880. The Pictorial New Testament for the Young, according to the Authorized version, with . . . notes and references . . .
  Elliot Stock, for Benjamin West : London. [1880.] 13·5 × 8 cm.

Text ends on D 31 b.

1273.

1880. The Book of Psalms, with an explanatory and critical commentary, by G. H. S. Johnson . . . C. J. Elliott . . . F. C. Cook . . .
  C. J. Clay, University Press : Cambridge, for J. Murray :
        London. 1880. 24·5 × 16 cm.

New and revised edition, reprinted from the Speaker's Commentary (see No. 1275, 1881).

Pp. xxxi, 340.

1274.

1881. The Holy Bible, according to the authorized version (A.D. 1611); with an explanatory and critical Commentary, and a revision of the translation; by Bishops and other Clergy of the Anglican Church. Edited by F. C. Cook . . .
  C. J. Clay, University Press : Cambridge, also W. Clowes
   and Sons : London, for John Murray :
      London. 1871–81. 24·5 × 16 cm. 10 vols.

The preparation of this edition was undertaken in 1864 at the suggestion of the Right Hon. J. Evelyn Denison, Speaker of the House of Commons, afterwards Viscount Ossington. From the circumstances of its origin it is generally known as 'The Speaker's Commentary.'

An important feature of this work was the numerous revised renderings contained in the notes to the text.

O. T. in 6 vols. (vol. 1 is divided into two parts); N. T. in 4 vols. The volumes bear various dates from 1871 to 1881.

 — Another copy of vol. 1.

 —— Another copy of vol. 2.

1275.

1881. The New Testament . . . translated out of the Greek : being the version set forth A.D. 1611 compared with the most ancient authorities and revised A.D. 1881. Printed for the Universities of Oxford and Cambridge.
  University Press : Cambridge. 1881. 25 × 16 cm.

The 'Revised Version' is distinguished from all its predecessors by the fact that it originated in the Convocation of Canterbury. In May 1870, the report of a Committee, appointed three months earlier, was adopted, to the effect 'that Convocation should nominate a body of its own members to undertake the work of revision, who shall be at liberty to invite the co-operation of any eminent for scholarship, to whatever nation or religious body they may belong.' Shortly afterwards two Companies were appointed for the revision of the Old Testament and New Testament respectively, with Dr. Harold Browne, Bishop of Ely, and Dr. Ellicott, Bishop of Gloucester and Bristol, as their chairmen. In the Old Testament revision thirty-seven scholars took part, of whom twenty-seven remained at its completion. In the New Testament revision twenty-eight scholars took part, of whom twenty-four remained at its completion. The rules laid down for the Revisers' guidance directed that alterations in King James' version should be as few as possible, consistently with faithfulness to the original, and that they should be made in the language of that and earlier English versions; also that no changes in the text should be retained in the final revision, unless approved by two-thirds of the Revisers then present.

In the year 1871-2, at the invitation of the English Revisers, a Committee of American scholars was formed to co-operate in the work. The American Old Testament Revisers numbered fifteen, and the New Testament Revisers numbered seventeen, of whom two and four respectively died before the completion of their undertaking. For full details see *Historical Account of the work of the American Committee of Revision . . .*, and *Documentary History of the American Committee on Revision* (privately printed), New York, 1885.

The revision of the New Testament occupied about ten and a half years, and the result was published on 17 May 1881. Four years later the Old Testament was ready, and the Revised Bible was published on 19 May 1885. A preface to each Testament described the principles on which the Revision had been carried out. In an appendix to each Testament, the American Companies of Revisers placed on record certain renderings which they preferred to those adopted by their English associates.

A revision of the Apocrypha was afterwards undertaken by four committees appointed by the English Revisers from their own number, and the new version appeared in 1895 (see No. 1302).

In 1898 a new edition of the Revised Bible, including the Apocrypha, was published with a carefully amended set of marginal references (see No. 1315).

In 1900-1, some survivors of the American Revision Committee issued a recension of the Revised Bible (see No. 1331).

Pica Royal 8°. Pp. xxv, 606.
The Preface is dated 'Jerusalem Chamber, Westminster Abbey, 11th November 1880.'
Text printed in paragraphs. The page- and chapter-headings (which originally it was proposed to revise) and the dates, are omitted, but the titles to the Books remain unaltered. Alternative renderings, etc. in margins.

1276.

1881. The New Testament . . . revised A.D. 1881 . . .
University Press: Cambridge. 1881. 18 × 12 cm.
Long Primer Crown 8°. Pp. xxii, 496.

1277.

—— ANOTHER EDITION.
Printed at the *University Press, Oxford.*

1278.

1881. The New Testament . . . revised A.D. 1881 . . .
University Press: Oxford. 1881. 16 × 10·5 cm.
Brevier 16°. Pp. xxi, 419.
Error in 1 Cor. iii. 5, the word *Lord* is displaced.

1279.

1881. The New Testament . . . revised A.D. 1881 . . .
University Press: Cambridge. 1881. 13·5 × 10 cm.

Nonpareil 32°. Pp. xviii, 332.

—— ANOTHER EDITION.
Printed at the *University Press, Oxford.*

1280.

1882. The Holy Bible . . .
Printed for the B. F. B. S. by C. J. Clay, University Press: Cambridge. 1882. 16·5 × 11·5 cm.

Nonpareil 16°. *Price Tenpence.* Pp. 876.
Error in 2 Sam. xiv. 33, *and the King hissed Absalom,* for *and the King kissed Absalom.*

1281.

1882. The Parallel New Testament. The New Testament . . . being the authorised version set forth in 1611 arranged in parallel columns with the revised version of 1881 . . .
University Press: Cambridge. 1882. 20·5 × 14 cm.

The left-hand column contains King James' version, with its marginal matter, 'reproduced, substantially, as it was first given to the public [in 1611], no notice having been taken of the changes which were made from time to time (without known authority) in subsequent editions.' Typographical errors and false references, however, are corrected, and some inconsistencies in the employment of capitals and in punctuation are removed. The right-hand column contains the revised version of 1881, with its marginal matter.
Prefixed are an Advertisement, and the Revisers' Prefaces, and annexed is a table giving the renderings preferred by the American Committee.
Minion Crown 8°. Pp. xxii, 552.

1282.

1882. The New Testament Scriptures in the order in which they were written: a very close translation from the Greek text of 1611, with brief explanations. The First Portion: the six primary Epistles, to Thessalonica, Corinth, Galatia, and Rome, A.D. 52-58. By the Rev. Charles Hebert . . .
E. Pickard Hall, and J. H. Stacy: Oxford, for H. Frowde, etc.: London. [1882.] 19 × 12·5 cm.

Apparently no more was published.
Pp. xii, 140.

1283.

1883. The Minor Prophets; with a commentary explanatory and practical, and introductions to the several books. By . . . E. B. Pusey . . .
Gilbert and Rivington, for Walter Smith: London. 1883. 32 × 25·5 cm.

Dr. Pusey (1800-1890) was Regius Professor of Hebrew at Oxford from 1828 until his death.

The Preface is dated 1860. Pp. iv, 623.

1284.

1883. The New Covenant. According to Matthew, with explanations of the translation, and Songs of Deliverance.
Edward Alexander Guy, Cincinnati, Ohio, U.S.A. [1883.] 16 × 11·5 cm.

Electrotyped at the Franklin Type Foundry, and printed at the Aldine Printing Works, Cincinnati.
Title on paper cover, as above; followed by half-title, with *Greeting* (dated 6th day, 10th month, 1883) on verso. Text, with foot-notes and appended *Explanations*, 72 pp. Hymns, with some tunes, 24 pp. See No. 1298, 1888.

1285.

1885. The Holy Bible . . . translated out of the original tongues: being the version set forth A.D. 1611 compared with the most ancient authorities and revised. Printed for the Universities of Oxford and Cambridge.
Henry Frowde, Oxford Warehouse; C. J. Clay and Sons,
Cambridge Warehouse: London. [1885.] 26·5 × 17·5 cm.

With this volume was completed the revision of the Old and New Testaments, begun in 1870. The revised Apocrypha did not appear till 1895. See note on No. 1276, 1881.

The Preface, dated 10 July 1884, deals with the work of the Old Testament Revision Company.

The last page bears the imprint of the *University Press: Oxford*. Published 19 May 1885.
Small Pica 8°. Pp. x, 940; xv, 276.

1286.

1885. The Parallel Bible. The Holy Bible . . . being the authorised version arranged in parallel columns with the revised version . . .
University Press: Oxford. 1885. 26·5 × 18·5 cm.

Texts printed in parallel columns, the 'authorised' on the left, and the revised on the right. Besides the usual matter, the left-hand margin contains within square brackets the more important variations between the first edition of 1611 and the current text of King James' version.
Minion Crown 4°. Pp. x, 1024; xii, 310.

1287.

1885. The Holy Bible . . . translated out of the original tongues: being the version set forth A.D. 1611 compared with the most ancient authorities and revised. Printed for the Universities of Oxford and Cambridge.
University Press: Oxford. 1885. 20·5 × 13·5 cm.

Revised version.
Minion 8°. Pp. x, 696; xv, 204. With maps.

1288.

1885. The Holy Bible . . . translated out of the original tongues: being the version set forth A.D. 1611 compared with the most ancient authorities and revised . . .
University Press: Oxford. 1885. 14 × 10 cm.

Revised version.
Pearl 16°. Pp x, 696; xv, 204. With maps, and index of place-names.

1289.

1885. A translation of the Old Testament Scriptures from the original Hebrew; by Helen Spurrell.
Ballantyne, Hanson, and Co. : Edinburgh and London, for
J. Nisbet and Co. : London. 1885. 23 × 14 cm.

Translated ' from the unpointed Hebrew.'

In the preface the translator acknowledges her special obligations to B. Boothroyd's ' Biblia Hebraica.'
Pp. 837.

1290.

1885. The Gospel according to Matthew, Mark and Luke.
Ballantyne, Hanson, and Co. : Edinburgh and London, for
Kegan Paul, Trench and Co. : London. 1885. 16·5 × 10 cm.

Pp. 293. Printed in paragraphs without the verse-numbers.

1291.

1885 ? The New Testament . . . American Bible Union Version. Improved edition.
American Baptist Publication Society :
Philadelphia. [1885 ?] 15·5 × 10 cm.

A new edition of the revised Testament first published in 1865 by the American Bible Union (see No. 1192, 1854). This present edition, prepared by A. Hovey, J. A. Broadus, and H. G. Weston, was issued in two forms—one with the rendering *baptize* for the Greek βαπτίζω, the other with the rendering *immerse*.

Printed in paragraphs, with alternative renderings, etc. at the bottom of the page. Pp. 590.
With the rendering *baptize*.

1292.

1887. The Holy Bible . . .
Printed for the B. F. B. S. at the University Press :
Oxford. 1887. 21 × 16 cm.

'This Edition of the Holy Bible was printed to commemorate the Fiftieth Year of the Reign of Queen Victoria 1887.'

Pica 16°. Thin. Pp. 1660, 520.
Printed on India paper. Bound in four volumes, in a case inscribed ' The Queen's Jubilee Bible 1887.' A specially bound copy of this edition was presented to Her Majesty by the Bible Society.

1293.

1887. The New Testament . . .
Printed for the B. F. B. S. at the University Press :
Cambridge. 1887. 13 × 8·5 cm.

A specimen of the Bible Society's Penny Edition of the New Testament, of which eight million copies have been sold between its first issue in July 1884, and October 1903.

Ruby 24°. *Price One Penny.* Pp. 240.
A special edition, having the binding stamped with a device, and the inscription, ' Jubilee V. R. 1887.'

1294.

—— ANOTHER EDITION.

Printed at the *University Press: Oxford.*
A special ' Jubilee Edition,' with the binding stamped like No. 1294.

1295.

ENGLISH

—— ANOTHER EDITION.

A special edition, with the binding stamped 'The Queen's Jubilee' and 'Victoria.' Inserted opposite the title is a facsimile of the words from Luke ii. 14, specially chosen by Her Majesty, and written in her own hand, for reproduction in these Testaments, which were presented to pupils in the Secular State Schools in Australasia. The original autograph is preserved in the Bible House Library. 'On Earth peace, Good will toward men. Victoria R. I. Windsor Castle. March 8. 1887.'

1296.

1887. The Gospel of St. John; a verbatim translation from the Vatican MS., with the notable variations of the Sinaitic and Beza MS., and brief explanatory comments. By F. A. Paley . . .
Hazell, Watson, and Viney: London and Aylesbury, for
Swan Sonnenschein, Lowrey and Co.: London. 1887. 22·5 × 14 cm.

A literal version, made from the Vatican MS. alone.

Pp. xii, 168. With foot-notes.

1297.

1888. The New Covenant. According to Matthew, with explanations of the translation, and Songs of Deliverance. Second edition.
Edward Alexander Guy, Cincinnati, Ohio, U.S.A.
[1888.] 18·5 × 12·5 cm.

See No. 1285, 1883. The title on the cloth cover is *The New Covenant. Part I. Matthew.* Preface dated 24.9.88. Pp. 72, 24.

1298.

1890. St. Paul's Epistles in modern English; translated direct from the original Greek texts, with the Apostle's own division of the subject matter restored; by Ferrar Fenton . . .
Alfred Green: Dewsbury, for E. Stock:
London, etc. 1890. 18 × 12 cm.

Translated by Ferrar Fenton of Batley, Yorkshire. See No. 1352, 1903.

'Third issue. Price one shilling.' First published in 1884.
Dedication to Professor J. S. Blackie, dated 1884, followed by Preface. Text, 84 pp.

1299.

1891. B. See 1892.

1892. The Holy Bible . . . revised . . .
University Press: Oxford. 1892,91. 17·5 × 12·5 cm.

General title dated 1892; N. T. title dated 1891.
Ruby 16°. Pp. x, 696; xv, 204.

1300.

1894. A translation of the Four Gospels from the Syriac of the Sinaitic Palimpsest, by Agnes Smith Lewis . . .
J. Palmer: Cambridge, for Macmillan and Co.:
London, etc. 1894. 19·5 × 13 cm.

Translated from the text in the manuscript discovered in the Convent of St. Katherine on Mount Sinai by Mrs. Lewis in 1892, and subsequently transcribed and published in facsimile by R. L. Bensly, J. R. Harris, and F. C. Burkitt. The manuscript was written ' not later than the fifth century.'

Pp. xxxvi, 239.

1301.

1895. The Apocrypha, translated out of the Greek and Latin tongues, being the version set forth A.D. 1611, compared with the most ancient authorities and revised A.D. 1894. Printed for the Universities of Oxford and Cambridge.

University Press : Oxford. 1895. 22 × 14 cm.

The last portion of the revision of King James' version, begun in 1870. See No. 1276, 1881.

The inclusion of the Apocrypha in the scheme of revision was mainly due to the University Presses, who had acquired the copyright of the whole revised version.

The preface describes how the work was divided between three small committees, formed from the New Testament Company in 1879, and a fourth committee chosen from the Old Testament Company in 1884. The Americans took no part in the revision of the Apocrypha.

'Considerable attention was paid to the text ; but the materials available for correcting it were but scanty.' The revisers, however, were able to use Professor Bensly's reconstruction of the Latin text of 2 Esdras, and to incorporate the ' missing fragment,' ch. vii, 36-105.

The work was completed in 1894, and published early in 1895.

Pica Demy 8°. Pp. xi, 516.

1302.

1895. The Story of the Kings of Israel and Judah. A compilation of Bible narratives arranged consecutively. By Henry Hill.

Elliot Stock : London. 1895. 20 × 13 cm.

Contains the matter of the books of Samuel, Kings, and Chronicles, with certain historical passages from Isaiah, Jeremiah, etc., harmonised into a continuous narrative. The wording of the revised version has been generally adopted.

Pp. xi, 255. With Chronological Table.

1303.

1895. A Harmony of the Four Gospels in the revised version ; chronologically arranged in parallel columns, with maps, notes, and indices, by S. D. Waddy, Q.C. Second edition, revised and enlarged.

J. and C. F. Clay, University Press : Cambridge, for C. H. Kelly : London. 1895. 22·5 × 15 cm.

Pp. xc, 244.

1304.

1896. The Art Bible, comprising the Old and New Testaments, with numerous illustrations.

Ballantyne, Hanson, and Co., for George Newnes : London. 1896. 25 × 16·5 cm.

Illustrated from well-known paintings, modern drawings, and photographs. Pp. 1022, 313.

1305.

1896. The Holy Bible . . .
*University Press : Glasgow, for David Bryce and Son :
Glasgow, and Henry Frowde : London.* 1896. 4·5 × 3 cm.

A miniature facsimile edition.
The title bears the words 'Printed by authority'; and on verso is a copy of the licence granted to D. Bryce to publish this edition of 25,000 copies, with the following note: 'The Publishers beg to thank the Oxford University Press for enabling them to produce in this tiny form a facsimile of their Nonpareil 16° Bible, printed upon the very thinnest Oxford India paper ever made, and Messrs. S. Bagster and Son for the use of twenty-eight illustrations by C. B. Birch, A.R.A.'
Pp. 876. The exact size of the page is 42 × 28 mm. A magnifying glass is supplied in a pocket inside the cover.

—— Another copy.

1306.

1896. The New Testament . . .
*Robert Maclehose, University Press : Glasgow,
for David Bryce and Son : Glasgow, and Henry Frowde :
London.* 1896. 2 × 1·5 cm.

A miniature facsimile edition, corresponding to the Bible published by D. Bryce and Son in the same year, No. 1306.
The title bears the words 'Printed by authority,' and on verso is a copy of the licence granted to D. Bryce to publish this edition of 25,000 copies. On the page opposite the title is the following note : 'The Publishers beg to thank the Oxford University Press for enabling them to produce in this tiny form a facsimile of their Pica 16° New Testament, printed upon the very thinnest Oxford India paper ever made.'
Pp. 520. The exact size of the page is 18 × 15 mm.

—— Another copy.
Enclosed in a metal case with magnifying glass.

1307.

1896. (The Four Gospels.)
*T. and A. Constable : Edinburgh, for Archibald Constable and Co :
Westminster.* 1896. 16·5 × 10·5 cm.

The Four Gospels, each with separate title, printed in paragraphs, without the verse-numbers. Pp. 88, 55, 94, 68.

1308.

1897. The Holy Bible . . .
Printed for the B. F. B. S., at the University Press : Oxford.
1897. 17 × 11 cm.

Ruby 16°. Refs. Pp. 1000. With maps.
A special edition, bound in purple leather, stamped 'In Commemoration of Sixty Years' Reign V. R. 1837 ★ 1897.'

1309.

1897. The Holy Bible . . .
Printed for the B. F. B. S., at the University Press : Cambridge.
1897. 14 × 10 cm.

Diamond 16°. Refs. Pp. 1000. With maps.
A special edition, bound in purple leather, stamped like No. 1809.

1310.

1897. The New Testament . . . With two hundred illustrations of Bible scenes and sites, chiefly from photographs . . .
T. Nelson and Sons: London, etc. [1897.] 18 × 18·5 cm.

On verso of title is printed a *Licence* giving permission for an edition of 5000 copies to be printed at Edinburgh.
Pp. xi, 576.

1311.

1897. The New Testament . . .
Printed for the B. F. B. S., at the University Press: Oxford.
1897. 14 × 9 cm.

Ruby 24°. *Price Two Pence.* Pp. 240.
A special edition, bound in purple cloth, stamped like No. 1309.

1312.

1897. . . . The New Dispensation. The New Testament translated from the Greek by Robert D. Weekes.
Funk and Wagnalls Company: New York and London.
1897. 21·5 × 15·5 cm.

An original version.

'An effort has been made . . . to ascertain, if possible, the thought of the writers, and then to express such thought correctly, in language which should be acceptable to both the ordinary reader and the scholar, with as little deviation from a literal rendering as practicable, at the same time retaining in good measure the familiar style of the older version.' 'The Greek text of Westcott and Hort has been followed in general, but not exclusively.'
Pp. viii, 525. With short foot-notes.

1313.

1897. The Gospels and the Acts of the Apostles . . .
Printed for the B. F. B. S. at the University Press: Oxford.
1897. 15 × 12 cm.

Brevier 16°. Pp. 225. Text divided into paragraphs.
A special edition, bound in red cloth, stamped like No. 1309.

1314.

1897. B. See 1902.

1898. The Holy Bible . . . revised . . .
University Press: Oxford. 1898. 22 × 15 cm.

During the course of the New Testament revision, an elaborate body of references to the New Testament text was compiled, mainly by Dr. F. H. A. Scrivener and Dr. W. F. Moulton, for the use of their colleagues. This material was afterwards placed at the disposal of a small committee, representing both Universities, formed in 1895 to superintend the preparation of a new set of references for the complete revised Bible. See Preface to the Bible.

Minion 8°. Refs. With the Apocrypha. Pp. xiv, 732; vii, 182; xv, 224. With maps, and index.

—— Another copy.

Without the Apocrypha.

1315.

1898. The Holy Bible . . . being the revised version set forth A.D. 1881–1885, with revised marginal references. Printed for the Universities of Oxford and Cambridge.
The Riverside Press : Cambridge, Mass., U.S.A., for the
Oxford University Press, American Branch, and the
Cambridge University Press, James Pott and Co., Agents :
New York. 1898. 21·5 × 15 cm.

An American edition of the Revised Bible of 1885 with the new marginal references. The Apocrypha are not included.

'Copyright, 1898, by Oxford University Press American Branch.' 'Electrotyped and printed at the Riverside Press . . .'
Bourgeois 8°, References. Pp. xvi, 909; xiv, 268. Text printed in double columns, with the references in the margins, and the alternative renderings, etc. placed at the foot of the page. With maps, preceded by an index ending on p. 276.
An edition very similar to this was published in England in 1903. See No. 1350.

1316.

1898. The Holy Bible . . . being the revised version set forth A.D. 1881–1885 with the readings and renderings preferred by the American Revision Companies incorporated in the text, and with copyright marginal references. Printed for the Universities of Oxford and Cambridge.
The Riverside Press : Cambridge, Mass., U.S.A., for the
Oxford University Press, American Branch, and the
Cambridge University Press, James Pott and Co., Agents :
New York. 1898. 21·5 × 15·5 cm.

The first edition of the revised Bible of 1881–1885, issued under the authority of the two University Presses, in which the American preferences are incorporated in the text and in the margins, while the corresponding English renderings are relegated to the Appendixes.

According to a Memorandum drawn up by the Vice-Chancellors of the two Universities in January 1899, 'several such editions of the Revised New Testament had already been published without authority.'
'The aim of those to whom the work was committed has been to carry out the wishes of the American Revisers, and the directions formulated by them and recorded by the Revision Companies have been faithfully obeyed.' These directions were exceeded in only one point : in the removal of archaisms 'it has been thought permissible to extend, though cautiously, to the New Testament the further rules drawn up for the Old Testament, so as to give the whole Version a greater degree of uniformity.'
'Copyright, 1898, by Oxford University Press American Branch.' This edition was published in America, simultaneously with the corresponding Bible, No. 1316, in November 1898.
Bourgeois 8°. References. Pp. xvi, 909; xiv, 267. With maps and index (ending on p. 276).

1317.

1898. The Holy Bible . . . revised . . .
University Press : Oxford. 1898. 21 × 14 cm.

Minion 8°. Pp. x, 696; xv, 204. With maps, and index.

1318.

1898. Linear Parallel Edition. The Holman comparative self-pronouncing S. S. Teachers' Bible, containing, in combined text, the authorized and revised versions of the Old and New Testaments.
A. J. Holman and Co. : Philadelphia. [1898.] 22 × 15 cm.

A combination of King James' version with the revised Bible of 1885, arranged according to the ' Linear Parallel Method.'

'It presents, in a single large type line, the texts of both versions, where they read alike. Wherever a difference occurs, whether in the reading, spelling, typography, capitalization, idiom, parenthesis, punctuation or otherwise, the same is directly shown, and in place, by upper and lower parallel lines, or proper designations, in smaller type . . . the chapter and verse divisions of the authorized version have been preserved for the sake of convenient reference. In Biblical poetry, the metrical showing of the revised version is preserved by means of the initial capital letters. In thus combining the two versions, numerous marginal readings in each were found to be identical with the corresponding texts in the other. In such cases of identity, the marginal readings have been omitted, their full significance being preserved in the combined texts. In other respects, effort has been made to preserve the best marginal readings of both versions. In many instances, where the light of modern interpretation warranted, new marginal readings have been entered; and all such old readings, referring to English coins, weights, measures, etc., have been Americanized.'

'Copyright, 1898, by A. J. Holman and Co.'

Small Pica 8°. Pp. 1156, 361. With Publisher's Preface, Revisers' Prefaces, 'A Key to the Pronunciation of Scripture Proper Names,' lists of the members of the O. T. and N. T. Companies of Revisers, both English and American, and appendixes of the renderings preferred by the American Revisers. The pronunciation of proper names is marked throughout the text. An 'Analytical and Comparative Concordance . . . by James P. Boyd . . .' (pp. 256) is appended, together with maps and index.

1319.

1898. The Twentieth Century New Testament. A translation into Modern English, made from the original Greek (Westcott and Hort's text). In two parts. Part I.—The five historical books.

W. and J. Mackay and Co : Chatham, for the publishers, Mowbray House, Temple: London. 1898. 18 × 12·5 cm.

An attempt to translate the New Testament into simple, modern English. The version was made from Westcott and Hort's Greek text 'by a company of about twenty persons, including Graduates of several Universities and Members of various sections of the Christian Church.'

According to the Preface, this was put forth as a 'Tentative Edition.' The Translators' constant effort was 'to exclude all words and phrases not used in current English,' though they used 'an older phraseology in the rendering of poetical passages and quotations from the Old Testament, and in the language of prayer.' Quotations and borrowed phrases from the Old Testament and Apocrypha are distinguished by italics. Measures of space and time and the value of coins are given in their nearest English equivalents. Fourteen passages, judged by Westcott and Hort 'not to have originally formed part of the work in which they occur,' are placed within square brackets. The usual grouping of the books is retained, but the books in each group are given in what is considered to be their chronological order.

The New Testament was completed by the publication of two more parts in 1900 and 1901 (Nos. 1329 and 1340). Though severely criticised in some quarters in regard to style, and even scholarship, this version has met with remarkable popularity.

Text printed in paragraphs. Pp. vi, 254.

1320.

1899. The Holy Bible, Two-version edition, being the authorised version with the differences of the revised version printed in the margins, so that both texts can be read from the same page.

University Press : Oxford. [1899.] 21·5 × 14·5 cm.

The Preface (dated November, 1899) by the Bishop of Gloucester states that this book 'owes its origin to a suggestion of Mr. Alfred F. Buxton, and it is to his generous support that its final publication is mainly due.'

An 'Explanatory Key,' and a note on the 'Abbreviations in the New Testament,' make clear the symbols employed in the volume to mark the differences between the two versions.

The preliminary matter includes the Translators' Preface of 1611, as well as the Revisers' Preface (dated 1884).

Brevier 8°. Refs. Pp. xxviii, 1384. Text printed in double columns, with the differences of the R.V. in the two margins, and the references placed in a central column. With maps.

1321.

1899. The New Testament . . .
    Printed for the B. F. B. S. at the University Press :
                                      Oxford. 1899. 13·5 × 8·5 cm.

Ruby 24°. *Price One Penny.* Pp. 240.
A special edition. The brown linen binding bears the royal arms stamped in red with the words 'South Africa, 1900.' A specimen of the 'Khaki Testaments,' prepared by the Bible Society for distribution among the soldiers who sailed for South Africa during the late war.

1322.

1900. Holy Bible: the Gospel of Jesus Christ the Son of God ; also the Old Testament containing the promises of God, through His Prophets of the ancient Hebrew race.
    Sunday School Supply Co. : London. [1900.] 15 × 10 cm.

In 'An Apology,' placed before the text, the editor, J. K. Starley of Coventry, gives his reasons for placing the New Testament before the Old.

In two parts: (1) The Gospel . . . (i.e. the New Testament), 276 pp. ; (2) The Old Testament . . ., 900 pp. With references, index, Bible helps, maps, etc.
The back of the binding is stamped ' Christian Edition.'

1323.

1900. The New Testament . . .
    Printed for the B. F. B. S. by Eyre and Spottiswoode :
                                      London. [1900.] 13·5 × 8·5 cm.

Minion 24°. Text ends on M 8 *b*.
A special edition, bound in black leather, stamped ' C. I. V.' Prepared for presentation to the ' City Imperial Volunteers.' A copy of this book, together with a copy of the special ' Khaki ' edition of St. John's Gospel, was presented by the Bible Society to each member of the ' Lord Mayor's Own ' before they embarked for South Africa in 1900.

1324.

1900. The New Testament . . .
    Printed for the B. F. B. S. by Eyre and Spottiswoode :
                                      London. [1900.] 13 × 8·5 cm.

Minion 24°. Text ends on M 8 *b*.
A ' Khaki ' edition, bound in buff-coloured cloth, stamped with the royal arms and the words ' South Africa, 1900.'

1325.

1900. The New Testament in modern English . . . newly translated direct from the accurate Greek text of Drs. Westcott and Hort, by Ferrar Fenton . . . with some critical notes. Second edition of the Gospels, and sixth of St. Paul's Epistles, translated afresh.
    Bradbury, Agnew, and Co. : London and Tonbridge, for
         H. Marshall and Son, etc. : London. [1900.] 19 × 12·5 cm.

A revision of the first edition, published in 1895. See No. 1352, 1903.
Pp. 254. The Gospel and the First Epistle of St. John are placed together at the beginning of the book.

1326.

1900. St. Paul's Epistles in modern English, newly translated . . . by Ferrar Fenton . . . with a critical introduction . . . Sixth edition.
Bradbury, Agnew, and Co., for H. Marshall and Son :
London. [1900.] 18·5 × 12 cm.

First edition published in 1884. See No. 1352, 1903. Pp. viii, 69.

1327.

1900. The Holy Gospels. With over 350 illustrations from paintings by the Italian, Flemish, German and French Masters of the xivth, xvth, and xvith centuries; notes on the pictures by Eugène Müntz . . . and a chronological and biographical list of the painters . . .
Christian Knowledge Society : London. 1900. 35 × 27 cm. 2 vols.
Pp. 148, xxxi; 196.

¶ Bound in one volume.

1328.

1900. The Twentieth Century New Testament . . . In three parts. Part II.—The Apostle Paul's Letters to the Churches.
W. and J. Mackay and Co. : Chatham, for H. Marshall and Son :
London ; *The Fleming H. Revell Co. :*
New York and Chicago. 1900. 18 × 12·5 cm.

See No. 1320, 1898.
What was intended to be the second part was divided into two, thus making three parts in all. 'Preface to Part II' dated November, 1900.
A short introduction precedes each book. The pagination is continued from Part 1 and carried to p. 380.

1329.

1900. The Gospel according to Saint John . . .
Printed for the B. F. B. S. at the University Press : Oxford. 1900.
11 × 7 cm.

A specimen of the 'Halfpenny Gospels' issued by the B. F. B. S.

Brevier 32°. *Price One Halfpenny.* Pp. 80.
A 'Khaki' edition, with the binding stamped 'South Africa, 1900.'

1330.

1900. B. See 1901.

Accession of King Edward VII: 22 January 1901.

1901. The Holy Bible . . . being the version set forth A.D. 1611 compared with the most ancient authorities and revised A.D. 1881–1885. Newly edited by the American Revision Committee A.D. 1901. Standard edition.
J. S. Cushing and Co., Berwick and Smith : Norwood, Mass., U.S.A., for
Thomas Nelson and Sons : *New York.* 1901,00. 22 × 17·5 cm.

The English University Presses, in acquiring the copyright of the revised version, had stipulated that for fourteen years every copy issued should contain in an Appendix the renderings preferred by the American Revisers, who undertook on their part to sanction no other version during the same period. It became obvious, however, that this would not be accepted as a permanent arrangement in the United States; and accordingly in 1898 the University Presses issued an edition of the revised Bible, in which the American preferences were incorporated in the text and margins, while the corresponding English renderings were relegated to the Appendixes (see No. 1317). Notwithstanding this, certain survivors of the American Committee combined independently to prepare what they finally published as an American recension of the revised version.

'This Standard American Edition of the Revised Version of the Bible, and editions in conformity with it published by Messrs. Thomas Nelson and Sons and certified by this indorsement, are the only editions authorized by the American Committee of Revision. George E. Day, Secretary of the Committee, and of the Old Testament Company. J. Henry Thayer, Secretary of the New Testament Company.' 'Copyright, 1901, by Thomas Nelson and Sons.'

The list of preferred renderings, drawn up in 1885 by the American revisers, omitted many which a two-thirds majority of their number had recommended as important. Nearly the whole of these were now transferred into the text; and still further steps were taken towards securing uniformity of rendering and modernisation of diction. At the same time, certain minor changes, which the revisers who remained in 1900 deemed expedient, were also introduced.

The principal alterations may be briefly summarised as follows:—

1. The uniform substitution of *Jehovah* for *Lord* and *God*, *Sheol* and *Hades* for *the grave, the pit*, etc., and *Holy Spirit* for *Holy Ghost*; the use of *who* and *that*, instead of *which*, when relating to persons; the substitution of *are* for *be* in indicative clauses; the omission of *for* before infinitives; the change of *an* to *a* before 'h' aspirated; and the uniform adoption of modern spelling in place of antiquated forms—these alterations were all contained in the original Appendixes giving the American preferences.
2. (i) The American revisers now revert in some instances to the rendering of King James' version, e.g. in Ex. xx. 4, 13, Ps. xlviii. 1, etc. (ii) They recede in a few cases from proposals formerly made in the Appendixes, e.g. *be ashamed* is not uniformly changed to *be put to shame*, but is often retained, and sometimes altered to *be confounded*, (iii) In order to be consistent, they 'go beyond the literal requirements of the Appendix': thus *judgment* is very often changed to *justice*, or *ordinance*, as the context requires; *spoil* is altered to *despoil*, *plunder*, etc.; *vanity* to *falsehood*, and so on. For the sake of euphemism *bowels* and *reins* are changed to *heart*, etc., when used in a psychological sense.

The remaining minor alterations are detailed in the preface to this 'American Edition,' which appears to be widely current in the United States.

The Apocrypha are not included in any editions of this American revision.

General title dated 1901; N.T. title dated 1900. Pp. xiv, 970; xvi, 295. Text printed in double columns, with references in a central column; alternative renderings etc. and references to cited passages in margins; subject-headings at top of page. An Appendix to each Testament gives a full list of the differences between the revision of 1881-5, and this recension. With maps and index.

1331.

1901. The Holy Bible . . .
Printed for the B. F. B. S. at the University Press: Cambridge. 1901.
15·5 × 11·5 cm.

Ruby 16° Central Refs. Pp. 921. With maps.
A special edition, with the binding stamped 'Edward VII R. & I. Crowned June 26, 1902. God Save the King.' Prepared for the date originally fixed for the Royal Coronation, which was eventually postponed to Aug. 9.

1332.

1901. The Holy Bible . . .
Printed for the B. F. B. S. at the University Press: Cambridge. 1901.
14·5 × 10 cm.

Diamond 16° Refs. Pp. 1000. With maps.
A special 'Coronation Edition,' with the binding stamped like No. 1332.

1333.

1901. The Holy Bible . . .
Printed for the B. F. B. S. at the University Press : Oxford. 1901.
14 × 10 cm.

Pearl 16° Refs. Oxford Facsimile Series, No. 6. Pp. 1000. With maps.
A special edition, having the binding stamped 'Centenary Edition 1804-1904,' together with the Society's monogram and a representation of 'The Sower.'

1334.

1901. The Holy Bible . . .
Printed for the B. F. B. S. at the University Press : Oxford. 1901.
14 × 9 cm.

Ruby 32°. Pp. 1024. With maps.
A special 'Coronation Edition,' with the binding stamped like No. 1332.

1335.

1901. The Holy Bible . . .
Printed for the B. F. B. S. at the University Press : Oxford. 1901.
14 × 9 cm.

A specimen of the 'Sixpenny Bible,' first issued by the Bible Society in 1864.

Ruby 32°. *Price Sixpence.* Pp. 1024.

1336.

1901. The New Testament . . .
Printed for the B. F. B. S. at the University Press : Oxford.
1901. 13·5 × 9 cm.

Ruby 24°. *Price Two-pence.* Pp. 240.
A special edition, bound in purple cloth stamped 'In Memory of Her Gracious Majesty Queen Victoria. 1837-1901.'
A facsimile of the Queen's autograph (see No. 1296, 1887) is inserted as a frontispiece.

1337.

1901. The Five Books of Moses, being volume the first of the Bible in modern English, translated direct from the Hebrew, Chaldee, and Greek languages into English, by Ferrar Fenton . . .
Bradbury, Agnew, and Co., for Messrs. S. W. Partridge and Co.:
London. [1901.] 19 × 12·5 cm.

See No. 1352, 1903.
Pp. viii, 214.

1338.

1901. The First Book of Moses called Genesis. Edited by A. H. Sayce, D.D., LL.D.
J. M. Dent and Co.: London ; J. B. Lippincott Co. :
Philadelphia. 1901. 14 × 11 cm.

The first volume of the series known as the 'Temple Bible.'

Each volume contains a frontispiece, an introduction, the text (King James' version, divided into paragraphs), and notes, with tables, chronological matter, maps, and a list of 'Biblical references in English Literature.'
Pp. xxii, 170.

1339.

1901. The Twentieth Century New Testament . . . In three parts. Part III.—
The Pastoral, Personal, and General Letters ; and the Revelation.
W. and J. Mackay and Co.: Chatham, for H. Marshall and Son:
London, etc. 1901. 18 × 12·5 cm.

See No. 1320, 1898.
With 'Preface to Part III,' dated November, 1901. Text ends on p. 513.

1340.

1902. The Emphasised Bible. A new translation, designed to set forth the exact meaning, the proper terminology and the graphic style of the sacred originals ; arranged to show at a glance narrative, speech, parallelism, and logical analysis, also to enable the student readily to distinguish the several Divine Names ; and emphasised throughout after the idioms of the Hebrew and Greek tongues. With expository introduction, select references, and appendices of notes . . . By Joseph Bryant Rotherham . . .
Bradbury, Agnew, and Co.: London and Tonbridge, for
H. R. Allenson: London. 1902, 1897. 24·5 × 18 cm.

'This version has been adjusted, in the Old Testament, to the newly revised " Massoretical-critical " text (or assured emendations) of Dr. Ginsburg ; and, in the New Testament, to the critical text (" formed exclusively on documentary evidence ") of Drs. Westcott and Hort.'

The Introduction explains fully the plan and scope of the work.
The New Testament, dated 1897, is a rewritten edition of the version first printed in 1872, and reissued in a revised form in 1878. A portion of the work, 'The Gospel according to Matthew with Notes,' was published as a tentative issue as early as 1868.
Pp. 920, 272.

¶ Inserted are : (1) a Prospectus (8 pp.) of the 'Emphasised Bible ' ; and (2) a two-page pamphlet entitled : 'A brief account of the origin and design of the work, compiled by J. George Rotherham (son of the translator).'

1341.

1902. The Holy Bible . . .
Printed for the B. F. B. S. at the University Press:
Oxford. 1902. 17 × 11 cm.

Ruby 16° Refs. Oxford Facsimile Series No. 5. Pp. 1000. With maps.
A special ' Coronation Edition,' with the binding stamped like No. 1332.

1342.

1902. The Holy Bible . . .
Printed for the B. F. B. S. at the University Press:
Cambridge. 1902. 14 × 10 cm.

Diamond 16° Refs. Pp. 1000. With maps.
A 'Centenary Edition,' with the binding stamped like No. 1334.

1343.

1902. The New Testament . . .
Printed for the B. F. B. S. at the University Press:
Oxford. 1902. 13·5 × 8·5 cm.

Ruby 24°. *Price Two-pence.* Pp. 240.
A ' Centenary Edition,' with the binding stamped like No. 1334.

1344.

1902. The Bible in modern English. Vol. II: The History of the People of Israel, by Isaiah-Ben-Amoz, the Prophet . . . from the conquests of Joshua to the death of King Hezekiah. (In VI Books.) Translated direct from the Hebrew into English, with a critical introduction and notes, by Ferrar Fenton . . .
Bradbury, Agnew, and Co., for Messrs. S. W. Partridge and Co.:
London. [1902.] 19 × 12·5 cm.

See No. 1352, 1903.
Contains Joshua–2 Kings. Pp. xv, 187.

1345.

1902. The Bible in Modern English. Vol. III: containing the Books of the Prophets, direct from the original Hebrew into English, and in verse, in the Hebrew metres of the prophets, or in prose, as originally written; translated by Ferrar Fenton . . . with an introduction and critical notes.
Bradbury, Agnew, and Co., for Messrs. S. W. Partridge and Co.:
London. [1902.] 19 × 12·5 cm.

See No. 1352, 1903.
Contains Isaiah, Jeremiah, Ezekiel, and the Minor Prophets. Pp. ix, 245.

1346.

1902. The Book of Job, translated direct from the Hebrew text into English by Ferrar Fenton . . . assisted by Henrik Borgström . . . rendered into the same Metre as the original Hebrew word by word and line by line.
H. Marshall and Son: London, etc. [1902.] 18·5 × 12·5 cm.

First published in 1899. See No. 1352, 1903. Pp. 47.

1347.

1902. The 'Revised English' New Testament; being the authorized version re-revised and grammatically corrected; with the Words of Jesus in a distinct type . . .
Philpott's Library Press: Surbiton, for S. Bagster and Sons:
London. [1902.] 24 × 18 cm.

An attempt to present King James' version with corrections of the grammar and rendering. Prepared by George Washington Moon.

'Preliminary specimen pages of the Tentative Edition shortly to be published by one of the Life Governors of the British and Foreign Bible Society, to mark its Centenary in the year 1904.' 'Rough advanced Proof, for private perusal, and criticism.'
With foot-notes. Pp. 72.

1348.

1903. The Holy Bible . . .
Printed for the B. F. B. S. by Eyre and Spottiswoode:
London. [1903.] 14 × 9 cm.

Ruby 32°. Pp. 1032. With maps.
A 'Centenary Edition,' with the binding stamped like No. 1334.

1349.

ENGLISH

1903. The Holy Bible, the revised version, with revised marginal references. Printed for the Universities of Oxford and Cambridge.
Henry Frowde; C. J. Clay and Son: London. 1903. 21 × 14·5 cm.

This edition of the revised version very closely resembles that issued in America in 1898. See No. 1316.

Bourgeois 8° Refs. Pp. xvi, 909; xiv, 268; with index (ending on p. 276) and maps.

In this edition, and in those published by the Bible Society in the same year (see Nos. 1351, 1354, 1357, and 1358), an error in 1 Cor. xii. 9 was corrected, *the strength of Christ* being altered to *the power of Christ*. The earlier rendering *power*, which had been retained by the revisers, was wrongly printed *strength* in all editions of the R. V. from 1881 on till 1903. The two-version edition of 1899 (No. 1321) rightly implies that the correct R. V. reading is *power*.

1350.

1903. The Holy Bible. The Revised version, without the marginal notes of the revisers; printed by order of the Universities of Oxford and Cambridge, and issued in connexion with the Centenary of the British and Foreign Bible Society, 1904.
Printed for the B. F. B. S. at the University Press:
Oxford. 1903. 16·5 × 11·5 cm.

This Bible, and a New Testament of the same date (No. 1354), were the first editions of the revised version of 1881-5 published by the Bible Society. Two more editions of the revised Bible were issued in the autumn of 1903 (see Nos. 1357 and 1358).

At a special General Meeting of the Society held in the Library of the Bible House, 9 Oct. 1901, the following resolution was unanimously passed: 'That henceforth Law I of the Society shall read as follows:—" The designation of the Society shall be the British and Foreign Bible Society, of which the sole object shall be to encourage the wider circulation of the Holy Scriptures, without note or comment. *The only copies in the English language to be circulated by the Society shall be either the Authorized Version of 1611, or the Revised Version of 1881-1885, or both.*" ' By this change in its law the Society was for the first time enabled to issue an English Bible other than King James' version.

The following alterations were adopted in these special editions: (1) the revisers' prefaces, marginal matter, and list of American revisers' preferences, were omitted; (2) the space between consecutive verses in the paragraphs was slightly increased.

The price of this Bible was fixed at 10*d*.
Nonpareil 16°. Printed in double columns. Pp. 607, 176.

1351.

1903. The Holy Bible in modern English, containing . . . the Old and New Testaments, translated into English direct from the original Hebrew, Chaldee, and Greek languages, by Ferrar Fenton . . . with introductions and critical notes.
Bradbury, Agnew, and Co., for Messrs. S. W. Partridge and Co.:
London. [1903.] 19 × 12·5 cm.

'The Complete Bible in Modern English,' translated by Ferrar Fenton, containing the New Testament and the four parts of the Old Testament, published 1900-3. For the plan and scope of this original version see the prefaces to the separate parts.

The translator—a direct descendant of Bishop Ferrar, and also of Roger Fenton (1565-1615) who assisted in making King James' version of 1611—received a certain amount of help from Henrik Borgström of Finland, the Rev. J. Bowen, and others,

See Nos. 1299, 1326, 1327, 1338, 1345-7, and 1356.
The books of the O. T. are given in the order in which they 'were arranged by the Editorial Committee appointed by the Great Sanhedrim, called at Jerusalem for the purpose, in the Third Century before Christ.'

1352.

1903. The New Testament . . .
  Printed for the B. F. B. S. by Eyre and Spottiswoode :
    London. [1903.]   13·5 × 8·5 cm.

Minion 24°. Text ends on M 8 *b*.
A 'Centenary Edition,' with the binding stamped, like No. 1334.

1353.

1903. The New Testament . . . The Revised version, without the marginal notes of the revisers; printed by order of the Universities of Oxford and Cambridge, and issued in connexion with the Centenary of the British and Foreign Bible Society, 1904.
  Printed for the B. F. B. S. at the University Press :
    Cambridge. 1903.   15·5 × 11·5 cm.

See note on No. 1351.
Brevier 16°. Sold at 4*d*. Printed in double columns. Pp. 346.

1354.

1903. The New Testament in Modern Speech; an idiomatic translation into every-day English from the text of 'The Resultant Greek Testament'; by the late Richard Francis Weymouth . . . edited and partly revised by Ernest Hampden-Cook . . .
  Butler and Tanner : Frome and London, for
    J. Clarke and Co. : London. 1903.   19 × 12·5 cm.

An original version, designed chiefly ' to furnish a succint and compressed running commentary (not doctrinal) to be used side by side with its elder compeers.'
R. F. Weymouth, at one time Headmaster of Mill Hill School, edited 'The Resultant Greek Testament,' the text of which is followed in this version.

Preface dated July, 1902. Text, with introductions and foot-notes. Pp. xvi, 674.

1355.

1903. The Bible in modern English. Vol. IV : containing the Psalms, Solomon, and Sacred Writers, in the original Hebrew order of the books, translated direct from the Hebrew and Chaldee texts into English by Ferrar Fenton . . . with an introduction and critical notes.
  Bradbury, Agnew, and Co., for Messrs. S. W. Partridge and Co. :
    London. [1903.]   19 × 12·5 cm.

The publication of this fourth volume of the O. T. completed the translation of the Bible into modern English made by Ferrar Fenton. See No. 1352.
Pp. viii, 346.

1356.

ENGLISH

1903. The Holy Bible : the revised version without the marginal notes of the revisers. Printed by order of the Universities of Oxford and Cambridge and issued in connexion with the Centenary of the British and Foreign Bible Society 1904.
Printed for the B. F. B. S. at the University Press :
Cambridge. 1903. 24 × 15 cm.

This Bible and the following—the third and fourth editions of the revised version issued by the Bible Society—were published in the autumn of 1903, while the last sheets of this Catalogue were passing through the press.

See No. 1351.
Small Pica 8°. Sold at 2s. and 3s., according to the binding. Pp. 931, 268.

1357.

1903. The Holy Bible : the revised version with revised marginal references. Printed by order of the Universities of Oxford and Cambridge and issued in connexion with the Centenary of the British and Foreign Bible Society 1904.
Printed for the B. F. B. S. at the University Press :
Oxford. 1903. 16·5 × 10·5 cm.

The first edition of the revised version with the revisers' prefaces and marginal matter issued by the Bible Society. The renderings preferred by the American Committee are not appended.

See No. 1351.
Nonpareil 16°, refs. Sold at 2s. and 2s. 6d., according to the binding. Pp. xv, 1033; xiv, 303. With maps.

1358.

THE BRITISH AND FOREIGN BIBLE SOCIETY, FROM ITS INSTITUTION IN MARCH 1804 DOWN TO THE PRESENT DATE, OCTOBER 1908, HAS ISSUED OVER SEVENTY-FIVE MILLION COPIES OF THE SCRIPTURES IN ENGLISH.

APPENDIX

This Appendix contains:—

(i) a few editions omitted by mistake, or acquired since the early sheets of the Catalogue were sent to press; together with additional notes on certain editions.

(ii) a list of the books of the Bible which were translated into provincial dialects of English for Prince Louis Lucien Bonaparte.

OMITTED EDITIONS, ETC.

1525. Note on the distribution of Tindale's Testaments.

Copies were smuggled into England from the Continent chiefly by Antwerp merchants, and sold secretly by the private enterprise of such men as Robert Barnes and Simon Fish of Gray's Inn. These dealers in a contraband book were known as 'New Testamenters.' Certain passages in works like Strype's *Ecclesiastical Memorials* enable us to obtain some idea of the methods of this traffic, and the prices at which the volumes were sold. In March 1528 John Pykas, a baker of Colchester, confessed before Tunstall that 'about a Two yeres last past, he bowght in Colchestre, of a Lumbard of London, a New Testament in English, and payd for it Foure Shillinges.' Barnes, while in the custody of the Austin Friars in London, received a visit from two men, to whom he sold a Testament for 'iijs. ijd,' 'and desyred them, that they wold kepe yt close.' Robert Necton deponed that he 'sold fyve of the said New Testaments to Sir William Furboshore Synging man, in Stowmarket in Suffolk, for vii or viii Grotes a pece.' He also 'sold Sir Richard Bayfell two New Testaments unbound, about Cristmas last; for the which he payd iijs. iiijd.' 'About Cristmas last, there came a Duche man, beyng now in the Flete, which wold have sold this Respondent ij or iij Hundreth of the said N. Testaments in English.' They were to have been bought at 'ixd. a pece.' Some of these were 'New Testaments of the biggest'; others were copies 'of the smal Volume.' These prices should be multiplied by fourteen or fifteen to obtain approximately their equivalent value in the money of to-day.

See Strype's *Ecclesiastical Memorials* (London, 1721), vol. i. p. 79, and App. xvii and xxii.

1537. Note on Matthew's Bible. No. 17.

The two variant leaves mentioned at the top of p. 17 are probably merely reprints. They occur in a copy of this Bible in the Cambridge University Library, and may perhaps be found in other copies. In these two leaves the comma is substituted for the virgule, or stroke, which is generally used throughout the volume.

1539. Note on the first edition of the 'Great Bible.' No. 25.

In Ps. cxlvii, v. 3 is omitted, though the catchwords *He healeth* remain at the bottom of D D iij *a*. In the small folio of April 1540 (No. 29) this verse is printed *He healeth the contryte in herte, and remedieth theyr sorowes*; but the large folio of April 1540 (No. 30) reads *He healeth those that ar broken in harte & gyveth medycine to heale ther sycknes*.

1539. Note on the octavo Taverner Testament. No. 28.

A few more leaves of this edition have recently come to light. These were discovered in the binding of a book in the Library of Queens' College, Cambridge, and the duplicates have been presented to the University Library, Cambridge, and to the British Museum.

1551. Note on the folio Bible printed by N. Hyll. No. 64.

In the list of printers for *John Whyte* read *John Wyghte*.

1560. Note on the first edition of the 'Geneva Bible.' No. 77.

The influence of the revisers of Olivetan's French Bible is strikingly shown by the fact that the 'Arguments' to the Books of Job and Psalms in this English edition are translated almost word for word from those found in the French octavo Bible printed at Geneva in 1559. We are indebted for this information to Mr. W. Aldis Wright.

1568 ? (The New Testament.)
                                    [*R. Jugge : London.* 1568 ?]   8°.   B. L.
Bishops' version.

A hitherto unnoticed edition, without verse-divisions. It resembles the two editions described by Fry at the end of his work on the Tindale Testaments (*A Bibliographical Description* . . ., pp. 173–8), but is quite distinct from both. One of Fry's editions adopts the text of the quarto Bible of 1569; the other follows the folio of 1572. The present edition, unlike any other, agrees with the first folio of 1568, and therefore probably preceded those mentioned by Fry. Thus it appears to be the earliest known edition of the New Testament of the Bishops' version.

Undoubtedly printed by Jugge; in 1568, or possibly in 1569. As the only known copy is incomplete at the beginning and end, it is impossible to give a full description.

DESCRIPTION. St. John's Gospel ends on X 3 *b*; Acts ends on Dd 1 *b*, and is followed by 7 pp., containing the map and *The order of tymes*; 2 Corinthians ends on Ll 1 *a*; 2 Timothy ends on Pp 8 *b*.

Signatures in eights. A full page contains 36 lines. No verse-divisions. Text, chapter-contents, notes after chapters, and marginal references, in black-letter. Arguments, head-lines, and marginal notices of Epistles and Gospels, in roman type. Words not found in the original Greek are printed in roman type within round brackets.

As in the two kindred editions described by Fry, the arguments, notes, and other accompanying matter, are taken from Jugge's revision of Tindale's Testament.

The cut of St. Paul, figured in Plate 73 of Fry's book, occurs before Romans, 1 Corinthians, Ephesians, and Hebrews. The initial P (containing the letters *M C*), also given by Fry, is placed before 2 Timothy.

See the *Athenæum*, 15 August 1903.

¶ 130 × 86 mm. Very imperfect: wanting all before S 1 (John v. 31), and all after Rr 6 (Heb. xi. 4); also Hh 8.

1359.

After **1572.** Note on the quarto Testament of the Bishops' Bible printed by R. Watkins. No. 97.

There seems reason to believe that this New Testament was published in 1575,

APPENDIX 405

simultaneously with the folio Bible of 1575, inasmuch as the minute of the Stationers' Company which records the granting of the special licences (see No. 103) bears that date.

1575. Note on the small folio edition of the Bishops' Bible. No. 103.

For *R. Jugge* as printer of this edition, read [*R. Jugge* ?].

1599. Novum Testamentum . . . Syriace, Ebraice, Græce, Latine, Germanice, Bohemice, Italice, Hispanice, Gallice, Anglice, Danice, Polonice. Studio et labore Eliæ Hutteri . . .
Norimbergæ. 1599. f°. 2 vols.

The English text (Geneva version) is included in Hutter's Polyglot New Testament 1599 (*q.v.*).

—— Another copy.
Imperfect.
1360.

1632. The Holy Bible . . .
Barker and Assigns of Bill: London. 1632,31. 8°.

Text ends on Kkk 8 a.
General title and colophon dated 1632; N. T. title dated 1631.
Not identical with any of the many varieties enumerated under the dates 1631 and 1632.

¶ 162 × 106 mm.
With Genealogies (1633).
With Prayer Book (? date), and Metrical Psalms (1633).
1361.

1640. P. 187, last line: for *Preface* read *Introduction*.

1795. The Holy Bible . . . with a few select notes and embellished with engravings.
T. Heptinstall: London. 1795. 4°. 2 vols.

'Published by the late W. Heptinstall and sold by the Proprietor T. Heptinstall, No. 131 Fleet St.' The date is taken from the frontispiece 'London, Published Jan. 12, 1795, by T. Heptinstall, Leather Lane, Holborn.' Some of the plates are dated 1794.
Vol. 2, which has a second copy of the general title, begins with Isaiah. No Apocrypha. The collection of short notes is appended, together with the list of books, and directions to the binder for placing the 21 illustrative plates.
Without signatures or pagination. The words generally printed in italics are distinguished in this edition only by a dot placed under the first vowel, as in Macklin's edition of 1800 (No. 982)

¶ 362 × 390 mm. Imperfect, wanting preliminary leaves, and the notes. Bound in one volume.
This copy belonged to Thomas Campbell, the poet (1777–1844), whose autograph appears on the first page of Genesis. It contain's Campbell's bookplate, and a family register.
1362.

1810. The Holy Bible . . .
Hudson and Goodwin: Hartford, Connecticut. 1809,10. 17 × 11 cm.

General title dated 1809; N. T. title dated 1810.
Text ends on Ll 12 a. One page of tables after the O. T., and another after the N. T.

¶ The fly-leaf is inscribed 'This Bible is presented to the British and Foreign Bible Society as a specimen of those purchased for gratuitous distribution by the Connecticut Bible Society. Price sixty cents each.'

1363.

1810. The Holy Bible . . .
    Hudson and Goodwin : Hartford, Connecticut. 1810. 17 × 11 cm.

Like No. 1363, but with both titles dated 1810.

¶ The fly-leaf bears an inscription similar to that in the copy of No. 1363.

                                                                      1364.

1818. The Holy Bible . . .
    Stereotyped by E. and J. White, for the American Bible Society :
                                      New York. 1818. 22·5 × 14 cm.

The American Bible Society was founded in 1816.

The binding of this and similar editions generally bears the stamp of the publishing Society.
Stereotype edition. Printed by *Daniel Fanshaw*, No. 20 Sloat-lane.
Pp. 705, 215. One page of tables after O. T.

                                                                        1365.

1818. The Holy Bible . . .
    Published by the American Bible Society :
                                      New York. 1818. 18 × 10·5 cm.

Stereotyped by *E. and J. White*; printed by *D. Fanshaw*.
Pp. 832, 254. Tables on verso of N. T. title.

                                                                        1366.

1819. The Holy Bible . . .
    D. Fanshaw, for the A. B. S. : New York. 1818,19. 22·5 × 14 cm.

Stereotyped by *E. and J. White*.
Like No. 1365, but with the N. T. title dated 1819.

                                                                        1367.

1819. The Holy Bible . . .
    D. Fanshaw, for the A. B. S. : New York. 1819. 24 × 14·5 cm.

Stereotyped by *E. and J. White*.
Like No. 1365, but with both titles dated 1819.

                                                                        1368.

1819. The Holy Bible . . .
    D. Fanshaw, for the A. B. S. : New York. 1819. 19 × 11 cm.

Stereotyped by *E. and J. White*.
Like No. 1366, but with the dates altered to 1819.

¶ The binding bears the stamp of the 'Massachusetts Bible Society' as well as that of the A. B. S.

                                                                        1369.

1819. The Holy Bible . . .
    D. Fanshaw, for the A. B. S. : New York. 1819. 19 × 11·5 cm.

Stereotyped by *D. and G. Bruce*.
Pp. 837. One page of tables after O. T.

                                                                        1370.

1819. The New Testament . . .
  D. *Fanshaw, for the A. B. S.: New York.* 1819. 18·5 × 11 cm.

Stereotyped by *E. and J. White.*
Pp. 254. The N. T. of No. 1369 issued separately, with the omission of the table on verso of title.

1371.

1819. The New Testament . . .
  D. *Fanshaw, for the A. B. S.: New York.* 1819. 19 × 11·5 cm.

Stereotyped by *D. and G. Bruce.*
Pp. 312.

1372.

1821. The Holy Bible . . .
  Stereotyped by *E. and J. White, for the Auxiliary New York Bible and Common Prayer-Book Society:*
  New York. 1821. 19 × 12 cm.

'New York stereotype edition.'
Pp. 676, 208.

1373.

1824. The New Testament . . .
  A. *Paul, for the A. B. S.: New York.* 1824. 28 × 14 cm.

Stereotyped by *A. Chandler.*
Pp. 429.

1374.

1827. The New Testament . . .
  Printed for the B. F. B. S. by S. Collingwood and Co.,
  Clarendon Press: Oxford. 1827. 18·5 × 11 cm.

Brevier 12°. Text ends on O 1$\frac{3}{2}$ b.

¶ This copy belonged to Lord Teignmouth (1751–1834), the first President of the Bible Society, and was used by him during his last illness. Presented to the Library by his granddaughter, Mrs. Ayscoghe Floyer.

1375.

1847. The Holy Scriptures . . . faithfully translated from the Hebrue and Greke by Myles Coverdale . . . 1535. Second modern edition.
  S. Bagster and Sons: London. 1847. 26·5 × 20 cm.

See No. 7, 1535. The first modern reprint appeared in 1838; see No. 1152.
With ' Memoir of Myles Coverdale ' added after Preface.

1376.

1877. The Holy Bible . . .
  University Press: Oxford. 1877. 17 × 11·5 cm.

'The Oxford Caxton Celebration Edition.' Above the title are the words ' In Memoriam Gul. Caxton '; and the leaf opposite bears the inscription ' Wholly printed and bound in twelve hours, on this 30th day of June, 1877, for the Caxton Celebration. Only 100 copies were printed . . .'

For a full description of this feat of printing and binding see H. Stevens, *The Bibles in the Caxton Exhibition,* pp. 141–7.
Minion 16°. Text ends on Kk 14 a.

¶ This copy is No. 37, presented to the Bible Society's Library by the Oxford University Press.

1377.

VERSIONS IN ENGLISH PROVINCIAL DIALECTS.

The following is believed to be a complete set of the books of the Bible translated into provincial dialects of English for Prince Louis Lucien Bonaparte, who presented a copy of each to the Society. They are catalogued in the following order: (i) 'Saxon English,' (ii) provincial dialects of England, arranged under counties, in alphabetical order, (iii) Lowland Scotch.

Unless the contrary is stated, each edition consisted of 250 copies privately printed at the expense of Prince Louis Lucien Bonaparte.

SAXON ENGLISH.

1862. The Song of Solomon in Saxon English; from the authorised English version, by George M. Green.
Strangeways and Walden: London. 1862. 13·5 × 10·5 cm.

The sole peculiarity of this version lies in the fact that 'words derived from the Saxon or German' are substituted for all words from Latin or Greek which occur in the authorised version: this is added on the opposite page throughout for comparison.

Pp. 31.

1378.

CORNISH (LIVING).

1859. The Song of Solomon in the living Cornish dialect; from the authorised English version.
George Barclay: London. 1859. 13·5 × 10·5 cm.

Pp. 19.

1379.

CUMBERLAND.

1858. The Song of Solomon in the Cumberland dialect; from the authorised English version, by John Rayson.
George Barclay: London. [1858.] 13·5 × 10·5 cm.

Pp. 19.

1380.

CUMBERLAND (CENTRAL).

1859. The Song of Solomon in the dialect of Central Cumberland; from the authorised English version, by William Dickinson.
George Barclay: London. 1859. 13·5 × 10·5 cm.

Pp. 19.

1381.

DEVONSHIRE.

1860. The Song of Solomon in the Devonshire dialect; from the authorised English version, by Henry Baird.
George Barclay: London. [1860.] 13·5 × 10·5 cm.

Pp. 19.

—— Another copy.

1382.

1863. The Gospel of St. Matthew, translated into Western English as spoken in Devonshire, by Henry Baird.
Strangeways and Walden: London. 1868. 18·5 × 10·5 cm.
Pp. 126.

1383.

DEVONSHIRE (EAST).

1860. The Song of Solomon in the East Devonshire dialect; from the authorised English version, by George P. R. Pulman.
Strangeways and Walden: London. [1860.] 18·5 × 10·5 cm.
Pp. 19.

—— Another copy.

1384.

DORSET.

1859. The Song of Solomon in the Dorset dialect; from the authorised English version, by the Rev. William Barnes.
George Barclay: London. 1859. 18·5 × 10·5 cm.
Pp. 19.

1385.

DURHAM.

1859. The Song of Solomon in the Durham dialect, as spoken at St. John's Chapel, Weardale; by Thomas Moore.
George Barclay: London. [1859.] 18·5 × 10·5 cm.
Pp. 19.

1386.

LANCASHIRE (NORTH).

1860. The Song of Solomon in the North Lancashire dialect, as spoken north of the Wyre; from the authorised English version, by James Phizackerley.
Strangeways and Walden: London. 1860. 18·5 × 10·5 cm.
Pp. 19.

—— Another copy.

1387.

LANCASHIRE (BOLTON).

1859. The Song of Solomon in the Lancashire dialect, as spoken at Bolton; from the authorised English version, by James Taylor Staton.
George Barclay: London. 1859. 18·5 × 10·5 cm.
Pp. 19.

1388.

1863. The Song of Solomon in the Lancashire dialect, as spoken at Bolton; from the authorised English version; translated for Prince Louis Lucien Bonaparte, by James Taylor Staton.
John Heywood: Manchester. 1868. 19 × 12·5 cm.

An unauthorised reprint of the preceding edition.
Sold also by *F. Pitman: London.* Pp. 16.

¶ This copy has a note in red lettering on verso of title: 'This Edition was printed, to the extent of at least 2000 copies, without my knowledge or consent. The unsold copies, being nearly the entire impression, have come into my hands, and most of them have been destroyed. On each copy preserved by me this Notice has been printed; and the total number saved is not more than about 250, including those that had been sold before my interference. L. L. B.'

1389.

NORFOLK.

1860. The Song of Solomon in the Norfolk dialect; from the authorised English version, by the Rev. Edward Gillett, vicar of Runham.
   Strangeways and Walden: London. [1860.] 18·5 × 10·5 cm.
Pp. 19.

—- Another copy.

1390.

NORTHUMBERLAND.

1860. The Book of Ruth in the Northumberland dialect; from the authorised English version, by J. P. Robson.
   George Barclay: London. 1860. 11 × 7 cm.
Pp. 24.

1391.

1860. The Song of Solomon in the Northumberland dialect; from the authorised English version, by Joseph Philip Robson . . .
   George Barclay: London. [1860.] 18·5 × 10·5 cm.
Pp. 19.

—— Another copy.

1392.

NORTHUMBERLAND (NEWCASTLE).

1858. The Song of Solomon in the Newcastle dialect; from the authorised English version, by John George Forster.
   George Barclay: London. [1858.] 18·5 × 10·5 cm.
Pp. 19.

—— Another copy.

1393.

1859. The Song of Solomon in the Newcastle dialect; from the authorised English version, by Joseph Philip Robson . . .
   George Barclay: London. [1859.] 18·5 × 10·5 cm.
Pp. 19.

—— Another copy.

1394.

NORTHUMBERLAND (TYNESIDE).

1860. The Song of Solomon, versified from the English translation of James of England into the dialect of the colliers of Northumberland, but principally those dwelling on the banks of the Tyne, by J. P. Robson . .
   George Barclay: London. 1860. 28·5 × 22 cm.
Pp. 28.

1395.

SOMERSET.

1860. The Song of Solomon in the Somerset dialect; from the authorised English version, by J. Spencer Baynes, LL.B.
            Strangeways and Walden: London. [1860.] 18·5 × 10·5 cm.
Pp. 19.

—— Another copy.
1396.

[A list of languages and dialects, drawn up by Prince L. L. Bonaparte in 1881, mentions a version of Ruth in the West Somerset dialect, which was not published by him.]

SUSSEX.

1860. The Song of Solomon [in] the dialect of Sussex: from the authorised English version, by Mark Antony Lower, M.A., F.S.A.
            George Barclay: London. 1860. 18·5 × 10·5 cm.
Pp. 19.

—— Another copy.
1397.

WESTMORLAND.

1858. The Song of Solomon in the Westmorland dialect; from the authorised English version, by the Rev. John Richardson, M.A., Head Master of Appleby School.
            George Barclay: London. [1858.] 18·5 × 10·5 cm.
Pp. 19.
1398.

WILTSHIRE (NORTH).

1861. The Song of Solomon in the Wiltshire dialect; as it is spoken in the northern division; from the authorised English version, by Edward Kite.
            Strangeways and Walden: London. [1861.] 18·5 × 10·5 cm.
Pp. 19.

—— Another copy.
1399.

YORKSHIRE (NORTH).

1860. The Song of Solomon in the North Yorkshire dialect; from the authorised English version, by the author of 'A Glossary of Yorkshire words and phrases collected in Whitby and the neighbourhood.'
            George Barclay: London. [1860.] 18·5 × 10·5 cm.

Giving the dialect as spoken in the east part of the North Riding, particularly in the neighbourhood of Whitby.
Pp. 19.

—— Another copy.
1400.

YORKSHIRE (WEST).

1860. The Song of Solomon in the West Riding of Yorkshire dialect; from the authorised English version, by Charles Rogers . . .
            George Barclay: London. [1860.] 18·5 × 10·5 cm.
Pp. 24. With notes at the end.

—— Another copy.
1401.

YORKSHIRE (CRAVEN).

1859. The Song of Solomon in the dialect of Craven, in the West Riding of Yorkshire; from the authorised English version, by Henry Anthony Littledale.
George Barclay: London. 1859. 18·5 × 10·5 cm.
Pp. 19.

1402.

YORKSHIRE (SHEFFIELD).

1859. The Song of Solomon in the Sheffield dialect; from the authorised English version, by Abel Bywater . . .
George Barclay: London. 1859. 18·5 × 10·5 cm.
Pp. 19.

—— Another copy.

1403.

LOWLAND SCOTCH.

1856. The Gospel of St. Matthew in Lowland Scotch; from the English authorised version, by H. S. Riddell.
Robson, Levey, and Franklyn: London. 1856. 19 × 12 cm.

A note after the titleleaf states that 'this Scottish version of the Gospel of St. Matthew has been executed at the expense of His Highness Prince Louis Lucien Bonaparte solely for linguistic purposes, and the whole number printed appropriated as follows :—I. *Bibliothèque Impériale, Paris.* II. *Library of the British Museum.* III. *Bible Society* . . . Two copies (one of which is unique on thicker paper) bear no number and belong to the Prince.' Only 18 copies were printed.
Pp. 136.
A few verses (ch. xiii, vv. 3 to 9) were reprinted in a polyglot edition of the 'Parable of the Sower' in seventy-two European languages, printed for the Prince in 1857.

1404.

1857. The Book of Psalms in Lowland Scotch; from the authorised English version, by Henry Scott Riddell.
Robson, Levey, and Franklyn: London. 1857. 21 × 13·5 cm.
Pp. 145.

1405.

1858. The Song of Solomon in Lowland Scotch; from the authorised English version; by Henry Scott Riddell.
George Barclay: London. 1858. 28·5 × 22 cm.
Pp. 11.

1406.

1860. The Song of Solomon in Lowland Scotch; from the authorised English version, by Joseph Philip Robson . . .
George Barclay: London. 1860. 18·5 × 10·5 cm.
Pp. 19.

—— Another copy.

1407.

1860. The Song of Solomon in Lowland Scotch; from the authorised English version.
    Strangeways and Walden: London. 1860. 18·5 × 10·5 cm.
Pp. 19.
                         1408.

——. Another copy.

1862. The Song of Solomon in Lowland Scotch; from the authorised English version, by George Henderson.
    Strangeways and Walden: London. 1862. 18·5 × 10·5 cm.
Pp. 19.
                         1409.

1862. The Gospel of St. Matthew, translated into Lowland Scotch, by George Henderson.
    Strangeways and Walden: London. 1862. 18·5 × 10·5 cm.
Pp. 8, 124.
                         1410.

[A list of languages and dialects drawn up in 1881 by Prince L. L. Bonaparte, mentions versions of Ruth and of Isaiah in Lowland Scotch, which were not published by him.]

INDEX

This three-fold index of names gives:—
  (i) Names of Translators, Revisers, Editors, etc.
  (ii) Names of Printers, Publishers, etc., down to 1824.
  (iii) Names of Places of Printing, Publication, etc., down to 1824.

I. NAMES OF TRANSLATORS, REVISERS, EDITORS, ETC.

ADDY, WILLIAM, 688
Alen, Edmund, 45, 46
Alexander, William, 1119
Alford, Henry, 1202, 1204, 1205, 1211, 1220, 1237
Allen, William, 134, 231
Alley, W., 89
Anderson, H. T., 1234
Andrewes, Lancelot, 240
Arber, Edward, 1248
Asher, David, 1, 1174

BABER, H. H., 1014
Baird, Henry, 1382, 1383
Bale, John, 43
Barham, Francis, 1242–1244, 1252, 1253, 1256
Barlee, Edward, 1151, 1160
Barnes, William, 1385
Barrow, J., 1202, 1204, 1205
Baynes, J. Spencer, 1396
Becke, Edmund, 47, 66
Bell, Alexander, 1226, 1257
Belsham, Thomas, 1007, 1008
Benjoin, George, 971
Bentham, T., 89
Beza, Theodore, 109, 524
Bilson, Thomas, 240
Birks, T. R., 1255

Blackader, Robert B., 1182, 1226
Blayney, Benjamin, 885, 887, 936
Blyth, Francis, 796
Bois, John, 240, 403
Bonaparte, Louis Lucien, p. 408
Boothroyd, Benjamin, 1102, 1187
Borgström, Henrik, 1347, 1352
Bosworth, F., 1226
Bowen, J., 1352
Bradshaw, Matthew, 895
Brenton, Lancelot Charles Lee, 1169
Briscoe, —, 1245
Bristow, Richard, 134, 231
Broadus, J. A., 1292
Broughton, Hugh, p. 185
Brown, John, 996, 1041, 1045, 1054, 1071
Brown, Joseph, 879, 990, 1009
Browne, E. Harold, 1276
Büdinger, M., 1174
Buxton, Alfred F., 1321
Bywater, Abel, 1403

C., J. See J. Calvin
—— See J. Canne
—— See J. Cawood (printer)
—— See J. Cheke
Callander, John, 927
Calvin, John, 68, 102, 1145

Camerarius, Joachim, 109
Campbell, Alexander, 1158
Campbell, George, 1158
Canne, John, 438, 541, 612, 665, 672, 968, 969
Carter, Charles, 1240
Cartwright, Thomas, 282
Caryl, Joseph, 457, 467
Challoner, Richard, 796, 824, 825, 829
Cheke, John, 58, 1167
Cheyne, T. K., 1267
Clark, Samuel, 643
Clarke, R. L., 1267
Clay, William Keatinge, 1159
Cobbin, Ingram, 1155
Coggin, Thomas, 1177
Coit, T. W., 1153
Coleman, John Noble, 1222, 1231, 1239, 1251
Conant, Thomas J., 1195, 1200, 1230
Conquest, J. T., 1163, 1168
Cook, F. C., 1274, 1275
Cotton, Henry, 1199
Coverdale, Miles, 7, 13-16, 19-23, 25, 26, 29, 30, 45, 46, 52, 55, 57, 71, 1152, 1376
Coxe, Leonard, 45, 46
Coxe, R., 89
Cranmer, Thomas, 30
Creighton, James, 978
Cruttwell, Clement, 987
Cue, John, 978
Cumberland, Richard, 679, p. 248

D., H. See H. Danvers
Danvers, Henry, 547, 727
Davies, B., 1269
Davies, R., 89
Day, George E., 1331
Dickinson, William, 1381
Doddridge, Philip, 870, 1158
D'Oyly, George, 1072
Driver, S. R., 1267
Du Jon, F. See Franciscus Junius

EDWARDS, JUSTIN, 1183
Ellicott, C. J., 1202, 1204, 1205, 1211, 1276

Elliott, C. J., 1274
Erasmus, Desiderius, 18, 82, 41, 45, 46, 50, 58, 59

FAWKES, FRANCIS, 884
Fenton, Ferrar, 1299, 1326, 1327, 1338, 1345-1347, 1352, 1356
Finch, John, 1189
Forshall, Josiah, 1178, 1213
Forster, John George, 1393
Fortescu, Alexander, 910
Foxe, John, 95
Fulke, William, 156, 202, 278, 371
Fry, Francis, 2, 4, 447, 655, 1212, 1215, 1216, 1223

GELL, JOHN PHILIP, 1272
Gilby, Anthony, 77
Gillett, Edward, 1390
Girdlestone, R. B., 1249, 1261, 1268
Good, —, 408
Good, John Mason, 1029, 1191
Goodman, G., 89
Goodwin, A., 1267
Goodwin, James, 1167
Gotch, F. W., 1246, 1269
Grashop, T., 119
Greaves, Alexander, 1120
Green, George M., 1378
Green, S. G., 1269
Greenfield, William, 1113
Grindal, E., 89
Guest, E., 89
Gurney, J., 1269
Gurney, W., 1053
Guy, Edward Alexander, 1285, 1298

H., R. F. See R. Harrison
Haak, Theodore, 518
Hale, Nathan, 1125
Hammond, Henry, 501
Hampden-Cook, Ernest, 1355
Harding, John, 240
Hare, Edward, 1258
Harrison, Robert, 123
Haweis, Thomas, 965

INDEX

Hawkins, E., 1202, 1204, 1205, 1211
Haydock, George Leo, p. 829
Heath, Nicholas, 84, 86
Hebert, Charles, 1283
Henderson, E., 1184, 1191, 1194, 1201, 1203
Henderson, George, 1409, 1410
Henry, Matthew, 720, 856, 1140, 1147
Henshall, Samuel, 1002
Hereford, Nicholas of, 777, 1014, 1164, 1178
Herrey, R. F.   See R. Harrison
Hervey, A., 1292
Hill, Henry, 1303
Hollybushe, Johan, 20
Hopkins, John, 94
Horne, R., 89
Hovey, A., 1292
Howard, Luke, 1117, 1118, 1121, 1123
Humphry, W. G., 1202, 1204, 1205, 1211
Hunt, Robert, 1262
Hutter, Elias, 1360
Hychyns. See W. Tindale, and pp. 1 and 5

JACOB, G. A., 1246, 1269
Johnson, G. H. S., 1274
Jones, John, 1089
Junius, Franciscus [François du Jon], 172

KAY, WILLIAM, 1221, 1254
Key, Thomas, 45, 46
Kite, Edward, 1399

LAWRENCE, GILES, 89
Leeser, Isaac, 1225
Leo Juda, 45, 46
Lewis, Agnes Smith, 1301
Lewis, John, 777
Littledale, Henry Anthony, 1402
Lively, Edward, 240
Lloyd, William, 678, 854
Locke, H., 698
Loseler, Villerius P.   See L'Oyseleur

Lower, Mark Antony, 1397
Lowth, Robert, 926
Lowth, William, 767
L'Oyseleur, 109

MCCALLUM, GILBERT, 1217
Mace, William, 773
McFarlan, James, 1173
Maclear, G. F., 1270
McClellan, John Brown, 1266
MacKnight, James, 1067, 1158
McLane, James W., p. 362
MacMahon, Bernard, 1015
McRae, David, 1049
Madden, Frederic, 1178
Malan, S. C., 1214
Mant, Richard, 1072
Martin, Gregory, 134, 231
Mary, Princess, 45, 46
Matthew, Thomas, 17, 47, 48, 64, 66, p. 45
Mead, —, 403
Moberly, G., 1202, 1204, 1205, 1211
Moon, George Washington, 1271, 1348
Moore, Thomas, 1386
Morley, Lord.   See H. Parker
Moulton, W. F., 1315

NARY, CORNELIUS, 744
Newberry, Thomas, 1241
Newcome, William, 1007, 1008, 1115
Newton, Samuel, 898

OFFOR, GEORGE, 1149
Olde, John, 45, 46

PALFREY, J. G., 1125
Paley, F. A., 1297
Paris, Thomas, 854
Parker, Henry, 38, 39
Parker, Matthew, 89, 95
Parkhurst, J., 89
Parsons, John, 988
Patrick, Simon, 756, 765–767
Pearson, A., 89

Penn, Granville, 1150
Perkins, S., 727
Perne, A., 89
Perowne, J. J. S., 1270
'Philalethes,' 1089
Phillips, William, 1115
Phizackerley, James, 1387
Pick, A., 1186
Pitman, Isaac, 1242
Pont, R., 119
Porteus, Beilby, 969
Proby, W. H. B., 1263, 1264
Pulman, George P. R., 1384
Purver, Anthony, 862
Purvey, John, 777, 1014, 1164, 1178
Pusey, E. B., 1284

RAFFLES, THOMAS, 1071
Rainolds (or Reynolds), John, 240
Rayson, John, 1380
Reeves, John, 985, 1017
Rich, Jeremiah, 529, 676
Richardson, John, 1398
Riddell, Henry Scott, 1404–1406
Robson, Joseph Philip, 1391, 1392, 1394, 1395, 1407
Rodwell, J. M., 1224
Rogers, Charles, 1401
Rogers, John, 17
Rogers, William, 1260
Rotherham, Joseph Bryant, 1341
Roye, William, p. 1

SAMPSON, THOMAS, 77
Sandys, E., 89
Sayce, A. H., 1339
Scarlett, Nathaniel, 978, 979
Scott, Daniel, 803
Scott, Thomas, 907
Scott, Thomas, 952, 1147
Scrivener, F. H. A., 1258, 1259, 1315
Selby, P., 727
Sharpe, Samuel, 1247, 1250
Shaxton, Nicholas, 15
Sibson, Francis, 1145
Simon, Richard, 775
Smith, Miles, 240

Southwell, Henry, 908
Speed, John, 240
Spurrell, Helen, 1290
Starley, J. K., 1323
Staton, James Taylor, 1388, 1389
Stebbing, Henry, 1161
Sternhold, Thomas, 94
Stokes, George, 1147
Street, Stephen, 949

TALBOT, MATTHEW, 983
Taverner, Richard, 24, 27, 28, 38, 39, 53, 54, 60, 65, 66
Taylor, Alexander, 1265
Taylor, Edgar, 1162
Thayer, J. Henry, 1331
Thompson, —, 945
Thomson, Charles, 1006
Tindale, William, 1–6, 8–12, 18, 41–44, 50–52, 57, 58, 61, 63, 66, 67, 69, 70, 74, 75, 80–83, 87, 1149, 1212, 1223, 1248
Tischendorf, Constantine, 1288
Tomson, Laurence, 109
Townsend, George, 1137
Trail, S., 1226
Travers, Smith, 1086
Tregelles, Samuel Prideaux, 1164, 1171
Tunstall, Cuthbert, 34, 36

UDALL, NICHOLAS, 45, 46
Ussher, James, 678

VIDLER, WILLIAM, 978
Villerius, P. Loseler. See L'Oyseleur

W., T., 1131
Waddy, S. D., 1304
Wakefield, Gilbert, 983
Walsh, P., 1056
Ward, —, 403
Webster, Noah, 1183
Webster, William, 775
Weekes, Robert D., 1318
Wesley, John, 1157

Weston, H. G., 1292
Weymouth, Richard Francis, 1355
Whiston, William, 813
Whittingham, William, 76, 77
Williams, W., 1028
Wilson, Thomas, 937
Witham, Robert, 776, 784
Wordsworth, Christopher, 1258
Worsley, John, 895

Worsley, Samuel, 895
Worswick, John, 1025
Worthington, Thomas, 231
Wycliffe, John, 777, 1014, 1164, 1178, p. 2
Wynne, Richard, 864

YOUNG, ROBERT, 1219

II. NAMES OF PRINTERS, PUBLISHERS, ETC. DOWN TO THE YEAR 1824

ADAMS, O., 892
Adams, Thomas, 278
Aitken, Jane, 1006
Aitken, R., pp. 303, 304
Anderson, Andrew, 571, 575
    Heirs and successors of, 666, 692, 710, p. 759
Appleby, T., 892
Arbuthnot, Alexander, 119
Archdeacon, John, 877, 881, 886, 889, 891, 894, 904, 906, 914, 920, 923, 925, 930, 935, 938, 941, 947, 950, 954, 960, 962, 968, 973
Ash, Francis, 171
Aylmer, Brabazon, 643

B., G., 447
Badius, Conrad, 76
Bagster, Samuel, 1081
Baines, Edward, 983
Baldwin, H., 985
Baldwin, R., 870, 882, etc.
Baldwin, Richard, 655
Bankes, Richard, 38, 39
Barber, John, p. 254
Barker, Christopher (i), 105–107, 109–111, 114–118, 120–133, 135–150, p. 254
    Deputies of, 151–158 160–171, 173–196, 364
Barker, Christopher (ii), 463, 466, 531–533, 535, 539, 542–546, 549–552, 554, 555, 572–574, 580, 582, 591–593
    Assigns of, 549–551, 554–556, 558–560, 563–565, 569, 570, 572, 573, 576–579, 593, 603
Barker, Robert (i and ii ?), 197, 200–212, 214, 215, 219–230, 232, 234–277, 280, 282, 283, 289, 328–330, 333–363, 366, 369, 373–382, 384, 386, 388, 390–394, 398–401, 404–417, 419–421, 423, 425–437, 439–441, 445, 446, 448, 451, 461, 462, 465, 562, 1361
    Deputies of, 196, 216–218, 281
Barnard, —, 1071
Baskerville, John, 857
Baskett, John, 716, 722, 723, 726, 728, 730, 732, 733, 735–742, 745–749, 753–762, 764, 768, 769, 771, 772, 779, 780, 782, 783, 785–790, 792, 795, 797, 799, 802, 804, 805, p. 254
Baskett, Mark, 852, 855, 858–860, 863, 865, 869, 871, 872, 875, 876, 880, 890, p. 285
Baskett, Robert, 805, 810–812
    Assigns of, 815, 819, 821, 822, 826, 830, 834, 835, 838, 840, 842, 845, 846, 851, 852, 858, 859, 865, 871, 872, 875, 876, 880, 890
Baskett, Thomas, 805, 810–812, 815, 816, 819–823, 826, 827, 830, 832, 834, 835, 838–842, 845, 846, 849–851, 855
Bassandyne, Thomas, 119
Bathurst, Charles, 817
Baylis, —, 985
Beecroft, John, 867, etc.
Beecroft, T., 920, etc.
Bellamy, —, 952
Bensley, T., 961, 966, 976, 977, 980, 982, 985, 987, 992, 993, 1001, 1003–1005, 1013, 1016, 1022, 1024, 1028, 1031–1033, 1063, 1064, 1066, 1070 1072, 1078, 1079, 1083

Bentham, Joseph, 807, 817, 847, 848, 853, 854, 866, 867
Bentley, William, 459, 471
Berthelet (or Barthlet), Thomas, 24, 27-29
Bible Society, British and Foreign [B.F.B.S.], *passim* after 1806; p. 318
Bill, C., 615, 620, 624, 633, 634, 640, 644-647, 652-654, 656, 657, 660, 661, 665, 667-674, 679, 680, 682-686, 688-691, 693-696, 701-703, 706, 708, 709
Bill, John (i and ii ?), 281, 283-293, 295-306, 308-321, 323, 325-329, 336, 531, 533, 539, 542-546, 549-552, 554, 555, 572, 573, 582, 588-593, 596
    Assigns of, 330, 333-335, 337-363, 366, 369, 373-382, 384, 386, 388, 390-394, 398-401, 404-417, 419-421, 423, 425-437, 439-441, 445, 446, 448, 451, 461-463, 466, 549-551, 554-556, 558-560, 562-565, 569, 570, 572, 573, 576-579, 593, 597, 599-603, 608, 611, 613, 615, 619, 620, 622-625, 627, 629, 630, 656, 684, 1361
Binauld, William, 725
Bishop, George, 102, 156
Black, —, 1029
Blair, D. Hunter, 1010, 1011, 1019, 1021, 1026, 1027, 1036, 1043, 1050, 1052, 1055, 1101, 1103
Blair, J. H., 981
Bleckley, W., 955
Blow, Daniel, 868
Blow, James, 886
Boden, N., 892
Bodley, John, 84
Bonham, William, 64
Booker, J., 1051
Boulter, D., 955
Bowyer, R., 961, 967
Brewman, —, 898
Brightly, —, 1041, 1054
Broerss, Joost, 438, 444
Brown, —, 994, 1056, 1084
Brown, William, 763, 770

Bruce, D. and G., 1870, 1872
Bruce, J., 981, 1010, 1011, 1019-1021, 1026, 1027, 1036, 1043, 1050, 1052, 1055, 1101, 1103
Brudenell, Thomas, 481
Buck, John, 324, 331, 332, 365
Buck, Thomas, 324, 331, 332, 365, 385, 396, 402, 403, 418, 422
Buckland, James, 907, 917
Burges, John, 960, 962, 963, 971, 973, 975, 984
Byddell, John, 24
Bynneman, Henry, 102

C., G., 447
C., J. See J. Cawood
Cadell, T., 895, 926, 936, 1066
Calvert, Giles, 457, 495
Cambridge University Press, 974
Cambridge University Printers, 397. See also under printers' names
Campbell, —, 1044
Canin, Isaac, 213
Carey, —, p. 308
Carmarden, Richard, 86
Carmichael, Alex., 794
Cawood, John, 58, 79, 88, 90-92
Chalmers, J., 928
Chandler, A., 1874
Chapman, T., 965
Childs, 1041, 1054
Chiswell, Richard, 643
Churchill, A., 698
Churchill, J., 698
Clark, S., 862
Cockerill, Thomas, 638
Coghlan, J. P., 903
Coldock, Francis, 103
Collingwood, S., 1016, 1022, 1024, 1031-1033, 1063, 1064, 1070, 1072, 1078, 1079, 1083, 1087, 1088, 1094, 1098, 1099
Conder, Thomas, 983
Cooke, J., 884, 908, 936, 966, 976, 977, 980, 987, 992, 993, 1001, 1003-1005, 1013, 1016, 1022, 1024, 1031-1033, 1063, 1064, 1070, 1072, 1078, 1079, 1083, 1087, 1088

Copland, William, 59
Corrall, C., 1059, 1065
Coustourier, John, 370, 387
Cowke, Symon, 8–10
Cox, —, 985
Coyne, Richard, 994, 1056, 1090, 1091
Crafoorth, Thomas, 191, 364
Crispin, John, 94
Crom, Matthew, 8–10, 17, 22, 23, 26
Crouch, Samuel, 638
Crowder, J., 985
Crowder, S., 882, etc.
Cruttwell, R., 987
Curry, William, Jun., 1104

DANIEL, ROGER, 385, 396, 402, 403, 418, 422, 454, 458, 465, 475–480, 502, 503, 510, 515
Darby, John, 765
Darton, —, 955
Davies, W., 1066
Davis, J., 949
Dawson, W., 931, etc., 959, 966, 976, 977, 980, 987, 992, 993, 1001, 1003–1005, 1013
Day, John, 43, 47, 51, 53, 54, 57, 60, 61, 63, 65–67, 95
Deighton, John, 971, etc.
Dexter, Robert, 172, 199
Dilly, C., 930, etc.
Dilly, Edward, 867, etc.
Dobson, Eliphal, 725, 752
Dod, Benjamin, 847, 848, 854, 866
Dodsley, J., 864, 926
Dodsley, R., 864
Dugdale, B., 945
Dumæus, Godefridus. See Govaert van der Haghen

EDWARDS, RICHARD, 986
Edwards, Richard, 1014
Edwards, —, 1071
Emperowr. See Keyser
Endhoven, Christopher, 8–10
Etherington, C., 879
Evans, Richard 1045
Evans, T., 898

Eversden, Henry, 529
Eyre, Charles, 900, p. 254
Eyre, George, 900, 997, 1080, 1085, 1037–1040, 1042, 1046, 1057, 1059, 1060, 1065, 1068, 1069, 1073–1076, 1082, 1085, 1095, 1097, 1100
Eyres, William, 933

FABIAN, THOMAS, 688
Fanshaw, D., 1365–1372
Farley, —, 1071
Fawne, Luke, 457, 467
Fenley, John, Jun., 988
Field, John, 469, 470, 492, 494, 496–500, 508, 509, 511, 512, 514, 516, 517, 519–523, 525–528, 530, 531, 534–538, 540, 544, 548
Field, Richard, 172, 199
Fielding, John, 980
Fittler, J., 961
Fitzpatrick, H., 1015
Flesher, J., 501
Fletcher, J., 884
Flint, W., 996
Fogny, John, 134
Foulis, Andrew, 927
Freebairn, Robert, 791, 793
Froschover, Christopher, 7, 55, 57, 71
Fry, Joseph, 921, 922
Fry, William, 1086

GARDNER, E., 1016, etc.
Gaultier, Thomas, 58
Ged, William, pp. 318, 320
Gill, W., 882, 885, 887, 888, 893, 896, 899, 901, 902, 905, 909, 911, 913, 918, 924
Gillet, T., 978, 979
Godfray, T., p. 12
Goodwin, —, 1104
Goodwin, —, 1363, 1364
Gosnel, S., 985
Gowghe, John, 8–10
Grafton, Richard, 17, 21, 25, 30–32, 34, 36, 37, 73, p. 67
Graisberry, —, 1044
Green, W., 994

INDEX

Greig, —, 1067
Grierson, Boulter, 843, 868, 883, 897
    Assignee of, 929
Grierson, George (i), 798, 800, 801, 806, 831, 836
Grierson, George (ii), 1092
Grosse, John, Heir of, 814
Gunne, R., 752
Guy, Thomas, 585-587, 594, 595, 598, 605-607, 609, 610, 618, 621, 628, 631, 635-637, 641, 642, 648, 649, 652

HALL, ROULAND, 77
Hamillon, C., 86
Hamilton, A., 931, 932, 934, 940, 942, 943, 951, 953, 956
Hamilton, S., 1009
Harris, William, 910
Harrison, Lucas, 102, 103
Harrison, Richard, 85
Hart, Andrew, 233
Harvey, —, 955
Hay, David, Executors of, 929
Haydock, Thomas, p. 329
Hayes, John, 553, 561, 568, 581, 604, 614, 617
Heaton, —, 1025
Heptinstall, J., 648
Heptinstall, T., 1362
Heptinstall, W., 1362
Hester, Andrew, 55
Hett, R., 895
Hills, Henry, 518, 519, 526, 527, 532, 533, 582, 588-591, 596, 603, 608, 615, 619, 620, 623-625, 627, 629, 630, 633, 634, 640, 684, p. 254
    Assigns of, 597, 599-602, 611, 613, 622-625, 656, 709, 711-713, 716, 717, 719, 722, 723, 726, 728, 730, 732, 733, 737-740, 742, 748, 749, 754, 756, 764, 769, 778, 779, 788, 795
Hudson, —, 1363, 1364
Hunter, Rowland, 1089
Hutchinson, R., 1049
Hyde, J., 752
Hyll, Nicholas, 64, 68
Hyll, William, 48

JACKSON, W., 882, etc., 931, 932, 934, 940, 942, 943, 951, 953, 956, 959
Johnson, —, 879
Johnson, J., 1009
Johnson, Joseph, 933
Johnston, William, 862, 870
Jones, J., 1053
Judson, John, 103
Jugge, Richard, 69-71, 74, 75, 80-83, 87-89, 93, 96, 98-101, 103, 104, 108, 112, 113, 1359

KEATING, —, 994, 1056, 1084
Keene, Martin, 1092
Keith, —, 917
Kele, Richard, 103
Kellam, Laurence, 231
Kerr, Charles, 948, 957, 964, 968, 969, 972
Kerr, Mark, 948, 957, 964, 968, 969, 972
Keyser, Martin de, 4-6
Kincaid, Alexander, 844, 861, 873, 874, 878, 968, p. 315
    Assigns of, 989, 944
Kinnersley, T., 1041, 1054
Kirton, Joshua, 518
Knaplock, R., 767
Knapton, J., 856

LANG, W., 1049
Lawrence, I., 638
Lawrence, J., 720
Leake, Ann, 605
Leake, William, 585-587, 594, 595, 598, 605-607, 609, 610, 652
Legate, John, 159
Lesson, T., 879
Letterman, —, 1017
Lewis, M., 917
Longman, —, 1080, etc.
Lowndes, W., 990
Lucas, Martin, 341
Luckman, T., 879
Luft, Hans, 3
Lunn, W. H., 971

Macklin, Thomas, 982
McNamara, J. A., 1056
March, John, 777
Marler, Anthony, pp. 26, 30
Marshall, John, 676
Marshall, William, 638, 676
Mathewes, Augustine, 371
Mawman, J., 984, &c.
Merrill, J. and J., 980, etc.
Merrill, T. and J., 867, etc.
Millar, Alex., 794
Miller, G., 457
Moir, John, 970, 994
Moore, Isaac, 915, 916
Moore, J., 744
Moore, William, 1102
Mortlock, George, 727
Mosman, John, 763, 770
Mount, William, 777

Newbery, John, 837, 882
Newcomb, Thomas (i and ii), 582, 588–591, 596, 603, 608, 615, 619, 620, 623–625, 627, 629, 630, 633, 634, 640, 644–646, 653, 684, p. 254
    Assigns of, 597, 599–602, 611, 613, 622–625, 656, 709, 711–713, 716, 717, 719, 722, 723, 726, 728, 730, 732, 733, 737–740, 742, 748, 749, 754, 795
    Executrix of, 647, 652, 654, 656, 657, 660, 661, 665, 667–674, 679, 680, 682–686, 688–691, 693–696, 701–703, 706, 708, 709
Newman, Dorman, 638
Nichol, G. and W., 985, 1017, 1018
Nichols, J., 926
Noon, J., 803
Norton, Bonham, 281, 283–293, 295–306, 308–321, 323, 325–328
Norton, William, 103
Nosche, Joachim, 455
Nycolson, James, 13–16, 19, 20, p. 8

Ogden, Hester, 371
Ogilby, J., 525
Ogilvy, D., 996

Oswen, John, 62
Overton, Henry, 457, 467
Owen, R., 752
Oxford University Printers (The Theatre, etc.), 566, 567, 585–587, 594, 595, 598, 605–607, 609, 610, 618, 621, 628, 631, 632, 635–637, 639, 641, 642, 648, 649, 658, 662–664, 677, 678, 681, 687, 697, 699, 704, 705, 707, 714, 715, 718, 721, 724, 771, 986
    See also under printers' names

P., C., 452, 456
Page, Thomas, 777
Parker, Peter, 585–587, 594, 595, 598, 605–607, 609, 610, 628, 632, 639, 642
Parker, William, 777
Parry, —, 1029
Parsons, John, 988
Pasham, J. W., 919
Paul, A., 1874
Peake, Robert, p. 171, etc.
Pemberton, John, 775
Petyt, Thomas, 27–29, 42, 44, 64
Pine, William, 912
Pitt, Moses, 585–587, 594, 595, 598, 605–607, 609, 610
Powell, William, 41, 50, 78
Preston, —, 1025
Prince, D., 986

Quentell, Peter, 1

Rawlins, J., 643
Raynalde, Thomas, 48
Redman, Robert, 18, 29, 33
Reeves, John, 985, 1017, 1018, p. 297
Regnault, Francis, 21, 25
Rhames, A., 725, 752
Richards, —, 1089
Richardson, W., 862
Rickaby, T., 946
Rivington, Charles, 775
Rivington, John, 867, etc.

INDEX

Rivingtons, 870, 920, etc.
Robarts, —, 952
Roberts, J., 773
Robinson, Jonathan, 643
Rothwell, John, 457, 467, 518
Royal Printers (Edinburgh), 367, 368, 372, 383, 448
   See also under printers' names
Royal Printers (London)
   Assigns of, 778, 779
      See also under the printers' names
Royston, Richard, 501

SANDERS, ROBERT, 650, 651
Scarlett, Nathaniel, 978, 979
Scatcherd, —, 946, 1017
Schoeffer, Peter, 2
'Scintilla.' See Michael Sparke
Seeley, L. B., 998, etc., p. 319
Seldenslach, James, 294
Seres, William, 43, 47, 51, 53, 54, 57, 60-62
Simmons, —, 917
Smith, J., 999, 1000, 1012, 1023, 1047, 1048, 1058, 1061, 1062, 1077, 1080, 1096
Smith, R., 655
Society for Promoting Christian Knowledge, 992
Sparke, Michael, pp. 171, 189
Stafford, Thomas, 424, 449
Stam, John F., 191, 864
Stationers, The Company of, 279, 322, 464, 468, 472-474, 483-491, 493
   A Society of, 504-507
      See also 103 ; and 'Scintilla,' pp. 189-194
Stevenson, M., 955
Stewart, —, p. 308
Stockdale, John, 1028
Story, Peter, 638
Strahan, Andrew, 997, 1030, 1035, 1037-1040, 1042, 1046, 1057, 1059, 1060, 1065, 1068, 1069, 1073, 1074-1076, 1082, 1085, 1095, 1097, 1100
Strahan, William, 900
Streater, John, 513

Swart, Stephen, 557, 583, 584, 616
   Widow of, 626, 675
Syers, Oswald, 1034

T., E. See Evan Tyler
Taylor, —, 985
Taylor, Richard, 1007, 1008
Thomas, Isaiah, 958
Tomlins, Richard, 518
Tooke, Benjamin, p. 254
Toye, Robert, 64
Tyler, Evan, 442, 443, 482, 504-507, 524
Tylle, William, 44

UNIVERSITY PRINTERS. See Cambridge University Printers, Oxford University Printers

VALLANCE, —, 917
Van der Haghen, Govaert, 6
Van Meteren, Jacob, pp. 5, 7
Van Ruremonde, Hans, 8-10
Vautrollier, Thomas, 105
Vervliet, Daniel, 198
Vint, M., 990
Vogel, J. B. G., 1093
Vorsterman, William, 8-10

W., R., 447
Wade, Samuel, 655
Walker, —, 1067
Walker, —, 1071
Walley, John, 103
Walthoe, J., 766
Ware, Richard, 758, 768, 839, etc.
Watkins, Adrian, 828, 833
Watkins, Richard, 97
Watkins, Richard, 808, 818
Watson, James, 729, 734, 743, 750, 751
   Assigns of, 770
Watts, R., 989, 991, 995, 998, 1029, 1081
Waugh, James, 867

Wayly, John, 59
Whitaker, —, 946
Whitchurch, Edward, 17, 21, 25, 30, 32, 34-37, 40, 45, 49, 56, 72
White, Benjamin, 867, etc.
White, E. and J., 1365-1369, 1371, 1373
White, J., 960, 984, 1002, 1053
White, Robert, 481
Whittingham, C., 1017, 1018
Wilkes, John, 910
Wilks, —, 985
Wilson, Andrew, 1051, 1092, pp. 318, 320
Wogan, —, 1015
Wolfe, Reynolde, 52
Woodfall, G., 997, 1035
Wright, T., 882, 885, 887, 888, 893, 896, 899, 901, 902, 905, 909, 911, 913, 918, 924
Wyghte, John, 64

YOUNG, ROBERT, 367, 368, 372, 383, 389, 395, 448

INDEX

III. NAMES OF PLACES OF PRINTING, PUBLICATION, ETC. DOWN TO THE YEAR 1824

ABERDEEN, 928
Amsterdam, 188-193, 307, 364, 424, 438, 444, 449, 452, 453, 455, 456, 541, 557, 583, 584, 612, 616, 626, 675, 700, 731, 774, 781
  See also Holland
Antwerp, 4-6, 8-12, 17, 22, 23, 26, 198, 294

BATH, 937
Belfast, 868
Birmingham, 892
Bristol, 912, 986, 988
Bungay, 1041, 1054

CAMBRIDGE, 159, 324, 331, 332, 365, 385, 396, 397, 402, 403, 418, 422, 454, 458, 465, 475-480, 516, 517, 525, 534, 536-538, 540, 544, 548, 553, 561, 568, 581, 604, 614, 617, 807, 817, 847, 848, 853, 854, 857, 866, 867, 877, 881, 886, 889, 891, 894, 904, 906, 914, 920, 923, 925, 930, 935, 938, 941, 947, 950, 954, 960, 962, 963, 971, 973, 974, 975, 984, 989, 991, 995, 998, 999, 1000, 1012, 1023, 1047, 1048, 1058, 1061, 1062, 1077, 1080, 1096
Cologne, 1
Coventry, 879

DONCASTER, 879
Dort, 194, 213
Douai, 231, 776, 784, 796
Dublin, 725, 744, 752, 798, 800, 801, 806, 824, 825, 829, 831, 836, 843, 860, 868, 883, 897, 929, 945, 994, 1015, 1044, 1056, 1090-1092, 1104, p. 278

EDINBURGH, 119, 233, 367, 368, 372, 388, 389, 395, 442, 443, 448, 482, 571, 575, 659, 666, 692, 710, 722, 729, 734, 743, 750, 751, 759, 761, 763, 770, 772, 791, 793, 808, 818, 828, 833, 844, 861, 873, 874, 878, 939, 944, 948, 957, 964, 968-970, 972, 981, 994, 1010, 1011, 1019-21, 1026, 1027, 1036, 1043, 1050, 1052, 1055, 1067, 1101, 1103

GENEVA, 76, 77, 84, 94
Glasgow, 650, 651, 794, 927, 1049

HARTFORD (Connecticut, U. S. A.), 1363, 1364
Holland. For a list of editions between the dates 1599 and 1746, which are known, or conjectured, to have been printed in Holland or elsewhere on the Continent, see note on p. 194
Huddersfield, 1102

LEIPZIG, 814
London, *passim*

MALBOROW [Marburg], 3
Manchester, 1034

NEWCASTLE-UPON-TYNE, 1025
New York, 1365–1374
Nuremberg, 1360

OXFORD, 566, 567, 585–587, 594, 595, 598, 605–607, 609, 610, 618, 621, 628, 631, 632, 635–637, 639, 641, 642, 648, 649, 658, 662–664, 677, 678, 681, 687, 697, 699, 704, 705, 707, 714, 715, 718, 721, 722, 724, 730, 732, 734, 735, 740, 741, 745–747, 753, 755, 757, 758, 760, 762, 768, 771, 779, 786, 797, 799, 802, 805, 811, 812, 816, 820, 823, 827, 832, 839, 841, 849, 850, 855, 860, 863, 869, 882, 885, 887, 888, 893, 896, 899, 901, 902, 905, 909, 911, 913, 918, 924, 931, 932, 934, 936, 940, 942, 943, 951, 953, 956, 959, 966, 976, 977, 980, 987, 992, 993, 1001, 1003–1005, 1013, 1016, 1022, 1024, 1031–1033, 1063, 1064, 1070, 1072, 1078, 1079, 1083, 1087, 1088, 1094, 1098, 1099

PARIS, 21, 25
Philadelphia, 803, 804, 1006, 1086, p. 808

RHEIMS, 134
Rouen, 86, 370, 387

SOUTHWARK, 13–16, 19, 20
Stamford, 813

WARRINGTON, 933
Winchester, 910
Worcester, 62
Worcester (Massachusetts, U.S.A.), 958
Worms, 2

YORK, 879

ZURICH, 7, 55, 57, 71

www.ingramcontent.com/pod-product-compliance
Lightning Source LLC
Chambersburg PA
CBHW071225290426
44108CB00013B/1292